Revelation and Authority

THE ANCHOR YALE BIBLE REFERENCE LIBRARY
is a project of international and interfaith scope in which
Protestant, Catholic, and Jewish scholars from many countries
contribute individual volumes. The project is not sponsored by
any ecclesiastical organization and is not intended to reflect
any particular theological doctrine.

The series is committed to producing volumes in the tradition
established half a century ago by the founders of the Anchor
Bible, William Foxwell Albright and David Noel Freedman.
It aims to present the best contemporary scholarship in a way
that is accessible not only to scholars but also to the educated
nonspecialist. It is committed to work of sound philological and historical scholarship, supplemented by insight from
modern methods, such as sociological and literary criticism.

John J. Collins
General Editor

THE ANCHOR YALE BIBLE REFERENCE LIBRARY

Revelation and Authority

Sinai in Jewish Scripture and Tradition

BENJAMIN D. SOMMER

 Yale

UNIVERSITY

PRESS

NEW HAVEN

AND

LONDON

Published with assistance from the foundation established in memory of James Wesley Cooper of the Class of 1865, Yale College.

The author gratefully acknowledges permission from Schocken Publishing House Ltd. of Tel Aviv to quote several lines from the poetry of Yehuda Amichai at the end of the last chapter of this book and permission from Hana Amichai and the Estate of Yehuda Amichai to provide his own translation of those lines.

Yale University Press books may be purchased in quantity for educational, business, or promotional use. For information, please e-mail sales.press@yale.edu (U.S. office) or sales@yaleup.co.uk (U.K. office).

Set in Adobe Caslon type by Newgen. Printed in the United States of America.

Library of Congress Cataloging-in-Publication Data

Sommer, Benjamin D., 1964–
    Revelation and authority : Sinai in Jewish scripture and tradition / Benjamin D. Sommer.
        pages cm. — (The Anchor Yale Bible reference library)
    Includes bibliographical references and index.
    ISBN 978-0-300-15873-1 (cloth : alk. paper)
    1. Revelation on Sinai.   2. Bible. Old Testament—Criticism, interpretation, etc.   3. Rosenzweig, Franz, 1886–1929—Influence.   4. Heschel, Abraham Joshua, 1907–1972—Influence.   5. Rabbinical literature—History and criticism.   I. Title.
    BM612.S66 2015
    296.3′115—dc23   2014032429

A catalogue record for this book is available from the British Library.

This paper meets the requirements of ANSI/NISO Z39.48-1992 (Permanence of Paper).

10 9 8 7 6 5 4 3 2 1

לבתי

שרה גילה

בהגיעה למצוות

For Sarah Gilah

on her reaching the age

of the commandments

Contents

Preface, ix

Acknowledgments, xiii

List of Abbreviations, xvii

Introduction: Participatory Theories of Revelation, 1

1. Artifact or Scripture?, 11

2. What Happened at Sinai? Maximalist and Minimalist Approaches, 27

3. Command and Law in the Participatory Theology of Revelation, 99

4. Scripture as Tradition, and Tradition as Scripture, 147

5. Event, Process, and Eternity, 188

6. A Modern Jewish Approach to Scripture, 209

Conclusion: Innovation, Continuity, and Covenant, 241

Notes, 253

Bibliography, 365

Subject Index, 403

Index of Ancient and Medieval Sources, 413

Preface

In this book, I address several audiences at once: biblical scholars, specialists in modern Jewish and Christian thought, theologians, clergy, religious educators, and—not least—lay readers who wonder about the place of the Bible in their lives and in the life of their communities. I hope my close readings of biblical texts show scholars of theology that the Bible is more subtle and more interesting than they may have realized, or interesting in ways they never considered. By drawing at once on studies of the Bible's ancient Near Eastern context and on constructive theology, this book should convince religious Jews and Christians that biblical criticism need not be hostile to religious readings of scripture, and that attempts to see the Bible in its own cultural setting equip the theologian and the person of faith with important tools. Conversely, many biblical critics shun Jewish thought and Christian theology as irrelevant to their area of study. I intend the chapters that follow to demonstrate to my colleagues in the guild of biblical studies that sensitivity to the concerns of later religious thinkers enriches our understanding of the biblical texts themselves. I focus on two modern Jewish thinkers, Franz Rosenzweig and Abraham Joshua Heschel, but the suggestion that interaction between biblical scholarship and theology will be fruitful for both applies to many other thinkers as well.

Striking a balance between providing necessary background and moving new arguments forward is an elusive goal. This is all the more the case in a book that draws on several disciplines and speaks to varied audiences. At times I pause to explain matters that some readers already have studied, and I hope these readers will be forbearing as they skim the relevant paragraphs. Where necessary I refer readers to useful overviews of scholarship in the endnotes.

Otherwise the endnotes are intended for academic specialists in one field or another. I use them to respond to potential objections to my argument that involve technical issues specific to particular academic subdisciplines. Many readers will prefer not to look at the notes at all, and even specialists will look at some and not others. It is for this reason that I have made them endnotes and not footnotes. Although the endnotes are lengthy, taking up about a third of the book, they are quite selective in their references to secondary literature. The topics I address are fundamentally important and also quite broad; they invoke scholarship from several areas of specialization, one of which has flourished since the early nineteenth century. Consequently, they have generated an enormous amount of secondary literature in a variety of languages. For most of the items in the bibliography, specialists can immediately think of several additional articles or books I might have cited. I make no attempt at being comprehensive in my references to these literatures.

Translations are my own, unless I specifically indicate otherwise in an endnote or in the bibliography. I refer to biblical verses using the numbering system found in the Hebrew (Masoretic) text. On occasion, the numbering in some English translations varies by one or two verses.

Some issues of terminology: The God of ancient Israel, like all deities of the ancient Near East, has a personal name, spelled in Hebrew with the four letters *yod*, *hey*, *waw*, and *hey*. Most translations render this name in English as "LORD," in uppercase letters, to differentiate it from the noun "Lord," but by rendering a personal name with this noun, these translations miss something crucial in the original text. I prefer simply to transliterate this name. Following Jewish tradition, however, I never pronounce this name out loud, instead substituting some other Hebrew word, such as *Adonay* or *Hashem*, wherever the four-letter name appears in a text, and as a sort of precaution I do not spell it with its vowels, either. Therefore, this name always appears as "Yhwh" in this book, even when I am citing the title of an article or book that spells it with the vowels.

The term "Israel" in this book always refers to the whole nation that goes by that name—that is, to the Jewish people, and not to the northern kingdom, to the character Jacob, or to the modern state.

I discuss various terms with which Jews, Christians, and academics refer to Hebrew scripture in chapter 1, and various meanings of the word "Torah" in chapter 4. To anticipate my comments there, I can note that "the

Bible" in this book refers specifically to Jewish scripture and not to the New Testament. In the fourth chapter, I discuss the various conceptions of Torah in classical rabbinic literature. When I want to refer to the Five Books of Moses, I usually employ the term "Pentateuch." I use the term "Torah" more broadly, to refer to Judaism's religious teachings through the ages.

Acknowledgments

The earliest kernel of what eventually became this book was a session I gave during Shavuot, the holiday of lawgiving, at the Hillel Foundation in Chicago's Hyde Park neighborhood. The session took place in the middle of the night, as is customary for that holiday, in 1993 or thereabouts. I remain grateful to the Hillel Foundation's rabbi, Daniel Leifer, of blessed memory, for the invitation to teach that night, for his enthusiasm for the topic, and for his friendship. Over the subsequent two decades, I presented material that found its way into this book to many audiences in the United States and Israel. The comments, questions, and challenges I received from laypeople, rabbis, and academics at those sessions greatly enhanced what is in front of you. I pursued much of the research and thinking behind this book while I served on the faculties of Northwestern University and the Jewish Theological Seminary, while I was a fellow at the Shalom Hartman Institute, and while I was a visitor in the Department of Bible at the Hebrew University; all these institutions provided ideal settings in which to study and teach this material.

The bulk of the writing took place during the years I spent at the Tikvah Center for Law and Jewish Civilization at the New York University Law School and at the Israel Institute for Advanced Studies at the Hebrew University. In both institutions I found an environment in which conversation, reflection, and research encouraged thoughtful, engaged scholarship. Without the support of Tikvah/NYU and the Israel IAS, I would never have finished this multidecade project. The flexibility of the Jewish Theological Seminary in allowing me two successive years of research leave reflects the seminary's unwavering commitment to scholarship. It is a pleasure to thank JTS's chancellor, Arnold Eisen, and its provost, Alan Cooper, for the many types of support they provide.

I am indebted to various *ḥevrutas* with whom I studied texts central to this project: Michael Balinsky, with whom I read Heschel's תורה מן השמים באספקלריה של הדורות; Yehoyada Amir and Job Jindo, with whom I read Rosenzweig's *The Star of Redemption*; and Lawrence Kaplan, with whom I read Naḥmanides's commentaries on the Torah's narratives of revelation. I discussed many aspects of this project with these colleagues, and their impact on the book has been significant. Michael helped me to see some of the most important implications of my own thinking in ways that became crucial to this project. Over the years Michael has been both רב and חבר, as he officiated at my wedding (along with Danny Leifer, who helped me plant that first seed a few years earlier), as we learned together, and as we shmoozed about Torah and other topics.

Detailed comments on the manuscript by Marc Brettler and Gary Anderson improved the book considerably. Starting in my undergraduate years, and ever since, I have learned what it means to be a scholar and a teacher from Marc. When writing, a professor (that is to say, a former grad student) often imagines a particular teacher as a reader. Marc is that audience for me, and the effect on my work is always beneficial. As a religious Jew, I am very pleased to acknowledge how much Torah I have learned over the years from Gary, whose ability to integrate piety and scholarship I admire, and whose deep Catholicity grounds and enhances his impressive catholicity. Richard Tupper, Harman Grossman, and Hillel Ben-Sasson also provided me with detailed and useful feedback on the manuscript, for which I am grateful. If my audience finds the book both readable and thoughtful, they share my debt to all five of these friends.

I have discussed the material found in these various chapters with many people, to all of whom I am obliged: Judith Alexander, Joel Baden, Joshua Berman, Erhard Blum, David Carr, Joseph Davis, Eliezer Diamond, Arnie Eisen, מורי ורבי Michael Fishbane, David Flatto, Yoni Garb, Jan Gertz, Shimon Gesundheit, Neil Gillman, Suzanne Griffel, Moshe Halbertal, Moshe Idel, Joan Katz, Richard Kieckhefer, Bernard Levinson, Yair Lorberbaum, Shaul Magid, Alan Mittleman, Danny Nevins, Alexander Rofé, David Rosenberg, Konrad Schmid, Avraham Sommer, André Ungar, Joseph Weiler, Ira Youdavin, and Yair Zakovitch. Conversations with Baruch Schwartz over the years have been especially important to this project.

I am happy to thank John Collins for inviting me to submit a book to the Anchor Yale Bible Reference Library, for his suggestions on the manuscript, and for his flexibility in accepting a book that is as much concerned with modern Jewish thought as it is with the Hebrew Bible. It was a pleasure working on the preparation of the manuscript for publication with Jennifer Banks, Heather Gold, Jay Harward, and Katherine Faydash, who were friendly, patient, sensible, and professional, and with Leslie Rubin, who did an outstanding job preparing the indexes. I am also happy to thank my friends Joyce Newmark and Richard Tupper for their help with proofreading the galleys.

Most of all, I am indebted to my family: my wife, Jennifer Dugdale, and our children, Avraham, Sarah, and Eliana. As I researched and wrote, Sarah's delightful good humor, sensible advice, and readiness to try new things (like moving to Jerusalem and going to a new school for a year—twice) made my life much easier. As I said recently at her bat mitzvah, Sarah loves many activities, but I think her favorite is reading. And she's not just a reader; she is that much more important thing: a rereader. Somehow Sarah has always known that if a book is really good, it's worth going back to again and again. As a result, she has both what we call in Hebrew בקיאות and עיון, broad familiarity and deep knowledge. She can tell you where some tiny detail toward the end of book 2 in the Harry Potter series turns out to mean something quite different from what we thought when we get to a paragraph in the middle of book 6. The book you are now reading is concerned with texts and teachings that our family has been rereading and re-rereading for more than two millennia. This book is also, and above all, about מצוה and חיוב, commandment and obligation; as it happens, it was being completed as Sarah arrived at the age of the commandments. Thus it is the perfect book to dedicate to her, with love and pride.

Abbreviations

AJSR	*Association for Jewish Studies Review*
b.	Babylonian Talmud
BDB	F. Brown, S. R. Driver, and C. Briggs, *A Hebrew and English Lexicon of the Old Testament*
CAT	M. Dietrich, O. Loretz, and J. Sanmartín. *The Cuneiform Alphabetic Texts from Ugarit, Ras Ibn Hani, and Other Places*
CJ	*Conservative Judaism*
DDS	Moshe Weinfeld, *Deuteronomy and the Deuteronomic School*
FRHLT	Franz Rosenzweig, *Franz Rosenzweig: His Life and Thought*, edited by Nahum Glatzer
GKC	E. Kautzsch, *Gesenius' Hebrew Grammar*
HALOT	Ludwig Koehler et al., *The Hebrew and Aramaic Lexicon of the Old Testament*
HBT	*Horizons in Biblical Theology*
HT	Abraham Joshua Heschel, *Heavenly Torah as Refracted through the Generations*, edited and translated into English by Gordon Tucker
HTR	*Harvard Theological Review*
HUCA	*Hebrew Union College Annual*
JAAR	*Journal of the American Academy of Religion*
JANES	*Journal of the Ancient Near Eastern Society*
JAOS	*Journal of the American Oriental Society*
JBL	*Journal of Biblical Literature*
JJS	*Journal of Jewish Studies*

JJTP	*Journal of Jewish Thought and Philosophy*
JM	P. Joüon and T. Muraoka, *A Grammar of Biblical Hebrew*
JQR	*Jewish Quarterly Review*
JSOT	*Journal for the Study of the Old Testament*
LXX	The Septuagint
m.	Mishnah
MJ	*Modern Judaism*
MT	Masoretic Text
OJL	Franz Rosenzweig, *On Jewish Learning*, edited by Nahum N. Glatzer
OrTr	*Oral Tradition*
RelSRev	*Religious Studies Review*
t.	Tosefta
TmH	Abraham Joshua Heschel, *Torah min Hashamayim B'aspaqlarya shel Hadorot* [in Hebrew]
VT	*Vetus Testamentum*
y.	Jerusalem Talmud
ZAW	*Zeitschrift für die alttestamentliche Wissenschaft*

Revelation and Authority

Introduction: Participatory Theories of Revelation

The relationship between revelation and authority in Judaism has been discussed by scholars, preachers, philosophers, and mystics throughout Jewish history. It has been the subject of commentaries and treatises, poems and sermons, discussions and debates. The chapters that follow examine this relationship from a vantage point that is surprisingly rare. I focus on the biblical texts themselves, especially ones that raise the issue of religious authority while narrating God's act of revelation, and I connect those biblical texts to later Jewish understandings of lawgiving at Sinai. My thesis is a simple one. Many biblical texts that describe the giving of Torah move simultaneously and without contradiction in two directions: they anchor the authority of Jewish law and lore in the revelation at Sinai, but they also destabilize that authority by teaching that we cannot be sure how, exactly, the specific rules found in the Pentateuch relate to God's self-disclosure. On the one hand, these biblical texts insist that duties emerge from the event at Sinai: the religious practices performed by members of the nation that witnessed revelation are matters not of choice but of obligation. These texts ground the law's authority in the divine will, which God deliberately made known to a group of human beings. On the other hand, these texts also problematize the notion of revelation by making their readers unsure as to precisely what occurred at Mount Sinai. These narratives provoke their audience to wonder, did the teachings and laws that result from the event at Sinai come directly from God's mouth, or are they the product of human intermediation and interpretation? These biblical texts suggest that revelation involved active contributions by both God and Israel; revelation was collaborative and participatory.

1

Throughout this book I use the terms "participatory theory of revelation" and "participatory theology" to speak of approaches to revelation that view the Pentateuch (and Jewish tradition generally) as the result of a dialogue between God and Israel. According to the participatory theology, the Pentateuch not only conveys God's will but also reflects Israel's interpretation of and response to that will. This view of revelation puts a premium on human agency and gives witness to the grandeur of a God who accomplishes a providential task through the free will of human subjects under God's authority.[1] We may contrast participatory theologies with a better-known view of revelation, which I term "the stenographic theory of revelation." According to the latter theory, God dictated all the words of the Pentateuch to Moses, and Moses recorded God's words without altering them. In the stenographic theory, all the words of the Pentateuch are God's. In the participatory theory, the wording in the Pentateuch is a joint effort involving heavenly and earthly contributions; or the wording may be an entirely human response to God's real but nonverbal revelation. Especially in the second chapter of this book, I argue that the Pentateuch itself gives voice to both stenographic and participatory theologies of revelation.

The Bible is the first Jewish book that valorizes yet questions revelation, but it is not the last, because certain medieval and modern Jewish thinkers make similar moves. Among modern Jews, this trend is evident in the work of the great German philosopher Franz Rosenzweig (1886–1929), the influential Polish American theologian Abraham Joshua Heschel (1907–1972), and the British scholar and communal leader Louis Jacobs (1920–2006). To some degree, it also evident in the writings of the German philosopher Hermann Cohen (1842–1918), the Romanian British American scholar and communal leader Solomon Schechter (1847–1915), and the French philosophers Emmanuel Levinas (1906–1995) and André Neher (1914–1988). Elements of this trend, we shall see, can be found among medieval Jewish mystics and philosophers, and in classical rabbinic texts of the talmudic era.

That medieval and rabbinic precursors can be found for what is usually thought of as a modern understanding of revelation has been argued by others, especially by Heschel himself in his three-volume masterpiece, *Torah min Hashamayim Be'aspaqlaria shel Hadorot*,[2] and by Yoḥanan Silman in his book *Qol Gadol Velo Yasaf: Torat Yisrael bein Shleimut Lehishtalmut*.[3] More recently, Eran Viezel has argued that several medieval biblical commentators, especially ibn Ezra and Rashbam, regard the wording of the Pentateuch as a mixture of divine and human elements that include not only God's own words but also, and more frequently, Moses's own words. Viezel further maintains that what I call the stenographic theory of revelation is less common among the talmudic rabbis than is generally assumed, and that it became the standard in Jewish thought only starting in the thirteenth century CE.[4] But scholars and theologians have not noticed the ways in which the Bible anticipates later Jewish thinkers who put forth a participatory theology and the extent to which biblical authors themselves probed the connections between revelation and authority. There are two main reasons scholars failed to observe the Bible's subtlety on this matter. First, scholars of Jewish thought and Christian theology tend not to engage in close literary readings of the biblical texts. Rather, they cite biblical verses as background before moving on to their own fields of specialty. (Rosenzweig and Heschel constitute exceptions to this trend, as does Martin Buber, whose view of revelation and authority is very different from the one that concerns me in this book. The most important exception to this trend among modern Christian theologians is Karl Barth.) Second, the complexity of biblical portrayals of lawgiving communicates itself most clearly when we read the Bible as the anthology of ancient Near Eastern texts that it is, and thus see biblical texts as their first audiences in ancient Israel saw them—in other words, when we examine the Bible through the lenses of modern biblical criticism. (By "biblical criticism" I mean the sort of biblical study carried out by professors in modern universities, colleges, and seminaries; I discuss the methods and assumptions of this field in more detail in the chapter that follows.) Theologians, both Jewish and Christian, have tended to shun biblical criticism, regarding it either as inimical or (what is worse) irrelevant to theological concerns. I hope to show, however, that it is precisely when we respect biblical texts enough to go through the labor of re-creating their original contexts that they emerge as religiously relevant to modern readers.[5] The biblical critical analyses I present will help us to discern powerful continuities between the biblical texts that describe revelation and the traditions that follow them.[6]

This book, then, has two topics. It is a book about the Bible, because I present interpretations of biblical passages, and I use those interpretations to reconstruct ancient Israelite attitudes toward religious authority. For this reason the book belongs to the field of biblical scholarship; it grounds close readings in rigorous philology, and it makes a contribution to the history of Israelite religious ideas. At the same time, I attempt to show that the modern theologians I have mentioned were less radical, less original than one might presume, because biblical texts already intimate an approach that leads toward theirs—and here we should recall that in theological discourse, showing a constructive thinker to be unoriginal is high praise. As a study of the connections between revelation and religious authority, this book belongs to the field of modern Jewish thought.[7] This is the case throughout the book, even where I do not engage in lengthy analyses of particular theologians' work. Whenever I interpret a biblical passage or discuss historical background that allows us to understand an ancient Israelite idea more fully, I am also talking implicitly about certain modern thinkers. The proper place of these thinkers in Jewish tradition becomes clear once we achieve a deeper understanding of the biblical material.

More specifically, this book is about the work of Franz Rosenzweig and Abraham Joshua Heschel. It would be possible to expand the scope of this study to treat the other figures I mentioned: Schechter, Jacobs, Neher, Levinas, and Cohen, who, in varied ways, present revelation as dialogical or essentially interpretive in nature. Further, one might examine notions of revelation, tradition, and authority in the work of the nineteenth-century Ḥasidic master Zadok Ha-Kohen, the early twentieth-century mystic and rabbi Abraham Isaac Kook, the mid-twentieth-century ultra-Orthodox leader Isaac Hutner, and the contemporary Israeli religious feminist Tamar Ross. The writings of all four of these thinkers disclose surprising areas of congruence with the approach of Heschel, as well as crucial differences from it. (Ha-Kohen, Kook, Hutner, and Heschel share much in their Eastern European background, especially in the mixture of Ḥasidic and rationalist influences that shaped all four.) I choose, however, to focus on Rosenzweig and Heschel. Their approaches to revelation, authority, and the nature of religious law, we shall see, are especially congruent with many biblical texts. I hope that scholars with more expertise in Jewish philosophy in western Europe and in the intellectual history of Jewish thinkers from Eastern Europe and Israel will delve further into these other connections. Several books could be written on those connections, none of which I am qualified to write. It seems best to limit my discussion to a smaller number of thinkers, lest the book extend beyond my competence, and lest its length render it unreadable.

I have distinguished thus far between two academic fields: biblical studies and Jewish thought. But I argue in this book that the Bible is itself a work of Jewish thought, a repository of ideas and questions that stands in direct continuity with the rabbinic, medieval, and modern texts. Thus, at a more fundamental level, this book has a single topic, not two that are historically linked. As a result, I often bring together what most of my academic colleagues keep separate: over the course of a few pages, I discuss a biblical passage viewed in its ancient Near Eastern context and a medieval philosophical text that attends to a similar idea; in a single paragraph I refer to scholarship by Semitic philologists alongside studies of modern theology. Some of my colleagues may object to this practice, as if I were illegally crossing an intellectual boundary by citing in adjacent endnotes works by scholars who do not attend meetings of the same academic societies and who write for different journals. One of the points I attempt to make in the present work, however, is that the boundaries that divide these fields are inappropriate—not only intellectually inappropriate but also religiously inappropriate. Both the P writers in the Pentateuch and Abraham Joshua Heschel produced works of Torah, and it is entirely right that a student of Torah will discuss them in a single sentence. (I use the term "Torah" not to refer to the Pentateuch or Five Books of Moses, but, as often in Jewish discourse, to refer to Jewish religious teaching, regardless of whether it appears in the Bible or in postbiblical literature. In chapter 4, I return to the varied uses of this term in Jewish culture.) Similarly, close study of a development in medieval philosophy or halakhah (rabbinic law) can allow us to gain a more precise understanding of the multiple voices present in a book from the Bible; consequently, it is both religiously fitting and academically expedient that we compare the medieval and the Iron Age texts. A core supposition of this book is that the work of an Assyriologist (that is, a scholar of ancient Babylonian and Assyrian culture) can help a Jewish or Christian thinker to understand a verse from scripture in a way that is theologically relevant, even as philosophical readers of scripture have a great deal to teach biblical critics. I think that scholars who keep an open mind will find my movement back and forth between disciplines not dizzying but enlightening. The major methodological goal of this book is to reconceive the Bible—and in particular, the Bible as understood by modern biblical critics—as a work of Jewish thought that should be placed in dialogue with medieval and modern works. Thus, this book contributes to what I call dialogical biblical theology, which compares, contextualizes, and contrasts the Bible with postbiblical Jewish tradition. Such a theology can recover biblical voices that were lost or obscured as a consequence of the way biblical books were edited in antiquity, and it places those voices in the longer trajectory of Jewish thought.[8]

In addition to contributing to two areas of study that can be viewed as one, the following chapters engage in two types of discourse. On one level, this is a study in the history of ideas: I attempt to demonstrate an affinity between ancient texts and modern thinkers. On this level, I undertake a descriptive project. But I also attempt a constructive—indeed, a polemical—project: I argue for the authenticity of the theologies of Rosenzweig and Heschel within Jewish tradition. One might view their approaches to religious authority as modern attempts to square a circle, as failed efforts to retrieve some notion of revelation that might validate an ersatz Judaism in the modern West. Heschel once remarked that Spinoza attempted to expand the concept of revelation so as to deny it.[9] One can imagine that some critics might make the same claim about Heschel and Rosenzweig themselves. A critic from the left might argue that these two thinkers display a failure of nerve by not rejecting a traditional notion of revelation the way that Spinoza did; such a critic would claim that Heschel and Rosenzweig do not go far enough. A critic from the right might argue that they go too far and leave behind the traditional concept of revelation. Against these not entirely imaginary critics, I maintain that these two thinkers reformulate and expand a concept of revelation already found in the Bible. Their proposals pick up threads that biblical authors and editors wanted readers to pick up. In fact, as we shall see, biblical authors and editors expended considerable ingenuity weaving those threads into biblical accounts of the events at Sinai.

From all this it becomes clear that I speak not only as a biblical critic or historian of ideas but also as a religious Jew. My goal is not merely to describe and analyze but to defend and advocate. In pursuing this constructive goal, I make a second polemical claim: the biblical texts that problematize revelation nonetheless assert the authority of the laws that emerge from it. As a result, I contend, the covenant that came to be known as the Jewish religion necessarily entails a robust notion of law, so that no Jewish theology can dispense with the concepts of חיוב (ḥiyyuv, duty or obligation) and מצוה (mitzvah, commandment). The notion of legal obligation that emerges from the biblical theology I discuss will be flexible in some respects. It involves a degree of doubt that renders religious practice tentative and searching rather than apodictic and self-confident. It ought to lead to that most important religious virtue, humility, rather than promoting a characteristic less rare among religious people than one would hope, self-righteousness. But the fact of obligation cannot be avoided, and thus I argue that any constructive proposal in Jewish thought that does not embrace these categories is at best imperfectly loyal to the revelation the Bible describes and to the tradition that grows out of it.[10]

This is, then, a book about authenticity. By examining what the Bible says about revelation and hence about its own authority, this study shows that participatory theologies of revelation, the theologies of Rosenzweig and Heschel, come not from Frankfurt or Warsaw or New York, but from Sinai.

In what follows I ask how biblical texts conceive of revelation and hence of their own status.[11] This question leads to an examination of how both they and later Jewish texts understand the relation of scripture to religious traditions not found in biblical texts—in other words, to the question of canon, and thus to the place of the Bible in the wider world of Jewish thought. I begin my treatment of these questions in chapters 2 and 3, where I discuss the status of scripture and law in light of the ways in which biblical, rabbinic, medieval, and modern texts recall the giving of Torah at Mount Sinai. In chapter 2, we will see that similarities between theories of revelation in the Bible and in the work of Rosenzweig and Heschel become evident when one reads the biblical texts with a source-critical eye—that is, when one is open to the claim of modern biblical scholars that the Pentateuch brings together varied and sometimes contradictory documents from ancient Israel. The redactors responsible for the Sinai narratives in the Pentateuch and some of their underlying sources encourage their readers to wonder about the extent to which the texts resulting from revelation are divine in origin and the extent to which their wording is the work of human beings. Postbiblical interpreters from antiquity to modern times react to this encouragement in various ways, some of which culminate in the modern approach to revelation with which we are concerned. In chapter 3, I suggest that some biblical authors conceive of revelation not only as an act in which God conveys something to Israel but also as a process in which Moses translates that something into a human language that the Israelites can understand. Although a theory of prophecy as translation is most clearly spelled out in rabbinic and medieval texts, biblical texts themselves already propose such a theory, though of course they do so in the allusive language and with the implicit rhetoric that typifies speculative thought from the ancient Near East. Chapter 3 further discusses the development of this notion in the work of Heschel and Rosenzweig and its relationship to the law's place in the covenant that is Judaism. These thinkers share with the Pentateuchal sources a pronounced emphasis on that binding authority. The chapter concludes by using ancient Near Eastern notions of authorship to examine whether modern approaches to the composition of the Torah present any real challenge to religious readers of scripture. Together, chapters 2 and 3 attempt to show that a traditional understanding of the authority of Jewish law can emerge from what many people regard as a less traditional or innovative understanding of revelation.

In chapter 4, I argue that the participatory theology of revelation implies that the very category of scripture is a chimera, and that the participatory theology resituates—and, surprisingly, resuscitates—the Bible as a work of tradition. This approach implies that for Judaism there really is no such thing as scripture; there is only tradition, which begins with and includes the Pentateuch, the Prophets, and the Writings. Although works by Rosenzweig and Heschel lead us toward this realization, neither of these thinkers admitted this implication of his own work; indeed, comments by both of them suggest they would be troubled by the downgrading of the Bible that my use of their work suggests. But the conclusion that the Bible is another form of tradition is less unsettling than it appears. By folding scripture into tradition, my proposal in chapter 4 renders modern attacks on scripture far less harmful to Judaism. Further, both the Bible and rabbinic literature work hard to erase, or at least to blur, the boundaries between scripture and tradition. As a result, some central voices within rabbinic tradition undermine the very category of scripture, dissolving texts found in the closed biblical canon into a larger Jewish canon that knows no closure. Thus, the conclusion I reach regarding the status of the Bible is less disruptive than one might suspect. Chapter 4's discussion of Israel's response to revelation as beginning in the Bible but continuing into post-biblical texts raises another central issue in the work of Rosenzweig and Heschel: the question of whether revelation is ongoing throughout Jewish history. I examine that issue in chapter 5. There we shall see that Rosenzweig and Heschel's discussions of this issue contribute to a debate that was already occurring among the various voices found in the Pentateuch. Chapter 5 points out a trajectory that moves from biblical texts, through kabbalistic and Hasidic thought, into the work of our modern theologians. Appreciation of that trajectory deepens our understanding of the theme of temporality in both the ancient and the modern texts.

In chapter 6, I attend to the main constructive teachings suggested by the treatments of revelation and canon found in this book. There I examine what it means to read scripture in light of these treatments, and I argue (against scholars like Brevard Childs, and against Rosenzweig himself) that for a Jewish religious approach to scripture, readings oriented toward the final form of the biblical canon need not take pride of place. On the contrary, the atomistic readings that typify a great deal of biblical criticism are religiously as legitimate as, and sometimes more interesting than, readings that presume a biblical book constitutes a literary whole. I also take a close look at a conclusion that emerges from chapters 2, 3, and 4: to wit, that the canon is imperfect and scripture flawed. This realization, I argue, has weighty and surprisingly positive implications for modern Judaism. In the conclusion, I address the relationship between innovation and continuity in light of the participatory theology of revelation. I examine how the recontextualization of scripture as tradition and the idea of revelation as an eternal event justify the right of Jewish communities deeply committed to covenantal obligation to modify some specifics within the law. By modifying some specifics, contemporary communities and their sages can rejuvenate that law and render it more compatible with the modern world. But the fact of these modifications does not undermine the binding authority of the law itself. In spite of their many differences, all the Pentateuchal sources (J, E, P, and D) agree that the event at Sinai was not merely revelation but lawgiving. While they differ regarding many of the specifics of individual laws and furnish evidence that these specifics developed over time, the Pentateuchal sources speak with one voice in regard to the centrality of divine command in the religion that the event at Sinai created. It follows that my methods and my conclusions are not as liberal as one might be tempted to believe; on the contrary, the approach to sacred texts I lay out in this book undermines certain modern constructions of Judaism and strengthens a highly traditional understanding of what an authentic Judaism demands. I can restate this final point using rabbinic language: this book demonstrates that one can reject the simplest and most common understanding of תורה מן השמים (revelation) without weakening one's commitment to עול מלכות שמים (the yoke of divine sovereignty) and עול מצוות (the yoke of the commandments).

Before turning to close readings of texts that recall and question the revelation at Sinai, I need to explain why, as a religious Jew, I depend not only on traditional Jewish interpreters of the Bible but also on modern critical methods of analysis. In chapter 1, I acknowledge the tensions between biblical criticism and religious exegesis, and I discuss how these modes of analysis differ both in terms of their methods and, more fundamentally, in terms of how they conceive of the Bible. The most crucial differences between biblical critics and many theological interpreters of scripture occur not in the ways they read but in decisions they make before they begin reading at all. Having examined these differences, I go on to suggest why the tension between them need not be a fatal contradiction and how biblical criticism can become useful for a constructive theologian. It is to these foundational matters that we now turn.

1 Artifact or Scripture?

A reader may approach the anthology that is the Hebrew Bible with two very different expectations. Religious Jews and Christians approach the Hebrew Bible as *scripture*—that is, as a document that relates to them at an existential level. Its teachings demand a response, whether in thought or action, through self-definition or participation in a community. It is a sacred text, perhaps deriving from human authors but also connected to a divine source. Biblical critics, in contrast, approach the Hebrew Bible as an *artifact*—that is, as a collection of Northwest Semitic texts from the Iron Age and shortly thereafter. These texts furnish insight into a particular culture that existed near the eastern edge of the Mediterranean over the course of several centuries. It is interesting for the same reasons that any cultural expression produced by human beings is interesting: because it contains attempts by human beings to explore fundamental questions. Some readers, including biblical critics, approach the Hebrew Bible as a particular type of artifact: as a *classic*, a great work that provides a model for a later culture's literature and thought even as it epitomizes the culture that produced it.[1] As one of the foundational documents of Western civilization, the Hebrew Bible sheds light on Western writing and art. It attracts interest from many Jews, because it contains the earliest literary expressions of a nation with whom they identify. A humanistic thinker, a student of Western culture, or a Jew may find the Hebrew Bible to be of vital concern without, however, regarding it as scripture: that is, without attributing to it some ontological status that differentiates it from other cultural artifacts. The ancient and varied traditions of Judaism and Christianity provide habits of reading and ritual that allow people to embrace biblical texts as scripture, and the more recent yet impressively diverse traditions of the modern university supply tools for understanding these texts as artifact.

The difference between these two conceptions of the Bible can also be seen as a question of how the audience of these texts is defined. For many biblical critics, it is an axiom that the Hebrew Bible does not address those of us who live in the modern world, or even those who lived in the medieval world. These scholars tell us that the texts found in the Hebrew Bible addressed a group of people who lived in certain parts of the Near East during the first millennium BCE. People who are committed to reading the Bible as scripture, however, remind us that this anthology defines its own audience more expansively: it speaks to the family of Abraham, Isaac, and Jacob throughout the generations.[2] From the first mention of those characters in Genesis, the Hebrew Bible is concerned with their progeny (see, for example, Genesis 12.2). Passages throughout the Hebrew Bible were composed, proclaimed, preserved, and redacted in order to address a whole nation that exists through time and whose future members are a special concern of these texts.[3] As a result, those of us who regard ourselves as being, in one way or another, the seed of Abraham, Isaac, and Jacob have an obligation to read the Bible as speaking to us. Now, fulfilling that obligation may be easy for people who reject the findings of modern biblical criticism—that is, for people who are ignorant, or who strive to become ignorant, of the abundant evidence amassed by biblical critics that these texts first of all addressed people living in the Iron Age, the Persian era, and the Hellenistic era.[4] But fulfilling the obligation to listen to these texts as scripture is more difficult for those of us who accept the methods and conclusions of modern scholarship. Members of this second group have to confront the question of how these ancient documents, written in the highlands of Canaan and in a diaspora of people who originated there, address us, for conceiving the Hebrew Bible as addressing us in addition to its original audience is essential to reading it as scripture.[5] Some critics might argue that my proposal to read these texts as addressing us today requires an anachronism, but the anthology itself encourages that anachronism: as long as the family (families?) of Abraham, Isaac, and Jacob exist, the text intends to speak to them.

For people who regard themselves as part of that group and who furthermore do not ignore what modern scholarship has discovered, it is inevitable that the Hebrew Bible must be read both as artifact and as scripture. Moreover, it will not do to read the Bible serially, sometimes as artifact and at other times as scripture. Such a choice would require one to partition oneself, so that one has a secular mind and a religious soul coexisting uneasily in a single body but not communicating with each other. In contrast, scripture commands the people it addresses to serve God בכל לבבך ובכל נפשך ובכל מאדך (Deuteronomy 6.5)—with all one's mind, with all one's soul, with all that one is. A person whose intellect believes that biblical criticism makes valid claims but whose religious self pretends otherwise renders service to God that this verse regards as fragmented and defective. An intellectually honest person addressed by the Hebrew Bible today must read the Bible at once as artifact and as scripture.

Is this project in fact possible? Can the Hebrew Bible, understood as artifact, continue to be read as scripture? One can answer this question only from a particular place. Among the communities that regard the Hebrew Bible as scripture, there has never been a universal notion of what scripture is—that is, of how it functions in the community, how it should be read, or how it can be used in ritual. While scholars have identified a shifting set of features that typify what has been termed scripture in religions throughout the world,[6] all conceptions of scripture are local; they are specific, in the case of the anthology with which we are concerned, to a particular type of Judaism or Christianity.[7] Consequently, one cannot discuss how artifact relates to scripture generically; one can discuss their relationship only in a given tradition. In this book, I discuss the Hebrew Bible as a Jewish scripture, and I speak from an unabashedly local perspective. (Consequently, from this point on, I refer to the anthology simply as "the Bible," rather than using the neutral, nondenominational term common in academic settings, "the Hebrew Bible.")* To speak from this local perspective, however, does not mean that the discussion involves only Jewish voices. On the contrary, just

---

* Scholars in the contemporary academy use the term *Hebrew Bible* to refer to the anthology that Christians call "the Old Testament" and Jews call "the Bible" (or, in Hebrew, *Miqra* or *Tanakh*). The term *Old Testament* causes some contemporary Christians discomfort and some Jews offense, but for no good reason. Only in modern Western culture, with its idolization of youth, would one think that the word *Old* implies some insult to Jewish scripture. In fact *Old* in the term *Old Testament* primarily means "venerable," not "antiquated." (The assertion in the New Testament's Epistle to the Hebrews 8.13 that the Old Testament is obsolete is exceptional in Christianity. After all, by preserving these texts and encouraging their use in study and prayer, Christian believers since antiquity have demonstrated their confidence that the Old Testament remains a vital source of religious guidance.) On the integrity of the use of the term *Old Testament* by Christians, see Seitz, *Word*, 61–74, and the remarks of Harrington and Brettler in Brettler, Enns, and Harrington, *Bible and the Believer*, 82 and 119, respectively.

as Christian readers will, I hope, find what I have to say stimulating, useful, and instructive, so too I find contributions of non-Jewish scholars relevant and enlightening. Consequently, I engage work by Christian biblical exegetes and theologians, as well as work by scholars of the Bible and the ancient Near East who might be described as post-Christian or ex-Christian.

This book, then, situates itself in two academic fields, one nondenominational and descriptive, the other parochial and constructive: biblical criticism[8] and modern Jewish theology.[9] In this respect it departs from the model envisioned by most of the scholars who have called themselves biblical theologians in the past two centuries. With a few exceptions, these scholars have pretended that their work eschewed confessional stances.[10] In fact, however, these earlier attempts at biblical theology usually perpetuated Protestant readings of Hebrew scripture. As a result they strike non-Protestant readers as self-contradictory and, insofar as they imply that only Protestant readings are loyal to the text, offensive.[11] Paradoxically, biblical theology of a decidedly denominational nature can make contributions not only to the denomination from which it emerges but also to the wider guild of religious studies and to the construction of creed or identity in other denominations.[12] The local context within which I read the Bible helps me uncover connections between biblical Israel and postbiblical Judaism that turn out to be suggestive outside Judaism as well. Without the local context, these connections might otherwise have gone unnoticed. Hence this study of Jewish scripture will open up unexplored features of Israelite thought that will interest not only people who want to read the Bible as Jewish scripture but also those who approach it as Christian scripture, as well as those who analyze the Bible as artifact and as classic.

In the chapters that follow, I propose an approach that allows modern Jews to study the Bible in good faith as both scripture and artifact. A deeper understanding of the Bible as artifact, we shall see, can trouble yet enrich our embrace of the Bible as scripture. Before embarking on this project, I need to explain why the tension between artifactual reading and scriptural reading exists and to introduce some core terms and concepts that will be helpful throughout the book.

Artifact Opposed to Scripture

The core question underlying the distinction between artifact and scripture involves the Bible's sanctity: does the Bible have a special status that sets it apart from other texts? This question can be helpfully rephrased: Is the Bible in some way unique, or at least essentially different from works of literature and culture produced throughout the world? Is it entirely the product of human writers, or does it have an origin that goes beyond this world? For most ancient and medieval readers, both Jewish and Christian, the answers to these questions were obvious. The Bible was sacred because it came from heaven. The words of the Five Books of Moses, according to most classical Jewish thinkers, were composed not by Moses or any human beings but by God. The remaining books of the Bible were also of heavenly origin, in their content, if not their precise phrasing. The question of whether the anthology was an artifact or scripture could not have arisen for these readers.[13]

This consensus began to break down in seventeenth-century Europe. Several freethinkers (for example, the philosophers Thomas Hobbes and Baruch Spinoza, followed a century later by David Hume) began to question whether the Bible really was sacred—literarily unique and stemming from a heavenly source. In their wake, scholars, most of them Protestant, primarily in France and Germany, investigated the origins of these texts, and they doubted that they were in fact literary unities at all, much less divinely written and perfect ones. The Book of Genesis, they showed, contains what seem to be earlier works, which contradicted one another on a number of narrative details. The author (or better, editor) of Genesis had brought together these older documents without reconciling the contradictions among them. Since the author-editor was relying on older documents that contradicted one another and could not be authoritatively reconciled, it seemed clear that this author-editor was not an omniscient, otherworldly being. These earliest scholars presumed that the author-editor in question was Moses, but it was not long before scholars realized this method of analyzing the origins of Genesis also worked for Exodus, Leviticus, Numbers, and Deuteronomy, which told the story of Moses himself. Once it was clear that the whole Pentateuch was composite in origin, the notion that the author-editor of this work was Moses became untenable; after all, Moses would not have needed to rely on multiple and contradictory sources to narrate recent events in which he was the major character.

Scholarship on the origins of the Pentateuch (which is often referred to as source criticism, because it attempts to discover the sources from which the Pentateuch has been put together) developed slowly from the seventeenth through the nineteenth centuries. Scholars put forth several theories that delineate how many sources there are, which verses and chapters belong to which sources, how these sources relate to one another, and how they were put together. The most famous of these theories, known as the Documentary Hypothesis, crystallized in the mid-nineteenth century. According to this hypothesis, there are four main sources within the Torah, which biblical scholars label J, E, P, and D. For our immediate purpose, it will matter only a little whether, as some proponents of the Documentary Hypothesis maintain, these sources can be further split into additional subsources (J_1 and J_2; a subset of P to be labeled "H"), and whether, as some speculate, some texts in the Pentateuch are to be attributed to sources or supplements in addition to J, E, P, and D. Similarly, it is of relatively little import whether, as many scholars in the late twentieth century proposed, an alternate theory better explains the textual evidence in the Pentateuch in its present form—for example, a theory according to which the Torah grew from some original kernels to which a series of supplements were added.[14] What matters is that modern scholars explain the origin of the Pentateuch not only in a manner that differs from classical Jewish and Christian teachings but in a manner that casts doubt on its unity and its connection with an omniscient and perfect being. (One question that will matter theologically, we shall see later, is the attitude of the Pentateuch's editors to their sources; at the proper time, we will delve further into that question.)

Many Jews feel that biblical critics attack the root of the Jewish religion in asserting that Genesis, Exodus, Leviticus, Numbers, and Deuteronomy are not books at all but a mélange of originally separate, post-Mosaic, and to some degree contradictory texts. Similar theories were developed in regard to other books, showing, for example, that Isaiah could not have written all of the Book of Isaiah and that Jeremiah's original prophecies were supplemented by various texts that later scribes or editors attributed to him.[15] Claims of this type regarding the Prophets and Writings (the second and third sections of the Bible) also caused discomfort among many Jews, although these latter claims are not usually perceived as attacking the root of the Jewish religion. But the discovery that the laws found in Exodus through Deuteronomy were not in any literal sense Mosaic and the realization that the Pentateuch contains contradictions and thus imperfection were greeted with dismay by many Jews over the past two centuries. The Five Books of Moses, the very core of Jewish scripture, were not put together, much less written, by Moses; and, since they contradicted one another, they could not have one author, much less One Author.

As Baruch Schwartz and others show, modern Jews have focused their scriptural anxieties especially on theories pertaining to the authorship of biblical texts.[16] In addition, some Jews have regarded biblical criticism as unnerving because it casts doubt on the historical reliability of biblical texts. This issue, however, has been much more pressing for Christians—especially modern Protestants—than for Jews.[17] The extent of this second challenge for believers who are not overly concerned with minutiae has been vastly exaggerated. Contrary to what one sometimes reads in the popular press or hears from less learned pulpits, there are no archaeological or historical reasons to doubt the core elements of the Bible's presentation of Israel's history: namely, that the ancestors of the Israelites included an important group who came from Mesopotamia; that at least some Israelites were enslaved to Egyptians and were surprisingly rescued from Egyptian bondage;[18] that they experienced a revelation that played a crucial role in the formation of their national, religious, and ethnic identity; that they settled down in the hill country of the land of Canaan at the beginning of the Iron Age, around 1300 or 1200 BCE; that they formed kingdoms there a few centuries later, around 1000 BCE; and that these kingdoms were eventually destroyed by Assyrian and Babylonian armies. To be sure, the fact that there are no reasons to doubt these basic elements of the biblical story line does not prove that one *should* believe them, either; my point here is simply to alert my readers to the specious nature of claims that any of these elements is contradicted or even undermined by what archaeologists have or have not found. People who put forward claims of this sort seem to be unaware of the evidence actually available; even more importantly, they are unschooled about the nature of the evidence—that is, about what the evidence can and cannot prove.

To my mind, however, biblical criticism's greatest challenge to religious belief stems from the ways in which the historical approach of biblical criticism has undermined theological concerns. This has resulted in what John Barton terms "the death of scripture," at least for many of those who accept historical criticism. (Barton goes on to argue cogently that historical criticism need not have this effect for believers with a serious, nuanced, and flexible faith.)[19] Similarly, Michael Legaspi (in a book whose title summarizes its thesis: *The Death of Scripture and the Rise of Biblical Studies*) shows that German biblical scholars of the nineteenth century "seemed to delight in creating scientifically reconstructed alternatives to the familiar salvation history (*Heilsgeschichte*) of the Christian tradition; these allowed them and their students to perceive more clearly the political dynamics, historical forces, and human contours of the ancient societies that produced the Bible."[20] A great many biblical scholars, for example, interpret almost all the laws and narratives in the P source of the Pentateuch as motivated by the desire to glorify the Aaronide Priestly caste responsible for P. They see the Book of Deuteronomy as ministering to the economic needs and social prestige of the Levitical caste from which Deuteronomy's authors are thought to have stemmed. According to an extreme but common version of this type of interpretation (which we scholars of religious studies term *reductionism*), the Priestly texts and Deuteronomy are not really about religion or God at all; they merely encode social, political, and economic claims of specific groups of people. This encoding is all the more effective precisely because the audiences of these works *thought* they were about God; indeed, even their authors may have believed they were about God. But the modern reductionist scholar claims to see through the delusions that ensnared both the authors and premodern readers.[21] By providing alternate interpretations of historical events narrated in the Bible, modern scholars relativize the Bible's own explanations: where the Bible tells us, for example, that God brought the Persian emperor Cyrus to punish Babylon and restore Judean exiles to their land (see Ezra 1.1–11; 2 Chronicles 36.22–23; Isaiah 44.28–45.6), the modern historian of biblical Israel may speak of geographic, economic, or perhaps even environmental factors that led to the decline of Babylonian power and the rise of Persian hegemony over the Near East. Biblical criticism allows (or requires) historical and natural forces to displace divine causality.[22]

Attention to all these forces yielded a sense that the Bible is less than one thought: rather than transmitting heavenly wisdom, it reflects the political, social, economic, and psychological contingencies of this world. An anthology that contradicts itself, that serves the ideological needs of particular groups or individuals, and that puts forward questionable interpretations of history is, in the eyes of many readers, clearly a collection of literary artifacts, not scripture. The Bible as illuminated by historical scholarship shrank into a motley accumulation of historically dependent, culturally relative textual scraps.[23]

Severing the Bible from Judaism

The Bible's role as Jewish scripture suffered a further blow at the hands of modern biblical criticism. Some modern biblical critics attempted to sever, or at least weaken, the Bible's connection to the Jewish religion and the Jewish people.[24] The goals behind this move are varied, and not in all cases objectionable. They stem not only from the ill-disguised anti-Judaism of some biblical critics but also from scholars' admirable determination to achieve historical distance from their subject matter and a desire to avoid anachronistic interpretations. The very core of modern biblical criticism consists of an attempt to understand biblical texts as their first audiences understood them in ancient Israel. If we are to see a biblical text as ancient Israelites saw it, we cannot automatically accept classical Jewish or Christian interpretations of the text, since these interpretations were composed centuries or millennia after the texts came into being. Just because Rashi or Augustine said that this passage or that verse has a particular meaning, it does not follow that the original audience of the text understood it that way.[25] Rather than seeing the Bible through the eyes of the rabbis or the church fathers, modern biblical critics attempt to see the Bible in the context of its own cultural world. That is why we biblical critics spend so much time in graduate school learning languages like Ugaritic and Akkadian and immersing ourselves in the cultures of ancient Canaan, Babylonia, and Assyria. We immerse ourselves in order to achieve literary competence so that we can read texts from the ancient Near East sympathetically, noticing what ancient readers are likely to have noticed and reacting as they reacted.[26]

To achieve this goal (and skeptical postmodern thinkers might be surprised at how spectacularly successful these attempts are, to judge from consistent patterns of insight this literary competence produces), Jewish and Christian scholars must make a considerable effort to forget what their traditions teach them about a given text. To take a famous example, Western readers of scripture have long assumed that the story of Adam and Eve in Genesis 2–3 describes the origin of sin and humanity's fall from grace. This reading, already known in some ancient Jewish sources (Sirah 25.24; 2 Baruch 17.3, 19.8, 23.4, 54.19, and 56.6; 4 Ezra 7.11–15), became standard in Christianity and hence in Western culture generally as a result of the influence of Paul and other New Testament writers who champion it (see, for example, Romans 5.12–19; 1 Corinthians 15.20–23; 1 Timothy 2.13–14).[27] Yet there is reason to believe that authors and audiences in ancient Israel did not find any idea of original sin or a fall in the Eden story. In spite of the eagerness of biblical narrators to label certain actions sinful, Genesis 3 contains none of the many words that mean "sin" in biblical Hebrew.[28] On the contrary, some modern scholars, including James Barr, Moshe Green-berg, and Michael Fishbane, have argued cogently that the story involves an ascent to moral agency rather than (or, as much as) a fall from grace.[29] Others, especially Bruce Naidoff and Carol Meyers, claim that the story is not a rumination on the existential nature of humanity generally but an attempt to explain and justify agricultural conditions prevalent in the highlands of Canaan in the Iron Age.[30] The job of the biblical critic is to find interpretations of this sort, which seem new to us but in fact may represent much older understandings consonant with the Bible's original, Near Eastern setting.

Similarly, texts that classical Jewish commentators understand in one way are read entirely differently by modern biblical scholars. Dozens of verses in Psalms and Isaiah are read by classical Jewish interpreters as look-ing forward to a Messiah. The rabbis understand these verses to predict the arrival at the end of days of a descendant of King David who will re-establish a monarchy in the Land of Israel. Such verses can be found in Isaiah 9–11, as well as Psalms 2 and 72, to name but a few of the most fa-miliar texts (see Midrash Tehillim to these psalms, as well as b. Sanhedrin 96b–99a).[31] But many biblical critics doubt that these verses refer to the reestablishment of Davidic monarchy or to the complex of messianic ideas widespread in postbiblical Jewish thought. Rather, these verses pertain to the pre-exilic Davidic monarchy. According to this interpretation, texts like Isaiah 9–11 and Psalms 2 and 72 predict that the Davidic dynasty will never fall. For the authors of these texts there was no imaginable reason for it to be reestablished.[32]

The gulf between traditional rabbinic interpretations and biblical criti-cal ones is especially clear in regard to legal texts. Exodus 21.2–6 and Deu-teronomy 15.12–18 contain divergent laws requiring Hebrew slaves to be set free after six years of service. In spite of their differences on important de-tails (for example, whether female slaves can benefit from this right), both laws allow slaves to renounce their right to freedom and instead to become slaves to their master "forever" (לעולם)—that is, for all their lives. Leviticus 25.39–43 also addresses the situation of Israelites sold into the service of a fellow Israelite, but it does so in a very different way. This passage states that Israelites have the right to go free not after their sixth year of service but in the Jubilee year—that is, the last year of a nationally standardized fifty-year cycle, regardless of when that year falls in one's term of service. Leviticus 25 makes no provision for an Israelite to renounce this right. Rabbinic law harmonizes these laws by asserting that the word לעולם in Exodus 21.6 does not have its normal meaning of "forever" but here intends "until the Jubilee year" (see Mekhilta deRabbi Yishmael, Neziqin §2; b. Qiddushin 15a, 21b and parallels). This reading may seem strained, but to a reader for whom it is axiomatic that the Bible does not contradict itself, it may very well be inevitable: if we know that the Bible contains no self-contradictions, then לעולם in Exodus 21.6 cannot mean "forever," and it must mean something else. For biblical critics, however, the rabbinic interpretation of these verses and the axioms on which it is based have no authority. Biblical critics believe that one part of the Bible can contradict another, because they were written by different authors. (In the case of Exodus 21, Deuteronomy 15, and Leviticus 25, the texts stem from E, D, and P [more specifically, the H supplement to P], respectively). Instead biblical critics endeavor to read these passages in their own cultural contexts. In fact varied laws concerning the manumission of slaves are known from other ancient Near Eastern law codes (for example, *Laws of Lipit-Ishtar* §§14, 25–26, *Laws of Ḥammurapi* §§117–20, 280). Consequently, it is not surprising to find variations on the theme of manumission in ancient Israel as well.[33]

In short, a fundamental goal of the modern scholarly interpretation of the Bible is to distinguish between what the Bible says and what the classical rabbis and the church fathers say the Bible says. In chapter 4, I address the extent to which the differences between classical and modern interpretations must produce tensions for religious Jews. For the moment, I want to note that many biblical scholars expanded this goal of distinguishing between the Bible and classical Jewish interpretation of the Bible. These scholars went on to distinguish between the Bible and Judaism altogether, insisting that the Bible is not really a Jewish book at all. Assuming an either-or model of textual identity, they asserted that since the Bible is an ancient Near Eastern book, it cannot also be a Jewish book. Many biblical critics, first Christians and subsequently Jews, created a firewall between biblical religion and Jewish culture, between Israel and Judaism.[34] In their writing and even more in their teaching, they maintain that it is illegitimate to use rabbinic lenses to look at the Bible, that it is perverse to think about the Bible in terms of classical Jewish ideas or values.[35] This emphasis among some scholars on discontinuity between the Bible and Judaism is not really new; it is not an invention of the modern world. It is a new form of ancient and medieval supersessionism—that is, the idea (repudiated by many modern Christians, most famously and magisterially by the Catholic Church at the Second Vatican Council[36]) that with the emergence of Christianity, the Jewish people are no longer the covenantal community witnessed to and created by the Bible; rather, the church has replaced the Jews as the true Israel and the true inheritor of the Bible. What is bizarre, in light of this fact, is that so many Jewish biblical critics have bought into what we might call the firewall mentality.[37]

While the idea of the firewall is applied especially to Judaism, it is possible to apply this sort of thinking to Christianity, as well, and at a less formal level it is sometimes applied to both religions. When applied to both postbiblical traditions, this sort of thinking is not specifically anti-Jewish. But it is, at least in effect, anti-religious in the sense that it deprives both religions of scripture.[38] The effect, especially on clergy who have studied in modern seminaries, can be devastating. Several generations of liberal Protestant and Jewish clergy have gone forth to their pulpits convinced that anything of a religious nature they might say about scripture was probably wrong, and that any attempt to relate scripture to their congregants' lives would be anachronistic, naive, and intellectually dishonest.[39] The effect on Protestants may have been the most severe; Jews and Catholics who are deprived of scripture still have a robust tradition on which to base their religious beliefs and practices, but undermining scripture in a community in which *sola scriptura* is a byword leaves the religious believer dangerously adrift.

In either form, anti-Jewish or anti-religious, the firewall mentality stresses that the Bible is an ancient Near Eastern artifact and that Judaism relates little to its original meanings. It is not surprising, then, that most traditionalist Jews view biblical criticism—that is, the artifactual mode of reading the Bible—as inimical to Judaism. Conversely, there are modern Jews who, having embraced modern methods of analyzing the Bible, find it impossible to see the Bible as Jewish scripture. (More precisely, they do not see it as scripture, and some may not even see it as Jewish.) Both these groups assume that the Bible cannot be both artifact and scripture: either it is subject to methods of study appropriate for a historically contingent product of the Iron Age, or it is an ontologically unique composition to which normal models of interpretation and analysis do not apply.

Modern approaches to studying the Bible have done much to undermine the Bible's claim to a status that sets it apart from other products of human culture. As a result, the Bible's claim to be a sacred text presents a quandary for Jews who are open to historically oriented, academic ways of studying Judaism. Because they are not quite able to regard the Bible as revealed or inspired in the manner it was (and is) for premodern forms of Judaism, many such Jews tend to regard this anthology as a historical artifact, as a classic, or as an object of nostalgia. Their relationship with the Bible is ethnic and national in nature; it may also be intellectual and humanistic; but it is not religious. Jews who subscribe to this approach do not connect the Bible with God, nor do they use it to connect themselves to God. They may accord these texts an honored place as the oldest literature of the Jewish nation and an important role in Jewish secular culture, but their conception of the Bible does not allow for a serious form of Jewish religiousness, for it no longer has any revealed status.[40] Other modern or postmodern readers attempt to forge a religious relationship with the Bible by temporarily renouncing their own historical consciousness so that they can read the Bible with a sort of feigned naïveté. For proponents of this option, attending to the Bible as artifact would preclude attending to it as scripture. Consequently, they may decide that the findings of modern biblical scholarship have to be denied in order to save the Bible as religiously relevant, or that they have to be ignored. In the latter case, they turn off their ability to think critically and their knowledge of history whenever they activate their religious identity. This option is deeply problematic, because it proposes to build Jewish belief on a foundation of bad faith and erects a barrier that separates truth from religion.[41]

The decision to renounce one's historical consciousness and pretend that the findings of biblical criticism do not exist is problematic for another reason. It reads not only the biblical critic out of the ongoing formulation of Jewish thought, but—more troublingly—the first Jews as well. Jewish thought is famously dialogical in nature, focusing less on a conclusion one may reach regarding a given question and more on the process in which one learns from revered figures who have addressed it. Whether one agrees with, say, the divergent opinions of Maimonides or Isaac Luria regarding השגחה פרטית (the extent to which divine providence attends to individual human beings) is less important in Jewish tradition than studying the issue in the writings of these thinkers. If dialogue and debate, talmudic שקלא וטריא, provide the proper model for Jewish theologizing,[42] then the participants seated at the table should include not only the postmodernist thinker, the neo-Kantian philosopher, the mystical pietist, and the mishnaic sage. Room must be made for ancient Israelites as well. Moreover, those Israelites must not be limited to the late figures who edited older texts into the biblical books as we know them. They must also include the authors whose writings are embedded within the final edition of the canon, and perhaps also the oral tradents who stand behind those authors. To exclude the findings of biblical criticism from modern Jewish thought, however disturbing they may be, is also to exclude the first Jews and to acquiesce to the supersessionism that separates the Bible from Judaism. It is precisely these Israelites whose voices are recovered by modern biblical scholarship.

Both Artifact and Scripture

In the chapters that follow, I suggest how the Bible as recovered by biblical critics can serve as scripture for contemporary Judaism. Further, I propose a specifically theological approach to the Jewish Bible, which investigates the correlations between the Bible and the religions it produced and the ways that the Bible and later religious thought challenge, nuance, correct, and enrich one another.[43] Surprisingly, these goals remain relatively rare even among religiously oriented Jewish biblical scholars, and they tend not to be explicit when they do appear among them.[44] Attempting to integrate the conclusions of biblical criticism into a constructive theological project, to be sure, can seem daunting or counterintuitive. As Uriel Simon has noted, "The late, foreign, and sometimes hostile origin of biblical criticism renders it a difficulty for an authentic religious system, but this is a psychological problem, not a problem of principle; it is possible and necessary to overcome it."[45] My method for overcoming this problem involves two strategies.

First, I read biblical texts in order to see what they have to contribute to our own discussions about authority, revelation, tradition, and canon. When addressing these issues, biblical texts do not articulate propositions in the explicit manner of Western thinkers. Rather, they speak in the concrete terms that typify most ancient Near Eastern speculative thought, employing a rhetoric that is nonsystematic though self-consistent.[46] Thus, sensitivity to ancient Near Eastern modes of thought and expression will enable us to notice how biblical texts explore issues that are at the core of modern theological discussions.

Second, I emphasize a broad sweep of Jewish thought that connects biblical and later Jewish literature. This broad sweep emerges, paradoxically, when we utilize methods that highlight discontinuity and diversity within the Bible itself to find multiple levels of authorship and redaction within biblical books. Because these methods discover a variety of voices in biblical texts, they allow us to notice predecessors of postbiblical thought that were less obvious or altogether hidden before the rise of historical criticism. It follows that by atomizing biblical texts, biblical critics also renew them. Unlike many works of biblical theology in the twentieth century, the theologically oriented Jewish reading of scripture I propose does not privilege work of the editors who created biblical books by combining older documents. Rather, it creates space for those who composed the older documents—for J and D and P and others whose voices are mere echoes in the first written texts of the Jewish people. This reading reveals surprising connections and unites long-lost soul mates. The most contemporary discussion of Jewish theology will come into focus precisely when we look to the most distant interlocutors. This dialogue between modern and ancient religious authorities becomes possible when we insist, in an unfashionably historicist manner, that modern biblical scholarship allows one to hear forgotten voices of Jewish creativity and consequently that biblical critics must be placed alongside the familiar rabbinic interpreters of the Middle Ages and the classical midrashic collections. By creating a dialogue among these ancient, medieval, and modern interpreters, I hope to show those familiar with any one type of literature on which I rely that the others are just as interesting. Modern historicist methods of reading that religiously oriented readers often eschew help us recover dichotomies of great interest from a theological point of view. It follows that critical scholarship can serve as a powerful tool for modern theologians, because it resurrects forgotten voices of religious creativity from ancient Israel.

A great deal of historical critical study of the Bible devotes itself to recovering divergent voices from multiple authors in texts most religious readers have regarded as unities. The goal of many modern biblical scholars is to undo the binding that holds the anthology together. But my use of historical criticism focuses on continuity in Jewish culture from the Bible onward. I show that the dichotomies modern critics discern in biblical texts generated, or at least foreshadow, similar dichotomies in rabbinic and medieval Jewish literature. By linking diachronically oriented biblical criticism with the study of the history of exegesis, this book delineates trajectories that link pre-redacted Israelite traditions to postbiblical Jewish literature. If we are willing to pay the price of losing the Bible's binding, we will be more than amply rewarded by a renewed ability to see the essential unity of scripture and tradition.

I use modern academic methods, then, to argue against the attempt to separate the Bible from Judaism. Thus, I return to a goal that motivated some Jewish scholars from the very beginning of the modern study of Judaism. Here it is worth pausing to recall a comment made in the late 1800s by Solomon Schechter, one of the most influential modern scholars of classical Judaism, in an essay he wrote about Leopold Zunz, the mid-nineteenth-century scholar who is regarded as the founder of the modern study of rabbinic literature and Jewish liturgy. Alluding to the neo-supersessionist firewall mentality I described earlier, Schechter noted that among German Protestant scholars,

> the Talmud and the Midrashim were considered as a perversion of the Pentateuch and the books of the Prophets, and the Jewish liturgy a bad paraphrase of the Psalms. . . . To destroy these false notions, to bridge over this seemingly wide and deep gap, to restore the missing links between the Bible and tradition, to prove the continuity and development of Jewish thought through history, to show their religious depth and their moral and ennobling influence, to teach us how our own age with all its altered notions might nevertheless be a stage in the continuous development of Jewish ideals and might make these older thoughts a part of its own progress—this was the great task to which Zunz devoted his life.[47]

As David Fine has noted, it is surely no coincidence that these words describe Schechter himself; the essay on Zunz is in part a disguised autobiography.[48] Schechter's statement summarizes a central goal of the book you are currently reading as well.[49] This is the case even though Schechter would have regarded my embrace of Pentateuchal source criticism with surprise or perhaps dismay; for him the method was inseparable from anti-Judaism that wore an academic disguise.[50] By the end of this book, I hope to show that the more regrettable motives of some source critics can be separated from the method itself. Appreciation for the variety of voices within the Pentateuch can enhance a traditionalist attitude toward scripture: it shows us how the Bible is part of Jewish tradition and how it engenders Jewish tradition. The thematic leitmotif of my work, then, is continuity, its surprising modes and its unexpected manifestations.

2 What Happened at Sinai? Maximalist and Minimalist Approaches

In the previous chapter, we saw that the modern critical study of the Bible poses several challenges to the idea that the Bible is sacred. These challenges are largely literary, philological, and historical in nature, and biblical scholars, theologians, and historians of religion have discussed them at length. But another, even more important challenge to the status of scripture requires our consideration. Some modern readers become aware of the Bible's human origin because of those biblical passages that cannot be reconciled with a God who is merciful or just, much less a deity who is both. The Bible appears to be all too human not only because it has trouble deciding whether Noah took two or seven of the clean animals onto the ark, but more importantly because it describes a God who sweeps away the innocent along with the guilty—if not in the Noah story (which tells us that all humans other than Noah were blameworthy), then surely in the Exodus narrative, in which God slays firstborn Egyptians who had no say in Pharaoh's labor policies. Even more disturbingly, the Bible commands humans, if only in a few specific cases, to imitate God in disregarding justice and mercy: all Amalekites, even children, are to be slaughtered (Deuteronomy 25.17–19); genocide or expulsion is the fate of all Canaanites who do not submit to Israel (for example, Deuteronomy 7 and 20).[1]

It matters only a little that rabbinic commentators through the ages have ruled that the laws regarding Canaanites applied only to the time of Joshua and not in perpetuity, so that nobody living after Joshua's era has the right, much less the obligation, to apply them. (According to rabbinic law, the category of "Canaanite" has not existed since the days of the Assyrian emperor Sennacherib, and thus all laws applying to Canaanites are void;

see, for example, m. Yadayim 4:4, t. Qiddushin 5:6, b. Berakhot 28a, b. Yoma 54a; Maimonides, *Mishneh Torah*, "Laws of Kings," 5:4.)[2] Similarly, a person who wants to regard the Bible as scripture receives only a little comfort from the suggestion that these laws don't mean what they seem to mean but are to be construed metaphorically. The Talmud proposes this idea when it grapples with the disturbing law in Deuteronomy 21.18–21 that allows parents to execute a rebellious son. In b. Sanhedrin 71a and t. Sanhedrin 11:2, the rabbis maintain that this law is in the Torah only so that we can receive a reward for interpreting it away.[3] This well-known teaching does not fully solve the moral problem that passages such as these raise. The fact remains that the Torah at the very least gives the appearance of encouraging cruelty and injustice in these verses (or, in the case of the Canaanites, the Bible appears to have done so for a single generation). These texts diminish the ability of many religious people to accept the notion that the Bible in its entirety was composed by God: a just and merciful God would not write a Torah that seems unjust, even in a small number of passages, even on a surface level.

Modern scholars describe these passages as "troubling texts," and they have received considerable attention in recent decades.[4] For many contemporary readers, the Bible's pervasive sexism and its attitude toward homosexuality pose similar problems. An example appears at the very end of the Decalogue, in which a man's wife seems to be classified along with other types of property, such as his house and (another troubling text!) his slaves. Some moderns maintain that the Bible is less sexist than other literature of the ancient Near East and more compassionate to slaves; it presents, we are told, an advance, and the direction in which this advance moves embodies the scriptural teaching relevant for contemporary readers. I am not positive that Hebrew scripture is consistently less sexist than most Mesopotamian or Canaanite literature; in any event, even if it is, there is no denying that almost all biblical texts that touch on the subject of gender are thoroughly patriarchal, though rarely downright misogynist, in outlook.

It is the presence of texts such as these, more than the existence of the contradictions noticed by source critics, that precludes me from believing in the traditional Jewish and Christian view of the Bible's revelatory origin.[5] Moral issues rather than historical-philological ones pose the most disturbing challenge to the Bible's status as scripture. I am not alone in this respect. To many a modern Jew, the Tanakh is a hallowed book but also an embarrassing one. However much we revere it, we are aware of its human side. How can a contemporary Jewish theology come to terms with obedience to the tradition based on this text along with the need to construct correctives to it? How can a theology express both love of Torah and readiness to study it critically and with an open mind?

An influential resource for answering these questions can be sought in the stream of twentieth-century Jewish thought associated with Franz Rosenzweig and Abraham Joshua Heschel. These thinkers have suggested that the Bible, along with all of Jewish tradition, is a response to God's act of revelation. The content we find in the Bible mixes divine and human elements. Alternatively, God's act of revelation may not have conveyed specific content, so that all the words and laws we find in the Bible are human interpretations of revelation.[6] Heschel conveys ideas of this sort repeatedly, especially in *God in Search of Man: A Philosophy of Judaism*:

> Judaism is based upon a minimum of revelation and a maximum of interpretation, upon the will of God and upon the understanding of Israel. . . . There is a partnership of God and Israel in regard to both the world and the Torah: He created the earth and we till the soil; He gave us the text and we refine and complete it.

He writes elsewhere:

> As a report about revelation the Bible itself is *a midrash*.

And:

> The Bible contains not only words of the prophets, but also words that came from non-prophetic lips. . . . There is in the Bible . . . not only God's disclosure but man's insight.[7]

In the first two quotes, Heschel seems to suggest that some of the Bible's language or specific laws may come directly from heaven; the third may intimate that the Bible is entirely a human interpretation of the divine self-disclosure, in which case all the wording we find in the Bible is human.[8] Rosenzweig is more definitive in assigning all the Bible's words to the human interpreters:

> The primary content of revelation is revelation itself. "He came down"—this already concludes the revelation; "He spoke" is the beginning of interpretation, and certainly "I am."

Also:

> All that God ever reveals in revelation is—revelation. Or, to express it differently, he reveals nothing but himself to man. The relation of this accusative and dative to each other is the one and only content of revelation.[9]

Rosenzweig refers to the Bible as being, in this respect, "human through-out"—even though, he asserts that it is possible, if only for a moment now and again, to sense "the divine in what is humanly written."[10] All the words, then, were authored by humans, but at crucial moments they contain some-thing divine. For Rosenzweig and Heschel the Bible remains holy as a re-sponse to God's self-manifestation, but its wording (or most of its wording) is the product of human beings. In this view, the event of revelation is real, and the Bible's status derives from that event; but the Bible's specifics are not absolutely authoritative as they would be had the Bible's text come directly from heaven. Is this view so radical that it goes beyond the bounds of authentically Jewish discourse on the sacred? I hope to show that it does not: for the model of revelation this line of thinking entails has very deep roots. To trace them, let us begin an exegetical journey at the moment of revelation itself, at Sinai.

Exodus 19–24

What, exactly, did the Israelite nation hear and see at Sinai? This is no merely academic query. The event that transpired at Mount Sinai some three months after the Exodus belongs to the threefold cord that is fun-damental to all Jewish existence. Along with the redemption from slavery and the gift of the Land of Israel, the experience at Sinai created the amal-gam of religion and ethnicity that we now call Judaism.[11] Jewish liturgy says repeatedly: God gave Torah to the Jewish people; the wisdom tractate of the Mishnah, Pirkei Avot, begins: Moses received Torah at Sinai and passed it on, which is to say, made it a tradition. But what do these crucial verbs—God *gave*, Israel *received*—mean? The authority of Jewish law and the sacred status of the Bible rest on these verbs, and so a thorough inquiry into their sense is warranted. Most modern Jews, including many who ob-serve halakhah (rabbinic law), cannot regard the stenographic theory of revelation (God spoke, Moses took dictation word for word, and the Five Books record God's utterances exactly) as compelling.[12] Theologically, this theory is possible, but it limits the notion of revelation severely: surely the divine can make itself known in other forms and in more complex ways. Moreover, the Pentateuch's lack of narrative cohesion, its consistent differ-ences of language and outlook, and (most of all) its passages containing moral difficulties irreconcilable with belief in a just and merciful God establish the Five Books to be the product of multiple human authors. What, then, makes these books holy? Jewish law rests its claim to authority on its divinely revealed status, and thus the question of whether the Pentateuch's laws can truly be described as revealed demands a response.[13]

The debate regarding what precisely was heard and seen at Sinai is not an exclusively modern one. Questions moderns ask were already present in the earliest strata of Jewish thought, not only in texts that interpret the Bible but also in the biblical accounts themselves. Thus, the construction of a contemporary Jewish theology of revelation can start with the Bible's own accounts of the origin of its laws. To be sure, biblical texts present no systematic theology of revelation and religious authority; by and large, biblical texts do not articulate abstract generalizations in the manner of Western philosophy. But when the Bible narrates how the nation Israel came to know the divine will, it makes claims regarding its own religious authority. A close reading of those narratives will show that they advance self-consistent and surprising ideas about the relationship between Israel's sacred traditions and their heavenly source. Some of these texts suggest that what Israel knows and practices—that is, what biblical texts themselves teach and require—does not come directly from heaven but results in part from interpretation by the human beings who provide religious leadership to Israel. To use the terminology I suggested in the introduction, some biblical texts express a participatory theory of revelation.

Let me turn, then, to biblical accounts of revelation at Sinai, focusing on the questions: What did Israel experience at Sinai? What sights and sounds entered the escaped slaves' eyes and ears? In answering these questions, we will proceed in two stages. First, a synchronic reading of these chapters will reveal patterns of ambiguity that are of great consequence for modern Jewish theology. Second, an examination of the teachings of the older texts and traditions from which the Book of Exodus was built will allow us to study two further issues: the surprising extent to which post-biblical understandings of revelation match precanonical teachings of the sources that constitute the Pentateuch and the distinctive contribution of the final form of the text, which results from the ways its editors utilized, reacted to, reformulated, and tempered the teachings they inherited from older Israelite schools of thought.

The story of revelation in Exodus 19–24 defies a coherent sequential reading. Even more than most passages in the Pentateuch, Exodus 19 is full of ambiguities, gaps, strange repetitions, and apparent contradictions, as many scholars have shown.[14] These oddities multiply when one reads the subsequent two narratives that treat theophany at Sinai: Exodus 20.18–22* and Exodus 24. These texts present a bewildering aggregate of verses describing Moses's ascents and descents on the mountain.[15] Moses seems not to be located at the right place when the Decalogue is given: God tells him to descend the mountain and then re-ascend with Aaron (Exodus 19.24), whereupon he descends (19.25); but before he reascends, the revelation of the law takes place (20.1).[16] Similarly, we may ask, where is God located before and during the revelation? According to Exodus 19.3, God is on the mountain several days before this event, but according to 19.11, God descends to the mountain immediately prior to the theophany (in agreement with 19.18); yet in 19.20 Yhwh comes down to the summit again. (Other biblical texts describe God as speaking from heaven, not the mountain; see Exodus 20.22, Deuteronomy 4.26, and possibly Exodus 24.10. The tension among these verses is reflected in the self-contradictory harmonization in Nehemiah 9.13: "You came down on Mount Sinai and spoke to them from heaven.")[17] God's instructions in some parts of the chapter are hard to reconcile with directions in other parts. Moses tells God in Exodus 19.23 that God's charge in the immediately preceding verses, according to which Moses should prevent the Israelites from coming forward to see God on the mountain, makes little sense in light of God's earlier instruction in 19.12, according to which the people aren't allowed even to approach the edge of the mountain; God never responds to Moses's query. These oddities can be resolved, after a fashion, through harmonistic exegesis, but their

---

* There are several systems for numbering the verses of Exodus 20 and Deuteronomy 5, resulting from the different cantillation systems used for the Decalogue within Masoretic tradition. One is associated with private study, a second with public reading, and a third represents a variant of the second; see Mordechai Breuer, "Dividing." As a result of these differences, Bibles variously number the first verse after the Decalogue in Exodus as verse 14, 15, or 18 and in Deuteronomy as 18, 19, or 22. Throughout this book, I number the first verse after the Decalogue in Exodus as 20.18 and in Deuteronomy as 5.22. For an authoritative chart distinguishing the private and public traditions, see p. 295 of Breuer's article or Bible editions published by Mossad Ha-Rav Kook. Most other printings (e.g., those in the JPS Torah Commentaries, the Koren editions of the Tanakh, and most תקוני קוראים) contain an error in the public version.

presence already intimates that the extraordinary event chapter 19 describes was witnessed through a fog, or that the narrative of that event could not be articulated in human words; further, one senses that the text combines multiple recollections of an essentially unreportable event.[18]

Nevertheless, regarding aural and visual experience, Exodus 19 seems fairly clear. The theophany was accompanied by, or consisted of, loud noises and radiant sights: in Exodus 19.16 we read of "thunder and lightning," a "very heavy cloud on the mountain," as well as "a mighty sound from a horn." The entire mountain was covered with "smoke" and "fire," and God's descent caused it to "tremble"—that is, the theophany also involved an earthquake (19.18; cf. 20.18). The fire in 19.18 in fact *was* the theophany, for it embodied the deity (באש 'ה ... ירד; the letter *bet* is the *bet essentiae*[19]). The cloud, too, may have been a bodily manifestation of God, who told Moses as the Israelites prepared for the event, "I am about to come to you in the form of the thick cloud" (19.9). Alternatively, God may be inside the thick cloud but not the same as the cloud.[20] The visual imagery remains the same even if the theology differs. In short, the theophany involved storm and earthquake imagery.

Similar language appears in other biblical descriptions of Yhwh's manifestation, especially those that make specific connections to Sinai or the wilderness south of Canaan. Thus, Judges 5.4–5 also associates an earthquake with God's appearance at that mountain:

> [4]Yhwh, when You came forth from Seir,
> Marched from the fields of Edom,
> The earth trembled;
> Yes, the heavens poured,
> Yes, the clouds poured water,
> [5]The mountains flowed like a stream,
> In the presence of Yhwh, the One from Sinai,[21]
> In the presence of Yhwh, the God of Israel

The earthquake and storm are connected to God's presence at Sinai in Psalm 68.8–10 as well:

> [8]O God, when You went forth before Your people,
> When You marched through the wilderness,
> [9]The earth shook,
> Yea, the heavens poured,

> In the presence of Yhwh,[22] the One from Sinai,
> In the presence of Yhwh, the God of Israel.
> [10]You shook down rain, masses of rain,
> You calmed the land, once languishing, that you bequeathed them.

The connection between this sort imagery, God's appearance, and commands known from the Decalogue also appears in Psalm 50.1–7. Similar imagery—lightning, fire, and earthquake, all of them signifying numinous power that is destructive and frightening—portrays God's appearance in the wilderness south of Canaan in Habakkuk 3.3–6, though without mentioning Sinai specifically. A subtler evocation of the events at Sinai appears in Psalm 114. This poem intimates that the miracle at the Reed Sea, the nation's entry into Canaan, and the Sinai theophany constitute, at the deepest level, a single event.[23] The earthquake induced by the theophany, the psalmist tells us, makes the mountains dance and leap, even as God's appearance causes the sea to rush away, as in a tsunami. Similar imagery connects Sinai, revelation of Torah, fire, and lightning in Deuteronomy 33.2–4, though there without the earthquake.[24] Other biblical texts associate Yhwh's theophany with earthquakes and storms, though without specific reference to Sinai or the wilderness south of Canaan—for example, Psalms 18, 29, and 97.[25]

As many scholars have noticed, this sort of portrayal of divine appearance is not unique to Yhwh or to the Bible; theophanies in Canaanite and Akkadian literature are described in very similar terms.[26] In particular, the Canaanites praised Baal using remarkably similar terminology. Thus, one song of praise to Baal (also known by the name Hadad) reads:

> He opens a window in his house,
> A sluice in his palace,
> Baal opens a rift in the clouds.
> Baal lets out his holy voice [or thunder],[27]
> Baal Ṣaphon repeats the utterance of his lips.
> His holy voice shatters the earth,
> The utterance of his lips made mountains shake with fear.
> . . . high places of the earth totter.
> Baal's enemies flee to the forests,
> The haters of Hadad to the sides of the mountain.
> Great Baal declared:
> Enemies of Hadad—why do you shake?
> Why do you shake, O armed ones of Demaron?
> Baal's eyes are toward the east;

His hand—yes!—it shakes.
A cedar is in his right hand.
So Baal sits enthroned in his house![28]

Another song states:

Baal sits, his mountain like a throne,
Hadad the Shepherd, as on the Flood.
In this midst of his mountain, divine Ṣaphon,
On the peak of his victory.
He casts seven bolts of lightning,
Eight peals of thunder,[29]
A spear of lightning in his right hand.[30]

In short, the imagery that characterizes God's self-revelation in Exodus 19—thunder, lightning, storm, clouds, and earthquake—is typical of the revelation of high deities of the Canaanite and Mesopotamian cultures out of which Israelite culture developed. This background will become relevant as we consider the development of the tradition of Yhwh's revelation in the Bible.

Did the People Hear the Lawgiving?
A Pattern of Ambiguity

Alongside the stereotypical portrayal of the theophany in Exodus 19–20, our text repeatedly introduces ambiguities concerning the sounds experienced by the Israelites. These ambiguities, five in number, lead the reader of our text to wonder: Did the nation actually hear commands being proclaimed by God? Or did they receive all the laws that resulted from the theophany through Moses? In other words, the text of Exodus 19–20 forces us to reflect on the question of the laws' origins and the extent to which they are and are not heavenly.

The first of these ambiguities centers around the word קול (qol), which allows several translations.[31] It often means "voice"—that is, the sound a human being makes when uttering words.[32] But it also can mean "thunder," especially when it is accompanied by other terms that denote thunder, by a term for lightning, or by other meteorological vocabulary. Finally, the term can be part of an idiom—that is, part of a combination of words in which literal senses of qol are less important. In particular, the phrase שמע בקול denotes obedience in biblical Hebrew.[33]

Appearing seven times in Exodus 19–20, *qol* serves as what Martin Buber and Franz Rosenzweig call a *Leitwort*, or "guiding word." This term refers to a word or verbal root repeated in a biblical passage, sometimes with variations; the repetition or variation reveals, clarifies, or emphasizes something crucial to that passage.[34] Which meanings does this guiding word carry in the Sinai narrative? At the beginning of 19.16 and at the beginning of 20.18, *qol* clearly refers to thunder, because it appears next to a term meaning "lightning." In the middle of 19.16, at the beginning of 19.19, and in the middle of 20.18, it refers specifically to the sound of a horn (קול השופר). In its first occurrence, at 19.5, the term is part of the idiom שמע בקול, "to obey," and thus it refers to the Israelites' compliance with God's covenant. As part of this standard phrase, the term does not literally refer to a voice, though it does imply some command or commands with which the Israelites are to be compliant. Because our term becomes associated with obedience very early in this chapter, the audience may hear an echo of this idea when the word appears later in the text; as is often the case in biblical narrative, the guiding word picks up a meaning in one verse that it drops off later on.

The most important case—because the least clear—occurs in the second half of 19.19: משה ידבר והא־להים יעננו בקול: "Moses would speak, and God answered him with a *qol*." Does this mean that God answered Moses with thunder, or with a voice that spoke specific words? On the one hand, the two cases in which *qol* clearly refers to thunder before and after 19.19 may lead the audience to assume that *qol* means thunder here as well. The presence throughout chapters 19–20, and especially immediately before our verse in 19.18, of lightning, clouds, and an earthquake (which, acquaintances from California tell me, sounds like thunder) may lead us to presume that "thunder" is the default value of *qol* in this narrative. On the other hand, the context at the end of our verse is one of speaking and answering—activities that are normally associated with a voice and with words. In short, both translations are legitimate,[35] but the difference between them is significant. Did God communicate with Moses using a human voice or a very loud noise? Our understanding of revelation's nature and its very content changes drastically depending on which understanding we adopt. If *qol* is a voice, the Israelites heard God providing specific information to Moses. If it is thunder, then what occurred at Sinai was an overwhelming experience, but not necessarily one in which Israelites acquired distinct teachings directly from God. The stenographic theory of revelation grows out of the former translation; participatory theories can align themselves with the latter.

The second ambiguity also raises the question of whether and to what extent the nation heard the revelation of specific laws. It emerges when we read the passage immediately after the Decalogue, Exodus 20.18–22. The content of these verses is straightforward: the people are frightened by what they have already heard, and they ask Moses to approach God so that they do not have to continue experiencing something so terrifying, whereupon Moses calms the people and agrees to serve as intermediary. What is not clear is when this conversation takes place. One might assume that the people spoke to Moses after the giving of the Decalogue, since the verses in question follow the text of the Decalogue (Exodus 20.2–17). In that case, the people heard the Decalogue in its entirety; and thus they seem to have heard not just loud noises but a humanlike voice emanating from the divine. Hearing this voice (or the noises that accompanied it) was an ordeal. When the Decalogue ended, the nation asked to be spared any more direct revelations, pleading that Moses notify them of subsequent communications from God. Moses approves this plan, and consequently he is alone when he goes into the presence of God. Upon doing so he receives additional laws, presumably those found in Exodus 20.23–23.33. The rest of the laws will be the product of Mosaic mediation; but the people did hear, directly from the mouth of God, one group of commands.

But one can read the order of events in Exodus 19–20 differently. It is possible that the discussion described in Exodus 20.18–22 took place during the revelation rather than after it. In that case, the people were quickly seized by terror, and they asked Moses to intervene even as God proclaimed the Decalogue. This reading is suggested by the initial verb in 20.18, which is not a past tense, as many translations imply,[36] but a participle, which identifies the actor without indicating any information about the timing of the event: "the people were/are the ones witnessing."[37] The absence in 20.18 of the typical past tense of biblical narrative (the *waw*-consecutive) is unusual, and the syntax here (*waw* + noun + participle) normally indicates that the event reported was simultaneous with a previously narrated occurrence.[38] The syntax suggests that the conversation between Moses and the people took place during the giving of the Decalogue; the narrator avoids interrupting the text of the commandments, however, and thus the narrative does not begin again until Exodus 20.18.[39] According to this understanding of the narrative sequence in Exodus 19–20, the nation heard only part (which part?) of the Decalogue; Moses, upon approaching "the thick cloud where God was" (20.21), was vouchsafed the text of the remainder. Further, on subsequent occasions Moses obtained additional legislation, including the laws found in Exodus 20.23–23.33, as well as those in the remainder of the Pentateuch.

Another possibility exists: the events in Exodus 20.18–21 follow temporally on Exodus 19.19 or 19.25, so that the people did not hear any of the Decalogue at all. The people's fear may have resulted from the extraordinary seismic and meteorological events that were already occurring prior to the lawgiving, in which case they must have urged Moses to approach God on their behalf before the lawgiving began. This assertion may seem odd, since it ignores the sequence of verses in the text of the Pentateuch, but ancient and modern interpreters alike recognize that the order in which biblical narratives present material does not always mimic the order of the events they describe.[40] As Naḥmanides (a deeply influential thirteenth-century biblical commentator, halakhic authority, and kabbalist) points out in support of this reading in his commentary to Exodus 20.18–19, the people do not say to Moses, "Let not God speak to us any more, lest we die," or "Let not God continue speaking to us," but simply, "Let not God speak to us, lest we die." Further, the syntax, *waw* + noun + participle, in Exodus 20.18 reports an event simultaneous with something previously narrated—which may have taken place in chapter 19 rather than 20.[41] If this is the case, then the nation did not hear the Decalogue at all; the entirety of that text, along with all the other commandments in the Torah, came to the nation exclusively through Moses.

A third ambiguity occurs in Exodus 20.1: "God spoke all these words, saying." This sort of phrasing (namely, "God/Yhwh spoke/said . . . saying") is exceedingly common; verses with the subject God or Yhwh and the *waw*-consecutive verb *spoke* (וידבר) or *said* (ויאמר) occur 339 times in the Bible. In every occurrence other than Exodus 20.1, the text uses the word אל or the particle –ל to tell us explicitly whom God addressed (thus, "Yhwh spoke to Moses, saying," or "God said to Moses and Aaron, saying").[42] Only in the verse introducing the Decalogue in Exodus is there any doubt about the recipient of divine speech. This fact is jarring to an audience whose ears are familiar with the hundreds of cases of the normal form.[43] It bothered ancient translators: the Septuagint (a translation of the Bible into Greek prepared by Hellenistic Jewish communities in Egypt in the third and second centuries BCE) adds the words, "to Moses,"[44] while the Old Latin translation (used in the Western church in the first centuries CE) adds "to the people." It is striking that this ambiguity crops up precisely at the central case of divine revelation in the entire Bible. One might view all previous revelations as leading to the event at Sinai and all subsequent ones as echoing it, repeating it, building upon it, or pointing toward its importance; certainly this is the way Jewish tradition has come to regard the Sinai revelation.[45] As a result, the absence of a prepositional phrase indicating the recipient of the revelation commands our attention. The unprecedented phrasing calls us to wrestle with the question, from whom did Israel receive the text of the Decalogue?

The fourth ambiguity results from the fact that one can punctuate the crucial verses where chapter 19 leads into chapter 20 in two different ways. One might understand Exodus 19.25–20.2 as follows:

> [25]Moses came down to the people and spoke to them. [1]Then God spoke all these words, saying, [2]"I am Yhwh your God who took you out of Egypt, out of the house of bondage ..."

But it would be just as defensible to render these verses as follows:

> [25]Moses came down to the people and said to them, [1]"God spoke all these words, saying, [2]I am Yhwh your God who took you out of Egypt, out of the house of bondage ...'"

In the former rendering, we first hear the narrator's voice, and then we hear the narrator quoting God's voice. Thus understood, the text reports that the people hear God's voice pronouncing the Decalogue. In the latter rendering, however, the text informs us that the Israelites hear Moses reciting the Decalogue, which he had heard earlier from God.[46] In that case the nation received the Decalogue only through human mediation. Both translations are legitimate—and both have strikes against them. Against the former, we can note that the verb that appears in 19.25, ויאמר, typically introduces direct speech. It is properly translated as "he said" (rather than what I suggested in the first rendering, "he spoke"), and it is normally followed by the words that the verb's subject utters.[47] But we can also find faults in the second rendering. The phrase "God spoke" in 20.1 is formulated using a *waw*-consecutive. This formulation suggests that God's act of speaking came immediately after Moses's act of speaking. If that is so, then the phrase "God spoke" are the words of the narrator, not of the character Moses.[48] Further, it would have been odd for the character Moses to begin a new statement with a *waw*-consecutive, which correctly is the *continuation* of a narration that was already taking place in a previous sentence.[49] In short, this phrasing forces us to debate whether God or Moses uttered the Decalogue to the nation, and it precludes us from bringing the debate to any definite conclusion.

The fifth ambiguity focuses our attention on the mode of the nation's perception at Sinai. Exodus 20.18 reads: "All the וְכָל־הָעָם רֹאִים אֶת־הַקּוֹלֹת וְאֶת־הַלַּפִּידִם וְאֵת קוֹל הַשֹּׁפָר וְאֶת־הָהָר עָשֵׁן people had seen the voices/thunders and the blazing lightning and the sound of the shofar and the smoke from the mountain." The verb רֹאִים normally means "to see." For this reason, commentators such as Rabbi Akiva (a second-century sage who is one of the greatest authorities in the Mishnah) and Rashi (an eleventh-century sage who is the most influential and beloved Jewish biblical commentator) point out that the verse presents us with the paradox of visible sound.[50] Thus, it suggests that whatever act of cognition took place during the lawgiving was singular; it was not the sort of cognition that takes place when one human being talks to another.[51] To be sure, other commentators, including Rabbi Yishmael (a contemporary of Akiva and also one of the most influential mishnaic sages) and ibn Ezra (a twelfth-century biblical commentator renowned for his linguistic precision and independent judgment) reject the notion that the phrasing is paradoxical. Yishmael claims that the verse means to say that the Israelites saw the visible but heard the aural.[52] Ibn Ezra points out that the verb ר″א″ה sometimes means "perceive" in a general sense, not just "perceive through the eyes."[53] This proposal is not entirely persuasive. In Genesis 2.19, Genesis 27.27, Jeremiah 33.24, and Habakkuk 2.1, ר″א″ה does not refer to sight, but there the verb means "think about," "attend to," or "understand," rather than "perceive non-visually."[54] Further, even if ibn Ezra's explanation is valid, the narrator's decision to use the verb ר″א″ה in a rare sense ("perceive through any sense organ, including the ear") rather than its most typical sense ("perceive through the eye") encourages the reader to slow down and to ponder how, precisely, the perceived matter came into the people's mind. A modern Italian Israeli scholar, Umberto (Moshe David) Cassuto, also attempts to downplay the oddity, but in a different way. He suggests that the phrase involves zeugma—that is, the use of this verb is suited to some of its direct objects (the lightning and the smoke from the mountain) but not to others (the various sounds).[55] Even if Cassuto is correct,[56] the narrator's decision to put the inappropriate accusative first rather than one of the accusatives that matches the verb focuses our attention on something that, at least initially, appears paradoxical.[57] It seems reasonable to agree with Nahum Sarna, who maintains that "the figurative language indicates the profound awareness among the people of the mystery of God's self-manifestation. It is an experience that cannot be adequately described by the ordinary language of the senses."[58]

These five ambiguities raise a single issue: the manner and extent to which the Israelites were in contact with the divine at Sinai, and, more specifically, the nature of their apprehension of the lawgiving. These ambiguities force the audience to contemplate two related questions: (1) What was the basic nature of the revelation the nation experienced? Did it consist of an overwhelming event without communicating specific content (*qol* means "thunder"), or did it involve specific words that enunciated the laws known from the text of Exodus 20.1–17 (*qol* means "voice")? (2) Did the nation Israel hear the text of the Decalogue (or parts thereof) directly from God, or did they hear them exclusively as the product of prophetic mediation? Three answers emerge regarding this second question: they heard all of the Ten Commandments (if we understand the textual location of Exodus 20.18–22 as reflecting temporal sequence), they heard some of them (if we understand the conversation in 20.18–22 as occurring during the lawgiving), or they heard none of them (if we understand the conversation as preceding the lawgiving). This second question might be recast: to what extent was the lawgiving a private event involving Moses, and to what extent was it a public one involving the whole nation?[59] Our five ambiguities are manifestations of a single concern, which the text poses insistently. Exodus does not want the audience to know whether the lawgiving was direct, mediated, or a mix of the two. The book does, however, encourage the audience to wonder about this issue, to think through various possibilities, to see their strengths and weaknesses, and perhaps to think about their implications. Exodus endorses a question, but not an answer; a debate, not a resolution.

The Evidence of Chapter 24

Exodus 24 picks up the story of the revelation at Sinai, and we need to examine how it relates to the events described in chapters 19–20. Commentators have long debated whether Exodus 24 narrates the same events as chapters 19–20, events that immediately followed them, or even events that preceded them. An early midrashic work, the Mekhilta deRabbi Shimon

Bar Yoḥai (in its comments to Exodus 24.1), points out that in both texts God directs Moses to "come up" to God along with Aaron (19.24, 24.1); in both the people are "far off" (20.18, 24.1); both specify that only Moses "approached" God (20.18, 24.2). The Mekhilta concludes that chapters 20 and 24 describe a single event.[60] But the eleventh-century commentator Rashi concludes that chapter 24 narrates events that preceded the giving of the Decalogue and partly overlap with chapter 19. One might also read the chapter as it appears in the final form of Exodus as an appendix to the Sinai narrative that preserves additional or alternative memories of the events at Sinai.[61]

How does chapter 24 address the ambiguities regarding what the people perceived at Sinai? Significantly, this chapter does not portray the people as hearing anything at all. The auditory imagery that appears so prominently in 19–20 is completely lacking here. Likewise absent are any other aspects of the trembling of nature associated with Baal's theophany in Canaanite literature and found in texts such as Judges 5; Habakkuk 3; or Psalms 18, 29, 68, and 114. The chapter lacks *qol* in either sense: the people hear neither thunder nor words. Rather, the revelation is visual; the elders and Moses are vouchsafed the sight of Yhwh. The question of public versus private revelation is also handled radically differently from what we found in 19–20. Instead of sometimes hinting that the direct revelation involved the whole nation and sometimes implying that it involved only Moses, this chapter moves to a third option: the nation as a whole was not present for the vision. Only the elders and members of Moses's own family saw Yhwh; and Moses alone received laws. Further, because Exodus 24.11 portrays the elders as eating and drinking during or immediately after the vision, one does not have the sense that the revelation was a tremendously overpowering event. This chapter takes the audience of the Book of Exodus in new directions, suggesting a completely different understanding of revelation: the theophany was first and foremost an experience of God. Taken alongside chapters 19–20, the chapter adds to our sense that the events at Sinai can be conceptualized or recalled in fundamentally different ways. This sense will be sharpened as we move away from a synchronic reading of these chapters to attend to the historically diverse sources from which the final form of Exodus has been built.

Ambiguity and the Participatory Theology of Revelation

The implications of this pattern of ambiguity for Jewish conceptions of religious authority receive attention in subsequent chapters, but it is worth pausing at this point to sketch out what is at stake in the equivocation that centers around the people's perception and Moses's mediation. For the many Jewish thinkers who subscribe to the stenographic theory of revelation, Jewish law is based on the actual words of God found in the Torah, which were revealed to Israel at Sinai. To be sure, the law as observed in rabbinic communities follows specifics found in talmudic literature; while those specifics are built upon human interpretations of Pentateuchal texts, the texts being interpreted (according to the stenographic theory) contain God's actual words precisely as God dictated them to Moses. According to the participatory theory developed by thinkers such as Rosenzweig, Heschel, and Louis Jacobs, the biblical texts themselves are largely or even entirely products of human beings who respond to the revelation at Sinai.[62] Now, the extent to which human beings might feel free to alter or correct laws based on revelation at Sinai will be limited if one believes those laws are rooted in a legislation whose wording came down from heaven. But it may be less limited if one believes that the biblical texts themselves were already the product of human interpretation, so that their wording is the work of Moses and those who followed him.[63] If human intermediaries wrote the laws found in the Torah, even those in the Decalogue, as an attempt to translate God's nonverbal *qol* into human language, then the authority behind the law in general remains fully divine, but the specifics of any given law are human.

The insistent focus of Exodus 19–20 on the question of Mosaic mediation represents an attempt by biblical authors themselves to raise the sorts of questions central to the work of Rosenzweig, Heschel, Jacobs, and kindred thinkers. If the nation Israel heard the Decalogue in its entirety directly from God, then we know that God does indeed speak with a voice, using words found in a human language—specifically, in the dialect of ancient Canaanite we call Hebrew. In that case, it is possible that other laws found in the Torah were also literally the word of God; when the text reports that God "spoke" to Moses and gave him this or that commandment (as the Torah does throughout the Exodus, Leviticus, and Numbers), "speaking" can reasonably be interpreted as speaking in the sense that one human speaks to another. The people, having heard one sample of divine speech in human language, can presume that the laws they subsequently received through Mosaic mediation were conveyed in words, as the Ten Commandments were. It follows that Moses, when acting as God's intermediary, is functioning as a stenographer, not as an interpreter, or to use Heschel's terminology, as a vessel rather than a partner.[64] In contrast, if the nation never heard the Decalogue from God but experienced an overwhelming sense of God's presence, then all the laws they received from Moses may in fact have been Moses's own formulation of God's nonverbal communication. In this case, whatever the Israelites know of the laws, they know from a fellow human and not from God. It remains possible that when the narrator says that God "spoke" to Moses, the narrator means that God literally uttered words to Moses (in which case we can return to the stenographic theory of revelation), but it is also possible that "spoke" in such a sentence (perhaps: in any sentence where God is the subject) refers to a communication that Moses had to translate into human language. If the people never heard any of the Ten Commandments, then they could not know which theory of revelation is correct; and neither can we. We can go a step further: because Exodus repeatedly calls attention to the question of mediation without allowing us to be certain about its answer, the book forces us to hover between two models for understanding revelation. The audience of Exodus must contemplate each possibility seriously but skeptically, without rejecting either one.

One might argue against my whole line of reasoning by pointing out that, regardless of the complexities of chapters 19–20, the Torah tells us hundreds of times that God "spoke" (וידבר) to Moses and "said" (ויאמר) certain words to him. The crucial question we confront throughout the Torah, however, is what these verbs mean when their subject is God (as we learn from the most influential of all Jewish philosophers, Maimonides, who lived in Spain and Egypt in the twelfth century, and whose views we will examine in greater detail toward the end of this chapter[65]). The purpose of the ambiguities in chapters 19–20, which are at once insistent and consistent, is to render sentences that link this subject to those two verbs problematic: the pattern of ambiguity suggests we should think carefully about such sentences, because they may contain more than one might initially assume or something different from one might think. These chapters, then, shed light on all cases of divine speech—or, more precisely, they set a dark cloud over them. One cannot use the frequent occurrence of verses like "God spoke to Moses, saying," to show that God really does talk in human language. The Pentateuch encourages us to conclude from the web of ambiguities in Exodus 19–20 that we are unsure whether God talks, even to Moses, in human language.[66] In so doing, the Pentateuch problematizes its own authority without in any way renouncing that authority. The Pentateuch's project of self-problematization has important implications for, and affiliations in, postbiblical Jewish thought, and I discuss these later on; but these brief remarks are necessary here to give a sense of why the exegetical journey in which we are engaged matters.

Lawgiving in the Torah's Sources

We have found that Exodus 19–20 and 24 are full of gaps, discontinuities, and contradictions. Some of these textual phenomena result from the subject matter of the text: human language cannot encompass an event in which heaven comes to earth and the transcendent becomes immanent. These phenomena, however, also result from the combination of several originally separate documents describing the event. Are the ambiguities we have noted peculiar to one particular source, common to several, or are they the product of the redactor who brought the sources together? To answer these questions, I will discuss the E, P, and J documents, as they have been reconstructed by late-nineteenth-century source critics and by contemporary proponents of the Documentary Hypothesis.[67]

These three narratives of revelation preserved in Exodus—along with a fourth, from the D source in Deuteronomy—were written centuries after the event at Sinai, and each one preserves memories going back to it.[68] Because the revelation was so overwhelming, the way people perceived it as it was happening must have varied; different Israelites noticed, and missed, different aspects of what took place. The differences among the conceptions of what happened at Sinai grew during centuries of transmission, as historical memories diverged even more significantly from each other. We should not regard this variety of perception, or the even greater variety of historical accounts that followed, as an error or a problem. Rather, it may be God's intentional strategy of overcoming the limits of human perception, which could not assimilate the extraordinary event.[69] Further, this strategy yields the human participants in the event and its aftermath the gift of interpretive freedom. By isolating each of the sources, then, scholars have recovered older voices from the history of Israelite theology, voices that are able to speak more distinctly when we hear each one by itself. The varied memories found in the Pentateuchal sources serve as religiously valuable testimonies that provide guidance to people for whom the Bible functions as scripture.[70] Attending to these testimonies allows us, first, to sense the extent to which teachings about revelation were already subject to rich debate in the biblical period itself and, second, to see how the modern debates about revelation recall and reenact this older debate.

In this second stage of our exegetical journey, I study the individual memories found in each of the Pentateuchal sources. This second stage is more speculative than the close reading of the whole we undertook in the first stage, because it builds on what can only be hypotheses, albeit widely accepted ones, regarding the precursor texts from which the Pentateuch was formed.[71] Readers who are skeptical of the whole attempt to find these older sources might even prefer to skip this section of the current chapter altogether. It would be possible to do so without destroying this book's larger argument, since the patterns of ambiguity we find in the first stage already provide a precursor to the participatory theory of revelation found in modern Jewish theology. Yet doing so would cause a reader to lose sight of the extent to which the questions that exercised later Jewish thinkers were already a source of controversy among the biblical authors themselves. Even though some of my colleagues in biblical studies can propose alternate theories regarding precisely how that debate transpired in ancient Israel, the fact that such a debate occurred remains clear, and it will be worthwhile for us to develop a detailed and textured sense of how the conversations and disputes concerning this issue developed in its most ancient stages.

Revelation in E

The E source provides the bulk of the material in Exodus 19–24. According to Baruch Schwartz, it consists of Exodus 19.2b–9a, 19.16.aα–17, 19.19, 20.1–23.33, 24.3–8, 24.11bβ–15, and 24.18b. The Sinai story in E according to Schwartz continues in Exodus 31.18 (minus a few words), 32.1–8, 32.10–25, 32.30–35, 33.6–11, 34.1, 34.4–5a, and 34.28. (Most source critics propose largely identical descriptions of the E material in these chapters, but we shall see that in one crucial respect some critics' analyses differ from Schwartz's.)[72] The verses read perfectly well as a continuous narrative. What theology of revelation do they present if we read them as the coherent unit they appear to be? What religious teaching can we recover by accepting E as a teacher of *torah*?

First, this narrative puts a strong emphasis on the idea of the law as the main, indeed the sole, expression of the covenant between God and Israel. E presents this law as the way the nation acknowledges the benefaction God granted them by taking them out of Egypt. In this respect the nation's observance of the law is oriented toward the past.[73] Further, the law provides a means for Israel to maintain its special relationship with God, and in this respect observance is oriented toward the present and the future. E introduces this conception of covenant as law at the very outset of its Sinai passage. As is often the case when biblical writers narrate especially momentous events, E slows down the narration by employing a stately, rhythmic prose that, with its parallel clauses and use of synonyms, moves in the direction of classical biblical poetry:[74]

> ³Moses went up to God.[75] Then Yhwh called Moses from the mountain,
>   saying,
> Thus you should say to the House of Jacob,
>   thus say to the children of Israel:
> ⁴You yourselves saw what I did to Egypt,
>   how I carried you on eagles' wings,
>   how I brought you to Me.
> ⁵So now—
>   if you all truly obey My voice
>   and adhere to My covenant (בריתי),
> you will be My personal treasure[76] from among all nations.
> Indeed, all the world is Mine,
>   ⁶but you will become My kingdom of priests,
>   My holy people. (Exodus 19.3–6)

The covenant or ברית the text mentions does not automatically exist; it is something that the Israelites have to uphold. The covenant for E simply means the observance of the law; note the parallelism between obedience and adherence to the covenant in verse 5. It results in the their becoming God's unique possession from among all God's nations. Observance is first of all a response to what God has already done for Israel. The Hebrew construction in verses 4–5 posits a cause-and-effect relationship between the people's recollection of what God did for them by taking them out of Egypt in verse 4 and the requirement that they obey the covenant in verse 5.[77] The laws are specified later in the text; they consist not merely, or even primarily, of the Decalogue but of the collection of laws found in Exodus 20.23–23.33, which biblical scholars often call "the Covenant Code."[78] It is that collection of laws to which the people formally assent in 24.3–7, both verbally and through ritual action.

The E narration contain some of the most important elements of the story of the lawgiving as it appears in the canonical form of Exodus. The ancient Near Eastern imagery of theophany appears prominently in E, which tells of thunder, lightning, and the thick cloud (19.9a, 16.aα, 20.18).

Further, several of the ambiguities that lead us to wonder about the extent to which revelation was mediated occur in E. The repeated use of *qol* (thunder and/or voice) belongs entirely to E: all seven occurrences of this guiding word belong to E, as do verses that provide contextual clues for its various meanings.[79] The ambiguities present in E also include the paradoxical, or at least arresting, phrasing in 20.18, which suggests visual perception of a sound. Thus, already in E we find a biblical author drawing our attention to the question of Mosaic mediation and the question of whether the legal teachings associated with Moses are heavenly or earthly in origin.

Two additional ambiguities may also be present in E, though their presence depends on whether, with many but not all Documentary critics, we believe that the Decalogue was already part of the E text. The first of those elements is the syntax of 20.18, which, we saw earlier, forces us to wonder whether the people heard all, some, or none of the Decalogue. The second is the absence of the words "to Moses" or "to the people" in 20.1, which leaves us unsure as to the recipient of the divine speech. Schwartz, whose meticulous reconstruction of the E source I adopt, follows the view of classical source critics such as Julius Wellhausen, August Dillmann, and Samuel Rolles Driver, who maintain that an early version of the Decalogue was originally part of E in its present location.[80] According to this view, the Decalogue in E immediately followed Exodus 19.19 (since 19.20–25 is assigned by classical source critics to J[81]) and then led directly to Exodus 20.18.[82] Other scholars, however, maintain that the Ten Commandments were originally located in E *after* the conversation between Moses and the people in Exodus 20.18–21, so that having "approached the cloud where God was" (20.21), Moses was allowed to hear the text of the Ten Commandments as well as the Covenant Code that followed them.[83] According to a third group of scholars, the E narrative never contained the Ten Commandments; instead, they were added secondarily as the Book of Exodus came into being.[84] If either of the latter schools is correct, then the original E text will have moved seamlessly from 19.19 to 20.18—and in fact a text that goes immediately from 19.19 to 20.18–21 would read extremely well.[85] While I regard the classical position (according to which the Decalogue was already part of E in its current location) as strongest,[86] it is difficult to decide among these possibilities with as much confidence as one would desire. For this reason, it is useful to think through how the presence, absence, or altered position of the Decalogue affects a reading of E.

If the Decalogue was already part of E in its current location (between 19.19 and 20.18), then the reading I suggested above for the final form of Exodus 19–20 as a whole remains intact. E confronts us with four ambiguities that force us to wonder whether the nation heard the whole, part, or none of the Decalogue as distinct words from God's voice. (In this case, E lacks only one of the ambiguities discussed earlier: the lack of clarity concerning the proper punctuation of the last verse of chapter 19 and the first two verses of 20.) It is possible in this reading of E that the people heard the entirety of the Decalogue, although such a reading would force us to ignore the equivocal syntax in 20.18, which pointedly does not represent the conversation between Moses and the people as happening after God spoke the Decalogue. In contrast, our text in Exodus may attempt to revive that possibility in 20.1, which states that "God spoke *all* these words, saying . . ." While it is still unclear to whom God spoke, the presence of the word *all* may at least hint at the possibility that the people heard the Decalogue in its entirety.[87] But the effect of E's text as a whole is neither to prove that the people heard all of it nor to show they heard a part or none; it is to force us to wonder.[88]

What if the Decalogue was not part of E at all, but was added to Exodus only at the time that the various sources were combined, or even after the sources were combined but before the Book of Exodus as we know it achieved its final form? In that case, the people could not have heard the Decalogue in E, and E is less richly ambiguous. An E that includes the Decalogue provides fodder to both a stenographic theory of revelation and a participatory theory even as it problematizes both, but an E without a Decalogue leans more heavily in the direction of the participatory, since in that case the people can have heard the Decalogue only from Moses. Nonetheless, even if the Israelites did not receive the Decalogue directly from God, one might read 19.19 ("Moses would speak, and God would answer him in a *qol*") as describing the nation overhearing God speaking specific words to Moses. If this is so (and, to be sure, it would be odd that the text fails to quote the words in question), then there remains a possibility that E portrays God's "speaking" at Sinai as identical to human "speaking." In that case, one could still maintain that 19.19 validates subsequent cases of Mosaic mediation as potentially stenographic in nature: since the nation heard God conversing with Moses using human language in 19.19, they can understand God as having spoken specific words to Moses in later cases.

Nevertheless, this reading seems weaker than another one in which 19.19 provides validation for Moses as an interpreter rather than a stenographer. An E that contains no Decalogue allows for a range of possible readings even as it leans toward emphasizing Moses as intermediary, because the ambiguity regarding *qol* (thunder or voice?) remains.

To my mind, the least likely possibility is that E contained the Decalogue, but that it originally followed 20.21, since that suggestion depends on a conjectural rewriting of our text. But even that reconstruction of E leads more or less inexorably in the direction we have already seen. In such an E, it is clear that God spoke the Decalogue to Moses but that the people did not overhear that event. Since God proclaimed the Decalogue only after Moses approached the dark cloud in 20.21, the nation—and their successors, the audience of our text—have no way of knowing whether the divine *qol* consisted of human-type speech, loud noises, or something else entirely. The authority of the specifics of the law has to rest in the reliability of Moses as intermediary; the people have no way of knowing precisely what went on between Moses and the deity. Here again, E may lean toward a participatory theology, but E hardly rules the stenographic theory out. In short, all three reconstructions of E provide support for the participatory theology without fully subverting the stenographic. The first reading of E emphasizes the need to think about both possibilities, but all of them encourage debate. No matter whose reconstruction of E we adopt, E at once endorses ambiguity and helps the reader see the legitimacy of a participatory theology.

Verses elsewhere in E play a critical role in adjudicating between the two theories of revelation. Three of these verses concern the tablets of stone that Moses brought down from the mountain. The first of these verses, Exodus 24.12, occurs as E narrates Moses's ascent to the mountain to spend several weeks alone with God: "Yhwh said to Moses: Ascend the mountain toward Me, and stay there so that I can give you the tablets of stone, and the teaching, and the commandment that I have written to teach them." The second, 31.18, occurs in the original text of E only a few verses later (though in E's time frame, it took place forty days later). As it stands in the final form of Exodus, this verse combines overlapping material from E and P, but in Schwartz's plausible (though by no means certain) reconstruction of E, it reads: "He gave Moses two tablets of stone written with the finger of God." The third passage, 32.15–16, occurs a bit later in the narrative, when Moses leaves the mountain; the E version of the verse reads: "Moses turned and descended the mountain, with two tablets in his hand, tablets with writing on both sides; on this side and that they had writing. The tablets were God's work; the writing was God's writing, inscribed into the tablets."[89] (Again, E and P are mixed; some might quibble with the reconstruction of E's precise wording, but the differences among scholarly reconstructions are not material to the point I am making.) All of these E verses push us significantly toward viewing the specific wording of the laws as coming directly from God. They emphatically portray God as writing the tablets, and one presumes that what God wrote consisted of words rather than pictures or abstract lines. (The verb used in all these verses, כתב, refers to inscribing words, not to drawing.)[90]

And yet, E tells us, the nation (and E's audience, who are in the same position as the nation within the world of the text) has no direct knowledge of what was written on those tablets, since Moses alone saw them. Before any Israelites could look at them, Moses shattered them after he came down the mountain and saw the golden calf (32.19). God directs Moses to replace them in 34.1, where the divine plan is that the new set of tablets will be the result of cooperation between Moses and God: "Yhwh said to Moses: Carve two tablets of stone like the original ones, and I shall write down on the tablets the words that were on the original tablets you broke." Here, the act of writing is supposed to be God's, not Moses's.[91] Yet when Moses prepares the second set of tablets in 34.28, the information E provides in somewhat unclear: "He was with God forty days and forty nights; he ate no bread and drank no water; and he wrote on the tablets the words of the covenant, the Ten Utterances." The subject of the verb *wrote*, like the subject of the preceding three verbs, is Moses.[92] This verse contradicts the plain sense of God's command in 34.1. Many scholars, ancient, medieval, and modern, attempt to avoid this problem by asserting that the real subject of the verb *write* in 34.28 must be God, even though the syntax and wording of the verse do nothing to indicate a change in subject.[93] Several midrashim and medieval commentators, however, show greater fidelity to the wording of the verse by maintaining that it depicts Moses, not God, as writing the second set of tablets.[94] These commentators typically explain the contradiction between 34.1 and 34.28 by suggesting that in 34.1 God does not intend literally that God will write the second set but that Moses will do so on God's behalf. According to this reading, the verb in 34.1 is in the first person to show that God will approve what Moses writes or that God will provide Moses with strength or aid to carry out the writing.[95]

Some modern scholars attempt a source critical solution, suggesting that 34.1b (with its reference to God writing the new tablets) is E while 34.28 is J.[96] But Joel Baden provides cogent reasons for viewing both these verses as E in their entirety.[97]

The contradiction between 34.1 and 34.28 is not surprising within E. It reflects the tension we saw throughout chapters 19–20: E repeatedly complicates the relationship between the words of the Decalogue and God. According to 34.1, the second set of tablets will result from cooperation between Moses (who carved the tablets out of stone) and God (who added a text to them). But 34.28 allows us to understand that both the tablets and the writing are the work of Moses. As several medieval rabbinic commentators (Isaiah of Trani; *Moshav Zekeinim*) note, 31.18 tells us that the writing on the first tablets was divine: they were "written with the finger of God. . . . The tablets were the work of God, and the writing was God's writing, incised into the tablets." But the text refrains from providing this information in regard to the second set of tablets.[98] This contrast weakens the attempt to import God as an unspoken subject into 34.28. It is understandable that scholars have debated who actually wrote in that verse, God or Moses. What is most significant for our purposes is not to determine which answer is correct. On the contrary, E seems not to intend us to come to a conclusion; had it so intended, it could have phrased itself with a level of clarity easily achievable within the norms of Hebrew grammar and syntax. We ought not strive, then, for the perspicuity that scripture denies us; rather, we should recognize that the description of the second set of tablets—the tablets actually given to the Israelites—fits E's pattern of ambiguity. The tension between 34.1 and 28 forces us once again to contemplate a tension between stenographic and participatory theories of revelation without coming to any definite conclusion.

Two additional E verses may suggest that God spoke to Moses using human language. Exodus 33.11 describes how, after the events at Mount Sinai, Moses would repair on occasion to a special tent outside the Israelite camp, where he would talk to God: "God would speak to Moses face-to-face, as a man speaks to his fellow." Similarly, in Numbers 12.8 we learn that God speaks to Moses "mouth-to-mouth." The phrasing in these two verses may be an idiom meaning "directly, without mediation": Moses enjoyed access to God unique even among the prophets. But the phrases could be taken more literally, to explain what "speak" means when God is the subject and Moses the recipient of the divine communication: in that specific situation, it has the same meaning it has when we use human beings as the subject.

In all these verses, however, it is significant that the nation Israel does not hear or see the divine words that Moses receives. The Israelites never gained access to the original tablets written by God. In theory, they might have seen the second set (though in fact we are never told that the tablets were displayed in public), but even then it appears to be the case in 34.28 that for some unspecified reason Moses wrote the second set rather than God. God regularly spoke to Moses at the Tent of Meeting, but the people were unable to overhear these exchanges. The Tent, we are told, was "some distance from the camp" (34.7), so that the people saw Moses from afar but could not hear what took place there. These E verses from Exodus 33 and Numbers 12, like their predecessors in Exodus 19–20, move in two directions. They direct us toward a stenographic theology, because they may suggest that God spoke or wrote in human words when communicating with to Moses; but they always put distance between the nation and those words. The Israelites (both as characters in the text and as E's audience) cannot be sure what transpired between Moses and God; they hear the divine communication only through Moses, and they never overhear God's voice or see God's writing on their own. E maneuvers its audience into a position that lacks clarity. Like Israel at Sinai, E's audience can only wonder about the exact nature of what Moses reports. They cannot know how much of what one hears in the sacred text is human in its phrasing and how much might be divine.

Revelation in P

There is widespread agreement about the extent of P's Sinai narrative, which consists of Exodus 19.1–2a, 24.16b–18a, 25.1–31.18, 34.29–35; and Exodus 35.1–Numbers 10.28. (The final section I list here includes the end of Exodus, the entire Book of Leviticus, and the first part of Numbers.)[99] To someone familiar with the Sinai narratives found in the redacted Book of Exodus or in Deuteronomy, P's Sinai narrative is almost unrecognizable.[100] P says nothing about thunder, lightning, or an earthquake. In Exodus 24.15–17, P describes God's body (the כבוד, or *kabod*) as consisting of a substance that looked like fire,[101] and it explains that when the *kabod* came down onto Sinai, the mountain was covered by a cloud (הענן). Here, however, the firelike substance and cloud are not meteorological accompaniments, predecessors, or reactions to the theophany; the fiery substance *is* the actual body of God, which the cloud surrounds like clothing.[102] P does not use any storm-related language to describe this cloud or the fire, and P mentions no earthquake.

A plot summary of P's Sinai narrative is useful for two reasons. First, readers of the final form of Exodus are so familiar with the E narrative (which takes up much more of Exodus 19–24) and with the similar narrative in Deuteronomy 4–5 that they are unaware of the very different course of P's story. Second, this Priestly story includes many nonnarrative passages of considerable length that provide legal, ritual, sartorial, and architectural information. As a result, it is difficult for most readers to pick out the trajectory of this narrative. In fact, many readers have a hard time noticing that this block of material has a narrative trajectory at all.[103]

P tells us that Israel arrived at Sinai (Exodus 19.1–2a), whereupon the cloud covered the mountain and the *kabod* descended on it (24.15b–16). On the seventh day of the *kabod*'s stay on the mountain, God called to Moses, and Moses ascended the mountain into the cloud itself (24.16–18a). God then gave Moses detailed plans for a Tent-shrine that the people were to build (25.1–31.17); God also gave Moses some physical object (called the עדות or '*edut*) that served as the token of the covenant between God and Israel (31.18). Having received the building plans, Moses descended, unaware that his face was radiating an uncanny light that resulted from his extraordinary proximity, upon entering the cloud, to the firelike substance that is God.[104] This radiance frightened Aaron, the elders, and everyone else, but Moses eventually convinced them to approach him (32.16, 34.29–35). He then directed the assembled people to build the Tent-shrine according to the exacting specifications he had received, and over the course of ten months they did so (Exodus 35.1–40.32). When the shrine was ready, the *kabod* (which apparently had spent the ten months waiting on the mountain, since we never hear that It returned to heaven[105]) entered the shrine (Exodus 40.33–38), called from inside the shrine to Moses (Leviticus 1.1), and imparted to him the laws of sacrifice (Leviticus 1.2–7.38).[106] The completion of the Tent, God's entry into it, and the presentation of the laws of sacrifice occurred on the first day of the first month of the second year of the Israelites' stay in the wilderness, ten months after the Israelites arrived at Sinai (see Exodus 40.17, and cf. 19.1). Once regulations concerning the proper procedure for sacrifices had been received, the formal dedication of the Tent-shrine began. (They could not begin earlier, since the dedication ceremonies themselves involved sacrifices.) This formal dedication lasted eight days and was marred by the death of two of Aaron's sons on the final day (Leviticus 8.1–10.20). After the dedication, God resumed the revelation of laws that had begun immediately prior to the ceremonies; this lawgiving continued through the end of the month (Leviticus 11–25 and 27). During this month Moses also received a series of warnings concerning the failure to obey these laws and a description of the benefits that would accompany their strict observance (Leviticus 26). The month-long lawgiving that began at Leviticus 1.1 and recommenced (apparently on the ninth of the month) at Leviticus 11.1 came to an end at in Leviticus 27.34, but Moses received additional laws at the Tent-shrine while Israel encamped at Sinai during the first three weeks of the second month of the nation's second year in the wilderness (Numbers 5–6). The Israelites left Sinai on the twentieth day of that second month (Numbers 10.11–12). Throughout subsequent years, Moses received additional laws at various locations as the Israelites traversed the wilderness (for example, Numbers 18–19, 27.1–11, and 28.1–30.16) and in the plains of Moab across the Jordan River from Jericho (Numbers 35–36).

Thus, P's memory of the location where Moses received the law differs from the better-known story found in E. P's Moses received no laws on top of Mount Sinai; instead, he received blueprints. He used those blueprints to build the Tent-shrine, and it was at that shrine that the lawgiving took place.[107] To be sure, the Tent was located at the foot of Mount Sinai for a period of seven weeks, during which all the laws in Leviticus and several in Numbers were given; for this reason, Leviticus 7.38, 25.1, 26.46, and 27.34 can speak of laws and statutes given "at Mount Sinai." But this does not mean on top of the mountain; it refers to acts of lawgiving when the Tent was located at the foot of the mountain.[108] Furthermore, the lawgiving at the Tent continued even after the Israelites (and the Tent) left Sinai.[109] That post-Sinaitic laws were imparted at the Tent is clear from Numbers 27.5, which tells us that Moses brought the legal query of Zelophehad's daughters "into God's presence." In P, "God's presence" is no metaphor, but a reference to the *kabod*'s physical location, which is found in the Holy of Holies of the Tent-shrine. For that reason the shrine is termed both the משכן ("Tabernacle," or more precisely, "dwelling place") and אהל מועד ("Tent of Meeting," since God met Israel there).[110] It was from this place that God provided Moses with the new law that addressed the daughters' inquiry. The spot all moments of lawgiving share was not Sinai but the

Tent.[111] More specifically, God communicated with Moses from the back room of the shrine, where God sits on a golden throne above the ark.[112] It is from that space that God reveals all the law (Exodus 25.22).[113]

P's conception of the lawgiving's timing also differs from that of E.[114] Whereas for E the lawgiving took place during a brief period shortly after the exodus, for P the lawgiving commenced fully ten months after the nation's arrival at Sinai and a year after the exodus itself. Much of the lawgiving took place during the first month of the nation's second year in the wilderness, but it continued sporadically thereafter until shortly before Moses's death many years later. Furthermore, for E, lawgiving was punctual. All the laws were given to Moses in two bursts that took place one after the other at Sinai: in the Decalogue, God provided a sample from a wider set of laws (or perhaps a statement of basic principles of the wider set[115]); subsequently, God communicated the wider set itself in Exodus 20.23–23.33. For P, lawgiving was frequentative: it took place over many years, always at the Tent of Meeting but in various locations in the wilderness and Moab. Usually it involved only Moses, but in a few cases it included Aaron or Aaron's sons.[116] The ongoing nature of lawgiving in P comes to the fore especially in the various stories in which Moses approaches God with legal queries. In these cases he receives both specific responses and general statements of law for the ages (Leviticus 24.10–23, Numbers 9.1–14, 15.32–36, 27.1–11, and 36.1–9).[117] Here we note a basic difference between conceptualizing lawgiving as a onetime event (E) and seeing it as ongoing process (P).[118] This difference will become a major issue in later Jewish thought. It reemerges, for example, in rabbinic texts as a debate between R. Yishmael and R. Akiva (see b. Ḥagigah 6a–b and parallels).[119] We will examine this debate's afterlife and implications in chapter 5.

It is not only the timing and location of lawgiving that distinguishes between E and P. The sources describe the very purpose of the lawgiving in their own ways. For E, the law itself is the goal of the event at Sinai. By giving the law, God initiates a covenant with the nation; by accepting it, the people ratify the covenant. The law, as Schwartz emphasizes, *is* the covenant for E.[120] But for P, the covenant is essentially a divine promise, and it has already existed since the time of Abraham.[121] What happens at Sinai is not the creation of a covenant but a result of it: The people to whom God promised a land are now responsible for providing an abode for God. They will then be responsible for maintaining conditions that allow the transcendent deity to remain immanent. To provide that abode, they build the Tabernacle. To facilitate divine immanence, they observe the law—especially the laws of ritual purity and sacrifice, but also laws pertaining to ethics.[122] The observance of these laws enables a being who never dies and never acts sexually to take up residence among beings who do, for the purity regulations require Israelites, when approaching God at the Tabernacle, to divest themselves temporarily of traces of their mortality and sexuality.[123] At its core, then, P's Sinai narrative is not about lawgiving. The goal of the events at Sinai as P describes them is divine immanence, and the laws are but the means to that end.[124] It follows that the many modern scholars who speak of P as essentially legalistic or as glorifying the law misrepresent this document.[125] P's main concern is not law but the divine presence that observance of the law makes possible. (Thus, for P, observing the law is an act of theurgy—and thus P contains the seeds of classical kabbalah.)[126] It is in fact E that represents true legalism, if by that term we mean a belief that the law is the very essence of revealed religion.[127]

Here we see how different concepts of revelation reflect a fundamental difference regarding the purpose of ritual practice and the nature of religious authority. This difference calls to mind a remark Franz Rosenzweig made in a letter he wrote in 1922 to Rudolph Hallo: "Judaism is not itself law; it creates law. But in itself it is not law. It 'is' simply being Jewish."[128] On this particular issue, Rosenzweig resembles P and rejects the position found in E. For Rosenzweig the commandments provide "an opportunity to behold God's presence . . . they are a locus for the theo-human encounter."[129] One also sees Rosenzweig's similarity to P regarding the purpose of revelation in a letter he wrote in 1927 to Jacob Rosenheim, where he states, "Mount Sinai in smoke and the chapter of the thirteen *middot* [the principles revealed at Sinai in Exodus 34.5–7] are not enough to teach us what revelation is; they must be interwoven with the *mishpatim* [laws in Exodus 20–23 and 34] and with the Tent of the Presence [in Exodus 25–31 and 35–40]."[130] Here Rosenzweig, like P, merges the issues of revelation, law, and Tent (which is to say, divine presence). For Rosenzweig (and no less for Heschel), revelation is not an end in itself, an I-thou encounter for its own sake, nor is it the delivery of a law that is an end in itself.[131] Rather, revelation involves both the law and the institutions that allow God to dwell within the nation.

A further difference between E and P involves sense perceptions. E emphasizes that the whole nation heard a great deal at Sinai. To be sure, E forces us to wonder whether or not the sounds they heard included specific words from the divine mouth, but the aural nature of the event was central. (Thus, E both thematizes and problematizes the aurality of revelation.) For P, the people's experience was largely visual: standing at the bottom of the mountain, they saw the *kabod* far away, on top of the mountain. The language of 24.16–17 ("Yhwh's *kabod* dwelt on Mount Sinai, and the cloud surrounded it. . . . The appearance of Yhwh's *kabod* was like a devouring fire at the top of the mountain in the sight of all Israel") suggests that the *kabod* was so intensely effulgent that the people could see some of It through the cloud. Presumably, had they seen the *kabod* directly without the cloud to screen Its intensity, they would have died. The people saw the *kabod* again on the final day of the dedication ceremonies for the Tent. This second time, they saw not the entirety of the *kabod* but some emanation from It that briefly left the Holy of Holies to consume the sacrifices on the altar immediately outside the Tent (see Leviticus 9.4, 6, 23–24). P's emphasis on sight is found throughout the Sinai narrative.[132] For example, the people are frightened by the radiance emanating from Moses's face when he descends from the mountain in Exodus 34.29. This visual phenomenon serves to authenticate Moses's prophetic status not only on this one occasion but each subsequent time that Moses conveyed laws to the nation,[133] just as in E the audible communication between Moses and God at once frightens the people and authenticates Moses's status (19.19). P underscores the visual especially at the beginning of the long passage presenting the plans for the Tent. There God says to Moses:

> They shall make Me a sanctuary, and I will dwell in their midst. You shall build it in accordance with all that I cause you to see [מַרְאֶה]—that is,[134] in accordance with the design of the dwelling and the design of all its furnishings . . . See [רְאֵה], and build, according to the design that you are shown [מָרְאֶה, literally "you have been caused to see"] on the mountain. (Exodus 25.8–9, 40)

This emphasis on what God caused Moses to see continues throughout the plans for the Tent (Exodus 26.30, 27.8, and Numbers 8.4; cf. Exodus 31.2). In fact, one wonders whether the revelation of the plans on the mountain was verbal in nature at all.[135] When P tells us that God "spoke" to Moses, P intends the verb in the sense of "communicate," and this section's repeated use of רא"ה as a guiding word suggests that the communication was visual rather than oral. Whatever took place between God and Moses on top of

Sinai was clearly sui generis in human history; after all, when Moses went into the cloud, he came closer to the *kabod* than any other human before or after. One need not be a strict Maimonidean to propose that "speak" in this context means something sui generis and hence nonverbal as well.[136]

Nevertheless, P does not focus our attention on the question that so concerns E: was there any unmediated lawgiving between God and Israel? For P all lawgiving was mediated (usually through Moses, and rarely through Aaron or Aaron's sons). The whole issue of public witnessing—both E's emphasis that the whole nation *perceived*, and also E's calculated ambiguity about *what* they perceived—is largely absent in P.[137] Instead, P makes mediation a process with multiple steps, as Victor Avigdor Hurowitz points out. Upon descending from the mountain with the directions for building the Tent, Moses speaks first to Aaron and the chieftains and only afterward to the nation as a whole (34.31–32).[138] This suggests that P leans toward a participatory theology of revelation, since the people receive all religious law through a human being rather than directly from God. For the most part, however, P does not focus our attention on this issue in the way that E does. It is E's work of thematizing and problematizing revelatory authority that prompts the audience to wonder to what extent the law is a divine product and to what extent a human one. By and large, P does not encourage us to ponder the nature of the lawgiving.

An exception to this general rule occurs in Numbers 7.89, which describes what transpires between God and Moses when Moses is at the Tent of Meeting:

> When Moses came to the Tent of Meeting to speak with Him, he heard the voice מִדַּבֵּר [on the translation of this term, see below] to him from above the covering that was on top of the ark of the covenant, from between the two *kerubim* [golden statues of a sphinx-like animal with wings], and He spoke to him.

The textual setting of this verse at the end of Numbers 7 shows that it does not narrate a particular event. Rather, the verse explains the meaning of God's "speaking" with Moses from within the Tent generally and provides the audience a picture of what happens each time that Moses approaches it to receive the law.[139] The *kabod* sits on the throne created by the outstretched wings of the *kerubim* above the ark in the Holy of Holies, and it is from there that the deity communicates with Moses, who (to judge from the evidence of Leviticus 16) is located inside the Tent but outside the Holy of Holies. Thus, this verse presents P's own commentary on earlier P verses like Exodus 25.22 and Leviticus 1.1, which describe God's lawgiving from the Tent. The word מִדַּבֵּר here is unusual.[140] Related to the verb that usually means "to speak," מִדַּבֵּר appears only in this verse, in two additional verses closely related to P (Ezekiel 2.2, 43.6, where they also describe communication between God and a prophet), and in 2 Samuel 14.13. The grammatical construction of the verb is known as the *hitpa'el*, which can have a few types of meaning. A *hitpa'el* can describe a reciprocal action, so that מִדַּבֵּר may refer to communication that moves back and forth between God and Moses.[141] Alternatively, the *hitpa'el* may intend ongoing action, which suggests that we translate the phrase, "he would hear the voice continually speaking to him," "he would hear the voice as it went on speaking to him."[142] The construction can also be reflexive, which leads Rashi to suggest that this voice "would speak to itself, and Moses would hear on his own"—that is, at the Tent, Moses somehow attained access to God's internal ruminations. P's use of the verb to explain what takes place when God communicates with Moses from the throne in the Tent suggests that this communication was not a simple matter of speaking in the way that humans speak.[143] A voice that allows for continuous rather than punctual communication or the overhearing of internal dialogue is not a voice speaking in any normal sense of the word.[144] These senses of our verb here suggest that the verb וידבר elsewhere in P means something different when God is its subject.[145] This implication is especially strong in one other possible meaning of our verb. The *hitpa'el* construction can denote simulation—that is, it can be used when the subject of the verb acts *as if* he were doing something (for example, התחלה means to feign illness in 2 Samuel 13.5, and התנכר, to act like a stranger in Genesis 42.7 and 1 Kings 14.5, 6).[146] If this sense of the verbal construction is intended, then the Priestly narrator is intimating that "speaking" is not something that the deity really does, and when the narrative attaches the verb *speak* to the subject God, it intends something different from that verb's usual meaning. God's "speaking" is something that only a prophet has experienced, and therefore something for which there is no word among us nonprophets who make up the narrative's audience. My use of quotation marks in the previous sentence, in fact, may be exactly what the Priestly authors (and Ezekiel) intend when they use the strange *hitpa'el* form of this verb: it reminds us that God's "speaking" is not really speaking at all.

Revelation in J

Schwartz identifies J's Sinai narrative as consisting of Exodus 19.9b–16a, 18, 20–25; 24.1–2, 9–11a; perhaps 32.9, 26–29; 33.1–5, 12–23; 34.2–3, 5–17, and perhaps 18–26 or an earlier version thereof.[147] But our level of confidence in turning to this material as a consistent whole cannot be what it was for the E and P material, which read well as complete stories on their own. In fact, for both E and P, the source by itself flows much better as a narrative than the redacted text. J, however, may be more fragmentary. It appears to assume that a terrible sin occurred at Mount Sinai and reacts to it at two points (32.9 and 32.26–28), but it does not narrate that sin. Parts of J, then, may have been left out of the redacted Book of Exodus, perhaps because those parts closely paralleled one of the other sources.[148] Further, it is possible that parts of what critics identify as J may include passages that were composed to supplement E or P or an early version of the Book of Exodus. Because of what may be the fragmentary nature of what we have of J's Sinai story, it is difficult to be sure how parts of this material relate to other parts. If some of the verses are post-J scribal additions or if parts of J are missing, then it is not possible to reconstruct J's view of revelation and lawgiving at Sinai as we can for the other sources. On the basis of what remains, however, it is worth noting a few themes that seem to come to the fore in J.

J, like P, emphasizes the visual aspect of the revelation. Joel Baden notes this pattern in J passages even before Exodus 19:

> The theophanies in Exodus are explicitly visual. First, there is Yhwh's appearance to Moses in the burning bush: "Moses hid his face, for he was afraid to look at God" (Exodus 3:6); then the theophany before all Israel at Sinai: "On the third day Yhwh will come down in the sight of all the people" (19:11); also in the theophany to the elders alone: "They saw the God of Israel" (24:10); and, famously, in the individual theophany to Moses on Sinai: "I will take my hand away and you will see my back" (33:23). This is to name only a few of the more prominent passages in which sight plays a significant role in J. Throughout the document, starting from the tree in Eden, sight is equated with knowledge and understanding: to see something is to know it more intimately, to comprehend it more fully.[149]

Whereas J accentuates the visual, the auditory plays little role, at least in what remains of J. Some of the imagery so prominent in E also appears in J, who tells us that "Mount Sinai was entirely covered with smoke, because

Yhwh alighted upon it in the form of fire, and its smoke ascended like the smoke of a furnace, and the whole mountain trembled greatly" (Exodus 19.18). In its stress on the visual, J recalls P, though with an interesting difference: P, rather more democratically, reports that the whole nation see the *kabod* (both when It comes down on Sinai in Exodus 24 and when It flares out of the Tabernacle to consume the sacrifices in Leviticus 9), but J adopts a more elitist attitude: only a small number of elders and leaders see God in Exodus 24.[150]

Further, J portrays the theophany as something the nation might find appealing or exciting as opposed to frightening.[151] E tells us that the Israelites were terrified by the sounds and sights that accompany the theophany (Exodus 20.18); D repeats this claim at greater length (Deuteronomy 5.23–27); and in P, the people—at the very least awed but perhaps also frightened by the appearance of the *kabod*—shouted and fell on their faces (Leviticus 9.23–24).[152] These three sources emphasize (to use the still useful conceptualization of Rudolph Otto) the element of *tremendum* in God's manifestation—that is, the extent to which the holy, in its overpowering majesty, is absolutely unapproachable, inspiring dread and fear.[153] Only J accentuates what Otto terms the *fascinans*—that is, the ways in which the holy is also attractive, alluring, and entrancing.[154] J's God is concerned that the people might endanger themselves by breaking through to see God from too close. God repeatedly warns Moses not to allow the people as a whole to come into physical contact with the mountain during the theophany (19.12–13, 21–22, 24). Similarly, in J sections of chapters 33–34, Moses and the people desire God's presence deeply. Without it, Moses claims, they cannot move forward on their journey toward the Promised Land (33.15), and the Israelites go into mourning when they learn that the full-fledged divine presence will not accompany them (33.4). God has to warn them of the danger divine presence poses to a stiff-necked people prone to sin (33.3).

As in the other sources, the issue of direct as opposed to intermediated revelation has a place in J. At least in what remains of J, however, the issue does not achieve the central place it has in the E source. J straightforwardly portrays access to the theophany as graduated. The whole nation witnesses Yhwh's descent onto the top of the mountain, but from a distance; the people are not allowed to come close to the base of the mountain, much less to approach the summit where God is. But representatives of the nation (Moses, Aaron, two of Aaron's sons, and seventy elders of Israel) are permitted to ascend the mountain and to genuflect "from afar" (24.9). In spite of this distance, the elders and Moses's close male relatives are able to see God with impressive clarity (24.10); the text notes that they were not killed by the sight, which indicates that they enjoy without danger a type of proximity rare for humans but not unheard for prophets. (One can compare Isaiah 6.1–5, for example, in which a prophet, having seen God directly, receives the surprising though welcome news that the sight will not kill him.)[155] Moses alone approaches God (in 24.2 and in again 33.21–22, 34.2–3, 5–8). Even he, however, is unable to see the full manifestation of God's presence, instead seeing God's back but not God's face or *kabod* from the front (33.18, 23).

What happened in J when Moses approached God? Did Moses receive laws, and if so, in what form and through what sort of cognition? As it stands, J does not preserve its own law collection of the sort we find in Exodus 20.23–23.33 (E), Leviticus 1–27 (P), or Deuteronomy 12–26 (D). Older critics argued that the short legal passage in Exodus 34.10–26 stems from J, but it is now clear to scholars on both sides of the divide separating neo-Documentarians and proponents of newer European theories that these verses contain at least some post-J material. Exodus 34.12–14 is clearly a secondary addition to the redacted Torah, and it is impossible to be sure whether 15–17 is the original continuation of the J material that ended at 11 or part of the later insertion.[156] Similarly, almost all contemporary scholars agree that the laws pertaining to holy days in Exodus 34.18–26 are not J but a postredactional addition to an early version of Exodus that already contained J, E, P, and D.[157] If all these verses are additional, then only verses 10–11 belong to J. We can speculate that other legal material appeared in this part of J's original Sinai narrative, but we cannot build a characterization of J's theology on the basis of that speculation.[158]

Nevertheless, it is clear that for J, law is a crucial aspect of Israel's relationship with God, whether it contained a discrete law code or not. In Exodus 34.27 God directs Moses to write a document that forms the basis of the covenant between God and Israel: "Yhwh said to Moses, 'Write these words down, because it is on the basis of these words that I form a covenant with you and with Israel.'" While we cannot be sure what "these words" refer to, this covenant does rest on specific words. This is even more explicit in 34.10–11, where God tells Moses, "I hereby form a covenant. . . . Carry out what I command (מצוך) you this day." Further, as Shuvi Hoffman has argued, at several places J narrates the origins of an Israelite ritual practice. These narratives provide grounds for observing each of these laws.[159] For example, in Exodus 16.4–5, 16–30, J narrates a story that teaches about the manner, origin, and importance of Sabbath observance.[160] J provides a description of circumcision and a narrative that shows how much it matters in Exodus 4.24–26.[161] Stories about Cain and Abel, Noah, the patriarchs, and the appointment of the Levites provide information on proper behaviors in cultic matters.[162] It may well be, as Hoffman argues, that instead of a legal collection, J provides repeated narrative justifications for individual laws.

Lawgiving in D and the Beginnings of Biblical Commentary

As we turn from the three Pentateuchal sources found in the Book of Exodus to the fourth source, D, we find ourselves making a move that is crucial for any Jewish attempt to wrestle meaning from the Bible. The D authors are responsible for all of Deuteronomy 1–31, a few brief interpolations notwithstanding. These authors reformulate material found in earlier books of the Torah, and in so doing, they clarify ambiguous statements, revise material, and react to ideas the older sources express. Thus, Deuteronomy is the oldest Jewish commentary on the material we have examined from Book of Exodus.[163] In a sense, Exodus becomes Jewish scripture only in Deuteronomy, because Jews study scripture as Jews within a community of readers that includes earlier Jews whose interpretations are available in classical commentaries. A specifically Jewish reading of scripture emerges from that community. Thus, Deuteronomy, by commenting on and engaging material we know from Exodus, constructs that material as sacred and authoritative from a Jewish point of view.

Deuteronomy's exegetical tendency is especially prominent in its depictions of the lawgiving in chapters 4 and 5.[164] (These two chapters come from a later and an earlier stratum of D, respectively, but they approach all the issues I discuss here from a single perspective.)[165] Joel Baden shows in exquisite detail that Moses's speeches in Deuteronomy 4 and 5 rework the E source, from which they borrow material word for word; they also react to material from J, though less frequently and without word-for-word borrowing.[166] In Deuteronomy 4, a later writer has Moses, addressing the people Israel shortly before his death, recall:

> [10]the day you stood before Yhwh your God at Ḥoreb, when Yhwh said to me, "Assemble the people to Me so that I may cause them to hear My words, which they should learn so that they will hold Me in awe all the days

that they live on the earth, and so that they will teach their children." [11]Then you drew near and stood at the base of the mountain; the mountain burned with fire to the very heart of the heavens—there was darkness, cloud, and fog. [12]Yhwh spoke to all of you from within the fire; you were hearing a voice of words (קול דברים), but you saw no form—just a voice. [13]He declared His covenant to you, which He commanded you to carry out—the ten utterances. Then He wrote them down on two stone tablets. [14]As for me, Yhwh commanded me at that time to teach you laws and statutes so that you carry them out in the land that you are entering so as to own it. [15]So be very careful, for this is a life-and-death point: for you saw no form on the day Yhwh spoke to you at Ḥoreb from the midst of the fire. (Deuteronomy 4.10–15)

These verses were written with two specific questions in mind, which are precisely the questions that emerged in our study of Exodus 19–20—and, it seems, from the Deuteronomists' study of this material as well: (1) What does the word *qol* in those chapters mean? (2) How much of the Decalogue did the Israelites hear? Deuteronomy 4.12 informs us that the nation heard a קול דברים, a sound of words. D's addition of the clarifying word דברים ("of words") to E's *qol* responds to an ambiguity we noticed in Exodus: the *qol* was a voice articulating sounds to communicate meaning. Further, this speech makes clear that the whole people, not just Moses, heard the Decalogue. Second-person plural forms fill in the gap we noticed in Exodus 20.1, which left out the recipient of the Decalogue text: "Yhwh spoke to all of you (אליכם). . . . You (אתם) were hearing a voice of words. . . . He declared His covenant to you (לכם), which He commanded you (אתכם) to carry out—the ten utterances . . . on the day Yhwh spoke to you (אליכם) at Ḥoreb" (the rhetorical effect of the second-person plural forms is lost in English; I attempt to regain it once by translating "all of you" at its first appearance[167]). To be sure, in verse 14 Moses was commissioned to act as intermediary, but only for subsequent legislative disclosures.[168]

In addition to clarifying the ambiguities in E, the Deuteronomists in this passage also take issue with a view found in J and in P. In 4.12 and 4.15, D insists that the people "saw no form" of the divine body, thus repudiating the view found in J verses such as Exodus 19.11 and 24.10–11, as well as P verses such as Exodus 24.17 and Leviticus 9.4–24. It is characteristic that D puts a voice in place of a visual form, for Deuteronomy's is a "religion of the ear and not of the eye" (to borrow a phrase Paul Tillich used to characterize Protestant Christianity in distinction from Catholicism and Orthodoxy).[169] Deuteronomy insists that the Temple contains not God's bodily presence (which is located exclusively in heaven and never on earth) but a symbol of God's presence that D terms God's "Name."[170] D emphasizes verbal symbolism rather than cultic sight as an avenue to God when, in texts like Deuteronomy 6.4–5 and 31.10–13,[171] it requires Israelites to listen to God's teaching on a regular basis.[172] This substitution of voice for picture speaks volumes not only about D's understanding of revelation but about D's theological project altogether. The neo-Kantian Jewish philosopher Hermann Cohen describes what he calls Deuteronomy's "reflective repetition" on the preceding books, insightfully connecting the replacement of form with voice to D's abhorrence of anthropomorphism:

> [T]he criticism of this reflection penetrates even deeper in that it considers above anything else those doubts in regard to revelation that must be raised from the point of view of God's spirituality. . . . The danger of a material conception of God was concealed in the theophany itself. It is very instructive to learn how Deuteronomy strives to avert this danger.[173]

And here Cohen quotes our passage from chapter 4 (specifically, verses 15–16).

As part of this move away from sight toward sound, the D authors redeploy the verbal root רא״ה throughout chapter 4 (and also in chapter 5). The texts we examined in Exodus use verbs and nouns from this root to denote the vision of God that the people or the elders see; so in both J (Exodus 3.3, 19.21, 24.10) and P (24.17); a similar idea occurs with the term לעיני ("in the sight of," or, more literally, "in the eyes of") in J (19.11) and P (40.38). P also uses the root רא״ה when speaking of the plan for the Tabernacle that God showed Moses in Exodus 25.9, 25.40, 26.30, 27.8, and Numbers 8.4. This verb appears throughout the Deuteronomic authors' Horeb narratives, but there the object seen is never God. Rather, D repeatedly finds new uses for the verb, which now refers to what the people learn in an abstract sense (Deuteronomy 4.5, 4.25), to what the nation did *not* see (to wit, the deity, 4.12, 4.15), and to enticements that might lead them astray if they pay too much attention to what they see (4.9, 4.19). Only twice in Deuteronomy's Horeb narratives does this verb refer to what Israelites really saw with their eyes (4.36 and 5.24). These verses make clear that what they saw were accompaniments of theophany but not God's bodily manifestation. Moreover, both of these verses go on to use שמע ("hear"), as if the verb רא״ה ("see"), by itself and unchaperoned by a more responsible verb, might get the Israelites into troubling situations. In fact in 4.36 "hear" appears once before "see" and again after it, so that the audience contextualizes seeing within a context controlled by hearing. Similarly 5.24 specifies that what the people *saw* is that God *speaks*; thus, רא"ה here—and also, D wants us to realize, in any case where it is used with something divine as the object—really means "understand," not "see with one's eyes." The Deuteronomists move the verb's meaning away from sight toward something of a verbal and intellectual nature, thus making רא"ה subservient to שמ"ע, and emptying the former of its central meaning to make more room for the latter.[174] This tendency to put hearing where other Israelite thinkers put seeing also appears in 4.33, where, in contrast to the biblical norm, it is the sound of God's voice rather than the sight of God's body that poses a mortal danger to human beings.

Moses's speech in Deuteronomy 5 responds to the ambiguities of Exodus 19–20 in similar ways:

> [2]Yhwh our God formed a covenant with us at Ḥoreb. [3]It was not with our parents that Yhwh formed this covenant, but with us, all of us, we who are here today, we who are alive! [4]It was directly[175] that Yhwh spoke with you at the mountain from within the fire, . . . saying:
>
> "[6]I am Yhwh your God, who led you out of the land of Egypt . . .
>
> . . .
>
> [21b] . . . You shall not desire your neighbor's house, his field, his worker, his maid, his ox, his ass, or anything that belongs to him."
>
> [22]It was these words that Yhwh spoke to your whole congregation on the mountain from within the fire, the cloud, and the fog—a great voice (קול), which did not continue. Then He wrote them down on two tablets of stone and gave them to me. [23]And it came about that when you all heard the voice (קול) from within the darkness—and the mountain was on fire—that the leaders of your tribes and the elders drew near to me, [24]and you said, "Look, Yhwh has shown us His glory[176] and His greatness; it was His voice (קולו) that we heard from the midst of the fire; today we saw that God can speak with a human, and the human lives. [25]So now, why should we die? For this huge fire will devour us! If we continue to hear the voice (קול) of Yhwh our God any more, we will die! [26]For who among all flesh has heard the voice of the living God speaking from the midst of the fire like us, and then lived? [27]You go, and hear whatever Yhwh our God may say; *you* can tell us all that Yhwh our God tells you, and we will listen, and we will carry it out." (Deuteronomy 5.2–27)

Deuteronomy 5 stipulates in verse 25 that the people heard a *qol* that "speaks," not just a *qol* that accompanies lightning and clouds. In fact, the guiding word *qol* appears in close proximity to the word *speak* in three of its four occurrences in the passage just quoted. The passage also resolves the oddity in Exodus 20.18, which told us that the people "saw the voices/thunders [קולות] and the blazing lightning and the sound of the shofar and the smoke from the mountain." Like Rabbi Yishmael in the midrash cited earlier, Deuteronomy 5.24 clarifies that the people saw the visible but heard the aural by adding verbs from the root רא"ה ("see") in its paraphrase of the verse from Exodus: "Yhwh has let us see [הראנו] His glory and His greatness; it was His voice (קולו) that we heard from the midst of the fire; today we saw [ראינו] that God can speak with a human, and the human lives." This verse closely tracks the vocabulary and imagery of Exodus 20.18 while removing any element of paradox.[177]

Furthermore, our passage addresses the question insistently raised in E concerning how much of the Decalogue the nation heard. Deuteronomy 5.23–31 echo Exodus 20.18–21 (where the people request that Moses act as intermediary), but the verses in Deuteronomy are not phrased ambiguously.[178] Exodus 20.19 did not specify whether the people heard the revelation: "Let not God speak to us, lest we die." But Deuteronomy 5.25 makes clear they did: "If we *continue* to hear the voice of Yhwh our God *any more*, we shall die."[179] (D has Moses repeat the same point in Deuteronomy 18.16, where we again find the crucial terms "continue" [אסף] and "any more" [עוד].) Moses's task on his own is to receive the remainder of the legislation, which 5.31 calls "the *whole* command."[180] The events recounted in 5.23–31 follow the giving of the Decalogue not only textually but also temporally; by using *waw*-consecutive verbs in verse 23 the Deuteronomist eliminates the possibility that the people heard only part of the Decalogue or none of it. D insists that this revelation involved not just Moses or elders but "the *whole* congregation" (5.22). To the same end, Deuteronomy revises the line introducing the Ten Commandments: while Exodus 20.1 stated merely, "God spoke all these words, saying," the parallel sentence in Deuteronomy 5.4–5 reads, "Yhwh spoke to you [עמכם; the Hebrew is plural, addressing the nation] . . . saying." Like the Septuagint and Old Latin translations of Exodus 20.1, the Deuteronomist attempts to remedy the earlier verse's failure to specify the addressee of the divine speech. Finally, D stresses that the people had direct contact with God in 5.4.[181] The revelation was public, not mediated; on this point Deuteronomy is both insistent and clear.

Clear—yet equivocal. Deuteronomy 5.5 contradicts the verse that comes before it (as well 4.12–13 and 5.19–20). Immediately after the vivid description of the unmediated meeting of God and Israel in Deuteronomy 5.4, there follows a comment announcing that Moses acted as intercessor:

> ⁴It was directly that Yhwh spoke with you at the mountain from within the fire—⁵I was standing between Yhwh and all of you at that time, so as to tell you God's word, for you were afraid of the fire, and you did not go up the mountain—saying: "⁶I am Yhwh your God."

The medieval commentators Rashi, Rashbam, and ibn Ezra point out that the word לאמר ("saying") in verse 5 belongs to the sentence found in verse 4, since it completes the phrase in verse 4 which begins with the words "Yhwh spoke."[182] This renders the remainder of verse 5 parenthetical. We can go a step further than these commentators: verse 5 (other than the word "saying") is a later addition to the text. It includes the formula, "at that time," which (as Samuel Loewenstamm has demonstrated) consistently serves in Deuteronomy to indicate scribal interpolations.[183] This interpolation reintroduces Exodus's idea of a mediated revelation into Deuteronomy. Exodus 19–20 (and already the E text preserved therein) forced the audience to contemplate the possibilities of direct, public revelation of the Decalogue and a mediated one. Deuteronomy 5, acting as a commentary on (more precisely, a revision of) these passages in Exodus, decides in favor of the view that revelation at Sinai was direct. However, a glossator who agrees with the older notion (which was one of the options E allows, and the only possibility in J and P) acts as a supercommentator, adding a line that eliminates both D's notion of public revelation and E's equivocation so that the text agrees with the position that we know from J and P—but only in the gloss itself, since the surrounding context remains intact. In the end, both Exodus and the final form of Deuteronomy present two possibilities, but it is important to notice the difference between them. In Exodus, we find ambiguity, whereas in Deuteronomy, we find מחלוקת or debate. The former contains a pattern of verses that could be understood in more than one way, each one self-consistent. This pattern focuses our attention on the question "Did they hear all or part or none?" but makes it impossible to give a definitive answer. The original text of Deuteronomy 5, in contrast, provides one answer to the question: they heard all, without mediation. But the gloss in 5.5 gives the other answer: they heard none directly and received Torah only through mediation. The final form of Deuteronomy converts deliberate indeterminacy into multivocalic disputation.

By utilizing the formula "at that time," the supercommentator in 5.5 has clearly marked his interpolation as such. Like a page in a midrashic collection or a rabbinic Bible, Deuteronomy 5 presents more than one reading of Exodus 19–20. As a result of the interpolation, the final version of the text contradicts itself: Deuteronomy 5 in its present form does not achieve the univocal clarity D originally sought.[184] In this way the final form presages a tendency that will become prominent in later Jewish literature: texts that attempt to reduce complex traditions to definitive compendia are typically subject to commentaries that reinscribe the earlier complexity.[185] This was the fate of the Mishnah, whose clarity and brevity are followed by the Gemaras' intricate and extended discourses. It was also the fate of Maimonides's code, which became canonical only alongside the whole literature of commentary and supercommentary it attracted. Maimonides's decision to borrow a traditional Jewish appellation for Deuteronomy, *Mishneh Torah* ("repetition of the Torah"),[186] for his code was unintentionally apt, for Maimonides's code came to share a particular type of multivocality with Deuteronomy 5. I refer here to comments found throughout almost all editions of Maimonides's *Mishneh Torah*. Known as the השגות or *Reservations*, these passages were written by Rabbi Abraham ben David of Posquières (known as the Rabad) and are now printed within the text of the *Mishneh Torah*, usually in a different typeface, or indented into Maimonides's own text. In the *Reservations* the Rabad often disagrees with Maimonides's rulings; he presents alternatives to them and transmits rulings from earlier rabbinic texts that Maimonides had rejected. In a strikingly similar fashion, the interpolator in Deuteronomy 5.5 puts forward precisely the view that D rejected. Indeed, the literary genre of 5.5 might be termed a השגה or "reservation," and we may dub the unknown scribe who wrote the verse "Proto-Rabad." The parallel between D and Maimonides's code goes further. The *Mishneh Torah* that became canonical and authoritative in Judaism was less Maimonides's *Mishneh Torah* than the *Mishneh Torah* of tradition: what Jews study as a central part of the curriculum of rabbinic Judaism are editions of the *Mishneh Torah* that include Rabad's *Reservations* interpolated into Maimonides's text along with a host of commentators positioned around Maimonides's text. These commentators reinstated the disputes, discourses, and legal derivations that Maimonides intended his *Mishneh Torah* to render avoidable.[187] Precisely the same dynamic is at work in Deuteronomy's depiction of Sinai: what serves as Jewish scripture is not D's Deuteronomy but tradition's; the canonical version of Deuteronomy includes both D and the tradition-restoring interpolations of Proto-Rabad.[188] Thus, Deuteronomy is a classical Jewish text—one might be so bold as to call it a rabbinic text—for two reasons: first, because it functions as commentary and revision;[189] second, because already in the biblical period it is subject to commentary and revision.[190]

One other element of D's view of lawgiving requires attention. We saw earlier that P and E differ in regard to the very purpose of the law: for P the law is a means to divine immanence, but for E the law is an end in itself. D's position shares elements of both while moving in its own directions. In the bulk of chapter 4 we find an emphasis on the law for its own sake.[191] But already in chapter 4 and increasingly in chapter 5, we find that the law is also instrumental for D, but not in P's sense of allowing God to dwell on Earth. On the contrary, D rejects the possibility that the transcendent God would dwell anywhere other than in heaven. But the law for D is instrumental because, as Thomas Krüger shows, D's law helps Israelites to become wise and thus to live safe and successful lives (see, for example, 4.1–9, 29.1–8).[192] Thus, D is a predecessor to Maimonides (in this regard as in so many others[193]): both D and Maimonides believe the law has an essentially pedagogical task. The law is not only a response to God's beneficence and thus oriented toward the past; it also encourages the creation of a well-functioning society and thus is oriented toward the future.[194] Furthermore, as James Kugel points out, the law in D plays a role analogous to that of the Temple in P: it allows Israelites to come close to God in spite of the danger of divine presence. In this conception,

> God is served in His temple via the sacrifices offered by His priests, but He is also served by the general populace observing His laws. . . . The laws of Deuteronomy do not omit the priesthood and the temple—they hardly could have!—but these are meshed into a book that clearly presents the ordinary Israelite's obedience to divine law as the primary form of piety. . . . It is observance of the laws that allows Israel to "cling" and "hold fast" to Him (Deuteronomy 13:5; 30:20; etc.). Evidently, obedience to these laws is thus a form of piety parallel to the sacrificial cult; both are ways of serving, *la'abod*, this God.[195]

For D, observance of the law outside the Temple becomes an alternative but powerful cultic service.[196] Following Moshe Weinfeld, Kugel notes that D uses the verb לעבוד, often reserved in biblical texts for sacrificial service performed by priests, to refer to the people's loyalty to Yhwh, which expresses itself through obedience to Yhwh's law.[197] From D's perspective, this alternative form of cultic service becomes necessary for two reasons. On a practical level, by commanding the centralization of the sacrificial cult in a single Temple, D removes the Temple from the religious lives of most Israelites, and therefore it must provide other rituals to take the place of the local temple or altar. (Thus, long before the rabbis, D had already created forms of religious expression for what became, in the day-to-day life of most Judeans, a religion without a temple. What many recent scholars regard as the rabbinic revolution necessitated by the destruction of the Second Temple was in fact accomplished by D prior to the destruction of the First.) Further, on a more theological level, it is not only the Temple that is distant from most Israelites but also God, for D's God dwells exclusively in heaven. Thus, where P sees a need for practices that enable the dangerous paradox of divine immanence, D sees a need for practices that bridge the gap between heaven and earth. Once again we see that D is a predecessor to Maimonides. As Kenneth Seeskin has memorably put it, a central task of Maimonides's thought is to search for a distant God.[198] This search, I submit, began with D's coupling of the avowal that God is distant with the assertion that the law allows us to connect ourselves to God nevertheless.

The Effects of Redaction

Having examined the sources individually, we need now to attend to the redacted text. This is important to us both as religious readers (since the canon presents the final form to us as scripture) and as historical critics (since the final form is an artifact no less important than its predecessors). Reading the final form, however, cannot mean simply returning to the canonical text as if we did not know about its components and history. While harmonistic or holistic readings prove themselves appropriate in some texts, in light of our knowledge of the seams that source criticism discovers we cannot pretend the text is a harmonious whole, or even that the redactors intended it to be a harmonious whole. An intellectually honest modern reader of scripture will regard some redacted texts less as the product of synthesis than as a record of debate and polemic. The case of the Sinai and Horeb traditions in the Pentateuch strikes me as such a case. When we read the whole, we need to ask: How can we evaluate the memories found in each of the sources in new ways once we see how they differ from one another? How do J, E, P, and D implicitly comment on one another?[199] How does R, the redactor of the Torah, comment on all of them and on the very notion of revelation?

What is most remarkable when we compare the Pentateuchal sources to the Pentateuch itself is the difference between the narrative consistency and thematic unity of the former and the disarray of the latter. Each source presents its story about the giving of the law without any sense that other laws were given at some other point in time. In E and D, God gives the law to Moses on the mountain immediately after the giving of the Decalogue, whereas in P God gives Moses the law many months later in the Tabernacle. Moreover, P makes clear that *all* the laws were given at the Tabernacle in Exodus 25.22. That verse renders it impossible to read the legislation in Leviticus and Numbers as the product of a second lawgiving that supplements an earlier one, which took place shortly after the Exodus—yet the redaction of the Torah forces us to do just that. Similarly, while E and D date Moses's receipt of the law to the same time right after the Exodus, they differ regarding the time when Moses passed the law on to them. In E, Moses read the laws to them shortly after he received them (Exodus 24.3–7), whereas in D Moses does not convey the law to them until forty years later.[200]

If anything, this contrast between the sources' unity and final version's disarray is even stronger on a thematic level. Both P and D have very clear and consistent positions about the lawgiving. (To be sure, Proto-Rabad's Reservation or השגה in Deuteronomy 5.5 undermines that consistency, but the original attempt still comes through clearly.) It is difficult to generalize about J because of its possibly fragmentary nature, but what we have of J repeatedly shows several main motifs. Even E is consistent, though in a deliberately perplexing way. Its ambiguity is (it is safe to say in light of its frequency) intentional and also instructive. But when the redactors combined the sources, thematic unities were obscured. For E and D, lawgiving was punctual, while for P it was a process that lasted decades. In the redacted text the former point of view has been undermined, since the final version depicts multiple moments of lawgiving. All the sources want to locate these important events in a single place, whether at Sinai, at Ḥoreb, or at the Tent that moves around the wilderness. But the unity of place each source championed is gone from the redacted text. J and P left us no doubt that all lawgiving was mediated; but D insists that God revealed the Decalogue directly, in its entirety, to the whole people. On this issue, the viewpoint of E has won, albeit in a new form, since the ambiguity that E crafted so carefully has given way to the redacted text's self-contradiction. The most crucial differences involve the purpose of the theophany. Is the law an end in itself, the very content of the covenant (E and D), a pedagogical tool (D), or a means to the end of divine immanence (P)? Or is the theophany most of all a matter of basking in a vision of God (J), so that legally obligatory rituals may aim to preserve or recall the experience of that vision? For the original sources, what we learn about revelation and from revelation is set and unalterable—written in stone, if you will. But the redacted Torah relativizes the sources, replacing their clarity with cacophony.

By presenting a jumbled set of memories as to what happened at the lawgiving, how it happened, why and when and where it happened, the final version of the Pentateuch forces us to wonder about revelation and to contemplate its nature. A reader of any one source has a specific picture of the revelation in her head, but a reader committed to accepting the whole witness of scripture cannot produce any such picture without doing damage to parts of the text or ignoring large swaths of it. This lack of clarity extends to a question as basic as whether there was a Decalogue at all (P: no; D: yes; E: depending on how one reconstructs this source, yes or no, but if—as is most likely—yes, the question remains open as to whether the people received it from God, Moses, or maybe partly from God and partly from Moses; J: we cannot be sure but probably no). The person who attends only to a single source can achieve that most dangerous of things in religion, certainty; the premodern reader of the final form of the text, constitutionally unable to become aware of the self-contradictions the text contains, might also achieve certainty, though only after a fair amount of exegetical struggle that undermines the sense of certainty. The modern reader who accepts the Pentateuch as scripture while recognizing its artifactual nature embraces its importance and sanctity but cannot privilege any one source over others. That reader is forced to accept that lawgiving occurred, that it is vitally important, but that we can never be sure precisely what it entails. In this respect, the final form, in its broad thematic sweep, most closely resembles E, though it goes even further than E in the direction of equivocation. What the Pentateuch presents to us is not univocality but argument, not clarity but perplexity.[201] Its final form highlights revelation as the central theme of the Pentateuch; much more of the Pentateuch is devoted to revelation and lawgiving than, say, the exodus from Egypt, the wandering through the wilderness, the creation of the world, or the lives of the Patriarchs.[202] Yet the final form undermines our ability to truly know about the revelation with any certainty. This combination of traditions, whether by design or by its refusal to decide among its sources, both emphasizes and problematizes the lawgiving.[203] This tendency is a hallmark of the Torah as a theological document: the Pentateuch accentuates a theme's importance even as it bewilders us with self-contradictory positions.

Maximalist and Minimalist Interpreters

Modern Jewish interpreters of Tanakh as scripture can attend to the torah of each source as well as to the Torah that combines them into a restless whole. But such readers cannot stop there. To produce a Jewish reading of scripture, they must listen to the torah of those who came after the redactor as much as to the torah of those who came before. When we study the history of interpretation in light of the history of composition, we will find that the pre-redacted sources reassert themselves. This is the case because the final form of the Torah, though it studiously refrains from giving us a clear picture of what happened at Sinai, presents us with a central question: to what extent did the people participate in revelation? The sources answer this question differently: D is maximalist, asserting that the whole nation heard the whole Decalogue. P and J are minimalist, asserting that all lawgiving was mediated through Moses (and, for P, through Aaron and his sons on a few occasions). E above all prompts the audience think about the tensions among maximalist, minimalist, and in-between positions. Studying classical Jewish interpretations of revelation at Sinai involves following the developments of these positions in postbiblical literature and noticing how older points of view reassert themselves in newly productive or surprisingly extreme ways. Doing so discloses an overarching unity that connects biblical and postbiblical Judaisms in spite of—indeed, because of—the Torah's lack of internal consistency.

Midrashic Interpretations and Medieval Biblical Commentators

We have seen that the first Jewish commentators on texts from the Book of Exodus, the authors of Deuteronomy, respond to precisely those questions that the E source in Exodus emphatically raised: How much of the Decalogue did the people hear, if any? What was the *qol* they heard—a voice, thunder, or something else? What did the people perceive at Sinai, and which senses were involved? Postbiblical commentators sensed these problems as well. In rabbinic exegesis of Late Antiquity and the Middle Ages, the maximalist and minimalist schools of thought developed further.[204] The maximalist school highlights the sequence of texts in Exodus 19–20. The people expressed their fear in Exodus 20.18 *after* the revelation, and thus they heard all of the Decalogue. These commentators, in other words, follow in the interpretive path initiated by Deuteronomy (minus the interpolation in Deuteronomy 5.5). Commenting on Exodus 20.18, an early midrashic collection, the Mekhilta deRabbi Yishmael, Baḥodesh §9, presents this reading:

> "And they said to Moses, 'You speak with us so that we may hear'" [Exodus 20.18]. This tells us that they did not have enough strength to receive any more than the Decalogue, as it is said, "If we continue to hear Yhwh our God any more, we shall die" [Deuteronomy 5.25]. Rather, [they said,] "You go near and hear" [Deuteronomy 5.27]. From that time forth Israel merited that prophets would appear from among them, as it is said, "I will repeatedly raise a prophet for them" [Deuteronomy 18.18].

The Mekhilta turns our attention to Deuteronomy 5.25's paraphrase of Exodus 19.19. The paraphrase makes clear that they did hear God by adding the words *continue* and *any more*: the people lacked strength to hear "any *more* than the Decalogue"—in other words, they did hear that much. One of the greatest of the contextual/linguistic commentators of medieval rabbinic tradition, the twelfth-century French rabbinic sage Rashbam, makes a similar point in his commentary on Exodus 20.18:

> And after they heard the Decalogue, they said to Moses, "You speak to us . . ." And if they had not said this, one must conclude that the Holy One would have told them all the commandments directly.[205]

The same reading is mentioned by Rashbam's Sephardic contemporary, the great rationalist-linguistic scholar Abraham ibn Ezra, in his long commentary to Exodus 20.18; it is also found in the commentary of an influential sixteenth-century Italian rabbi, Obadiah Seforno, to Exodus 20.1. While Rashbam and ibn Ezra are maximalist in their reading of the Decalogue itself, Viezel shows that they are minimalist in regard to the rest of the Pentateuch: both regard the Decalogue as the only case of pure divine speech in the Bible and view the wording of the rest of the Pentateuch as largely the work of Moses.[206]

But others view the conversation between Moses and Israel in Exodus 20.18–21 as having taken place *during* the revelation. According to these minimalist interpreters, the nation heard only the First and Second Statements of the Decalogue. (Here and in what follows I follow Jewish tradition in referring to the Ten Statements [דברות] rather than Ten Commandments.)* Thus, we read in a passage from the Talmud, b. Makkot 23b–24a:

> Rabbi Simlai expounded: 613 commandments were spoken to Moses—365 negative commandments, equal to the days of the solar year, and 248 positive commandments, corresponding to the limbs in a human being. Rav Hamnuna said: from what text do we learn this? [From the verse in Deuteronomy 33.4:] "Moses commanded us torah . . ." In gematria, [the numerical value of the word] "torah" is 611 [and thus Moses commanded us 611 commandments]. Thus it is evident that we ourselves [that is, the Israelite nation as a whole] heard "I am Yhwh" and "You shall have no other gods" [the First and Second Statements in the Decalogue, Exodus 20.2 and 20.3–6] directly from God.

Essentially the same midrash appears in a well-known midrashic anthology, in Shemot Rabbah 33:7, where the rabbis as a group are quoted rather than R. Hamnuna specifically, and in Bereshit Rabbati Lekh Lekha 17:19. In the version from b. Makkot, Rav Hamnuna deftly solves two questions, only the first of which is stated explicitly: (1) How do we known that there

---

* Several systems exist for dividing this text into ten commandments or statements. In this book I use the system most widespread in rabbinic Judaism, in which the First Statement is "I am Yhwh your God" (20.2), and the Second is "You shall have no other gods . . . You shall not make any image . . . You shall not bow down to them" (20.3–6). In another system, which is found in the פסקאות (ancient Jewish paragraph markings) in Torah scrolls, all of 20.2–6 constitutes the First Statement or Commandment. This system was adopted by Rabbi Yishmael and by Catholic and Lutheran churches. In a third system, used by most Protestants and Eastern Orthodox Christians and found in the work Philo and Josephus, "I am Yhwh your God" (20.2) is an introduction to the Decalogue as a whole; the First Commandment is "You shall have no other gods besides Me" (20.3); the Second consists of "You shall not make any image . . . You shall not bow down" (20.4–6). In the first and third systems, the Tenth Statement or Commandment forbids coveting; in the second system, the Ninth forbids coveting one's neighbor's house, and the Tenth forbids coveting one's neighbor's wife and property.

are 613 commandments? After all, it is possible to count them differently. (2) How do we explain the oddities of Exodus 20.18–21, whose syntax and wording, as we saw in the previous chapter, imply that the people heard only part of the Decalogue? Rav Hamnuna concludes from Deuteronomy 33.4 that Moses himself taught 611 commandments to Israel, since one might read that verse as "Moses taught us 611 (= torah)." This is two fewer than the traditional rabbinic calculation of the commandments. The missing two, then, must have been heard directly by the nation, since they were not among those that "Moses taught us." The unmediated commandments must have been transmitted at Sinai, which is the only legislative scene in the Bible where the whole nation was present.

Both sides of the debate are represented in a passage found in Shir Hashirim Rabbah 1:13 (commenting on Song 1.2); the midrash also appears in Pesiqta Rabbati 22:5:

> Rabbi Joshua ben Levi and the rabbis disagreed. Rabbi Joshua said: Israel heard two Statements from the mouth of the Holy One, blessed be He: "I am" [the First Statement, in Exodus 20.2] and "You shall not have" [the Second Statement, Exodus 20.3–6]. That is what is meant by the verse, "Let Him kiss me with some of the kisses of His mouth" [Song of Songs 1.2]. Some of the kisses, and not all of them. [Rabbinic interpreters understand the Song of Songs to describe the meeting of God and Israel at Sinai. Songs 1.2, then, tells us that Israel had direct contact with God at Sinai; the "kisses" represent divine utterances that come from God's mouth. But the text in Song of Songs reads "some of the kisses."[207] Hence the nation was in direct contact with God only for some divine utterances.] But the rabbis say that Israel heard all the Statements from the mouth of the Holy One, blessed be He. Rabbi Joshua of Sikhnin passed on a teaching of Rabbi Levi, explaining the reasoning of the rabbis as stemming from the verse, "They said to Moses, You speak with us, so that we can hear" [Exodus 20.19; the rabbis' position can be supported if we read this verse as narrating what happened exactly where the verse is located—after the text of the entire Decalogue]. How does Rabbi Joshua ben Levi handle this verse [since he argues that Israel heard only two statements]? He disagrees [with the rabbis' use of the verse, instead pointing out that] there is no early or late in the Pentateuch. [The order of material in the text of the Pentateuch does not always mimic the order of events they describe, so that a later event can be described in the text before one that took place earlier.[208]] But perhaps the Israelites spoke the words, "You speak with us, so that we can hear," after three Statements? [That is, strictly speaking, Rabbi Joshua's interpretation

does not stipulate that the people heard two Statements; rather, they heard "some"—more than one but less than ten. How, then, do we know that they heard only the first two?] Rabbi Azariah and Rabbi Judah ben Simon support the viewpoint of Rabbi Joshua ben Levi by citing the verse, "Moses commanded us Torah" [Deuteronomy 33.4]. The whole Torah contains 613 commandments. In gematria, the numerical value of "Torah" is 611 [and thus Deuteronomy 33.4 shows that Moses relayed 611 commandments to Israel]. However, Moses did not relay "I am" and "You shall not have" [the First and Second Statements] to us; we heard them directly from the mouth of the Holy One, blessed be He.

The opinion that the nation heard only the first two commandments is also attributed to Rabbi Yishmael in another talmudic passage, b. Horayot 8a.[209]

The interpretive deductions on the basis of which the minimalists in these talmudic and midrashic passages arrived at their conclusion may strike modern readers as far-fetched, but a twelfth-century French commentator supports the same opinion on the basis of reasoning that modern readers will appreciate readily.[210] Rabbi Joseph Qara is quoted in the commentary of Joseph Bekhor Shor on Exodus 20.1:

> The rabbis[211] said that the people heard the First and Second Statements directly from God and the rest from Moses. Rabbi Joseph Qara of blessed memory explained that Scripture itself proves this, because the first two are spoken as if He Himself was speaking to them [that is, God refers to Himself there in the first person: "I am Yhwh."]. But from the Third and on, it is as if He speaks through a messenger [because the Third Statement refers to God in the third person]. . . . Thus it says, "For He will not acquit," not "I will not acquit"; "Yhwh made the world in six days," not, "I made the world in six days," etc.[212]

According to the minimalist position, the people heard God's *qol* in the sense of "voice" only briefly. For the most part, what they experienced was an overwhelming event, not the communication of specific content.[213] Further, the First and Second Statements primarily involve theology or first principles rather than legislation: even the Second Statement is as much a theological assertion regarding exclusive loyalty to one deity as it is a statute. In claiming that the nation heard only the first two statements, the minimalists within rabbinic tradition in effect prefer E over D—and they opt for a particular reading of E, in which the people did hear God's voice speaking actual words, albeit quite briefly. They do not embrace the more radical possibility that E allows—that the people heard nothing at all of the

Decalogue and that the divine *qol* they heard was not verbal in nature.[214] Thus, these commentators move in the direction of a participatory theory of revelation, but they do not articulate it fully.

Maimonides as Minimalist

Later minimalist commentary limited the verbal content of the revelation experienced by the nation even more, thus moving toward the more radical reading and adopting a full-fledged rejection of a stenographic theory of revelation. This is the case in the most influential work of Jewish philosophy, the *Guide of the Perplexed*, by the twelfth-century Spanish-Egyptian rabbi, legal authority, and philosopher Maimonides. Because of the notorious difficulty of pinning down Maimonides's true opinions in the *Guide*, we need to pause to read through relevant passages quite carefully.[215]

In his discussion of revelation at Sinai in the *Guide* at II:33, Maimonides seems initially to agree with the less far-reaching minimalism of the talmudic sages Joshua ben Levi, Yishmael, and Hamnuna, and of Maimonides's older contemporaries, Rashbam and ibn Ezra:

> The *Sages, may their memory be blessed** . . . have a dictum formulated in several passages . . . : *They heard "I" and "Thou shalt have" from the mouth of the Force.* They mean that these words reached them just as they reached *Moses our Master* and that it was not *Moses our Master* who communicated them to them. . . . The texts and dicta of the *Sages* permit considering as admissible that all *Israel* only heard at that *Gathering* one *voice* one single time—the *voice* through which *Moses* and all *Israel* apprehended *I* and *Thou shalt not.* . . . As for *the voice of the Lord,* I mean the created voice from which the *speech* [of God] was understood, they heard it once only, according to what the text of the *Torah* states and according to which the *Sages* make clear. . . . This was *the voice* . . . through which *the first two commandments* were apprehended.[216]

But Maimonides goes beyond the minimalism of the classical rabbis in several respects. Maimonides claims that the divine voice the people heard in the First and Second Statements of the Decalogue was not a voice in the

---

* Maimonides wrote the *Guide* in Arabic, but he frequently included words, phrases, and quotations in Hebrew. Shlomo Pines (from whose translation I quote) italicizes material that appears in Hebrew in Maimonides's original.

regular sense of the term; even in those two statements the Israelites did not hear actual speech directly from God. They heard the words of Exodus 20.2–6 only when Moses repeated the Decalogue's components to them one by one:

> Know that with regard to that *voice*, too [namely, the sound of the First and Second Statement that they heard directly from God] their rank was not equal to the rank of *Moses our Master*. I shall draw your attention to this secret, and I shall let you know that this is a matter that is transmitted by tradition in the religious community and known to its men of knowledge.[217]

Maimonides goes on to point out that the authoritative translation of the Pentateuch into Aramaic by Onqelos supports his thesis: whenever God speaks with Moses, Onqelos translates with the verb מליל, but when Exodus 20.18 refers to the people hearing the voice at Sinai, Onqelos translates with the verb יתמלל. The distinction, Maimonides claims, shows that the people's perception of the first two statements did not match Moses's perception. Thus, Maimonides argues that the people did not truly hear God's voice in the sense of words; what they experienced was something less specific.[218] Maimonides shares this view with one possible reading of E, and he differs from D. Nonetheless, he attempts to support his position by citing, and radically limiting, a D verse:

> About hearing this great voice, it says: . . . *Ye heard the voice of words, but ye saw no figure; only a voice* [Deuteronomy 4.12]. It does not say: *Ye heard the words*. Thus every time when their hearing words is mentioned, it is their hearing the *voice* that is meant, *Moses* being the one who heard words and reported them to them.[219]

Maimonides seems troubled by the phrase "the voice of words," in Deuteronomy 4.12, which was intended by D to answer the question that E raised in Exodus 19–20 ("What is the *qol*?") and to preclude a possibility that E intimates (namely, that the *qol* is thunder or an overwhelming noise but not a voice speaking words). Contrary to the grain of the verse from Deuteronomy, Maimonides argues that the presence of the phrase "voice of words" rather than just "words" shows that the nation heard a sound but not words directly. Thus, he attempts to read a minimalist position into this verse from Deuteronomy, which was intended to clarify Exodus 19 according to the maximalist one.[220]

Maimonides's pursuit of the minimal does not stop there. He explains that even what Moses heard was not speech in any normal understanding of that word. Granted, Maimonides initially seems to suggest that Moses really did hear God's voice articulating words in the last passage I quoted ("*Moses* being the one who heard words and reported them to them"). But later in the same chapter Maimonides intimates that what Moses heard did not in fact consist of words at all:

> It is impossible to expound the *Gathering at Mount Sinai* to a greater extent than [Onqelos and the rabbis] spoke about it, for it is one of the *mysteries of the Torah*. The true reality of that apprehension and its modality are quite hidden from us, for nothing like it happened before and will not happen after. Know this.[221]

Here, too, Maimonides hints at a reading that goes beyond the minimalism of the rabbis. This implication becomes clearer in two passages elsewhere in the *Guide*, I:65 and II:48. (The "mystery of the Torah" to which Maimonides refers at the end of II:33 is "hidden" not in some abstract sense but hidden elsewhere in the *Guide* itself.) There Maimonides intimates that even Moses's experience of God at Sinai could not have been verbal. Indeed, it cannot be audial in any sense, because, Maimonides insists, speech cannot be attributed to the incorporeal God any more than walking or eating can.[222] In his discussion of divine speech in I:65, Maimonides rightly points out that the Hebrew verbs that mean "speak" (דבר) and "say" (אמר) can refer not only to making the sound of words with one's mouth but also to two abstract, nonphysical processes: first, thinking, and second, willing, desiring, or intending. He then states categorically:

> Now in all cases in which the words *saying* and *speaking* are applied to God, they are used in one of the two latter meanings. . . . They . . . denote either will and volition or a notion that has been grasped by the understanding having come from God. . . . The terms in question never signify that He, may He be exalted, spoke using the sounds of letters and a voice, nor that He, may He be exalted, possesses a soul into which notions are impressed so that there would subsist in His essence a notion superadded to that essence. For these notions are attached to and related to Him in the same way as all other actions. As regards volition and will being denoted by the words *saying* and *speaking*—this . . . is one of the meanings because of which these words are equivocal. In this case too they are used by way of likening Him to us. . . . The term "command" is figuratively used of God with reference to the coming to be of that which He has willed.[223]

When the Torah describes God as talking, it does not mean that God communicated using a voice and words. Indeed, for Maimonides, it cannot and must not mean that. It refers only to volition or thought. Further, it cannot refer to an *act* of volition or thought that Moses could receive through some sort of extrasensory perception. For if God acted at a given moment to think a specific thought or to express a particular wish (such as "I don't want Israelites to eat pork"), then God is not eternal and unchanging. Whatever happened to Moses at Mount Sinai, it did not involve his ears hearing God speaking any words to him, or even his mind "hearing" God silently expressing specific volitions. Both Moses and Israel had some intellectual experience of God at Sinai; but in light of Maimonides's statement in I:65, even Moses's deeper perception there did not involve the medium of language, even silently.

A similar conclusion about Maimonides's real intention in his discussion of Sinai in II:33 arises from a consideration of his comments at the end of the second book of the *Guide*, at II:48. He lets the reader know that he is about to hint at something that is at once very important and, for many Jews, very unsettling: "Listen to what I shall explain in this chapter and consider it with particular attention, with an attention exceeding the attention with which you consider the other chapters of the Treatise." Having indicated that what he is about to say will require careful thought and a certain degree of intellectual and religious fortitude, he proceeds:

> Know that all proximate causes through which is produced in time that which is produced in time . . . are ascribed in the books of the prophets to God, may He be exalted. And according to their manner of expressing themselves, it is said of such and such an act that God did it or commanded it or said it. For all these things the *expressions to say, to speak, to command, to call*, and *to send* are used. This is the notion to which I wished to draw attention in this chapter. For inasmuch as the deity is . . . He who arouses a particular volition in the irrational animal [that is, the animals other than human beings] and who has necessitated this particular free choice in the rational animal [human beings] and who has made the natural things pursue their course . . . it follows . . . that it may be said with regard to what proceeds necessarily from these causes that God has commanded that something should be done in such and such a way or that He has said: Let this be thus. . . . Accordingly . . . in order to designate the shaping of the causes in whatever way they are shaped . . . these five terms are used—namely, *to command, to say, to speak, to send, to call*. Know this and reflect upon it regarding every passage that fits it.[224]

The Pentateuch's laws and its Sinai narratives constitute a "passage that fits" this conception of divine speech. One needs to "consider" this teaching "with particular attention" because it has an extraordinary bearing on (among other issues) the question of where the law to which Maimonides was so deeply committed originates. The terms he discusses here—*send, speak, command*—are always to be understood as radically figurative when applied to God. To say that God commands is to say that God is the ground for the fact that a good and rational command has been perceived by a wise human; it is not to state that God literally uttered the command.[225]

If this is the case, then what does it mean to say that God called Moses, that God sent Moses, that God spoke to Moses, and that God commanded Israel through Moses? In other words, what does it mean to say that God gave the Torah and that Moses received it? An extraordinary answer to these questions is provided in a series of studies by specialists on Maimonides's thought. While others could be mentioned in this connection, I will focus on four. Alvin Reines, Kalman Bland, Lawrence Kaplan, and Micah Goodman provide detailed readings of the *Guide* showing that Maimonides viewed the verbal content of the Torah to be the work of Moses, not of God. Further, they demonstrate that when composing the laws, Moses was not acting as a prophet—and certainly not on his unique level as a prophet who goes beyond all other prophets. Reines describes Maimonides's view as follows:

> At Sinai, Moses attained a prophetic revelation in which he acquired the greatest knowledge possible of God—the negative theology and the theology of divine actions. . . . Inasmuch as Moses' prophetic apprehension was intellectual or conceptual, he did not learn the particulars of divine government in his prophecy but its abstract essence. With the essence of the ideal law apprehended by his reason to guide him, Moses then wrote the Torah, creating the particular laws that reify the essence of the ideal law and which serve best to order society and further the spiritual and physical well-being of man. In writing the Torah, which was not prophecy, Moses employed his imagination to fulfill the twofold function of divine law: the teaching of true theological beliefs; and the establishment of the just and moral society.[226]

Here we see a picture of Moses reminiscent of E's and opposed to D's. Moses was the mediator of the law, not its transcriber, and a highly active mediator at that. He apprehended something divine that no other human had apprehended, and on the basis of that apprehension Moses composed the law. Whereas maximalists beginning with D insisted that the whole people received a sample of the laws in verbal form when they heard the whole Decalogue, Maimonides adopts and extends the logic of the minimalist tradition in his belief that neither Moses nor the nation heard specific laws from the mouth of God. E, we have seen, allows the possibility that the people heard no laws at Sinai and permits us to speculate that the divine *qol* Moses "heard" was not verbal. If the people heard none of the Ten Commandments, then they cannot verify that the wording of the laws comes from God through Moses, rather than simply from Moses. By emphasizing Moses's intermediary role, E creates space for an interpretive option in which Moses's role was so major as to include the actual formulation of the law, even though that law is attributed to God for serious but rhetorical purposes. Using circumspect language, Maimonides revives and extends E's understanding of lawgiving when he emphasizes Moses as intermediary.

Kalman Bland also focuses our attention on the robust nature of Moses's intermediary role according to the *Guide* and claims that for Maimonides the law of Moses was not the law of God:

> The Mosaic law and other laws are conventional . . . laws. . . . Since the laws are conventional, they cannot be ascribed to God unequivocally. . . . Maimonides denies that the Mosaic law is natural law, and therefore we may deduce that Maimonides did not think that it existed as such in God's mind. . . . Maimonides . . . does not believe that Moses ever received the particulars of his Law in revelation. . . . According to the logic of his arguments, Maimonides does not believe that God could have transmitted the particulars of the Law to Moses. . . . Maimonides considered Moses to have been the direct author of the Law.[227]

Bland goes on to remind us that "this does not imply, however, that the Law is not divine,"[228] since Moses composed the law based on his unique apprehension of the nature of the world and of the human personality. This apprehension resulted from the divine overflow that Moses alone among humanity was graced to receive. As a result, Moses's law has a divine imprimatur in a way that no other law known to humanity has; but its specifics were created by Moses, not God. The text of the Torah is a product of this world, the work of a particular person who lived at a particular historical juncture; it is for this reason that, against rabbinic tradition, Maimonides does not believe that the Torah preexisted the world.[229]

Lawrence Kaplan presents a similar thesis: "For Maimonides, . . . Moses' primary act of *Imitatio Dei* . . . was Moses' formulation of the Law,

Moses' legislation of the Law, or, to state the matter boldly, Moses' 'author-ship' of the Law."[230] Kaplan explains that for Maimonides, Moses's prophecy differs from all other prophecy because Moses's prophecy was purely intel-lectual and did not in any way call upon the faculty that medieval philoso-phers call the "imagination," which allows humans to conceive of physical realities that are not immediately present to their senses (see *Guide* II:45 as well as II:36).[231] But Maimonides elsewhere states (II:37, II:40, III:27) that all legislation must involve the imagination for complex reasons we need not go into here.[232] It follows that, when he wrote the law, Moses could not have been acting on the unique prophetic level he enjoyed, even though what he composed was decisively influenced by what he alone among all humanity knew. Thus, Kaplan demonstrates that for Maimonides the Torah is not a prophetic or revealed book!

> If, according to Maimonides, Mosaic prophecy does not involve the activity of the imagination while Mosaic Law does involve the activity of the imagi-nation, it follows that one must differentiate between Mosaic prophecy and Mosaic Law. Mosaic Law, while related to Mosaic prophecy, is not to be equated with it. . . . [In *Guide* III:39] Maimonides almost openly states that Mosaic Law is not to be identified with Mosaic prophecy . . . but *follows* from it.[233]

Similarly, Reines explains:

> The Mosaic experience [at Sinai] was twofold: prophetic and subprophetic. A subprophetic experience is defined as one that is not prophetic but which bears a special relation to prophecy. The Torah was produced by Moses as a subprophetic experience. Accordingly, Maimonides' admonition that the true nature of the Sinaitic revelation is one of the "secrets of the Law" can be well understood.[234]

More recently, Micah Goodman has addressed the issue, and his phras-ing of the question comes close to answering it: "Did Maimonides believe that God wrote a book? Is it likely that the thinker who freed God from the fetter of religious language and from the limitations of religious beliefs took God out of the Torah as well?"[235] Employing a detailed reading of sections of the *Guide* that differ from those on which Reines, Bland, and Kaplan focus, Goodman comes to an identical conclusion. He shows that for Maimonides the Torah was written by Moses as an imitation of nature:

> The analogy between Torah and nature is the hidden principle that or-ganizes Maimonides' conception of the Torah. Moses scrutinized nature,

understood the depths of divine wisdom [it contains], and translated it into laws that shape the ideal society and ideal human beings. . . . God created nature, and Moses wrote the Torah. And yet, because Moses wrote the Torah as a reflection of nature, it is appropriate to conclude that the divine wisdom found in nature has been copied into the Torah successfully. In sum, it is appropriate to say that even though God did not write the Torah, the Torah is divine.[236]

It will come as a surprise to many that Maimonides expressed such a view of the origin of the Torah.[237] After all, in a famous passage from his *Commentary to the Mishnah* (specifically, in his comments to the tenth chapter of the Mishnah's tractate Sanhedrin), Maimonides lays out his Thirteen Principles that a Jew must believe. The Eighth Principle might be understood to reject the view of the Torah's origin found in the *Guide*, especially in this principle's image of Moses as a secretary taking dictation:[238]

> The eighth Principle of Faith: That the Torah has been revealed from heaven. This implies our belief that the whole of this Torah found in our hands this day is the Torah that was handed down by Moses and that it is all of divine origin. By this I mean that the whole of the Torah came unto him from before God in a manner which is metaphorically called "speaking"; but the real nature of that communication is unknown to everybody except to Moses (peace to him!) to whom it came. In handing down the Torah, Moses was like a scribe writing from dictation the whole of it, its chronicles, its narratives, and its precepts. It is in this sense that he is termed מחוקק = "lawgiver." In the opinion of the Rabbins, [the wicked Judean king] Manasseh was the most renegade and the greatest of all infidels[239] because he thought that in the Torah there were a kernel and a husk, and that these histories and anecdotes have no value and emanate from Moses.

From this passage, one can receive the impression that according to *Commentary to the Mishnah*, the author of the *Guide* is a heretic. Thus, Kaplan writes:

> It should be noted that if our interpretation is correct, it follows that Maimonides' esoteric view of Mosaic Law [in the *Guide*] differs from his exoteric view as set forth in his . . . Eighth Principle [in his commentary to Mishnah Sanhedrin]. . . . The difference between Maimonides' esoteric view—assuming that Reines, Bland and I have understood him correctly—viz., that Moses "authored" the Law, and his exoteric view, viz., that Moses received the Law word for word from God like a scribe taking down dictation, cannot be glossed over.[240]

Kaplan does not quite spell out the implication of this difference, but it seems clear: the *Guide* is, from the point of the of the Thirteen Principles, a heretical work.[241] Maimonides could not have believed the Principles to be entirely true, though they were largely true and always useful.[242] A similar conclusion seems necessary regarding the ruling in Maimonides's *Mishneh Torah* (Law of Repentance 3:8) that condemns one who holds that "the Torah is not from God" (שאין התורה מעם ה').[243] One might attempt to harmonize this passage with the *Guide* by suggesting that the word *from* (מעם) in this statement is subject to interpretation. But in what follows, Maimonides adds that his condemnation applies even to one who makes such a claim even about a single verse or word in the Torah, and this phrasing undermines such a harmonization. The emphasis in Repentance 3:8 on the Torah's specific wording, like the understanding of the Eighth Principle as just outlined, supports a stenographic theory of revelation.[244] The *Guide*, in contrast, posits a major participatory role for Moses in the creation of the Pentateuch.

Yet it is possible to read at least the Eighth Principle differently.[245] Although the image of Moses as scribe taking dictation is a famous aspect of the Eighth Principle, the sentences before and after this image undercut it. Maimonides writes that "the whole of the Torah came unto him from before God in a manner which is metaphorically called 'speaking'" and that "the real nature of that communication is unknown to everybody except to Moses."[246] Thus, Maimonides gives us of a picture of Moses taking down dictation, but only after reminding us that this dictation did not involve any "speech" at all, since he uses that term figuratively. Further, Maimonides may distance God from the role of the person giving dictation in the simile, since the verb for dictation is passive and without a subject in Maimonides's Arabic original. By telling us that nobody understands how the Torah came to Moses, Maimonides makes clear that the image he provides of the scribe is just that: imaginary. He does not claim that this image depicts the historical event as it actually occurred.[247] Further, the Eighth Principle's strong rejection of the possibility that the Torah's contents "emanate from Moses"[248]—that is, that Moses wrote the Torah on his own—may be consonant with the *Guide*. While the latter work hints that Moses was not functioning as a prophet when he composed the Torah, it also makes clear that Moses wrote the Torah on the basis of his perfect understanding of the nature of God's works in the world. The Torah's wording is Mosaic and nonprophetic, but the ideas it embodies and encourages are indubitably divine, as Reines, Bland, and Goodman all take pains to state.[249]

In short, a careful reading shows that even in the Eighth Principle Maimonides does not condemn the view that Moses, rather than God, wrote the Torah. Indeed, as Yehoyada Amir points out to me, not only does Maimonides not regard the view that God did not utter the words found in the Torah as heresy; he would regard the view that God did utter those, or any, words as heresy, because the nonphysical God (of whom nothing can be predicated) uses words no more than this God walks or eats. Finally, readers surprised at the reading of the Eighth Principle I have just outlined will find it useful to recognize the nature of popular restatements of the Thirteen Principles with which they may be more familiar. (I think here, for example, of the "Yigdal" hymn recited at the end of many Sabbath and holiday services and the "Ani Ma'amin" statement found in many prayer books.) As Menachem Kellner points out, the principles as found in these restatements and in their reception among most Jews tend to be "simplified, even debased."[250] When compared with the more careful, detailed, and subtle formulations by Maimonides himself, Marc Shapiro writes, "these popularizations . . . vulgarize, and at times distort, a philosophically sophisticated text."[251] Thus, the flexible version of the Eighth Principle I lay out may be less surprising to people who read Maimonides's own formulation than it is to those who know the principles only through popular intermediaries.

The Rymanover Rebbe, the Ropshitzer Rebbe, and the Prophet Elijah

It is not only in the rationalist tradition that we find minimalist interpretations. A Ḥasidic rebbe, Menaḥem Mendel of Rymanov (d. 1815), proposed an especially fascinating understanding of the revelation at Sinai. Two of his students, Naftali Tzvi Horowitz of Ropshitz (d. 1827) and Horowitz's brother-in-law, Asher Isaiah Lipman, report Menaḥem Mendel's view, which is nowhere found in his own writings.[252] In his book, *Zera' Qodesh*, the Ropshitzer rebbe quotes the Rymanover as follows:

> I heard from the mouth of our master, teacher and rabbi from Rymanov, Menaḥem of blessed memory, discussing the verse "One thing God spoke, Two I heard" [Psalm 62.12] that it is possible that we heard from the mouth of the Holy One, blessed be He, only the letter *aleph* of *anokhi* [that is, the

first letter of the Hebrew word *I* that begins the First Statement in Exodus 20.2]. How beautiful are words from the mouth of a Sage! (*Zera' Qodesh*, 2:40a)

The Ropshitzer refers again to this teaching in *Zera' Qodesh* 1:72, where he does not mention Menaḥem Mendel of Rymanov; there he explains that the Israelites heard the *aleph* along with its vowel (a *qametz*, pronounced by eastern European Jews as an "au" sound that one finds in the name "Saul" or in the first syllable of "Boston"). The version of the Rymanover's teaching that appears in Lipman's *Or Yesha'*, also reports that the nation heard the letter *aleph* along with its vowel. According to the Rymanover's teaching, the Israelites hear not the first two statements, or the first, or even the first word. They hear only the first syllable of the first word of the First Statement, which is nothing more than a neutral vowel, since the Hebrew letter *aleph* makes no sound of its own but allows simply for a vowel to follow. The ears of the Israelites, then, did sense a noise, but, by itself, it was nothing other than that: a pure noise, without any meaning—a rush of air without even a consonant.[253] At Sinai, Israel heard nothing specific, but it did experience a revelation, a wordless signification of God's commanding presence.[254]

For Menaḥem Mendel of Rymanov and Naftali Tzvi of Ropshitz, the Sinaitic *aleph* constituted a genuine breakthrough of the divine into the human consciousness. Their understanding of God's oral but nonverbal disclosure is not identical to the suggestion of those modern biblical scholars who, arguing that the Decalogue was not originally part of the Sinai narrative, claim that in some biblical traditions the people did not experience direct revelation at all.[255] According to the Ḥasidic rebbes, the Israelites did hear something that came from or even embodied God, even though that something was not a word. In the view that results from the Rymanover's saying, the tension between understanding *qol* as voice and *qol* as noise or thunder is resolved by integrating both options into a single interpretation: what the people heard was a voice making the sound, "au"—a sound, but not a word. Another ambiguity that characterizes the E account of revelation is echoed quite literally by this reading. The Ropshitzer writes that the *aleph* heard by the people at Exodus 20.1 is referred to again in Exodus 20.18:[256] "all the people saw the sounds (*qolot*)." What can it mean to "see a sound," in particular to see the sound of the letter *aleph*? Addressing this well-known textual conundrum,[257] Naftali Tzvi explains that the shape of the letter *aleph* (א) consists of the letter *waw* surrounded by two *yods* (יוי = א). The numerical value of the letters *yod-waw-yod* equals twenty-six, which is also the numerical value of the divine name Yhwh (spelled with the letters *yod*, *he*, *waw*, and *he*). The *aleph* the people experienced thus amounted to God's name or presence. Further, Naftali Tzvi spells out, these letters resemble a face; the *yods* are the eyes, the *waw* the nose (ייו). Hence Deuteronomy 5.4's statement that "Yhwh spoke face-to-face" with Israel; Israel saw the divine countenance at Sinai, not as a form but as a sound (that is, as an *aleph* that was at once a face and the equivalent of God's name). Naftali Tzvi explains that his concept of seeing God not as form but as sound accords with Deuteronomy 4.12 ("you heard the sound of words but perceived no shape—nothing but a voice") as well as, or in combination with, Exodus 20.18. Indeed, he goes on to argue (employing even more complex reasoning based on gematria) that the *aleph* in some sense contained in latent form all 248 positive and 365 negative commandments.[258] However different Naftali Tzvi's interpretive norms are from our own, it is clear that for him the revelation through an indistinct syllable at Sinai was a genuine disclosure of God's being, of God's "face" or "presence," to Israel, and moreover a perception of divine command. That syllable was much more than the sort of a syllable that a human utters, and the process of hearing it involved vastly more than regular hearing. And yet it was not itself a word or a sentence, much less the whole text we know as the Decalogue.

Menaḥem Mendel goes beyond the rabbinic notion that the nation received only part of the Decalogue; he proposes a final, radical, variation of the minimalist position that was found in Shir Hashirim Rabbah, b. Makkot, and Joseph Qara's comment on Exodus 20.1. Yet Menaḥem Mendel's extreme minimalism in relation to Exodus 19–20 is not new in Jewish tradition. It returns us to a much earlier interpretation of the Sinai events. For this interpretation we need to turn to the culmination of the Elijah narratives in the Books of Kings. In 1 Kings 18, Elijah the Tishbite achieves a victory over the prophets of Baal and Asherah at Mount Carmel. His demonstration of the powerlessness or nonexistence of these Canaanite deities infuriates Queen Jezebel in chapter 19, and Elijah therefore flees to Mount Horeb. Elijah's experience there patterns itself after stories of Moses at the same mountain, as many commentators have pointed out (notice, for example, the motif of a forty-day fast in 1 Kings 19.7, which recalls Moses's fast at the same mountain in Exodus 34.28).[259] As a result of these patterns, the story of Elijah at Horeb becomes a potential locus for reflecting on stories of Moses and Israel at Horeb; a biblical writer might invite us to compare what he says about Elijah at Horeb with narratives concerning Moses at the same mountain, and through the juxtaposition of the stories a reaction to or a reading of the older story can emerge. Several lines in the Elijah narrative concern us in particular. 1 Kings 19.11–12 are marked off in the text because the phrasing that precedes them is repeated immediately after them as well. Such repetitions in biblical texts indicate the literary integrity of the section in between; in most cases, these sections are later additions to the text.[260] Thus, the verses in question appear to be an addition to the finale of the Elijah cycle that engages two motifs found in the story as a whole: the conflict with Baal and the comparison with the Sinai revelation. The crucial verses read:

> [God] said [to Elijah], "Go out, and stand at the mountain in Yhwh's presence." And—look!—Yhwh was passing by, but before Yhwh there was a great and mighty wind tearing mountains apart and smashing stones; Yhwh was not in the wind. And after the wind, an earthquake; Yhwh was not in the earthquake. And after the earthquake, fire; Yhwh was not in the fire. And after the fire, a sound (qol) of thin silence [or: of hushed rustling] (דממה דקה). When Elijah heard, he covered his face with his mantle, went out, and stood at the entrance of the cave. (1 Kings 19.11–13a)

This passage recalls and comments on other Israelite conceptions of theophany. It reuses images and vocabulary found in the Sinai stories in J, E, and D, including elements known from the depictions of theophany generally in ancient Israel and the ancient Near East—and especially, we saw earlier, in the appearance of the Canaanite god Baal: the mighty wind (recalling the storm), the earthquake, and the fire. It also recalls motifs and vocabulary specific to the Pentateuch's texts: the crucial word qol; the word "pass by" (עבר, which appears four times in Exodus 33.19–34.6); and most of all, the location, a cave or cleft in the rock at Mount Horeb.

By using these motifs to call to mind the stories of lawgiving at Sinai and the theophany genre more broadly, this passage critiques the former's use of the latter. This interpolation in Kings argues against the Canaanite model of theophany we saw earlier in this chapter. In that model Yhwh utilized storms and earthquakes as instruments of self-revelation. To our interpolator, this model makes Yhwh too similar to Baal for comfort.

(Recall that this section of the Book of Kings tells the story of Elijah's successful battle against Baal worship.)[261] In arguing against this understanding of theophany, our interpolator also contests, or at least refines, the portrayal in E and D of the event at Ḥoreb centuries earlier.[262] Yhwh's manifestation is not a matter of loud noises and spectacular natural phenomena, though, to be sure, those phenomena may precede or accompany revelation. Rather, God becomes known through a sound that is דממה.[263] This term has two possible meanings: it may refer to a soft breathing sound, or it may denote complete and utter silence.[264] God has a voice, but it is either difficult or impossible to hear it amid what prepares the way for it. (It is no coincidence that both Exodus 20.18 and 1 Kings 19.12 mark the perceptual field of revelation as enigmatic or even paradoxical, the former with a mysterious sound or voice that the people "see," the latter with its "thin silence" that Elijah "hears.") One might object that God does speak with a normal voice in other verses nearby (1 Kings 19.9 and 15–18). Those verses, however, belong to the original Elijah story; our short theological interpolation is limited to 11–13a. Reminiscent of the J passages in Exodus, this interpolation discards the notion, so central to E in Exodus 19–20, that God becomes manifest through storm and thunder and earthquake. But 1 Kings 19.11–13a goes further, eschewing visual revelation as well.[265] These verses depict God as becoming present not through something that can be seen, nor through loud noises or words, but through a soft murmur.

If one had to spell the hushed sound that God makes in this passage, one could only use the letter *aleph* and some vowel (or, if one interprets דממה as utter silence, an *aleph* by itself). Our examination of 1 Kings 19, then, demonstrates that the reading of Sinai advanced by Menaḥem Mendel of Rymanov is not a new one, nor is it only a logical extension of the interpretations found in Shir Hashirim Rabbah, b. Makkot, and the remarks of Joseph Qara. Menaḥem articulates a view already found in the story of Elijah—who, as the one who brings tidings of comfort in Jewish tradition, might also be termed "Menaḥem," which means "comforter": for the *aleph* the Rymanover believes Israel heard at Sinai is nothing other than a קול דממה דקה, the hushed sound of 1 Kings 19.12. Both our Menaḥems, then, the Tishbite and the Rymanover, imagine a peculiar type of perception, one that listens to a sound at once present and still, a consciousness that attends to the slight noise that introduces the "I" that is God but does yet not constitute it.

While 1 Kings 19.11–13 contains the Bible's strongest statement on this model of revelation, similar ideas appear elsewhere. Job 4.16 uses language nearly identical to 1 Kings 19.11–13 to describe a revelation. It may be significant that Ezekiel 1.25 associates a *qol* with God but does not describe its sound or volume, in contrast to the loud *qolot* of the heavenly creatures in 1.24. As in 1 Kings 19.11–13, the *qol* of Yhwh there is preceded by tumultuous noises but is distinct from them. Just as Yhwh is revealed amid silence, so too Israel's most intense communication with Yhwh occurs in silence: "To you, God in Zion, silence (דומיה) is praise" (Psalm 65.2).[266] Yehezkel Kaufmann famously argues that worship at the altar according to Priestly legislation was conducted in silence.[267] Finally, it seems appropriate that the God who is manifest in a sound of thin silence is known by the names Yhwh and Yah, which consist entirely of sounds that are barely sounds at all: the liquid glides *Y* and *w* (consonants that are almost vowels) and the mere rush of air that is the *h*.[268]

Let us return to the two questions we posed toward the beginning of this chapter's exegetical journey. First, was the revelation Israel experienced at Sinai an overwhelming event devoid of content, or did it involve distinct words? In the Tishbite-Rymanover reading, the answer is neither. Revelation was not verbal. Yet it was not an overwhelming event, or it was overwhelming only in a way that differs materially from the Canaanite-influenced imagery of Exodus 19 and Deuteronomy 4–5. Second, how much of the Decalogue did the nation hear? They heard no words, just as they saw no form, because there were no words to hear. The revelation was no more and no less than a signification of divine communication, an intimation of something beyond words or shapes, a trace that discloses a commanding presence.[269]

Does the idea of a silent revelation mean that there was no command in the divine self-disclosure? One can readily imagine a theology based on such a notion of theophany: it would emphasize the communion of God and humanity, but not regulations that might come out of the event. Indeed, one can find this non-nomian theology in the work of Martin Buber. But biblical and rabbinic texts move in the opposite direction: from revelation inexorably to law. This is the case not only in D (for whom revelation was verbal) but also in E (who plays with the idea that the *qol* did not involve a voice stating words). In spite of their differences, E closely resembles D in emphasizing law as the very essence of the covenant, even though E allows for the possibility that God did not literally speak the laws to Moses. This is also the case for P (who does not even consider the possibility that the people heard any words, all of which came exclusively through Moses or, in a few cases, other members of Moses's family), and J (for whom revelation seems most of all to have been a visionary experience but who also refers to a covenant commanded by God in Exodus 34.10–11 and narrates the origins of various laws). In the next chapter, I examine the necessity of command in the traditions that describe revelation at Sinai.

Pushing Too Hard?

The Torah's accounts of revelation at Sinai consistently raise the issue of how the nation Israel came to know the law. Did they hear God's commands directly, or exclusively through Moses's mediation, which inevitably involves some degree of interpretation? This question points to several larger ones: Is God's voice similar to a human voice, or does God communicate in nonverbal ways even with the intermediator himself? If God does not speak in any human sense, where do the specifics of the Torah's law originate? These questions received attention not only from texts in Exodus but from two traditions of interpretation that began within the Bible, especially in Deuteronomy and in the story of Elijah at Ḥoreb. These traditions, one maximalist and one minimalist, developed further among the rabbinic interpreters in antiquity and among commentators and philosophers in the Middle Ages. I have emphasized a family of answers to these questions that I variously call the participatory theory of revelation and the minimalist reading. Biblical texts inaugurate this family of answers when they raise the possibility that the people heard no words at the lawgiving. Rabbinic, medieval, and Ḥasidic texts follow them when they emphasize Moses's intermediary role and the nonverbal nature of the lawgiving. The theologians I discussed at the outset of this chapter, Rosenzweig and Heschel, build on an implication of nonverbal revelation by proposing that the specific words found in scripture are a human response to God's commanding but nonverbal self-disclosure. In the coming chapter I explore this implication of the minimalist tradition by addressing the relationship between a revelation that involved few or no words and the many words that constitute the Torah.

Before doing so, I need to scrutinize the hermeneutic character of the category of thought we call implication.[270] A critic of the argument I am developing might argue that I place too much weight on a few elements of the texts in Exodus 19–20 and their interpreters. In attempting to trace a trajectory that leads from E to the theologies of Rosenzweig and Heschel, I am, such critics would maintain, pushing too hard, because most of the ancient and medieval sages I categorize as minimalist did not in fact believe the Torah's words to be the product of multiple human authors. Further, to posit a connection between E's use of the guiding word *qol* and Maimonides's thesis concerning the radical inappropriateness of divine speech may seem unrealistic. Maimonides's ideas reflect the philosophical culture of his time and place; they are neo-Platonic and Aristotelian in a way that E's ideas about the *qol* could not have been. In a thoughtful critique of my proposal, Jerome (Yehudah) Gellman argues that the Ropshitzer Rebbe did not view the *aleph* of *anokhi* as devoid of content. Consequently, for the Ropshitzer the laws cannot consist exclusively of Israel's interpretive reaction to the *aleph*. Rather, Gellman writes,

> there is good indication in the text that the Ropshitzer did not have in mind a midrashic enterprise, rather than cognition of a transmitted content. . . . We find in the Ropshitzer a conception of revelation in which specific content pours out of the ineffable point of the *aleph* with the vowel *kamatz*.[271]

Gellman is right to note the difference between the Ropshitzer and the view of Rosenzweig and Heschel I champion. As I note earlier,[272] for the Ropshitzer the *aleph* in some sense contained all the commandments. He claims that law pours out from God's *aleph*, where in a Heschelian or Rosenzweigian reworking of the Ropshitzer's image, the *aleph* is a vessel God gave us so that we can pour law into it.

I take the ideas of the premodern minimalists further than they did when I connect their minimalism with that of twentieth-century theologians. Doing so, I submit, is entirely legitimate. Thinkers sometimes do not articulate or even realize crucial implications of their own ideas.[273] This phenomenon is well known to any teacher who attempts to convey material of a certain complexity. On occasion, I have known a student to make a comment that shows she understood what I said better than I did. At other times, students have asked questions I was able to answer immediately— but my answer entailed ideas I did not know until the student asked the question. The existence of unrealized implications is an inevitable feature in the history of ideas, for changing circumstances and new conversation partners create new vantage points from which to observe and extend earlier observations.[274] One thinker may have an insight that cannot be easily expressed or even fully understood in the conceptual language of his own day, but a later author, equipped with habits of thought unavailable earlier, can take up that insight, grasp it more thoroughly than the thinker who first propounded it, and articulate it in ways the original thinker could not imagine.[275] To use Aristotelian terminology: the new formulation actualizes a potential that was present in the original insight. The inability of the earlier thinker, using the tools of his own day, to imagine all the consequences of the insight hardly vitiates the link between that insight and the later author's proposals. (Here it is useful to recall the distinction that the historian of religion Wilfred Cantwell Smith draws between continuity and unchangingness.[276] The former, I think, is essential to authenticity of a religious tradition; the latter is inimical to its endurance.) As the Catholic theologian Yves Congar teaches, within a tradition, a doctrine may contain the solution to a problem not yet encountered when the doctrine emerged.[277] We may add that the solution might surprise the sages who first propounded the doctrine; this does not mean, however, that the solution is any less organic to the tradition in question.

This phenomenon of unstated or unrealized implications that emerge only as a tradition evolves is especially important in religious discourse—and one does not have to be associated with progressive movements to recognize this. One theologian not reputed to harbor an overenthusiastic love of radical change has explained this phenomenon especially well. Joseph Ratzinger (Pope Benedict XVI) writes that "it is necessary to keep in mind that any human utterance of a certain weight contains more than the author may have been immediately aware of at the time." This is especially the case when we speak of a scripture, Ratzinger explains, because in scripture

> older texts are reappropriated, reinterpreted, and read with new eyes in new contexts. They become Scripture by being read anew, evolving in continuity with their original sense, tacitly corrected and given added depth and breadth of meaning. This is a process in which the word gradually unfolds its inner potentialities, already somehow present like seeds, but needing the challenge of new situations, new experiences and new sufferings, in order to open up. . . . The author is not simply speaking for himself on his own authority. He is speaking from the perspective of a common history that sustains him and that already implicitly contains the possibilities of its future, of the further stages of its journey. . . . The author does not speak as a private, self-contained subject. He speaks in a living community, that is to say, in a

living historical movement not created by him, nor even by the collective, but which is led forward by a greater power that is at work.[278]

Thus, a religious thinker may begin to perceive, and to express, some aspect of a divine reality whose significance cannot be fully understand in her own day, and this tentative perception may bear fruit many generations later. It is just such a latent possibility that E experiments with; and as Solomon Schechter rightly notes, "No creed or theological system which has come down to us from antiquity can afford to be judged by any other standard than by its spiritual and poetic possibilities."[279] The fact that minimalist thinkers I cite in this chapter would not have agreed with all the participatory implications I find in their words is of no relevance for evaluating the validity of my claim that those implications grow out of scripture. It is the very nature of scripture that it illuminates crucial matters for later audiences in ways the first authors and audiences did not foresee. In the following chapters, we will examine several sparks from scripture and from tradition that grew into a flame centuries later.[280]

3 Command and Law
in the Participatory Theology
of Revelation

In the previous chapter I sketched out the development of what I called the participatory theory of revelation. According to this line of interpretation, at Mount Sinai God communicated with Israel and Moses but spoke little or not at all. The account of the revelation in the Book of Exodus and especially the version of this narrative found in the E source furnish a basis for the participatory theory. They encourage their audiences to wonder how the Decalogue came to Israel: directly from God, entirely through the mediation of Moses, or in part directly and in part through Moses? This ambiguity points toward the further question of what Mosaic mediation involved, especially if we are to understand that when some biblical texts describe God as "talking," they may not intend that God uttered specific words the way that humans do. Texts in Exodus permit us to speculate that God may not have conveyed distinct words at Sinai, so Moses's role in the lawgiving may have been substantial. We can describe this approach to the divine element in revelation as minimalist. At the same time, however, these texts from Exodus allow the possibility that the whole nation heard God speaking at least some specific words and perhaps the entire Decalogue. One of the earliest interpretations of texts from Exodus attempts to render this second option the only possible reading. The recollections of lawgiving in Deuteronomy 4–5 (with the exception of one verse) eschew the sort of ambiguity so pronounced in Exodus 19–20, maintaining instead that God uttered words that the whole nation heard. Consequently, we characterized Deuteronomy's approach to revelation as maximalist. Another of the earliest reactions to the Sinai traditions found in Exodus moved in the opposite direction: the theological reflection in 1 Kings 19.11–13a intimated that God became manifest in silence or in a nonverbal whisper at Ḥoreb. These interpretive options continued into the work of rabbinic and medieval sages, some of whom took the logic of minimalism quite far. For Maimonides in *The Guide of the Perplexed* revelation was supralingual, so that the actual wording of the Torah must have been produced by Moses rather than God. For Menaḥem Mendel of Rymanov and his followers (especially the Ropshitzer Rebbe, Naftali Tzvi Horowitz), the aural aspect of revelation involved a single syllable—in fact, a single vowel. What the people heard was a sound, not a word. The passages by Franz Rosenzweig and Abraham Joshua Heschel with which we began the second chapter represent the fruition of the participatory theology, not its inception.

Having traced the development of the participatory theology, we now turn to the challenges of that theology for traditional Judaism. In this chapter I address questions that the minimalist interpretations of God's specific contribution to revelation raise: Does the extreme version of the minimalist interpretation imply that revelation, because it is nonverbal, has no content? If so, how can it produce a law? If Moses or the nation Israel produced a law in response to God's self-disclosure, why should later generations of Israel remain bound by a law whose particulars are human in origin? Finally, can we take seriously a law that is attributed to Moses once we realize that its historical development was complex and that its connection to the historical Moses is, at best, subject to radical doubts? In answering these questions in this chapter, I argue that a Jew who acknowledges the validity of biblical critical theories concerning the origin of the Pentateuch can—in fact, must—accept what rabbinic tradition calls עול מלכות שמים and עול מצוות—the yoke of divine sovereignty and the binding authority of the commandments. Underlying this argument is a particular conception of biblical prophecy found in medieval Jewish thought and intimated in some biblical texts, to which we now turn.

The Implications of Minimalism: Prophecy as Translation

In theory, a nonverbal revelation might be contentless and purely experiential or emotional. It might limit itself to establishing an intense connection between God and a human being. But a nonverbal revelation might just as well have a sort of content that is not fully reducible to language; as Shai Held puts it, there is no reason to assume that "'verbal revelation' and 'revelation with content' are overlapping categories, and that to reject the former is to reject the latter." On the contrary, Held rightly notes that the core of Abraham Joshua Heschel's view of revelation at Sinai is that human words can give voice to content that is divine in origin: "The humanness of the words [found in the Bible] does not entail, for Heschel, the sheer humanness of the ideas conveyed."[1] This sort of revelation—nonverbal but full of content—is precisely what we find in the biblical texts that intimate the minimalist approach and their more explicit successors in rabbinic tradition. All these texts link revelation with a particular kind of content: God's will that Israel behave in accordance with a set of commandments. In the E narrative the revelation leads first to the Decalogue in Exodus 20 and then to a law code in Exodus 21–23. Even if we conclude that humans formulated the wording of these regulations, the fact that E moves immediately from the revelation to law tells us something about E's view of God's self-disclosure. For the participatory theology as it is found in Exodus, revelation engendered a sense of commandedness, which required paraphrasing in the form of law. Israel's encounter with God yielded a normative claim, which Israel was entrusted with shaping into a more specific content. God's self-disclosure also led to descriptions of God's nature and activity in the world, especially in chapters 33 and 34 of Exodus. The moment of revelation may have included no verbal content, but what followed in its wake is full of content, both legal and theological. The minimalist interpreters in talmudic and medieval texts we discussed in the previous chapter are no less committed to the whole system of halakhah (rabbinic law) than the sages who championed the maximalist point of view. In *The Guide of the Perplexed*, Maimonides regards the law as the work of Moses, not God, but he is quite clear that it is a perfect law that binds all Israel. Observance of the law, for Maimonides, is a necessary condition for beginning to become as close as possible to God, even though it is not sufficient to bring a person to that closeness.[2] Thus, it is no surprise that Maimonides, in some ways one of the most extreme minimalists, was a great scholar of halakhah and the author of one of the most influential law codes in the rabbinic tradition. Similarly, the Ropshitzer Rebbe, immediately after quoting the Rymanover's dictum on the *aleph* of *anokhi*, explains how that one syllable managed to imply all the commandments, whose strict observance the *aleph* requires. The minimalist position in Judaism is not an antinomian one, or even a non-nomian one. Silence for these thinkers hardly means emptiness. How, then, do divinely decreed laws come out of nonverbal communication? How does content attach itself to such a revelation?

An answer to this question emerges from the work of many Jewish thinkers who discuss non-Mosaic prophecy and whose approach can also become relevant, we shall see, to the Pentateuch itself. Already in the rabbinic period and the Middle Ages, Jewish thinkers articulated the belief that the words of biblical prophets other than Moses were the product of the prophets themselves. The prophets received a message from God, but the formulation of that message in human language was left to the individual through whom God sent the message. Examples of this viewpoint in rabbinic and medieval Judaism have been collected by several scholars, in particular, Abraham Joshua Heschel in *Torah min Hashamayim*,[3] and Menaḥem Kasher in *Torah Sheleimah*.[4] Further, analyses of many of these texts appear in Moshe Greenberg's article "Jewish Conceptions of the Human Factor in Biblical Prophecy" and in Alan Cooper's essay "Imagining Prophecy."[5] These scholars show that some rabbis from the talmudic era (for example, R. Isaac in b. Sanhedrin 89a) and medieval Jewish thinkers (Isaac Abarbanel, Menaḥem Meiri, Joseph Albo, Profiat Duran, Rashi) affirm that biblical prophets received numinous and hence ambiguous (probably nonverbal) communications from God, which they rendered into Hebrew. According to these sages, the proclamation of a prophetic message involves what we may term an act of translation. The prophet converts a supralingual, transcendent communication into a verbal one, and in so doing, the prophet inevitably puts his or her own stamp on it. Because Heschel, Kasher, Greenberg, and Cooper have treated these texts at length, we need not pause to summarize them here. Rather, I would like to discuss the way that some modern thinkers echo and expand on this understanding of prophecy by applying it to Moses himself. This expansion, we shall see, has predecessors in premodern Jewish tradition, and it was intimated by medieval authorities including ibn Ezra and Rashbam.[6] (Elsewhere, I have shown that the conception of prophecy as an act of translation is already intimated in several prophetic texts in the Bible itself; I will not restate my arguments here.)[7]

The belief that there is a significant human element in prophecy (to use Greenberg's phrase for this conception) or significant human participation in revelation (to use the phrasing I use throughout this book) appears among both Jewish and Christian thinkers in the modern era. This belief constitutes a middle way between the stenographic theory and the theory that prophets are essentially poets, creative thinkers endowed with minds allowing them to formulate powerful ideas. In the stenographic theory,

God employed language of the sort normally used by humans to speak specific words to prophets; the prophets then repeated these words verbatim to the audience.[8] In the theory of prophecy as poetry, the divine element of prophecy involves the creation of persons with strong imaginative, rational, and moral faculties, and God does not have particular moments of contact with a prophet.[9] In between lies our participatory theory of prophecy as translation. Among Christians this approach appears especially among biblical scholars such as Samuel R. Driver, Gerhard von Rad, and Harold H. Rowley.[10] Related points of view appear among some Protestant theologians (most recently, Keith Ward and David Brown),[11] and in the work of Catholic thinkers (including one prominent scholar of Christian theology who has also involved himself in practical issues of church governance).[12] According to this approach, prophets are bound by a divine commission yet enjoy a degree of freedom. Heschel introduces the apt terms of *vessel* (כלי) and *partner* (שותף) in his review of rabbinic and medieval material: the prophet is not merely a vehicle God uses to convey a message but also a participant who helps to shape it.[13] Other thinkers suggest similar metaphors. H. H. Rowley says of Paul, "He was the ambassador, not the postman."[14] Already in 1854, William Lee argued that the writers of scripture were "God's penmen, not His pens."[15] Several scholars have used the metaphor of translation to describe this approach.[16] These thinkers are not identical to one another. Some deny that there is any verbal element in the original divine communication; others maintain that a verbal element is possible while still rejecting a dictation theory that encompasses all prophetic texts. Christian thinkers tend to place less emphasis on the interpretive nature of prophetic activity than Jewish thinkers. (Some liberal Protestant thinkers speak of the need to interpret God's activities in history; for them, historical events can act as symbols pointing toward the nature of God. This interpretation of history, however, differs from prophetic interpretation of nonverbal communications from God to a particular individual.)[17] Nevertheless, the similarity of the modern thinkers cited here to the rabbinic and medieval figures I have mentioned is clear: they all assert that scripture results from the interaction of God and a human being; God communicates the divine will to the prophet, and the prophet shapes that communication for presentation to a larger community.

Among Jews, this approach is especially well known from the work of Heschel and of Franz Rosenzweig.[18] This is clear from the brief passages I quoted at the beginning of the previous chapter. For Rosenzweig, revelation itself does not yet involve content. Rather, he maintains in his later writings that content emerges only with the human interpretation that translates the revelatory event into language.[19] (Thus, for Rosenzweig revelation by its nature is always dialogical.)[20] To be sure, earlier, in *The Star of Redemption*, Rosenzweig's formulation allowed two fundamental elements of content: God's self-identification, "I am the Lord," and God's command, "Love Me"—that is, the content found in various biblical verses including the opening of the Decalogue (Exodus 20.1 and Deuteronomy 5.6) and the beginning of the central text of Judaism's daily liturgy, recited each morning and evening, the Shema (Deuteronomy 6.5).[21] One can debate whether or not his later writings evince a change. Compare the *Star*, which Rosenzweig completed in 1919:

> Revelation commences [*anhebt*] with "I the Lord" as the great Nay of the concealed God. This "I" accompanies revelation through all the individual commandments.[22]

And a letter to Martin Buber in 1925:

> The primary content of revelation is revelation itself. "He came down" [on Sinai]—this already concludes the revelation; "He spoke" is the beginning of interpretation.[23]

On the one hand, the later phrasing might be seen as overturning the earlier. In the *Star*, the opening words of the Decalogue begin the revelation, while in the letter to Buber, they come immediately after revelation has ended and constitute the beginning of the human interpretation or response. On the other hand, in both formulations revelation was primarily a matter of self-identification. To say, with the later Rosenzweig, that God "reveals nothing but himself to man"[24] is not terribly different from saying that the idea represented by the words "I am the Lord" was revealed. If the Rosenzweig of the *Star* allows us to understand that the content "I am the Lord" was revealed nonverbally, and that the wording we find in Exodus 20.2 is already a translation of that self-identification, then the earlier and later formulations in fact agree.[25] In any event revelation involves contributions from both sides.[26] Similarly, the notion that all the laws of the Torah are attempts to flesh out the essential command, "Love God," also brings us into the realm of translation: Israel concretizes this abstract demand first of all by creating the Torah's laws and then by observing them; in that case none of the words found in the Bible is itself directly from God.[27] This focus on love as the one command that all other instructions in the Bible flesh out is congruent with Rosenzweig's claim in the *Star* that "the analogue of love permeates . . . all of revelation. It is the ever-recurring analogy of the prophets. But it is precisely meant to be more than analogy."[28]

The extent of the divine and human roles in the theological correlation becomes a more vexing issue for Heschel than for Rosenzweig.[29] Rosenzweig views all the specific wording of scripture as a human reaction, perhaps making an exception for "I am Yhwh" (Exodus 20.2) and "Love Yhwh your God with all your might" (Deuteronomy 6.4). But Heschel evinces a more ambivalent position on this issue, especially in relation to Mosaic revelation. When he speaks of a "minimum of revelation,"[30] he does not make clear whether this minimum contains verbal content. We can find hints in his oeuvre that support both possibilities. At times he suggests that we would be naive to assume that the event at Sinai involved specific words on God's part—for example, when he suggests that the frequent biblical phrase "God spoke" should be taken in a special sense:

> *Indicative* words . . . stand in a fluid relation to ineffable meanings and, instead of describing, merely intimate something which we intuit but cannot fully comprehend. . . . Their function is not to call up a definition in our minds but to introduce us to a reality which they signify. . . . Words used in this sense must neither be taken literally nor figuratively but *responsively*. . . . They are not portraits but *clues*, serving us as guides, suggesting a line of thinking. This is our situation in regard to a statement such as "God spoke."[31]

If this is the case, then we need not interpret "God spoke" as entailing the syllables, words, and sentences that characterize language. Presumably this is the case throughout the Bible, including Exodus 20.1. Heschel gives the same impression when he writes:

> The words of Scripture are . . . neither identical with, nor the eternally adequate rendering of, the divine wisdom. As a reflection of His infinite light, the text in its present form is, to speak figuratively, one of an endless number of possible reflections. . . . The prophets bear witness to an event. The event is divine, but the formulation is done by the individual prophet. According to this conception, the idea is revealed; the expression is coined by the prophet.[32]

Some might presume that this restatement of the rabbinic and medieval idea of prophecy as translation is not intended to refer to Mosaic revelation—yet in the footnote to the last sentence, Heschel cites Abraham ibn Ezra's comment on the variants between the Decalogues in Exodus and

Deuteronomy as evidence for the idea that the specific and varying phras-ing of the Decalogue is a human paraphrase.[33] Thus, he links the idea of translation to the very heart of Mosaic prophecy. He goes on in this passage to state that "the expression 'the word of God' would not refer to the word as a sound or a combination of sounds."

In other passages, however, Heschel leans in the other direction: "The word is the word of God, and its understanding He gave unto man,"[34] he writes, in a sentence whose first half seems to acknowledge that actual wording does come from heaven, even if, in the next sentence, he adds that "the source of authority is not the word as given in the text but Israel's un-derstanding of the text." Similarly: "God is not always evasive. He confided Himself at rare moments to those who were chosen to be guides. . . . God expresses His will to us. It is through His word that we know that God is not beyond good and evil."[35] This ambiguity or, perhaps, this sense of wanting to have it both ways, comes across especially in his comment that "*mitzvoth* are both expressions and interpretations of the will of God."[36] Heschel's characterization of commandments as "expressions" accords with a more maximalist understanding of revelation, while the word "interpreta-tion" moves toward a minimalist understanding. In short, at times Heschel gives the impression that he sees the Bible's wording as wholly human, and at other times he seems to allow for the possibility that some of the words (which ones, he does not venture to say) come from heaven.[37] Heschel does not allow himself to be pinned down on this issue, whether because of his own vacillation; because of a certain rhetorical sloppiness on his part (evi-dent in his contradictory use of the adverb *figuratively* in two of the pas-sages quoted earlier in this paragraph); or because of his principled refusal to resolve an issue that he feels human beings cannot, with intellectual and spiritual honesty, resolve.

Before discussing the main implication of the translation theory of prophecy or of the participatory theory of revelation, I must acknowledge the respect in which the modern version of this theory goes beyond its an-cient and medieval predecessors. When talmudic sages and medieval Jew-ish thinkers affirm the human factor in biblical prophecy, they are speaking of non-Mosaic prophecy: prophets *other than Moses* invariably gave linguis-tic shape to the communications they received from God. (In this regard the talmudic and medieval sages are loyal to their biblical predecessors, many of whom regard Moses as without parallel among the prophets.)[38] The sages claim that this is clear from the way the prophets often introduce proclamations: with the words "Thus says Yhwh [כה אמר ה']." In the sages' view the word *thus* points not to exact quotation but to an attempt to convey the main purport of a communication.[39] By and large the sages and the medievals believed that Moses differed: he received precise linguistic communications from God. (Some sages believed that at times, especially in Deuteronomy, Moses interpreted or extended God's messages before passing them on, and to the extent this was the case, Moses resembled other prophets—but only in Deuteronomy.)[40] Moses, then, achieved the exalted status of stenographer, while all other prophets were mere translators. By implicitly demoting Moses from stenographer to translator, Heschel, Rosenzweig, and kindred thinkers introduce a new idea.

Yet the idea is not entirely without precedent. A comparison between two passages that discuss what we might call the Mosaic distinction shows that some rabbis in the talmudic era were already blurring the line between Moses as prophet-stenographer and the prophet-translators. In Numbers 12, Miriam and Aaron complain about Moses's prestige, pointing out that they, too, are prophets. God then conveys this rebuke:

> Listen to My statement: If your prophet is a prophet from Yhwh, it is through a mirror [בַּמַּרְאָה] that I make Myself known to him; I speak to him through a dream. Not so My servant Moses! He is trusted throughout My household. I speak to him directly, clearly [וּמַרְאֶה] and not in riddles. He gazes on the form of Yhwh, so why do you not fear to speak against My servant, against Moses? (Numbers 12.6–8)

These verses use a subtle play on words to express the difference between two types of prophecy. Moses sees God "clearly"—literally, he is in contact with the actual sight (וּמַרְאֶה—*mar'eh*) of God, whereas other prophets see God by means of a "mirror" (מַרְאָה—*mar'ah*). Here we need to recall that mirrors in the ancient world were not like our own. Generally small and handheld, they were made of copper, and they had slightly uneven surfaces rather than the perfectly smooth surfaces our mirrors have. As a result, the image one saw in a mirror was tiny, reddish, and a bit blurry. Where Moses sees God, other prophets see a poor reflection. Further, what non-Mosaic prophets learn from God is like a dream or a riddle, and dreams and riddles are famously in need of interpretation. Thus, as Jacob Licht explains in his commentary on this passage:

> What a dream and a riddle have in common is that their meaning is never spelled out; they need to be elucidated or interpreted in order to be

understood, and of course it is possible to err when elucidating them. A normal prophet takes in God's word in a clouded fashion. . . . He cannot know whether his interpretation is correct, even if he receives the divine word while awake and in what seem to be clear utterances. In contrast, Moses had the great privilege to see in a way that did not resemble a riddle, and his prophecies came to him already spelled out.[41]

Numbers 12 maintains that there is a pronounced human factor in biblical prophecy, but in Moses's case, the human factor disappears.[42] But several rabbinic texts draw a different sort of contrast between Moses and other prophets, which suggests that the idea that even Moses is a translator has precedent in Jewish thought prior to modernity. Thus in a midrash, Wayiqra Rabbah 1:14, we read:

> How did Moses differ from all the prophets? Rabbi Judah son of Rabbi Ille'ai and the Sages expressed their opinions. Rabbi Judah said: All the prophets saw through nine *aspaqlariyot* . . . but Moses saw through one *aspaqlariyah*, as it is written, "Clearly and not in riddles" (Numbers 12.8). The Sages said: All the prophets saw through a dirty *aspaqlariyah*, . . . but Moses saw through a polished *aspaqlariyah*.

Variants on this teaching are found elsewhere in rabbinic literature; thus the Talmud, in b. Yebamot 49b, tells us that Moses saw through a bright *aspaqlariyah* and the prophets through a dim one. An *aspaqlariyah* refers either to a mirror or to a pane of glass.[43] In either case, looking through one of these in ancient times meant that the image one sees was at least somewhat distorted; when the rabbis thought of a pane of glass, what they had in mind differed from a modern window; it was bumpier and less clear. In the course of reaffirming a distinction between Moses and other prophets, then, this rabbinic teaching also alters it. In Numbers, Moses sees God directly, while the prophets see through something that distorts the image. But in Wayiqra Rabbah and its variants both Moses and the prophets see through something that distorts; the question is how distorted the image is. For the sages, the image Moses sees is flawed, but it suffers from the distortion introduced by a single mirror or glass, whereas the image prophets see is much more significantly warped.[44] Similarly, for Maimonides in the *Guide*, Moses saw God more clearly than other prophets, yet even Moses could not apprehend God's essence.[45] Various Jewish mystical texts, both prekabbalistic and kabbalistic, suggest something analogous: Moses's perfect sight extended only to the lower manifestations of God, not to the higher ones.

For these thinkers, Moses did not act as stenographer; rather, he was a uniquely great translator. This is especially clear in Maimonides's view of the law. We saw in the previous chapter that according to Maimonides, Moses himself composed the Torah on the basis of his pure apperception of the divine will; he did not receive its precise words from heaven. For example, Lawrence Kaplan summarizes Maimonides's view of the origin of the Torah thus: "The laws of the Torah are an imaginative *translation*, an *imitation*, of the divine cosmic law."[46] Micah Goodman, Alexander Even-Chen, and David Novak also use the term *translation* to characterize Moses's composition of the Torah according to Maimonides.[47] For Maimonides, the distinction between Moses and other prophets, at least in this regard, is one of degree.[48] Insofar as Rosenzweig and Heschel imply that Moses was translator, they are elaborating a theme found in classical sources rather than inventing a completely new doctrine.

Correlational Theology, Theurgy, and Minimalism

Heschel emphasizes what I call translation, using it as the ground for his powerful amplification of the participatory theory. Speaking of the roles of God and humanity, he writes, "His is the call, ours the paraphrase."[49] He explains the nature of prophetic discourse by affirming that

> the prophet is not a passive recipient, a recording instrument, affected from without without participation of heart and will, nor is he a person who acquires his vision by his own strength and labor. The prophet's personality is rather a unity of inspiration and experience, invasion and response. . . . Even in the moment of the event he is, we are told, an active partner in the event. His response to what is disclosed to him turns revelation into a dialogue. In a sense, prophecy consists of a revelation of God and *a co-revelation of man*.[50]

This emphasis on dialogue characterizes not only Heschel's view of prophecy but his approach to religion as a whole. One sees this in statements he makes about several issues: religious life ("Religion consists of *God's question and man's answer*"[51]); an appropriate approach to scripture ("We cannot sense His presence in the Bible except by being responsive to it"[52]); and, more fundamentally, what it means for the Bible to be scripture and not merely literary artifact ("We must learn to respond before we may hear; we must learn to fulfill before we can know. . . . Unless we respond, the Bible ceases to be Scripture"[53]). One need not even open Heschel's books to sense the importance of this theme throughout his career; it suffices to read their titles: *God in Search of Man; Man's Quest for God; Man Is Not Alone; Between God and Man.* The *Leitmotif* that emerges here is one of connectivity between heaven and earth. Heschel's approach to revelation in particular and to religion in general emphasizes simultaneously God's movement toward humanity and humanity's movement toward God.

We might sum up Heschel's approach with the phrase "correlational theology." This term is famously associated with the liberal Protestant theologian Paul Tillich, who used it to describe the way he links insights from revelation, scripture, and the history of Christian thought with questions prompted by the study of philosophy and psychology.[54] But it also appears in Jewish thought. Already the late nineteenth- and early twentieth-century Jewish philosopher Hermann Cohen, whose influence on Rosenzweig and Heschel was immense, spoke of revelation as stemming not only from heaven but from the heart of man, and especially (here recalling Maimonides) from man's verbal and rational capacity. For Cohen, duties are not simply imposed from above but embraced by humans who use a divinelike rational capacity to realize what duty should be.[55] Cohen uses the term *correlation* to describe this aspect of revelation. Correlation plays an important role in Cohen's thought, which stresses both humanity's duties and humanity's autonomy. Because revealed duties become evident from the correlation between God and the human being, Cohen concludes, accepting duty does not impugn a person's autonomy.[56] The term *correlation* has also been used by Moshe Idel to describe a core theme of kabbalah. This theme, Idel argues, was neglected in the work of Gershom Scholem:

> In lieu of the remoteness of the deity . . . [which Scholem's] scholarly approach assumes, and of its reflection in symbols as the sole mode of perceiving it, I propose a much more correlational theology. My understanding of this term is less related to the presence of God and the dynamism of this presence in things, or the birth of the new being, as is the case in Paul Tillich's existential theology of correlation, but the possibility of the reciprocal impact of God's and man's deeds on each other.[57]

Heschel's work evinces all these senses of correlational theology—Tillich's intellectually oriented conception,[58] Cohen's emphasis on partnership between heaven and earth,[59] and Idel's behaviorally oriented proposal. In particular, it is remarkable how well Heschel's thought expresses the themes Idel identifies as core elements of kabbalah and its rabbinic forerunners. Idel stresses that kabbalah involves not only "descending vectors" from the transcendent realm but also "ascending vectors" that involve human ritual and ethical activity.[60] Indeed, he defines kabbalah as "a set of practices designed to enhance a series of 'ontic continua,' or 'connecting metaphysical continua.'"[61] Thus, Idel's conception of kabbalah emphasizes ritual practices involving correlation at least as much as it focuses on theosophical speculation.

It is hardly a coincidence these elements of kabbalistic thought as described by Idel are so evident in Heschel's concept of Judaism. Heschel was deeply shaped by the Ḥasidic communities in which he grew up and in which his relatives have served as rebbes for generations. He was decisively influenced by the kabbalistic literature studied in Ḥasidic circles, especially the Cordoverian stream that Idel's conception of kabbalah emphasizes.[62] One can even find in Heschel's work traces of an idea that other modern Jewish thinkers and scholars have ignored, avoided, or ridiculed: the notion of theurgy, or human ritual activity that affects, influences, or changes God. Theurgy is central to medieval kabbalah, and (as Heschel himself already noted) it is prominent in certain rabbinic texts that served as precursors to classical medieval kabbalah.[63] Idel defines theurgy at it broadest as "the impact of human acts on the divine realm,"[64] and in this sense theurgy plays a role in Heschel's work. Thus, Heschel writes that God

> is in need of the work of man for the fulfillment of His ends in the world.... *God is beseeching man* to answer, to return, to fulfill.... Life consists of endless opportunities ... to redeem the power of God from the chain of potentialities.[65]

One of Heschel most famous theological ideas is his concept of divine pathos, according to which God "is moved and affected by what happens in the world, and reacts accordingly."[66] This idea emerges in a more classically kabbalistic form when Heschel contrasts customs, ceremonies, and religious symbolism, on the one hand, with the observance of Jewish law, on the other:

> The primary function of symbols is to express *what we think*; the primary function of the *mitzvoth* is to express *what God wills*. . . . Symbols have a psychological, not an ontological, status; they do not affect any reality, except the psyche of man. *Mitzvoth* affect God.[67]

To be sure, it is unlikely that Heschel intended these phrases to mean precisely what they would mean if uttered by a Ḥasidic master such as, say, the Apter Rebbe or the *Admor* of the Kopitzhinitzer Ḥasidim. Similarly,

Heschel's approach to religious observance completely lacks the idea of a sexual effect on the deity, which is prominent in the theurgical conception of the commandments in the *Zohar* (which is widely regarded as the central text of kabbalistic mysticism).[68] Nevertheless, his emphasis on God-focused commandments rather than communally focused customs or personally meaningful ceremonies echoes the theme of theurgy that characterized the milieu in which he grew up.[69] Heschel embraces this theme to underscore God's personhood, and he transforms it into a central motif in his oeuvre, the idea of partnership between heaven and earth. Partnership, after all, entails the idea that one person has an impact on the other. Although scholars have shied away from exploring this aspect of Heschel's thought,[70] it plays an important role throughout his writings. When it expresses itself in relationship to the issue of revelation, Heschel links it with the older Jewish notion that there is a human factor in prophecy: revelation is dialogue, in which each side influences and is influenced.

The theme of theurgy also appears at the very end of Rosenzweig's *Star*, where Rosenzweig makes its connection to kabbalah explicit.[71] While this theme is less pervasive in Rosenzweig's work than in Heschel's, its climactic placement near the very end of the *Star* is significant. Further, Idel argues that "the surrender of God to man, or his 'selling Himself' to man, is a basic idea that appears over and over in Rosenzweig's work, and seems to be rooted in the kabbalistic idea about the Shekhina."[72] But in developing a correlational theology out of the idea of theurgy, Heschel and Rosenzweig are not only picking up a theme from kabbalah; they also recall P's conception of law. We saw in the previous chapter that for P the purpose of the law was to maintain the conditions that allow God's presence on earth. By observing the law Israel helps the transcendent deity remain immanent. Thus, for P the law is fundamentally theurgical in nature. The ritual activity of Israel and its priesthood are, to echo Idel's definition of kabbalah, a set of practices that enhance the metaphysical continuum between the divine and the earthly, a continuum that P localizes in the Tabernacle. More specifically, for P the law is an instrument of what Idel, discussing kabbalistic and proto-kabbalistic ritual, calls "drawing-down theurgy." P's rituals do not, however, involve what Idel calls "augmentation theurgy."[73] Thus, Yehezkel Kaufmann is not quite correct when he maintains that P's cult "is not intended to bring a mysterious overflow or emanation of power [המשכת שפע כח מסתורי] upon the divinity by magical or mythological means."[74] Here Kaufmann chooses vocabulary drawn from the realm of kabbalah, thus emphasizing a gulf between Priestly and kabbalistic ritual. But in light of Idel's description of the importance of "drawing-down theurgy" in kabbalah, it becomes clear that when Kaufmann goes on to describe the goal of P's cult as bringing about the indwelling of God's presence in Israel (שריית השכינה בישראל), he describes a goal that is no less proto-kabbalistic. The theme of correlation in Jewish ritual, then, begins neither with Hermann Cohen nor with the kabbalists but with P.

Heavenly and Earthly Torahs

It is not only in the notion of theurgy that correlational theology in Heschel and Rosenzweig links itself with kabbalah and with proto-kabbalistic elements in rabbinic literature. The conception of prophecy as translation recalls an understanding of revelation that distinguishes between the Torah known in this world and a Torah that exists beyond this world. While this view of the Torah is especially associated with kabbalah, a major concern of Heschel's *Torah min Hashamayim* is to show that it is also well developed in talmudic and midrashic literature.[75] Among the rabbis the belief was widespread that the Torah existed before the world (see, for example, Midrash Tehillim 93:3; Bereshit Rabbah 1:4; b. Nedarim 39b) and that God used the Torah as a blueprint in creation (m. Avot 3:18; Bereshit Rabbah 1:1).[76] Consequently, Heschel shows, the question arose among the rabbis: To what extent is this preexistent Torah identical with or parallel to the earthly Torah? If they are not identical, does the earthly Torah fall short of the heavenly? As Gordon Tucker demonstrates,[77] Heschel begins a crucial chapter in *Torah min Hashamayim* by denying the dualistic or gnostic position that the true Torah is in heaven and that the one below is lowly.[78] But, Tucker notes, as the chapter progresses, Heschel begins to point toward differences between these Torahs as conceived of in rabbinic literature. The differences become pronounced when Heschel quotes a midrashic teaching from Bereshit Rabbah 17:5 concerning נובלות, a term referring to fruit that falls from a tree before fully ripening. The midrash uses the term metaphorically to refer to less developed phenomena that originated from something fuller:

> Rabbi Ḥanena bar Isaac said: There are three cases of fallen fruit/inferior fruit/lesser versions (נובלות). The inferior fruit/lesser version of death is sleep. The lesser version of prophecy is a dream. The lesser version of the World to Come is the Sabbath. Rabbi Avin adds: The lesser version of

the supernal light is the sun. The lesser version of the supernal wisdom is Torah.[79]

This type of question recurs again in *Torah Min Hashamayim* when Heschel asks: is the primordial, heavenly Torah identical to the written Torah found on earth, or does the heavenly Torah exist solely in the mind of God?[80] If the former, then the Torah as we know it was brought down from heaven; Heschel sums up this notion with the well-known phrase תורה מן השמים ("Torah from heaven"). If the latter, the Torah as we know it results from a transformation that brought the divinely cogitated Torah into physical form; to describe this Torah, Heschel coins the phrase תורה שבשמים ("Torah that is in heaven").[81] In the latter case, the earthly Torah is an incarnation of a heavenly prototype. Many sages expressed the former view, which Heschel characterizes as "extreme and inflexible" (קיצונית ותקיפה) and which corresponds to the stenographic theory of revelation. This became the best-known view in rabbinic culture; one can rightly call it the standard theology. The main goal of the second volume of *Torah min Hashamayim* is to demonstrate that a more "interpretive and moderate" (פרשנית ומתונה)[82] view is found among the classical rabbis, to defend it, and to explore the implications of the tension between it and the more common view. For me to summarize Heschel's work of collecting and analyzing the relevant rabbinic texts is unnecessary, but some readers may find a few samples indicative. Qohelet Rabbah 11:12 states the distinction between the Torah available on Earth and the ideal Torah quite boldly: "The Torah one learns in this world is emptiness compared with the Torah of the Messiah." That the primordial Torah has no earthly form is expressed also in a dictum found in Midrash Tehillim (Buber) 90:12 and elsewhere, according to which the primordial Torah is written in fire.[83] The comparison of Torah to fire is suggestive: fire is real yet insubstantial, perceptible but not quite physical, ever-changing yet oddly constant. Further, this is no ordinary fire, since the Torah is written in black fire on white fire. By comparing the heavenly Torah to something that does not exist on earth, the midrash intimates that it is wholly other, analogous to but distinct from anything known to humanity, and hence not identical to the Torah in Israel's hands.

Similar ideas are widespread in kabbalistic texts. Scholem provides a pithy summary, explaining that for some kabbalists,

the Wisdom of God . . . forms an "Ur-Torah" in which the "word" rests as yet completely undeveloped in a mode of being in which no differentiation of the individual elements into sounds and letters takes place. The sphere in which this "Ur-Torah" (torah kelulah) comes to articulate itself into the so-called Written Torah, where signs (the forms of the consonants) or sounds or expressions exist—that sphere is already interpretation.[84]

The Zohar teaches that the narratives and laws that comprise the biblical text are outer garments that Torah wears. They are to Torah as people's clothes are to their bodies (Zohar 3.152a [on Numbers 9.1]).[85] The idea of various manifestations of Torah, some of greater purity and some more enmeshed in the physical world, is also found in teachings of the Zohar and other kabbalistic works focusing on the sephirot. (The sephirot in kabbalah are ten manifestations of God [or, alternatively, powers emanating from God] that enter the created world. Each of the sephirot [sing., sephirah] embodies or reflects an aspect of God, such as Wisdom, Justice, Mercy, or Royalty.) In most kabbalistic systems, the second sephirah, Hokhmah or Wisdom, stands for the primordial Torah; the sixth sephirah, Tif'eret or Beauty, stands for the Written Torah; and the last sephirah, Malkhut or Kingship (also known as Shekhinah or Indwelling), is associated with the Oral Torah.[86] Similarly, the founder of Hasidism (the eighteenth-century teacher Israel ben Eliezer, better known as the Besht) distinguished between "the Torah of God" and "the Torah of Moses." The former is "a hidden light" which few humans have attained, while the latter is the Torah revealed to Israel.[87] We can link this heavenly Torah, upon which the verbal garments that are the Penta-teuch lie, to the "hushed rustling noise" or "sound of thin silence" in 1 Kings 19.12 and thus also to aleph of anokhi in the Rymanover Rebbe's teaching I discussed at the end of chapter 2. In Kantian terms, the only Torah we can know is a phenomenon, a product of human perception and interpretation; but this Torah reflects a noumenon that is at once real and unrealizable.

My summary of Torah min Hashamayim's second volume fails to do it justice; readers interested in rabbinic theology, the rabbinic roots of kab-balistic notions of Torah, and Heschel's own thought will want to study the book themselves. What is crucial for my project is to take his point a step further. In speaking of a distinction between the Torah as it exists for God and the Torah that Moses brings Israel, the rabbis do not invent a new trope; they develop an idea with roots in Exodus's Sinai narrative. As we saw earlier, the original tablets containing the Decalogue written with the finger of God (Exodus 31.18, 32.16) were shattered by Moses (32.19), and consequently the Israelites never received the original, heavenly tablets in a readable, intact form. The whole and readable tablets placed into the ark resulted from a collaboration between heaven and earth; they were carved, and probably also written, by a human intermediary. The final form of the Decalogue physically available to Israel is the product both of what Idel calls descending and ascending vectors. Thus, the narrative about the tablets in Exodus suggests a distinction between purely heavenly tablets and collaborative ones. The former did not—could not?—endure on earth, but the latter, provided by Moses with God's aid, did.[88] Much later, the classical rabbis would develop this distinction into the idea of heavenly and earthly Torahs; kabbalists would amplify it further; and Heschel makes it the centerpiece of his masterwork. But in a very sketchy form, the distinction can be found, at least in regard to the physical tablets of the Decalogue, already in the Book of Exodus. Indeed, since the narrative regarding the first and second tablets seems to consists entirely of E material, we can say that the roots of the distinction are older than the Pentateuch itself.[89]

It might strike some readers as unlikely that biblical authors already intimate the notions I am attributing to them. Can a notion of prophecy as translation and a distinction between earthly teachings and heavenly prototypes really appear in the ancient Near Eastern text that the Pentateuch is? Am I importing into the Bible much later rabbinic, kabbalistic, or modern notions—or, in the case of the heavenly prototype, a Platonic idea? Studies of scribal practices from antiquity show that ancient Near Eastern cultures do express comparable distinctions between prototypes and secondary manifestations. Prophets are a type of messenger, and in the ancient Near East it was the norm that messengers would shape the message they conveyed. This was true whether the message came from a human or a deity. We have extensive records from Mesopotamian and Egyptian scribes, who composed letters for various human clients, especially kings, and who also passed on wisdom deriving from the divine sphere.[90] Karel van der Toorn describes the practice of these scribes:

> The transformation of speech into scripture was not a mechanical recording in writing of the oral performance. As the scribe committed the spoken word into writing, he adapted it to meet the conventions of the written genre. In the ancient Near East the most common genre for which scribes acted as transcribers was the letter. . . . To judge by cuneiform letters that have been preserved, scribes did leave their imprint on the text dictated to them. Trained as they were in the niceties of the epistolary genre, the terminology and phraseology the scribes used were proper to the art of their profession as well as their personal talent; their style was hardly a reflection

of the rhetorical gifts of their patrons. . . . Scribes, even in their most instrumental of roles, impose their style, language, and ideas on the text. Acting as secretaries and transcribers, they are not phonographs in writing; they mold the material that reaches them orally.[91]

Messengers typically rendered the source in a manner that made it appropriate for the recipient. This does not on its own prove that biblical prophets translated heavenly communications into earthly language, but it does show that the notion that messengers construe, structure, and paraphrase messages that come from a higher ranking party is entirely at home in the world of the Bible. Further support for this idea emerges from biblical stories in which one character repeats the words of another, or in which narrators have occasion to repeat their own words. In such cases, the repetition typically alters the original. George Savran studied such repetitions in biblical narratives, and he points out that in some cases the repetition introduces minor stylistic changes that have no bearing on the meaning of the passage, while in others subtle variations carry great significance. He speaks of "a finely graded scale moving from repetition to reinterpretation."[92] What remains constant is these texts' assumption that when reporting something that has already been said, one may paraphrase the original rather than repeating it verbatim.[93] In a culture with such a norm, the idea of prophecy as translation is not inevitable, but it is likely.[94] For this reason, Jeremiah 36.32 regards it as perfectly normal that the replacement of an older prophetic scroll that had been destroyed would contain not only the original text but also new material resembling the old.[95]

The idea of a mixture of divine and human elements can also be detected in Mesopotamian textual tradition. Scholars there, especially in the second millennium and the first centuries of the first millennium BCE, did not generally claim that the exact wording of their texts came from heaven.[96] Rather, scribes understood their craft to be a gift from the gods (especially from Ea, and later from his grandson Nabu), while the actual composition of texts was their own work. In the prologue to his famous legal collection, Ḥammurapi does not claim to have received laws from the gods. Rather he declares he acquired authority from the gods Anu, Enlil, and Marduk and wisdom from Shamash, which allowed him to compose the laws.[97] In this ancient Babylonian text we find a distinction between heavenly authority and wisdom, on one hand, and earthly legislation, on the other. The former were abstract entities, while the latter existed in verbal and physical form. It becomes clear, then, that the sort of distinction so central to Heschel is native not only to his kabbalistic and rabbinic sources but also to the ancient Near Eastern culture from which the Bible emerged.

Divine Command, Human Law

Rabbinic and medieval Jewish notions of heavenly and earthly Torahs provide an analogue for a distinction that plays a crucial role in the work of Rosenzweig. Already in the *Star* Rosenzweig maintains that revelation consists of a divine command (*Gebot*), but not a specific law (*Gesetz*).[98] He returns to this distinction frequently in his later writings. According to Rosenzweig's conception, the specifics of the law—that is, the actual legal directives found in the Pentateuch and in the rabbinic system of halakhah—do not come from God. They are rather interpretations of revelation that attempt to flesh out the primal command to love God. Divine command yields, but is not identical with, the laws authored by humans: the Jewish people transform *Gebot* into *Gesetz*—more precisely, into *Gesetze* (laws) in the plural. Though Rosenzweig himself did not suggest the analogy, *Gebot* and *Gesetz* are comparable to heavenly and earthly Torahs respectively, especially if we view the heavenly Torah as a supralingual phenomenon, given to Israel either in silence or in a single vowel that is not a word. The *Gebot* consists of a commanding presence, the election of Israel, and the call to love God. But this *Gebot* need not have been a text. The sentiment, "acknowledge me, know me, love me," can be conveyed without words. Indeed, among humans, this sentiment is expressed in its most genuine and heartfelt way—between infant and parent, between lovers—with a look, with a cry, with a caress, but without words. What Rosenzweig calls *Gebot* consists of the *ah* of *anokhi* at Sinai, perhaps merely the *aleph* or glottal stop that precedes sound but is not itself a sound.[99] The *Gebot*'s demand for loyalty, affection, and obedience is the whole of the heavenly Torah as God delivered it to Israel. The *Gesetz*, consisting of laws and teaching Israel creates in response to God's self-identification, is the earthly Torah.

Heschel does not use the terms *Gebot* and *Gesetz* (or consistent English or Hebrew equivalents) throughout his writings, but he also distinguishes between a charge that comes from heaven and duties that Jews on earth understand as flowing from that charge. "To Judaism," he writes, "religion is . . . an *answer* to Him who is asking us to live in a certain way. *It is in its very origin a consciousness of duty.*"[100] This sentence rephrases Heschel's famous statement that the Bible itself is a midrash,[101] construing its message in terms of practice: God's presence at Sinai is a question about behavior, and the Jewish religion (in the basic sense of "action or conduct indicating belief in, obedience to, and reverence for a god [or] gods")[102] is an answer. This notion of religion as action rather than mere faith, and moreover as action that provides humanity's answer to a divine question, appears often in his work: "The root of religion is the question of what to do with . . . awe, wonder and amazement. Religion begins with a consciousness that something is asked of us."[103] Thus, Heschel distinguishes between the practices of Judaism, spelled out in the *mitzvot* or commandments,[104] and the divine question that called them forth. This does not mean, however, that Heschel believes that halakhah is a matter of customs and ceremonies invented by human beings. On the contrary, Heschel belittles the modern Jewish affection for "customs and ceremonies" as opposed to traditional Jewish obedience to *mitzvot*; the former are merely meaningful or gratifying, while the latter ultimately derive binding authority from God:

> Jewish piety is an answer to God, expressed in the language of *mitzvot* rather than in the language of "ceremonies." The *mitzvah* rather than the ceremony is our fundamental category. . . . Ceremonies . . . are required by custom and convention; *mitzvot* are required by Torah. . . . Ceremonies are folkways; *mitzvot* are ways of God. Ceremonies are expressions of the human mind. . . . *Mitzvot*, on the other hand, are expressions or interpretations of the will of God.[105]

As interpretations of God's will, the commandments are formulated by humans, but they are also expressions of divine will, so that their origin in some way goes back to God. The abstract nature of the heavenly, ineffable Torah that so concerns Heschel identifies it as *Gebot*, while the specific nature of the earthly, verbal Torah shows it to be *Gesetz*.

Command and Law in the Ḥoreb Narrative

The distinction between heavenly command and earthly law that plays such a major role in twentieth-century Jewish thought corresponds to a theme we saw in the Book of Exodus, and especially in the E source. The *Gesetz* (for Rosenzweig) or the earthly Torah (for Heschel) is the product of human mediation. In E, and in one likely reading of Exodus 19–24 as a whole, it is possible that the people never hear specific commandments directly from God; rather, all law, including even the Decalogue, comes to them from Moses. Similarly, in Exodus 34, E distinguishes between the short-lived heavenly tablets containing the Decalogue and the enduring earthly ones produced by Moses. The Horeb narrative uses a series of ambiguities to encourage its audience to ponder the dynamics that connect God, Moses, law, and Israel. It thus initiates a tradition of deliberation about the relationship between divine presence and the law. These ambiguities were by no means inevitable. It would have been perfectly easy for the texts in Exodus to make clear that the words found in the Decalogue came directly from God, so that the Israelites in the narrative (and their descendants reading that narrative) could understand that God spoke and wrote the law in human words. Had the Israelites distinctly heard at least some of these words with their own ears from God prior to receiving them from Moses, then they would have reason to presume that subsequent laws they heard from Moses came verbally from heaven. (That conveying such a conception of revelation was possible is evident from the fact that Deuteronomy succeeds in conveying it—or at least succeeded, until the addition of Proto-Rabad's scribal gloss or השגה in Deuteronomy 5.5 undermined D's clarity and self-consistency.) But E's Horeb narrative and the final form of Exodus 19–24 eschew a straightforward narrative. It is for this reason that I locate the beginning of the participatory theory of revelation in E. The ancient version of the participatory theory revels in ambiguity, but it also makes clear that a revelation did occur and that it involved command. For the sages who composed E, as for our two modern sages, Moses was not a stenographer, but he was not an author, either; he was a translator.

Here we have arrived at the central point of this book: *the bold notion of revelation that we find in the work of Franz Rosenzweig and Abraham Joshua Heschel recapitulates one of the most ancient Jewish understandings of revelation and the law.* The interpretation of these two thinkers returns us to the root of Jewish thought and creativity, the texts preserved in the Bible; indeed, it returns us to some of the prebiblical texts and traditions from which the Bible was created. The notion of *Gebot* and *Gesetz*, of the Bible as midrash, is (to use a traditional Hebrew term) פשט (*peshat*), a valid contextual reading of the oldest texts we have.[106] It is not the only *peshat* interpretation of the Torah's several accounts of revelation, for it flies in the face of Deuteronomy's approach to these questions. But the very fact that Deuteronomy insistently reacts to a conception of revelation similar to that found in Rosenzweig and Heschel demonstrates that this conception is much older than the twentieth century—older, in fact, than Deuteronomy itself. Nor is this notion limited to the E text in Exodus. As David Frankel points out, the distinction between a humanly authored law that corresponds broadly to a divine command also appears in Joshua 24.25–28 (where Joshua composes the law) and 1 Samuel 10.25 (where Samuel composes it).[107]

Several implications of this old/new idea of divine command and human law demand attention. Before turning to them in subsequent chapters, however, I need to respond to several potential critiques of the core assertion I have articulated here. Two of these critiques come from the left and one from the right; a fourth might be asked, perhaps with differing intonations, from the left or the right. The remainder of this chapter addresses these four challenges:

(1) In the previous paragraphs I used the terms *revelation* and *divine command* more or less interchangeably. Throughout this book I have regarded law as the necessary outcome of revelation at Sinai. I thus have hinted at an idea that I mentioned explicitly in the introduction: law is essential to Judaism, and no authentic form of the religion that emerges from the events at Sinai can dispense with an idea of covenantal obligation or חיוב (*ḥiyyuv*). The participatory theory of revelation maintains that Jewish tradition results from the work of teachers starting with Moses who struggle to echo, amplify, and reify God's voice. According to this theory, these teachers struggle to do so precisely because the divine voice imparts no content yet does command. Those last three words, "yet does command," require defense. Why must a Jewish theology of revelation involve law? Why is divine presence itself insufficient for a genuinely Jewish conception of revelation?

(2) Some readers of Rosenzweig may be surprised that I bracket him with Heschel on the issue of law and halakhic obligation or *ḥiyyuv*. While Heschel's commitment to a traditional notion of halakhic obligation is clear, Rosenzweig has been interpreted as lacking a notion of *ḥiyyuv* that encompasses the whole Jewish people—that is, an obligation that applies to all Jews, and not only to Jews who choose to be obligated. Does Rosenzweig really endorse an encompassing, binding halakhah?

(3) Turning to a defense against potential critics to my right, I defend the distinction between *Gebot* and *Gesetz* as an authentic one in Jewish thought. In my arguments for the centrality of law in Judaism I lean heavily on precedent in Jewish intellectual history. Consequently it behooves me to ask if precedent really allows for a distinction between command and

law. Can a law authored by human beings be sacred and authoritative in Judaism?

(4) Finally, I need to address the relationship between the Pentateuch's idea of Mosaic mediation and the more expansive idea of prophetic mediation required by the modern version of the minimalist tradition. Even if one agrees that some of the Torah's narratives (and also Maimonides) may regard Moses, not God, as the author of the wording found in the Pentateuch's laws, one might still maintain that modern biblical criticism undermines the authority of those laws, because biblical critics attribute their composition neither to God nor to Moses but to anonymous scribes and sages who lived centuries after the events at Sinai. In light of the tight connection between Moses and the law both in the Bible and in postbiblical Jewish traditions, can a modern view of the law as post-Mosaic really support a robust and authentic notion of halakhic obligation? To answer this question, I will examine what the Torah's sources mean when they attribute their own laws to Moses.

The Centrality of Law

I have made clear that I regard the notion of legal obligation as indispensable to any Jewish theology. The responses of the Jewish people to revelation at Sinai, from biblical texts at least until the advent of the modern era, have unanimously expressed themselves in terms of law. From the consistency of this response, we can learn that Jews apprehended the God of Sinai not merely as presence but as commanding presence. This remains the case even though we recognize that a community of human beings fashioned (and fashions) the specific mandates found in the Bible and later Jewish texts. Israel completes the sentence that begins "God commands us to," but God remains the subject, and the verb does not lose its basic meaning of requiring obedience.

That Israel's response to Sinai always involved a sense of commandedness, of ḥiyyuv, was the case even before the redaction of the Pentateuch. We saw in chapter 2 that all four Pentateuchal sources present us with a set of laws justified by their narrative settings. Both E and D provide us with the Decalogue, and both go on to present a law code with cultic, criminal, and civil laws. In P the lawgiving was a thirty-nine-year process that began one year after the exodus. Because P's laws were given over many years, they are found in several large groupings in Leviticus and Numbers along with a few brief passages in Exodus and one in Genesis; here again, the laws mix cultic, criminal, and civil matters. J differs in not having a discrete law code, but J contains several passages that narrate the origins of crucial cultic laws of ancient Israel and thus provide justifications for their observance. Further, in at least one passage (Exodus 34.10–11,27), J tells us that God directed Moses on Mount Sinai to write a document that forms the basis of the covenant between God and Israel; while we cannot be sure what this document included, it is at least clear that in J a covenant was formed on the basis of commandments written down by Moses at Sinai.

In three cases (P, E, and D), laws are grouped together and justified by the narratives that surround them, while in one case (J), sundry laws appear throughout the narrative rather than in one or more blocks.[108] In each of the four sources, then, law is justified in one way or another by narratives, including especially a narrative that takes place at Sinai. This consistent pattern suggests the best definition of the genre "Torah": a combination of law and narrative in which the latter comes to authenticate, cultivate, and motivate the former.[109] Taken as wholes, all four sources belong to the genre "Torah" in this sense, as does the redacted Pentateuch.[110]

While the four sources disagree in considerable ways in regard to lawgiving—where it happened, when it happened, why it happened, and most of all what the actual law is—they agree on the importance of law.[111] For each of the four, Sinai was not merely about theophany or God's self-disclosure; it was about command. It is worth pausing to note this, because one could of course imagine revelation in other ways, and some biblical texts outside the Pentateuch do so. A few poetic texts refer to Sinai as a place where God appeared to Israel for the sake of the manifestation itself, regardless of lawgiving (Habakkuk 3.3–6; see also Psalm 114, which alludes to Exodus 19 subtly while conjoining the event at Sinai and the event at the Reed Sea but does not mention law specifically). Others speak of Sinai or similar locations south of Canaan as the place from which God went forth to wage war on behalf of His people (Judges 5.4–5; Psalm 68.8–10). A similar understanding of Sinai plays a role in Exodus 3–4, where Moses experienced God's presence in the form of a strange flame inside a bush. There God revealed the divine name (Yhwh) and commissioned Moses to serve as Yhwh's lieutenant in the war of liberation against Israel's Egyptian overlords. One may ask, then, who appeared at Sinai—God the lawgiver; God the warrior; or, quite simply, God? While there need be no contradiction among these three possibilities, different texts emphasize them differently.[112] The section of the biblical canon that came to be most authoritative in all forms of Judaism, however, accentuates the legal aspect of revelation. (This statement is equally true of rabbinic and Karaitic Judaism, and it was valid for Qumran Judaism as well. It applies even more strongly for the Samaritans, who regard only the Pentateuch as canonical and do not accept the Prophets and Writings in their scripture.) Within the Tanakh it is specifically the Pentateuch that is normative for Jews, and the Pentateuch (in this respect following each of its main predecessor texts) consistently interweaves lawgiving with revelation. In Judaism's core canon, God's self-manifestation took place not only to teach theology or to establish relationship but also to command.[113] (Of course, texts in the other sections of the canon also connect revelation, lawgiving, and imagery reminiscent of Sinai; see, for example, Psalm 50.1–7. But other sections of the canon do so less consistently.)

The very existence of the Pentateuch as a literary unit emphasizes the centrality of law. This becomes clear when we compare the Pentateuch with a work concerning which biblical scholars have engaged in debate for well over a century, the Hexateuch. Since the nineteenth century, scholars have speculated, quite plausibly, that in ancient times there may have existed a literary unit that began with what we know as Genesis and ended with what we call Joshua, or perhaps several pre-redactional works that narrated a history from creation through the death of Joshua. Such a literary work would have stressed not only the promise of the land found in stories about the patriarchs and recurring in the narratives of the exodus but also the fulfillment of the promise with the conquest of Canaan.[114] The difference between these two literary units is consequential. Joel Baden sums up the issue that concerns us:

> Given the trajectories of the J, E, and P documents, it is highly likely that each included at least the history of the settlement of the promised land, for it is to this end that the patriarchal promises point. The compiler [of the Pentateuch], however, has ended his work before the ends of his source documents. He ends it, pointedly, with the final laws and the death of the law-giver, Moses. Once the laws were set down in their entirety and, with the death of Moses, the possibility of any further laws was eliminated, the compiler's work was complete. The compiler produced a law book.[115]

Scholars debate how and when the longer work or works that closed with Joshua's death gave way to the shorter unit ending with Moses's passing.[116] What is important for our purposes is the different theme emphasized by the shape of the work that became canonical:[117] rather than the Hexateuch's story of promise and fulfillment, the Pentateuch gives us a story of promise, hope, and law. The very fact that all forms of Judaism revere the latter and not the former underscores the law's centrality.[118] (At the same time, I ought not overstate the contrast; the Hexateuch is hardly antinomian or non-nomian. The last chapter of Joshua narrates the covenant ratification under the leadership of Joshua, who gives the nation a law and commandment, written down in a book, whose binding force the people explicitly take upon themselves [Joshua 24.24–26]. The difference between the Pentateuch and the Hexateuch is primarily one of emphasis.)

The belief that law is an indispensable mode of Jewish response to revelation remains consistent throughout Judaism until the advent of the modern era. Prior to the nineteenth century, we never find wholesale rejection of legal-covenantal obedience among Jewish sages, with the exception of radical antinomian thinkers like Paul or some of the followers of the seventeenth-century false Messiah, Shabbetai Tzvi. Over the course of time, the Jewish community unambiguously rejected such thinkers. My argument for the necessity of ḥiyyuv for any authentic Judaism, then, grounds itself in the history of the Jewish people. On a theoretical level, a scholar might make a serious textual argument for the legitimacy of Paul or antinomian Sabbateans as authentic Jewish thinkers, or for the exclusion of Maimonides from that category. Paul and the Sabbateans, after all, were deeply committed to sacred Jewish texts (in the latter case including the Zohar and Lurianic texts) and enmeshed in the exegetical practices employed by Jews of their age. Maimonides's abstract and nonpersonal notion of God, on the other hand, was a radical departure from biblical and rabbinic Judaism,[119] even as his conceptualization of scripture and midrash rejected the ways Jews had understood those collections until his day.[120] But theoreticians, scholars, and פוסקים (halakhic authorities) do not determine who is a Jewish sage and what is a Jewish practice. Rather, Jewish communities with deep commitments to Jewish tradition of the past and of the future define what is and is not Jewish.[121] Such communities have rejected exegetically interesting but antinomian Jews such as Paul and the Sabbateans, even as they have embraced theologically radical but reliably nomian Jews such as Maimonides. To be sure, in the past two centuries, segments of the Jewish community have flirted with a wholesale rejection of the notion of a binding legal authority. This is a recent development when viewed in the long trajectory of the Jewish people's existence, and it is too early to say whether this approach will endure within the nation Israel. Previous flirtations with antinomianism suggest that it will not.

In making this argument, I apply a notion known from the Talmud in b. Berakhot 45a, b. Eruvin 14b, and b. Menaḥot 35b: פוק חזי מאי עמא דבר ("Go out and see what the people are doing"). The sages apply this principle to halakhic controversies not resolved among the sages: if the sages cannot decide whether a law is implemented in this way or that, then the behavior of Jews observing that law determines which opinion is correct. (The yardstick used when applying the principle of פוק חזי consists of Jews committed to the halakhah, not Jews generally. The principle in its talmudic contexts provides a way to resolve a disagreement concerning which of two possibilities is the proper way to observe a given law. Only by watching Jews who actually follow the law can one know whether option A or option B is valid. Jews who practice neither option are irrelevant when applying this principle.)[122] I am applying this principle on a much broader scale: committed Jews, in the long run, define what Judaism is. For more than two millennia, they have defined Judaism in terms of law. Whether attempts to define Judaism in a new, nonlegal way will endure remains to be seen, but the voice of precedent is unanimous on this issue.

A commitment to ḥiyyuv, however, does not necessarily mean a commitment to the classical halakhic system of talmudic Judaism. While the centrality of legal obligation has been constant in Judaism since Sinai, the actual legal system involved has varied. Indeed, the Pentateuchal sources that narrate what happened at Sinai agree on the principle that Israel's response to God expresses itself through law, but they differ on what that law actually is. The legal systems that emerged within various forms of Judaism in the Second Temple period based themselves to varying degrees on the combination of those sources, but none of them was identical to any of those sources. The halakhic system of the classical rabbis emerged gradually in the postbiblical period, but there is no reason to think that Israel's legal obligation will eternally express itself through that particular system. On the contrary, history suggests that other systems will evolve to take its place. Rosenzweig addresses this issue explicitly, acknowledging that since the Enlightenment of the late eighteenth and early nineteenth centuries, the unity of the Jewish "way" (Straße, roughly equivalent to the rabbinic term halakhah) has loosened; where once there was one way with some side paths and bridges, now one can speak only of a unity of landscape.[123] In other words, he is open to multiple halakhic systems, out of which a single street may eventually reemerge. But saying that there may be multiple legal systems in Judaism is not the same as saying that no legal system is binding, for the latter would effectively be saying that there is no legal system at all.

Obligation and Autonomy in Heschel and Rosenzweig

My emphasis on the binding nature of the law will strike some readers as unexpected in light of the central role Rosenzweig and Heschel play in the participatory theory of revelation. To what degree are these modern liberal theologians committed to halakhic obligation? This question is more easily answered in Heschel's case than in Rosenzweig's.

A robust notion of *ḥiyyuv* plays a central role in Heschel's thought.[124] This is especially clear in his essay "Toward an Understanding of Halacha" (which he delivered as an invited speaker at the annual meeting of the Reform rabbinate in North America in 1953).[125] His argument for the indispensable position of halakhah in Judaism, present throughout the essay, becomes quite pointed at the end, as Heschel issues a frank, heartfelt denunciation of the Reform view that Jewish law is no longer to be regarded as binding—in other words, that it is no longer law at all.[126] Heschel's tone throughout the essay is gentle and often self-critical, and his surprisingly open censure of Reform ideology in the last pages strikes me as wistful rather than harsh.[127] Heschel's notion of *ḥiyyuv* appears elsewhere in his work, when he emphasizes submission, and when he insists that lawgiving is the essential core of a Jewish concept of revelation. It appears rather more subtly in his discussions of God's will and God's way, and in his descriptions of Judaism's commitment to a personal God rather than belief in a philosophical principle.[128] Of course, his strong emphasis on halakhic obligation does not mean he feels that stringency in legal matters is preferable to leniency,[129] or that the law can never change.[130] Heschel rejects the reduction of Judaism to legalism, for he regards the law as a means rather than an end.[131] But Heschel makes clear that consistent commitment to this particular means is indispensable for any authentic Jewish life.

Of course, it is possible to misrepresent Heschel by selectively misquoting him.[132] One needs simply to pay attention to only one half of what he says on the subject. Heschel frequently condemns legalism or exclusive devotion to halakhah without a commitment to aggadah, only to emphasize the importance of the law immediately thereafter. Seemingly left-wing and right-wing statements follow each other constantly; some readers, of course, will tend to underline only the one or the other in their copies. Thus, Heschel sounds similar to the rigorously Orthodox philosopher Yeshayahu Leibowitz when Heschel speaks approvingly of "Israel's *supreme acquiescence* at Sinai," telling us, "At the beginning is *the commitment, the supreme acquiescence.*"[133] Yet he goes on in the same chapter to insist that "what obtains between man and God is not mere submission to His power or dependence upon His mercy. The plea is not to obey what He wills but to *do* what He *is*."[134] Examples of this dialectic in regard to law and piety, כוונה and קבע (intention and fixed structure) abound throughout the third section of *God in Search of Man*. The dialectic is evident from successive chapter titles alone: "A Science of Deeds" (chapter 28), "More than Inwardness" (29), "Kavanah" (= intention, 30), "Religious Behaviorism" (31), "The Deed Redeems" (40), "Freedom" (41), and, most characteristically, "The Problem of Polarity" (32). This insistence on accepting both sides of what others regard as a polarity occurs not only in his attitude toward practice but also in his understanding of interpretation. Heschel could be taken to regard Judaism as infinitely malleable when he writes, "The source of authority is not the word as given in the text but Israel's understanding of the text."[135] Yet a few paragraphs later, Heschel reminds us that proper understanding of the Bible "requires austere discipline and can only be achieved in attachment and dedication, in retaining and reliving the original understanding as expressed by the prophets and the ancient sages." For Heschel, there is such a thing as the original understanding; Judaism is not primarily a matter of our own interpretive creativity and innovative spirituality but, as he puts it, of austere discipline, attachment, and dedication.[136]

While Heschel's commitment to law and structure as an indispensable means for any Jewish response to God is clear, Rosenzweig prompts more debate. The issue of religious authority looms large in his thought, but his views are difficult to pin down.[137] Many scholars read Rosenzweig as articulating a much less traditional attitude toward halakhic obligation. His liberal attitude toward the law, we are told, can be seen in his emphasis on autonomy, his celebration of personal choice, and his assertion that each individual must perform those *mitzvot* that the individual has accepted. Thus, Zvi Kurzveil writes that for Rosenzweig,

> the ultimate decision as to the acceptance or non-acceptance of *Mitzvoth* rests with the individual, and the only criterion is "the choice of ability" . . . that is, the inner readiness of the individual to choose the precept and "bless"

it. . . . Rosenzweig's attitude to the Law must lead to an arbitrary adoption or rejection of precepts on the part of the individual Jew.[138]

The sense that Rosenzweig endorses the notion that each Jew should create her own halakhah also emerges in Paul Mendes-Flohr's reading of Rosenzweig's work: "The ba'al teshuvah, the modern Jew seeking to return to the Tradition, as Rosenzweig taught and exemplified in his own life, finds within this landscape his own path—that set of mitzvot—in which he personally hears the commanding voice of God."[139] Similarly, Arnold Eisen links Rosenzweig more closely with Buber than with Heschel on this issue: "Both Buber and Rosenzweig *shifted the authority of observance from a commanding God to the individual self* who hears the commandment. . . . Both thinkers . . . *presumed that diverse selves would hear and practice differently.*"[140] But other scholars, including Isaac Heinemann, Nahum Glatzer, Steven Kepnes, and Norbert Samuelson, read Rosenzweig on the law as much more of a traditionalist.[141] The debate is difficult to resolve for several reasons. Rosenzweig did not live long enough to write the more comprehensive work on Jewish law he hoped to write,[142] and thus we have to glean his approach to the law from relevant passages in the *Star* (which nobody has ever characterized as an easy book to read), later essays (especially "The Builders"[143]), and various letters he wrote.[144] Further, his views on the Law developed over one-and-a-half decades (consistently, it should be noted, in the direction of greater observance), and thus it may be illegitimate to expect complete agreement between the *Star* and the later writings.[145] In spite of these difficulties, I think it is possible to show that Rosenzweig was a traditionalist in his attitude toward *ḥiyyuv*. Evidence that he subscribed to a choice-based approach to law rather than an obligation-based one is based on two misunderstandings.

First of all, it is imperative that one take into account the audience whom Rosenzweig addresses in his essays and letters concerning the law, which consisted of people from a background like his own: assimilated Jews distant from Judaism who were taking their first steps toward embracing a tradition in which they had not grown up. What he presents in his letters and in his famous essay "The Builders" (itself an open letter to Martin Buber) was not a general theory of Jewish law. He was speaking to בעלי תשובה, "returnees," Jews on a path back to a place they had never been. Such returnees could not suddenly carry out all the dictates of the halakhic system. Each returnee, Rosenzweig proposed, needed to find his or her own way into that system. He did not believe there was a single manual spelling out how every person can successfully adopt the law. Consequently, it would be neither productive nor fair to criticize the way another person advances on this path. A returnee decides to progress according to her particular ability:

> A decision based on ability cannot err, since it is not choosing, but listening and therefore only accepting. For this reason, no one can take another person to task, though he can and should teach him; because only *I* know what *I* can do; only my own ear can hear the voice of my own being which I have to reckon with.[146]

This is not a statement of universal principle but one of practicality. Rosenzweig speaks here as what he claimed to be in a Jewish context: an educator. Rather than attempting to define the essence of Judaism, he writes to draw his fellow western Jews into Jewish practice, a home they had really never entered.[147] This is clear, for example, when he writes to four friends, "What can be expressed marks the beginning of our way. This is peculiar to our situation. . . . The situation of the Jew who never left the fold is different. . . . Our way has led back to the whole, but we are still seeking the individual parts."[148] An individual's inability, for the time being, to embrace parts of the whole does not mean that the whole is not binding. The notion of a system of commandments is divine in origin, and we can look forward to expressing our belief in that system increasingly over time by practicing more and more of the system's humanly authored specifics. This is very different from the view that commandments are a menu of actions that are potentially meaningful and potentially meaningless, so that each individual has the task of deciding which are which within her own life. Rather, the returnee is thinking of accepting the whole law in principle but cannot yet observe each law in practice. To that person Rosenzweig says: Go ahead and observe the law imperfectly. That is the way in. "We are still seeking the individual parts"—that he has not yet found all the parts does not mean that they are not *Gesetze* or are any less a response to divine *Gebot*.

In short, Rosenzweig's talk of choice may lead to a misunderstanding. He does not exalt individual choice as the essence of Jewish action but sees it as a path toward Jewish action, which ideally will come to encompass the whole. Thus, he wrote to his friend, the art historian Rudolph Hallo:

> So you see: there is no choice, in the sense that *you* mean. . . . There is very little "choice" in it all. . . . One must *want* to see a bit of the inner "*Must*" approaching. While one wants to live with others of both the past and the

present, and searches for a way to do so, one seizes opportunities, and then it is not inert, so that at some point one makes due with a "Can"—then, where the "Can" is, the "Must" will readily join it.[149]

Choosing Jewish practices, then, is not itself the end of the path; accepting happily that one must observe is. Mistaking Rosenzweig's map of the path's beginning for his understanding of its destination yields only misunderstanding. As he wrote in the "Builders," "What I myself have to say about [the question of the Law] is not based on the experience of having reached the goal but on that of seeking and being on the way."[150]

A second misunderstanding arises from Rosenzweig's emphasis on autonomy. Rosenzweig insists that in observing *mitzvot* what matters is not how many *mitzvot* one practices but how one practices them. Law "must consciously start where its content stops being content and becomes inner power, our own inner power. Inner power which in turn is added to the substance of the law. Whatever is being done shall come from that inner power."[151] In the letter to Hallo quoted earlier, Rosenzweig maintains that it is only when one observes a *Gesetz* due to an "inner 'Must'" that it truly becomes *Gebot*; and at that point, because there is no external compulsion involved in the obedience, the obedience is truly free.[152] The concept of autonomy Rosenzweig expresses here goes back to Immanuel Kant, and thus it is in light of Kant's definition of autonomy that Rosenzweig needs to be read. Kenneth Seeskin explains that for Kant,

> divine commands do not become binding until I accept divine sovereignty. . . . From a moral perspective the real decision rests with me, not with God. Kant writes: "The will is thus not only subject to the law, but subject in such a way that it must be regarded also as self-legislative and only for this reason as being subject to the law (of which it can regard itself as the author)."[153]

For Kant, truly observing law means accepting a command. Doing so requires that we accept God's sovereignty and right to command, rather than observing due to fear, hope of reward, or social expectation. It is in this sense that Rosenzweig says he cannot observe until he feels commanded: If one lights Shabbat candles only out of nostalgia or communal feeling, then one is not lighting them as a *mitzvah* at all. If one lights them hoping for a reward (whether a psychological reward in terms of one's well-being, a reward in terms of belonging to a community, or even a reward from God), one is still not practicing a *mitzvah*. Only if one lights because one must, because one is obligated, is the action truly a *mitzvah*. In making this observation, I am saying nothing threatening to a traditional Jewish point of view. On the contrary, this definition of *mitzvah* recalls such arch-traditionalists as Yeshayahu Leibowitz, Maimonides, and the Pharisaic sage Antigonus (whom the Mishnah quotes in Avot 1:3).

Further, as Seeskin notes, in a Kantian ethic, "having imposed the law on myself, I am not at liberty to repeal it. If I were, obeying the law would cease to be an obligation and become a preference."[154] As Seeskin goes on to point out, for Kant the moral autonomy to which we should strive is not personal but universal and necessary. It is autonomous in the sense that it is free of personal, contingent influences—that is, autonomy is the opposite of what the words *individual autonomy* often imply in modern American English: "For Kant a free will is a will under law. Clearly he is not thinking of freedom as the ability to do whatever one wants. . . . There is no reason to think that he took the formula of autonomy as a way of inviting creativity."[155] Read in this light, Rosenzweig's call for performing *mitzvot* with autonomy hardly exalts personal choice above religious obligation.[156] Rosenzweig is far from saying that each Jew should decide which *mitzvot* she wants to observe—even though he acknowledges that the Jew returning to tradition must decide which *mitzvot*, for the time being, she *can* observe. The Kantian autonomy Rosenzweig assumes is a universal and not a personal autonomy, and for this reason it is far more enriching to traditional Jewish notions of *ḥiyyuv* than many have assumed.[157]

Partial Fulfillment of the Law: Rosenzweig, Heschel, and Paul

Rosenzweig's attitude toward partial fulfillment of the halakhic system is especially useful for helping us understand his approach to *ḥiyyuv* and his relation to other thinkers who discuss the Law. In his 1922 letter to Hallo, he rejects the suggestion that if he accepts the Law, he must immediately obey all the laws. Instead, he argues, "something" is an authentic option, whereas "nothing" is illegitimate and "everything" is simply impossible. In fact, perfection is not even a useful goal for someone who, like him, is "only beginning."[158] Heschel addresses this issue in "Toward an Understanding of Halacha," where he, too, rejects the view that "either you observe all or nothing" and confutes the prediction that "if one brick is removed, the whole edifice must collapse."[159] Both thinkers reckon calmly with the fact of human imperfection, acknowledging that no human succeeds in obeying all the law. "Where," Heschel asks, "is the man who could claim that he has been able to fulfill literally the *mitzvah* of 'Love your neighbor as yourself?'"[160]

Of course, Heschel and Rosenzweig are not the first thinkers to address this issue. In the New Testament, Paul, too, avers that no one can fully keep the law, but for Paul this means that the law can only lead to failure—a pedagogically useful failure that brings one to Christ:

> For all who rely on the works of the law are under a curse; for it is written, "Cursed is everyone who does not observe and obey all the things written in the book of the law." Now it is evident that no one is justified before God by the law; for "The one who is righteous will live by faith." (Galatians 3.10–11, New Revised Standard Version [NRSV])

The word "all" (πᾶσιν) in Paul's version of Deuteronomy 27.26 (which he quotes here) is crucial to Paul's argument; interestingly, the Septuagint translation of the Bible includes the word (as does the Samaritan Pentateuch), but the Hebrew of MT (which is authoritative for rabbinic and Karaite Jews alike) does not. Paul maintains that if one fulfills 612 out of 613 commandments, one has fulfilled none: "Circumcision indeed is of value if you obey the law; but if you break the law, your circumcision has become uncircumcision" (Romans 2.25 [NRSV]). Paul goes on to make clear that anyone who attempts to observe the law in fact breaks the law: "All have sinned and fall short of the glory of God" (Romans 3.23 [NRSV]; cf. 7.14–25).[161] Rosenzweig and Heschel, in contrast, regard whatever we do achieve as worthwhile. If a person fulfills one commandment, that person has embarked on the right path, and this is praiseworthy. The fact that nobody achieves the entirety need not mean that the project of the law is doomed. For Paul, the cup that is nine-tenths full is effectively empty. For Heschel and Rosenzweig, a cup that is one-tenth full represents an accomplishment.[162] Their attitude is an ancient one. The mishnaic sage Rabbi Tarfon preaches the same message in m. Avot 2:15–16. Initially, he sounds a pessimistic note reminiscent of Paul: "The day is short, and the workload is immense, but the laborers are lazy." But he goes on to note that the goal is not perfection in any event: "It is not incumbent on you to finish the work, but neither are you free to desist from it."

In their attitude toward the worthiness of imperfect observance (which is the only type of observance), Heschel and Rosenzweig were precursors to late-twentieth-century Ḥabad Ḥasidim, who, in their own way, have also been interested in encouraging assimilated Jews to return to Jewish tradition.[163] In Ḥabad missionary (קירוב) ideology, as in the thought of Rosenzweig and Heschel, any *mitzvah* observed is worthwhile, even though Ḥabad Ḥasidim would prefer to see two observed rather than one, and 613 best of all. One of the reasons that Ḥabad Ḥasidim are genuinely pleased when an otherwise nonobservant Jew lights Shabbat candles or puts on תפילין (phylacteries used during daily prayer) even a single time is that they believe each individual *mitzvah* is an effective act of theurgy. That one ritual act, however small or infrequent, has cosmic value and could provide God with the extra amount of human-given power necessary to redeem the world. Given that Heschel and Rosenzweig are unique among modern liberal Jewish thinkers in espousing some notion of theurgy, it may be relevant that the two of them similarly emphasize the value of "something" while rejecting the idea of "all or nothing."

In defending his position in his letter to Hallo, Rosenzweig quotes the rabbinic adage that one should "live by the commandments, not die by them,"[164] and then explicates the significance of this line for the beginner or returnee: "This principle must stand over our observance of the law today, if any principle at all should do so. For what is possible for me may be impossible for another; what is freedom for me may be compulsion for another."[165] Now, we have seen that some interpreters believe Rosenzweig endorses the view that each individual should decide what parts of the halakhah, if any, to observe. If this were the case, then Rosenzweig would be rejecting the traditional Jewish notion of the halakhah's binding and universal authority. But the continuation of the letter makes clear that this is not the case:

> Even though my way for now is only *my* way, I know myself to be the brother of anyone who is going on his own way—so long as he *is* on the way; so long as he does not merely content himself with the supposed goal of his supposed "Everything"; so long as he does not just wait in the inert "Nothing" for the call to begin, which of course will *never* come.

Rosenzweig clearly believes a Jew has a responsibility to begin the way; and the way moves in a particular direction—toward greater observance and, one hopes, toward accepting the *Gesetz* as *Gebot* in the context of the act itself. His view of the goal is not undermined by his recognition of the fact that one beginner's something will differ from another's; for me, putting on *tefillin* daily will seem the right beginning, while for you observing the Sabbath once a month will be appropriate. The fact that each individual's "something" may work only for that individual does not mean that there is no universal *ḥiyyuv* encompassing the whole Jewish people. But, Rosenzweig teaches, whatever fraction of the halakhah's "everything" one uses to embark on a journey to the whole is praiseworthy. Here, again, the comparison with contemporary Ḥabad Ḥasidim is surprisingly useful. Nobody familiar with Ḥabad would argue, on the basis of the emphasis on single *mitzvot* one frequently encounters among Ḥabad missionaries (שלוחים), that they do not believe that the whole halakhic system is binding. Such an argument would grossly (indeed, comically) misrepresent their understanding of Jewish law. Ḥabad missionaries value the single *mitzvah* both for pedagogical reasons (especially when speaking to the potential returnee) and for ideological and theurgical reasons, but this does not mean that they fail to regard other *mitzvot* as obligatory. Rosenzweig's approach is similar: speaking as a returnee and to returnees, he values the commandment that he can do, not because he sees it as meaningful in place of the whole but because it is his way toward the whole.

Traditional Judaism and the Distinction between Command and Law

In arguing for the centrality of legal obligation in Judaism, I pointed out that no Jewish thinker before the nineteenth century denies the binding nature of the law; the only exceptions, such as Paul, were written out of Jewish tradition altogether. My argument is historical in nature: I learn what is authentically Jewish from over two millennia of precedent. It behooves me, then, to ask whether, by adopting Rosenzweig's distinction between divine command and human law, I am being inconsistent. After all, even though the distinction maintains the integrity of the covenantal legal system as a whole, it also radically downgrades the status of any given halakhic practice; for someone who accepts this distinction, *Gebot* is divine and hence authoritative, and the *Gesetze* taken together are crucial, but any one *Gesetz* is understood to be the product of human sages rather than God. My argument would be fatally inconsistent, then, if the distinction between *Gebot* and *Gesetz* is also absent until modernity. But this approach is not completely absent in earlier Jewish traditions, even though Rosenzweig uses new terms and takes this approach further than his predecessors. A few words on the coupling of uncompromising adherence to divine command with a flexible approach to specific laws, then, are in order.

Some earlier sages accept the divine authority of the legal system as a whole while regarding particular Pentateuchal laws as having a status that was not unalterable. It has been widely noted that the rabbis of the Talmud effectively overturn some biblical legislation. Examples include the rebellious son from Deuteronomy 21.18–21, other laws involving the death penalty and corporal punishment, and the possibility of conversion by Moabite males. These cases have attracted a great deal of attention from scholars of rabbinic thought and historians of halakhah in recent decades.[166] The sages of the Talmud all but abrogate these biblical laws by means of extremely narrow definitions of terms or extraordinarily demanding laws of evidence. What the Pentateuch seems to present as real laws become inoperative as the sages in effect forbid us from enacting them, but nobody would suggest that the talmudic sages were antinomian or even lukewarm in their enthusiasm for law. Rather, they set aside several ancient rules in favor of later ones. In the realm of specifics, the sages create room for flexibility, but they are far from doubting the facticity of the divine command and Israel's eternal acceptance of its force.[167] On the contrary, the sages allow surprising leeway in terms of detail within the legal system precisely because they never countenance any question regarding the binding nature of the system as a whole. The specifics are analogous to what Rosenzweig terms the *Gesetze*, while the binding nature of the system as a whole involves *Gebot*.

It is not only in literature from the Middle Ages and antiquity that we find phenomena of this sort. The redactors of the Pentateuch themselves relativize specific laws even as they emphasize the centrality of legal obligation. The redactors combined Priestly, Deuteronomic, and other laws that blatantly contradict one another. In presenting us laws along with their narrative justification, the redactors emphasize the binding status of law, but they require us as interpreters to exercise considerable judgment regarding specifics. Let me take a very simple example involving Passover. Both Exodus 12 and Deuteronomy 16 require all Israelite families to slaughter and consume an animal as a Passover ritual. But they differ on details: Exodus 12.5 stipulates that the offering must be a lamb or a kid, while Deuteronomy 16.2 allows one to bring the offering from the flock or the herd—that is, in addition to sheep and goats, large cattle are permissible. Whereas Exodus 12.8 directs Israelites to roast the offering, Deuteronomy 16.6–7 require that the offering be boiled.[168] Now, it is clear that the redactors who put both passages into the Pentateuch want Israelites to obey a law regarding the Passover offering. But no matter how we do so, we will end up *disobeying* one version of the law or the other. If we roast the offering, we adhere to the law from Exodus, which is Priestly in origin, but we disobey Deuteronomy's version. If we boil it, we live up to the standard of the Deuteronomists but disappoint the Priestly authors. If we somehow roast it and boil it simultaneously (as 2 Chronicles 35.13 mysteriously suggests in its harmonization: "They boiled the Passover offering in fire, in accordance with the law"),[169] or if we first roast it and then boil it, we still disobey the P verse in Exodus 12.9, which tells us, "Do not eat any of it raw or boiled in any way in water, but roasted in fire." Here the redactors force us to ignore some specific law that they themselves include in the Pentateuch, even though they could not be more clear on the importance of obedience to the Passover laws. The redactors' general principle is that we should obey; but the redactors give us some latitude on which version or harmonization we obey. Indeed, the redactors impose that latitude upon us, since we are forced to ignore either the stricture against boiling in Exodus or the requirement that we should boil it in Deuteronomy.

Biblical and rabbinic texts, then, permit what we might call tactical flexibility regarding specific laws; but obedience to the legal system remains firm as their core strategy. Similarly, the most important Jewish philosopher makes a subtle distinction between a heavenly command and the specifics of actual laws obeyed by Jews on Earth. As we saw in the previous chapter, several scholars show that in *The Guide of the Perplexed*, Maimonides regards the wording of the Torah to be the work of Moses, not the work of God. (To be sure, Maimonides is careful to make this surprising claim in a circumscribed manner. As a result, one must read the *Guide's* several chapters treating Mosaic revelation synoptically to uncover it.) Yet Maimonides did not believe that Moses invented a law without authority or guidance from the divine realm. Though the scholars who present this reading of the *Guide* do not make a comparison with Heschel or Rosenzweig explicit, the language they use to describe Maimonides's view is strikingly reminiscent of both twentieth-century thinkers. This is especially so in the work of Alvin Reines, who summarizes Maimonides's approach to the law as follows:

> Thus the essence of the Torah is divine, since it is the essence as well of the divine actions that govern man, but the particulars of the Law are human, having been created by Moses. . . . Maimonides distinguishes between the essential character of the Law and its particular manifestations. . . . For the essence of the Law is concretized by the structure of the Law as a whole and not by any given particular law. Hence individual laws may be meaningless,

antiquated, and even injurious, yet inasmuch as particular laws of one kind or another are necessary, and the immutability of the total Law is necessary to make the particular laws efficacious, the totality of the Law as the concrete manifestation of the divine essence is good and must be observed absolutely.[170]

In short, Reines detects in the *Guide* a distinction between the Torah's divine essence and its human particulars. This recalls the distinction between what Rosenzweig, borrowing Kantian terminology, calls *Gebot* and *Gesetz*, and what Heschel, employing rabbinic and kabbalistic concepts, characterizes as heavenly Torah and earthly Torah. As Reines notes in the last sentence of the quotation just above, this distinction does not in any way undermine the authority of the halakhic system. Maimonides's commitment to rabbinic law could not be more pronounced; it is evident throughout his writings, and not only in his voluminous legal works. Nor does this distinction contradict Maimonides's condemnation, in his Eighth Principle, of those who think that the Torah has "a kernel and a husk."[171] Maimonides's choice of vocabulary there is telling: one goes through a husk, a shell or a peel to arrive at what really matters, but, having done so, one throws the husk away; indeed, to get to what matters, one must destroy the husk. The halakhah's particulars for Maimonides are something else altogether. They always serve as the necessary condition for coming close to God; one cannot leave them behind, although to come closer, one must supplement them with philosophical thought. For this reason Maimonides maintains that even in the messianic era they will remain in force. This idea of the law's immutability is expressed both in Maimonides's Ninth Principle and in the discussion of the messianic era in his introduction to the Thirteen Principles,[172] where Maimonides makes clear that the law's authority endures in perpetuity. The law cannot be discarded even by the few enlightened ones who understand its true purpose. On the contrary, precisely those enlightened ones achieve the most through observing the law.[173]

All this is not to suggest that Rosenzweig's distinction between *Gebot* and *Gesetz* existed already in antiquity precisely as he conceived it or that his suggestion lacks originality. Rather, Rosenzweig's idea and the similar notion found in different wording in Heschel have predecessors in biblical, rabbinic, and medieval Jewish thought. Well before the modern era, authoritative Jewish texts intimated that divine command abides even if occasional laws are changed or ignored. Thus, we can, without inconsistency, use tradition to learn about the centrality of covenantal obligation in

Judaism while also sharpening and extending an inchoate distinction between obligation writ large and particular requirements. Rosenzweig took
that distinction further than previous thinkers had done, and I will suggest
in the conclusion of this book that we can find weighty implications in this
distinction that Rosenzweig himself did not spell out. Unlike the rejection
of Jewish law in the work of some liberal Jewish thinkers over the past century and a half, however, Rosenzweig's line of thought does not represent a
decisive break in Jewish tradition.

The Laws of Moses?

One of the foundational claims of biblical criticism is that the Pentateuch was written by diverse scribes who lived centuries after the Mosaic
era. These anonymous sages credit the legal passages they composed to Moses; to use the technical term, they practiced *pseudepigraphy*. In chapter 2 of
this book I discussed the question of God's relationship to the Torah, but
we also need to ask: How can a modern approach to the Bible as scripture grapple with the contradiction between the Pentateuch's claims that
its laws are Mosaic and the modern view that they are post-Mosaic? By
acknowledging a view of these laws' origin and date that differs from what
the Pentateuch itself says about them, does the modern approach force us
to view the Pentateuch as mistaken or even dishonest, thus undermining
its authority?

Many thinkers characterize the Torah's attribution of its own laws to
Moses as a pious fraud.[174] This characterization misunderstands the nature
of authorship and pseudepigraphy in the ancient world.[175] Modern people
tend to see pseudepigraphy as an indication of the real author's mendacity, but in its own cultural setting pseudepigraphy was an act of humility.
Because writers in our cultural world value originality, they strive to create
their own unique voice. As Walter Jackson Bate and Harold Bloom have
shown, poets since the romantic era have attempted to cover up the extent
to which they are indebted to their predecessors.[176] Ancient and medieval
authors, however, saw their writings as valuable only if they contributed to
a mighty stream that predated and transcended them. Where a modern
author (to borrow language from T. S. Eliot) emphasizes individual talent,
the ancients found meaning in tradition.[177] They believed in all sincerity
that anything of merit in their writing was the product of insight they
culled from earlier authorities and of skills they learned from their masters.

In that case, to take credit for a composition would be a type of theft. It would be more honest to credit the work to the wise people truly responsible for whatever worth it had. Of course the names of these earlier sages were often unknown, and there were a great many of them in any event, so ascribing a work to all of them was impossible; typically one such figure sufficed. In ancient Israel, especially in regard to legal traditions, that figure was Moses.[178] (For poetic prayers, David came to play that role, and thus many psalms and ultimately the whole Book of Psalms were attributed to him.[179] Already 2 Chronicles 23.18 and Ezra 3.2,10 reflect this division of labor.) This does not mean that scribes were unaware of the fact that they had written a new law, or even (in the case of Deuteronomy, for example) a law that departed in certain ways from earlier laws. But the ancients were for the most part sure that the qualities of the new or updated law derived from predecessors greater than themselves and ultimately from God, and the way to avoid the hubris of taking credit for those qualities was to acknowledge Moses as, in a deeper sense, the true conduit for what was valuable in the text. To attribute a teaching to Moses, then, was to attribute it to a sage in the Mosaic tradition.[180] "The claim of Mosaic authorship," Brevard Childs explains, "functioned . . . within the community of faith to establish the continuity of the faith of successive generations with that which had once been delivered to Moses at Sinai."[181] If one judges that claim by the norms of modern notions of authorship, one simply misunderstands it.[182]

Furthermore, most ancient texts did not have any one author in any event; legal, narrative, poetic, and cultic texts crystallized over generations. In a culture where every new copy of a text was made by hand, scribes could alter a text they copied, and careful examination of multiple copies of the same text from antiquity shows that scribes not infrequently did so.[183] Some psalms, narratives, or laws as we know them from the Bible passed through many hands that added to or revised the text, and it would have been deceitful for any one scribe in this chain of transmission and transformation to claim authorship. The very idea of an author in premodern times was radically different from what it is today.[184] Until recently it was difficult to explain premodern notions of authorship, but the rise of the Internet, email, and wikis has made it much easier for people in the contemporary world to understand this phenomenon. Around the time I came up for tenure as a junior faculty member at Northwestern University, several friends sent me an email that floated around the Internet back then: "Why God Could Not Get Tenure at a University."[185] These emails listed several reasons: He only has one publication; it has no footnotes; it is in Hebrew; when one experiment went amiss, He tried to cover it up by drowning all the subjects; and (relevant to our concerns, incidentally) some doubt He even wrote His one publication Himself. Aside from making me laugh out loud several times, these lists fascinated me as a scholar specializing in textual transmission and transformation, because each list that showed up in my inbox was a little bit different from the others. They never contained precisely the same eight or ten reasons. Six or seven of the reasons were common to all the emails, but the rest varied, and even the ones that showed up in several lists were sometimes phrased a little differently. Because anyone who forwards an email can alter the text, various people (whether my friends, or the people who sent it to them, or some unknown person in the chain before that) had introduced small modifications, additions, and subtractions. Some people must have said to themselves, "It would be even funnier if I rephrase this one a little," "Here's a good one I thought of myself," "I can take a joke as well as the next guy, but this one's just sacrilegious." Even though it was clear that people who passed the lists on often intervened in the text, I never saw anyone's name attached to a list as author, even as partial author. It would have been ridiculous for someone who made a minor alteration to claim that status. The situation of biblical scribes, mutatis mutandis, was similar. A scribe who added a line, even rephrased a sentence, or combined two texts did not regard himself as the author, and no one person was the "real" author. As a desire to attribute texts to particular authors became more common over time in ancient Israel,[186] scribes connected texts with specific figures, but putting their own names on texts they were transmitting would have been grossly inappropriate. In such a situation, attribution to a respected symbolic figure from the past was culturally sensible.

Pseudepigraphy was widespread in the ancient world, and among Jews the attribution of new laws to Moses came to be especially prominent. Hindy Najman refers to this practice as "Mosaic discourse," and she points out that it spans the biblical and postbiblical eras.[187] (The phenomenon of Mosaic discourse helps to break down the artificial scholarly distinction between biblical religion and postbiblical Judaism I discussed in chapter 1.) Mosaic discourse is well known from rabbinic literature. It occurs, for example, in the many passages that claim that all of later Jewish teaching was already revealed to Moses at Mount Sinai (for example, b. Berakhot 5a, b. Megillah 19b, y. Pe'ah 4a [6:2], Shemot Rabbah 47:1). We also find it in passages asserting that several laws not known from the Pentateuch

and not supported by any exegesis of biblical texts were originally given to
Moses at Sinai. (Tannaitic examples include m. Yadayim 4:3, m. Pe'ah 2:6,
and t. Sukkah 3:1–2 [cf. the nonlegal example in m. Eduyot 8:7]; amoraic
literature employs the phrase forty-six times in the Babylonian Talmud and
nineteen in the Jerusalem Talmud.)[188] Medieval rabbinic thinkers take up
this notion in their own ways as well.[189] Mosaic discourse is not only a rabbinic phenomenon. It appears frequently in literature of the Second Temple
period. For example, the creators of both the Temple Scroll from Qumran
and the Book of Jubilees attributed their new versions of Pentateuchal laws
and narratives directly to Moses. It also occurs, Jacob Milgrom has pointed
out, in Second Temple texts found within the Bible itself.[190] In 2 Chronicles
30.16, priests and Levites at the Temple take "their accustomed stations in
accordance with the Torah of Moses, the man of God." Milgrom points
out that "no such stations are attributed to priests and Levites in the Torah.
However, the priests and Levites did have stations in the Tabernacle, albeit
different ones (Numbers 3:5–10; 18:6–7)." Thus, the stationing of priests and
Levites described in the passage was not literally a Mosaic law, but it could
plausibly be described as rooted in a similar law associated with Moses,
and this sufficed to allow the Chronicler to describe the practice as Mosaic
in origin.[191] Another case involves the compact between God and Israel in
Nehemiah 10.1–40. Its laws were said to have been given "by the agency
(ביד) of Moses, God's servant" (10.30). Now, it is clear that the author of
this passage in Ezra-Nehemiah, a very late biblical book, knew the Pentateuch in more or less its current form. This author recognized that most of
the compact's specific provisions, which are listed in Nehemiah 10.31–40,
are not in fact found in the Pentateuch. Nonetheless, because some of them
are derived from Pentateuchal law, they can be described as having been
given through Moses. The intention of the Chronicler and the author of
Ezra-Nehemiah, both of whom were writing for audiences familiar with
the Pentateuch, was not literally to assert that the historical Moses wrote
all these laws but to claim that the post-Mosaic law continues in Moses's
own path.[192]

Mosaic discourse is also found in the Pentateuch itself. The sages who
produced E, P, and D recognized, no less than the authors of rabbinic texts,
Jubilees, the Temple Scroll, Chronicles, and Ezra-Nehemiah, that the laws
they committed to writing were the product of their own pens. But these
scribes also knew that the laws they wrote continued a tradition that went
back to revelations in the Sinai desert, and for this reason E, P, and D could

rightly, if broadly, attribute their own laws to Moses.[193] Edward Greenstein describes this decision of the Pentateuch's authors especially well:

> Throughout the course of its history, Israel developed forms of religious observance that were additional to the laws already existing or that differed in their interpretation or understanding from the laws of earlier periods. . . . The traditions of the Torah, then, encompass the records of revelation experiences from many periods of Israel's growth. But the biblical tradition "telescoped" the accumulated revelations of Israel into one great revelation, beginning at Sinai and continuing through the career of our greatest teacher-leader, Moses. "Telescoping" is a common technique used in passing on traditions. Many events occurring over a long period of time are viewed as occurring at one, prime moment, usually the first great moment in the tradition. . . . Israel's responses to God's presence in later generations were telescoped into the Mosaic age as though . . . they had existed from the first meeting of God and Israel at Sinai.[194]

There is no reason the telescoping that Mosaic discourse represents should be troubling to people committed to the halakhic system. Traditional Jews have long recognized that most of the practices they carry out on the basis of medieval halakhic codes are not literally Mosaic in origin, and this recognition does not attenuate the authority of the legal system as a whole (even though it may at times allow for flexibility regarding the status or immutability of a specific practice). The same is true in regard to legal passages in the Pentateuchal itself. Acknowledging that E, P, and D regard the laws as Mosaic in a broad sense, as a result of the processes that Greenstein calls "telescoping" and Najman calls "Mosaic discourse," in no way undermines the central place of *Gebot* in Jewish life, even as it allows us to see the human and thus potentially malleable nature of a given *Gesetz*.

Read in its ancient context, the Torah claims to be written by "Moses" more than by Moses, by a collective of older, mostly anonymous authorities rather than by a particular historical figure. In acknowledging this, we in no way deflate the book's dignity. In fact, the opposite is the case, for reasons eloquently expressed by Joseph Ratzinger (Pope Benedict XVI), who writes of biblical authors:

> These authors are not autonomous writers in the modern sense; they form part of a collective subject, the "People of God" from within whose heart and to whom they speak. Hence, this subject is actually the deeper "author" of the Scriptures. And yet likewise, this people does not exist alone; rather, it

knows that it is led, and spoken to, by God himself, who—through men and their humanity—is at the deepest level the one speaking.[195]

Similarly, the contemporary Jewish theologian Steven Kepnes asserts, "As a collective cultural artifact it is impossible to think of [revelation] as springing from an individual. Rather, as the tradition suggests, it is a gift which comes from the outside, from a transcendent source."[196] Such a Torah, written by a collective rather than an individual, may claim an enhanced religious status. For modern people who are more conscious of the fallibility of all human individuals, a Torah written by one person can seem limited. Torah is bigger than any one individual, and acknowledging that a collective that encompasses generations produced it indeed protects the Torah from being belittled. The ancients referred to that collective as "Moses."

Ex Post Facto Holiness

One might object to accepting the laws of "Moses" as authoritative. At some point, most of these laws lacked a connection to Moses, and thus they once lacked the "Mosaic" authority I claim they should retain. It is clear, after all, that many laws came to be seen as Mosaic over time in the biblical period; as Avigdor Hurowitz has shown, earlier biblical texts are much less likely to refer to legal traditions as Mosaic than later ones.[197] Does this secondary authority, an ex post facto holiness, suffice? Since laws were written down by "Moses" rather than Moses, do they really matter to Judaism?

They do, because Jewish tradition takes ex post facto holiness quite seriously. According to a rabbinic teaching attributed to Rabbi Joshua ben Levi in b. Makkot 23b, to the sages in Ruth Rabbah 4:5, and cited by R. Shmuel in b. Megillah 7a, among other sources,[198] human beings enacted three laws that were confirmed after the fact by God. These include, most famously, the commandment to read the Scroll of Esther on the holiday of Purim—clearly a post-Mosaic innovation, since the events the holiday commemorates date to an era a full millennium after the era of Moses. The scroll attributes the institution of the holiday to two post-Mosaic authorities, Mordechai and Esther (Esther 9.20–23, 29, 31, 32; the whole Jewish people are also described as committing themselves and their descendants to observe the holiday in 9.23 and 27). In spite of its human origins, the liturgical recitation of the book during Purim is preceded by the formula praising God "who sanctified us through His commandments and commanded us to read the Scroll." This is possible because, as b. Makkot 23b and its parallels teach, God gave divine authority to the requirement after the human beings promulgated it. Similarly, it was a group of postbiblical authorities (namely, the Hasmonean rulers of Judah) who ordained that Jews must observe the holiday of Ḥanukkah, yet each night of the holiday Jews light the menorah only after praising God for "commanding us to kindle lights of Ḥanukkah." Similarly, rabbinic texts discuss several teachings the sages regard as having been instituted by Moses "on his own," without divine guidance. God subsequently agreed with Moses's innovations, and therefore they are fully authoritative in spite of their human origin (see b. Shabbat 87a, b. Yebamot 62a, Bemidbar Rabbah 19:33).[199] The same notion appears in the work of Rebbe Naḥman of Bratslav, who wrote:

> The *zaddikim* (saintly ones) are "Mighty of strength who make His word" (Psalm 103.20), for they make and build the word of the Holy One Blessed be He. . . . When *zaddikim* wish to hear the word of God, they first make the word and build it. . . . When [*zaddikim*] want to hear speech from God first they make the speech, and afterward they hear it from the holy One blessed be He.[200]

Jerome Gellman points out an implication of this passage: "The saintly make God's word. Then they hear it. . . . .God speaks to us after we create God's speech."[201]

    This model of religious authority is known in Hebrew by the shorthand קיימו וקבלו ("[humans] established and [God] accepted"), from the phrase in Esther 9.27 that the talmudic sages use to anchor this idea.[202] It can be extended to refer to all the *Gesetze*: Israel responds to God's command at Sinai by authoring specific laws, which, having endured for generations, can be understood to have been accepted and even legislated by God.[203] We may further understand that God did not accept, or did not continue to accept, laws that did not endure. The same is true of whole legal systems that disappeared, such as the extensive nonrabbinic laws of the Qumran community. *It is entirely possible in traditional Judaism to view a legal system as divinely decreed even though it is not divinely written.* The participatory theory of revelation can anchor a robust notion of obligation, and it is precisely this sort combination of aggadic flexibility and halakhic rigor that one finds as early as the E document and as late as Heschel.[204] Here the theme of theurgy returns: *Israel's observance of the law helps God to grant the law the status of divine bidding, just as Israel's intensive, committed, ongoing study of scripture helps God to speak through it.*

Conclusion

How does the divine Torah relate to the earthly Torah or Pentateuch? Our earthly Torah is an interpretation, a reflection, a deeply human attempt at approximation. The divine presence in the biblical text consists not of its words but in the *qol* that is not yet a word, in the *aleph* of God's presence that hovers beneath the biblical text and invites it into being. The words in that text are signposts pointing toward a transcendence that cannot be apprehended, but they are not synonymous with or written by that transcendence. Such a view explains why the all-too-human documents we know as the Pentateuch are indeed sacred even as it attenuates claims that they are ontologically distinct from all other texts. Further, this view removes the distinction between the Pentateuch and the rest of Jewish literature. The Pentateuch, like Midrash Sifre and Rashi's commentary, like Rosenzweig's essays and a worshipper's questions made during a synagogue's Torah discussion, is one of many human interpretations—in fact, a collection of several such interpretations. It follows that all of Jewish tradition, including the Bible itself, constitutes what the classical rabbis call Oral Torah: that is, tradition, commentary, and reflection. In breaking down the ontological distinction between the Five Books and the rest of Jewish creativity, I introduce what may seem to be the most radical aspect of this book. In the next chapter, I will develop this suggestion that there is no distinction between the Bible and later Jewish literature. By studying the notions of Written Torah and Oral Torah (or scripture and tradition) as they appear in rabbinic literature, I will attempt to contextualize my proposal and to argue that it should be far less unsettling than one might initially assume. In fact, doing away with the distinction between the two Torahs of classical Judaism will prove theologically constructive, especially for religious Jews committed to hearing the divine command in the modern world.

4 Scripture as Tradition, and Tradition as Scripture

Religious Jews have always acknowledged that rabbinic texts combine human and divine elements. The words found in the Mishnah, the Talmuds, and the midrashim were composed by the rabbis, but what they say derives, sometimes more directly and often less, from the revelation at Sinai. In light of modern biblical criticism and the work of thinkers like Rosenzweig and Heschel, we can make the same assertion about the Bible, and even about the Pentateuch itself. If the Pentateuch was not revealed in the stenographic sense but results from a dialogue between God and Israel, then its words, as human formulations, are tentative and searching rather than definitive. It follows that the distinction between what rabbinic culture calls Written Torah and Oral Torah falls away entirely. Scripture is simply another form of tradition.

The participatory theology I discuss in this book, then, implies a new understanding of Judaism's canon: *there is no Written Torah; there is only Oral Torah, which starts with Genesis 1.1.* Given the centrality of the doctrine of two Torahs in rabbinic religion, this sentence may seem shocking. In the present chapter I propose that it need not be. Many of the rabbinic texts that introduce the distinction between the two Torahs also subvert it. Similarly, while some biblical passages distinguish between dynamic oral traditions and fixed written texts, many of these passages also minimize that distinction. Consequently, Jews may legitimately regard Written Torah as but one manifestation of Oral Torah.[1] The participatory theology teaches that God's will comes to the Jewish people through a tradition that includes but is not limited to the Bible.

Before I defend this thesis, it will be useful for me to summarize the rabbinic doctrine of the two Torahs. Doing so is necessary because this doctrine entails ideas about canon radically different from Protestant notions that many modern people, including many Jews and Catholics, assume to be universal.

Torah and Torahs, or the Extracanonical Canon

The Bible is not the only canonical anthology for rabbinic Judaism. The twenty-four books of the Jewish Bible or Tanakh never stand on their own but are canonical only within a larger matrix of texts. There are, famously, two Torahs according to rabbinic literature: תורה שבכתב, or Written Torah, and תורה שבעל פה, or Oral Torah.[2] Both Torahs stem from revelation at Sinai.[3] The former consists of the Pentateuch along with the Prophets and Writings; the latter consists of rabbinic literature. Now, let me pause to explain how I use these terms, since some of them can have confusingly overlapping referents. The term *Written Torah* refers to the twenty-four books of the Jewish Bible and not merely its first five books.[4] When I intend to refer to the first five books in this chapter, I use the term *Pentateuch*, rather than the term *Torah*. When referring to the other two parts of the Jewish Bible, the Prophets (נביאים) and Writings (כתובים), I use the Hebrew acronym, Nakh (נ״ך). This not only saves a few syllables but underscores the fact that the Prophets and Writings are essentially a single bloc of material in the Jewish biblical canon, which, functionally speaking, is bipartite rather than tripartite.[5] By *Oral Torah*, I mean rabbinic literatures. This term includes the classical works of the early sages known as tanna'im (who lived from the early first century CE to the mid-third century) and those by slightly later sages known as amora'im and sabora'im (mid-third to mid-sixth centuries): the Mishnah, the two Talmuds (or Gemaras), and the various midrashic and aggadic compilations. (I refer to tanna'im, amora'im, and sabora'im as a group with the phrase "the classical rabbis.") But the term Oral Torah as typically used also includes later works. Post-talmudic texts and teachings, whether from the geonic period (the sixth through eleventh centuries), the Middle Ages, or the current era, can fall under the rubric of Oral Torah. To be sure, the boundaries of Oral Torah are vague. The Mishnah is clearly in, while Masechet Sofrim (an extracanonical tractate sometimes published along with but not quite as a part of the Talmud) lies near the border, perhaps on the outer side rather than the inner. Both the Jerusalem Talmud and the *Nefesh Haḥayyim* (a nineteenth-century scholastic work) are in, but the former is somehow more in than the latter. But the existence and importance of Oral Torah, however large its periphery may be, are quite clear.

The idea of Oral Torah has been discussed comprehensively in scholarship,[6] and an extensive summary of the rabbinic texts that describe the duality of Torah need not be repeated here. Two issues, however, call for brief discussion in order to avoid some misapprehensions: (1) the extent to which Oral Torah really is oral at all; and (2) the different forms that the notion of dual Torah takes in rabbinic literature.

First, the classical works of Oral Torah have long been available in written form. Recently, scholars have investigated the orality of this body of learning during the first millennium CE. The important questions they ask,[7] however, are not relevant to the project at hand. For many centuries Oral Torah has consisted first and foremost of written documents, even though the term continues to include oral learning as well, if only in the sense of exchanges between teacher and student. Oral Torah, in short, is not exclusively oral, and for our purposes it does not matter to what extent it ever was. The "orality" of Oral Torah, we will see, is a matter of ideology, not of actual transmission or reception. For the moment, it will suffice to cite Emmanuel Levinas's apt comment:

> Even written down, . . . the oral Torah preserves in its style its reference to oral teaching; the liveliness provided by a master addressing disciples who listen as they question. In written form it reproduces the diversity of opinions expressed, with extreme care taken to name the person providing them or commenting upon them. It records the multiplicity of opinions and the disagreements among scholars. . . . The Talmudic texts, even in the physiognomical aspects that their typography takes on, are accompanied by commentaries, and by commentaries on and discussions of these commentaries.[8]

Second, rabbinic works conceptualize the relation between Oral Torah and revelation in more than one way.[9] In the concept's most fully developed form, Moses received the *entire* Oral Torah at Sinai—including all of rabbinic literature and even what keen-witted students of the Torah would one day expound before their teachers: this idea appears in several talmudic and midrashic texts, for example, y. Pe'ah 4a (2:6), y. Ḥagigah 2d (1:8), b. Megillah 19b, Shemot Rabbah Ki Tissa 47:1; Wayiqra Rabbah 22:1; and Qohelet Rabbah 1:29 and 5:6. The texts expressing this maximalist idea tend to be later; they are amoraic, not tannaitic.[10] Other rabbinic texts make less comprehensive claims. Some passages in tannaitic midrashim come close to the amoraic position, claiming that laws found in rabbinic literature come from God, without insisting that all their details were revealed to Moses; this is the case in Sifra Shemini 1:9, Mekhilta de-Rabbi Yishmael Vayyisaʻ §1, and Sifre Devarim §48 and §351.[11] Other tannaitic or early amoraic texts make quite clear that some aspects of Oral Torah were unknown to Moses and arose only after his day, even though some such later teachings were rhetorically linked to Moses; so, for example, in the famous story told by Rav in b. Menaḥot 29b.[12] The Mishnah and Tosefta ascribe only three non-Pentateuchal laws to Moses at Sinai (see m. Yadayim 4:3, m. Pe'ah 2:6, and t. Sukkah 3:1–2; a nonlegal tradition is also ascribed to Moses at Sinai in m. Eduyot 8:7).[13] In short, there are varying degrees to which rabbinic literature ascribes authoritative traditions outside the Written Torah to revelation,[14] and this degree increases over time.[15] (In this regard rabbinic literature resembles biblical literature, which, we saw in chapter 3, displays an ever-increasing tendency starting in the late preexilic period toward what Hindy Najman calls "Mosaic discourse," the attribution of laws to Moses.) Because the expansive formulation from some amoraic texts is so well known in rabbinic culture, it is useful to recall that a less expansive (and earlier) claim appears as well: Oral Torah (but not *all* of the Oral Torah) was given to Moses at Sinai; this Oral Torah developed further as scribes and sages interpreted and enacted new laws throughout the generations.[16]

   In view of the fact that rabbinic tradition attributes more and more teachings from the Oral Torah to revelation, it is important to recall that even the most traditionalist of Jewish thinkers continue to acknowledge the human element in the Oral Torah. Jewish thinkers from antiquity through modernity do not view works of rabbinic literature as being in their entirety divine or infallible. Some medieval Jewish thinkers, such as Yom Tov Ishbili (the Ritba) and Nissim Gerondi (the Ran), regarded the disagreements and multiplicity of opinion that resulted from this mixing of human and divine elements as ennobling; in the twentieth century, several rigorously Orthodox thinkers, including Yitzchok Hutner and Abraham Isaac Kook, put special emphasis on the human nature of Oral Torah, as David Bigman has pointed out.[17] Granted, other medieval Jewish thinkers, including no less an authority than Maimonides, regarded this mixing and the resultant multiplicity of views as the tragic result of human forgetfulness, which impaired the tradition's preservation of the original divine message.[18] But all agree on the fact of the Oral Torah's mixed character. Indeed, what makes the notion of Oral Torah distinctive in the history of religions is precisely this combination of divine and human provenance in a single literature.[19] Oral Torah is, we may say, the Gilgamesh or Akhilleus of religious literature, part human and part divine. It is a literature at once sacred and fallible. That its actual wording originates with human sages does not detract from its authority, but it may allow for a more nuanced or flexible notion of authority. The participatory theology of revelation forces us to acknowledge that the same characteristic applies to the Bible, even to the Pentateuch. It is this sense of Oral Torah that I have in mind when I say that for modern Jews there is no Written Torah but only Oral Torah: the Pentateuch is sacred but not perfect, because it includes human and divine elements.

Blurring the Boundary in Rabbinic Literature

To collapse Written Torah into Oral Torah may seem to move beyond the norms of rabbinic Judaism and its doctrine of two Torahs. In practice, however, doing so is not as radical as one might imagine. Some rabbinic sources themselves blur the boundary between Oral Torah and Written Torah, and others effectively eliminate it. Thus, the move I am suggesting emulates and extends a trend already found in many rabbinic texts.

One begins to sense the blurring of this boundary from the simple fact that in rabbinic Judaism both Torahs were revealed to Israel, both are sacred, and both carry authority. The idea that Oral Torah, like Written Torah, is revealed appears elsewhere in rabbinic literature with great frequency: in the Talmuds (b. Shabbat 31a, y. Ḥagigah 2d [1:8]), in the midrashim (Sifra Beḥuqqotai 8:12), and in aggadic works (Avot deRabbi Nathan A 15/B 29 [31a–b]), to cite only a few examples. For our purposes it is necessary to quote just one such source. Commenting on the verse "The Levites will teach your laws to Jacob and your teachings/Torah/Torahs to Israel" (Deuteronomy 33.10), the midrash Sifre Devarim §351 states:

> The words "Your Torah[s] to Israel" (ותורתך לישראל) teach that two Torahs were given to Israel, one orally and one in writing. A Roman official named Agnitus asked Rabban Gamaliel, "How many Torahs were given to Israel?" He replied, "Two, one orally and one in writing."

(In the unvocalized written text of Deuteronomy, the noun *torah* could be read as either singular or plural.)[20] Note that the Torah mentioned first is the Oral Torah, not the Written Torah; there seems to be no assumption here that the Written Torah has priority.

Other rabbinic texts go a step further. They point toward a deeper unity that joins the two Torahs and suggest that the distinction between them is unimportant or misleading. An amoraic comment in b. Berakhot 5a reads:[21]

> R. Levi bar Ḥama passed on a saying of R. Shimon ben Laqish: What is the aggadic teaching that can be derived from the verse in scripture, "And I shall give you the tablets of stone, and the Torah (והתורה), and the command-ment (והמצוה), which I wrote to teach them" (Exodus 24.12)? "The tablets"—this refers to the Decalogue. "Torah"—this refers to the Pentateuch.[22] "And the commandment"—this refers to the Mishnah.[23] "Which I wrote"—this refers to the Prophets and the Writings. "To teach them"—this refers to the Gemara.[24] This teaches that all these were given to Moses at Sinai.[25]

It is significant that components of Oral Torah and Written Torah are mixed together in this passage. The order in which the text presents the material is not, as we might expect, "Pentateuch, Nakh, Mishnah, Gemara," but "Pentateuch, Mishnah, Nakh, Gemara."[26] This passage points toward a notion of canon that goes beyond scripture (Pentateuch and Nakh) to encompass rabbinic literature (Mishnah and Gemara). One does not sense that either type of literature as a whole takes precedence, has greater im-portance, or makes a stronger claim on our loyalty.[27] If anything, the or-der in which Levi bar Ḥama and Shimon ben Laqish mention the various texts might lead one to conclude that the Mishnah, a component of Oral Torah, takes precedence over Nakh, a component of Written Torah. Clas-sical commentators on this passage in fact make precisely that claim. An early medieval commentator on Berakhot 5a states, "From this passage one concludes that the Mishnah and also the Gemara, which explains the Mishnah's laws, have greater sanctity than the Prophets and Writings . . . for the biblical verse puts 'the commandment,' which is the Mishnah, be-fore 'which I write,' which are the Prophets and Writings."[28] Similarly, the *Iyyun Yaakov* (a commentary by Yaakov Reischer, a late-seventeenth-cen-tury halakhic authority)[29] on this passage from b. Berakhot maintains that the verse from Exodus mentions Mishnah first to teach that one should study Mishnah before one studies Nakh. A nineteenth-century rabbinic commentator, Abraham of Minsk, in his *Ahavat Eitan*,[30] refers to a teach-ing from elsewhere in the Babylonian Talmud, Nedarim 22b, to explain the placement of Mishnah before Nakh in Berakhot 5a. According to Nedarim 22b, if the Israelites had never sinned, only the Pentateuch and the Book of Joshua would have been revealed to them; God would not have needed to give the remainder of the Nakh to a perfectly righteous Israel. This is because (as the fourteenth-century commentary of Nissim Gerondi, or the *Ran*, to Nedarim 22b explains) the Pentateuch contains laws that will be in effect in perpetuity, and Joshua 13–22 stipulate how land should be allocated among the Israelite tribes in Canaan for all time. Thus, both the Pentateuch and Joshua had to be revealed whether or not the Israelites sinned. In contrast (the *Ran* avers), the remaining books of the Nakh merely contain exhortations and warnings to sinful Israelites regarding the need to observe the Torah's laws. The *Ahavat Eitan*, commenting on our passage from Berakhot 5a, makes clear that in this regard the Mishnah resembles the Pentateuch, not the Nakh: the Mishnah would have been revealed even if Israel had not sinned, presumably because it contains rulings and explanation of law.[31] Thus, sacred texts containing law (the Pentateuch and Joshua from the Written Torah, and the Mishnah from the Oral Torah) are of primary value, while the remaining texts of the Written Torah are merely of contingent value.[32]

The primacy of Oral Torah over parts of Written Torah emerges even more strongly in other rabbinic texts.[33] Take the following passage, which appears in b. Gittin 60b, y. Pe'ah 4a (2:6) and in many other sources:[34]

> R. Ḥaggai passed on a saying of R. Shmuel bar Naḥman: [Sacred] words have been expressed orally and [sacred] words have been expressed in writing, and we would not know which of them is more precious, except for the fact that it is written, "For in accordance with (כי על פי—literally, "according to the mouth of") these words I establish My covenant with you and with Israel" (Exodus 34.27). This proves that those that came orally are more precious.

The sense that Oral Torah takes precedence becomes unmistakable in some medieval and modern discussions of curriculum. There is an agreement in principle that ideally a Jew should study both Written Torah (in particular the Pentateuch) and Oral Torah, but some authorities maintain that one can fulfill this dual obligation by studying Oral Torah alone. After all, rabbinic literature quotes scripture quite often, so by studying the rabbis, one kills two birds with one stone. Some medieval authorities, especially among Ashkenazim, went so far as to discourage the study of the Bible, mentioning it alongside heretical works![35] The notion that Talmud alone is worthy of study became, and to some degree remains, fairly widespread in the great Lithuanian yeshivot founded in the nineteenth and twentieth centuries.

While other authorities within medieval and modern rabbinic culture have defended the study of the Bible,[36] nonetheless the Bible in traditional rabbinic culture is always studied alongside rabbinic texts, or through rabbinic texts, when it is studied at all. Never in rabbinic Judaism do we find the converse opinion, that Written Torah is important and Oral Torah is not.[37]

Some rabbinic works barely distinguish between Written and Oral Torah at all. Two central documents of rabbinic tradition, the Mishnah and Tosefta, never refer to the duality of Torah; the terms "Oral Torah" and "Written Torah" do not even appear in these works. Rather, they use the term *torah* to refer to all authoritative Jewish learning with its roots at Sinai (reserving the term *hatorah*, with the definite article, to refer to the Pentateuch).[38] Thus, the opening passage of Mishnah Avot simply says that Moses received *torah* at Sinai and passed it on, ultimately, to the rabbis.[39] A stronger statement of the unity of scripture and tradition can hardly be made. Other rabbinic texts similarly maintain that *torah* (and not just Written Torah or Pentateuch) constitutes a unity.[40] Sifre Devarim §306 suffices as an example: "The words of *torah* are a unity that includes scripture, repeated tradition [*mishnah*], discussions of tradition [*talmud*],[41] laws [*halakhot*], and lore [*aggadot*]."[42]

Other rabbinic documents admit the distinction but minimize it. A midrash preserved in Shemot Rabbah 47:1 and many other texts regards the division of Torah into written and oral components as nothing more than a practical measure:[43]

> When the Holy One, Blessed be He, revealed Himself at Sinai in order to give Torah to Israel, He dictated it to Moses in sequence: scripture, repeated traditions, discussions, and lore, as it is said, "God spoke *all* these things" (Exodus 20.1). At that moment, God told Moses even what a student would one day ask a teacher. Once Moses learned it from God's mouth, God said, "Teach it to Israel." Moses responded, "Master of the Universe! I shall write it down for them." God said, "I don't want to give to them in writing, for I know that the nations of the world will rule over them and will take it from them, and they will be degraded among the nations. Rather, I will give them scripture in writing, and I will give them repeated traditions, discussions, and lore in oral form. This way, when they come to be oppressed by the nations, they will still be distinct from them."[44]

According to this comment, all Torah was originally Oral Torah. Only after it was given to Moses was one part of it transmuted into Written Torah, in deference to Moses's request. This midrash does not indicate that there is any essential difference between the sections of Torah God consigned to writing and the sections God kept oral. The point was to divide the precious inheritance so that no other nation could take it in its entirety. Other nations could usurp the written sections (and in the view of the rabbis the Christians did exactly that[45]). But one who has only a part of Torah has nothing of it at all, for Torah is a unity, its apparent division into written and oral sections notwithstanding.[46]

This view of the relationship between Oral and Written Torah was extended by Samson Raphael Hirsch, a deeply influential rabbi of the mid-nineteenth century and the leader of the most rigorously Orthodox communities within German Jewry. Whereas most thinkers assume that the role of the Oral Torah is to explicate the Written Torah and to fill in its gaps, Hirsch maintains that the role of the Written Torah is only to provide notes and samples of the larger whole so as to prompt the memory of the reader. Alan Levenson explains that

> for Hirsch, the Written Torah provided the Cliffs Notes to the Oral Torah, which God taught Moses directly at Mount Sinai and which Moses then transmitted perfectly to the sages from Joshua onward. For a full forty years [up until Moses wrote the Written Torah down shortly before his death], then, the Oral Torah existed as living Judaism without the Written Torah at all! Even after the Written Torah was given to Israel before Moses' death, it in no way supplanted the Oral Torah.[47]

In Hirsch's view, the Oral Torah does not depend on the Written Torah, in spite of its midrashic-exegetical form. Rather, as Jay Harris explains:

> For Hirsch, the written Torah never existed as a distinct source requiring supplementation and explanation. There was one sweeping, comprehensive oral revelation of all the laws incumbent on Jews by divine command, a small number of which, usually exceptional or distinctive cases, were set to writing, and were formulated in linguistically unusual ways. For Hirsch, then, the ubiquitous talmudic question [regarding legal rulings in the Mishnah and Talmud], "How do we know this?" is not asking for the source of the law [in the Pentateuch]. . . . Rather, the question must mean . . . "What written verse . . . calls attention to the larger constellation of laws of which the law under discussion is an integral part?" We wish to know the answer to this question so that we can more readily preserve the entire corpus of traditional laws.[48]

Harris claims that Hirsch's view of the relationship between the two Torahs was unprecedented,[49] but I think this overstates the case. The idea that
Torah began as Oral Torah and that parts of it were transferred to writing
for practical reasons is the clear meaning of the midrash found in Shemot
Rabbah 47:1 and in many parallels.[50]

It follows that Oral Torah has a conceptual and even temporal priority over Written Torah.[51] Since the default value of Torah is oral, Written
Torah can be seen as a subset of Oral Torah. Scripture and tradition are not
parallel; rather, scripture is but one form of the larger entity that is tradition.[52] This point emerges from the opinion of the amoraic sage Shimon
ben Laqish in b. Gittin 60a, according to whom Moses memorized the
various sections of the Torah as they were given to him during the forty
years in the desert and wrote down the Pentateuch only at the end of his
life.[53] As David Kraemer explicates the passage, "According to [Shimon ben
Laqish] . . . Written Torah was originally oral. In effect, the only difference
between Written and Oral Torah during the life of Moses was what they
one day would become; for most of that period the form of the two Torahs
was literally identical."[54]

These texts espouse what we might term a *transcanonical canon*—that
is, a canon that goes beyond the twenty-four books of the Jewish Bible to
encompass rabbinic literature. Moreover, they make clear that this canon
contains not only the Mishnah and Gemara but oral discourses that continue into the present and the future. The midrash from Shemot Rabbah
47:1 tells us that the revealed Torah includes questions students would one
day ask their masters. Other versions of this text (y. Pe'ah 4a [2:6]; Wayiqra
Rabbah 22:1; Qohelet Rabbah 1:29 and 5:6) tell us that what keen-witted
students would one day teach in the presence of their masters is also part
of the revealed Torah.[55] Oral Torah includes the living words of students in
every generation.

This transcanonical canon is further evinced by the fluidity of the border separating the Torahs. The classification of a particular work as part of
Written or Oral Torah seems straightforward: biblical books such as Genesis and Judges belong to the former, while talmudic tractates like Berakhot
and Bekhorot belong to the latter. Nonetheless, many teachings found in
works classified as Oral Torah are derived exegetically from biblical verses.
Consequently, one might consider those teachings to belong, deep down,
to Written Torah, reserving the term Oral Torah for the small number of
traditions independent of and parallel to Written Torah. (In fact, accord-

ing to Rashi's commentary, this is precisely the view of Rabbi Elazar in b. Gittin 60b.)[56] And yet teachings that are distinctly articulated in a work of Oral Torah might also be considered part of Oral Torah. (This more common view lies behind the comment of Rabbi Yoḥanan in Gittin 60b, according to the Maharsha's commentary there.)[57] The latter approach seems sensible in light of the fact that many teachings derived exegetically from Written Torah are not self-evident from Written Torah alone. R. Naḥman points out in b. Qiddushin 66a that any literate person can *read* the Written Torah, but no one can fully *understand* it without the sages—that is, without the insights and techniques of Oral Torah.[58] Since such teachings of the Written Torah depend on Oral Torah, they can sensibly be classified as Oral Torah. Many teachings, then, are simultaneously part of both Torahs, and these teachings probably include the bulk of Jewish law and belief.

A similar point emerges from m. Ḥagigah 1:8:

> Laws concerning the annulment of vows are fluttering in the air; they have nothing on which base themselves. Laws concerning the Sabbath, offerings for the festivals, and misappropriation of property belonging to the Temple are like mountains suspended by a hair; they have a bit of Bible and a great deal of law. Laws concerning monetary matters, sacrificial service in the Temple, ritual purity and impurity, and forbidden sexual relations have something on which to base themselves; they are the very body of Torah.

This passage recognizes that Judaism's laws have varied origins: some are firmly based in scripture, some have only a minor or nominal basis in scripture, and some have no basis in scripture whatsoever. This mishnaic passage does not claim that laws without scriptural support have no authority, nor does it suggests that those with only a little scriptural support have only a little authority. On the contrary, throughout its many tractates the Mishnah lays out the requirements of all three types of law in great detail.[59] This passage merely proposes an academic classification of laws and their origin. If we correlate the passage's categorization with those rabbinic texts that (unlike the Mishnah) speak of two Torahs, we may regard the first group of laws, those "fluttering in the air" without any basis in scripture, as Oral Torah; laws firmly based in scripture are Written Torah; and those "suspended by a hair," with precious little basis in scripture, are at once Oral and Written Torah—the former, according to the view of Maharsha explaining Yoḥanan in b. Gittin 60b, the latter according to the view of Rashi explaining Elazar there.

The last sentence of this passage seems to create a hierarchy within this categorization: while all the laws are in force, the most scripturally based laws are described as "the very body of Torah." The Gemara, however, is uncomfortable with the implication that laws having a firmer basis in scripture are somehow more essential. In b. Ḥagigah 11b the Gemara asks regarding the Mishnah's phrase "These are the very body of Torah" (הן הן גופי תורה—literally: "these—*these*—are the very body of Torah"), "Are we to understand that these [the last category, those laws with a firm basis in the Bible] are the very body of Torah while those [the less scriptural categories] are not? Rather, understand the text this way: These *and* these are the very body of Torah"—in other words, all three categories are equally part of Torah. Thus, the Gemara accepts the classification of three types of law but rejects the suggestion that, even on a merely theoretical level, those with the closest relationship to scripture have a special status. Instead, the Gemara insists that all laws, even if they have no basis in scripture, are essential to Torah. This reading of the last line in m. Ḥagigah 1:8 becomes the standard understanding in rabbinic Judaism. The commentaries of Rashi, Maimonides, and Bartenura (the late-fifteenth-century author of a standard commentary on the Mishnah) give it as the correct understanding even for the passage in the Mishnah itself.[60]

What emerges from these texts is that many laws and teachings belong to more than one category. Laws that one might assume are part of one Torah can also be conceptualized as part of the other. Indeed, one of the main projects of the Gemaras and the halakhic midrashim is to demonstrate that mishnaic material that seems to belong to the Oral Torah also belongs to the Written; the Gemara and halakhic midrashim accomplish this by connecting mishnaic rulings to biblical verses through midrashic interpretation.[61] One might even view the very distinction between two genres, halakhic midrash and mishnah, as a מחלוקת or rabbinic debate. The genre of halakhic midrash claims that law is primarily derived from Written Torah, while the genre of mishnah, with its relative absence of scriptural citation, claims that for a law to be a law, it is sufficient that it has been transmitted as part of a collection going back to Sinai; a connection to scripture is unnecessary.[62] Significantly, neither the Mishnah on its own nor the halakhic midrashim on their own became the central text of rabbinic Judaism. That role belongs to the Talmud, which includes both genres: it presents nonscriptural laws in the Mishnah, followed by midrashic grounding of those laws in the Gemara. In the end, rabbinic Judaism insists that most Jewish laws and teachings are authoritative both because they are transmitted in the chain that started at Sinai and because they are exegetically rooted in scripture. The religion based on the Talmud (rather than just the Mishnah or the halakhic midrashim) is a belts-and-suspenders religion. The result of studying the full range of classical rabbinic genres is that one recognizes the considerable overlap between the two Torahs, so that the very separation between them seems artificial.[63]

It follows that the English term *scripture* is misleading in a Jewish context, because it obscures the extent to which traditional Judaism conceptualizes the Bible as both oral and written.[64] In fact, the former conceptualization takes pride of place. Rabbinic literature refers to the Bible as the Written Torah, but a far more common term for the Bible among the classical rabbis is מקרא (*miqra*), which means not "scripture, what is written" but "what is called aloud, what is chanted." The term *Written Torah* (תורה [ש]בכתב) appears thirty-eight times in tannaitic and amoraic literature, while *miqra* appears 657 times.[65] For centuries, most Jews knew the Bible primarily from hearing it chanted. Many Jews memorized large parts of it (and here it is useful to recall that the Hebrew word for memorizing "by heart," על פה, literally means memorizing "by mouth"). The technology through which one comes to know information shapes how we use that information, and the Bible was at least as much an aural/oral document for Jews throughout the ages as a written one. When scripture was primarily memorized, recited, and chanted, it functioned in one set of ways, and people searched it for certain types of information or guidance. When it became more widely available in printed editions, changes occurred in the ways it was interpreted and the sorts of information people tried to get from it.[66] Even then, the aurality of "scripture" continued to play an important role; Jews chant and memorize the Pentateuch and selections from the prophets in synagogue and educational settings to the present day.

The rabbinic texts we have examined overturn the presumption that Oral Torah's authority is derivative, flowing from the Written Torah that it explains. Although some thinkers suppose that the authority of rabbinic law is based on the Written Torah,[67] in fact the opposite is the case.[68] The authority and stature of the Written Torah is a teaching of the Oral Torah; as the rabbis themselves put it in Wayiqra Rabbah 11:7: "Without the sages, there is no Torah."[69] Granted, it is on the basis of a biblical passage, Deuteronomy 17.8–11, that the classical rabbis claim authority to legislate and to rule on matters of law. But this claim is itself based on the somewhat peculiar way the rabbis interpreted the passage. In its biblical context this passage does not deal with legislating at all, or even with ruling on existing questions of law. Rather, it requires judges throughout the land to travel to the Temple in Jerusalem to receive oracles in difficult cases that cannot be decided locally.[70] If this passage from the Written Torah provides a basis for the authority of Oral Torah, it does so only when we see it through the eyes of the Oral Torah. The Pentateuch itself never creates procedures for the interpretation, reform, or updating of law, and thus it does nothing to provide a basis for the authority of Oral Torah.[71] Ultimately, rabbinic law carries authority because it comes in some sense from God, and this underlying norm applies equally to laws found in either Torah. Authority in Judaism stems from revelation, and the question of which Torah records a given element of revelation is not relevant.[72]

One might object to this assertion by invoking rabbinic Judaism's distinction between דאורייתא and דרבנן commandments—that is, between laws that come directly from the Pentateuch and those instituted by the rabbis.[73] The two categories are governed by different legal rules; for example, in cases of doubt, a halakhic authority should rule more stringently in regard to the former and more leniently in regard to the latter.[74] The distinction between these categories is itself a trope of the Oral Torah, and decisions concerning which laws belong to which category are entirely governed by rabbinic texts. Many דאורייתא, or "Pentateuchal," commandments are the product of midrashic reading; they have little or no basis in the contextual-philological meaning of the Pentateuch itself.[75] Thus, it remains the case that many דאורייתא, or "Pentateuchal," commandments are effectively part of the Oral Torah in the sense that their content and the very existence of the category are known from rabbinic literature. The category "Written Torah" is not equivalent to דאורייתא-"Pentateuchal," and "Oral Torah" is not the same as דרבנן-"rabbinic."

To be sure, not all sages in rabbinic tradition would agree with the assertion that the line between the Oral Torah and the Written Torah is nonexistent or unimportant. Some sages accord greater priority to the Written Torah.[76] Azzan Yadin has argued that sages associated with the school of Rabbi Yishmael in the period of the Mishnah regard scripture (and hence exegesis of scripture) as the only source of authority, so that for them authoritative traditions parallel to and independent of scripture are all but nonexistent.[77] A comparable view, as Elliot Wolfson points out, is espoused by the influential thirteenth-century biblical commentator, halakhic scholar, and kabbalist Naḥmanides. In the introduction to his *Sepher Hamitzvot*, Naḥmanides avers that everything found in Oral Torah is already implied and genuinely present in Written Torah.[78] But the opposite point of view, which valorizes Oral Torah on practical and conceptual levels or regards the boundary between the two Torahs as insignificant, also exists in rabbinic culture. Because it is tradition that preserves scripture and passes scripture on to us, this point of view is especially persuasive. Consequently, my assertion at the outset of this chapter (to wit, that the participatory theory of revelation in modern Jewish thought requires us to admit that the Written Torah is just another form of Oral Torah) is far less threatening to traditional Judaism than one might initially assume.

Blurring the Boundary in Biblical Literature

It is perhaps not surprising that rabbinic texts valorize Oral Torah. After all, rabbinic texts are themselves the main component of Oral Torah, so the cynics among us (רחמנא ליצלן) will contend that the rabbis' assertions about Oral Torah's primacy are nothing more than a self-aggrandizing power grab. But it is not only rabbinic texts that blur the boundary between written and oral structures of authority; biblical texts do so as well, and thus prove themselves proto-rabbinic. The distinction between a flexible oral tradition and a fixed written scripture is foreign to biblical texts and the culture that produced them. Scripture emerged from tradition and was often subject to modification on the basis of tradition. Consequently, eliminating the distinction between Oral and Written Torah is loyal not only to significant elements within rabbinic Judaism but to biblical religion as well. This becomes clear in several distinct ways: from the study of inner-biblical exegesis, from the study of the composition and crystallization of the Bible, from the ways the Bible itself uses the term *torah*, and from the nature of scribal practice in biblical Israel and the ancient Near East.

Just as teachers within rabbinic literature disagree with one another, question one another, and supplement one another, so too biblical authors revise, interpret, and even reject other biblical authors. Chronicles retells the historical narrative found in its main source, the Books of Samuel and Kings.[79] Deuteronomy retells narratives found elsewhere in the Pentateuch and reformulates laws found in Exodus, while also responding to Priestly traditions.[80] Within the Priestly literature of the Pentateuch, texts from the Holiness School supplement the Priestly Torah, preserving its wording while altering some of its teaching.[81] Prophetic texts contain allusions and reactions to earlier biblical texts, so that their own wording and imagery are to a great extent based on earlier texts.[82] Throughout biblical literature one finds scribal glosses that reflect on or modify a given text. In short, the Written Torah is itself an exegetical document and hence also a form of Oral Torah.

It will be worth looking at two brief examples that exemplify this exegetical aspect of scripture, in which a single passage contains both a base text and an interpretive expansion.[83] It is likely that Exodus 22.24 originally read, "If you lend money to My עם, do not act toward them as a creditor; exact no interest from them." Now, the Hebrew word עם usually means "nation," but it can also mean "the poor" or "impoverished folk, peasantry" (see Isaiah 3.15, 10.2; Micah 3.3; Psalms 14.4, 72.2, perhaps 94.5–6; Nehemiah 5.1). Since the meaning of עם as "nation" was more common, a scribe worried that without clarification the verse would be misread. To make it apparent that the lesser-known sense was to be understood, the scribe added the words "to the poor among you" immediately after עם, yielding the verse as we know it.[84] Thus, in addition to serving as the basis for the lengthier, separate law code in Deuteronomy 12–26, the Covenant Code in Exodus 21–23 was itself subject to additions over the course of time that elucidated and at times altered its legislation. Another example of an exegetical comment inserted into a biblical text occurs in the Priestly law of Passover in Exodus 12.[85] The opening verses of this law are somewhat uneven, because at times they refer to the Israelites in the third person, while at others they refer to them in the second person. A fascinating pattern emerges when we separate the second-person verses (which I put in italics in the following translation) from the third-person verses (which are in roman type). At the outset of the passage I treat one second-person phrase as part of the third-person section:[86]

> [1]Yhwh said to Moses and Aaron in the land of Egypt: [2]This month shall be the head of your months.
> *It shall be the first of the months of the year for you.*
>
> [3]Tell the whole community of Israel that on the tenth of this month each of them should take a lamb for a family, a lamb for a household. [4]But if the household is too small for a lamb, it should share one with a neighbor dwelling nearby.
> *You should contribute for the lamb according to what each household will eat, in proportion to the number of persons. [5]Your lamb should be without blem-*

ish, a male one year old; you may take it from the sheep or from the goats. ⁶You should keep watch over it until the fourteenth day of this month.

The whole assembled congregation of the Israelites should slaughter it at twilight. ⁷They should take some of the blood and put it on the two doorposts and on the lintel of the houses in which they eat it. ⁸They should eat the flesh that very night; they should eat it roasted over the fire, with unleavened bread and with bitter herbs.

⁹You may not eat any of it raw, or boiled with water, but roasted—head, legs, and entrails—over the fire. ¹⁰You may not leave any of it over until morning; if any of it is left until morning, you should burn it. ¹¹This is how you shall eat it: your loins girded, with sandals on your feet, and with your staff in your hand. You should eat it hurriedly.

It is a passover offering to Yhwh.

The sections that use the third person (in roman type above) read perfectly well on their own, and it is likely that they constitute the original Priestly text of what we know as Exodus 12. The verses using the second person provide additional information that explains or clarifies the laconic directions from the original text. A reader of the original version might have wondered what the phrase "the head of the months" meant; a later priest paraphrased this potentially ambiguous phrasing, telling us that it means "the first of the months of the year." Similarly, one might wonder how to work things out when sharing the lamb with a neighbor's family; the later material explains that the amounts contributed to the meal should be proportional to the size of the two families involved, rather than a fifty-fifty split that ignores the relative size of the two groups. To a person who has studied the halakhic midrashim of the classical rabbis, the biblical text as laid out above will look and sound very familiar. After each older passage we find a brief comment that clarifies the base text, expands on it, or provides additional detail necessary for applying it with confidence that one is conducting the ritual properly.

Analysis that attends to phenomena of this sort—that is, the study of inner-biblical exegesis, allusion, and revision—has weighty implications for our understanding of the nature of scripture.[87] This field of study sheds light on how biblical texts functioned in the biblical period, and how those functions relate to the place of scripture in postbiblical Judaism and Christianity. The authors of the Bible, we now realize, were at once readers and writers; more precisely, they were writers through being readers. Biblical authors commented on other biblical texts; argued with them; alluded to them; revised them; applied their principles to new situations; borrowed from their authority; and, by quoting them, underscored their prestige. In this they resemble later Jewish and Christian sages, who often create new works by recasting language and themes they find in the Bible. The religion that generated the Bible, then, foreshadowed the religions generated by the Bible. Biblical authors bequeathed their successors not only a text but also ways of relating to that text.[88] Thus, the study of inner-biblical exegesis breaks down the implicit hierarchy that separates primary text and belated commentary. As Bernard Levinson puts it:

> The ingenuity of the interpreter operates even in the formative period of the canon, while those texts that will subsequently win authoritative status are still being composed and collected. . . . Interpretation is constitutive of the canon; it is not secondary to the canon in terms of either chronology or significance.[89]

The Bible is to a very great extent an interpretive anthology, just as Oral Torah is an evolving interpretive literature. What later Jews and Christians came to know as scripture was in fact Oral Torah for the ancient Israelites who created it.

Nowhere is this more importantly the case than in the Book of Deuteronomy. Jean-Pierre Sonnet has noted that this book, in contrast to other legal collections from the ancient Near East, presents itself as being first of all an oral document. This tendency is evident from the book's very first verse, "These are the words that Moses spoke (דבר) . . .":

> Deuteronomy's opening ushers in a distinctively oral communication. . . . Outside the Bible . . . no mention has been found indicating that in the ancient Near East collections of laws were promulgated orally . . . without the mediation of a written record. Yet Moses does precisely that, conveying orally, without any written reminder, an extensive collection of laws (that YHWH revealed to him at Ḥoreb forty years ago!).[90]

To be sure, Moses's Oral Torah, like the rabbis', is eventually written down, as the last chapters of the book make clear (27.3–8, 28.58–61, 29.19–26, 30.10).[91] But its opening words lead us to understand it as something other than Written Torah. The suggestion that Deuteronomy is first and foremost an oral teaching is not merely a modern proposal of a biblical critic. One Ḥasidic commentator in the nineteenth century, Avraham of Sochochow, described the Book of Deuteronomy as Oral Torah; another, Zadok Ha-kohen of Lublin, described Deuteronomy as the "root" of the Oral Torah. As Yaakov Elman has noted, both Avraham of Sochochow and Zadok of Lublin base themselves on Naḥmanides, the thirteenth-century kabbalist and halakhic authority.[92] In his Pentateuch commentary Naḥmanides maintains that the laws in Deuteronomy fall into two classes: some were originally dictated by God to Moses, who memorized them and wrote them down years later; the rest consist of Moses's explanations of laws written down earlier in the Pentateuch. Naḥmanides implies a basic similarity between Deuteronomy and Oral Torah in two respects: parts of Deuteronomy were originally oral, like the Mishnah; other parts are commentaries, like the midrashim. Other medieval and early modern works, including the *Zohar*, Isaiah Horowitz's *Shenei Luḥot Haberit*, and Elie Benamozegh's *Em Lamiqra* also refer to Deuteronomy as Oral Torah, in distinction from the first four books of the Pentateuch.[93] A functionally similar assertion appears in the work of the modern Jewish philosopher Hermann Cohen, who points out that Deuteronomy contains both revelation and a reflection on revelation that moves beyond an earlier naïveté.[94]

For all these classical Jewish thinkers, Deuteronomy is at once Written Law and Oral Law. Coming from a completely different method of analysis, the biblical scholar and Assyriologist Karel van der Toorn makes a strikingly similar claim: from D's perspective the Ten Commandments were Written Law, which was supplemented by an authoritative Oral Law, which Moses received from God and ultimately wrote down as Deuteronomy 12–26. Thus, van der Toorn suggests, "What is adumbrated here [in the development of the Book of Deuteronomy] is the doctrine of the Torah *šebbe'al-peh*," of the Oral Torah.[95] A great many biblical critics—including S. R. Driver, Moshe Weinfeld, Michael Fishbane, Bernard Levinson, Timo Veijola, and Eckhard Otto[96]—have laid out in great detail the ways that the authors of Deuteronomy rewrite narratives and laws from earlier sources that eventually became part of what we know as the Pentateuch. Both classical Jewish thinkers and modern biblical critics soften the distinction between Oral Torah and Written Torah by pointing to a significant overlap between them, which includes an entire book of the Pentateuch.

The study of inner-biblical exegesis and revision demonstrates that tradition is historically prior to scripture; in fact, tradition creates scripture. Further, while modern scholars propose varied models to explain how the Pentateuch came into being, they agree that the process involved the redaction of originally independent texts and a greater or lesser degree of supplementation of those texts by later scribes. These scholars uncover varied and dynamic traditions that preceded the canonization of scripture. The philological work of modern biblical critics has broken down the artificial distinction between scripture and tradition: rather than speaking of early written traditions that are subject to later interpretations, we need to speak of an ongoing dialectic between scripture and tradition in ancient Israel. Through this dialectic, tradition created scriptures; the new scriptures required interpretation; the new interpretations were passed on, becoming traditions in their own right; some of these traditions became scripture.[97] We saw earlier that many rabbinic texts view Oral Torah as having priority over Written Torah on a conceptual level (since Oral Torah defines what Written Torah includes and guides its interpretation) and on a temporal level (since God originally gave the whole Torah orally and only later allowed Moses to write parts of it down). We can add now that this rabbinic view matches the historical relationship of tradition and scripture.[98]

The ways the Bible uses the term *torah* also anticipate the fluid border between Oral and Written Torah in rabbinic Judaism.[99] There is no biblical term that precisely matches our word "revelation," but *torah* comes close, meaning, in many cases, that which God revealed. But as Norman Solomon has rightly noted, "the biblical style of revelation . . . is an *encounter with God*, rather than the *dictation of a book*."[100] Thus, it is no surprise that the term *torah* in the Bible need not mean a written text. In Priestly literature (for example, Leviticus 6.2, 7.37, Numbers 31.21), *torah* denotes specific teachings, especially those pertaining to ritual matters. *Torah* in this sense probably referred to both oral and written teachings. Joachim Begrich argued that Priestly torahs were originally communicated orally.[101] Indeed, P (to an even greater degree than D) regards its own laws as oral in nature. P never refers to Moses writing these laws down, even at the end of his life. The only reference to writing by Moses occurs in Numbers 33.1–2, where God directs Moses to write down the itinerary of the nation during their forty years in the desert. As Schwartz notes, P makes "no reference to any written Torah at all . . . P relates that Moses received the laws in a series of audiences with God . . . but nowhere is he charged with writing them down, and nowhere is it related that he did so."[102] Thus, not only the Book of Deuteronomy but also the Priestly texts were originally Oral Torah.

Even when biblical texts use the term *torah* to refer to a specific book, the dynamic and expansive nature of the term comes to the fore. This becomes evident in late biblical texts such as Ezra-Nehemiah that use the term to refer not only to a specific Pentateuchal text but also to interpretations based on a Pentateuchal text.[103] Nehemiah 8.14–15 is quite instructive in this regard. The exilic community in Jerusalem, this passage tells us,

> [14]found it written in the Torah that Yhwh commanded through Moses that the Israelites should dwell in booths during the holiday in the seventh month, [15]and that they should make a public announcement in all the cities and in Jerusalem as follows: "Go out to the hills to get olive branches, oil trees, myrtle, palms, and all kinds of trees to build the booths," as it is written.

Verse 14 restates the regulation regarding the holiday of Sukkot found in Leviticus 23.42: "You should dwell in booths seven days; all Israelite citizens should dwell in booths." Verse 15, however, enumerates two regulations not explicitly found in Leviticus 23: that a public announcement about building the booths is commanded, and that branches of certain trees should be used to build the booths. The latter regulation may be inferred from an ambiguous command regarding tree branches in Leviticus 23.40: "On the first day, take the fruit of a *hadar* tree, branches from a palm tree, boughs from leafy trees, and willows of the brook, and rejoice for seven days before Yhwh your God." This verse does not explain precisely what one should do with these branches, boughs, and fruit in order to rejoice. The exilic readers described in Nehemiah 8 attempt to fill in this gap: basing themselves on the proximity of this verse to the requirement two verses later that Israelites must dwell in booths, these readers plausibly infer that one should take the branches in order to build the booths.[104] (This interpretive leap in Nehemiah 8.15 is no more unlikely than the leap made by the classical rabbis and their forebears, according to which one uses the fruit, branches, and boughs to fashion a handheld ritual object that one shakes in all directions during the holiday liturgy.)[105] Here we see that the Book of Ezra-Nehemiah describes as "Moses's Torah" not only what is clearly written in Leviticus but also exegetical extensions thereof. More surprisingly, the first regulation in Nehemiah 8.15 (that one should make a public announcement concerning the holiday) has no basis in the written text of Leviticus whatever. Yet Nehemiah 8 calls it Torah as well.[106] Thus, in Ezra-Nehemiah, a practice may be ascribed to the Torah of Moses if it appears explicitly in a Pentateuchal text, if it is exegetically derived from the text, or if it is based on an authoritative teaching outside the Pentateuch but somehow parallel to it.[107] Here we see precisely the three categories of m. Ḥagigah 1:8: Torah is a unity encompassing written texts, exegesis of those texts, and extra-textual tradition.

Similarly, Jon Levenson discusses the meaning of the term *torah* in Psalm 119, and he shows that "the author of Psalm 119 recognizes three sources of *tôrâ*: (1) received tradition, passed on most explicitly by teachers (vv 99–100) but including perhaps some sacred books now in the Hebrew Bible, (2) cosmic or natural law (vv 89–91), and (3) unmediated divine teaching (for example, vv 26–29)."[108] In short, in biblical times, no hard and fast distinction existed between authoritative teaching and emerging teaching, between mediated and unmediated revelation, between Written Torah and Oral Torah.[109]

The fluid boundary between these categories in the Bible should come as no surprise, because the cultural world from which the Bible emerged knew no firm division between written and oral sources of authority. In ancient times the use of written texts was largely an oral-performative affair.[110] Written texts were primarily aids to memory for texts that people learned and passed on orally. David Carr explains:

> Many ancient texts were not written in such a way that they could be read easily by someone who did not already know them well. . . . The visual presentation of such texts presupposed that the reader already knew the given text and had probably memorized it to some extent. . . . Such written copies were a subsidiary part of a much broader literate matrix, where the focus was as much or more on the transmission of texts from mind to mind as on transmission of texts in written form. . . . Societies with writing often have an intricate interplay of orality and textuality, where written texts are intensely oral, while even exclusively oral texts are deeply affected by written culture.[111]

Written texts served alongside memorization as a means of preservation comparable to electronic recordings in modern times. To study or enjoy a text, one had to "play" the recording out loud. One accomplished this not by pressing a button on a machine but by having a trained scribe chant the text, and whether the scribe did so from his own memory or from a written copy was immaterial. This variation was comparable to our choice of whether to listen to a recording from a CD or an MP3—it sounds more or less the same either way.

The orality of all reading in the ancient world becomes clear when we recall that the verbs קָרָא in Hebrew, קְרָא in Aramaic, and *šasâ'u* in Akkadian, which are often translated as "read," in fact mean to "call out loud." Rare exceptions notwithstanding, silent reading did not exist in antiquity, and it is important to realize how oxymoronic the idea of silent reading—that is, "silent calling aloud"—would have seemed to an ancient Israelite, Aramean, or Babylonian.[112] Even a scribe who studied a text by himself generally did so out loud, so that information went into the reader's mind not solely through the eye, as it does for us, but through the ear by way of the mouth. (Two institutions preserve this practice of textual study in the contemporary world: the Jewish *beit midrash* and the Muslim *madrasa*—in both one studies a text by murmuring or chanting it.) All written texts were also oral texts, and thus it is not surprising that scribes often committed to memory texts that were also written down. This is the case, for example, in Deuteronomy 31.19, where God commands, "So now, write this song down and teach it to the Israelites; put it in their mouths."[113] Preserving the song is a matter of both instruments, the pen and the tongue. Reproducing it for an actual audience, however, needed to involve only the latter.

Avigdor Hurovitz, Yaakov Elman, and Karel van der Toorn point out that oral and written manifestations of a given tradition often influenced each other.[114] Some scribal texts from ancient Mesopotamia include explanatory comments that are marked with the Akkadian phrase, *ša pi ummâni*, "from the mouth of the sage," which probably originated as oral clarifications of a master scribe in the classroom that scribes recorded in new copies of the text.[115] This phenomenon probably explains the origin of explanatory glosses in the Bible as well, such as the clarification of the word עם's meaning ("nation" or "poor person"?) in Exodus 22.24. Because both oral and written texts were authoritative in the ancient Near East,[116] biblical scribes rarely sensed opposition between them. For this reason biblical texts often mention oral and written versions of a text alongside each other. At the lawgiving, Geoffrey Miller points out, the Israelites

> offer explicit consent [to the law] twice, with a slight variation: once in response to Moses' oral recitation of the law (Exodus 24:3) and once in response to Moses' reading of the written law (Exodus 24:7). . . . The acceptance of the oral recitation allows for greater flexibility in adapting the law to changing circumstances.[117]

This double consent is not a function of a redundancy that results from the combination of two sources. Both 24.3 and 24.7 are part of the E narrative, which regards it as normal that Moses first conveys his own oral report of God's will and then reads a written version aloud. E further emphasizes the overlap of the categories by having the people say "We will listen" specifically to the written version, rather than to the purely oral one that preceded. The inseparability of oral and written versions of a text shows the distinction between canon and exegesis to be foreign in the world that produced the Bible.[118] Carr describes this relationship:

> Written biblical texts in general were but the numinous, written reference points for a predominantly *oral-cognitive* process of writing the traditions on the minds of elite Israelites, and later Israelites in general. . . . Writing and orality are parts of a deeper and more important writing-supported, performance-oriented process: shaping elite subgroups (and later broader groups) through writing . . . ancient traditions on their hearts.[119]

Carr and others demonstrate that writing in ancient Israel does not run parallel to oral tradition; rather, writing was part of a larger oral tradition in which it played subservient and limited roles. Carr's historical point is an analogue to the theological point I am making: Written Torah is not a parallel teaching alongside Oral Torah, much less the source of Oral Torah. It is a subset of Oral Torah.

Are All Canons Equal?

On reflection, it is clear from both biblical and rabbinic viewpoints that the distinction between scripture and tradition is misleading. Both Torahs are canonical; both are revealed, sacred, and authoritative. One may ask, nevertheless, whether they are canonical in different ways or to different extents. Does Written Torah have any greater degree of canonicity, so that the demotion of Written Torah to the status of Oral Torah has troubling results for rabbinic Judaism? In what follows, I examine the canonicity of each Torah from several perspectives to ascertain whether there is any real difference between the status of each.

First, one perspective is suggested by the very helpful discussion of canon by Moshe Halbertal in *People of the Book: Canon, Meaning and Authority*. Halbertal distinguishes among several senses of the term *canonical*. For our purposes, the distinction between what he calls *normative* and *formative* canons is especially important. Texts that are canonical in the *normative* sense are obeyed and followed; they provide the group loyal to the text with guides to behavior and belief. Texts that are canonical in the *formative* sense are "taught, read, transmitted and interpreted. . . . They provide a society or a profession with a shared vocabulary."[120] In this latter sense, canon overlaps with the notion of curriculum. In the ancient world,

scribal curricula embodied, as Carr observes, "a body of recollections transmitted in organized ways to participants in a given group, recollections of
values and views that shape each individual into a member of the group."[121]
Halbertal suggests in passing that scriptures are canonical in the normative
sense, but I think that in practice this is not the case. In Judaism Written
Torah is taught and read, transmitted and interpreted, but it is not the location of legal norms that Jews follow. When one wants to know whether a
pot is kosher, whether a business transaction is acceptable, or what time the
Passover Seder must begin, one does not open up a Bible. One turns instead
to works of Oral Torah.[122] Crucial beliefs regarding messianism, resurrection, and the nature of God are also articulated in rabbinic and postrabbinic
texts rather than the Bible.[123]

Not only is Judaism's normative canon found within the Oral Torah
more than the Written; even within Oral Torah the situation is complex.
The core texts of Oral Torah—the Mishnah and the Gemaras—are, like
the Bible, more formative than normative. When answering legal questions, halakhic decisors rely primarily on recent law codes and responsa
literature, not on tannaitic or amoraic texts. A basic principle of halakhic
jurisprudence is הלכתא כבתראי: the law as practiced follows the later authorities. Both the Written Torah and the classical works of the Oral Torah
(that is, Mishnah, Gemara, and midrashic collections) are canonical in the
formative sense. But these texts are not in practice authoritative. Granted,
the Pentateuch once played a role in creating legislation: the tanna'im and
amora'im created law or decided legal questions on the basis of (or at least
with reference to) Pentateuchal texts. But that role of the Written Torah
became a thing of the past in the early Middle Ages; by and large, from the
close of the amoraic era on (and in practice even much earlier), decisions
on questions of halakhah have been made by referring to other texts in the
Oral Torah, not texts from the Written Torah.[124] Similarly, while medieval
and modern decisors of Jewish law consult the Mishnah and Gemaras,
there are areas of Jewish law in which we now follow later codes or responsa
that differ from the Talmud.[125]

Gary Knoppers and Bernard Levinson suggest a distinction similar to
Halbertal's: "It is perfectly imaginable . . . that the Pentateuch could have
been regarded as sacred Scripture in the sense of embodying a set of much-
respected didactic tales and edifying laws. It is another thing for those laws
to be regarded constitutionally as legally binding norms for all members
of the community."[126] In fact it is the first of these two possibilities that

describes the role of the Pentateuch in rabbinic Judaism and even in the biblical period itself: it is didactic and edifying, not prescriptive. As Raymond Westbrook and Jean Bottéro have pointed out, ancient Near Eastern law collections such as Ḥammurapi's were not codes at all, in the sense of a source that judges and practitioners of law consulted to determine what the actual law must be. Rather, they were intellectual exercises to be studied for principles concerning how laws can or should work.[127] All the less should we expect to find such a code in the Pentateuch's assemblage of contradictory legal collections![128] Consequently, I disagree when Knoppers and Levinson claim, "Whatever its origins and original status, the Pentateuch did eventually become prescriptive law normative for all Jews and Samaritans."[129] The Pentateuch brings together motley selections from older legal traditions and fuses them with narratives to motivate loyalty to covenantal law in principle. But the Pentateuch ignores many topics crucial for any functioning system of civil, criminal, and ritual law. The Pentateuch does not function as a prescriptive code, simply because a self-contradictory and incomplete legal anthology cannot so function.[130] The realm of prescription always consisted of a wider tradition from which the Pentateuch emerged and to which the Pentateuch gives selected and somewhat random witness. The Pentateuch came to serve as a foundation for making decisions about prescriptive law in the Second Temple and rabbinic periods. But it did so only because legal authorities in those periods supplemented the Pentateuch with material from that wider tradition, even as they found ingenious ways of harmonizing the Pentateuch's contradictory laws. In so doing, they converted the Pentateuch from an educational tool to a text underlying (but still not constituting) the genuine legislation found in the Mishnah.

Let me return to our central question. Given that Written Torah and Oral Torah are both canonical, are they canonical in similar or different ways? In light of Halbertal's distinction between normative and formative canons, the Bible and Talmuds turn out to be similar. Both are canonical primarily in the formative sense: by studying them Jews enact and define their Jewish identity. The most crucial texts in the Oral Torah (the Mishnah and Gemaras) once were normative, but as a result of the principle of הלכתא כבתראי, they ceased being fully normative in the Middle Ages. Only the most recent texts within the Oral Torah are truly normative, and they, like the Mishnah and the Pentateuch before them, will become less authoritative as time goes by and newer halakhic works take their place.

Second, while Halbertal's categories suggest a basic similarity between each Torah's canonicity, the perspective suggested by Jewish ritual practice turns up a difference. The Pentateuch is chanted during synagogue services, in its entirety and following a set of very exact rules. Similarly, selections from the Nakh are also chanted following specific rules. Some rabbinic texts are recited as part of liturgy, but they are not chanted as part of a formal and legally regulated lectionary.[131] (Here we should recall that to be bound by halakhic ordinance is the highest honor in rabbinic thought; that which is less rule-bound is less important in the rabbis' eyes.) Further, the Pentateuch serves as a ritual object in a way that rabbinic texts do not.[132] The scroll of the Pentateuch is carried about in formal procession during the synagogue service. Pentateuchal texts are put on the doorpost of a Jew's house (the *mezuzah*) and are worn during prayer (the *tefillin*). The common Jewish practice of reciting psalms is also ritual in nature: what matters to most people who recite psalms on behalf of the sick or for some other purpose is not contemplating the text but pronouncing it.[133]

This ritual use of the Written Torah is not an innovation of rabbinic Judaism. Karel van der Toorn points out that already in the Bible, and especially in Deuteronomy, the written text of scripture serves as a sacred object.[134] Deuteronomy directs Israelites to install words of Torah on the doorposts of their homes and to wear words of the Torah on their arms and foreheads (Deuteronomy 6.6–9, 11.18–20).[135] According to Deuteronomy, a copy of Deuteronomy itself was to be kept in the ark, which ultimately rested in the Jerusalem Temple. Thus, during the biblical period Israelites used holy scrolls in nearly the same manner that Mesopotamians and Canaanites used cult statues (which were placed in temples and also in homes) and amulets. Written texts for Israelites and cult statues for other ancient Near Eastern peoples "were each an embodiment of the sacred, and both were perceived as incarnations of God," van der Toorn writes. "Like the icon, the Book is both a medium and an object; as a medium, it refers the reader to a reality beyond itself, whilst as an object, it is sacred in itself."[136] The use of sacred text as icon, already present in the seventh century BCE, deepened and intensified in rabbinic Judaism. It remains central to Jewish worship today. In short, Written Torah functioned and functions not only as a text to be taught or obeyed, but also as a sacred object. Oral Torah, in contrast, does not have so pronounced a ritual function in Jewish practice.[137]

A third lens through which to compare the status of the two Torahs involves a distinction articulated by John Barton. Barton points out that in first-century Judaism, "there was 'Scripture' but no canon."[138] As Barton uses the terms, *Scripture* refers to sacred texts, whether normative or formative or both. He uses the term *canon* in its narrow sense, to refer to a finite list of such texts. For rabbinic Judaism, both Written and Oral Torah are scripture in the sense Barton implies: they are holy, in some way authoritative, worthy of study and contemplation. But only the Written Torah is canon, or closed and delimited: it has twenty-four books, no more and no fewer. In contrast, new teachings and texts continue to be added to Oral Torah throughout Jewish history. From this perspective, a difference exists between the two Torahs: one is static, and one dynamic.

Fourth, the issue of authorship raises the clearest distinction between the status of each Torah in rabbinic Judaism. According to the dominant view found among the classical rabbis, the Written Torah, or at least the Pentateuch, was revealed in its entirety. The ideas and the precise wording found in the Pentateuch come directly from God. (Other views concerning Pentateuchal revelation are expressed or at least hinted at in rabbinic literature, but this stenographic theory was the most common.)[139] Similarly, the Nakh frequently quotes God, prefacing many passages with words like "Thus says Yhwh." As a result, Written Torah constitutes what Michael Wyschogrod has called "the primary document of revelation."[140] Oral Torah was also revealed, but because it was never closed, it continues to grow and evolve.[141] Consequently, it is a mix of human and divine elements, which cannot be definitively disentangled, and it does not repeatedly claim to quote God verbatim.[142] Both Torahs, then, are revealed, but the Oral Torah is a highly mediated form of revelation. In Oral Torah human beings have restated the divine teachings, supplemented them, extrapolated from them, and perhaps even forgotten or perverted some of them.[143] The distinction between direct revelation in Written Torah and mediated or derived revelation in Oral Torah provides the strongest affirmative answer to the question whether there is any difference between the status of the two Torahs.[144] Significantly, this distinction is the least applicable for the modern Jew who accepts the participatory theory of revelation even with regard to the Pentateuch itself.

Related to the issue of authorship is an issue of attitude. Classical rabbinic thinkers do not openly disagree with Written Torah, but they do display some openness to disagreeing with texts from Oral Torah, at least those with which they are roughly contemporaneous.[145] A medieval rabbi may argue against an older medieval text. An amora may disagree with a tanna, at least if he can find another tannaitic tradition to bolster his claim. But neither will argue that scripture itself is wrong. I doubt, however, that this difference of attitude has a major impact in the construction of Jewish law and thought. Disagreements with Written Torah are not absent in rabbinic Jewish literatures; they are merely cloaked as interpretations, interpretations that we today would characterize as strong misreadings. Practically, then, there seems to be relatively little difference between the attitudes toward Written Torah among premodern and modern Jewish thinkers. Granted, the ancients and medievals maintained that such a difference existed, since they did not see themselves as practicing misreading at all. In many cases they genuinely believed that their interpretations delved deeper in the text rather than erasing it.[146] But modern thinkers are affected (or, some would have it, infected) by historical and hermeneutic consciousness, and consequently we cannot with intellectual honesty maintain the distinction between disagreement and strong misreading. From our vantage point, the belief in different types of authorship between Written and Oral Torah produces a difference of style but not of substance in the way that classical Jewish thinkers utilized each corpus.

I have addressed the question of the unity of canon in Jewish tradition by asking how the canonicity of Oral Torah differs from that of Written Torah.[147] The differences primarily involve attitude: the rabbis regard one Torah as the product of mediated revelation, and the other as the product of direct revelation. Consequently, they feel free to disagree with the one openly, and they are constrained to mask their disagreements with the other as interpretations. (Lest we accuse them of mendacity, we should note that in the vast majority of cases they were genuinely unaware of the extent to which they disagreed with the biblical texts; they probably could not imagine that the biblical text meant what we read it to say.) Further, because Written Torah is a product of direct revelation, every handwritten Torah scroll constitutes what Mircea Eliade calls a hierophany, a manifestation of the sacred (something that is rooted in a wholly different realm) in an object that is an integral part of this mundane world.[148] It therefore becomes a sacred object with ritual uses. Copies of rabbinic texts are not treated as hierophanies in quite the same way, and the Oral Torah has a much more limited ritual function. In short, Written Torah enjoys a greater degree of prestige. Yet in terms of the ongoing formulation of Jewish thought, there is little difference between them. In the realm of aggadah both spur new ideas and provide prooftexts for them. In the realm of practice, Written Torah might be compared to a constitutional monarch: hers are the honor and the ceremony. But we all know that the Oral Torah, as the prime minister, holds the power.

The Nature of Oral Torah

Up until this point in the chapter, I have defended the reclassification of Written Torah as a type of Oral Torah. It now behooves me to discuss some characteristics of Oral Torah, for only by understanding the nature of Oral Torah can we understand what it means to say that the Bible is part of it. In discussing these characteristics, I begin to speak of Oral and Written Torah not only as collections of texts but as categories of thought. What concerns us now is the very idea of Oral Torah in rabbinic Judaism: what does it mean to assert that a body of teaching is primarily oral, even if to a significant degree it is also written down?

Walter Ong has described a core aspect of oral culture that sheds light on the rabbis' insistence that revelation is preserved in an oral teaching: "Sounded words are not things, but events. . . . The oral word is essentially a call, a cry . . . from someone to someone, an interpersonal transaction."[149] Ong's characterization of the sounded word helps us to understand Oral Torah as a theological idea in three ways. First, Oral Torah is not just a body of texts (a thing, as Ong puts it). It is a process as much as a vessel containing content. Second, the Oral Torah involves an interpersonal transaction.[150] Thus, it requires either teacher and student or study partners. Third, to assert that a teaching is part of Oral Torah is to assert that this teaching is revealed in the present. Oral Torah happens now; it does not merely record something from a time gone by.[151] In this section of this chapter I discuss the first two implications of Ong's characterization of orality. The third implication will bring us back to the depiction of revelation in biblical and midrashic texts as well as in Rosenzweig and Heschel; that implication will form the subject of the next chapter.

Tradition is a process and not only a body of texts. Orality is dynamic and fluid in a way that writing is not, because with each new statement an oral text can change. Of course in the ancient world each new copy of a written text could be changed as well; consequently, we have seen, even the written texts of antiquity functioned as what Ong would call an oral text.

The distinction we are examining involves not a polarity but a continuum from dynamic to static, and in the biblical period written tradition was close to the former side. Van der Toorn captures the changes in the nature of religious authority as a culture moves from oral to written models of textuality:

> In the civilizations of the ancient Near East, knowledge from revelation is in origin oral lore; predictions, oracles, and instructions are found in the mouth of religious specialists: diviners answer their clients' queries, prophets deliver their oracles as the divine inspiration moves them. . . . In its oral manifestation, revelation is lodged and anchored in its human transmitters. Matters change to the extent that we may speak of a paradigm shift when written texts supplant the oral tradition as the main channel of information. When the notion of revelation is transferred from the spoken word to the written text . . . , revelation denotes a product rather than an interaction. Since the written text has an objective existence outside its producers and consumers, it is a source of authority by itself. Where, before, religious specialists derived their legitimacy from the revelation they possessed in person, they now have to refer to the sum of knowledge laid down in a body of texts. . . . The art of interpretation supplant[s] the gift of intuition. . . . The oral lore does not die, but its authority is subordinate to that of the written texts. . . . [As] revelation became an object rather than an interaction, . . . the mediator became a mere channel; not an author and composer, but a scribe and transcriber.[152]

Van der Toorn provides an excellent description of written and oral loci of authority as ideal types. The paradigm shift he describes, however, never fully happened in biblical Israel or in rabbinic Judaism, for written texts did not supplant oral tradition. In the biblical period itself, new prophetic revelations were still available. Further, records of older revelations may have remained somewhat malleable in the hands of the scribes or disciples who wrote each new copy of those records. As a result, prophets, scribes, and priests in the biblical period functioned as both channels and authors. At some point in the Second Temple period prophecy ceased in Israel, and the text of the Bible became less flexible.[153] Nevertheless, traditions continued to evolve outside the biblical canon among Pharisees and tanna'im (who enthusiastically acknowledged the existence of these traditions[154]) and among non-Pharisaic groups (whose denial in this matter hardly shows that their own version of tradition did not exist[155]). Further, written scripture in postbiblical Judaism became available only through practices of recitation, interpretation, and contextualization. As a result, revelation remained a matter of interaction as much as a product, so that van der Toorn's portrayal of the oral authority fits a great deal of postbiblical Judaism.

Another way of describing the dynamism of oral tradition focuses on the difference between content and process. Michael Satlow uses the term *Oral Torah* to refer to the conceptual category that allows Jews to derive Jewish meaning from written texts; thus, *Oral Torah* refers not simply to particular texts but to orally transmitted reading practices peculiar to Jewish cultures through the ages.[156] Similarly, Yaakov Elman understands Oral Torah as a method of transmission, not just the content transmitted.[157] Steven Kepnes describes Oral Torah in all periods well when he writes that from the perspective of post-liberal theology,

> revelation would not be the ineffable religious experience of the noumenal or mystical realm by the individual. Rather, it would be the reception of the basic framework, the terminology, the vocabulary units and the principles and rules of their usage for the system within which the Jew acts and thinks. Revelation would be the reception and basic understanding of the language game, the context within which Jews live. . . . The written Torah provides the basic vocabulary units and the oral Torah the hermeneutical rules and *halakhot* (laws) through which the written Torah is understood and enacted in life.[158]

Oral Torah, then, is the body of rules, attitudes, and habits of thought through which Jews receive, understand, and pass on revelation. This aspect of tradition was captured especially well by the Catholic theologian Yves Congar, who taught that "in the first place tradition is something unwritten, the living transmission of a doctrine, not only by words, but also by attitudes and modes of action."[159]

Jews absorb these attitudes and habits through direct contact with teachers, not only through a solitary grappling with texts.[160] Thus, tradition (and hence scripture understood as a part of tradition) is inherently dialogical.[161] The rabbis emphasized that one could not know Torah simply by reading it on one's own; one learns Torah only by hearing it discussed by a master and by joining the discussion,[162] by finding a teacher and acquiring a study partner. As van der Toorn pointed out, in an oral setting religious instruction moves from person to person.[163] A purely Written Torah, if there were such a thing, would move directly from text to person. In valorizing the category of Oral Torah, and in sometimes folding Written

Torah into that category, the sages emphasize the importance of the human teacher. One can learn about an artifact from a book, by oneself. One receives scripture from a teacher, in a social setting.[164] "One acquires Torah only in community," b. Berakhot 63b tells us (cf. Seder Devei Eliyahu Zuṭa 17:4). For this reason, the sages teach that any time a Jewish community, no matter how small, comes together, no matter how briefly, without speaking words of Torah, a tragedy has occurred (see the comments of Ḥananiah and Shimon in m. Avot 3:3–4). Writing is a thing, whereas an oral text remains anchored in a community of human beings.[165]

In noting the personal, socially embedded nature of orality, I do not, of course, deny that written texts play a crucial role in Jewish cultures starting already in the biblical period. One of the most important points that emerges from the study of inner-biblical exegesis is that a highly textual model of authority already functioned in the First Temple period. But that same field of study shows that biblical sages who interpreted and revised older biblical texts had a dynamic relationship to scripture. Further, I do not deny that there are periods in Jewish history during which the role of a living human example recedes and the place of textual authority looms larger. In a series of essays Haym Soloveitchik has brilliantly demonstrated that among late-twentieth-century ḥaredim, or ultra-Orthodox Jews, imitating the human example of parents and teachers plays a smaller role. For contemporary ḥaredim, religious authority has come to reside more heavily in texts.[166] The transformation Soloveitchik describes exemplifies the paradigm shift that van der Toorn describes in the passage quoted earlier, in which written texts supplant oral tradition as the main conduit for information and authority, gaining an objective existence outside the sages who produce it.[167] The process Soloveitchik describes amounts to the conversion of Oral Torah (to wit, halakhic codes such as the *Shulḥan Arukh* and the *Mishnah Berurah*) into a written torah. This aspect of ultra-Orthodoxy represents a move away from traditional Jewish models of authority, though it also represents a tendency always available in Judaism and sometimes taken up—as demonstrated by the examples of the Sadducees in the late Second Temple period, the Qaraites in the Middle Ages, and to some degree even the school of Rabbi Yishmael in the mishnaic era.[168]

Several modern thinkers emphasize these aspects of orality in Judaism in general and in Jewish scripture in particular. I think especially of the twentieth-century philosophers Rosenzweig and his close associate Martin Buber, the nineteenth-century thinker Samson Raphael Hirsch, and the late-eighteenth-century philosopher Moses Mendelssohn. It is no coincidence that all these thinkers who focus attention on the orality of Jewish scripture were German Jews. In Germany, Jewish intellectuals absorbed Protestantism's emphasis on scripture along with its relative devaluing of tradition, or they had to react to it. Rosenzweig, Buber, Hirsch, and Mendelssohn chose the latter route. As Michah Gottlieb explains:

> Mendelssohn notes that rabbinic teaching was originally oral and that one function of its orality was to allow the teacher to "explain, enlarge, limit and define more precisely what for wise intentions and with wise moderation was left undetermined in the written law." Because one would learn how to practice the law not just by having teachers explain it but also by observing them, the practice of the law had a social, living dimension that helped prevent it from turning into a dead, rote practice. And since the student needed to seek instruction from a teacher . . . , he was naturally led ". . . to seek the instruction which his master considered him capable of absorbing and prepared to receive . . ." In a striking reversal of the Protestant critique of Judaism, he calls the ritual law a "living script." So for Mendelssohn, the oral nature of rabbinic teaching allows the Rabbis to infuse the practice of the law with spirit and vitality, thereby helping prevent it from turning into dead letter. . . . Hirsch follows Mendelssohn's reversal of the Christian charge of Jewish attachment to the dead letter by emphasizing the oral nature of the Talmud, which preserves the living spirit of biblical teaching.[169]

For Mendelssohn and Hirsch, Torah involves first of all a living teacher; Jews absorb written texts in an oral environment. Both spoke primarily of the Talmud, but their point applies equally well to biblical texts as studied in classical Jewish settings. Such study has always involved reading or chanting scripture aloud, translating or paraphrasing it, discussing it with a master, and above all attending to the ongoing conversation that takes place among the classical commentators with whom the Bible is read in a Jewish school.

Buber and Rosenzweig apply this emphasis on dialogue to the Bible more explicitly. In their translation of and writings about the Bible, Buber and Rosenzweig attempt to get back to the orality of scripture. This is the case in a practical sense: they wanted to compose a translation that would read well out loud. It is also the case in a philosophical sense: they wanted scripture to involve interaction between text and reader and thus to foster interaction between God and the individual.[170] Yehoyada Amir explains that for Rosenzweig and Buber, to read the Bible as scripture means to read in a process of exchange:

> The Bible reveals itself as a dialogical "I" and grants a person the possibility of approaching it again and again and saying, "Here I am." The responsiveness of the reader, who must be ready to be answered, allows for the dialogue; only from the personal viewpoint from which this responsiveness emerges can the ancient human text be transformed into the word of God that speaks directly to a person and commands him.[171]

This dialogical aspect of the Bible rests in its oral character. Buber and Rosenzweig believed, as Jonathan Cohen points out, that

> the living voice of God, carried through the events of meeting between God and Israel, and the enthusiasm of the human response to that voice have been preserved in a seemingly "frozen," written medium. The biblical narrative has been formed in such a way that, paradoxically, its written forms call forth its original "spokenness."[172]

Rosenzweig emphasized that this dialogical reading had to take place in a community. He meant this in two senses. One can hear the revelatory voice of scripture when one reads it aided by the community of readers Oral Torah provides: the manifold rabbinic commentators who cite, challenge, and disagree with one another. If one fails to read Written Torah through this lens, one allows it to speak only as artifact and not as scripture. (Rosenzweig reports that as a youth he read the Bible "without the help of tradition, hence without revelation.")[173] But he also valued community in a less abstract sense: he argued that Jews should study scripture with other contemporary Jews seeking to hear revelation, not by oneself, and not only in academic settings. It was precisely for this reason that, forgoing an academic career, Rosenzweig founded the Freies Jüdisches Lehrhaus in Frankfurt, which he continued to direct much longer than one would have thought possible during his struggle with amyotrophic lateral sclerosis.[174]

By locating revelation first and foremost in Oral Torah, Jewish thinkers from biblical times to modernity assert the organic, dynamic nature of the teaching that emerges from revelation. Modern biblical scholarship (especially in its analysis of the composition, redaction, and transmission of biblical texts and in the study of inner-biblical exegesis) recovers the Bible's multivocality and thus helps us to see the way that scripture behaves like Oral Torah.[175] Further, by emphasizing the primacy of Oral Torah, Jewish thinkers assert all Torah's intimate connection with the relationship between master and disciple, and with learning as something that occurs in community. Because the event that is Oral Torah requires the presence of a teacher or study partner, the revelation of Oral Torah cannot be confined to a particular instant in the past. The understanding of Torah that we have been developing, therefore, requires us to address the question of whether the stream of Jewish thought that concerns us regards the disclosure of God's will as continuing beyond the moment at Sinai and perhaps even into the present day. We turn to this question in the next chapter, but before doing so, one final aspect of the classification of scripture as a type of tradition requires attention: do the main proponents of the participatory theology in modern Jewish thought in fact acknowledge this implication of their own work?

Modern Thinkers' Attitudes toward Eliminating the Boundary between the Oral and Written Torahs

Both biblical criticism and the work of theologians like Rosenzweig and Heschel prompt the realization that for modern Judaism, there is no such thing as Written Torah; there is only Oral Torah, from which the Bible itself emerges and to which it belongs. I have argued that this conclusion is far less radical than it seems, because some traditional Jewish texts break down the boundary between the two Torahs, while others assert the temporal and conceptual priority of the Oral Torah. A final question needs to be asked before we draw this part of our investigation to a close: did Rosenzweig and Heschel themselves acknowledge this implication of their work? Given their love of the Bible and their intensive work to defend the Bible against reductionist, simplistic, or exegetically flat-footed treatments by biblical critics, one can imagine that they would resist the demotion of scripture that my thesis implies. It is true that neither Rosenzweig nor Heschel addressed the issue as directly as I do in this chapter. At no point, to my knowledge, do they directly say, "There is no more Written Torah." Nonetheless, in asides at various points in their work they move in this direction.

Already in the *Star* Rosenzweig blurs the line between custom and law.[176] Elsewhere he calls for custom to be accorded the same status as law: "The custom and the original intention of the law must have the same rank of inviolability as the law itself."[177] Rosenzweig addresses the issue of Oral

Torah more specifically in a letter to Jacob Rosenheim, a leader of German Orthodoxy. There Rosenzweig speaks of Oral Torah as the completion of or complement to the unity of the written text as it has been read in Jewish tradition. Thus, he implicitly acknowledges that the Written Torah on its own may lack unity, but when learned through Oral Torah it achieves it; and it is that Written Torah—the Written Torah as it has been learned in Judaism, which is to say the Oral Torah's version of the Written Torah— that is Rosenzweig's scripture.[178] In the letter to Rosenheim he does not subsume the Written Torah under the Oral Torah; he avers that both are wonderful, not that they must be taken as a unity to be seen as wonderful.[179] But he does suggest that what matters most is the Written Torah as learned through the Oral Torah, so that the Oral Torah receives priority. Similarly, Rosenzweig views the obligations incumbent on Jews as involving the whole rabbinic system; he does not regard laws from the Pentateuch as having greater weight than laws from the Talmud, or, for that matter, later customs.[180]

Heschel comes closer to articulating the thesis I have suggested here, though he does not focus attention on it by according it a particular chapter of its own. He points out in passing that parts of Oral Torah are older than parts of Written Torah, noting further that the covenant was concluded on the basis of both.[181] For Heschel the midrashic tradition is of prime importance, since it embodies the continually unfolding understanding of the Bible which takes the place of (or perhaps is a late manifestation of) prophecy in Israel.[182] Similarly, he stresses that without the sages there is no Torah, and that the sages responsible for the Oral Torah complete and perfect the Written Torah.[183] He acknowledges that the Bible itself "contains not only words of the prophets, but also words that came from non-prophetic lips. . . . There is in the Bible . . . not only God's disclosure but man's insight."[184] Heschel does not pause to note this, but a text that is a mixture of divine and human elements is by definition Oral Torah rather than pure Written Torah. Heschel refrains from specifying whether he includes the Pentateuch within this judgment, but passages elsewhere that speak of the Pentateuch and even the Decalogue as being formulated by an individual prophet suggests that he might do so.[185] Heschel comes closer to acknowledging that all Written Torah is Oral Torah in his famous assertion, "As a report about revelation the Bible itself is *a midrash*."[186] Midrash, after all, is a form of Oral Torah. But even here Heschel does not write that the Bible has the same status as rabbinic literature. One can perceive such an implication in that assertion, especially when it is read alongside others I cite in this paragraph, but it is not necessary to do so.

Other modern sages have acknowledged the collapse of Written Torah into Oral Torah more explicitly. Gershom Scholem discusses the consequences attendant on the understanding of revelation among some Jewish mystics in his essay "Revelation and Tradition as Religious Categories in Judaism." One consequence of this understanding, he writes,

> is so radical that it was taught only in veiled, symbolic terminology. It amounted to the assertion that there was no such thing as a Written Torah in the sense of an immediate revelation of the divine word. For such a revelation is contained in the Wisdom of God, where it forms an "Ur-Torah" in which the "word" rests as yet completely undeveloped in a mode of being in which no differentiation of the individual elements into sounds and letters takes place. The sphere in which this "Ur-Torah" (*torah kelulah*) comes to articulate itself into the so-called Written Torah, where signs (the forms of the consonants) or sounds or expressions exist—that sphere is already interpretation. . . . [Here Scholem cites the midrash on the preexisting Torah as black fire on white fire.[187] For kabbalists, the white fire is the Written Torah in which the letters are not yet formed; black fire is like the Oral Torah that gives the Written Torah form.] This would imply that what we on earth call the Written Torah has already gone through the medium of the Oral Torah and has taken on a perceptible form in that process. . . . We can perceive revelation only as unfolding oral tradition.[188]

Scholem is even more explicit in his essay "The Meaning of the Torah in Jewish Mysticism," where he discusses a passage from Naḥmanides's introduction to his commentary on Genesis:

> The mystical symbolism of this profoundly meaningful passage conceals the view that, strictly speaking, there is no written Torah here on earth. A far-reaching idea! What we call the written Torah has itself passed through the medium of the oral Torah, it is no longer a form concealed in white light; rather, it has emerged from the black light, which determines and limits and so denotes the attribute of divine severity and judgment. Everything that we perceived in the fixed forms of the Torah, written in ink on parchment, consists, in the last analysis, of interpretations or definitions of what is hidden. *There is only an oral Torah*: that is the esoteric meaning of these words, and the written Torah is a purely mystical concept. It is embodied in a sphere that is accessible to prophet alone. It was, to be sure, revealed to Moses, but what he gave to the world as the written Torah has acquired its present form by passing through the medium of the oral Torah.[189]

To be sure, kabbalists who express this idea did not mean by it everything that a biblical critic or a modern theologian might mean. For the kabbalist, all the Torahs, heavenly, written, and oral, were realms of perfection and divinity. For the modern version of the participatory theology I lay out (as we shall see in chapter 6), the Bible lacks perfection, precisely because it is a mixture of human and divine elements. But Scholem's distillation of kabbalistic attitudes suffices to underscore my main thesis in this chapter: that removing the distinction between the two Torahs has a rich pedigree in Jewish thought.

The similarity between Scholem's views and those of Heschel is even clearer in a précis of comments Scholem made at a meeting of intellectuals in Jerusalem organized by Judah Magnes (the first president of the Hebrew University) on July 13, 1939. According to brief summaries taken by an anonymous note taker,[190] Scholem began the evening's discussion by making the following points:

> Everything in the world, even a person, can be "Torah," but there never is Torah without supernal authority. The Torah is the Creator's dialogue with man, prayer is man's dialogue with the Creator. There is no Written Torah without the Oral Torah. Were we to desire to restrict the Torah to the Torah transmitted in writing, we would not be able to read even the Pentateuch, only the ten commandments. It follows that even the Torah is already Oral Torah. The Torah is understandable only as Oral Torah, only through its relativization. In itself it is the perfect Torah without a blemish, and only through its mediation, the Oral Torah, is it rendered intelligible.[191]

One would be tempted to cite Heschel's influence on Scholem, so Heschelian is this statement, were it not for the fact that Heschel had yet to begin publishing his own works of theology at this date. Alternatively, one might speculate that Heschel was present that evening and that he resolved to dedicate the rest of his life to fleshing out Scholem's remarks. In fact that same evening Heschel arrived in London, having escaped Warsaw a few weeks earlier. (He would first visit Jerusalem years later.) Nor had the men met in Europe; Heschel arrived in Berlin to study for his doctorate in 1927, four years after Scholem's departure for Jerusalem.[192] The similarity between their ideas on the meaning of Torah for modern Judaism points not to one's influence on the other but to the deep roots this line of thinking has in the rabbinic and kabbalistic traditions that, in their different ways, Scholem and Heschel spent their lives elucidating.[193]

The other modern sage who articulates a similar view is Solomon Schechter. Discussing the difficulty that the historical and philological analyses of biblical criticism had already caused for Jewish views of revelation by the end of the nineteenth century, Schechter wrote:

> The best way to meet this difficulty was found to be to shift the centre of gravity in Judaism and to place it in the secondary [or midrashic] meaning [of biblical texts], thus making religion independent of philology and all its dangerous consequences. . . . When Revelation or the Written Word is reduced to the level of history, there is no difficulty in elevating history in its aspect of Tradition to the rank of Scripture, for both have then the same human or divine origin (according to the student's predilection for the one or the other adjective), and emanate from the same authority. Tradition becomes thus the means whereby the modern divine seeks to compensate himself for the loss of the Bible, and the theological balance is to the satisfaction of all parties happily readjusted.[194]

It is precisely this balance that I have attempted to find in collapsing scripture into the larger category of tradition. Once we realize that the Bible is a part of Oral Torah, the sting of biblical criticism that I discussed in the first chapter of this book loses all its force. We recognize that the Bible is not entirely divine in origin, that its verbal formulation may be entirely human. But for Jews (and, I imagine, also for Catholic and Orthodox Christians[195]), this realization need not shake any foundations. Judaism has long recognized a realm of religious authority that is a mix of human and divine elements, and that realm is the main source of Jewish religious practice and belief. The Talmuds and related literature from the Oral Torah have played this role for centuries, and these texts' mixed parentage has not caused dismay. I see no reason that recognizing the same sort of mixed parentage for the Bible should present a problem for committed Jewish communities.

Conclusion

Schechter spoke of "the richness of the resources" that "an old historical religion like Judaism . . . has to fall back upon in cases of emergency."[196] The category of Oral Torah—a literature at once sacred and human, instructive and flawed, providing guidance to its audience and open to being reshaped by those who accept its guidance—is precisely such a resource.[197] By acknowledging that the Bible belongs to that category, we can admit its imperfections even as we embrace it as an authoritative guide for our practice, a crucial anthology for our study, and an essential source for our identity. Even for the modern Jew committed to the participatory theory of revelation, the Bible remains all these things, in the profound and dynamic ways that an evolving Oral Torah has always been for observant Jews.

People brought up on the stenographic theory of revelation typically suffer a wrenching loss when they become convinced that the Pentateuch includes, or consists entirely of, human words. The divine words that anchor their life, their beliefs, and their practices turn out to be human formulations, and the disappearance of the firm foundation a divine text provided can be devastating. But the participatory theology in fact posits a very similar relationship between revelation on the one hand and Israel's beliefs and practices on the other. Even for adherents of the stenographic theory, the actual laws one observes as a religious Jew are human formulations; they were debated in the Talmuds and are laid out in the medieval and modern law codes. The adherent of the stenographic theory might object: "Yes, the law as we observe it involves human formulations—but these human formulations are based on and derived from a heavenly text; they are rooted in God's own words." To this I respond: the participatory theory entails essentially the same structure of thought, and it merely pushes the heavenly origin back by a single step. Instead of an earthly talmudic law based on a heavenly Pentateuch, the participatory theory yields an earthly talmudic law based on an earthly Pentateuch that is in turn based on a heavenly, albeit nonverbal command. In both theories, Jewish law as we practice it ultimately but imperfectly reflects a divine revelation. The loss involved in recognizing the earthly nature of the Pentateuch is less momentous than one initially assumes. But the gains that follow from frankly acknowledging the human and thus at times flawed nature of the Pentateuch are considerable. I discuss the theoretical and practical implications of the participatory theory, in the realms of biblical theology and halakhic development, in the sixth chapter and in the conclusion of this book. Before doing so, however, I turn in the following chapter to one aspect of the realization that all Torah is Oral Torah: if Torah continues to grow, did the revelation at Sinai ever cease?

5 Event, Process, and Eternity

In the previous chapter, we saw that Oral Torah plays roles that scripture typically plays in many religions: it provides both norms of behavior and a common vocabulary that binds the community together. Thus, for Judaism, tradition is in effect a type of scripture.[1] But unlike the Bible, the Oral Torah never develops a canon in the sense of a closed list of texts. (To make this point differently, we might borrow Ismar Schorsch's phrasing to assert that Oral Torah is a canon without closure.)[2] Oral Torah never ceases to evolve. Further, we saw that Oral Torah is not only a body of texts and teachings but also an event that requires the presence of a living teacher or study partner. Consequently, Oral Torah cannot be confined to a particular instant in the past; it occurs in the present. These aspects of Oral Torah require us to ask how its development, transmission, and ongoing renewal relate to revelation. Does revelation take place in Jewish tradition after Sinai, or are all post-Sinaitic laws and teachings based on interpretations of what God finished communicating at Sinai? Is there such a thing as postbiblical inspiration or guidance that manifests itself in works of tradition?

A postbiblical tradition's claim to reliability, insight, and authority can rest on any of three pillars: (1) the tradition's preservation of teachings not recorded in scripture but nonetheless handed on over time; (2) the intellectual achievements of scholars whose interpretations of scripture the tradition preserves; and (3) an unceasing divine presence that inspires and informs the work of human sages who pass on, interpret, and supplement older texts. Jewish thinkers regard the first two of these pillars positively, but they tend to have a mixed attitude toward the third—that is, to the possibility that postbiblical tradition results from exegesis that is not only intellectual in original but divinely inspired.[3] Some Jewish authorities reject that possibility outright, and even those who see new ideas as resulting from a phenomenon akin to revelation tend to express this opinion with great caution. Several books address the approaches of classical and medieval rabbinic thinkers to the possibility that tradition might be guided by some form of inspiration; these include Heschel's *Torah min Hashamayim*, Yochanan Silman's *Qol Gadol Velo Yasaf: Torat Yisrael bein Sheleimut Lehishtalmut*, and Tamar Ross's *Expanding the Palace of Torah: Orthodoxy and Feminism*.[4] It is not necessary for me to review the findings of these volumes, all of which are crucial reading for anyone interested in the topic of this book. Instead, in this chapter I attend to biblical texts that bear on the question of ongoing revelation, to writings by Rosenzweig and Heschel that address this question, and to the relationship between the treatments of these issues in the biblical and the modern texts.

Before I move to this material, however, it is useful to note that in his review of classical and medieval rabbinic literature, Silman finds three attitudes toward the possibility of ongoing divine influence on Jewish sages through the ages. One attitude he terms the "Perfection (שלמות) Position";[5] it regards the Torah in our hands as entirely complete (I use the term *Torah* in the broadest sense, to include both the Written and the Oral). Sages who hold this position reject in principle the possibility of halakhic change, though they admit that because of human forgetfulness and fallibility some changes have, tragically, crept into the Oral Torah. In what Silman terms the "Being-Ever-Perfected (השתלמות) Position," human beings make original and positive contributions to Torah, which becomes more and more perfect over the ages. To the extent that human forgetfulness has caused some changes in the tradition, one can even speak positively of that forgetfulness, since that forgetfulness precipitates a desire for restoration, and that desire spurs human creativity that expands the Oral Torah.[6] A variation of this second position is the "Discovery (גילוי) Position," in which Torah as it exists in heaven is perfect, but the limited apprehension human beings have of the heavenly Torah is being continually perfected. When we apply Silman's categories to Rosenzweig and Heschel, it is clear that these thinkers fit the second or third positions. Rosenzweig's thought is especially close to the השתלמות or "being-ever-perfected" position, whereas Heschel's *Torah min Hashamayim* lays out the idea of a perfect heavenly Torah to which human beings strive to gain ever greater access.[7]

Punctual and Eternal Revelation
in the Pentateuchal Sources

In chapter 2, we saw that the Pentateuchal sources address the question of whether the revelation of the law took place at a particular moment or over time.[8] D and E regard lawgiving as a onetime event involving one super-prophet, Moses. For P, however, lawgiving was durative. It began before the Israelites arrived at Sinai, for they received laws concerning the Passover while still in Egypt (Exodus 12). In fact, the first time God conveyed a law the Israelites were to obey was much earlier, when Abraham received the command to circumcise himself and the males in his household (Genesis 16.10–11). According to P, Moses (and sometimes Aaron) received laws throughout the seven weeks during which the Tent of Meeting was at the foot of Mount Sinai, but additional laws were revealed to Moses, Aaron, and Aaron's son Eleazar during the following forty years. (This debate among Pentateuchal sources reemerges in b. Ḥagigah 6a–b as a debate between Rabbi Akiva, whose position recalls that of E and D, and Rabbi Yishmael, whose position essentially restates that of P.) The difference between these understandings of revelation is consequential. A punctual revelation allows for no improvement over time; because the canon of law was given in its entirety on a single occasion, the human role from that moment on is simply to preserve and pass on, and perhaps also to recover what was not correctly preserved and passed on. E and D in this regard prefigure Silman's "perfection" position. P is a predecessor for the "ever-perfecting" or "discovery" positions. Indeed, P may even allow for the possibility that lawgiving can continue into future generations, because it happens over time and it involves several human mediators.

D's attitude, however, is more complex than it initially seems. On the one hand, crucial verses in D emphasize the nondurative nature of the lawgiving. These include the verse that resumes the narrative immediately after the text of the Decalogue:

> It was these words that Yhwh spoke to your whole congregation on the mountain from within the fire, the cloud, and the fog—a great voice, which did not continue (קול גדול ולא יסף). (Deuteronomy 5.22)

According to this verse, what started at Ḥoreb finished at Ḥoreb. A similar message emerges from passages in which D warns its audience not to alter the text containing the laws:

Do not add (לֹא תֹסִפוּ) to the matter that I am commanding you, and do not take anything away from it, so that you keep the commandments of Yhwh your God that I am commanding you. (Deuteronomy 4.2)

As to the matter that I am commanding you—you should carry it out carefully; do not add (לֹא תֹסֵף) to it, and take nothing away from it. (Deuteronomy 13.1)

The word that God commands is fixed; once Moses has vouchsafed it to the Israelites, it cannot be changed. That all three passages employ some form of the verb יסף to articulate this theme reinforces our sense of its consistency within D. Lawgiving was an event, not a process. This approach fits D's theology of revelation, which denies a human element in the law and emphasizes its divinity. All these verses reflects what we might, anachronistically but accurately, refer to as D's anti-Rosenzweigian, anti-Heschellian aims.

But on closer inspection D evinces some ambivalence that leads us to wonder where its allegiance on this question really lies, because several verses hint at the opposite view. These include a verse that immediately precedes the text of the Decalogue and thus comes shortly before the verse in which D claims that God's voice does not continue:

²Yhwh our God formed a covenant with us at Ḥoreb. ³It was not with our parents that Yhwh formed this covenant, but with us, all of us, we who are here today, we who are alive! (Deuteronomy 5.2–3)

These verses contradict historical facts known both to the Israelites Moses addresses within the text and to the audiences D addresses through the text.[9] Moses delivers this speech at the very end of the Israelites' forty-year sojourn in the wilderness. By that time, Deuteronomy 1.33–39 tells us, all of the adults who had witnessed the lawgiving at Ḥoreb were dead (with the exception of Moses himself, his successor Joshua, and one other loyal member of that generation, Caleb).[10] Thus, God had formed the covenant with the audience's parents and not, on a literal level, "with all of us, we who are here today, we who are alive." (The anxious repetition of that phrase evinces the narrator's awareness that what is being asserted counters, on the most basic level, what the audience knows.)[11] D's Moses goes beyond history in 5.2–3, claiming that those listening to him saw what their parents saw a generation earlier. Moses makes similar claims throughout Deuteronomy: see 1.30, 4.34, 6.22, 9.17, 11.2–9, 29.1, and 29.13–14. In all these passages, the plural "you" whose experiences Moses recalls is not simply the audience in front of him on the plains of Moab; it includes the whole nation, future Israelites included.[12] Thus, August Dillmann characterizes D's practice of regarding the nation addressed throughout the book as constituting "an organic whole with a shared identity . . . a whole that became obligated at Horeb."[13] Similarly, Moshe Weinfeld points to "the blurring of generations concerning the covenantal commitment"; the result of this blurring is that "Israel throughout its generations is . . . presented in Deuteronomy as one body, a corporate personality."[14] In light of this trope, D's Moses intimates in 5.2–3 that while the covenant making happened at Horeb forty years earlier, at a deeper level it did not occur *only* forty years earlier. It also happens in the next generation—and, by implication, in every generation thereafter, for the point of the verses is that the covenant is ours and not our parents'. These verses encourage the reader to understand that God's voice does continue. Thus, Hermann Cohen points out that in 5.2–3,

> the whole historical thread is rejected with the strongest emphasis, and, yet, much less still is it abolished; rather, it is immediately attached to the men of the present. Thereby the spirituality of revelation is detached from the single event in primeval times, and in all clearness established in the living renewal of the national continuity.[15]

Another passage moving in the same direction appears toward the end of the book, when Moses addresses the assembled people shortly before his death and their entry into Canaan:

> [9]You—all of you—are standing here today in the presence of Yhwh your God: the leaders of your tribes, your elders, your officials, every Israelite man, [10]your children, your wives, and the stranger who is in the camp, from the one who cuts down trees to the one who draws water from the well, [11]so that you can enter into the covenant with Yhwh your God and into its sanctions, which Yhwh your God is making with you today, [12]so that He will raise you up today to be His people, and He will be your God, as He promised you, and as He swore to your ancestors, Abraham, Isaac, and Jacob. [13]It is not only with you that I am making this covenant, with its sanctions, [14]but with everyone who is here with us, standing in the presence of Yhwh our God today, and with everyone who is not here with us today. (Deuteronomy 29.9–14)

Here D makes explicit the implication about future generations in Deuteronomy 5.2–3. The covenant is made with every generation: those listening to Moses in Moab; the preceding generation, who stood at Ḥoreb forty years earlier; and all the generations thereafter.[16] ("You—all of you" in 29.9 is unusually emphatic,[17] and this emphasis points to the broadest possible sense of the words.) Classical rabbinic texts take up this notion from our passage. Several midrashim on 29.13–14 specify that the souls of all Israel were present at the lawgiving at Sinai, including those whose bodies had not yet been created (see R. Shmuel bar Naḥmani in Tanḥuma Niṣṣavim §4; R. Isaac in Shemot Rabbah 28:6).[18] The same point is emphasized by medieval commentators (for example, Rashi, ibn Ezra, and Bekhor Shor to 4.9). Two talmudic passages (b. Shevu'ot 39a; b. Shabbat 146a) add that the future generations of Jews present at Sinai include people who, centuries or millennia later, would convert to Judaism. This tradition invites comparison to the widespread rabbinic teaching that God revealed to Moses what students would ask and what scribes would innovate in later generations (y. Pe'ah 4a [2:6]; Wayiqra Rabbah 22:1; Qohelet Rabbah 1:29 and 5:6). The notion that all future Jews were present at the revelation is the other side of the same coin: just as Moses at Sinai heard into Torah's future, so too did Jews yet to be born arrive there to hear God's voice.

Deuteronomy 29 emphasizes in verses 11 and 12 that the covenant is made "today"—which means not only that it was made a generation earlier at Ḥoreb but also that it continues to be made into the narrator's present, and perhaps into the reader's, as well.[19] Insofar as the goal of the whole Book of Deuteronomy is to provide a law for the Israelites to observe once they move into the Land of Canaan, the covenant will continue to be renewed today, on the next "today," and in the "today" of every generation to come. In fact *today* (היום) is an important guiding word throughout Deuteronomy. It appears three times in chapter 5, where, on a literal level, it has more than one referent: in verses 1 and 3 *today* refers to the day of Moses's speech, shortly before his death, whereas in 24 it refers to the day at Ḥoreb forty years earlier. The effect of using *today* to refer to the narrator's present and to the narrator's past in the same passage is to blur the distinction between them: *today* refers to no one day in history but to a "today" that is always accessible and never ends, the "today" in which the nation ratifies the covenant and accepts the law.

The word *today* also occurs six times in chapter 4, and the phrase "which I command you this day" (אשר אנכי מצוך\מצוה אתכם היום) occurs no fewer than twenty-four times throughout Deuteronomy.[20] Generally, the speaker of this phrase seems to be Moses rather than God, because the surrounding verses usually refer to God in the third person. As a result, *today* in these verses must refer to the day Moses spoke to the people in Moab. Yet the audience reading or hearing Deuteronomy might assume, not unreasonably, that the "I" who commands them in these verses is Yhwh.[21] In that case the "today" could be understood to be the day of lawgiving at Ḥoreb, and the word becomes multivalent, referring to more than one moment in time. An especially revealing case occurs at 26.16–18, in which *today* occurs three times:

> [16]On this day (היום הזה) Yhwh your God commands you to carry out these laws.... [17]It is Yhwh whom you have declared to be your God today (היום) so that you will follow His paths and observe His laws and statutes and obey Him. [18]And it is Yhwh who has declared you to be His special nation today (היום), as He promised you, so that you observe His commandments.

Today must refer here on the most basic level to the day on which Moses is giving his speech on the plains of Moab. It is significant, then, that the subject of the verb *command* in verse 16 is God, not Moses: it follows that God is still commanding Israel in Moab, forty years after the event at Ḥoreb.

The same phenomenon is evident in the phrase "which I command you today" in 11.13. In the two verses that follow 11.13 God speaks in the first person ("I shall provide timely rain for you.... I shall provide grass for your cattle"), which suggests that the speaker in verse 13 is God. In 11.13, then, God commands the people "today," on the day of Moses's speech in Moab, and the divine lawgiving is not confined to the day the people stood at Ḥoreb forty years earlier. Alternatively, we may understand God's *today* of 11.13 as referring to the event at Ḥoreb forty years earlier. In that case, it is noteworthy that Moses uses the word *today* elsewhere in the same passage (11.8, 11.27, and 11.28) to refer to Moab, so that the shift between the *today* of Moab and the *today* of Ḥoreb breaks down the specificity of the word's referent. This repetition in chapter 11 disconnects the guiding word from any particular day in the past, allowing Deuteronomy's audiences through time to understand the word as referring not only to these two events in the past but to their own present.

Ultimately, the "today" of which D speaks includes the day of lawgiving at Ḥoreb, the day of covenant renewal in Moab, and the "today" of the book's audience—that is, the many "todays" of each person the text addresses. It is this last "today" that is most important for D. After all, D composed the text, and the tradition preserves it, so that it can command audiences throughout the generations.[22] Thus, the very same book that tells us that lawgiving was punctual also hints that lawgiving is ongoing. D's emphasis on the importance of the present is also evident when one compares Deuteronomy 5.3 with 11.2–8. In the former, it is not with the parents but with the present generation that God makes the covenant; in the latter, it is not the children but the present generation who witness God's miracles (though in fact the present generation is one generation removed from those events). D wants the audience's acceptance always to occur in the present, not in the past; religious meaning seems reserved for, or at least most intense in, a moment that knows neither past nor future, neither earlier generations nor later ones, but only an eternal now. We will encounter a similar attitude among more recent theologians a few pages hence.

This mixing of time frames also emerges from the distance between the day on which God gave the laws to Moses and the day, forty years later, when Moses passed this law on to the nation. (Deuteronomy 1.33–39 describes a gap of one generation between lawgiving at Ḥoreb and Moses's discourses in Moab; 8.2–4 and 29.4 speak more specifically of forty years.) In D's version of history, during the forty years in the wilderness, the people did not yet have the whole law, for at Ḥoreb they heard only the Decalogue; the remainder of the laws were vouchsafed to Moses alone.[23] Thus, God gave the law at Ḥoreb, but Israel received it in Moab.[24] And though they heard the details of the law later, they had already accepted them at Ḥoreb, when they said, "We will obey and we will carry it out" (ושמענו ועשינו) in 5.27; and they will accept it again in Canaan, when they carry out the ceremonies required by Deuteronomy 27. The creation of a covenant at Ḥoreb and the creation of a covenant in Moab are at once distinct events and overlapping ones. The forty-year time lag between Moses's receiving the Torah and Moses's bestowing it upon the people undermines D's emphasis on the punctual nature of the lawgiving. It creates a sense that giving and receiving law is durative, or at least subject to repetition. Deuteronomy itself highlights this gap in 28.69, which distinguishes between the covenant at Ḥoreb and the covenant of Moab—even though their content is identical.[25] The event at Mount Ḥoreb comes to completion only on the plains of Moab, and thus the sun sets on the "today" of Ḥoreb only at the end of the "today" in Moab. Insofar as the latter "today" brings the former to consummation, the text suggests a pattern in which every "today" can restore the "today" of Ḥoreb. Thus, the following summary that the philosopher Paul Franks provides for Rosenzweig's views in fact serves as a fine articulation of the teaching implied by Deuteronomy: According to Rosenzweig (and equally, I think, according to D),

> by invoking the demand that every day be seen as "today"—as the present moment of revelation—Rosenzweig effected, not the replacement of Sinai with the plains of Moab, but rather the situation of Sinai within a broader tradition originating with Deuteronomy. For, if Sinai was more than a merely political event that had occurred in ancient history, this was because of the Deuteronomic repetition of Sinai, and because of the accompanying call to make revelation ever-present by repeating Sinai again and again.[26]

Notwithstanding its own claim that the voice at Ḥoreb did not continue, D legislates the recurrence of that voice in Deuteronomy 31.9–13. That passage tells us that shortly before his death, Moses, for the first time, wrote down the Torah he had proclaimed orally. The passage goes on to require that this Torah be read aloud to the whole nation every seven years. That public reading (Jean-Pierre Sonnet tells us) "brings about nothing less than a new Ḥoreb . . . , enabling the Torah words to pervade Israel's future time and space."[27] The original revelation conveyed an Oral Torah, but Moses writes down that Oral Torah so that the teaching can be carried into the Land of Canaan after his death. It is precisely this belated Written Torah that enables the original Oral Torah revealed to Moses at Ḥoreb and conveyed to Israel in Moab to endure in the future.

The tension between the punctual nature of the lawgiving at Ḥoreb and the eternal "today" of the events that happened there parallels another tension in Deuteronomy. As we have seen, D twice warns the audience not to add to or subtract from its law (see 4.2 and 13.1). Yet, as Robert Polzin and Bernard Levinson have stressed, this warning from D is at odds with D's own revisionary project, for the law code in D represents an extensive and systematic rewriting of earlier Israelite laws, especially E's code in Exodus 20–23.[28] The very book that tells us not to add or subtract has, for example, added (in 15.12–18) to the law of the released slave (from Exodus 21.2–6) a requirement that the slave receive generous payment for years of service when the slave goes free; further, D subtracts the subsequent law regarding female slaves (Exodus 21.7–11) in its entirety, requiring instead that female slaves receive the same rights as their male counterparts. D, in short, sponsors precisely the sort of innovation that D claims to reject.[29] D would have us limit our use of D's own text to mere citation rather than reinterpretation—but, as Levinson shows, D's own example shows that the citation of tradition provides a means to rework tradition. Citation does not entail passive deference to the ostensibly authoritative—and canonical—source but rather critical engagement with it. That generalization holds true while the traditions of ancient Israel are still taking shape ... [and also] once the canon is closed.... Through various genres and periods of rabbinic literature, the citation either of a scriptural or of an earlier rabbinic source will mark the transformation or even domination of that source. Similar issues apply to the citation of the Hebrew Bible in the New Testament and at Qumran.[30]

To be sure, D camouflages its own innovative nature by attempting to supplant the earlier law code, rather than supplementing it or commenting on it.[31] But this attempt did not succeed, since the Pentateuch ended up including both D and its source in Exodus 20–23.[32] As a result, readers can contrast D's version of a given law with its predecessor earlier in the Pentateuch. The work of the redactor, then, removes the camouflage.[33]

Much the same fate overtook D's (halfhearted?) portrayal of the lawgiving as punctual rather than durative. Once E's laws in Exodus 20–23 and the various P and H laws in Exodus, Leviticus, and Numbers came to precede D's law in Deuteronomy 12–26, the model of a onetime lawgiving became impossible. The redacted Pentateuch leaves the impression that what Moses gives Israel on the plains of Moab is not *the* law but a supplement to earlier laws.[34] But, we have seen, the very fact that D admitted there had been a forty-year gap between the commencement of the lawgiving and its completion intimates that D's rhetoric concerning punctual lawgiving diverged from D's real view, even in whatever version of Deuteronomy existed independently before its redaction into the Pentateuch. Similarly, D's insistence that the reception of the law has to occur again and again in each audience's "today" works against D's prohibition on adding to and subtracting from the law, for every act of adoption in a new circumstance is likely to lead to some adaptation.[35]

One wonders how seriously D intended the strictures neither to add to its law nor to subtract from it. Deuteronomy 18.15–19 provides a law concerning future prophets whom God will raise up, and these prophets, D tells us, will receive commandments from God; note the word אֲצַוֶּנּוּ ("I will command him") in 18.18, which allows these post-Mosaic prophets' activities to enter the realm of commandment. Thus, D envisions divinely ordained additions to its own law through prophets other than Moses.[36] (In light of my repeated references to Deuteronomy as a precursor to

Maimonides, we should note the great difference between the two on this point. Maimonides insists that Moses was the only prophet in human history who legislated, and for this reason the term *prophecy* as Maimonides applies it to Moses and to all other prophets has two fundamentally different, if overlapping, meanings.)[37] Consequently, we are hardly disloyal to D if we read 4.2 and 13.1 with a grain of salt. The merely rhetorical purpose of these verses becomes even clearer when we recall that D does not present its audience with a workable law code. D treats a great many topics cursorily or not at all. To take but one famous example, Deuteronomy 24.1–4 presents a detailed subspecies of the laws of divorce—but Deuteronomy never presents us with a basic law of divorce, or, for that matter, with a basic law of marriage. As a result, one cannot live by Deuteronomy's laws while also being literally faithful to Deuteronomy 4.2 and 13.1.[38] One can accept Deuteronomy as binding law only if one supplements it with a legal tradition that exists outside the work.[39] (This circumstance, of course, reminds us yet again that scripture cannot function on its own but must participate in the wider tradition from which it is drawn.)[40]

In short, D is a work of Oral Torah that attempts (pretends?) to identify itself as a work of Written Torah. But both the reception of D by the redactor of the Pentateuch and D's own emphasis on the renewal of Torah through its ongoing acceptance undermine that attempt. It was inevitable that D's audiences through the ages learned as much from D's revisionary example as from D's more conservative admonitions. Later sages who continued D's work of adopting and adapting the law did not understand 4.2 and 13.1 to forbid all modification. Medieval commentators argue that these verses applies only to changes proposed by individuals, but that the sages as a body can legislate additions and modifications. Others, including Maimonides, maintain that the prohibition applies only to enactments that masquerade as interpretations by claiming already to be present in the biblical texts. For Maimonides, these verses do not prohibit additions intended as a fence around the law that extend or protect an existing biblical law. As Joel Roth points out, midrashic interpretation "makes abundantly clear that the prohibitions *do not apply to rabbinic interpretations*."[41] The rabbis' strong readings of Deuteronomy 4.2 and 13.1 go against the grain of the verses' own language, but they are also loyal to the wider context of these verses within the Book of Deuteronomy. These readings eviscerate the verbal meaning of the verses, but they import into the verses a meaning that is entirely consonant with Deuteronomy's larger revisionary project. Consequently, we might term the rabbinic readings of these verses a nonverbal *peshat*, or perhaps we might characterize them as a midrashic reading that accords perfectly with the intent of the original author—that is, the real intent, rather than the intent D affected.

Precisely the same can be said of the way Deuteronomy 5.22's phrase קול גדול ולא יסף was understood in rabbinic literature and in the Targums (ancient Aramaic translations of scripture that enjoy a privileged status in rabbinic culture). Earlier I translated this phrase as "a great voice, which did not continue," since the verb יסף means "to continue, to carry on."[42] But Targum Onqelos translates these words as קל רב ולא פסיק—"a great voice that never stopped." Other Targums provide similar renderings.[43] R. Shemuel b. Ammi puts forth the same interpretation in the Talmud (b. Soṭa 10b).[44] These sages interpret the verb יָסַף as if it were related to the noun סוף, "end," effectively revocalizing it as יָסֵף ("cease, stop").[45] This reading overturns the phrase's basic verbal sense; in fact, one can achieve the same effect reading simply by allowing יָסַף to retain its normal meaning and removing the word *not* from 5.22. Yet we saw above that Deuteronomy intimates that the covenant was formed not only at Ḥoreb but again a generation later, and that it will continue to be formed in generations to come. One of the passages that conveys this message of ongoing covenantal formation is 5.2–3, the introduction to the passage that includes 5.22 and its "great voice"! Consequently, in the wider context in Deuteronomy and even the narrow context in chapter 5, we might understand D's true intention as being the opposite of what 5.22 conveys on its most basic verbal level. Here again we may speak of a nonverbal *peshat*, or a midrash that respects the intent of the author with greater fidelity than the verbal *peshat* does. D presents a thesis (the moment at Ḥoreb was punctual, and the law cannot be changed) even as D intimates its antithesis (the moment at Ḥoreb endures into every "today," and the law in fact does change).[46] Thus, D bequeaths to Judaism not a specific contention but a dynamic, not an opinion but a *maḥloqet* (a dispute).[47] By claiming to support one thesis while consistently including subtle evidence for its opposite, D once again shows itself to be proto-Maimonidean.

"Today" in Rosenzweig and Heschel

The tension I have just described between D's surface claim that lawgiving was punctual and D's subtler intimation that the lawgiving has durative or repeatable aspects enjoys a rich afterlife in rabbinic literatures of Late Antiquity and the Middle Ages. Because Heschel's *Torah min Hashamayim* and Silman's *Qol Gadol* study both points of view in those literatures, there is no need for me to survey the relevant texts. Instead I move directly to a discussion of this theme in the thought of Rosenzweig and Heschel. These thinkers add greater complexity, and also greater precision, to the understanding of this productive tension.

For both thinkers, one of the most crucial phrases in Exodus 19's account of lawgiving comes in its first verse: ביום הזה—"On this day." Heschel uses the phrase as the title of a section in *Torah min Hashamayim*.[48] Similarly, in the section with the title "The Present" in the *Star* (immediately after "The Command" and before "Revelation"), Rosenzweig speaks of the "great today" in which command occurs, using the word *today* (*Heute*) six times in one brief paragraph.[49] For Rosenzweig this phrase focuses our attention on the fact that divine command must occur in a person's present. In his call for a renewal of halakhic observance and for the acceptance of law as emanating from a divinely ordained command, Rosenzweig writes (in "The Builders"):

> Whatever can and must be commanded is not yet commandment. Law [*Gesetz*] must again become commandment [*Gebot*] which seeks to be transformed into deed at the very moment it is heard. It must regain that todayness [*Heutigkeit*] in which all great Jewish periods have sensed the guarantee for its eternity.[50]

Similarly, he argues that it is not merely the historical fact that revelation occurred at a particular moment in the past that forms the ground for observance of the halakhah. The presence of that moment in the life of a Jew plays an essential role:

> Can we really fancy that Israel kept this Law, this Torah, only because of the one "fact which excluded the possibility of delusions," that the six hundred thousand heard the voice of God on Sinai? This "fact" certainly does play a part, but no greater part than all we have mentioned before, and all that our ancestors perceived in every "today" of the Torah: that the souls of all generations to come stood on Sinai along with those six hundred thousand, and heard what they heard.[51]

When *Gebot* is truly *Gebot*, it exists exclusively in the present; it has neither past nor future. Thus, Rosenzweig writes in the *Star*:

The imperative of commandment makes no provision for the future; it can only conceive the immediacy of obedience. If it were to think of a future or an Ever, it would be, not commandment [*Gebot*] nor order [*Befehl*], but Law [*Gesetz*]. Law reckons with times, with a future, with duration. The commandment knows only the moment; it awaits the result in the very instant of its promulgation. . . . Thus the commandment is purely the present. . . . All of revelation is subsumed under the great today. God commands "today," and "today" it is incumbent to obey his voice. It is in the today that the love of the lover lives, in this imperative today of the commandment.[52]

Heschel, too, speaks of the need for commitment to happen in a moment that is always present; this is true of commitments humans have to other humans, and no less so for one's acceptance of commitments to God:

Revelation lasts a moment, acceptance continues. . . . Is there any meaning to our being loyal to events that happened more than three thousand years ago? . . . Social relations . . . are initiated in an act or in an event *at a definite moment of time.* These relations can only endure if we remain loyal to the promise we have made or to the agreements into which we have entered. . . . People believe in the passing away of time; they claim that the past is dead forever. . . . And yet we are willing to regard it as if it were immortal. . . . We accept events that happened at moments gone by, as if those moments were still present, as if those events were happening now. . . . Sinai is both an event that happened once and for all, and an event that happens all the time. What God does, happens both in time and in eternity. Seen from our vantage point, it happened once; seen from His vantage point, it happens all the time. About the arrival of the people at Sinai we read . . . "In the third month after the children of Israel were gone forth out of the land of Egypt, on this day they came into the wilderness of Sinai" (Exodus 19:1). Here was an expression that puzzled the ancient rabbis: on *this* day? It should have said, on *that* day. This can only mean that the day of giving the Torah can never become past; that day is this day, every day. The Torah, whenever we study it, must be to us "as if it were given us today."[53]

In these passages, both thinkers link the idea of *ḥiyyuv*, or halakhic obligation, with the idea that lawgiving, to be a true lawgiving, must always occur in the present.[54] These passages also evince a tension between two themes that our thinkers stress: "today," which is by definition a particular moment, and eternity. According to the *Star*, commandment does not reckon with the future, with duration; it knows only the moment. Similarly, at times Heschel stresses that Sinai is an event, not a process, and consequently he rejects the idea of "continuous revelation" that is sometimes attributed to him:

> Whatever the motive or content, and whatever be the mode in which inspiration is apprehended, there remains always its character as an event, not a process. What is the difference between a process and an event? A process happens regularly, following a relatively permanent pattern; an event is extraordinary, irregular. . . . The term "continuous revelation" is, therefore, as proper as a "square circle."[55]

Similarly, he insists that prophecy involves

> a particular *act of communication*—one that took place not beyond, but within the consciousness of man, not prior to, but within the realm of his historical existence. . . . Prophetic inspiration must be understood as *an event*, not as *a process*. . . . A process happens regularly, following a relatively permanent pattern; an event is extraordinary, irregular.[56]

And yet Heschel also endorses the notion that the voice at Sinai lasts forever. He translates Deuteronomy 5.22 according to Targum Onqelos: "*a great voice that goes on forever*"[57] and emphasizes that the command from Sinai takes place above all "today." Both thinkers emphasize that revelation is punctual, but they also stress it is beyond time.[58] This duality is explicit in Heschel's statement, "Sinai is both an event that happened once and for all, and an event that happens all the time. . . . Seen from our vantage point, it happened once; seen from His vantage point, it happens all the time."[59]

There is no contradiction here. Heschel and Rosenzweig are not saying that the lawgiving happens in an ongoing or durative fashion; rather, it occurs in eternity, outside the realm of time altogether. Time, after all, is a category of human understanding that does not apply to God, and it is for this reason that both thinkers can see revelation as an event that was punctual but also eternal—the former from humanity's point of view, the latter from God's. Alexander Even-Chen relates this idea to the ongoing *ḥiyyuv* that comes out of the event at Sinai: what the event of revelation produces is a sense of commandedness, and by observing mitzvot the Jew reconstructs the *experience* of revelation and moves from the human to the divine point of view. In this way the punctual event becomes an eternal one.[60] As Rosenzweig puts it, revelation in the full sense of the receipt of the command to love God is an event that is entirely present, with neither past nor future; it is an occurrence in which time is no longer relevant.

Elliot Wolfson sensitively unpacks this notion as it appears in both rabbinic texts and in the work of Rosenzweig:

> The rabbinic understanding of an ongoing revelation that unfolds through an unbroken chain of interpretation is not based on a static conception of the eternity of Torah set in opposition to time and therefore resistant to the fluctuation of historical contingency. Rather, it is predicated on a conception of temporality that calls into question the linear model of aligning events . . . in a sequence. . . . The rabbinic hermeneutic champions a notion of time that is circular in its linearity and linear in its circularity. The study of Torah, accordingly, demands that one be able to imagine each day—indeed, each moment of each day—as a potential recurrence of the Sinaitic theophany. Each interpretative venture, therefore, is a reenactment of the revelatory experience, albeit from its unique vantage point. . . . The divine word reiterated with each reading of Scripture, therefore, is the word yet to be spoken. The phenomenological cornerstone of Rosenzweig's new thinking rests on the belief in the possibility of experiencing revelation as a genuine contingency at every moment.[61]

We may add that not only the act of interpreting Torah but also the act of carrying out a commandment allow one to experience revelation as occurring in an eternal present. Within the dimension of eternal time there are no divisions between past, present, and future, so that the moment at Sinai is always ready to be disclosed.[62] In this regard Heschel differs from Maimonides, for whom revelation continues forever, even though, because of a decline in human perfection over the ages, its voice is no longer heard. For Heschel, revelation is not an ongoing radio broadcast whose frequency we have lost. Rather, God communicated for a moment at Sinai in a manner never repeated, but through study and commitment, a Jew can reenter that moment.[63] (It follows that Heschel's belief in the persistence of prophecy into the Middle Ages and perhaps later, a view he expressed in an essay published in 1950,[64] is not essential to his thought. If one could convince Heschel that prophecy ceased in the early Second Temple period,[65] Heschel's claims about the unique but recoverable event beyond time at Sinai would require no alteration. To be sure, Heschel regards the sages as among the translators of revelation into Torah; consequently, as Alexander Even-Chen puts it,[66] for Heschel the sages work, whether knowingly or not, under divine inspiration. This viewpoint works well with his belief that prophecy did not fully cease, but one can still regard the sages as reacting to the eternal event at Sinai to which they have access, in spite of the end of prophecy, because of their presence at Sinai in Moses's day.) Heschel departs not only from Maimonides in his view of Sinai. Another rationalist philosopher with whom he disagrees is Hermann Cohen, for Heschel rejects the view that Sinai is a mythical archetype symbolizing God's relationship with Israel throughout time; rather, Heschel regards Sinai as a real historical event.[67]

Heschel takes very seriously the idea (associated with the rabbis but, we saw, already discernible in Deuteronomy 29) that all Jews, those born and those not yet born, were present at Sinai. If this is so, then every Jew can strive, through discipline, loyalty, study, attachment, and dedication,[68] to relive that event. From this point of view, the two translations of Deuteronomy 5.22 ("a great voice that did not continue / a great voice that never stopped") are both correct; in fact, they say the same thing. The voice at Sinai did not continue, because the revelation was an event and not ongoing. But insofar as Jews can return to that moment by accepting law as command, the voice is still available in all its strength. It is still possible to hear that voice in the present, and not only to learn about it as something from the past.[69] Similarly, the rabbinic notion that God showed Moses everything that would ever become Torah plays a crucial role in Heschel's thought. This notion implies that there are no חידושים or innovations in the realm of Torah. Jews can, however, recover an aspect of Torah that was revealed at Sinai but has been dormant ever since.[70] Elliot Wolfson aptly refers to this theme as "the paradox of discovering anew what was previously given."[71]

Given their similarity on this point, one might be tempted to see Rosenzweig's influence on his much younger contemporary Heschel. But in this arena the whole idea of early and late disappears, for Abraham Joshua Heschel articulated the point that lawgiving always occurs in the present before Rosenzweig articulated it—in fact, a century earlier. I refer here not to the Abraham Joshua Heschel who wrote *Torah min Hashamayim* and *God in Search of Man* but to his great-great-great-grandfather and namesake, the Ḥasidic sage known as the Apter Rebbe (1748–1825). In his book *Oheiv Yisrael* the earlier Heschel wrote that a Jew must

> always see himself, at every moment, as if he is standing at Mount Sinai to receive the Torah. For humans are subject to past and future, but God is not,[72] and each and every day God gives the Torah to the people Israel. Therefore when a person opens any book in order to learn, he should remember at that

time the standing at Sinai, as if he received the Torah directly from on high. Thus will he achieve a measure of reverence and awe, just as was the case when the Torah was given in fear and in trembling.[73]

Similar ideas occur in medieval and early modern works, including Isaiah Horowitz's *Shenei Luḥot Haberit*, Abraham Azulai's *Ḥesed Le'avraham*, and the *Zohar*, among other sources cited by the twentieth-century Heschel in his discussion of the great voice that did, and did not, stop.[74] The idea Heschel and Rosenzweig share concerning the eternal present of command is one that Heschel learned not from Rosenzweig but from kabbalistic and Hasidic sources that he studied as a youth in Poland.[75] Heschel arrived at his understanding of a punctual event that stands outside time on the basis of his immense learning in Jewish sources. What is extraordinary is that Rosenzweig arrived at this idea without a similar breadth and depth of textual knowledge. In the few years between Rosenzweig's initial steps toward Jewish learning immediately before the First World War and the composition of the *Star* during and immediately after it, Rosenzweig articulated ideas stunningly appropriate to Jewish tradition. How he was able to do so is one of the great mysteries of Jewish intellectual history. Rosenzweig's uncanny intuition may be enough to make one believe that the voice from Sinai never fully came to a stop.

Does Tradition Change?

One of the sources Heschel cites in this connection is a work that is still widely read, *Shenei Luḥot Haberit* by Isaiah Horowitz (c. 1565–1630). Horowitz's discussion of the eternal moment of lawgiving is strikingly similar to those of Rosenzweig and Heschel.[76] Horowitz addresses the benediction from Jewish liturgy in which successive lines praise God as "the one who gave (נתן) us His Torah" and as "the one who gives (נותן) the Torah." Both phrases are true, Horowitz explains, just as both understandings of Deuteronomy 5.22 (the great voice did not continue, and the great voice never ended) are true, since "in truth God already gave the Torah, but He is still giving the Torah and does not stop."[77] Horowitz writes that the "great voice" at Sinai contained ideas intended for certain individuals in certain ages. He alludes here to a midrashic interpretation of Psalm 29.4, according to which God spoke many messages to many individuals at Sinai, each one according to that person's strength and ability to comprehend, so that there were myriads of individual revelations at Sinai.[78] These messages potentially included individually tailored revelations not only to Israelites who left Egypt but to Jews of each and every generation. According to Horowitz, each idea revealed at Sinai has its own appropriate moment. On the day when God revealed Torah at Sinai, the right moment had not yet come for many an idea: "the matter depends on the level of wakefulness of mortal beings, on their essence and their quality, and on the level of the souls of each and every generation."[79] Throughout the centuries, sages who heard a particular interpretation of Torah when they were at Sinai subsequently awaken that teaching during their historical lifetime. These sages bring the interpretation from potential into actuality at that idea's right time. It follows, Horowitz insists, that new interpretations offered by sages are not new at all:

> It is not the case, God forbid, that the sages innovated based on their own opinions! Rather, they simply arrived at the conclusion that God had already expressed. Their souls, which stood at Mount Sinai (for at that event all the souls were present), received everything appropriate to the nature of their souls and their generation. . . . It follows that the Holy Blessed One gave the Torah at every time. At every hour the well that pours forth does not stop; what God gives (נותן) is what God gave (נתן) in potential.[80]

It is difficult to decide where Horowitz's teaching fits on a map of Jewish thinkers. Is he a reactionary, denying the very possibility of innovation? Or is he strikingly liberal, because he accords new interpretations that emerge in each generation the status of direct revelations from God at Sinai? Horowitz provides the liberal with a way to respond to the challenge of a conservative who objects to interpretations or legal rulings. The conservative might ask: "What right have you to alter what earlier generations fixed in place? Those who came before us were historically closer to revelation, and consequently our knowledge of God's will is faint compared to theirs."[81] But if we all stood together at Sinai, then the interpretation of a twenty-first-century sage or the ruling of a contemporary legal decisor is not necessarily on an altogether different level from an interpretation Akiva put forward in a classical midrashic collection or a decision the great halakhic authority Moses Isserles (1520–72) rendered in his renown legal writings. The contemporary sage stood at Sinai on the selfsame day that Akiva and Isserles did.[82] One can use Horowitz's teaching to solve the apparent contradiction between D's theoretical rejection of addition and subtraction and D's actual legal innovations: employing Horowitz's point of view, one can say that D did not innovate at all but actualized earlier teachings whose time had come. Such a reading of Deuteronomy is fitting, for the approach of *Shenei Luḥot Haberit* is indebted to the idea that all generations of Israel were present at the lawgiving—which stems from Deuteronomy 29.9–14.

These considerations recur when we study the following passage from the *Star*, in which Rosenzweig maintains that for the people Israel,

> custom and law, past and future, become two changeless masses; in this process they cease to be past and future and, in their very rigidity, they too are transmuted into a changeless present. Custom and law, not to be increased or changed, flow into the common basin of what is valid now and forever. A single form of life welding custom and law into one fills the moment and renders it eternal. . . . The law is supreme, a law that can be forsaken but never changed. . . . Every single member of this community is bound to regard the exodus from Egypt as if he himself had been one of those to go. Here there are no lawmakers who renew the law according to the living flux of time. Even what might, for all practical purposes, be considered as innovation must be presented as it were part of the everlasting Law and had been revealed in the revelation of the Law.[83]

What we asked of Horowitz can be asked of Rosenzweig: is he reactionary or liberal? At first blush, Rosenzweig seems to deny the very possibility of innovation and thus positions himself far to the right. But at the end of the passage, Rosenzweig makes clear that he does not deny that change ever occurs in Judaism. Rather, he insists that since Israel stands outside time, there is no before or after, and thus all the customs, laws, and beliefs exist in the same eternity. If this is the case, then an innovation has the same venerable antiquity as a practice that goes back millennia. One legal authority may urge us to allow women to lead prayers; another may respond that only men have led prayers since time immemorial, and therefore the innovation must be rejected. On the basis of Rosenzweig's notion of time—and, it seems to me, of the implication of Horowitz's notion of time as well—the argument that the older practice is preferable to the new one has little validity: a people who stand outside time cannot use chronology as a criterion for accepting or rejecting a law. If every Jew was at Sinai, we must reckon with the possibility that the new practice was sanctioned by God at Sinai, though it only has moved from potential Torah to actual Torah in our own day. It is characteristic that Rosenzweig does not even distinguish between law and custom in this passage; for him, customs that eventually become law are just as ancient, or rather just as Sinaitic, as laws expressed clearly in the Pentateuch.[84]

Of course this reasoning does not mean that all innovations are therefore legitimate. That God said many things to many Jews at Sinai does not mean that any idea a Jew comes up with is a part of Torah. (Indeed, Rosenzweig disliked many of the formalities German Reform rabbis introduced into Jewish worship in the nineteenth century and thus did not consider them true examples of Jewish custom.)[85] But it does mean that a surprising new element of Torah can be as old and as legitimate as an element long known to the community. Within Judaism as Rosenzweig and Horowitz describe it, there is no distinction between new and old; there is neither early nor late in Torah. To make our days new is but to bring them back to their ancient state, as Lamentations 5.21 implies. This point cuts both ways. If the ordination of lesbian women as rabbis turns out in the course of time truly to be Torah, then that practice is as Jewishly legitimate as any practice found in the *Shulḥan Arukh* (the most famous code of Jewish law, published in 1655) or in the P document: it represents a response of religious Jews to what they perceived at Sinai. But it is also the case that the justly revered twentieth-century Orthodox rabbis Joseph Soloveitchik and Moshe Feinstein act with complete authenticity when they attribute the law requiring separation between men and women at prayer to the Bible itself,[86] even though there is no historical evidence that this practice was required in talmudic, much less biblical, times.[87] In describing the separation this way, Soloveitchik and Feinstein are simply engaging in a modern form of what Hindy Najman describes as Mosaic discourse, which, we saw earlier, is a well-worn habit that Jews have hallowed for millennia. If revelation occurs in eternity, then the liberal is merely recovering a primordial truth; but the reactionary's views can never be termed outdated. We return to this tension between two truths and the question of tradition's relationship to change in the conclusion of this book.

6 A Modern Jewish Approach to Scripture

Is there a place for the Bible, and for modern biblical scholarship, in contemporary Jewish theology? In the eyes of many Jewish thinkers, biblical criticism confines itself to antiquities and is consequently irrelevant to constructive projects.[1] The philologist can ascertain the meanings of words; the comparativist can relate biblical beliefs and practices to those of other ancient Near Eastern cultures; the source critic and the tradition historian can recover older versions of the texts that the Israelites knew. But those are taken to be purely academic pursuits, no more connected to the tasks of the modern thinker and the concerns of the religious Jew than are artifacts dug up by an archaeologist. I argued earlier that this attitude should be deeply troubling to religious Jews, because it excludes the earliest members of the covenant community from the ongoing conversation that is Jewish thought. A major accomplishment of modern scholarship has been the recovery of ancient Israelite traditions and ideas in the Bible that were difficult to discern without the philological tools of the biblical critic. Both by identifying compositional layers within biblical texts and by contextualizing biblical texts in their own cultural setting, modern biblical scholarship has allowed us to hear a rich variety of voices that redaction and time had rendered silent.[2]

One may characterize the history of Jewish thought as a series of מחלוקות לשם שמים, disputes for the sake of heaven (to borrow a phrase from rabbinic literature, specifically m. Avot 5:19). Biblical critics allow us to study the earliest of these disputes, thus enlarging the realm of Torah. Religious readers who ignore the findings of biblical criticism, however, exclude the first Jews from our dialogue and perpetuate a new form of supersession-ism that separates biblical Israel from Judaism. The purpose of this book has been to reclaim the Bible as a Jewish book by uncovering the way that modern, medieval, and ancient discussions of one topic—revelation—are manifestations of a debate that occurs in the Bible itself. Attending to the trajectory of this ongoing debate made it possible to find a place for the Bible in modern Jewish thought: the Bible is the earliest, and in some ways the most influential, form of Oral Torah.

In this chapter, I explore what it means to read the Written Torah as Oral Torah. I discuss how such a reading practice relates to ways Jews have long interpreted and produced scripture, in medieval rabbinic interpreta-tion, in midrash, and in the revisions and redactions of biblical books that took place in the biblical period. I address how my proposal of reading Written Torah as Oral Torah differs from modern programs (associated with Franz Rosenzweig and with the great Protestant interpreter Brevard Childs) for recovering the Bible as scripture. Finally, I describe some theo-logical implications for the view of scripture as tradition that I propound. In so doing, I hope to demonstrate that traditional Judaism has nothing to fear from the findings of biblical criticism, and much to gain.

Tradition as Dialogue

As people in any culture receive and transmit a body of texts, ideas, and values, they both listen and speak; in repeating, they paraphrase and add. Rabbinic culture embraces this dialogical aspect of tradition, cherishing discussion and debate in many settings: in the classroom, of course, but also on the printed page, as sages from various generations engage, quote, and critique each other. Consequently, to study in a traditional Jewish setting entails the suspension of time and space. One listens to sages from past centuries, and one speaks back to them. A leading Jewish thinker and hal-akhic scholar of the twentieth century, Joseph Soloveitchik, describes this aspect of traditional study especially well:

> When I sit down to learn Torah, I find myself immediately in the company of the sages of the *masorah* [tradition]. The relations between us are personal. The Rambam [the twelfth-century Spanish-Egyptian philosopher and le-gal scholar also known as Maimonides] is at my right, [his older Franco-German contemporary] Rabbenu Tam at my left, Rashi [Rabbenu Tam's grandfather, the most beloved and widely studied of Jewish commentators,

who lived in the eleventh century] sits up front and interprets, Rabbenu Tam disputes him; the Rambam issues a ruling, and the Rabad [Abraham ben David of Posquières, a southern French commentator of the twelfth century] objects. They are all in my little room, sitting around my table. They look at me affectionately, enjoy arguing and studying the Talmud with me, encourage and support me the way a father does. Torah study is not solely an educational activity. It is not a merely formal, technical matter embodied in the discovery and exchange of facts. It is a powerful experience of becoming friends with many generations of Torah scholars, the joining of one spirit with another, the union of souls. Those who transmitted the Torah and those who receive it come together in one historical way-station. . . . When I solve a problem in the Rambam's or Rabbenu Tam's writings, I see their glowing faces. . . . I always feel as if the Rambam and Rabbenu Tam are kissing me on the forehead and shaking my hand. This is not a fantasy. . . . It is the experience of the transmission of the Oral Torah.[3]

Modern biblical scholarship allows us to include the earliest sages in the discussion this recent sage describes. In light of our new understanding of the multilayered nature of biblical texts, we can appreciate how they functioned during the biblical period as tradition. Scholars of inner-biblical exegesis demonstrate that biblical authors spoke to one another. Interpolations and glosses in various biblical texts explicate or react to verses within that text. Later texts respond to earlier texts or rewrite them altogether. The dialogical dimension of inner-biblical exegesis is especially vivid in what Yair Zakovitch calls the "boomerang" phenomenon, in which a later text reacts to an earlier text, and subsequently scribes insert material influenced by the later text into the earlier text, so that it now contains a response to a conversation it generated.[4] All this should seem familiar to traditional Jewish students of the Bible. On many a page from the *Miqra'ot Gedolot* (a traditional edition of medieval rabbinic commentators to the Bible, in which commentaries by various sages appear in their own columns surrounding the central column that contains the biblical text), an intergenerational, time-suspending discussion occurs. Scholars in one column cite or take issue with scholars in another, and a sage in a third column defends or clarifies the first. Thus, the twelfth-century commentator ibn Ezra criticizes a view of Rashi's, and the thirteenth-century commentator Ramban defends Rashi against ibn Ezra.[5] Similar time-suspending conversations occur on every page of the Gemara.[6] What we now see in light of the study of inner-biblical exegesis is that this sort of discussion takes place not only between one column of a *Miqra'ot Gedolot* and another but also within the central column itself: the Bible's authors engaged in conversations and debates that prefigured those of its interpreters.

In this book, I take this implication of a modern critical method one step further. Having recognized that the Bible is a work of tradition, I put the biblical authors into conversation not only with one another but with later Jewish sages as well. Thus, in chapter 2, I discussed a debate between the Pentateuchal sources E and D concerning mediated and unmediated revelation, and I uncovered an objection to D's view inserted into Deuteronomy 5.5 by an interpolator I dubbed Proto-Rabad. I further pointed out how the biblical-era debate continued into texts from the talmudic period and the Middle Ages. Maximalist interpreters (such as the Mekhilta, Rashbam, ibn Ezra, and Seforno) parallel D when they claim the whole nation heard the whole Decalogue. Minimalists (Hamnuna, Joshua ben Levi, Joseph Qara, Maimonides, the Rymanover and Rophshitzer rebbes, and ultimately Rosenzweig and Heschel) take up questions and hints found in E. (We also noticed that while Rashbam and ibn Ezra are maximalist in their view of the Decalogue, which they regard as God's exact words, they take a minimalist stance on the rest of the Pentateuch, whose wording they regard as for the most part Moses's rather than God's.) Here I spoke not only as a biblical scholar but as a scholar of Jewish thought more broadly, illustrating how biblical texts are part of a vital tradition that endures into modern times.

Removing the boundary between Written and Oral Torah opens up the conversation that is Jewish thought so that we can hear biblical and postbiblical interlocutors engaging one another. Treating the Bible as part of, rather than separate from, Jewish tradition allows us to appreciate the deep roots of later Jewish thought. Thus, the manner of reading I propose focuses our attention on continuity: it uncovers a long-term conversation in Judaism about the nature of revelation that goes back to the earliest period of Jewish history—that is, to the biblical period. I am able to trace this long-term coherence in Jewish thought only by recognizing the Pentateuch's lack of coherence. To understand how a medieval or modern minimalist develops an older point of view, I need to read E against P in Exodus 19, and I need to read Proto-Rabad against D in Deuteronomy 5. It is through embracing source criticism while conceptualizing Written Torah as Oral Torah that we discern overarching trajectories in Jewish intellectual history.

In short, I read the Pentateuch for disunity in order to find a greater unity in Jewish tradition. It will be useful to sketch out an additional example of this method. In an earlier book, *The Bodies of God and the World of Ancient Israel*, I described a view of divinity found in the ancient Near East, according to which deities differ from human beings because deities' selves are fluid and unbounded. These deities could have multiple bodies, located simultaneously in heaven and in several earthly locations. (This is especially evident from the ceremonies that brought the real presence of a deity into its cult statue; the ancient texts that describe these ceremonies make clear that they regarded the god as literally embodied by or housed in the statue. Because there were many such statues of a given deity in various temples at the same time, it follows that a god or goddess often had multiple bodies, that they were physically and not merely symbolically present in more than one house.) Further, a deity's self could fragment into more than one local manifestation. These manifestations, or *avataras* (to use the Sanskrit term), were distinct from one another and were even worshipped separately. Nonetheless, these local manifestations retained an underlying unity. Thus, there were several goddesses named Ishtar who were ultimately a single being, many Baals or Hadads who were one Baal Hadad. This conception, which I call the fluidity model, appears not only in ancient Mesopotamian, Canaanite, and Egyptian religions but also in the Bible, especially in J and E texts of the Pentateuch and in sundry passages in the Psalms, prophets, and Samuel. It also can be detected in several ancient Israelite inscriptions discovered by archaeologists in the past century, which speak of "Yhwh of Teman" and "Yhwh of Samaria," just as biblical texts speak of "Yhwh in Zion" and "Yhwh who is at Hebron." (Similarly, ancient Near Eastern texts speak of "Ishtar of Arbela" alongside "Ishtar of Nineveh" and of multitudinous local Baals.) In those texts the one God Yhwh has multiple cultic bodies; Yhwh can appear in small-scale manifestations that on the surface seem separate from the heavenly Godhead yet clearly overlap with the Godhead and never become autonomous beings. J, E, and related texts use several terms to describe the multiple bodies of God in various temples throughout ancient Israel. These include מצבה ("stone pillar"), ביתאל ("betyl" or "divine house"), and אשרה ("asherah" or "sacred tree, sacred wooden pole"), the first two of which also refer to earthly embodiments of a deity in ancient Near Eastern texts outside the Bible. These texts speak of Yhwh's *avataras* on earth as מלאך ה' (usually translated as "Yhwh's angel," though in J and E it often refers to a manifestation of Yhwh and not a messenger).

This entire way of thinking is completely rejected by the P and D authors, who insist that God has only one body. According to P and the closely related Book of Ezekiel, this divine body came to dwell in the Tabernacle and, later, the Jerusalem Temple. (Ezekiel 8–11 further narrates God's return to heaven shortly before the destruction of the Temple in 586 BCE.) According to D and the historical books from Joshua through Kings, which follow D's theology in many respects, God dwells eternally and exclusively in heaven. D insists that there is only one Yhwh, not several local manifestations in Teman and Samaria, Zion and Hebron (see Deuteronomy 6.4). Neither P nor D depicts small-scale manifestations, emanations, or *avataras* of God in their narratives. These authors forbid Israelites from using the cultic items believed to be embodiments of God in local temples—that is, the מצבות (stone pillars) and אשרות (sacred trees or poles)—and require them to be destroyed (Leviticus 26.1–2; Deuteronomy 7.5 12.3, 15.21–22). They insist that God's presence (or, for D a symbol of God's presence, since God is exclusively in heaven) can be encountered only in a single Temple, and thus sacrificial ritual can be practiced only there.

P and D are the dominant voices of the Bible. Together they account for about two-thirds of the Pentateuch,[7] and the schools that produced them edited many biblical books into their current form. As a result, it is exceedingly difficult to notice the Israelite fluidity tradition that they attempt to suppress. (For this reason I needed to devote eighty-one pages of *Bodies of God* to reconstructing that tradition.)[8] But the fluidity tradition does not disappear from Judaism. It reemerges in new forms, with new terminology, in Late Antiquity and the Middle Ages, especially in works of Jewish mysticism such as the *Zohar* (the thirteenth-century masterpiece that is one of the central texts of kabbalistic tradition). The kabbalistic doctrine of the *sephirot* in the *Zohar* and related works constitutes a highly complex version of the notion that the divine can fragment Itself into multiple selves that nonetheless remain parts of a unified whole. The *sephirot* are usually conceived of as ten manifestations of God in the universe, as opposed to the utterly unknowable essence of God outside the universe. While some kabbalists view the *sephirot* as created beings distinct from God, most classical kabbalistic thinkers see in them, as Moshe Idel puts it, "an organic part of the divine essence" whose complex interactions with one another constitute "intradeical dynamism."[9] These ten *sephirot* relate to one another in ways that seem to disclose a degree of individual existence. They interact in various ways, including sexual ones, and these interactions suggest their distinct identity. Yet kabbalists maintain that they are all part of the unity that is God. The whole doctrine of the *sephirot*, with their complex interactions that in no way compromise God's unity, is a late reflex of the ancient Near Eastern fluidity tradition. From the point of view of P, D, and, arguably, the redacted text of the Torah, the *Zohar*'s doctrine of God is dangerously novel. But when viewed in light of the distinct theological voices of J and E, the doctrine of *sephirot* returns to an earlier model; it is a massively ramified elaboration of an ancient idea.

Jewish philosophical texts, however, pick up and extend the Bible's anti-fluidity tradition, especially as it manifests itself in D. According to D, God has only one body, which is in heaven and never comes to earth. Thus God's body is basically irrelevant from the point of view of a human being in this world—which is the only world D ever speaks of. On a practical level it is a small step from the view that God's body is unrelated to our world to the view that God has no body at all, a view that first finds expression in Judaism in the writings of the medieval philosopher Saadia, and subsequently in the powerfully influential work of Maimonides.[10] Of course, in making this assertion, Maimonides does not consider himself to be joining a debate on the side of D against J and E; Maimonides regarded Moses as the only author of the Pentateuch, and he would have been appalled at the Documentary Hypothesis. But it is clear to us, eight centuries after his work was written, in a way that could not be clear to Maimonides himself, that Maimonides is a Deuteronomic writer. (Thus, it is quite appropriate that Maimonides cites Deuteronomy much more often than any other biblical book in his philosophical work *Sepher Hammadda'*—more often, in fact, than the other four books of the Pentateuch put together.[11] The same can be said of the Jewish philosopher Hermann Cohen, whose affinity to Deuteronomy is even more pronounced.)

A full discussion of the relationships among these biblical and medieval views is not my concern here. What is relevant to the project at hand is that biblical criticism in its source critical and comparative modes allows us to see the traditionalism of both the *Zohar*'s theosophy and Maimonides's rejection of divine embodiment—both of which might otherwise seem so radically new that one might dismiss the *Zohar* or Maimonides's thought as simply non-Jewish. As in the case of maximalist and minimalist understandings of the revelation at Sinai, it is source criticism that links torah from the mid-first millennium BCE with torah from the early second millennium CE. Appreciation of the varied theologies of embodiment in the Pentateuch encourages modern Jewish thought to grapple with aspects of God that it otherwise tends to ignore. Consequently, an interpretation based on source criticism is religiously enriching for a modern Jew.[12]

In the present book and in my earlier study of divine embodiment, then, I construe the Bible as a Jewish book in two senses. First, I associate the varied theological voices found in scripture with similar voices from rabbinic, medieval, and modern Judaism. Second, I read the Bible, and more specifically the Pentateuch, as a record of debate and thus as prototypically Jewish. Indeed, we may regard the Pentateuch, with its embrace of controversy and multiplicity, as the first Jewish book—or, to speak with greater precision, as the first rabbinic work. Here it is useful to recall the way that Shaye Cohen has characterized the late-first-century and second-century CE sages at the rabbinic academy in Yavneh who produced the Mishnah. Cohen speaks of the "major contribution of Yavneh to Jewish history" as consisting of

> the creation of a society which tolerates disputes without producing sects. For the first time Jews "agreed to disagree." The major literary monument created by the Yavneans and their successors testifies to this innovation. No previous Jewish work looks like the Mishnah because no previous Jewish work, neither biblical nor postbiblical . . . , attributes conflicting legal and exegetical opinions to named individuals who, in spite of their differences, belong to the same fraternity. The dominant ethic here is not exclusivity but elasticity.[13]

Moshe Halbertal resembles Cohen when he speaks of the Mishnah as "the first canon of its kind known to us, a canon that transmits the tradition in the form of controversy."[14] But I think Cohen and Halbertal err when they regard the Mishnah as the first Jewish work that brings together opposing positions. The Pentateuch, with its blatant and unresolved narrative and legal contradictions, enjoys this distinction. To be sure, the Pentateuch, unlike the Mishnah, does not identify the schools of thought that it preserves, but, no less than the Mishnah, it presents us with passages that openly disagree with one another. In one sense, the Pentateuch's transmission of disagreement is even more extreme than the Mishnah's: whereas the Mishnah often tells us which opinion is to be regarded as correct and which as incorrect, the Pentateuch provides no guidance on how to resolve its contradictions or how to decide which opinion to follow.[15] If the Mishnah can be said to constitute a first in Jewish literary history, it is in its consistent practice of attributing conflicting legal and exegetical opinions to named individuals. But in its embrace of the value of agreeing to disagree, the Pentateuch rather than the Mishnah must be regarded as the first Jewish book.[16] This conclusion reinforces the idea that we can find a place for Written Torah in Judaism by classifying it as Oral Torah.

Reading the Bible as a form of tradition enables us to accord the Bible greater prominence than it has in many forms of rabbinic Judaism without, however, demoting rabbinic tradition or denigrating midrashic interpretation. For this reason, the dialogically oriented biblical theology I propose differs from other modern Jewish attempts to return to the Bible. Several modern Jewish movements since the late eighteenth century have called for such a return: these include *haskalah* (the Jewish enlightenment in Germany and Eastern Europe), the early Reform movement, and secular Zionism. However, in these cases, greater emphasis on the Bible entailed a rejection of or a distancing from rabbinic literature and, in many cases, a condescending attitude toward midrash.[17] What I propose, in contrast, is a reintegration of Written Torah into the larger category of Oral Torah which preserves the importance of both. Indeed, my proposal endorses midrashic reading as much as it calls for *peshat* (the contextual and linguistic approach to biblical interpretation that emerged in medieval Judaism),[18] for two reasons. First, in some cases a midrashic reading that seems far from the *peshat* of a biblical text turns out to have a pronounced affinity to the *peshat* of a pre-redacted Pentateuchal source. The suggestion of the Rymanover and Ropshitzer rebbes that the nation Israel heard only a single vowel at Sinai but in some sense saw God's presence there recalls the views of J and P, in which the national theophany at Sinai was seen but not heard. Similarly, my previous book makes clear that some of the *Zohar*'s interpretations that depart radically from the *peshat* of the redacted Pentateuch uncannily revive a theological intuition found in J and E. Second, I emphasize that a view found in any Pentateuchal source is important for a reason that applies equally to all midrashic readings: any one source's viewpoint, just like that of the Pentateuch's final redactor (or R), is consequential simply because the source, like R, is a part of the Oral Torah. The opinion of E or P is worth recovering, even if it contradicts the *peshat* of the redacted text. Similarly, any midrashic reading has validity as a voice within tradition. Regardless of whether it agrees with the *peshat* of the final text, a midrash carries authority in precisely the same way that D and J carry authority: as a voice from the Oral Torah.[19]

In this model, then, modern Jewish thinkers will want to turn to the Bible for the same reasons they turn to rabbinic literature. (Readers unfamiliar with the norms of traditional Jewish learning should pause to note that the previous sentence suggests an upgrade for the status of the Bible on a practical level, not a downgrade.) I turn to the Bible not with the expectation that it always gives me propositional statements that convey accurate knowledge. Rather, the Bible's propositional statements and its allusive, associative discourse constitute the beginning of a discussion. For Jewish theology, specific propositions (whether made by the Bible's authors, by later voices in the tradition, or by ourselves) are less important than the process of discussing these propositions. That discussion, to be the fullest Jewish discussion it can be, should include Israel's earliest voices. This does not mean that a religious Jew must accept everything the Bible says as true, but it does mean that everything it says must be considered and demands a response.[20] In short, the Bible, like the Mishnah or *The Guide of the Perplexed* or *The Star of Redemption*, is *torah*, guidance. These works point us in specific directions, but they are not sources of dogma.[21] Indeed, they cannot be, since they present so many mutually exclusive ideas. As a biblical theologian I do not simply start with the biblical text and then go beyond it. Rather, the whole of Jewish thought, including the Bible, is the text to which I devote attention and upon which I build. I am not especially concerned with the fact that at some point, a redactor put some of the earliest material together as the Pentateuch, or that at another point, Rabbi Judah Hanasi put other parts together as the Mishnah. My project is to notice elements of conversation and continuity that go beyond the artificial boundaries that the various anthologizers over the ages have created.[22]

Centripetal versus Centrifugal Reading

How does the mode of reading I have proposed, which embraces biblical critical methods of analysis, compare to traditional Jewish ways of reading scripture? To answer this question, it is useful to contrast what we may call centripetal readings of the Bible with centrifugal ones. The centripetal mode strives for a center; it is holistic and seeks unity. The centrifugal mode flees from a center; it is atomistic and oriented toward multiplicity. Both forms of reading are known in Jewish biblical exegesis, but the centrifugal is especially prominent in rabbinic literature.

Midrashic reading is more centrifugal than centripetal, in two respects. First, the unity or coherence of biblical books has traditionally not been important for rabbinic (or other ancient Jewish) approaches to scripture. For the midrashic exegete, the next unit after the verse that matters is the Bible as a whole, or perhaps the section (Torah or Nakh), but certainly not the book. James Kugel explains:

> Midrash is an exegesis of biblical verses, not of books. . . . There simply is no boundary encountered beyond that of the verse until one comes to the borders of the canon itself—a situation analogous to certain political organizations in which there are no separate states, provinces, or the like but only the village and the Empire. One of the things this means is that each verse of the Bible is in principle as connected to its most distant fellow as to the one next door. . . . Indeed [the midrashist] sometimes delights in the remoter source.[23]

The rabbis believe that the main unit of expression in the Bible is the verse, or a group of two or three successive verses. They are not interested in larger literary units, such as a whole poem or a complete story, much less a whole biblical book. For the rabbis, the Bible is not a collection of songs, laws, and narratives. It is a collection of verses.[24] In this respect, midrash is a fragmentary mode of reading: it examines words, verses, or small collections of verses independently of their context in a given biblical book. True, midrash is concerned in its own way with context, but the context into which a midrashist puts a given verse is that of the entire Bible. Thus, there is no such thing as a midrashic commentary on, say, the Book of Genesis; nor is there such a thing as a midrashic commentary on a given passage.[25] Anthologies of midrashic comments on individual verses in the Book of Genesis have been brought together following the order of biblical verses, sometimes with some thematic thrust in mind. But such anthologies show no concern for the canonical shape of Genesis as a textual unit, or even for the coherence of a given narrative.[26] Rather, they are interested in the connections between a given verse and verses throughout the Bible. When discussing, say, Genesis 22.1, midrashic interpreters were not particularly interested in the relationship of this verse to Genesis 22.2 and 22.3, or even later verses from this chapter. More far-flung relationships interest them much more. Thus, in Bereshit Rabbah §55, the interpreters of Genesis 22.1 do not examine Genesis 22.1 within what postmidrashic interpreters call the story of the binding of Isaac. Instead, they overwhelmingly cite verses found far away: Psalms 60.6, 11.5, and 110.4; Ecclesiastes 8.4; Deuteronomy 23.21; Leviticus 19.18; Micah 6.6; 2 Samuel 7.18; and Proverbs 25.6 (to name but a few). Of the fifteen verses cited in the discussion of Genesis 22.1 in Bereshit

Rabbah §55, only two are from Genesis, and even those (Genesis 21.5 and 23.5) are from neighboring narratives but not from the story at hand itself.

From the point of view of the midrashic sages, the fact that Genesis 22.1 appears in a Torah scroll next to Genesis 22.2 and not right next to the verses from Psalms, Deuteronomy, Isaiah, Ecclesiastes, Micah, Samuel, and Proverbs that Bereshit Rabbah cites results from the limitations of the technologies with which humans write. It is not possible to put Genesis 22.1 next to all the verses related to it when writing on a leather scroll or, for that matter, when printing a book. Here we arrive at a crucial aspect of the midrashic conception of the Bible. For the rabbis, the Bible is not really a book at all. Rather, the Bible is a hypertext, a database with myriad internal connections spanning the whole canon. These connections link any one verse to many other verses, which in turn are linked to a large number of additional verses. Thus, a given verse has several literary contexts, each of which implies several additional contexts. The physical data-storage technologies available to humanity in the midrashic era (and also in subsequent eras up until the development of computer databases in the late twentieth century) allowed a verse to be contextualized next to only a few other verses. But in reality as the classical rabbis conceived it, any one biblical verse was part of a matrix of verses, each of which invoked additional matrices and thus encouraged new combinations of biblical verses and texts.[27] While writing could not accommodate the matrix, memorization of a text could do so, at least to some extent.[28] Here again we see the importance of orality-aurality in a genuinely Jewish conception of scripture.

Because midrash, as an atomizing form of reading, links words or verses from one part of scripture with words or verses from elsewhere, the notion of book is of little significance for a rabbinic approach to scripture.[29] The relative unimportance of the concept of book and its textual flow also emerges from the lectionary practices of Judaism—that is, from the way the Bible is chanted in synagogue. Jews do not hear prophetic books chanted from start to finish in the synagogue; instead, we listen to discrete passages from the prophets, so that most synagogue-attending Jews have no sense of prophetic books as wholes. Even in the case of the Torah, the context of the book as a whole is largely broken down liturgically. Although we chant the Torah sequentially in its entirety, this reading is accomplished piece by piece over the course of a year; and in some ancient communities (where a Palestinian rather than Babylonian lectionary cycle was in use) the reading was accomplished over three to three-and-a-half years.[30] Thus, religious Jews both ancient and modern have been encouraged by their liturgical practices to view scripture as a series of short segments that link up with one another across local contexts rather than as whole scrolls.

There is a second respect in which we may characterize midrash, and indeed the intellectual project of classical rabbinic Judaism as a whole, as centrifugal rather than centripetal. Midrashic collections string together alternate interpretations of a verse and record exegetical controversies among rabbis.[31] The *Miqra'ot Gedolot*'s presentation of debate among commentators in various columns achieves a similar effect. (The setup of the page in the *Miqra'ot Gedolot* is important when we consider Jewish perceptions of scripturality, since from the medieval era until recently the multivolume *Miqra'ot Gedolot*, with its multivocality and its mixture of scripture and interpretive tradition on each page, was the only Bible most Jewish scholars used. Single-volume editions containing only the Bible itself were rare among Jews until the twentieth century, and they remain somewhat rare among contemporary ultra-orthodox Jews.)[32] Argument and exchange are the focus of traditional Jewish Bible study. Similarly, the Talmuds consist largely of debates about a wide variety of matters, whether they are records of actual discussions that took place in the academies or literary creations.

The multiplicity that is essential to Oral Torah becomes especially clear in a phrase that appears in b. Eruvin 13b and b. Gittin 6b: אלו ואלו דברי א־להים חיים ("Both these and those are the living words of God"). This phrase bestows approval upon each side of a debate, however mutually exclusive the two sides are.[33] In light of this dictum, some rabbinic thinkers view revelation itself as open ended, since all sides of any debate found in the Oral Torah must have been revealed to Moses at Sinai. (Recall that for the rabbis God revealed to Moses everything that later students would ask and later masters would teach.)[34] Halbertal points out that for medieval rabbinic commentators such as Yom Tov Ishbili (known as the Ritba) and Nissim Gerondi (the Ran),

> controversy ... [was] rooted in the very structure of revelation. The body of knowledge transmitted to Moses was not complete and final ... but openended, including all future controversies as well. Moses [received at Sinai an Oral Torah that included disagreements,] passed on this multifaceted body of knowledge and left it to the court of each generation to constitute the norm.[35]

The high regard for multiplicity in rabbinic culture comes to the fore in a teaching attributed to the second-century-CE Rabbi Judah bar Ilai. According to this teaching, at Sinai God arranged for the whole nation Israel to hear Moses and God engaging in a debate, in the course of which God agreed to Moses's words (see Mekhilta deRabbi Yishmael, Baḥodesh §2; Mekhilta deRabbi Shimon 19:9). Thus, debate was part of revelation from the beginning—and God saw to it that the human recipient (or rather participant) in revelation won the debate.[36] Revelation at Sinai as understood by some classical rabbinic thinkers, then, was multiple in two senses. Two Torahs were given; but, even more importantly, from the beginning the Oral Torah revealed by God included conflicting opinions on many subjects. This view strongly underscores the dynamism and fluidity inherent in the very concept of Oral Torah. Because Oral Torah is not fixed, it never achieves the stasis that is characteristic of true unity; we cannot know what surprise the Oral Torah has in store for us tomorrow.

Midrashic reading, then, is radically different from holistic methods of reading that emphasize the integrity of literary units such as poems, stories, or whole books. This is not to deny that some elements of holistic reading occasionally appear in Oral Torah. In one respect, midrash has a strong harmonizing tendency: it often brings together two contradictory verses and proceeds to resolve the contradiction so that the two verses work together as a unity. Thus, midrash is at once atomistic and holistic: it reads individual verses rather than longer units, but it often does so in order to harmonize the verses.[37] Similarly, many medieval commentaries adopt the view that Talmud, too, should be free of contradictions, and therefore they work to harmonize passages from disparate books or tractates that seem to contain them. A whole literature of commentaries on the Babylonian Talmud, known as Tosafot, arose beginning in the late eleventh century; their main concern is to demonstrate the harmony of the whole talmudic corpus, and these commentaries play a central role in traditional study of Talmud. Further, not all rabbinic thinkers esteem disagreement among the sages. In contrast to those who, like the Ritba and then Ran, believe that controversy was inherent in revelation itself, medieval thinkers like Abraham ibn Daud maintain that revealed law, both Oral and Written, was originally unified. According to this point of view, multiplicity of meaning entered Oral Torah only as the result of human failure to recall the revelation correctly. Other thinkers (for example, Maimonides) view controversy as limited to laws that were not revealed at all but were created by the rabbis in the first place.[38]

A shift toward holistic reading occurs among some medieval Jewish interpreters of the Bible, especially from the French school associated with Rashi and Rashbam—who, not coincidentally, were father-in-law and son, respectively, of one of the first tosafists (as the authors of the harmonizing commentaries on the Talmud, the Tosafot, are known). In fact, Rashbam himself was also a prominent tosafist. These biblical commentators created *peshat* interpretation, which emphasizes what for rabbinic culture was the new idea of local literary context.[39] In the work of Rashbam and his circle, we find a centripetal approach closer to modern literary interpretation. But this approach developed late in the history of Jewish biblical interpretation, and it remained somewhat marginal. Rashbam and his emphasis on *peshat* were largely forgotten until Moses Mendelssohn began to emphasize his work in the late eighteenth century. Even since that time, *peshat* interpretations, though beloved of biblical scholars such as myself, have not taken center stage within the community of Jewish readers.[40] Nevertheless, in the enormously popular and influential commentary of Rashi, we find a mode of reading that combines midrashic data with an emphasis on local literary context and thus qualifies as centripetal even though his readings do not exemplify *peshat* in the typical use of the term.[41] In short, Jewish modes of reading scripture have included both atomistic, multiplicity-seeking trends and holistic, unity-seeking forces; but the former have been more widespread.[42]

The seeds of both trends go back to the Bible itself. On the one hand, the redaction of the Pentateuch appears unconcerned with literary unity or ideational harmony. As Baruch Schwartz stresses, the Pentateuch's redactors created a text whose plot is full of undisguised self-contradictions, and whose laws conflict with one another on questions that are both multiple and obvious. The redactor (or, to use Schwartz's term, the *compiler*) treats his four sources with extraordinary fidelity, altering their wording as little as possible so as to preserve the original texts to a maximal extent, even when this creates contradictions—not only between two texts at some remove from each other (as is the case with the legal materials) but also in a single narrative and within the space of a few verses.[43] Joel Baden summarizes this position and its implications:

> The extent of contradiction that the compiler allowed to stand in his combined text is extraordinary. The laws, for instance, with all of their

disparities, were left untouched. The competing notions of what and where the Tent of Meeting was; the competing numbers of animals Noah was to take onto the ark; the different names of Moses's father-in-law; the different names for the mountain in the wilderness—all of these and many more were evidently not deemed problematic enough to warrant correction. . . . The compiler's primary goal was not to resolve contradictions . . . [but] to retain as much of his source material as possible. . . . By preserving four discrete and distinct documents, each of which relates its own version of the early history of Israel and argues for a particular view of Israelite religion, the compiler has made an important theological statement. . . . No one viewpoint captures the entirety of the ancient Israelite religious experience. No single document describes the full panoply of ancient Israelite culture . . . The competing voices preserved in the Pentateuch are, in fact, complementary, even as they disagree. Only when they are read together is the picture complete. . . . To attempt to read the canonical Pentateuch as having a single theological message, be it that of the compiler or one of his sources, is to gravely misunderstand the meaning of the final form of the text, of the compiler's work.[44]

Thus, the method of the compiler marks the beginning within Jewish tradition of the attitude that both these and those are the living words of God. Openness to multiple viewpoints that are left as they are without harmonization is characteristic of rabbinic culture, but it dates back at least to the time of the Pentateuch's compilation.[45]

On the other hand, the centripetal approach typical of the tosafists is also known within the Bible. While the Pentateuch gives no indication that its laws need to be reconciled, historiographic literature of the Second Temple period nevertheless strives to harmonize among the various law codes. We saw in chapter 3 that Chronicles suggests how one can observe the laws of the Passover ritual meal as they appear in both Exodus and Deuteronomy. Thus, the Chronicler regards the Pentateuch as a legislative unity, not as a collection that preserves the wording of older sources within a broad if bumpy narrative framework. According to the Chronicler, one does not choose which law to observe; one attempts, through a somewhat forced exegesis, to observe a law that encompasses the wording of both. Similar exegeses are found in other passages of Chronicles, as well as in Ezra-Nehemiah. Scholars have shown that the authors of both these works engage in halakhic midrash to resolve contradictions in the Pentateuch's laws.[46] This also occurs, albeit less frequently, with narrative passages. A brief but telling example of the latter that is especially relevant to our concerns in this book occurs at Nehemiah 9.13, which values harmonization more than it fears oxymoron: "You came down to Mount Sinai to speak to them from the heavens." This verse creates a narrative that is difficult to picture but gives all the relevant verses from the Pentateuch their due: God descends to Sinai before the lawgiving in Exodus 19.3, 11, 18, and 20, while God speaks from heaven according to Exodus 20.22 and Deuteronomy 4.26.

On occasion, the centripetal point of view occurs even within the Pentateuch itself. Several scholars have shown that Exodus 34.18–26 is the product of a post-redactional addition to the Pentateuch—that is to say, it is one of the rare Pentateuchal texts that even neo-Documentary scholars do not attribute to J, E, P, or D. This legal text, which provides an overview of the festival calendar, is based on the older festival law in Exodus 23.14–19.[47] As Shimon Gesundheit writes,

> The two festival calendars in Exodus 23:14–19 and 34:18–26 . . . are not two separate texts; rather, the latter is but a midrashic revision of the former. The inner-biblical midrashic process has solved difficulties, eliminated obscure words and phrases, and drawn conclusions based on the juxtaposition of disparate elements in the earlier text. Archaic linguistic usages have been replaced by later ones, and the discrepancies between the ancient festival calendar [in Exodus 23] and those found in later Pentateuchal texts have been harmonized . . . [Exodus 34:]18–26 are not an independent document at all but rather a revision of extant materials; the secondary nature of this revision is reinforced by the presence of Priestly influence and Deuteronomic style.[48]

Gesundheit's use of the term *midrashic* is significant. While many modern scholars use this term sloppily, to mean "interpretive" (or, sometimes, "boldly interpretive"), Gesundheit uses it, correctly, in a more specific manner: to refer to biblical interpretation that brings together verses from disparate parts of the biblical canon to create a new narrative or law.[49] Gesundheit and others show that the passage in Exodus 34 represents a melding of legal passages from elsewhere in the Pentateuch. These verses represent a revision of E's festival law in Exodus 23 in light of festival and sacrificial laws in both P (Exodus 12.10, Leviticus 23.15) and D (Deuteronomy 4.38, 9.4–5, 12.20, 14.8, 18.12). This addition to the Pentateuch attempts to create a comprehensive *Pentateuchal* law of the festivals that borrows from and thus harmonizes the sometimes contradictory laws on the festivals elsewhere in the Pentateuch. In contrast to the compiler (who left intact several discrepancies among the festival laws in the Pentateuch's sources), the late interpolator responsible for Exodus 34.18–26 attempted to demonstrate that it is possible to bring language from varied traditions together in a way that entails no contradictions, or at least diverts our attention from them.

Such late additions are rare in the Masoretic Text, which is authoritative in Judaism. They appear more frequently, however, in the Samaritan version of the Pentateuch—especially in passages that describe the revelation at Sinai. This version of the Pentateuch (which is used by the Samaritan communities living near Ashdod and Nablus to this day) represents a later edition than what we find in the Masoretic Text, and it sometimes develops or alters material from earlier editions in such a way as to create a more harmonized literary work. The Samaritan edition inserts material from Deuteronomy 5.24–31 (which describes the immediate aftermath of the proclamation of the Decalogue) into the parallel passage after the Decalogue in Exodus 20. Further, it inserts verses from Deuteronomy 27.1–7 into the verses following the Decalogue in both Exodus and Deuteronomy. Finally, it harmonizes minor differences of language between the Exodus and Deuteronomy Decalogues. Thus, in the Samaritan Deuteronomy, the verb in the very last sentence is לא תחמד ("Thou shalt not covet"), as in Exodus, rather than MT Deuteronomy's לא תתאוה ("Thou shalt not desire"). Similarly, in the Samaritan Exodus the verb introducing the Sabbath commandment is שמור ("observe"), in agreement with Deuteronomy, rather than MT Exodus's זכור ("remember"). Whereas the Masoretic edition of the Pentateuch has two somewhat different accounts of the events immediately after the Decalogue, one in Exodus and one in Deuteronomy, in the Samaritan Pentateuch they resemble each other much more closely. Similarly, the Samaritan adds material concerning the appointment of magistrates and judges from Deuteronomy 1.9–17 into the parallel narrative at the end of Exodus 18. It is significant that, the example of Exodus 34 and perhaps a few other texts notwithstanding, midrashic harmonizations of this sort are rare in the version of the Pentateuch accepted as authoritative in Judaism. Thus Judaism, as opposed to Samaritanism, preserves a more pristine centrifugal voice in the most sacred part of its scripture (the Pentateuch), even as other parts of its scripture (Ezra-Nehemiah, Chronicles) foreshadow the harmonizing trends evident in some rabbinic documents.

These tendencies—one emphasizing unity, the other embodying multiplicity—are also evident when we consider how some biblical texts attempted, but failed, to replace earlier ones. We noted earlier that the D authors probably intended their legal collection to replace its predecessor in Exodus 21–23. After all, the point of revising the older collection was to present a new law that included the best of the older one while improving it in various ways. Once the new collection existed, what was unique to the old one could only lead one astray. Similarly, the Book of Chronicles encompasses a large amount of material taken more or less word for word from Samuel and Kings. Having taken everything of value from the older work while leaving out those parts they viewed as problematic or objectionable, the authors of Chronicles almost certainly intended the new work to supplant its sources. Deuteronomy and Chronicles were oriented toward unity in the basic sense that their authors wanted audiences to have single works presenting the law of Moses and the history of the monarchy respectively. But the attempts of D and the Chronicler did not succeed, since the Pentateuch ended up including both D and Exodus 21–23, while the Bible as a whole found room not only for Chronicles but also for Samuel and Kings. Thus, the final version of the canon presents us with multiplicity. Exodus 12 contains a smaller-scale but fascinating example of this dynamic, in which the intention of supplanting older traditions in order to produce a monovocal text has been overruled by an editor who, unable to abide by the loss of any traditional material, prefers multiplicity. Shimon Gesundheit shows that Exodus 12 originally included an older version of a passage that was recast to form what we know as vv. 12–14. Subsequently, Gesundheit explains, another editor restored the original version of the material underlying vv. 12–14, placing it as an appendix at the end of the chapter, where it now forms vv. 22–24.[50] Here again we move from revisionary unity to agglutinative variety.

It is significant that the Bible manifests both trends: On the one hand, D and Chronicles underscore a revisionary unity by attempting to supersede older material so that what remains is self-consistent. On the other hand, the Pentateuch's compilers and the process of canonization abhor the idea that a part of the tradition will be lost. Consequently, they present more than one understanding of the truth, however difficult or self-contradictory the resulting anthology may be. It is also significant that the parties who refuse to let go of older traditions and who favor multiplicity have the final say.

Rosenzweig, R, and Canon Criticism

Religious readers of scripture often look askance at biblical criticism because, they claim, religious readers seek unity in scriptural texts, whereas biblical critics atomize them. For example, both Rosenzweig and Brevard Childs, in his attempt to reclaim the Bible as Christian scripture, privilege the final form of the text as an integrated whole rather than the parts from which the whole was constituted. Neither Rosenzweig nor Childs denies the validity of compositional criticism, but both regard centrifugal modes of reading as carrying limited religious relevance. Indeed, Rosenzweig and Heschel acknowledge the intellectual legitimacy of biblical criticism while minimizing or effectively denying its import for religious readers. Rosenzweig and Heschel thus can avoid the charge of fundamentalism while remaining essentially unaffected by modern biblical scholarship regarding the composition and editing of biblical texts. The project of the book you are now reading is to move beyond this self-imposed (and, I think, self-contradictory) limitation by showing that a religious, traditionalist reading of Tanakh can acknowledge what Jon Levenson calls a "positive religious role [for] the new, post-Enlightenment modes of biblical study."[51] Such an acknowledgment is possible because the critique of diachronic, compositional scholarship as religiously uninteresting ought to have little traction for Jews who want to read the Bible in a Jewishly authentic way. After all, we have seen, the final form of scriptural books as wholes is not important for midrashic exegesis. Further, the realization that there is no ontologically distinct category of Written Torah undermines the claim that synchronic, centripetal reading should take pride of place. Unity within the narrow confines of the Bible matters little for the modern Jew committed to this realization; for such a Jew, a different sort of unity within the much broader category of Torah becomes significant. Because this reclassification of Written Torah as Oral Torah emerges from an implication of Rosenzweig's own work, it follows that Rosenzweig's theology of revelation, taken to its conclusion, challenges his hermeneutic for reading biblical texts.

Rosenzweig famously expressed his views on the proper way for Jews to interpret scripture in a letter to Jacob Rosenheim, a leader of Orthodox Jewry in Germany, concerning the German translation of the Bible that Rosenzweig wrote together with Martin Buber. In this letter (which was published as an article during Rosenzweig's lifetime), Rosenzweig explains that he and Buber regard the Pentateuch as a literary unity. To be sure, he clarifies, they do not accept the view that God gave the whole Pentateuch to Moses, and in principle they are open to the possibility that the Documentary Hypothesis or some similar theory correctly describes the historical development of the Pentateuch. But, he tells Rosenheim, that development is of little import for interpretation or theology. As a result, their mode of reading the Pentateuch is not so different from an Orthodox one:

> We too translate the Torah as one book. For us too it is the work of a single mind. We do not know who this mind was; we cannot believe that it was Moses. We name that mind among ourselves by the abbreviation with which the Higher Criticism of the Bible indicates its presumed final redactor of the text: R. We, however, take this R to stand not for redactor but for *rabbenu* ["our Rabbi"]. For whoever he was, and whatever text lay before him, he is our teacher, and his theology is our teaching. An example: let us suppose that Higher Criticism is right, and that Genesis 1 and Genesis 2 are in fact by different writers. . . . Even in that case, however, it would remain true that what we need to know from the account of creation is not to be learned from either chapter alone but only from the juxtaposition and reconciliation of the two. Indeed, it is to be learned only from the reconciliation of the apparent contradictions from which the critical distinction begins: the "cosmological" creation of the first chapter, which leads up to man, and the "anthropological" creation of the second chapter, which begins from man. Only this *sof mas'aseh ba-mahashabah tehillah* ["what was created last has conceptual priority," a quote from the Sabbath hymn *Lekhah Dodi*] is the necessary teaching.[52]

A similar point of view plays a central role in the work of Brevard Childs, the pioneer of canon criticism. In a programmatic essay, he wrote:

> It is [a] . . . grievous error for Christian scholars to assume that the reconstruction of the literature's historical development can now replace the study of the canonical shape of the Pentateuch. . . . Rather, the present shape of the Pentateuch offers a particular interpretation—indeed a confession—as to how the tradition was to be understood by the community of faith. Therefore, it seems to me important first of all to describe the actual characteristics of the canonical shape and secondly to determine the theological significance of this shape.[53]

Childs does not deny the findings of modern biblical critics regarding multiple layers of authorship and supplementation in the Bible, but he insists that the final form of the text reflects the work of the redactors and canonizers who have created a whole rather than a jumble of parts, and that final form is what the religious interpreter needs to read. The religious interpreter is not required to ignore what we know about the multiplicity of the text; on the contrary, a central goal of religious reading for Childs is to see how the redactor shaped a unity from diverse materials. The quest for this complex unity is the primary goal for Childs, not only in interpreting a given passage but in reading biblical books as wholes.[54] While the predilection toward unity-oriented interpretations plays an especially important role for Childs and his followers, it also appears in the work of biblical theologians who are not canon critics. Many biblical theologians regard one of their most crucial tasks as finding the center of scripture, the idea that holds scripture together, or the group of texts out of which other texts flow.[55] Biblical theologians often use the German term *Mitte* to describe this central element. Thus Walther Eichrodt structures his theological analysis of the Old Testament around the idea of covenant.[56] For Gerhard von Rad, the idea of salvation history and the process of transmission and transformation of biblical material work together to form the pivotal concern of the canon and its theological interpreter.[57] Samuel Terrien centers Christian scripture around the interplay between divine manifestation and absence.[58]

This quest for unity is fitting for Protestant readings of scripture, because Protestant Christianity has often assumed that the Bible speaks as a unity.[59] (In light of both the history of theology and comparative religions, this assumption is somewhat unusual.)[60] From a Protestant point of view, when one crosses the boundary of the canon, one moves into a different, and lesser, realm, and therefore what is within the boundary must have a conceptual integrity or singularity. But rabbinic forms of Judaism, like Catholic and Orthodox Christianity, emphasize the authoritative status of tradition alongside or even more than that of scripture. Thus, the literary integrity of the entities on each side of the boundary can matter less. Because traditional Jewish interpreters of scripture are at least as centrifugal as centripetal in orientation, the emphasis that Rosenzweig and Childs place on textual unity appears extraneous for a Jewish reader.[61] Canon criticism, then, is of no particular relevance to Jewish theological appropriation of scripture; but what might be called tradition-critical approaches (under which source criticism can be subsumed) are.

As a result, I cannot see why, from a Jewish point of view, the redactor of the Pentateuch should have a more important voice than the P authors or the D authors who came before him, or than various commentators on the Pentateuch who came after.[62] In saying this, I am not claiming that all voices carry the same weight or that all opinions are equally valid. (Jewish tradition over the ages has made it clear, for example, that Rashi's commentaries on the Bible are more important than those of his rough contemporary Ḥazzequni, and that the Tosefta is part of Torah but the Book of Jubilees is not.)[63] I am merely pointing out that once we realize that the Pentateuch is as much an anthology as a book, there is no reason to see the anthologizer as more sacred, more authoritative, or even more interesting than the anthologized.

Further, the well-known passage about R that I quoted from Rosenzweig's letter is problematic from an exegetical point of view. Rosenzweig maintains that what is to be learned from Genesis emerges not from what either creation account says on its own but "only from the juxtaposition and reconciliation of the two." Yet the interpretation he sketches out—that creation is anthropocentric—could in fact be arrived at by reading either account by itself. In the first account, which stems from P, humanity is the goal and climax of creation, whereas in the second account, from J, humanity is the starting point. Both accounts emphasize the importance of humanity within the scheme of creation, though they express that emphasis in different ways. The interpretation Rosenzweig produces involves no reconciliation, since P and J agree on that matter.[64] By stressing this shared theme, however, Rosenzweig misses what it may be most interesting in the redacted text: the two accounts' very different portrayals of human nature and of God's relationship with humanity. In J, humanity is made from mud; in P, humanity is created in the image of God. In J, Yhwh is on Earth, personally blowing the breath of life into Adam's nostrils; in P, God is distant from the world God creates. The final form of Genesis gives us two theologies and also two anthropologies, and R provides no guidance as to how they might be reconciled or even any hint that they should be reconciled. Accepting that both these and those, however different, are torah is a perfectly good Jewish practice; harmonizing, or pretending to harmonize by noting what the two accounts have in common while ignoring their differences, is not a better method of reading, Jewish or otherwise.[65]

Rosenzweig gives a second example of the postcritical reading he proposes later in his letter to Rosenheim: "Mount Sinai in smoke and the chapter of the thirteen *middot* are not enough to teach us what revelation is; they must be interwoven with the *mishpatim* and with the Tent of the Presence."[66] Here, again, Rosenzweig's centripetally motivated emphasis on R gains us nothing even as it involves a loss. The interweaving of law and narrative is not a product of the redactor's work. It occurs already in P, E, and D, and in a different way in J. Further, P connects law to divine presence by making clear that a core reason Israel must observe the law is to allow God to abide in the Tent. Thus Rosenzweig's evocation of R does not accomplish anything that we might not have accomplished from a source critical point of view. Indeed, the theological point Rosenzweig finds in the text becomes stronger if we regard not only R but also J, E, P, and D as our rabbis. In that case, we are able to note their unanimity regarding the importance of the law, so that this teaching has greater force. It is not the opinion of one sage but a shared tenet of a several authors and schools.[67]

The problematic nature of Rosenzweig's approach to reading the Pentateuch is also evident in his review of the first volume of the German *Encyclopaedia Judaica*. There Rosenzweig criticizes the encyclopedia for segregating discussions of the Bible itself from treatments of biblical interpretation among the classical and medieval sages. He calls for a new form of biblical scholarship that he hopes to see in some future publication:

> This new biblical scholarship will not avert its eyes from critical problems of modern scholarship, but it will apprehend all problems comprehensively . . . from the viewpoint of the final redactor—or, to put it differently, from the viewpoint of the first reader. This new scholarship will rediscover a connection to Jewish biblical scholarship of the past, which . . . started out from a similar point of view—only a connection; not more than that; not submission to it. . . . Then, perhaps, some day an encyclopaedia will be able to put aside that fearful distinction separating what is in the Bible, what our Sages said, and what modern biblical criticism says![68]

It should be clear by now that a major purpose of the book you are reading is to put aside that fearful distinction. In that respect as in so many others, I follow Rosenzweig's path. Yet two problems mar Rosenzweig's comment. First, Rosenzweig equates the viewpoint of the final redactor with that of the first reader. He assumes that until R did his work, there was no scripture, and therefore there could be no interpretation of scripture. But one of the most important conclusions of modern biblical scholarship is that the Bible's first readers lived generations before its final redactors. D reads both E and J and reacts to them throughout Deuteronomy. Priests supplemented a law of Passover with clarifying remarks that transformed an older law into the text of Exodus 12 as we know it. Deutero-Isaiah read P and D—and reacts to them in very different ways that suggest this prophet knew them as separate documents.[69] Only after the earliest interpreters produced these readings were the sources combined to produce the first edition of the Pentateuch. Even then, subsequent readers added the legal passage in Exodus 34. Rosenzweig's decision to privilege the work of the redactor is based on his assumption that the most legitimate reading of the Pentateuch is one that returns to the experience of first readers; but to return to the first readers we must interpret pre-redacted sources underlying the Pentateuch and not the Pentateuch itself. Thus, if we follow Rosenzweig's advice by acknowledging the findings of biblical criticism rather than averting our eyes from them, we have to recognize that the there were Jewish readings of scripture before there was a Bible, and those scriptural readings were produced by sages whose teachings are part of Torah.

Second, here and in his letter to Rosenheim, Rosenzweig assumes that Jewish biblical scholarship should accentuate the unity of the text. Consequently, he regards modern atomizing readings as less relevant to Jewish concerns. These readings, Rosenzweig avers, are not meaningful for a Jewish reader who wants to find *torah* or guidance in the Bible, because the traditional interpreters bring the text together rather than splitting it apart. In fact, we have seen, a great deal of Jewish religious reading is atomistic. Midrash typically takes verses out of their immediate contexts and connects them with verses elsewhere to form what is in effect another text altogether.[70] Now, it should be evident that one could substitute the subject *source criticism* for *midrash* in the previous sentence, and the new sentence would remain true. Indeed, the exegetical spur behind the decontextualization and recontextualization of biblical verses in both midrash and source criticism is the same: both midrash and source criticism attempt to create coherence in a text that is often incoherent as it stands.[71] A midrashic mode of reading is in significant ways closer to Julius Wellhausen and Baruch Schwartz than it is to Franz Rosenzweig or Brevard Childs.

Theology and *Peshat*

We have arrived, then, at a surprising conclusion. Jewish traditions endorse an all-encompassing canonical unity that goes beyond the boundaries of the Tanakh to include rabbinic and postrabbinic literature. A modern Jewish idea of revelation intensifies that unity by collapsing Written Torah into Oral Torah—or rather, by returning Written Torah to the Oral Torah it originally was. But this Jewish canonical unity does not resemble the sort of unity sought by many biblical theologians. Centrifugal rather than centripetal in nature, it bids the Jewish thinker to contemplate the Torah's journey down paths not yet taken and to acknowledge that opposing ideas can be valid, and arguments sacred.[72]

The perspective I outline suggests an answer to a question often asked in religious settings: of what use are modern critical readings of biblical texts? Or, as the question might be phrased in a Jewish context: what is the religious significance of *peshat*, of the straightforward interpretations of scripture which are often opposed to midrashic exegeses found in the Oral Torah?[73] Many authorities deem readings not based on the exegeses of Oral Torah as irrelevant to a Jewish appropriation of scripture, even though those readings may be interesting and valid. Thus, Michael Satlow, in a sensitive discussion of what it means to read Jewish texts, maintains that one creates Jewish meaning out of Jewish texts by interpreting them through the orally transmitted lens of tradition—that is, through Oral Torah.[74] Of course, Satlow avers, one can read classical Jewish texts through other intellectually legitimate lenses, but the meanings one constructs through those lenses are not Jewish meanings.

Taken to the extreme, however, such a view might remove from the category of Jewish interpretation not only the readings of modern biblical scholars but also those of classic *peshat*-oriented medieval rabbinic figures such as Rashbam, ibn Ezra, and Radak. Exegetes such as these systematically disavow midrashic readings in favor of interpretations based on the linguistic and cultural contexts of the biblical texts themselves. Are such commentaries irrelevant to Jewish interpretation of Scripture? In light of our discussion it becomes clear that they are not. The biblical texts that these exegetes help us to understand in their own settings are themselves part of Jewish tradition; they are the oldest, and often the faintest, voices found in the Oral Torah. Thus, any attempt at hearing them more distinctly—in their own voice, in their own historical and philological contexts—generates Jewish meaning from a Jewish text. To take the most challenging example: Rashbam's interpretations of the Bible's legal texts often contradict explanations in the Talmud which form the basis for Jewish legal practice; indeed, Rashbam's interpretations of these biblical texts contradict Rashbam's own rulings in his writings on the Talmud.[75] But these interpretations do not overturn Oral Torah; rather, they shed light on an earlier voice in Oral Torah, albeit one that holds no legal authority. Rashbam engages in two separate discourses, one academic and one practical. Because the discourses are parallel and nonintersecting, they never contradict each other. What Rashbam does in such cases is no less Jewishly relevant than the decision of the Mishnah's redactors to include legal opinions already rejected by the sages. There was value to including the frequently rejected opinions of the first-century sage Shammai alongside those of his contemporary Hillel, even though the former are not the law. The same value attaches to Rashbam's nonrabbinic exegeses of the Torah's legal sections. Similarly, when Samuel Rolles Driver or Menahem Haran recovers, say, the J strand of a passage and interprets it in contrast to E, that commentator revives a lost voice of the Jewish tradition.[76] (That Driver, one of the greatest biblical exegetes of the past millennium, was not himself Jewish hardly prevents him from teaching Torah to Jews.) These commentators contribute to our attempt to understand Jewish tradition in all its fullness.[77]

Peshat readings, including modern critical readings, are religiously significant because they enable us to hear religious teachings that might otherwise have been neglected. Those teachings may fortify, enhance, clarify, problematize, or undermine later voices in Oral Torah in useful ways.[78] Torah, we have seen, is a specific sort of teaching: it involves dialogue, debate, and growth. Critical readings that recover lost voices in that debate need not undermine that process. On the contrary, they expand the realm of Torah.

Flawed Scripture

In chapter 3, I developed the notion of prophecy as translation, which is the heart of the participatory theology of revelation. According to this conception, God reveals the divine will to Moses and the prophets in a manner that goes beyond language—indeed, beyond normal forms of perception and the categories of understanding associated with them. Moses, the prophets, and the sages translate this supralingual revelation into the specific words and laws we find in the Bible and Jewish tradition. Among the classical rabbis and medieval Jewish thinkers, the notion that all non-Mosaic prophecy involved what I call an act of translation is fairly common (though it is not the only view). Intimations that even Moses's prophecy in its own way involved translation are not unknown among the rabbis and medievals.

The idea of prophecy as translation has an important corollary that requires attention. No translation is perfect. At its best, a translation approaches the original, but it never precisely matches it.[79] This is true when we translate from one human language to another; it is all the more true when we translate from a supralingual divine communication into a human language. Scripture and tradition, as products of this act of translation, reflect the ways human beings understood God's self-revelation—and also the ways they misunderstood it.[80] Such misunderstandings are inevitable when the transcendent becomes immanent. As one contemplates this paradoxical mission of scripture, Wilfred Cantwell Smith points out,

> one . . . discovers—and this is decidedly healthy—that the particular form through which one's own group was being introduced to transcendence was in fact a particular, human, finite form; flawed, like everything human; mediating transcendence yet in perilously earthen vessels. . . . We human beings—each of us individually and all of us corporately—live in what I am calling the double context of mundane and transcendent: a mundane that is shot through with transcendence, a transcendent that we apprehend, although in always mundane—and often distorted, sometimes even demonic, always improvable—ways.[81]

The distortion inevitably present in scripture need not pervert the divine will,[82] but intellectual honesty and religious humility require us to recognize that sometimes it does. This fact explains the existence of the troubling texts I discussed at the beginning of chapter 2—that is, those texts that we feel cannot have been written by a God who is just and merciful. I can understand Deuteronomy 25.17–19's call to kill all Amalekite men, women, and children only as stemming from a gross misunderstanding of divine will. In that passage Israel's perception of the divine demand that Israel defend itself and that it bring malefactors to justice was exaggerated into a law of indiscriminate vengeance.

As so often with seemingly unprecedented ideas in the participatory theology as I articulate it, this admission is less novel than it might seem. Talmudic and medieval Jewish texts already reject the notion that the apparent sense of the biblical verses concerning Amalek and similar laws concerning the Canaanites expresses the true will of God; these authoritative legal traditions limit the applicability of the laws so radically that they effectively overturn them.[83] And yet precisely because these verses never lose their apparent sense, they remain dangerous.[84] That danger must be confronted and named; only by acknowledging these verses' failure to reflect God's will can a modern reader fully tame them. Doing so puts us into the position of condemning material from our own scripture, a position that is at once correct and uncomfortable, even if on a practical level our condemnation has substantial precedent within our tradition.

At this point the utility of the idea of Written Torah as Oral Torah becomes evident. A person who insists that by definition scripture must be perfect will find that the Bible, with its flaws and troubling texts, cannot function as scripture. (Nor can any other text known to human beings.)[85] Further, if a community in which scripture provides the sole authority loses scripture, it loses religion altogether. But when Jews who subscribe to the participatory theory of revelation confront the imperfection of scripture, they need not surrender faith or forswear motivation to perform the commandments. Jews have always located practical religious authority in Oral Torah, without losing sleep over the fact that it is a mixture of divine and human elements. Imperfections within the realm of Oral Torah are universally acknowledged, even though debates about their extent occur. Classifying the Bible as Oral Torah allows us to acknowledge its ethical flaws, to counterbalance them with material from within the tradition, and thus to neutralize the flaws.[86] This process of neutralizing one specific law here and another there leaves the status of the divine command underlying the halakhic system as a whole unaffected, just as the halakhic tradition's tendency to disregard occasional practices over time does not lead to apostasy or to the collapse of the covenant. The approach I describe here, in short, combines deep loyalty to the law with awareness that at times the law evinces its human side. This attitude was well described more than a century ago by no less a sage than Solomon Schechter. Speaking of the implicit theology of the historical school of scholars that began with Zunz and to which he himself belonged, he wrote: "On the whole, its attitude towards religion may be defined as an enlightened skepticism combined with a staunch conservatism which is not even wholly devoid of a certain mystical touch."[87] It is fascinating to note how well this line applies to Rosenzweig and Heschel—and also how well it applies to the E document, which insists on the centrality of covenantal law even as it forces us to wonder about the provenance of the law's details.

To what extent do disciples of the participatory theory acknowledge this corollary of their approach to scripture? It must be admitted, first of all, that Maimonides does not. Though in his *Guide of the Perplexed* he regards the specific wording of the Pentateuch as the product of Moses's pen rather than of God's (nonexistent) mouth, Maimonides does not dwell on its human, and hence less than fully perfect, form. For him, the law that Moses authored is, as Lawrence Kaplan puts it, "a perfect imitation in political terms of the idea of cosmic law cognized by Moses."[88] Rosenzweig, for his part, allows for this conclusion but does not focus our attention on it. By describing the Bible as "thoroughly human,"[89] he implies the idea of a flawed scripture, but he does not pursue the issue. Heschel's attitude toward the idea of a flawed scripture is more complex. In *God in Search of Man*, Heschel comes close to articulating this notion as he speaks of "harsh passages" that "seem to be incompatible with our certainty of the compassion of God."[90] But in the end he sidesteps the issue, maintaining that we don't understand these passages fully. This, to my mind, is a way of avoiding the issue rather than confronting it. His discussion of what we now call "troubling texts" has a defensive, evasive tone. When we think through Heschel's theology fully, we realize it leads us to recategorize Written Torah as Oral Torah; that recategorization may then prompt us to critique biblical passages more openly than had previously been the norm in Judaism. But Heschel does not express this corollary of his own work. His earthly Torah is still perfect, though not as sublime as the heavenly one.[91] It is the beginning of revelation and not the whole of it, but he does not quite admit that it is flawed.[92] And yet Heschel also focuses our attention on the extent to which the earthly Torah can be improved when he chooses the following line as one of the preambles to the second volume of *Torah min Hashamayim*: "When the Holy One, blessed be He, gave Torah to Israel, He gave it only as wheat from which flour could be gotten, and as flax from which clothing could be fashioned."[93] This line from a classical rabbinic text, Tanna DeVei Eliyahu Zuṭa 2:1, intimates that the Written Torah is an imperfect work, but also one from which something of greater value can be derived through the tradition of interpretation and reflection found in the ongoing process of Oral Torah.

One of the few modern sages who confronts this issue directly is David Weiss Halivni, who maintains that the Pentateuch we possess is, as he calls it, a "maculated" form of the original divine revelation.[94] According to Halivni, the original Torah was verbally revealed to Moses, but it was partially forgotten or impaired as a result of human sinfulness starting at the time of the golden calf. Much later the Torah was restored expertly, but not perfectly, by Ezra. Hence for Halivni, the Pentateuch as we have it is really Ezra's, not Moses's. Like the Oral Torah, this Pentateuch is infected by at least some degree of human fallibility. The fallibility Halivni describes involves not moral failings but self-contradictions and historical imprecision—in other words, the phenomena that led biblical critics to propose the Documentary Hypothesis and related theories of the Pentateuch's origins. Thus, Halivni's notion of a maculated Torah does not go as far as what I am suggesting here. Further, it does not start from the notion of a nonverbal revelation, and he is not as deeply invested in a participatory theory of revelation as Rosenzweig and Heschel are. Yet Halivni's approach does make clear why it is appropriate to apply critical tools to the Pentateuch and how the Torah that Moses received verbally from God (according to Halivni) could have yielded a document with the self-contradictions noted by source critics.

If scripture and tradition are flawed, then it behooves Jews to repair them, to work with the wheat in order to produce flour. Indeed, doing so is the essence of the participatory theology, for it is in receiving and transforming what is passed down that each generation of Israel participates in the dialogue at Sinai. The imperative to participate raises pressing questions concerning the relationship between innovation and continuity in the Sinai covenant, to which we shall turn in the conclusion of this book.

Jewish Biblical Theology?

A final implication of the participatory theology requires attention. If there is no Written Torah, and if Oral Torah begins at Genesis 1.1, it follows that there can be no Jewish biblical theology; there can be only Jewish theology. The attempt to construct teachings concerning God and God's relationship to the world solely or even primarily on the basis of biblical texts cannot be a Jewish activity, since any Jewish theology must prominently include both the revealed Torahs. For Jews, as for Catholics, religious thought is not based primarily on scripture, much less only on scripture. It can only be based on tradition along with scripture, or on a tradition that includes but is not limited to scripture.

My conclusion that there can be no Jewish biblical theology should come as little surprise. After all, the few Jewish scholars who have become active in the field of biblical theology spend much of their time pointing out how problematic the notion of Jewish biblical theology is.[95] What can serve as a Jewish theology is one that returns to scriptural documents, utilizing them alongside later sacred writings so that all these texts illuminate, challenge, relativize, and renew one another. This sort of undertaking might be called a biblically oriented Jewish theology rather than Jewish biblical theology.[96] Because it creates a dialogue between biblical and postbiblical texts, it might also be called a dialogical biblical theology.[97] Such a theology—the theology we have been pursuing in this book—focuses on biblical texts in novel ways and to a greater extent than has been the norm in the past several centuries. It brings biblical texts to bear on postbiblical theological questions. It shows that some modern concerns are not solely modern but were concerns of ancient authors as well. By fostering discussion between the first Oral Torah (that is, the texts embedded within the Tanakh) and later forms of Oral Torah, dialogical biblical theology creates new Oral Torah. And thus it rejuvenates the canon by enlarging its boundaries once again.

Conclusion: Innovation, Continuity, and Covenant

The core of the participatory theory of revelation is the realization that all Torah, ancient, medieval, and modern, is a response to the event at Sinai. Each generation receives the responses, the Torah, of earlier generations, but to some degree each generation also formulates its own responses, so the Torah evolves over time. Thus, the participatory theory forces us to confront the question of how innovation relates to continuity within the covenant formed at Sinai.[1] This question fascinates modern scholars, but it has been a stumbling block to them, because even the finest among them tend to overemphasize transformation at the expense of tradition.

An instructive case, precisely because it is so exegetically sensitive, occurs in the work of my friend Bernard Levinson, whose account of textual revision and religious renewal in biblical Israel I use in what follows as a backdrop for laying out my own view. Following Yochanan Muffs, Levinson notes that some biblical texts teach that God punishes the children and grandchildren of sinners for their forebears' sins (for example, Exodus 34.5–7, Numbers 14.14–19, Psalm 99.8), whereas others reject that view (for example, Deuteronomy 7.9–10, Ezekiel 18, Jonah 4.2, Psalm 103.8–10). The latter texts allude to some of the former, echoing their language even as they overturn parts of their teaching.[2] Consequently, Levinson notes,

> the conceptual breakthrough [of the latter texts] is grounded in the [former] . . . ; and the break with tradition presents itself in terms of continuity with tradition. . . . Successive writers were able to conceal the conflict between their new doctrine of individual retribution and the authoritative principle of transgenerational punishment. . . . [An] extensive repertoire

of sleights of scribal hand suggests the difficulty of innovation in ancient Israel. . . . Israel's concept of textual authority was thus profoundly dialectical: the break with tradition validates itself in the vocables of tradition. For all the rhetoric of concealment—the impossibility of making innovation explicit or of employing the human voice—the very act of concealment [through which the later writers hid the revisionary nature of the pronouncements] . . . reveals the innovator—the human author—at work.[3]

These "sleights of the scribal hand," Levinson maintains, occur in legal texts as well, whose exegetical and revisionary character he lays out in great detail in a series of publications.[4]

Levinson's phrasing—we hear of cultural change, a break with tradition, and the ways later scribes concealed a conflict between their new doctrine and authoritative principle—can give the impression that continuity was no more than a gesture for the biblical scribes, a rhetorical trope they used to ease their program of overturning tradition. While Levinson brilliantly depicts the techniques of inner-biblical revision and exegesis, the complexity of those techniques ought not blind us to the fact that the scribes were justified in stressing the place of the texts they composed within the tradition. After all, the authors who rejected the idea of transgenerational punishment agreed with the texts they reformulated on theological principles that were highly distinctive within the ancient Near East, such as monotheism and God's particular relationship with the nation Israel. Similarly, later legal texts reworked earlier ones, but both the revising texts and their predecessors concurred on a basic structure of thought and practice. They all affirm that Israel owes covenantal loyalty to one deity. They all declare that each Israelite must enact that covenantal loyalty by obeying a law. At the end of the day, it is somewhat trivial whether that law requires the Israelites to boil the ritual meal for Passover (as D maintains) or to roast it (as P insists). What matters is not the specific action the law requires but the fact that the law does require. Further, for the law to be genuinely a law and not a lifestyle, it is imperative that the decision about the specific practice be made not by each individual but by a larger entity that transcends the individual. At any given moment, the legal system serves as that entity; over time, as the system itself evolves, communities of observant Jews play that role, for ultimately communities decide which changes are acceptable and which are not.[5] When sages such as the authors of the Book of Deuteronomy alter certain specifics within the legal tradition, and when an observant community comes to accept, reject, or modify those alterations, they are hardly "breaking with tradition." That phrase, it seems to me, involves something more fundamental—for example, claiming that the law is not binding, that it does not require but recommends, which is to say that it is not law at all. Rejecting an occasional *Gesetz* is a normal activity within a tradition over time; truly subverting the tradition would involve rejecting the *Gebot*. (Here I refer once again to Franz Rosenzweig's distinction between *Gesetz* and *Gebot* in Jewish life: a *Gesetz* is a specific law or legal practice, which Rosenzweig regards as humanly authored, whereas *Gebot* is the nonspecific divine command that underlies all of the *Gesetze* in Judaism's legal systems.)[6]

Any revision of a specific law within a legal tradition is an act of continuity rather than of rupture, for such revisions make it possible for the legal tradition to endure. This remains the case even when the alteration bears weighty theological or practical ramifications. Early biblical documents (for example, Exodus 20.24–25) permitted Israelites to offer sacrifices at sundry altars throughout the Land of Israel. Later authors (for example, the D school in Deuteronomy 12) insisted that they be offered only at the one Temple in Jerusalem. In so doing, D rejected the ancient Israelite theology that I call the fluidity model, according to which God could be physically present at many cult sites simultaneously.[7] Further, by limiting sacrifice to one location, D effectively removed the sacrificial cult from the everyday life of the majority of the Judean population.[8] In short, the centralization of the sacrificial cult profoundly affected the beliefs and the religious experience of Judeans. And yet it would be misleading to portray the elements of continuity that the scribes work into Deuteronomy as nothing more than a mask whose purpose was to conceal a discrepancy between themselves and their predecessors. D's law, no less than the law from Exodus 20, provided Israel with a tool to express covenantal loyalty to the God Yhwh. The way most Judeans expressed that loyalty on a day-to-day level changed as a result of cult centralization; perceptions of Yhwh's nature changed as well; but D did nothing to break with covenant loyalty itself. In stressing disruption and characterizing elements of continuity as "a rhetoric of concealment . . . that served to camouflage the actual literary history of the laws,"[9] Levinson could create a misimpression. In this regard he typifies the way most scholars of religion describe the process of interpretation in the Bible and in rabbinic literature.

The overemphasis on novelty among modern scholars and their failure to notice continuity has been criticized by Jon Levenson (who, as another descendant of the ancient tribe responsible for the composition of D, has a last name that is inconveniently similar to that of Bernard Levinson, the scholar against whom I am using him as a foil). The truth is that the rabbis, even when innovating, were, as Jon Levenson puts it, "deeply conservative."[10] The same must be said of biblical scribes, for they limited their innovations to changes within the legal system. Consequently, it is problematic to speak of radical subversion of prior authorities. The root and trunk of E's law code is not subverted by the D authors or the rabbis after them. Those sages confine themselves to reorienting the branches, pruning some leaves, and grafting a new stalk here or there. The tree remains in place, strengthened rather than uprooted, still available to those who hold fast to it and support it.

Thus, I would characterize the theological implications of inner-biblical revision and exegesis differently than many of my colleagues.[11] The relationship between continuity and innovation in the Bible and in postbiblical tradition does not always involve tension. A similar conclusion emerges when we consider the source of the law's authority. Bernard Levinson points out that Mesopotamian legal collections attribute their laws to a human king, whereas biblical texts (whose legal collections closely resemble Mesopotamian prototypes in form and phrasing) attribute their laws to God. This attribution added the trope of divine revelation to an ancient legal tradition. "That trope of divine revelation," he suggests, "had a far-reaching impact upon the literary and intellectual life of ancient Israel. There is a clear relationship between textual voice and textual authority, so that attributing a legal text to God literally gives that text ultimate authority."[12] Jews to this day remain under the thrall of that trope, so much so that for many Jews questioning the divine nature of that voice leads to the breakdown of the halakhic system. What I have come to show in this book is that this questioning need not destroy the authority of the Torah's law. On the contrary, some of the same biblical authors who utilize this trope are the ones who began to undermine it: they not only attributed their legal traditions to God; they also problematized that attribution. Already in biblical times, the process of interpretation reintroduced humans into the creation of law and authority. The divinely attributed laws found in the Pentateuch first emerged out of human traditions of an ever-growing Oral Torah, and law continues to emerge from Oral Torah to this day. It is crucial to note the

paradoxical order in which the creation of law and the bestowal of authority proceed: Israel composes a law, which God then gives to Israel. We saw
earlier that this surprising order is already recognized, in specific cases, by
the rabbis (see b. Makkot 23b; b. Megillah 7a; Ruth Rabbah 4:5).[13] Scribes in
ancient Israel, who had notions of authorship very different from our own,
were aware of the mixture of human and divine elements underlying laws
they described as passing from God to Moses. Later readers can recover the
original notions of authority that animated the work of those scribes only
with some effort.

Bernard Levinson eloquently poses the problem raised by these considerations of revelatory and interpretive authority:

> In a legal and literary culture where the divine or prophetic voice has pride
> of place, what is the place of the human voice? ... How does a culture with a
> concept of divine revelation address the problem of legal change? How can
> legal texts, once viewed as divinely revealed, be revised to fit new circum-
> stances without compromising their—or God's—authority?[14]

The problem to which Levinson points becomes considerably less acute
when we are in the realm of what Idel (borrowing a term from Tillich, as
we saw in chapter 3) calls correlational theology. In that realm the vectors
connecting heaven and earth include not only descending ones that impart
authority but also ascending ones that respond to God's command by for-
mulating specific laws. The interplay of these vectors produced a tradition
that was both human and divine from the very beginning. Consequently,
the addition of another human voice poses no threat to the authority of
the divine voice. On the contrary, by responding anew to the divine call,
later Jews reaffirm the ongoing vitality of God's nonverbal command. The
emphasis of participatory theology on the human voice encourages us to
realize that covenantal law always involves dialogue. The possibility that law
may evolve—whether because new human voices enter the dialogue or because God corrects a misinterpretation of the divine will—is ever present.
Further, the fact that the Bible frequently portrays God as changing God's
mind encourages considerable doubt as to whether law given by this deity
really is unchanging. At least in the way God relates to humanity, the Bible
portrays God as fallible,[15] and this portrayal empowers not only a correlational theology but also a correlational halakhah.

But a correlational halakhah or an evolving law remains just that: law.
In spite of their many differences, all the Pentateuchal sources agree that

the event at Sinai or Ḥoreb was not merely revelation but lawgiving. While they present varied lists of *Gesetze*, they speak with one voice in regard to *Gebot*. This point warrants emphasis, because one can imagine some readers jumping to an unfounded conclusion based on the variety of views in the Pentateuch and in postbiblical Jewish thought regarding revelation. One might infer from this plurality of opinion that the boundaries of authentic Jewish thought are infinitely elastic. Such an inference betrays our sources. What unites the maximalist and minimalist schools of interpretation we discussed earlier is greater than what divides them: they agree that Israel must worship one God, no more and (this is the important point for the modern Jew) no less; they concur that Israel must express its loyalty to God by observing a binding covenantal law. Without these beliefs, no form of Judaism can claim to go back to Sinai or to be based on the Pentateuch, its sources, or its successors.

But the differences between maximalist and minimalist interpretations of the event at Sinai are consequential. For the maximalist, halakhic practice hinges on the notion that specifics of the law either came directly from heaven or follow from interpretations based on the precise wording of a text whose every letter, vowel, and cantillation mark were penned by God. If the *Gesetze* themselves are the work of God or, through exegesis, only a single step removed from God, then the extent to which human authorities can change them will be limited. Insofar as one of the details of the system is that Jews are to follow the rulings of each generation's sages,[16] the possibility of modest change within the system exists for maximalist sages. But they are likely to alter that system with great hesitancy. Furthermore, if I am sure that the details of the law I observe come from heaven, then I will believe my actions correspond precisely to the will of God. I may consequently develop an extraordinary spiritual confidence, which can easily devolve into arrogance. There is nothing quite so dangerous as human beings who think they know exactly what the deity wants—and nothing so lacking the humility that consciousness of our created status should engender. Empirical evidence abounds demonstrating the correlation between certainty regarding God's will, on the one hand, and arrogance, inflexibility, and intolerance, on the other.

The attitudes toward halakhic change and religious certainty that flow from the participatory theory of revelation will be entirely different.[17] People who regard the *Gesetze* as Israel's attempts to translate the *Gebot* will feel obligated to carry out the *Gesetze* even as they are aware that it is possible that the translation occasionally errs. As a result, halakhic observance among minimalist interpreters should avoid the arrogance that can mar observance among some maximalists. And yet, here lurks a grave danger. The virtue of observance that is unsure of itself, taken to an extreme, leads to the sin of nonobservance. Empirical evidence for this assertion is, alas, as abundant as evidence of the dangers that result from theological certainty. The question of the law's malleability also appears in a new light when seen from within the participatory theory. If the *Gesetze* from the outset were part of Israel's response to divine *Gebot*, then it is entirely appropriate that the nation Israel and its sages today should strive to hear God's will more clearly and to alter details of the *Gesetze*—but only so long as the *Gebot* remains unaffected. This caveat is crucial, because greater willingness to alter *Gesetze* in the modern period correlates very closely with the loss of a sense of *Gebot*. Consequently, even though the participatory theology provides a theoretical underpinning for a binding but malleable halakhic system, it also forces us to confront the practical question of how to change the law, how much to change it, and how fast to change it.

Does the participatory theology provide any guidance on the means and the extent of halakhic change? In chapter 3, I pointed out the importance of the talmudic dictum פוק חזי מאי עמא דבר ("Go out and see what the people are doing"; b. Berakhot 45a, b. Eruvin 14b, b. Menaḥot 35b). In consonance with this dictum, it is observant Jewish communities, even more than the sages of each generation, that ultimately determine what Jewish law is.[18] This idea was famously stated by Solomon Schechter:

> The centre of authority is actually removed from the Bible and placed in some living body. . . . This living body, however, is not represented by any section of the nation, or any corporate priesthood, or Rabbihood, but by the collective conscience of Catholic Israel. . . . The norm as well as the sanction of Judaism is the practice actually in vogue. Its consecration is the consecration of general use—or, in other words, of Catholic Israel.[19]

What Schechter presents here—at once an empirical observation and a religious prescription—follows naturally from the participatory theory of revelation. If Jews of all generations were present at Sinai, then Jews of all generations received the responsibility to participate in the response to revelation we call Torah. The authority that emanates from God at Sinai is offered to all those who witness the event. But the Catholic Israel that decides what is Torah does not include all Jews; it is limited to those Jews who observe the law. After all, the reason Catholic Israel or כלל ישראל can change the law is that God gives it to Israel, and one has some right to alter one's own property. The fact that God gives, however, does not mean that all Israel has received. Only those Jews who accept the law take ownership in it; and the only way to accept the law is to observe the law. (This statement is tautological. One does not, for example, accept law by studying it, because if one merely studies it, it is not yet law; it is merely an academic exercise.) One can imagine very radical changes being introduced into the law by communities that observe it—but only by those communities. Authority, which God offers freely to all Israel, belongs to a self-selecting subgroup. This observation has far-reaching ramifications for evaluating the legitimacy of halakhic changes proposed among contemporary Jewish communities.

The malleability of the law is appropriate, because we realize that our forebears' acts of translation were fallible. This principle, however, is a double-edged sword. Insofar as we, too, innovate, we, too, may err. Just as our ancestors and forebears in ancient Israel must have misunderstood God's will when they authored the law requiring us to kill Amalekite babies in Exodus 17 and Deuteronomy 25, so, too, is it possible that we are sometimes mistaken as we attempt to apply God's command to our time. If we lack the humility to admit this, we ought not alter the *Gesetze*. We have the right to change the tradition that is joint property we share with God and with our forebears, but only if we do so in fear and trembling. The awesome responsibility of interpreting and applying God's command cannot be an exercise in shaping the tradition in our own image, in making it hew to our predilections. Thus, the minimalist tradition can provide a foundation for halakhic change, but the humility so essential to the minimalist approach also tempers the pace and depth of change. The covenant formed at Sinai is correlational, but it is not a contract between equals. Modern Jews eagerly embrace the idea of a dialogical covenant; we are comfortable with, indeed delighted by, the notion that we are God's partners. We have failed, however, to acknowledge the covenant's hierarchical side. Consequently, we cannot claim to have fully embraced the Sinai covenant, for in this covenant, there is a master and there are slaves, and as Leviticus 25.42 and 55 state clearly, the Jewish nation are the slaves. God did not tell Pharaoh, "Let My people go, because freedom is a good thing," but "Let My people go, so that they may serve Me" (Exodus 7.16, 7.26, 8.16, 9.1, 9.13, 10.3). Redemption from Egyptian slavery carries little value on its own in the Pentateuch, which does not find the notion of Israel's slavery inherently bothersome. The Pentateuch is concerned, rather, with the question of whom the slaves serve, and how.

If revelation is a dialogue, then I need to recall that in a dialogue, mine is not the only voice. Participating in any dialogue requires at times that one stop talking so that one can listen—how much the more so in a dialogue in which we are mere vassals! Part of our job in the Sinaitic dialogue is to be silent in God's presence in order to be open to God's voice.[20] Further, we need to attend to the voices of the vassals who came before us. As we stand at Sinai, we remain in the presence of earlier members of Catholic Israel, whose voices in this dialogue continue to carry weight. The community of which we are part includes preceding generations, to whom we are responsible.[21] For this reason, it is appropriate to allow older texts to moderate the pace of change.[22]

While the participatory theology teaches that Jews create Torah, it does not suggest that every idea expressed by a Jew is Torah. According to Shemot Rabbah 47:1, any question a student asks a master is Torah; it was revealed to Moses at Sinai. But parallels to this passage (y. Pe'ah 4a [2:6]; Wayiqra Rabbah 22:1; Qohelet Rabbah 1:29 and 5:6) indicate that only some answers students provide are Torah—specifically, those stated by keen-witted or experienced students in the presence of their master. Answers from less experienced students and comments made outside the hierarchical community of Jewish learning are not included in what God showed Moses.[23] Together, these sources prompt the realization that there are no illegitimate questions—and this realization is important for contemporary Jews on the right. These sources also acknowledge that there are answers outside the bounds of Torah—and this acknowledgment is important for contemporary Jews on the left.

Some textual interpretations, legal rulings, and theological teachings are out of bounds. Which additions and alterations are Torah, and which go beyond the Oral Torah's invisible but real boundaries? Asking this question is crucial, but answering it on philosophical, theological, or hermeneutic levels is impossible.[24] And yet the realization that observant communities ultimately determine what is Torah shows that a reasoned answer is unnecessary, because on a practical level the answer is quite simple: Come back in five hundred years and look around. What are religious Jews doing? What are they studying? What shapes who they are? That is Torah. Which contributions of twenty-first-century Judaism have they discarded? Which ones have they never even heard of? That is not Torah. In the year 50 CE, there was no criterion that allowed one to say which forms of Judaism were the right ones. On a purely theoretical level nobody could prove that the traditions of the Pharisees and the earliest rabbis were Torah while the writings of the Qumran sect and the teachings of the Sadducees were not. But by the year 600, it had become clear that this was the case. There is no conclusive way to explain why the philosopher Philo's first-century attempt to fuse Plato and Judaism did not become Torah, whereas Maimonides's twelfth-century attempt to fuse Aristotle and Judaism did; but there is no denying that Philo's writings (which were not preserved by Jews but came down to us because they were copied by Christian clerics) are not Torah, whereas Maimonides's writings (despite all the opposition to them during his lifetime) are. Some people will not be satisfied by the simple answer I suggest for the question "Which of our innovations are really Torah?" since none of us will live to see the answer. But finding the answer is not expected of us. Our task is only to nurture, protect, and create Torah with as much honesty as possible, to live that Torah, to teach it, and to pass it on. We cannot complete that task, but we are not free to desist from it.

Ours is a time of tumultuous but uncertain change. We are aware of clamor all around us but unsure whether we can experience God's voice in the stillness that we hope will follow. We cannot know if we are expanding the bounds too much or too little, in the right direction or the wrong. I shall end, then, with two recent Hebrews texts that we can read as addressing the right proportion of innovation and conservation, of clamor and stillness. At least one of them was not intended to be a sacred text but (perhaps to its author's chagrin), it may well be subject to the heavenly decree of קיימו וקבלו ("Israel established and God accepted") that erases its pretense to be no more than a poem written by a human being.[25] We modern religious Jews find ourselves in the position of the speaker—or of the addressee?—to whom Yehudah Amichai gives voice:

Now, in the clamor and quaking before the silence,	עַכְשָׁיו בָּרַעַשׁ לִפְנֵי הַדְּמָמָה
I can tell you the things	אֲנִי יָכוֹל לְהַגִּיד לָךְ אֶת הַדְּבָרִים
That in the silence before the clamor I didn't say ...	אֲשֶׁר בַּדְּמָמָה לִפְנֵי הָרַעַשׁ לֹא אָמַרְתִּי...
See, we met where it was safe, in the corner	רְאִי, וְנִפְגַּשְׁנוּ בַּמָּקוֹם הַמֻּגָּן, בַּזָּוִית

Where history began to ascend,
quietly
and safely, faithfully, out of frightened hurried deeds.
And the voice began to tell a story in
the evening, by the children's bed.

My father was God and didn't know
it. He gave me
The Ten Commandments, not in
thunder and not in fury, not in fire
and not in a cloud
But gently and with love . . .
. . . And he said: I want to add
Two to the Ten Commandments:
The eleventh commandment,
"You shall not change,"
And the twelfth commandment,
"Surely you shall change." . . .[26]

בָּהּ הֶחֵלָה הַהִסְטוֹרְיָה לַעֲלוֹת, שְׁקֵטָה

וּבְטוּחָה מִן הַמַּעֲשִׂים הַנֶּחְפָּזִים.

וְהַקּוֹל הֵחֵל לְסַפֵּר בָּעֶרֶב, לְיַד מִטַּת הַיְלָדִים.

אָבִי הָיָה אֱ־לֹהִים וְלֹא יָדַע. הוּא נָתַן לִי

אֶת עֲשֶׂרֶת הַדִּבְּרוֹת לֹא בְּרַעַם וְלֹא בְּזַעַם,
לֹא בָּאֵשׁ וְלֹא בֶּעָנָן

אֶלָּא בְּרַכּוּת וּבְאַהֲבָה . . .
. . . וְאָמַר: אֲנִי רוֹצֶה לְהוֹסִיף
שְׁנַיִם לַעֲשֶׂרֶת הַדִּבְּרוֹת:
הַדִּבֵּר הָאַחַד־עָשָׂר, "לֹא תִּשְׁתַּנֶּה"

וְהַדִּבֵּר הַשְּׁנֵים־עָשָׂר, "הִשְׁתַּנֵּה, תִּשְׁתַּנֶּה" . . .

Notes

Introduction

1. My phrasing here borrows from my colleague Gary Anderson's summary of my approach.

2. Abbreviated hereafter in notes as Heschel, *TmH*; English translation, with very useful notes, available in Heschel, *Heavenly Torah*, which is abbreviated as *HT*. Heschel's Hebrew title can be understood as a phrase, in which case it defines the book's subject as a descriptive study: "Torah from heaven in the lens of the generations," or, less literally, "The notion of revelation as viewed through Jewish tradition." But the title can also be translated as a sentence that makes a constructive theological claim: "Revelation occurs through the lens of the generations"— that is, "Torah comes to us through the medium of tradition itself." No doubt Heschel intends both senses.

3. Silman, *Voice*. For the argument that the participatory theology of revelation is far more loyal to the traditions of medieval Jewish philosophy than most scholars have realized, see also Samuelson, *Revelation*, chaps. 2 and 7, esp. pp. 173–75. For the claim that Heschel's philosophy of revelation has deep roots in classical rabbinic literature, see Perlman, *Abraham Heschel's Idea*, 119–33; Even-Chen, *Voice*, 160–79.

4. See Viezel's articles, "Divine Content," "Rashbam on Moses' Role," and "Moses' Literary License," which attend, respectively, to the views of ibn Ezra, Rashbam, and Abarbanel. While Viezel primarily examines the work of medieval commentators, he also notes that texts of the talmudic era are much less concerned than is often assumed with the technicalities of how God's revelation was reduced to the written form we have in our Pentateuch, and he points out the paucity of texts within the rabbinic corpus that actually claim that God dictated the Pentateuch to Moses word for word. See "Rashbam on Moses' Role," 178–80; "Moses' Literary License," 606 n. 11. Nonetheless, the stenographic theory is articulated by some authorities in the talmudic era; see, for example, the view of Resh Lakish (y. Shekalim 6:1, 49d;

cf. b. Berakhot 5a [in manuscript versions]) that the entire Pentateuch (and not only the Decalogue) was written down on the tablets that Moses received at Sinai. Concerning this view, see Shweka, "Tablets," 363–66.

5. In characterizing compositional studies performed by biblical critics as fundamentally *respectful* toward the Bible, I argue against a fallacy prevalent among theologically and literarily inclined readers. Many of those readers regard biblical criticism as destructive, because (such readers believe) it undermines attempts to read biblical texts as coherent pieces of literature. This view misconstrues compositional criticism. As Barton, *Nature*, 43–44, astutely explains, the goal of compositional critics is to recover the coherence of biblical texts by reconstructing their underlying documents. Compositional criticism attempts to find harmonious, complete, integrated literary works that our biblical texts encompass. This goal is achieved especially by the earliest Documentary critics in the nineteenth century and by the neo-Documentary school of contemporary scholars such as Baruch Schwartz and his students. On the unreadability of the canonical Torah and the readability of its sources, see Schwartz, "Torah," esp. 214–15. On modern scholarship as motivated by respect for scripture, see Enns, *Inspiration*, 107, and Sharp, *Wrestling*, 45–75, esp. 49.

6. The same exegetical and historical claim—that is, that biblical critical analyses can uncover surprising continuities linking the Bible with later Judaism (and especially with kabbalistic theosophy)—is central to my book, Sommer, *Bodies*; there the topic is not revelation and authority but conceptions of divinity.

7. On the centrality of questions concerning religious authority for modern Judaism, see Eisen, *Rethinking*, 209–10. On its centrality throughout Heschel's work, see Eisen, "Re-Reading Heschel," 6.

8. For a programmatic discussion of this model, see Sommer, "Dialogical," which serves as the theoretical underpinning to this book. Several recent works similarly emphasize the theological and anthropological richness of the Bible's record of ancient Israelite conversation and debate: Goldingay, *Theological Diversity*; Brueggemann, *Theology*; Knohl, *Divine Symphony*; and Carasik, *Bible's Many Voices*.

9. See Heschel, *Prophets*, 525. Cf. similar remarks on Schleiermacher's problematic legacy for the notion of revelation in Rosenzweig, *Star* [Hallo], 99–101 = *Star* [Galli], 110–11.

10. Here it becomes evident why I focus attention on Rosenzweig rather than on his close associate Martin Buber. On the preferability, from a Jewish point of view, of Rosenzweig's view of revelation over Buber's precisely because Buber's view does not lead to command, see Samuelson, *Revelation*, 60, 74–75, and 111. Cf. Amir, *Reason*, 295.

11. On the neglected question of how scripture views itself and what biblical documents suggest about their place in the community they serve, see Hurowitz, "Proto-Canonization," 31–48, esp. 40.

Chapter 1. Artifact or Scripture?

1. On the relationship between the categories of scripture and classic, see Wilfred Cantwell Smith, *What Is Scripture*, 176–95; Stendahl, "Bible as a Classic."

2. In this regard, people committed to reading Bible as scripture come closer to describing its original aim better than those biblical critics who insist that the Bible does not speak to us. It is hardly surprising that an ancient text intends to speak to audiences beyond its own time; as Richard Tupper points out to me, Thucydides tells us he writes "not to win the applause of the moment but as a possession for all time" (Thucydides, *Peloponnesian*, 1:22).

3. On Torah as addressed to the whole nation Israel, see Greenberg, *Studies*, 11–24, esp. 11–12. See also the astute comments of Jacob Wright, "Commemoration," 443–44. As we shall see in chapter 5, Deuteronomy especially makes explicit that it addresses the whole nation, including generations not yet born.

4. This evidence includes respects in which the Hebrew Bible resembles other ancient Near Eastern literature. Literary conventions used by authors of the Hebrew Bible were typical of those of ancient Near Eastern literature. Further, biblical texts assume their audience holds views typical of ancient Near Eastern people—for example, these authors take it for granted that their audience believes that the earth floats atop a cosmic ocean and is anchored there by pillars.

5. My attempt to read the Bible at once as artifact and as scripture resembles Uriel Simon's effort to arrive at what he calls פשט קיומי, an existential reading of the Bible in its own literary and cultural context. People who seek פשט קיומי employ modern critical methods of reading while regarding themselves as an addressee of biblical texts. See Simon, *Seek Peace*, 44–45. On this correlation of descriptive and constructive concerns, see also the eloquent statement of Jon Levenson, "Religious Affirmation," 25–28.

6. See Wilfred Cantwell Smith, *What Is Scripture*; Graham, *Beyond*; and the brief but very insightful discussion in Graham, "Scripture." It is unfortunate that contemporary biblical scholars have for the most part failed to engage with these powerful and suggestive studies.

7. On the diverse understandings of what scripture is and how it functions in varied forms of these religions, see the essays in Holcomb, *Christian Theologies*, and Sommer, *Jewish Concepts*.

8. It comes as no surprise that scholars define *biblical criticism* in more than one way. My use of this term follows the characteristically insightful and balanced approach of Barton, *Nature*. I use the term to refer to a mode of reading that (1) is "concerned with the recognition of genre in [biblical] texts and with what follows from this about their possible meaning"; (2) shares with other branches of the humanities "a common concern for evidence and reason," as opposed to relying on authoritative religious tradition; and (3) "strives to be 'objective' in the sense that it tries to attend to what the text actually says and not to read

alien meanings into it," while recognizing the impossibility of perfectly attaining that objectivity or defining precisely what is alien (I quote from Barton, *Nature*, 5–7). Further, while biblical criticism shares with precritical and postcritical approaches "a desire to read the text in its coherence, . . . biblical critics do not assume that all texts can in fact successfully be read in this holistic way," and they may therefore conclude that a given text is composite in nature (Barton, *Nature*, 30). I would add that the biblical critical attempts to understand genre and to avoid imposing alien readings depend especially on situating biblical texts in the linguistic, historical, and literary context of the ancient Near East, and thus involves frequent comparison with ancient Canaanite, Mesopotamian, Egyptian, Hittite, Persian, and Greek cultures. On the importance of this contextualization for almost all forms of biblical criticism, see Collins, *Bible after Babel*, 4; cf. Barton, *Nature*, 80–86.

Barton rightly emphasizes that people who argue against biblical criticism (whether for religious or literary reasons) usually overemphasize the historical dimension of the field. In fact many biblical critics do not focus on diachronic issues; the heart of modern biblical criticism, rather, lies in the area of genre recognition. (See esp. *Nature*, 31–68; for the argument that biblical criticism is essentially literary and linguistic rather than historical in nature, see also Barr, *Holy Scripture*, 105–26.) The threats that religious believers perceive from biblical criticism, however, stem largely from the diachronic components of biblical criticism. For this reason I focus on these diachronic components. My concern with compositional and historical issues throughout this book should not be taken as an indication that these are the only important tasks of the modern biblical scholar.

9. For a similar (and, at least for me, deeply influential) programmatic statement about Tanakh theology as spanning two fields and two types of commitment, one scholarly and one personal, see Moshe Goshen-Gottstein, "Tanakh Theology," 629–30.

10. See Jon Levenson, *Hebrew Bible, the Old Testament, passim*, but esp. chs. 1, 2, and 4, and Sommer, "Dialogical," esp. 8–14. Biblical theologians' self-delusion that their work is primarily descriptive provides a neat equilibrium with the work of biblical historians, since, as Barton, *Nature*, 38–39, has noted, "Most biblical historians turn out to be theologians in disguise."

11. I think, for example, of the foundational assumption of Walther Eichrodt that the Old Testament has an "essential coherence" with the New Testament (Eichrodt, *Theology*, 1:31)—an idea that would require us to admit that Jewish readers are unable to comprehend the essence of their scripture, which for them remains incoherent. For further examples, see the discussions of Levenson in the previous note. Not all Protestant biblical theologians make assumptions of this kind; see Brueggemann, *Theology*, and Rendtorff, *Canonical*.

12. I think here especially of books such as Barr, *Biblical Faith*; Oeming, *Gesamtbiblische Theologien*; Jon Levenson, *Sinai and Zion*; Jon Levenson, *Creation*;

Anderson, "Necessarium"; Anderson, "Biblical Origins"; Anderson, "To See." All these openly denominational studies have much to teach any student of the Bible. On the benefit of work that stems from one standpoint for those committed to another, see Ward, *Religion*, 36–42.

13. That this consensus was widespread does not mean that it met no challenges whatsoever. On ancient and medieval doubts concerning the self-consistency and accuracy of biblical texts, and rabbinic responses to these doubts, see Solomon, *Torah*, 113–32. On rabbinic and medieval views that the Prophets and Writings were the products of divine-human interaction and that their specific wording originates with human beings, see the essay on Jewish conceptions of the human factor in biblical prophecy in Greenberg, *Studies*, 405–19. On the views of some medievals that the Pentateuch's wording is largely by Moses, see the various studies by Viezel I cite in the bibliography.

14. Many works introduce the Documentary Hypothesis and other theories regarding the composition of the Torah, describe the development of these theories, and assay the types of evidence that support them. For a compelling and elegant presentation of what has been called the neo-Documentarian approach (according to which there are four and only four sources that were brought together to form the Pentateuch, a few additional texts here and there notwithstanding), see Schwartz, "Torah," and Baden, *Composition*. A readable if quirky presentation of the Documentary Hypothesis is found in Richard Elliott Friedman, *Who Wrote*. A detailed study of the development of the Documentary Hypothesis and the reasoning it employs is found in the first volume of Carpenter and Harford-Battersby, *Hexateuch*. (Carpenter and Harford present the classic version of the Documentary Hypothesis, which distinguishes various strata within J and E, as opposed to the more elegant neo–Documentary Hypothesis associated with Schwartz.)

More recently, many scholars, especially in Europe, have questioned aspects of the Documentary Hypothesis and have put forward alternative models for understanding the crystallization of the Pentateuch, especially in regard to what Documentarians consider the J and E material. These newer theories emphasize not only the combination of originally separate documents but a series of supplements to older textual cores and scribal and/or editorial interpolations that bring together diverse material. Crucial works that paved the way for these newer approaches are Rendtorff, *Problem*, and Blum, *Studien*. An especially useful overview of these theories is found in Carr, "Controversy and Convergence." Another recent presentation sympathetic to these trends is found in Ska, *Introduction*. Overviews of both older theories and newer theories can be found in Rofé, *Introduction*, 159–298, and Gertz et al., *Handbook*, 237–351 (both of whom are sympathetic to the newer theories), as well as in Nicholson, *Pentateuch* (who defends the older theories from the attacks of the more recent scholarship). A detailed yet lucid defense of the neo-Documentary approach to the material that is the main source of contention between Documentarians and the newer models is found in Baden, *J, E, and the Redaction.* Essays representing both schools of thought are found in Dozeman, Schmid, and Schwartz, *Pentateuch: International Perspective.* A good sense of the debate between the two schools can be gained by comparing Baden, "Continuity," with Schmid, "Genesis and Exodus."

15. Overviews of these theories are legion. Especially useful for relatively brief overviews are standard dictionaries of the Bible, such as Sakenfeld, *The New Interpreter's Dictionary of the Bible;* Freedman, *Anchor Bible Dictionary;* and Sukenik et al., *Encyclopaedia Biblica,* as well as various introductions to the Bible, such as Rofé, *Introduction;* Brettler, *How;* and Collins, *Introduction.*

16. See Schwartz, "Pentateuch as Scripture." Among other studies, see especially trenchant comments throughout Jon Levenson, *Hebrew Bible, Old Testament, passim,* but esp. ch. 4; Cooper, "Biblical Studies and Jewish Studies"; Samuelson, *Revelation,* 85–89; Alan Levenson, *Making.* On a wide variety of responses to historical criticism among Jewish thinkers, see Solomon, *Torah,* 158–271. Scholars can gain considerable theological, historical, and psychological insight into effects of biblical criticism on traditional Jews, along with an example of one type of response to it, from Potok, *In the Beginning.*

17. On the importance of this threat in Christian denominations, see, e.g., Collins, *Bible after Babel,* 6–7; on its particular consequence for Protestants, see Enns's treatment in Brettler, Enns, and Harrington, *Bible and the Believer,* 149–56. On the lesser import Jews tend to accord to historical and scientific challenges to biblical narratives, see Brettler, Enns, and Harrington, *Bible and the Believer,* 51–53 and 164. Concern with scripture's historicity is a recent development; it is shared by fundamentalist Protestants and anti-religious skeptics, who are equally influenced, in their thoroughly modern view of scripture, by historical critics. On the innovative rather than traditional nature of fundamentalists' views of scripture and their close resemblance to historical critics, see Wilfred Cantwell Smith, *What Is Scripture,* 364 n. 54.

18. Biblical scholars will note my careful phrasing here. See Hendel, "Exodus," esp. 604–8, as well as Na'aman, "Exodus," both of whom suggest that biblical references to Egyptian bondage may be based on memories of enslavement to Egyptian overlords in Canaan during the Middle or Late Bronze Age. For a possible reference to Israelite enslavement within Egypt, see Rendsburg, "Date," esp. 517–18. For a devastating critique of contemporary claims that the Exodus cannot be based on historical memories, see Hoffmeier, *Israel in Egypt,* and Hoffmeier, *Ancient Israel in Sinai.* One need not agree with Hoffmeier's own positive conclusions, which go vastly beyond the available evidence, to recognize that Hoffmeier exposes the ignorance and faulty reasoning of those who deny a historical kernel to the Exodus story.

19. See Barton, *Nature,* 31–33. Barton proposes that historical criticism can also have a significant theological dimension without impairing its critical or historical

quality; see Barton, "Should," and cf. Barton, "Alttestamentliche Theologie." See further Barr, *Holy Scripture*, 23–48 and 105–26. Similarly, Ward, *Religion*, 197–200, 232–58, 342, lays out a middle way: he rejects the hubristic historicism that claims to render the founding of faith on any historical claim as indefensible; at the same time, he acknowledges historical criticism's contribution to religious self-understanding and humility.

20. Legaspi, *Death*, 30.

21. Examples of the reductionist approach to biblical texts, whose occasional validity as explanatory model does little to diminish its pervasive shallowness, are so common in biblical studies that citing examples in a comprehensive fashion would require a separate volume. To cite one well-known work: this phenomenon is found throughout Richard Elliott Friedman, *Who Wrote*. Friedman speaks of each of the four Pentateuchal sources exclusively in terms of the political, social, and economic needs each allegedly serves, without ever exploring the possibility that these texts might have some connection to religious or humanistic ideas. That the differences among the four sources might relate to the varied ways they perceive God, the world, and humanity is barely hinted at in the book, except in vague comments in the conclusion on the theological heterogeneity that resulted from the redactor's work (234–41). Friedman's reductionism is the more noteworthy in light of the fact that he elsewhere deals sensitively with religious and humanistic meanings of biblical texts, especially in Richard Elliott Friedman, *Disappearance* (reprinted as Richard Elliott Friedman, *Hidden Face*). For a lengthier discussion of this phenomenon in biblical studies generally, see Sommer, "Dating."

  Because source criticism of the Pentateuch is so often coupled with pseudo-historicist reductionism, it is worth emphasizing that one can be a Pentateuchal source critic without eschewing the search for literary meaning. Attempts at viewing the differences among the four Pentateuchal sources as reflecting larger differences in their theological and anthropological outlooks can be found, e.g., in von Rad, *Old Testament Theology*, vol. 1; Weinfeld, "Theological Currents"; Blum, *Studien*, 287–332 ; Schwartz, "Origin," 252–65; Mordecai Breuer, *Pirqei Bereshit*, especially the programmatic statements in 1:11–19 and 48–54; Sommer, *Bodies*.

22. In this regard, biblical criticism is simply one manifestation of broader historicist trends in modern Europe. On those widely studied trends and theological critiques of them in the work of thinkers like Ernest Troeltsch, see, e.g., Myers, *Resisting, passim* and esp. 2; on their relationship to biblical theology specifically, see Harrington's discussion of Troeltsch in Brettler, Enns, and Harrington, *Bible and Believer*, 94–95, as well as Ward, *Religion*, 232–35. Like Harrington and Ward, I reject the notion that historical study inevitably leads to reductionist and anti-transcendental results. For an example of anti-historicist thinking that nonetheless allows an important place for historiography, see Myers's discussion of Hermann Cohen's hope for nonhistoricist,

nonreductionist historical study at 40 and 50–51, and Sommer, "Dating," 104–7. As far as Cohen's approach to biblical monotheism goes, it is worth noting that Cohen's hope was realized in Kaufmann's massive *Toledot*, which is historical but nonreductionist. The congruence of *Toledot* with Cohen's conception of biblical monotheism has been widely noted; see esp. Schweid, "Biblical Critic."

23. This effect of biblical criticism is no coincidence. Diminishing the Bible (in particular, limiting its political influence) was a central goal of the earliest biblical critics, especially Spinoza and Hobbes. See, e.g., Alan Levenson, *Making*, 14, 19, 21; Legaspi, *Death*, 3–26.

24. On the separation between the (positively evaluated) religion of ancient Israel and the (lifeless, stagnant) religion of the Jews in the work of historical critics, see Jon Levenson, *Hebrew Bible, the Old Testament*, 42. On Michaelis's attempt to divorce postbiblical Jews and the Hebrew Bible, see Legaspi, *Death*, 84–93, who is disturbingly credulous in regard to Michaelis's claims.

25. Cf. Collins, *Bible after Babel*, 5, and cf. 10–11.

26. On literary competence as central to biblical criticism, see Barton, *Reading*, 10–19, and Brettler, *How*, 13–17. On the relevance of ancient Near Eastern literatures for achieving this goal, see, e.g., Greenstein, "Interpreting."

27. On the development of the idea that Genesis 2–3 deals with sin, see Anderson, *Genesis of Perfection*, esp. 197–99, 207–10.

28. So far as I know, the first person to note the importance of this absence was Fromm, *You Shall*, 23. A nuanced view of sin in this story is presented by Bird, *Missing Persons*, 191–93.

29. See Fishbane, *Text and Texture*, 18; Evans, *Paradise Lost*, 19–20; and Sommer, *Bodies*, 112–15. Even the death sentence the expulsion precipitates may be seen as a moral gift rather than a punishment; see Greenberg, *Al Hammiqra*, 218–20. For balanced accounts of the complexities of fall and ascent in Genesis 2–3, see esp. Jobling, "Myth," 20–24; Barr, *Garden*, 4–14; and Krüger, "Sündenfall?"

30. Naidoff, "Man"; Meyers, *Discovering*, 47–94, esp. 87–88.

31. For additional sources, see Urbach, *Sages*, 649–92, and Schäfer, *Studien*, 198–213.

32. See von Rad, *Old Testament Theology*, 1:308–23, 2:169–76. For a discussion of the tensions between biblical texts that regard God's promises to the Davidic monarchy as absolute and biblical texts that regard it as conditional, see Frisch, "Concept," 61–65. For a subtle discussion of the relationship between these readings of Davidic promise within biblical scholarship itself, see Watts, "Psalm 2," *passim* and esp. 74–76.

33. For additional parallels, see Paul, *Studies*, 46–52, and the brief but helpful discussion in Tigay, *Deuteronomy*, 147–50 and notes. Even if one does not go as far as David P. Wright, *Inventing*, by positing the Covenant Code's direct dependence specifically on Hammurapi's Laws, it remains clear that at the very least biblical law collections arise from the same legal tradition as Mesopotamian ones.

34. For an especially famous and influential example of this distinction, see Well-hausen, *Prolegomena*, 365–425, who maintains (or assumes) that Israelite religion in its earliest and purest form was fresh, natural, spontaneous, and the realm of the individual; later this religion shrank into the artificial set of ordinances and institutions seen in Priestly texts such as Leviticus. (I summarize Wellhausen's views with language borrowed from 411–12, 422. On Deuteronomy as the crucial pivot between these two religions, see 362.)

35. See, e.g., the disparaging use of the term *midrash* in ibid., 227. Later scholars, both Jewish and Christian, demonstrated that attention to the Jewish interpretive tradition is a crucial aid to the modern critical interpreter of the Bible. See, e.g., Childs, *Exodus*, x, xv–xvi (note his positive use of the term *midrash* in, e.g., Childs, "Psalm Titles"); Rendtorff, "Rabbinic"; Greenberg, *Understanding*, 4–7.

36. Especially in the document, *Nostra Aetate*, available at http://www.vatican.va/archive/hist_councils/ii_vatican_council/documents/vat-ii_decl_19651028_nostra-aetate_en.html. See in particular sec. 4.

37. Another factor that helps Jewish scholars to adopt the firewall mentality is the strong tendency of some parts of rabbinic culture to downplay the importance of biblical study. In traditional *yeshivot*, students devote little or (more typically) no time to studying the Bible; among Orthodox Jews, ordination as a rabbi depends on talmudic and above all halakhic learning, not on knowledge of the Bible. Thus, the supersessionist position of some modern biblical critics dovetails with the practices of some intensely religious rabbinic Jews for whom Judaism is the religion of the Talmud, not of ancient Israel. The firewall mentality contradicts basic teachings of Judaism regarding the continuity that links Abraham and (above all) Moses to a contemporary *rosh yeshivah*, but on a practical level it poses no real problem: the *biblical* Bible, as opposed to the midrashic Bible, had already been largely left outside the boundaries of many *yeshivot* in any event.

38. See Davis, "Losing a Friend," 83–94.

39. My thinking about this issue benefited from my time at the Wabash Center for Teaching and Learning in Theology and Religion, where I discussed the issue with colleagues from various seminaries in North America. For incisive reflections on this state of affairs, see Seitz, *Word*, 3–27, esp. 9–10, 14–15, 27.

40. Proponents of this postscriptural conception of the Bible, especially among Israeli secularists, speak with great seriousness and integrity. See, e.g., Zakovitch, "Scripture." See further the collection of documents in Shapira, *Bible and Israeli*, and, on the return to Bible in Zionist and early Israeli thought, Alan Levenson, *Making*, 96–132, and Amir, *Small Still Voice*, 200–201. For a person who strives to be a religious Jew, however, these attempts cannot be fully satisfying, even though they have much to teach the modern religious Jew.

41. See further Urbach, "Search," along with Uriel Simon's collection of rabbinic texts relating to this article at 28–41. See further Hartman and Buckholtz, *God*.

When I say that denying modern biblical scholarship is dishonest, I am speaking of modern Jews who, on an intellectual level, acquiesce to the validity of the main findings of biblical criticism but who, through a technique of compartmentalization or self-deception, pretend for religious purposes that they do not regard these findings as valid. I am not, however, referring to Jews who genuinely find the conceptions of scripture of Late Antiquity or the Middle Ages convincing. After all, much of the evidence used by modern scholars to argue, for example, that the Pentateuch is the product of multiple authors was known to midrashic interpreters. Given the assumptions those interpreters made in good faith about the nature of biblical language (on which see Sommer, "Concepts of Scriptural Language"), it was possible to explain away each individual textual oddity that centuries later led to the development of Pentateuchal source criticism. People who makes these assumptions honestly find that biblical criticism poses little threat. For those of us who do not fully share those assumptions, however, honesty requires that we confront the challenge of biblical criticism.

42. To be sure, not all ancient and medieval Jewish thinkers would agree with this "if" statement. Some thinkers, including Maimonides and Abraham ibn Daud, regard these disagreements as tragic results of human fallibility. On this question, see especially the helpful discussion in Halbertal, *People*, 54–64, 161–62.

43. For a similar attempt in a Protestant context (which is admirably open to the possibility of analogous attempts in non-Protestant contexts), see Oeming, *Gesamtbiblische Theologien*, 232–41, especially Oeming's proposal on 235 for a dynamic, back-and-forth discussion between biblical texts and later theology. (On scripture's crucial role of renewing tradition, see also Congar, *Meaning*, 125.) In starting from the conclusions of modern biblical criticism but insisting that we ought not stop there, I am suggesting a Jewish analogue to what Brevard Childs attempted and what his disciple Christopher Seitz achieves; see esp. Seitz, *Word*, 14–15.

44. Nonetheless, I am influenced by several predecessors, though they are less explicit about these goals than I am. See my discussion of three scholars (Moshe Greenberg, Jacob Milgrom, and Yochanan Muffs) whose impact on my own work is immense: Sommer, *Reclaiming*. Alan Levenson points out a similar project in the work of several Jewish scholars. His discussion of Benno Jacob is especially revealing in this regard; see Alan Levenson, *Making*, 65–71. See also the discussion of Yehezkel Kaufmann in Jindo, "Concepts," 231, 241–42. My work differs from several of these figures in my desire to recover the Bible for Jews not only as classic but as scripture. This goal is less pronounced in the work of most Jewish biblical critics, but it was central to Buber and Rosenzweig; see Jonathan Cohen, "Concepts." It is also central to the work of מורי ורבי, my own teacher, Michael Fishbane, most explicitly in *Garments of Torah* (esp. 33–36, 121–33) and in *Sacred Attunement* (esp. 46–107), but also implicitly in *Text and Texture* and *Biblical Interpretation*.

45. Simon, *Seek Peace*, 283. For illuminating descriptions of how modern approaches to biblical studies are difficult for many contemporary American Protestants, and for discussions that make clear that these problems are, at root, psychological and sociological rather than theological, see Sharp, *Wrestling*, *passim*, esp. 1–6, 45–48.

46. On the tendency of ancient Near Eastern thinkers not to articulate ideas abstractly but to exemplify them concretely and to intimate complexities through subtle variations, allusions, and puns, see Frankfort and Frankfort, "Myth and Reality," 6–15; Geller, *Sacred Enigmas*, *passim* and esp. 6; Geller, "Some Sound and Word Plays," 65–66; Geoffrey Miller, *Ways*, 16–20.

47. See Schechter, "Leopold Zunz," 98. For a similar emphasis on continuity that transcends the differences noted by more prosaic minds, see Rosenzweig, *FRHLT*, 233 (=Rosenzweig, *OJL*, 101).

48. See Fine, "Solomon Schechter," 17. Schechter's attempt to combat what I have called the firewall mentality also comes to the fore in his work on Ben Sira. For an engaging overview of this issue, see Hoffman and Cole, *Sacred Trash*, 43–61.

49. It is no coincidence that I am a faculty member at the Jewish Theological Seminary, which Schechter headed from 1902 to 1915, or that my children attend the Solomon Schechter School of Bergen County, having transferred there from the Solomon Schechter School of Chicagoland when we moved east.

50. See, most famously, his essay, "Higher Criticism—Higher Anti-Semitism," in Schechter, *Seminary Addresses*, 35–39. The views in this brief toast made at a dinner honoring Kaufman Kohler are not Schechter's most sophisticated statement on biblical scholarship. In subsequent chapters we will have occasion to quote more subtle remarks of his regarding the Bible's place in Judaism. Even in the toast Schechter objects not to methods of higher criticism, or even all its conclusions, but to their anti-Jewish use. On the complexities of his views, see further Fine, "Solomon Schechter."

Chapter 2. What Happened at Sinai?

1. On the ways different biblical sources treat the fate of these peoples, see Weinfeld, *Promise*. Contrary to what many Christian readers have assumed, the Torah does not consign all nations to this perdition; the vast majority of gentiles are not the object of these attacks. The Jewish Bible does not the divide the world into those chosen and those consigned to perdition; rather, it divides the world into those chosen (viz., Israel); those not chosen (the vast majority of humanity, who are not viewed negatively, and who often receive blessings identical to those promised to the chosen, as in the case of the descendants of Ishmael and Esau); the Canaanites, who are required to leave the land of Canaan to make room for Israel; and the tribe of the Amalekites, who are to be destroyed. On this categorization and its difference from the binary categoriza-

tion of the New Testament, see Kaminsky, *Yet I Loved*. Kaminsky's treatment is noteworthy because he exposes the tendentious misrepresentations of the biblical doctrine of election so common among liberal Christian thinkers, even as he avoids any evasion in his treatment of the laws of genocide.

2. On rabbinic and medieval attempts to ameliorate the moral sting of these passages by severely limiting them or effectively overturning them, see Greenberg, *Hassegullah*, esp. chs. 1 and 3; Greenberg, "Problematic"; Sagi, "Punishment"; Josef Stern, "Maimonides on Amaleq"; Lamm, "Amalek."

3. On rabbinic interpretations that effectively abrogate this law, see Halbertal, *Interpretive Revolutions*, 42–68.

4. See especially the articles in a special issue, in 1999, of *Textual Reasoning: The Journal of the Postmodern Jewish Philosophy Network*, with essays on this topic by Nancy Levene, Shaul Magid, Aryeh Cohen, and Michael Zank. For treatments of the issue by historical-critical scholars with keen interest in biblical theology, see Collins, "Zeal," and Moberly, "Election." For a comparativist who identifies the issue with honesty and sympathy, see Wilfred Cantwell Smith, *What Is Scripture*, 217, 224, 241. My sense is that Jewish scholars are more troubled by texts such as these in the Torah, while Christians attend to them more in the Psalms—which Jews barely address. On the latter, see, e.g., Zenger, *God of Vengeance*; Day, *Crying*, and Brueggemann, *Praying*. For Christian approaches to these issues outside the Psalter, see Brueggemann, *Theology*, 382–83 (on the Canaanites) as well as 359–62 (on the abusive God); Zenger, *Am Fuß*, 20–27; for a discussion of how Christian exegetes can wrestle with a troubling narrative from the Torah, see Stephen L. Cook, "Theological Exegesis." On premodern scholars' interest in these problems, see Solomon, *Torah*, 121–25, in addition to Solomon's own treatment at 248–59 and 318–20.

5. Similarly, Norbert Samuelson explains that moral problems of this sort make it philosophically impossible to believe in what I have called a stenographic theory of revelation. See Samuelson, *Revelation*, 96–101.

6. On differences between Rosenzweig and Heschel in this regard, see Neil Gillman, *Sacred Fragments*, 24–25.

7. Heschel, *God*, 274, 185, and 26, respectively.

8. It is difficult to pin Heschel down on the question of whether the Bible contains any wording or even specific content uttered by God. Even-Chen, *Voice*, 83, captures the duality and ambiguity well.

9. The first quotation is from Rosenzweig, *OJL*, 118 (in which he quotes Exodus 19.23 and 20.1 respectively), and the second from Rosenzweig, *FRHLT*, 285. Cf. Rosenzweig, *Star* [Hallo], 176–78 (= *Star* [Galli], 190–92). Nahum Glatzer expressed a kindred view of revelation, as Rosenzweig notes, *OJL*, 119 (= Rosenzweig, *FRHLT*, 242). A related idea appears in the work of Martin Buber, who understands scripture as a response to divine presence (but not divine command); I explain later why his approach is less relevant to my project here.

10. Rosenzweig, *Zweistromland*, 761. The crucial sentence from which I quote here is missing from the English translation in Buber and Rosenzweig, *Scripture and Translation*, 59.

11. Exodus, revelation, and the land are three elements of a single gift granted to Israel in the eyes of biblical thought; each element is meaningful only in relation to the other two. On the ineluctable connection among them, especially in the Pentateuch, see Frankel, *Land*, 2–17. Frankel discusses texts that differ, especially in Joshua, but he notes that the Pentateuchal model won out in Judaism; see 97–136. Eloquent discussions of the centrality of the Sinai narrative not only for the Torah but for Jewish culture as a whole are found in Greenstein, "Understanding," 275–76, and Fishbane, *Sacred Attunement*, 46–49. On the centrality of the Sinai narrative in the Hexateuch and in the conceptual world of the Bible, see further Geoffrey Miller, *Ways*, 151–53.

12. But see Norman Lamm's contribution to *The Condition of Jewish Belief*, 124–26 (see n. 13, *infra*), for an eloquent and serious, though to my mind unconvincing, defense of a stenographic theory.

13. For a sense of the centrality in modern Jewish thought of questions concerning the Pentateuch's revealed status, see *Commentary* magazine, *Condition*. On the centrality of the issue of religious authority to modern Jewish thought, see Eisen, *Rethinking*, 209–10. On the connection of the authority and revelation in modern Jewish thought, see Neil Gillman, *Sacred Fragments*, 1–62, and cf. Solomon, *Torah*, 294–98 and 322–24.

14. Crüsemann, *Torah*, 28, sums up the scholarly consensus: "The extent of the gaps and contradictions in the Sinai pericope in both larger outline and details is unparalleled elsewhere in the Pentateuch. . . . There are obvious (and intentional?) contradictions in the final product." Cf. Zenger, "Wie und wozu," 266; Toeg, *Lawgiving*, 13–14; Childs, *Exodus*, 244; Greenberg, *Studies*, 280–84; Blum, *Studien*, 45–72, 88–99, esp. 45–53; Schwartz, "What Really," 20–46, esp. 23–25.

15. For a detailed treatment of Moses's ascents and descents, which finds coherence in each of the individual source's accounts, see Schwartz, "What Really," 21 (on the final form of the text), 27 (E), 28 (J), and 29 (P).

16. Moshe (Umberto) Cassuto argues that it went without saying that Moses obeyed God's directive, and thus the text does not bother to mention his reascent specifically (Cassuto, *Exodus*, 162). This is unlikely, given the detailed descriptions of ascents and descents in the rest of the chapter. Further, other verses make clear Moses is with the people, not on the mountain, as the theophany begins; see Deuteronomy 5.18 and one possible reading of Exodus 20.18.

17. A similar embarrassment of riches involves the question of how the nation's acceptance of Torah is described in various Sinai texts. These texts present three distinct models for acceptance: by the whole people (Exodus 19.8, 24.3, and 24.7), by representatives of the people (19.7 and 24.10–11), and by the leader alone (Exodus 34). See Geoffrey Miller, *Ways*, 148–49.

18. Crüsemann, *Torah*, 28, suggests that the contradictions in Exodus 19 may be intentional. On what we may describe as the Sinai texts' thematization of its ambiguities, see further Greenberg, "Exodus, Book Of," 6:1056, 1060; Licht, "Revelation," 252–54; and Greenstein, "Understanding," esp. 277–78.

19. On this use of *bet*, see GKC, §119i.

20. In that case, 19.9 contains a *bet* indicating location, not a *bet essentiae*. Cf. the linguistically plausible reading of Cassuto, *Exodus, ad loc.*: "I shall be concealed in a thick cloud, as though in a disguise that the eye of man cannot penetrate."

21. The staircase parallelism suggests that זֶה סִינַי is an epithet, as suggested in Albright, "Song of Deborah," 30. (Concerning staircase parallelism, see Watson, *Classical*, 150–56; on staircase parallelism in Judges 5, see Albright, *Yhwh and the Gods*, 13–15.) Alternatively, Fishbane, *Biblical Interpretation*, 54–55 and 75 n. 30, suggests that we understand זֶה סִינַי as a gloss added by a scribe who interpreted this description of God's theophany in the desert south of Judah to refer to the event at Sinai. In either case the connection of imagery, theophany, and Sinai occurs—though if Fishbane is right, the connection was made not by the original poet but by a learned scribe, who, sensitive to the traditional language, makes explicit the connection with Sinai that he felt was already implicit in the poem.

22. MT reads "God," but the original is likely to have read "Yhwh," since this psalm is part of what is known as the Elohistic Psalter, which regularly substitutes the word *God* for the tetragrammaton.

23. Psalm 114.1 alludes to Exodus 19.1. Though the poem overtly mentions the exodus, it is in constant dialogue with the revelation narrative at Sinai in Exodus 19. See Weiss, *Scriptures*, 252–62; and Avishur's commentary in Sarna, *Olam Hatanakh: Tehillim*, 2:170–72.

24. On the presence of fire in MT *qere*'s מימינו אש דת ("fire flew from His right hand"), see Steiner, "דת and עין," 693–96; Lewis, "Divine Fire."

25. The rabbis interpret Psalm 29 as a description of the revelation at Sinai; see Mekhilta deRabbi Yishmael, Baḥodesh §§1, 5, and 7. The repetition of the word קוֹל (voice or thunder) throughout the psalm probably suggested to the rabbis that the psalm's storm-filled and earth-shaking theophany took place at Sinai. See Irving Jacobs, *Midrashic*, 77.

26. See, e.g., the comprehensive discussion of Cross, *Canaanite Myth*, 147–77 (emphasizing the Canaanite background of these motifs); Loewenstamm, "Trembling" (stressing the Mesopotamian parallels); Jeremias, *Theophanie*, 73–90, 174 (stressing both).

27. The Ugaritic noun קל can mean both thunder and voice. Pardee, "Ba'lu Myth," 262, captures both senses by translating these two lines: "Ba'lu emits his holy voice, / Ba'lu makes his thunder roll over and over again."

28. CAT 1.4.7, lines 25–42. The text is available in Dietrich, Loretz, and Sanmartín, *CAT*, 21, in Mark Smith, "The Baal Cycle," 136–37 (which also provides an En-

glish translation with notes), and in Smith and Pitard, *Baal*, 2:635–83 (with translation and extensive commentary, in which 672–83 is especially relevant to our concerns). These editions occasionally differ in their reading of the cuneiform; in the seventh line above, I follow the reading found in Dietrich, Loretz, and Sanmartín.

29. The tablet reads רעת. I follow the emendation to רעם proposed in Fischer and Knutson, "Enthronement," 159. Cross, *Canaanite Myth*, 148 n. 5, argues that רעת is correct but also means "thunder" (from the root רע"ד: *ra'adtu > ra'attu*).

30. CAT 1.101. See Dietrich, Loretz, and Sanmartín, *CAT*, 115–16; translation with notes in Wyatt, *Religious Texts from Ugarit*, 388–90.

31. The information in what follows can be found in almost any dictionary of biblical Hebrew. As is so often the case, the most thorough and subtle treatment is BDB, 876–77.

32. Especially clear cases of this word's association with human speech occur, e.g., in 1 Samuel 1.13, 24.17, 26.17; Judges 7.9; and Psalm 86.6, to mention only a few examples. It can also refer to the voice of God speaking what seem to be specific words (Isaiah 6.8).

33. On *qol* as command even outside this idiom, see Krüger, "Stimme," 2, and cf. 17.

34. I paraphrase the definition of the phenomenon found in Buber's essay "Leitwort Style," in Buber and Rosenzweig, *Scripture and Translation*, 114–28, esp. 114 . See further his essay "*Leitwort* and Discourse Type," at 143–50; Alter, *Art of Biblical Narrative*, 92–112; Hendel, "Leitwort Style."

35. On the unresolved nature of the ambiguity, see Childs, *Exodus*, 343. In light of Childs's discussion, any attempt to claim that קול must be translated one way or the other is unfaithful to the text.

36. E.g., NJPS, NEB, NRSV, KJV, Luther, Buber-Rosenzweig, Hirsch, Mendelssohn.

37. See S. R. Driver, *Exodus, ad loc*, and Cassuto, *Exodus*, 174–75. Neither Driver nor Cassuto fully follows the logic of this grammatical observation, which implies that the people did not hear the whole of the Ten Commandments. Childs, *Exodus*, 371, and Dillmann and Ryssel, *Bücher Exodus und Leviticus*, 245, also note the import of the participle. LXX attempts to preserve this difference, translating רואים with an imperfect (ἑώρα) and the other verbs in the verse with aorists (φοβηθέντες, reading וַיִּרְא, and ἔστησαν).

38. See, e.g., JM, §121f, and cf. §167h. Alternatively (as some of Joüon-Muraoka's examples in §121f show), the participle can indicate an action that was ongoing in the past and was followed by a new action. Thus the syntax of 20.18 may tell us that the people were witnessing the thunder for some time, and then they spoke to Moses—perhaps toward the end of the giving of the Ten Commandments, or even when it was complete. But the latter possibility is less likely; to indicate clearly that 20.18 took place after the giving of the Ten Commandments, *waw*-conversive could have been used.

39. See Ḥazzequni's commentary to Exodus 20.18.

40. See the famous dictum of the midrashists, "There is no early or late in the To-rah" (Sifre Bemidbar Beha'alotka ad 9.1; b. Pesaḥim 6b).

41. See JM, §118d, 166j.

42. Two apparent exceptions are not exceptions at all: 2 Kings 21.10 introduced the recipients of divine speech with (ביד), and Genesis 17.3 does so with את. As Richard Tupper points out to me, other exceptions occur in Genesis 1, in which God speaks the world into existence. In these cases, with the exception of verse 26, God is not addressing anyone at all; and in verse 26, the absence of the dative reflects the text's strategy of reminding us of the heavenly council while also belittling it.

43. See Toeg, *Lawgiving*, 62–64, though Toeg explains the reasons for the unusual phrasing here differently, on the basis of the theory (which I find unconvincing) that the Decalogue was added to the redacted text of Exodus much later than the narrative surrounding them.

44. More specifically, these words appear in the Codex Alexandrinus of the Septuagint.

45. On Sinaitic revelation as the mother of all subsequent revelations in Judaism, see the rabbinic texts that claim that all Jewish teachings through the ages were already revealed in some form to Moses at Sinai; see my discussion in chapter 4 and the literature cited in n. 10 there. Cf. Maimonides's Seventh Principle (in his commentary to Mishnah Sanhedrin 8:1), which describes Moses as "the father of all prophets who preceded him or who came after him." The importance of Sinai for all subsequent revelations is discussed throughout Brooke, Najman, and Stuckenbruck, *Significance of Sinai*. On the conviction in Second Temple Judaism that later revelations receive authority through their connection or resemblance to the Sinai revelation, see Najman, *Seconding Sinai*; on a similar idea in Jewish mysticism, see Scholem, "Revelation and Tradition," esp. 288–90. The importance of Sinai is not only a postbiblical development; Gesundheit, "Das Land Israels," 333, notes that Deuteronomy 18.15–19 sees all later prophecy as a continuation of the event at Ḥoreb. This connection was made already by several of the Dead Sea Scrolls: see 4QGen-Exodusⁱ, 4Qpa-leoExodusᵐ, 4QBibPar *ad loc.*, and see further Propp, *Exodus 19–40*, 115.

46. See ibid., 166.

47. In other words, אמר always takes an object, whether quoted material (in which case we translate אמר as "say") or a noun or a relative pronoun (in which case "mention, specify, designate"). See BDB, 55, sec. 1, under the rubric "*mention, name, designate.*" When the verb means "command," the object is sometimes implied (sec. 4 in BDB); even in these cases, one cannot translate the verb as "speak." Other than Exodus 19.25, there are only three cases in which the verb does not have an object stated or implied, and which thus suggests that the verb might be translated as "speak" (as argued by Propp, *Exodus 19–40*, 145). Two of these, Genesis 4.8 and 2 Chronicles 32.24, are textually suspect (see the criti-

cal commentaries *ad loc.*). The third is Judges 17.2, but the object *imprecation* is clearly implied by the immediately preceding verb. Thus, Exodus 19.25 presents at the very least an unusual use of the verb that avoids the clarity that could easily have been achieved by רבד. On this anomaly, see S.R. Driver, *Exodus*, 168 and 175.

48. Hence my literal translation of the וַיְ of the *waw*-consecutive in the first rendering as "then."

49. Propp, *Exodus 19–40*, 145 rightly notes: "If Moses were reciting the Decalog in Exod 20:1, he would surely begin, 'thus said Yhwh,' not, 'And Deity spoke.' That sounds like a narrator."

50. Mekhilta deRabbi Yishmael, Baḥodesh, §9 and (with even greater emphasis on the paradoxical nature of the phrasing) the parallel passage in Mekhilta deRabbi Shimon bar Yoḥai; Rashi to Exodus 20.18 and to b. Shabbat 88b. For additional rabbinic and medieval sources, see Kasher, *Torah Sheleimah*, 16:136–37 notes to §§131 and 143; for prerabbinic and rabbinic sources, see Fraade, "Hearing and Seeing," 250–61.

51. For overviews of the exegetical problem, see Carasik, "To See," 262; Bartor, "Seeing the Thunder," 13–14 and notes there.

52. See references in to his debate with Akiva in n. 50 above.

53. See both of ibn Ezra's commentaries to our verse. The same interpretation is found in Dillmann and Ryssel, *Bücher Exodus und Leviticus*, 245.

54. See BDB, 906 §6d, g and §7; *HALOT*, s.v. רא"ה §§2, 6e, 13; Seeligmann, *Studies*, 155–58.

55. Cassuto, *Exodus, ad loc.*; Noth, *Exodus*, 168; Propp, *Exodus 19–40*, 181. (This explanation essentially restates the position of Yishmael and the commentators discussed by Kasher on the top of 137; see above, n. 50.) For a different suggestion that attempts to explain the phraseological oddity on a rational plane, see Samson Raphael Hirsch, *Pentateuch*, 218, who maintains that the phrasing signifies that they were able to perceive that the lightning they saw and the voice they heard were coming from the same place.

56. Carasik, "To See," 262, notes that Cassuto himself does not seem fully convinced by his explanation, since he goes on to provide another one, to wit, that (following ibn Ezra) the verb רא"ה can mean "perceive" more generally.

57. The Samaritan Pentateuch reads the verb שמע here as the verb governing את הקולות ואת קול השופר (in addition to ראים as the verb governing את הלפידים ואת ההר עשן). This suggests that רא"ה is at least a *lectio difficilior* that calls out for exegetical attention.

58. Sarna, *Exodus*, 115. Cf. Alter, *Five Books, ad loc.*: "The writer presents the Sinai epiphany as one tremendous synesthetic experience that overwhelms the people." Similarly, Heschel, *God*, 249, 250: "The voice of God is incongruous with the ear of man. . . . We do not *hear* the voice; we only *see* the words in the Bible."

59. See Toeg, *Lawgiving*, 39–41, 48–59; Childs, *Exodus*, 351–60.

60. For additional correspondences, see Toeg, *Lawgiving*, 40–41, and see the similar conclusion of the Mekhilta deRabbi Yishmael, Beḥodesh §3.

61. On the very complicated traditional historical issues in this chapter, see Childs, *Exodus*, 499–502; Toeg, *Lawgiving*, 39–43; Blum, *Studien*, 90–99, in addition to my discussion of passages from the chapter in the next section.

62. This theme appears throughout Heschel's oeuvre, but of particular importance for understanding the practical and halakhic implications of Heschel's theology of revelation are Heschel, *TmH*, vol. 2, *passim*, and esp. 3:49–138 (= *HT*, 321–640 and esp. 680–769); his essay "Toward an Understanding of Halacha," in Heschel, *Moral*, 127–45; Heschel, *God*, 213–17. See also the discussion in Even-Chen, *Voice*, 154–79, and Eisen, "Re-Reading Heschel." From among Jacob's works, see esp. Louis Jacobs, *Tree*, and *Beyond*, 106–31. For other presentations of this sort of approach, see Neil Gillman, *Sacred Fragments*, esp. 39–62; Dorff and Rosett, *Living*; Dorff, *Unfolding*.

63. See further Eisen, "Re-Reading Heschel," 16–17.

64. I discuss whether Moses and other prophets were stenographers or took a more active role in shaping their proclamation in the next chapter. Heschel treats this especially in Heschel, *TmH*, 2:264–98 (= *HT*, 478–501).

65. Maimonides, *Guide*, I:65–67. On a proper, which is to say, nonidolatrous, understanding of the biblical phrase "God spoke," see also Heschel, *God*, 177–83; regarding the implied issue of idolatry in those pages, see Shai Held, *Abraham Joshua Heschel*, 268 n. 45.

66. My thanks to Dan Baras for encouraging me to express myself more fully on this point.

67. On contemporary debates concerning the Pentateuch's composition, see my discussion in note 14 of ch. 1 here, which provides a basic bibliography both for the classical Documentary Hypothesis and for newer theories that challenge it. I primarily follow the rigorous, massively detailed, yet elegant revision of the classical theory known as the neo–Documentary Hypothesis, available and defended in the works of Menahem Haran, Joel Baden, and above all Baruch Schwartz. Schwartz has written extensively on the Sinai traditions and their development; see his accessible introduction in Schwartz, "What Really," as well as his more detailed studies in Schwartz, "Origin," and most of all the tour de force in Schwartz, "Priestly Account." See also his theological reflections in Schwartz, "Giving." See further the important source-critical discussion in Baden, *Redaction*, 153–71. While I follow Schwartz and Baden regarding the source-critical isolation of the relevant verses, I propose my own interpretation of the sources, which in some respects contradicts theirs. For alternate theories concerning the composition of the Sinai pericopes in particular, see esp. Toeg, *Lawgiving*, and Dozeman, *God on the Mountain*.

68. Cf. Greenstein, "Understanding," 277–78, who points out that the differences among the memories preserved in Exodus 19–24 reflect not only different

perceptions of the event itself but also different ways of preserving, interpreting, and passing on those perceptions.

69. On revelation as something that "God has not, in the working-out of Divine providence, seen fit to do ... in ... [a] clear and unequivocal way" but rather in a way that produces argument and perplexity, see Ward, *Religion*, 22–23.

70. Source criticism is religiously valuable because it allows us to recover theologically meaningful views of the revelation that existed in ancient Israel, and these views are harder to see if we focus on the final form of a biblical text. For this argument, see Schwartz, "Origin," 254, and cf. Schwartz, "Torah," 213–18. The same point has been made in relation to other issues, such as conceptions of God in the Torah and the theme of the promises to the patriarchs; see Sommer, *Bodies*, 124–26, and Baden, *Promise*, 127–45.

71. Almost all modern biblical scholars agree on the division between the priestly and nonpriestly sections the Pentateuch, and most will be able to read my analysis of P's Sinai narrative without any significant disagreement about the extent and shape of that narrative. Debate will be more substantial in regard to what I describe as E, since many contemporary scholars, especially in Europe, do not believe that the E strand of the Pentateuch exists as a consistent, much less previously self-contained, block of material. For this reason, I take some trouble to examine several models of what the tradition in question does and does not include within the Sinai chapters. The question of whether and to what extent what I term E material within Exodus 19–34 links up with certain blocks elsewhere in the Pentateuch is of less importance for the exegetical claims I make here. Consequently, supporters of newer theories associated with Rolf Rendtorff, Erhard Blum, Konrad Schmid, David Carr, Jan Gertz, and Thomas Dozeman can evaluate my exegetical claims independently of our disagreement about the continuity or existence of a longer E strand. Regarding the remaining material in Exodus (i.e., regarding J), disagreement is much greater; many scholars will wonder about the extent to which that material is from a single school. For this reason, I invest less time on that material and present a less comprehensive reading of it.

72. See Schwartz, "What Really." Similar source critical analyses are found in Carpenter and Harford-Battersby, *Hexateuch*, 109–19; Dillmann and Ryssel, *Bücher Exodus und Leviticus*, 206–26, 245–58, 284–92.

73. On E's notion that the covenant is the law, and that this law serves as the nation's expression of gratitude toward God, see Schwartz, "Origin," 258–59.

74. Paran, *Forms*, 98–136, has described the tendency of priestly texts, both narrative and legal, to move from prose to poetry and back in a single passage, especially when momentous events are narrated. This tendency occurs in other prose sources as well, albeit less frequently. It is crucial to recall that prose and poetry in ancient Hebrew were not strictly distinguished and that a middle ground existed in which poetic features, such as parallelism and rhythm, appeared but

did not occur with regularity. See Kugel, *Idea*, 59–95, esp. 85–87, 94–95. The lines I quote here exemplify this middle ground, moving at times further toward the heightened language we usually call poetry in the Bible (I indicate these places by indenting the second and third parts of a parallel line), but also at times remaining in nonparallel lines typical of prose.

75. This syntax (*waw* + subject + suffix verb) is often used to begin a new narrative. Within the redacted text of Exodus 19, this syntax is difficult to explain: it does not begin a new narrative, and its other likely meaning—a parenthetical statement, especially in the past perfect—makes no sense here. This syntax is also used to emphasize the subject, in contrast to a previous subject, which is unlikely here, since there is no reason to think that the previous subject (Israel) would be going to see God or to be surprised that it was Moses who did so. But as the opening verse of the E Sinai narrative, the syntax makes perfect sense.

76. See Greenberg, *Studies*, 273–78, and cf. Moshe Held, "Faithful," 11–12.

77. This subtle cause-and-effect relationship is indicated by the term ועתה, which is used, Brown, Driver, and Briggs (BDB, 773 §2b) explain, for "drawing a conclusion, esp. a practical one, from what has been stated"—or, we might add, from what has been perceived. The practical conclusion for the immediate future is stated in an imperative or (as here) in a prefix form. On ועתה as introducing a consequence, especially (as in Exodus 19.2–6) in contexts concerned with the creation of covenant, see Brongers, "Bemerkungen," esp. 290, 293–94. A weak cause-and-effect relationship similarly appears when הנה introduces the first clause (which describes what has been noticed, like אתם ראיתם in Exodus 19.4) and ועתה introduces the second (which describes the result); see Lambdin, *Introduction to Biblical Hebrew*, 168–72.

78. See, e.g., Carpenter and Harford-Battersby, *Hexateuch*, 2:111; Haran, *Ha'asufah*, 2:130, 160–61; Schwartz, "Origin," 258; Baden, *Redaction*, 157–58.

79. See 19.5, 16 (twice), 19 (twice); 20.18 (twice). In addition, E uses *qol* once, in 24.3, to refer to the something the people themselves say. Some contextual clues in E—thick cloud (9a), lightning and cloud (16aα), fire and the mountain giving off smoke (20.18)—support the understanding of *qol* as thunder, while references to speech in 19.19 support understanding *qol* as voice. Fire, smoke, and earthquake also appear in J (19.18, 19.20); in the redacted text, these provide additional support for thunder.

80. Schwartz, "What Really," 25; Schwartz, "Horeb"; Baden, *Redaction*, 153–58. These scholars largely follow Dillmann and Ryssel, *Bücher Exodus und Leviticus*, 217, and S. R. Driver, *Exodus*, 168, 174, 201. Similarly, for Wellhausen, *Composition*, 86–89, Exodus 19.10–19 and 20.1–17 are a compositional unit, and the Decalogue was proclaimed to the people specifically in E (see Wellhausen's helpful summary on 95, and 329–30, where he adds that 20.18–21 are also from E).

81. Carpenter and Harford-Battersby, *Hexateuch*, 110–11; Dillmann and Ryssel, *Bücher Exodus und Leviticus*, 217–18; Schwartz, "What Really," 24–25. Some re-

cent critics (e.g., Blum, *Studien*, 48–49) assign these verses to an interpretive supplement.

82. The Decalogue in the original E text was almost certainly shorter than the one we know from Exodus, but the length or version of the Decalogue in E is immaterial to the question I am pursuing. Attempts to reconstruct such an original text, without Priestly or Deuteronomic or other accretions, are legion in modern biblical scholarship. See Carpenter and Harford-Battersby, *Hexateuch*, 2:111–12, and the standard critical commentaries, and cf. Blum, "Decalogue" (who reconstructs earlier versions of the Decalogue, though he does not associate them with E).

83. This suggestion was first put forward in 1881 in a Dutch publication by Abraham Kuenen (which I have not read), as noted by Wellhausen, *Composition*, 329–30, and Nicholson, "Decalogue," 423 n. 2.

84. The literature is voluminous; see, e.g., Noth, *Exodus*, 154–55 and 168, Toeg, *Lawgiving*, 17–26 (including a helpful review and critique of other interpretive options), 26–31, 61–64; Nicholson, "Decalogue," 423–27; Dozeman, *God on the Mountain*, 47–49. Cf. Carpenter and Harford-Battersby, *Hexateuch*, 111, who suggests that an earlier version of the Ten Commandments was part of E, though (somewhat confusingly) they add that even that earlier version may not have *originally* been part of E. Cf. an analogous point of view (which refrains from discussing E) in Blum, "Decalogue," 295, who argues that the Covenant Code and not the Pentateuch was the original goal of the Sinai narratives, thus regarding the addition of the Decalogue as secondary, though already assumed by the material in Exodus 32; see further Blum, *Studien*, 97–98.

85. Cf. Ḥazzekuni *ad loc.*

86. The main reason cited by scholars for regarding the Ten Commandments as an interpolation is that it breaks the narrative flow between 19.18–19 and 20.18, since the latter describes an event motivated by the frightening sights and sounds in the former. Further, these scholars presume that the Ten Commandments in their current place were heard by the entire nation, while 20.18–21 show they were to be heard directly only by Moses. (See, e.g., Nicholson, "Decalogue," 423; Noth, *Exodus*, 154; on the presumption that in their current place they must have been heard by the whole nation, see Toeg, *Lawgiving*, 61–62.) However, once we realize that the syntax of 20.18 shows the conversation in 20.18–21 took place during or before the revelation, these objections to the current location of the Decalogue lose all their force. In assuming that the current placement of the Ten Commandments requires us to conclude that the people heard the whole of that text, scholars like Nicholson not only fail to attend to the syntax of 20.18; they fail to notice the insistent ambiguity of chapters 19–20 as a whole in regard to the question of Mosaic mediation, and they import the view of Deuteronomy into Exodus (or into the E source in Exodus).

87. Another verse in Exodus that points in this direction is 20.22. This verse describes God as *speaking* to the Israelites, not merely impressing them with loud noises and extraordinary sights. Finally, the very next verse may be intended as a quotation or paraphrase of what God said to the Israelites—and thus it is significant that this verse ("Make no gods of silver or gold with Me") could be taken as a paraphrase of a crucial part of the Decalogue, Exodus 20.4 (see Nicholson, "Decalogue," 429–30). God's heavenly location in 20.22 contradicts several E verses in chapter 19 that describe Yhwh as having descended to the mountain prior to the revelation. Consequently, it seems to be not E (as Schwartz and many classical source critics maintain) but a scribal addition to the final form of Exodus (or perhaps to E itself?) that echoes Deuteronomy's version of revelation, in which God was exclusively in heaven. For defense of this suggestion, see Noth, *Exodus*, 141; Childs, *Exodus*, 465; Blum, *Studien*, 95–97; and Nicholson, "Decalogue," 428–29.

88. An additional question can be added to this scenario: if the nation did hear the whole Decalogue, were they able to discern specific words, or did they hear only loud noises that were unintelligible to them, though they were somehow intelligible to Moses? Schwartz, "Horeb," argues that "according to 19.19, the people heard only a voice . . . but apparently could not discern the actual verbal content. Moses' task was to relay it to them in the form of intelligible speech, one utterance at a time. . . . From the standpoint of the listener it must have seemed as if 'Each time Moses would speak [i.e., would utter one of the דברות], God would respond to him with voice.'" The purpose of the people overhearing the voice without understanding the words, Schwartz explains, is to validate the status of the prophet. In other words, already in E we see an author grappling with this question of authority as it relates to revelation. If Schwartz is right, E claims that God does really speak in words, but the people have access to these words only through the human intermediary, never directly. As a result, it seems to me (Schwartz may disagree), E at once suggests a stenographic theory of revelation (since God did speak in human words) and also pulls back from it (since our only access to those words, even at Horeb itself, was through an intermediary).

89. I follow Schwartz's reconstruction of E. The core of the reconstruction of these verses (32.15–16) and of 31.18 lies in the realization that elsewhere P never speaks of "tablets" (לחת) but only of an object called the עדות (25.16, 25.21, 40.20). Only where E and P are mixed do we hear of שני לחות העדות, "the two tablets of the covenant." See Schwartz, "Priestly Account," 126–27, esp. n 52.

90. On the complicated questions of what actually was on the tablets according to various sources and redactions and whether what is presented in our redacted text as the giving of the second set of tablets might originally have been an another narrative regarding the giving of the first and only set, see the overview in Crüsemann, *Torah*, 50–55.

91. This is the case in the MT and most copies of the LXX. Some LXX miniscules at 34.1 read not γράφω, matching the Hebrew text's וְכָתַבְתִּי ("I shall write"), but the aorist imperative γραψον, implying that we should read וכתבת ("You should write"); see Wevers, *Exodus . . . Göttingensis Editum*, 374. This reading probably results from an attempt by some scribes and tradents of LXX to harmonize between 34.1 and 34.27–28; it does not represent an original reading in E. See Sommer, "Translation as Commentary," 58 n. 47.

92. The Karaite commentator Abū al-Faraj Hārūn ibn Faraj, in his *al-Kitāb al-Kāfī*, pt. II, ch. 4, discusses the syntax we find here, explaining that in a series of verbs the subject remains the same unless a new subject is introduced; see Khan, "Biblical Exegesis," 146–47.

93. So Rashbam, Naḥmanides, and ibn Ezra; Dillmann and Ryssel, *Bücher Exodus und Leviticus*, 391; Propp, *Exodus 19–40*, 617; Baden, *Redaction*, 169. All these scholars cite 34.1 in support of their contention but provide no grammatical explanation for the unannounced shift in subject's in 34.28. Cassuto, *Exodus*, 167, suggests that ויכתב in 34.28 has an impersonal subject similar to a passive. While such impersonal verbs do occur in biblical Hebrew, this particular verb does not fit into that category, as the discussion of impersonal third-person masculine singular verbs in GKC §144b–d shows.

94. E.g., Shemot Rabbah 47:2.

95. On these midrashim and commentators, see Lieberman, *Hellenism*, 80–82, and Kasher, *Torah Sheleimah*, 22:126–27.

96. See S. R. Driver, *Exodus*, ad 34.1 and 34.28. The possibility is discussed in the notes in Carpenter and Harford-Battersby, *Hexateuch*, 2:134–35.

97. Baden, *Redaction*, 167–69.

98. See *Moshav Zekeinim* to 34.1 (in Sasson, *Sefer Moshav Zekeinim*, 216) as well as the discussion of these commentators in Kasher, *Torah Sheleimah*, 22:126–27.

99. See, e.g., Schwartz, "What Really," 24–27. Schmid, *Schriftgelehrte*, 143–58, suggests that several verses usually attributed to P are the work of a postredactional hand. Schmid explains the reasons for this judgment with admirable clarity, but the assumptions about the nature of reading on which he bases them are, I think, inappropriate for the analysis of narrative texts.

100. In what follows, I read P as an independent, self-standing text that can be, and was originally intended to be, read on its own. In this I follow Schwartz, "Priestly Account," esp. 105–9. For a clear discussion of the question whether P is a source that can be read independently or a redactional layer that supplements other sources, see also Carr, *Reading*, 43–47. Carr, too, emphasizes that P can be read as a discrete document. I reject the proposal of scholars who regard P as a redactional supplement to other material—most famously, Cross, *Canaanite Myth*, 294–319, and, with a different approach, Blum, *Studien*, 229–85. For a critique of Cross and Blum on this point, see Nicholson, *Pentateuch*, 197–218, and Schwartz, "Priestly Account."

101. Milgrom, *Leviticus 1–16*, 575, points out that P uses the word *like* in 24.17 to show that the *kabod* is not actually made of fire; rather, *fire* is the closest word P can think of to describe the unique, otherworldly substance of which the *kabod* consists. This is the case again in another crucial P verse, Numbers 9.15, and in Ezekiel 1 (which is also written by a priest).

102. On P's conception of the *kabod* as the actual body of God, see Weinfeld, "God the Creator," 113–20; Weinfeld, "Kābôd"; Sommer, *Bodies*, 59–62, 58–78, and 214–32. On *kabod* as simply equivalent to God, see Mettinger, *Dethronement*, 107. See further Hundley, *Keeping Heaven*, 39–52.

103. On the importance of recovering this trajectory, see Schwartz, "Priestly Account," 115–17, and Hundley, *Keeping Heaven*, 173–75.

104. On the origin of Moses's radiance in God's own radiance, see esp. Aster, *Unbeatable Light*, 337–51, and Seth Sanders, "Old Light," 404.

105. So Schwartz, "Priestly Account," 125.

106. Leviticus 1.1 narrates the event that follows immediately on the one narrated in the last verse of Exodus. There is no delay in narrative time between the last verse of Exodus and the first verse of Leviticus; see Dillmann and Ryssel, *Bücher Exodus und Leviticus*, 428; Milgrom, *Leviticus 1–16*, 139; Schwartz, "Priestly Account," 116. It is for this reason that we find a *waw*-consecutive verb at the beginning of Leviticus rather than one of constructions that begin a new narrative (e.g., ויהי followed by a temporal phrase; or *waw* + noun + suffix verb)—in other words, the Book of Exodus ends, and the Book of Leviticus begins, midsentence.

107. See, e.g., Wellhausen, *Prolegomena*, 353; Blenkinsopp, *Prophecy and Canon*, 76; Schwartz, "Priestly Account," 123–24.

108. As already noted in the commentary of Naḥmanides to Leviticus 7.38. See further Schwartz, "Priestly Account," 123 and n. 45 there.

109. See Toeg, *Lawgiving*, 154–57. Toeg points out that the tension between the idea of lawgiving at Sinai and lawgiving at the Tent of Meeting already attracted attention from the rabbis, who attempt to harmonize between these two options; see b. Ḥagigah 6a–b.

110. P stresses in Numbers 9.15–23 that the cloud and fire indicating the immediate presence of God were always located in or above this Tabernacle. The Tabernacle as described in P was the site of an unceasing and ever-accessible theophany. See Clements, *God and Temple*, 118; Milgrom, *Leviticus 1–16*, 574; Levine, "On the Presence," 76; de Vaux, "Ark," 146; Sommer, *Bodies*, 81–82. On the ritual implications of God's presence in the sanctuary, see Joosten, *People and Land*, 125–28.

111. See Schwartz, "Priestly Account," 115–16, 123–24; Licht, *Numbers I–X*, 111; Kaufmann, *Toledot*, 2:473. Similarly, Schmid, *Schriftgelehrte*, 146, notes the small role that Mount Sinai plays in the priestly narratives of revelation, though he uses this observation for diachronic-compositional purposes that differ from my thematic purpose here.

112. On the ark and its cover as God's footstool and throne respectively, see Haran, *Temples*, 236–53; de Vaux, "Ark," 147–48.

113. There are two exceptions. Some laws of Passover were given to Moses on the eve of the first Passover (Exodus 12); because this first Passover occurred prior to the erection of the ark, these laws had to be imparted elsewhere. Also, the command regarding circumcision was given to Abram in Canaan (Genesis 17.10).

114. See the very suggestive discussion of this issue in Toeg, *Lawgiving*, 154–58, as well as Schwartz, "Priestly Account," 124.

115. On this possibility, see Patrick D. Miller, *Way*, 3–36, and Rofé, *Deuteronomy*, 88–89 (with further references to medieval rabbinic commentators). Kratz, "Dekalog" argues that the Decalogue was written as a summary or abstract of the Covenant Code. Even if one does not agree with Kratz's diachronic conclusions, the connections he notes remain intriguing. The idea of the Decalogue as the conceptual root from which all other laws stem is also known in rabbinic sources. See Heschel, *TmH*, 2:75–79 (= *HT*, 371–73); Kasher, *Torah Sheleimah*, 16:201–13.

116. Kislev, "Numbers 36.13," points out that it is for this reason that hundreds of different laws in P are introduced by their own וידבר or ויאמר formulas: God communicated with Moses again and again over the forty years. In E and D, however, we do not repeatedly see this formula, since they know of only two legislative events.

117. See Fishbane, *Biblical Interpretation*, 98–102; Chavel, "Second Passover"; Chavel, "Numbers 15."

118. The debate is not only a debate between P on the one hand and D and E on the other; it may have taken place within the priestly schools as well. Baden, "Identifying," 20–23, shows that the original stratum of P regarded all law as having been given at the Tent at the foot of the mountain. But for later strata of the priestly writings (viz., H), lawgiving happened later as well (e.g., throughout Numbers), and even before Sinai (Exodus 12; on the H provenance of this chapter, see Knohl, *Sanctuary*, 20–21). It is not only in regard to lawgiving that the P views revelation as developing over time; Knohl has shown that P regards knowledge of God in the patriarchal era as incomplete in comparison to the fuller knowledge of God that emerged in the Mosaic era. See *Sanctuary*, 124–48. H has adopted P's view of continuing theological revelation and applied it to lawgiving as well.

119. In b. Ḥagigah 6a–b and parallels, R. Yishmael held that general principles were revealed at Sinai in the time frame narrated by Exodus 19–24; specifics of many laws were then revealed at the Tent of Meeting (starting at Leviticus 1.1). R. Akiva, however, maintained that both general principles and specifics were revealed to Moses at Sinai, repeated at the Tent of Meeting, and then repeated again on the plains of Moab in Deuteronomy 12–26). On this debate and its roots in the Pentateuchal sources, see Shamma Friedman, "What Does

Mount Sinai," esp. 399–400 and 417–18. Analogously, b. Gittin 60a debates whether the Torah was given scroll by scroll or in one fell swoop (though in this case Rashi and other commentators understand the latter option to refer not to the actual revelation but to Moses's act of writing the Torah down). On the relationship of the two debates, see Kasher, *Torah Sheleimah*, 16:256.

120. Schwartz, "Origin," 258–59.

121. On P's conception of covenant (ברית) as promise, see Zimmerli, "Sinaibund und Abrahambund"; Schwartz, "Priestly Account," 130–32; Knohl, *Sanctuary*, 141–47, 172–75; Nihan, "Priestly Covenant"; Weinfeld, "Covenant of Grant," 186, 188–89, 195, 200–203. A helpful review of literature, along with a nuanced presentation of the multivalent use of the term ברית in P and H (for whom the term can refer not only to the divine promise but also to the obligations that flow from that promise), see Stackert, "Distinguishing," 377–85.

122. The complex question concerning the layers within the priestly traditions that may add some of these laws does not affect the larger point I am making concerning revelation and authority. Whatever their differences, P and H share the notion that, as Joosten, "Covenant Theology," 163, puts it, the covenant "is a sacral bond between the god YHWH and the people of Israel designed to enable the former's dwelling, in an earthly sanctuary, among the latter."

123. By definition, certain ritual states (which are themselves in no way ethically or religiously objectionable) repel divine presence because they are the opposite of the undying and ungendered deity. People in these states (referred to in Hebrew as טמא, often translated into English as "impure" but more accurately rendered, as Cantor Yakov Hadash suggested to me, as "God-unready," as opposed to טהור, which means "God-ready") must not enter the Tabernacle where God lives or the area immediately around it. See further Hundley, *Keeping Heaven*, 179–92; for a useful overview of approaches, see also Klawans, "Ritual."

124. Cf. Toeg, *Lawgiving*, 158 and his important comment in n. 132 there, as well as Schwartz, "Priestly Account," 133, though he takes a somewhat different approach at 122–23. On the idea that the very concept of a temple is an attempt at rendering manageable the dangerous and intermittent yet highly desired phenomenon of divine presence, see Kugel, "Some Unanticipated," 9–10.

125. Note the infamous statement about the priestly law in Julius Wellhausen's article "Israel," in the ninth edition of the *Encyclopaedia Britannica* (reprinted in Wellhausen, *Prolegomena*, 509). For an excellent discussion of attitudes toward so-called priestly legalism among nineteenth- and not a few twentieth-century biblical theologians, see Blenkinsopp, *Sage*, 66–68, and *Prophecy*, 17–23. Blenkinsopp provides a useful critique of the very assumption that there was such a thing as priestly legalism.

126. See my discussion of theurgy in ch. 3 of this volume, esp. nn. 64 and 73 and references to Moshe Idel's work there.

127. This debate about what is the core of Torah, the law itself or the divine immanence in the sanctuary that the law makes possible, occurs elsewhere in the Bible and its reception. A fascinating example can be detected when we compare the 1 Kings 6 in the MT and the LXX. The older version of the text preserved in the LXX mentions only the importance of the sanctuary; MT adds verses 11–13 to stress the importance of the law itself, regardless of the sanctuary. The supplement's position is closer to that of E and (we shall see shortly) of D, while the original text's focus on divine presence's recalls P.

128. Rosenzweig, *Briefe und Tagebücher*, 762. In expressing this view, Rosenzweig rejects the view, going back to Spinoza (and, before him, to Paul, and also, at least terminologically, to the Septuagint translators, but evident already in E), that Judaism or Torah is to be equated with law. In this respect, Rosenzweig recalls Mendelssohn, for, as Paul Franks points out ("Sinai," 354), Mendelssohn responded to Spinoza by insisting "that the Torah was in part teaching (*didache*), and that the obligations of Judaism were best understood, not as laws, but rather as commandments, addressed by a personal God to a singular individual or to a singular people."

129. This is the explanation of Rosenzweig's remark by Mendes-Flohr, *Divided*, 299.

130. Buber and Rosenzweig, *Scripture and Translation*, 23.

131. Heschel insists on the central importance of the law, but he rejects the reduction of Judaism to legalism, explicitly denying that the halakhah is an end in itself. See Heschel, *God*, 323: "Judaism is not another word for legalism. The rules of observance are law in form and love in content. . . . The law is the means, not the end; the way, not the goal. One of the goals is 'Ye shalt be holy.' The Torah is guidance to an end through a law." See further Even-Chen, *Voice*, 158–59, and Tucker's remarks in *HT*, 720–21.

132. But not thereafter. As Milgrom, *Numbers*, 365–66, and Licht, *Numbers I–X*, 112, show, after the events at Mount Sinai Moses has aural, not visual, contact with God: he enters the Tabernacle but not the Holy of Holies where the *kabod* sits enthroned on the *kerubim*. Even Aaron doesn't see the *kabod* when he enters the Holy of Holies (Leviticus 16.2, 13).

133. Moses removes the veil whenever he tells the Israelites what he is commanded to tell them. On the iterative meaning of Exodus 34.34, see especially the end of Naḥmanides's remarks on verses 31–34. On the authenticating role of Moses's facial luminosity, see Haran, *Bible and Its World*, 404; Dozeman, "Masking." Similarly, in Leviticus 9.23–24 the *kabod* emanated from the Holy of Holies where the *kerub* throne was located, and it is from the same place that the sound of God's communication with Moses came forth in Numbers 7.89. For this reason, Gersonides argues plausibly, the emergence of the fire from the Holy of Holies in the sight of the whole people serves to authenticate Moses's prophetic status: what Moses heard or understood and what the people saw came from precisely the same place. See Gersonides's commentary

on Numbers 7.89 and his ninth תועלת to פרשת נשוא. Similarly, Toeg describes the event in Leviticus 9.23–24 as an authentication of the Tent of Meeting as God's dwelling (see Toeg, *Lawgiving*, 156); we might add that since Moses receives all his revelations there, the event that authenticates the Tent also authenticates Moses.

134. The words את and ואת in Exodus 25.9 mean "namely, specifically, that is." Fishbane, *Biblical Interpretation*, 48–51, discusses how scribes use the term to insert secondary clarifications to existing texts. The term can also be used by a single author as a clarifying remark; see examples collected in JM, §155j.

135. The plans may have consisted of drawings or as a three-dimensional model; see Propp, *Exodus 19–40*, 376–77. On the visual nature of the revelation see Dillmann and Ryssel, *Bücher Exodus und Leviticus*, 310. S. R. Driver, *Exodus*, 267, discusses an ancient Near Eastern parallel involving a visual model of a temple. Commenting on הראה in Exodus 27.8, Cassuto, *Exodus*, suggests that the details of the Tabernacle's construction were not sufficiently clear from God's oral communication, and thus God provided the visual model as well. See also his comment to 25.40, as well as Propp, *Exodus 19–40*, 345. Schmid, *Schriftgelehrte*, 147, notes that Exodus 35–40, which describes the building of the Tabernacle, refer back to the plans from Exodus 25–31 by using the phrase "as/which Yhwh commanded (צוה) you" no fewer than twenty-two times. He notes the possibility that the phrase might include nonverbal instructions, such as those involving the תבנית or model that Moses was shown.

136. Given P's emphasis on the visual revelation of information to Moses, it is noteworthy that P never refers to its teachings as written in Moses's day. Unlike J, E, and D, the P texts do not tell us that God directed Moses to write down the laws he received. See Schwartz, "Priestly Account," 132.

137. The motif occurs in passing, as noted by Toeg, *Lawgiving*, 155–57, who points to Leviticus 9.22–24 (and, he might have added, the similar verse in Exodus 24.17). But P accords the motif no prominence and presents no ambiguity about who heard God's commands (Moses) and who did not hear them in any form, verbal, thunderous, or otherwise (the nation).

138. Hurowitz, "Proto-Canonization," 37, who also notes that this model of multistaged mediation from deity to human cultural hero to elders or ritual specialists to later recipients also occurs in Mesopotamian literature. On the emphasis on mediation in P and the connection to Mesopotamian ritual texts believed to have been revealed through a multistage mediation, see also Lenzi, *Secrecy*, 384.

139. So Licht, *Numbers I–X*, 112; Levine, *Numbers 1–20*, 259. Ibn Ezra maintains that the phrase "When Moses went to the Tent of Meeting to speak with Him" refers back to Leviticus 1.1 (see also Bekhor Shor for this reading), and thus our verse in Numbers explains what precisely transpired on that first occasion of divine speech from the Tent and on all subsequent ones. Exodus 25.22, Le-

viticus 1.1, and Numbers 7.89 need to be read together to give us a picture of what happens when God reveals the law to Moses at the Tent; so Rashi and his sources in Sifre Bemidbar, Naso' §58. I must admit that the *waw*-consecutive וַיְדַבֵּר at the end of the verse argues against seeing this verse as a repeated action rather than a single punctual event. Most ancient versions, however, read that verb as indicating repeated action: LXX renders with the imperfect ἐλάλει, as if the Hebrew read the imperfect וִידַבֵּר (rather than what is the normal rendering of the *waw*-consecutive וַיְדַבֵּר, to wit, the aorist ἐλάλησεν). Onqelos and Pseudo-Jonathan render וידבר with מתמלל (precisely as they render מְדַבֵּר earlier in the verse, and unlike their normal rendering of the *waw*-consecutive וַיְדַבֵּר, to wit, ומליל), thus suggesting that they, like LXX, read the imperfect here.

140. The verse contains several stylistic anomalies that attract the attention of an audience familiar with the norms of narrative style, as noted by Alter, *Five Books*, 720.

141. The phrase used here, דבר אתו, means "converse, confer" (as opposed to דבר אל, "to speak to"), as noted by Milgrom, *Numbers, ad loc.* This phrasing strengthens the reciprocal reading.

142. See Levine, *Numbers 1–20*, 258; Fox, *Five Books*, 695. On the durative sense of the *hitpa'el*, see Speiser, "Durative."

143. Kellermann, *Priesterschrift*, 108, dismisses the evidence of the verb form as late Masoretic hairsplitting—as if an emphasis on fine distinctions were not at the very heart of the Priestly worldview!

144. This sense is reinforced by the fact that we cannot be sure whether to translate, "He would speak to him" or "he would speak to Him." On this ambiguity, see Milgrom, *Numbers*, 59; Alter, *Five Books*, 720; Levine, *Numbers 1–20*, 259, Kellermann, *Priesterschrift*, 107–8.

145. Alter, *Five Books, ad loc.*, speaks of "a theological impulse here to interpose some kind of mediation between the divine source of the speech and the audible voice that is spoken to Moses."

146. JM, §53i.

147. See Schwartz, "What Really," 24–26, but my list above reflects small changes in Schwartz's thinking since he wrote that piece.

148. Further, the Sinai narrative in J seems to lack a beginning, unless (as Schwartz suggests to me) 19.9b simply is a continuation of the J narrative that broke off at 17.7—in other words, in 17.7b tells us of the nation's question about God's presence, and Moses forthwith reports that question to Yhwh in 19.9b. In that case, the central theme of J's Sinai narrative is introduced in 17.7b.

149. Baden, *Promise*, 113. Baden further notes the prominence of seeing in J more generally, even outside of theophanies.

150. See Milgrom, *Leviticus 1–16*, 574.

151. Schwartz, "Priestly Account," 127–28.

152. On this parallel, see Weinfeld, "God the Creator," 119. Milgrom, *Leviticus 1–16*, 591, however, suggests that in these P verses the people shout for joy, not just out of fear, which is a philologically strong reading of the verb וירנו.

153. I borrow the concept and the terms from Rudolf Otto, *Idea of the Holy*, 12–24, esp. 20. In the sentence following this note, I borrow from Otto, 31–41, esp. 31.

154. This pattern is also present in the story of the burning bush. Moses's expression of fear (3.6) stems from E, while Moses's desire to see the mystery more closely (Exodus 3.3) belongs to J. (While Dillmann and Ryssel, *Bücher Exodus und Leviticus*, 29, mention מראה in verse 3 as a characteristic E word, its appearance in Genesis 2.9 and 39.6 makes clear that the word appears in J as well.)

155. On the lethal nature of divine presence, both in ritual contexts involving priests and in theophanic contexts involving prophets, see Savran, *Encountering*, 190–93; on the surprising exceptions to this tendency, see Savran, 193–203. Many biblical authors and characters express surprise that humans saw God but did not die, or fear that having seen God, they would die; see Genesis 32.31, Exodus 24.10–11, Judges 6.22–23, Judges 13.22, Isaiah 6.1–5; also perhaps Genesis 16.13, according to the likely emendation (הגם א־להים ראיתי וָאֶחְי) suggested by Ehrlich, *Randglossen*, 1.64–65.

156. As scholars have long recognized, Exodus 34.12 and following are glosses made by scribes influenced by Deuteronomy's ideology, and perhaps specifically by Deuteronomy 7.5, whose linguistic resemblance to Exodus 34.13 is pronounced. The conclusion that 34.12–13 belongs to a Deuteronomistic insertion is not only supported by recent critics who are quick to find deuteronomistic material in Genesis–Numbers and who doubt the existence of J and E (e.g., Blum, *Studien*, 69–70, 354, and Carr, "Method"). Even earlier critics who believe in J and E and are more hesitant to see later additions in them also regard the verses in question as deuteronomistic and not original to J or E. Thus, Carpenter and Harford-Battersby, *Hexateuch*, 2:118 and 134–35; Childs, *Exodus*, 460 and 486; Ginsberg, *Israelian*, 64. This tendency to expand legal material in Exodus 19–24 also occurs in the Decalogue itself, in which material in the style of both D and P occur; see Toeg, *Lawgiving*, 67, and references there. For a defense of the non-J provenance of these verses, see Sommer, *Bodies*, 210–12 n. 104. Note further that 34.12 and 15 both contain the phrase פן־תכרת ברית ליושב הארץ, which suggests the strong possibility that they constitute a *Wiederaufnahme*, so that we may confidently judge the secondary insertion to consist of the material between 12 and 15. It is precisely in that material, verses 13–14, that we find the Deuteronomic language and concepts that conflict with the surrounding context. On the *Wiederaufnahme* and its use in determining scribal insertions, see Kuhl, "Wiederaufnahme."

157. Gesundheit, *Three Times*, 12–43; Fishbane, *Biblical Interpretation*, 194–97; Carr, "Method."

158. Some critics attribute 34.28 to J, in which case J contained some form of the Decalogue; so Carpenter and Harford-Battersby, *Hexateuch*, 2:135. But Schwartz and Baden assign this verse to E and do not believe that J contained the Decalogue at all; see Baden, *Redaction*, 168–71.

159. Hoffman, "J's Unique." See also Chavel, "Biblical Law," 235.

160. Hoffman, "J's Unique," 82–93.

161. Ibid., 93–106.

162. Ibid., 63–80.

163. The exegetical nature of Deuteronomy has been widely discussed among biblical scholars in recent decades, but one might locate the first reference to this aspect of Deuteronomy in the fifth verse of the book: "On the other side of the Jordan, in the land of Moab, Moses began to explicate (באר) this Teaching, as follows" (Deuteronomy 1.5)—at least, if באר here means not "inscribe" (as it does in Deuteronomy 27.8) but "explain, expound," as it does in late Biblical Hebrew. The latter seems likely both in the context (in which the verb introduces a speech orated by Moses, not an act of writing in stone) and in light of the relatively late provenance of Deuteronomy 1–4. See further Tigay, *Deuteronomy*, 5 and 344 n. 17. On the learned, scribal, and exegetical dimensions of Deuteronomy and the Deuteronomistic literature more generally, see Levinson, *Deuteronomy and the Hermeneutics*; Eckart Otto, "Mose der erste"; Stackert, *Rewriting*; Veijola, *Moses Erben*, 192–240, and Veijola, "Deuteronomistic Roots."

164. Toeg emphasizes inner-biblical exegesis in Deuteronomy 4 and 5; see Toeg, *Lawgiving*, 57–58 and 52. n. 81. So also Childs, *Exodus*, 343. Similarly, Blum, *Studien*, 94, shows that Deuteronomy 4.36 and 5.25–26 set out to clarify the ambiguous term נסות in Exodus 20.20. A review of exegetical elements in the chapters appears in Brettler, "Fire."

165. On Deuteronomy 1.1–4.40 as a later deuteronomistic addition to the bulk of the D source that begins at 4.45, see, e.g., the brief discussion and further references in Baden, *Composition*, 130–32, and the classic treatment by Noth, *Deuteronomistic*, 29–33, as well as the standard introductions and commentaries (other than Driver, who does not view 1.1–4.40 as late).

166. Thus, the authors of Deuteronomy knew both E and J, but they know them separately, and they relate to them in very different ways. D's dependence on E is far greater and more often involves direct borrowing of words, phrases, and whole sentences. See Baden, *Composition*, 133–36, and, at greater length, Baden, *Redaction*, 153–72. This is true both of the earlier authors of Deuteronomy 4.45–11.31 (D1) and the later, supplementing authors of Deuteronomy 1.1–4.40 (D2). Baden maintains that in presenting Horeb narratives both these sets of authors refer to J narratives that highlight the disobedience of the Israelites, but they do not refer to J's Sinai material. It seems to me that the particular emphasis on the nonvisual nature of the revelation in 4.12 could be seen as a response to the emphasis on visual elements in J (Exodus 24.10–11)

and/or P (24.17). But these correspondences between D and J/P are much less verbally close than the ones Baden adduces between D and E. They could be D's response to traditional ideas about revelation, or they might be responses to specific J and P texts.

167. Though a native of New Jersey, I refrain from translating these forms as "yous"—even though that rendering is, technically, more accurate.

168. Further, this verse is likely to be a secondary addition, for reasons I adduce later; see the reference to Loewenstamm in n. 183, *infra*.

169. See Tillich, *On Art*, 215, as well as the useful discussion in Kieckhefer, *Theology*, 120. On aural/Protestant this tendency in D, Dtr, and prophetic traditions under their influence (e.g., Jeremiah), see Sommer, *Bodies*, 135.

170. On this theology in D, see Weinfeld, *DDS*, 191–209; Mettinger, *Dethronement*, 48–80; Geller, *Sacred Enigmas*, 30–61; Sommer, *Bodies*, 62–68. All these studies are indebted to von Rad, *Studies in Deuteronomy*, 37–44.

171. Non-D material appears in Deuteronomy from 31.14 on; the verses from 31 with which we are concerned, however, belong to D. See, e.g., S. R. Driver, *Deuteronomy*, 336–38; Wellhausen, *Composition*, 118; Baden, *Composition*, 146–47.

172. On cultic sight of the Temple as an avenue to God in (non-Deuteronomic) Israelite religion, see, e.g., Mark Smith, "Seeing God." On D's movement away from this form of religiosity, see Hendel, "Aniconism," and van der Toorn, "Iconic Book."

173. Hermann Cohen, *Religion*, 73. On this theme in Cohen's work and its anti-mythological tendency, see Erlewine, "Reclaiming," 188. On the philosophical context of Cohen's demythologizing reading of Deuteronomy, see Seeskin, *Autonomy*, 163–64.

174. On the use of ‏רא"ה‎ and ‏שמ"ע‎ as guiding words in Deuteronomy 4, see the brilliant treatment in Geller, *Sacred Enigmas*, 36–44, 52–53, esp. 39. Geller establishes that this chapter reverses the normal hierarchy of ancient Near Eastern wisdom: "hearing is promoted and seeing demoted in significance as regards revelation, and, by extension, all religious experience." On the hierarchical relationship of visual and aural knowledge in the Bible generally, see Seeligmann, *Studies*, 141–68, esp. 155–58. On the complex interplay of visual and aural elements in both Exodus 19–20 and Deuteronomy 4–5 and their relationship to the interplay of *fascinans* and *tremendum*, see further Savran, *Encountering*, 109–16.

175. Heb., ‏פנים בפנים‎. In light of Deuteronomy's theology of transcendence, which insisted that God dwells only in heaven and never comes to dwell on earth, it is clear that D intends this phrase idiomatically ("directly, without intermediary") and not literally ("face to face"). On the possibility that this phrase disturbed later Deuteronomistic tradents because of its implications if taken literally, and on their reaction to this problem, see Carasik, "To See," 263. For a compelling defense of my understanding of the phrase that does not

rely on reference to D's theology, see ibn Ezra's commentary to this verse. The difference between this phrase here and the same phrase as used by E in Exodus 33.11 is instructive. There E adds several words: "God would speak to Moses face-to-face, as a man speaks to his fellow." The added clause at the end may be intended to specify that the phrase is not merely an idiom intending "directly" but refers to genuine physical proximity, as indicated also by verse 9, which tells us that God (or at least a significant avatar of God) descended from heaven to the Tent of Meeting to speak with Moses. (On the notion of avatar in J and E, see Sommer, *Bodies*, 78, 232, 254.)

176. I do not capitalize *glory* here, because D, unlike P, does not use the word כבוד as a technical term for God's body. See ibid., 64.

177. I am indebted to Hillel Ben-Sasson for pointing out this exegetical aspect of Deuteronomy 5.24.

178. See Childs, *Exodus*, 351. Childs, 343, points out the ambiguity of *qol* in Exodus 19.19 and also notes that Deuteronomy 4.10, 4.33, 5.4, and 5.24 decisively resolve the ambiguity.

179. Naḥmanides notes this contrast in the opening section of his commentary on Exodus 20.18–19. He concludes that Exodus 20.18–19 and Deuteronomy 5.24 narrate two completely different events, the former before the revelation of the Decalogue and the latter after it. His solution differs from that of a modern scholar, but his literary sensitivity is an important tool for the modern scholar all the same. Similarly, he notes that in Exodus 20.18 the people are frightened by sounds and sights, while in Deuteronomy 5.23–26 they are frightened by the divinity's speech (דבור השכינה). Even if we do not agree that this shows the texts narrate different events altogether, Naḥmanides helps us to see that Deuteronomy unambiguously identifies the voice the people hear as God's, while in Exodus E forces us to wonder what the noise the people hear is and how (or whether) it relates to God's person.

180. Here we see another subtle difference between D and its source in E. Schwartz, "Horeb," explains that in D, "God's original intention was to impart to them the whole of his teaching, and that he . . . thought better of it only in light of their resistance. . . . In the Elohistic account, the assumption that the entire body of laws is going to be communicated to the people by means of a messenger is present from the beginning. In E, the purpose of the proclamation of the Decalogue from the outset is to establish the credibility of the prophet, whose task it will then be to convey the laws and statutes." In light of this contrast, it becomes clear that Rashbam imports the attitude of Deuteronomy into his reading of Exodus 20.19 (see his commentary *ad loc.*). In this regard Rashbam is a predecessor of many modern scholars, e.g., Nicholson, "Decalogue," 424–27; Crüsemann, *Torah*, 253; and Patrick D. Miller, *Way*, 4, 19–23.

181. Here again D neatens up E's enigmatic or messy categories. For D lawgiving at Horeb was entirely unmediated: the whole people heard the whole of the Ten Commandments; and all lawgiving thereafter was entirely private and mediated through Moses. E, on the other hand, portrays lawgiving at Sinai itself as combining public and private aspects, as partially mediated and partially direct, without letting us know how and when the public, national revelation gave way to the private, Mosaic lawgiving. See further Lenzi, *Secrecy*, 302, who points out that for D the people are never "distant" as they are in Exodus; they are either present and fully involved or entirely absent.

182. See their commentaries to Deuteronomy 5.5, especially ibn Ezra's discussion of the biblical narrative style as it relates to the displacement of לאמר.

183. See Loewenstamm, "Formula." Loewenstamm collects 14 other examples in chapters 1–10 in which context shows that the sections starting with the formula, "at that time," are secondary. Loewenstamm, 103–4, points out the contradiction between 5.5 and 5.4 in particular. For the view that 5.5 is a later interpolation that modifies the claim in 5.4, see also Krüger, "Stimme," 15–16; Rofé, *Deuteronomy*, 29–30.

184. S. R. Driver, *Deuteronomy*, 84, argues that 5.5 is not really contradictory: "the people heard the 'voice' of God, but not distinct words; the latter Moses declared (הִגִּיד) to them afterwards." Thus, Driver argues, Deuteronomy 5 as a whole, and not just Deuteronomy 5.5, agrees with Exodus 19.9 and 19.19. Weinfeld, *Deuteronomy 1–11*, *ad loc.*, and Krüger, "Stimme," 16, both adopt a similar reading, acknowledging that Deuteronomy 5.5 is an interpolation but arguing that it does not necessarily contradict 5.4. Similar attempts at reconciling verse 5 to its context appear in ibn Ezra, *ad loc.* (who argues that 5.5 refers to a later exposition of the law by Moses), and Hermann Cohen, *Religion*, 75–76. These interpretations are not compelling. They contradict Deuteronomy 4.12 (according to which the people heard not an indistinct noise but the "sound of words"). Further, they do not even agree with Exodus 19, since the Deuteronomy 5.4 still emphasizes the direct revelation that does not occur in the former.

185. On this tendency in Jewish learning, see Halivni, *Midrash, Mishna, and Gemara*, 108–15. On the parallel between the multivocality of postbiblical Jewish commentary and that of biblical texts generally, see Greenberg, *Al Hammiqra*, 345–49.

186. The term is borrowed from Deuteronomy 17.18, which directs future kings of Israel to write out את משנה התורה הזאת. Though often taken to be Deuteronomy's title for itself, in its own literary context the phrase in fact means "a copy of this Teaching." The text refers to itself here simply as "this Teaching"; the משנה (copy) of which the text speaks refers physical copy the king writes out.

187. The השגות of the Rabad have been a standard element of printed editions of Maimonides's Code since the Constantinople edition of 1509—that is, since very shortly after the invention of printing.

188. Proto-Rabad also inserts a Reservation at 1.18 that undermines D's belief that Moses delivered the law to the people only in Moab, at the end of the forty years of wandering; in this verse Proto-Rabad restores E's view that Moses provided legal instruction to Israel at the beginning of that period. In the Reservation found in 4.14 Proto-Rabad emphasizes Moses's intermediary role, again drawing the text closer to E's point of view.

189. Cf. the notion of Deuteronomy as a "proto-Mishnah" suggested by Weingreen, *From Bible to Mishna*, 143–54. The exegetical nature of Deuteronomy's repetition of the story of lawgiving is also evident in Deuteronomy's treatment of the tablets produced after the golden calf incident. We saw earlier that in Exodus 34.1 God announced that God would write the second set of tablets, yet in 34.28 the narrator allows the possibility—in fact, the likelihood—that Moses wrote them. The tension between those verses was typical of E, who, by introducing ambiguity as to the origin of the tablets, again encourages the readers to wonder about the provenance of the laws' wording and hints at a greater role for Moses. In Deuteronomy 10.1–4 D entirely eliminates the contradiction by stating clearly that God wrote the second set of tablets. Thus, D achieves the perspicuity that E studiously avoids when reporting this event. On the exegetical nature of D's treatment of the tablets, see Sonnet, *Book*, 42–45.

190. The question concerning D's relationship to its main legal predecessor in E's Covenant Code (Exodus 21–23) mentioned in chapter 5 n. 32, *infra*—to wit, did D intend the D law code to replace the Covenant Code or to be read beside it?—can be, and has been, asked of Maimonides's code. Whatever the intentions of the authors of both these *Mishnei Torah*, their works became canonical alongside the earlier works rather than instead of them. On the question of whether Rambam intended his code to supersede the Talmud (or, to use Moshe Halbertal's phrasing, whether the *Mishneh Torah* is a summary or a substitute for the Talmud), see Shamma Friedman, "Rambam and the Talmud," who provides very strong arguments that Rambam intended his code to supersede the Talmud. See further Halbertal, "What Is," esp. 97–111. Halbertal suggests that Maimonides himself was ambivalent, but he ultimately concludes, like Friedman, that "Maimonides' true position is [that] the composition is a replacement for the halakhic literature that preceded it" (109). Thus, Maimonides intended his work to be a normative canon (to use Halbertal's phrasing from Halbertal, *People*, 3), but the Jewish people accepted it and indeed revere it as formative canon (cf. Halbertal, "What Is," 100–104). The fate of Maimonides's *Mishneh Torah* is identical to its biblical namesake: it is canonical, but not in the way it was intended to be, and only alongside works it had intended to replace. On the connection between Maimonides's supersessionist attitude toward the Talmuds and his view of himself as a second Moses, see further Even-Chen, "'I Appear,'" 213–14.

191. On the differences between the approach to the law in Deuteronomy 5 and in the newer material at the beginning of chapter 4, which builds on the older material, see Toeg, *Lawgiving*, 131–33.

192. See the sensitive reading of Krüger, "Gesetz und Weisheit," 1–10, esp. 3–4 and 6. Cf. the comments of Toeg, *Lawgiving*, 134, on Deuteronomy 4's emphasis on the educational mission of the lawgiving.

193. See Sommer, *Bodies*, 134.

194. See Schwartz, "Origin," 264, though see further his contention on 265 that the law in D is not simply a practical measure but first and foremost the divine command. On D's orientation toward the future, both in this passage and generally, see also Savran, *Encountering*, 115–16, who further notes the near identity of divine voice and divine command in D.

195. Kugel, "Some Unanticipated," 10–13.

196. To some degree, this tendency is also noticeable in later strata of priestly writings (i.e., the Holiness School), which, like D, require the centralization of the cult and provide rituals for nonpriests to perform that allow them to have a cultic experience far from the Temple. See Knohl, *Sanctuary*, 175–97.

197. See Weinfeld, *DDS*, 332.

198. Seeskin, *Searching*.

199. In asking this question, I do not assume that D reacted to P, or that H reacted to D. The authors of any one of these schools may or may not have known about views found in another. In either event the redactor juxtaposed narratives and ideologies in such a way that we readers are forced to confront the doubt that one version of a narrative or an idea can shed on another.

200. The fact that each source intends to tell the one and only story of the lawgiving has been demonstrated especially convincingly by Schwartz; see, e.g., Schwartz, "Torah," 181–82.

201. Here I borrow phrasing from Ward, *Religion*, 22–23, from the section subtitled "The Ambiguity of Revelation."

202. Lawgiving at Sinai or Horeb and at the Tabernacle takes up Exodus 19–40, Leviticus 1–27, and Numbers 1–10, along with significant sections of the remainder of Numbers and Deuteronomy. The exodus narrative is found in Exodus 1–15; the wandering, in Numbers 13–36; creation, in Genesis 1–3; and patriarchs, in Genesis 12–50.

203. Something similar happens with the Pentateuch's three divergent pictures of divine presence, I have argued in Sommer, *Bodies*. A very similar debate occurs among D, P, and H in regard to holiness in the Pentateuch: Is it a characteristic of space or of people? Is it automatically granted by the divine presence, or is it something toward which Israelites must always strive? On this rich topic, see especially Kornfeld and Ringgren, "קדשׁ," 530–34; Knohl, *Sanctuary*; Joosten, *People and Land*; Japhet, "Some Biblical Concepts"; Schwartz, *Holiness* (and, more briefly, Schwartz, "Holiness of Israel"); Regev, "Priestly"; Anderson, "To See."

204. For this terminology, see already Heschel, *TmH*, 2:220–63 (= *HT*, 552–88), as well as Halivni, "Man's Role," and Halivni, *Peshat*, 112–19. The existence of these longer trajectories in rabbinic and medieval Jewish culture is a major theme in Heschel's work, as noted by Even-Chen, *Voice*, 173.

205. Rashbam sees it as lamentable that the nation declined the opportunity to receive additional revelations; Lockshin, *Rashbam's Commentary on Exodus*, 219 n. 27. In this one regard, Rashbam agrees with Deuteronomy and differs from the E verse he explicates. As Schwartz has explained, "In the Elohistic account, the assumption that the entire body of laws is going to be communicated to the people by means of a messenger is present from the beginning. In E, the purpose of the proclamation of the Decalogue from the outset is to establish the credibility of the prophet, whose task it will then be to convey the laws and statutes. . . . The idea that were it not for Israel's dread God would have preferred to speak directly to them is D's invention and D's alone" (Schwartz, "Horeb").

206. See Viezel, "Rashbam" and "Divine Content."

207. The letter *mem* in the word מנשיקות in Song of Songs 1.2 can mean "with," but it also can have a partitive meaning, "from among," "with some [but not all] of."

208. On this dictum in rabbinic exegesis, see *supra* note 40.

209. On the complex development of the interpretation that the people heard only the first two statements in the tannaitic and amoraic periods, see Schwartz, "'I Am.'"

210. Because this line of reasoning seems so much less fanciful and more text-immanent to modern eyes, modern readers might speculate that it is the unstated source of minimalist position in the midrashim and Talmuds. But Schwartz, "'I Am,'" 195, argues that this line of reasoning arose only in the Middle Ages and that the interpretation as it appears in midrashic and talmudic texts has a completely separate origin.

211. Note that "the rabbis" here refers not the unidentified maximalist rabbis of Shir Hashirim Rabbah 1:13 but to minimalist rabbis mentioned in Shemot Rabbah 33:7.

212. The same line of thought is summarized by ibn Ezra in his Long Commentary to 20.1, though he discusses the difficulties of this interpretation and goes on to reject it there as well as in the comment to 20.18. It is also mentioned by Naḥmanides to 20.7, who notes ibn Ezra's objection; he maintains that the people heard and understood the actual wording of the first two Statements; then they heard the sound of God's voice in the remaining eight, but they did not hear the words distinctly. Thus according to Naḥmanides the people heard the whole Decalogue but received the laws in the last eight Statements only from Moses. Rashi affirms that the people heard only the first two commandments in his commentaries to Exodus 19.19 and Numbers 15.22 and 31. However, commenting at Exodus 20.1 Rashi maintains that the people heard

all the statements from God directly. On this contradiction, see Schwartz, "I Am," 184–86, 193–95. On the various systems of midrashic and medieval exegetes for interpreting what the people heard at Sinai (e.g., distinct words of each statement or a great sound that included all of them at once) and from whom (God, or Moses, or both, or part from God and part from Moses), see the very useful categorization in Kasher, *Torah Sheleimah*, 16:221–22.

213. Qara's convincing reasoning raises an interesting question: does he prove that the reading of Exodus 20 according to which the people heard none of the Decalogue is incorrect? An answer to this question becomes clear in light of what the fifteenth-century sage Abarbanel wrote in chapter 18 of his *Rosh Amanah*: because the Bible often presents Moses as speaking in God's name, the first-person references to God in the first two statements could perfectly well have been spoken by Moses. See the discussion in Kellner, "Maimonides, Crescas," 141 and 145. This tendency occurs with prophets other than Moses as well; the speaker of many prophetic texts shifts between God and the prophet himself throughout the Bible. For a lengthy list of similar passages, see Heschel, *Prophets*, 397 nn, as well as Robinson, *Inspiration*, 166–70 (though see Robinson's discussion, at 184–85, of his difference on this point from Heschel).

214. For a discussion of these themes in additional midrashic texts, see Fraade, "Moses and the Commandments," who notes the debate between sages who "affirm Moses' role as passive recipient and transmitter of God's words/commandments" and those who regarded him as "play[ing] an intellectually active and independent role in the transmission of the commandments" (408). Fraade argues cogently that some sages saw God's approval of "Moses' rational arguments and legal innovations as a model for all times thenceforth" that provided "radical (yet also ambivalent) divine authorizations of rabbinic legal initiative" (421).

215. Maimonides intends the *Guide* for an intellectual-religious elite and deliberately avoids stating radical or unsettling conclusions in clear language. As a result, it is often necessary to construct Maimonides's view on a particular issue by combining and comparing statements he makes in multiple chapters, some of them on the surface less related to the issue at hand. On techniques of obscurity and disclosure in the *Guide*, see Halbertal, *Rambam*, 235–44; Halbertal, *Concealment*, 49–68; Goodman, *Secrets*, 17–46; Seeskin, *Searching*, 177–88. One particular approach to this issue is outlined in Strauss, "How," but, as Seeskin makes clear, one need not be a Straussian to realize that the *Guide* often conceals. In the introduction to the *Guide*, Maimonides himself states that he will not spell out his ideas clearly in this work; see Maimonides, *Guide*, 5–7. (All the quotations and page references I provide from the *Guide* are from Pines's translation.) Lorberbaum, "On Contradictions," shows that in many cases the nature of Maimonides's subject matter, rather than theological-

political considerations, leads (or rather requires) Maimonides to state certain ideas dialectically and thus with what appears to be contradiction; in these cases, his goal is not to conceal from the multitudes. Nevertheless, in some cases, Lorberbaum avers (735), Maimonides does use contradiction to conceal disturbing or destructive truths from the multitudes—and it seems likely that these cases include the issue of Mosaic prophecy.

216. Maimonides, *Guide*, 364–65.

217. Ibid., 365.

218. On the nonaudible, nonarticulate, and thus nonverbal nature of what the people heard in the first two statements, see the useful summary in Kreisel, *Prophecy*, 230–34.

219. Maimonides, *Guide*, 364.

220. What we see here happens elsewhere in rabbinic tradition: sages who support the position of one Pentateuchal source will quote and exegetically overturn the basic meaning of verses from another source that work against their position. See Sommer, "Reflecting on Moses," 614–21.

221. Maimonides, *Guide*, 366.

222. As Reines, "Maimonides'," 349–50, points out, for Maimonides "God did not 'descend' in space onto Sinai, and Moses did not 'ascend' in space to God, but the emanation or 'inspiration' that produces prophecy came to Moses, who had previously directed his thoughts to the lofty subject of metaphysical theology."

223. Maimonides, *Guide*, 158–59.

224. Ibid., 410–12.

225. Cf. Reines, "Maimonides'," 337.

226. Ibid., 354–55.

227. Bland, "Moses," 62–63.

228. Ibid., 64.

229. As Diamond, "Concepts," 128–29 points out, "Scripture, for Maimonides, does not antedate the world as in the midrashic and kabbalistic tradition but arrives on the historical scene to address an urgent human predicament. . . . The Torah, then, is neither the midrashic blueprint for the universe nor the kabbalistic mind or body of God but rather is a document that is thoroughly human in its concerns and language."

230. Kaplan, "'I Sleep,'" 139.

231. Ibid., 135. The same point is made by Reines, "Maimonides'," 332–33.

232. Kaplan, "'I Sleep,'" 133–35. Cf. Reines, "Maimonides'," 353–54.

233. Kaplan, "'I Sleep,'" 137 and 160 n. 40. For a different perspective, see Kellner, *Dogma*, 229 n. 93. While Kellner succeeds in showing that according to Maimonides, before one accepts the Torah one must accept the principle that prophecy exists, he does not, to my mind, demonstrate that Moses acted as a prophet when composing the Torah.

234. Reines, "Maimonides'," 328. On the Torah's subprophetic status, see further
     353–54. For a similar conclusion with a difference of emphasis stressing the
     similarity between Moses when writing the Torah and other prophets, see
     Even-Chen, "'I Appear,'" 212.

235. Goodman, *Secrets*, 170.

236. Ibid., 169–87; the summary quoted here is from 187.

237. It must be noted that he expresses it only indirectly; nowhere does he provide a
     statement that articulates the idea that Reines, Bland, Kaplan, and Goodman
     attribute to him in the passages I quoted earlier. One discovers Maimonides's
     belief that the Torah was written by a human being only by juxtaposing pas-
     sages from several different sections of the *Guide*, reading them carefully, and
     seeing how they add up to support for a thesis that is not quite stated. Indeed,
     it might be more accurate to say that when it comes to the origin of the law,
     Maimonides hides his view in the *Guide* than to say that he articulates it
     there. As Goodman, *Secrets*, 170, notes, "Maimonides did not leave us spelled-
     out statements in regard to this question. Nonetheless, from statements that
     he scattered throughout the *Guide* it is possible to reconstruct his confron-
     tation with the riddle of the Torah's origin." Cf. references in n. 215, *supra*.
     On differences between the exoteric and esoteric ideas of the Torah's origin
     in Maimonides (both of which were important and legitimate, the former
     because it is useful and the latter because it is true), see further Reines, "Mai-
     monides'," 348–49.

238. The following translation from Maimonides's Arabic original is by Abelson,
     "Maimonides," 54. For a reliable Hebrew translation, see Kafaḥ, *Mishnah*,
     4:143–44. My thanks to Simon Hopkins of the Hebrew University for clarify-
     ing important terms and phrases in the Arabic original.

239. The wording of Abelson's translation here follows Maimonides's original for-
     mulation in Arabic rather than the standard medieval Hebrew translation
     available in printed editions of the Vilna Shas. The latter, though more fa-
     miliar to Jews, departs completely from the original in these lines. See Kafaḥ,
     4:143 n. 67.

240. Kaplan, "'I Sleep,'" 161 n. 50.

241. Kaplan proves himself authentically Maimonidean by implying this conclusion
     without actually articulating it: even though Kaplan says the conclusion "can-
     not be glossed over" (ibid.) he does not in fact state what that conclusion is.
     Similarly, he asserts that the difference "should be noted" (ibid.), but he hides
     this assertion at the end of a lengthy footnote. Kaplan's Maimonidean circum-
     spection manifests itself in the article's title, which gives no hint of Kaplan's
     bold and unsettling thesis concerning the origin of the Torah. Indeed, Kaplan
     first introduces his thesis about a third of the way through the text. Only a
     person who makes an sustained intellectual effort and who exhibits forbear-
     ance will come to understand the central ideas that Kaplan at once conceals

and reveals. In noting the Maimonidean aspect of Kaplan's self-presentation in his 1990 article, one may further observe that though he refers to his predecessors Reines and Bland, he makes no reference to the writings of Goodman and Even-Chen. I presume Kaplan refrains from citing their work (published in 2005 and 2010) in order to intimate to perceptive readers that he does not claim prophetic status.

242. For the view that Maimonides did not believe the principles himself (in particular, with regards to the Fourth and Eighth Principles), see Shapiro, *Limits*, 118–21, and further references there. (I should note that Shapiro does not go as far as Kaplan regarding the nonprophetic origins of the Torah.) See also Kellner, *Dogma*, 53, who, in the course of arguing for the basic coherence of the *Guide* and the principles, clarifies that he does not "mean to imply that Maimonides accepted the beliefs included in the Thirteen Principles at their face value, the way he wanted the masses to accept them."

243. On the coherence between the longer discussion of the Thirteen Principles in the *Commentary to the Mishnah* and his briefer and less sophisticated discussion of main categories of heretical belief in the *Mishneh Torah*'s Laws of Repentance, see ibid., 21–24.

244. For this reading of the *Mishneh Torah* and the principles, see also Heschel, *TmH*, 2:98–99 (= *HT*, 384–86). See esp. Tucker's useful comment, 385–86 n. 46: Heschel cites Abbaye as an authority against what he sees as Maimonides's extreme and uncompromising position. On the divergence of the talmudic rabbis from Maimonides's views, see further Jon Levenson, *Hebrew Bible, the Old Testament*, 64; Shapiro, *Limits*, 91–121; Brettler, Enns, and Harrington, *Bible and the Believer*, 32–37.

245. For this reading of the Eighth Principle, I am indebted to Yehoyada Amir. On the congruity of the *Guide* and the Eighth Principle, see further Bland, "Moses," 65–66. The question of the relationship between the principles and the later writings has vexed scholars of Maimonides since the Middle Ages. For the view that the Thirteen Principles were an earlier formulation that Maimonides abandoned in later works, see Shapiro, *Limits*, 7–8, and references there. Alternatively, Maimonides may have phrased the Principles (at least the last seven Principles), along with parallel passages on foundations of belief in the *Mishneh Torah*, in a deliberately strict manner that need not be taken over-literally by the philosophically adept, so that the tension between the principles and the *Guide* involve a difference of audience and genre rather than a difference of substance. On this possibility (relevant especially for the last seven principles), see Kellner, *Dogma*, 42–53, who concludes (53) that it is not the case "that Maimonides accepted the beliefs included in the thirteen principles at their face value, the way he wanted the masses to accept them." This does not mean that Maimonides himself rejected the Thirteen Principles or thought they constituted useful lies while *Guide* embodies truth. It does

mean, however, that one should not take the view in the principles that seem to be in tension with the *Guide* in an overly literal fashion, and one should be sensitive to subtle phrasing in light of which the tensions can be resolved.

246. Translation from Abelson, "Maimonides," 53.

247. Seeskin, *Autonomy*, 113, astutely comments on the image of Moses as scribe: "The reference to dictation is also metaphorical since Maimonides insists that Moses' apprehension was entirely intellection." Similarly, Kreisel, *Prophecy*, 178, notes that Maimonides's phrasing "suggests that the speech is not audible speech at all. This is reinforced by the view presented in the previous principle that Moses' prophecy did not involve any of the senses." In light of Kreisel's close reading, it is not clear to me why he emphasizes (168) that for Maimonides every word of the Written Torah has divine origin; the fact that the "speech" (*kalām*) Moses perceives is not audible seems to allow this speech to be supralingual, even if it does not require it. Kreisel further speculates (195 n. 83) that in any event in *Mishneh Torah*, Yesodei Torah 9:1–5, Maimonides may move away from what Kreisel regards as the more conservative claim of the Eighth Principle.

248. Translation from Abelson, "Maimonides," 54. A more literal translation of the Arabic phrasing would be "they are from Moses."

249. See Bland, "Moses," 64, and Goodman, *Secrets*, 187. Cf. Reines, "Maimonides'," 357–58 n. 119 and 360. Cf. Shapiro, *Limits*, 115–16.

250. Kellner, *Must*, 69.

251. Shapiro, *Limits*, 3.

252. See Naftali Tzvi (Ropshitzer) Horowitz, *Zera' Qodesh*, 2:40a. Naftali refers to this teaching again in 1:72a, this time without mentioning Menaḥem Mendel. A different version of the tradition appears in Lipman, *Or Yesha'*, 7a. (My thanks to Daniel Matt and Michael Balinsky for helping me to locate these quotations.) For other references to this teaching in Ḥasidic literature, see Weisbaum, *Yalqut Menaḥem*, 158–59. The association between Mendel's interpretation and Maimonides's comments in the *Guide* is noted in Marcus, *Chassidismus*, 239, and in Scholem, *On the Kabbalah*, 30–31, both of whom attribute the Rymanover's teaching to the Rymanover's own work, *Torah Menaḥem* (also known as *Menaḥem Tzion*). In fact, the remark does not appear in any of the editions of that work, including the several editions from Scholem's own library, which I examined at the Jewish National and University Library at the Givat Ram campus of the Hebrew University. On Scholem's misattribution of the remark and its possible motivations, see further Idel, *Old Worlds*, 119–25.

253. This sounds similar to Buddhist notions of meaning; in fact, the "Perfection of Wisdom" or "Transcendent Insight" sutras (*Pranjaparamitasutras*) exist in a variety of longer and shorter versions, including one that reduces the sutra to the single syllable *a*. Some Buddhists designate this the single-syllable mother

of all sutras. See Wilfred Cantwell Smith, *What Is Scripture*, 149 and 310 n. 14, and see further 249 (on a possible Hindu parallel, see 307 n. 52). It is possible that the one God granted the same revelation, *a*, to Jewish and Buddhist communities, and it is fascinating to see how they developed that revelation in radically different ways.

254. If the wording in the Ropshitzer's *Zera' Qodesh* 2:40a is taken at face value, then the Rymanover would present a paradox that achieves this apogee of the minimalist reading: an *aleph* creates the verbal space for discourse, but it is not itself a sound. It is this understanding of the Rymanover's saying that is especially close to Maimonides's approach in the *Guide* and this understanding that excited Marcus and Scholem (see n. 252, *supra*). However, the *aleph* is vocalized rather than silent in almost all the other references to the Rymanover's teaching, including not only Horowitz's *Zera' Qodesh* and Lipman's *Or Yesha'* but other passing references to the teaching in Hasidic literature as well (on which see Weisbaum, *Yalqut Menaḥem*, 158 nn. 27 and 28). Indeed, the presence of the vowel in the combination *qametz–aleph* (the phrase famously spoken to Jewish children who are beginning to learn to read in the Eastern European ḥeder of yore) may be the core of the teaching's attempt to present God as the prototype of a child's first teacher; see Idel, *Old Worlds*, 123–24.

255. See references in n. 84, *supra*. Further (as Idel, *Old Worlds*, 121–25 stresses) the rebbes do not teach that revelation is contentless and silent, though it seems clear to me that the single syllable without a consonant that is the public revelation at Sinai is not verbal discourse; it is commanding and full of implication but non-specific. In this sense, the rebbes' teaching may be regarded as minimalist–but by no means nihilist.

256. Naftali Tzvi (Ropshitzer) Horowitz, *Zera' Qodesh*, 2:40b, and see also the brief summary on 1:71b. My thanks go to Shaul Magid, who helped me understand this text.

257. For discussion of this theme in the kabbalistic literature, see Wolfson, *Through a Speculum*, 345–55.

258. To give but one example of Naftali Tzvi's reasoning: God appeared to Israel through the "great aleph" of the word *anokhi*, and the numerical value of the "great aleph" (רבתי 'א) is 613. Through considerably more complex (and clever) reasoning, he shows that God's revelation through the aleph involves 248 positives and 365 negatives. In asserting that the Decalogue contained all 613 commandments, Naftali Tzvi elaborates an old mystical tradition, on which see ibid., 354–55, and note additional references in n. 96. For discussion of this theme in rabbinic texts, see Kasher, *Torah Sheleimah*, 16:203–5.

259. See, among others, Cross, *Canaanite Myth*, 192–93; Zakovitch, "Qol Demamah Daqah," 334–35, 345; White, *Elijah*, 4–11; and esp. the hermeneutically sensitive treatment in Savran, *Encountering*, 207–20.

260. This principle was identified by Kuhl, "Wiederaufnahme." Ernst Würthwein convincingly shows that 1 Kings 19.11–13a are a late addition to our text; see Würthwein, "Elijah," 160–62.

261. Many scholars have read this passage either as a polemic against either Canaanite influence in Israelite religion or as response to the stories found in Exodus 19; see, e.g., Cross, *Canaanite Myth*, 193–94; Jeremias, *Theophanie*, 112–15; Savran, *Encountering*, 86.

262. On this passage as an inner-biblical corrective of the notion of revelation in texts like Exodus 19, Deuteronomy 4, and Psalm 29, see Krüger, "Stimme," 13–14. This does not mean that the interpolation completely rejects the sort of imagery in Exodus, Deuteronomy, Psalms, and elsewhere, as noted by Würthwein, "Elijah," 158 and 164; rather, it represents "very subtle reflect[ion]" on the already existing tradition. Cassuto, *Exodus*, 159–60, also notes the connection between this text and Exodus 19, but he rejects the notion that the latter opposes the former. However, he goes on to claim (following Midrash Shemot Rabbah 29:9) that the Decalogue was given in total silence—i.e., that the various noises described in Exodus 19.16, 19 were no longer occurring during the theophany itself (at 162). Thus, Cassuto (and Shemot Rabbah) read the Elijan notion of theophany into the Exodus theophany. It was precisely such a reading of the older texts that the interpolator in 1 Kings 19 intended to foster. Richard Elliott Friedman, *Disappearance*, 23–24, suggests an alternative reading: this passage indicates the cessation of the process of divine revelation in the Hebrew Bible; the sort of clear divine manifestation that reached a high point at Sinai in Moses's day comes to a close in this passage. If this is the case, the passage is not a polemic against the view of revelation seen in Exodus 19. Friedman's reading works well in the context of a canonical interpretation, since (Friedman points out) the divine voice becomes less and less common in the Tanakh as one moves from the Pentateuch to the end of the *Ketuvim* (though he overstates his case in claiming that Yhwh no longer speaks in narrative passages after this one; see, e.g., Job 1–2 and 38). However, in light of the clearly polemical cast of 1 Kings 18–19 and the distinct nature of 1 Kings 19.11–13a, it is also justifiable to read these verses outside of the broad canonical context and within their context in Kings as a response to those models of revelation that describe theophany in Baalistic terms.

263. That the silent *qol* embodies God's presence made explicit in the Septuagint to 19.12, in Targum to 19.11, and in Radak's commentary on 19.12, see further Zakovitch, "Qol Demamah Daqah," 340.

264. See, in addition to the standard lexica, Jeremias, *Theophanie*, 114–15; Savran, *Encountering*, 219–20; and Eidevall, "Sounds." In Psalm 107.28–30, דממה is equated with the situation created by the verbs חשה and שתק, both of which mean "become silent"; this context supports the translation, "silence." Job 4.16 is ambiguous, since the relevant phrase can either be understood as a narrative

progression meaning "there was silence, and [then] I heard a voice" or as a case of a hendiadys meaning "a soft sound." The Septuagint's rendering of דממה in our verse as αὔραν ("breeze, air in motion") suggests a hushed but just barely perceptible sound (a rendering supported also by readers as sensitive as Ralbag and Yosef Qara). Texts from Qumran seem to associate the noun with silence (see 1QIsaᵃ 47.5; and the phrase קול דממת שקט in 4Q405 19.7). Similarly, rabbinic texts gloss it with שתיקה (Sifre Bemidbar Naso §58). Our inability to decide definitively whether the noun means utter silence or a sound that is only barely audible is not surprising; in other languages as well a single word can have both meanings (thus in English "quiet" can refer to the absence of sound as well as to a sound that is hushed).

265. On the anti-visual element of this story, see Savran, *Encountering*, 87 and 227–28, who further argues that the story supports the notion of aural revelation. It seems to me that Savran's sensitive reading misses the extent to which the interpolation in verses 11–13a rejects both visual and aural, or at least verbal, models of revelation.

266. On the understanding of this verse in Jewish tradition, see the commentators on the verse and also Rashi to Exodus 15.11. Cf. Psalm 4.5, 62.2, and see further Maimonides, *Guide*, 139–40 (= 1:59).

267. Kaufmann, *Toledot*, 2:477–78, Knohl, *Sanctuary*, 148–52.

268. On the trope of silence as "the sign not of an absence but, on the contrary, of a Presence" in biblical texts, with reference to many other passages, see further Neher, *Exile*, 9–128 (the quote is at 10). On silence as the apogee of religious experience in Maimonides, see Halbertal, *Rambam*, 250–55.

269. Cf. Scholem, *On the Kabbalah*, 30: "With his daring statement that the actual revelation to Israel consisted only of the *aleph*, Rabbi Mendel transformed the revelation on Mount Sinai into a mystical revelation, pregnant with infinite meaning, but without specific meaning. . . . In this light every statement on which authority is grounded would become a human interpretation, however valid and exalted, of something that transcends it."

270. My thanks to Yair Lorberbaum, who helped me think through this issue more carefully.

271. Gellman, "Wellhausen," 196, 198.

272. In this second paragraph of the subsection, "The Rymanover Rebbe, the Ropshitzer Rebbe, and the Prophet Elijah," and already on page 241 of Sommer, "Revelation," the article Gellman discusses.

273. Indeed, we shall see in chapter 5 that aspects of revelation in D contradict ideas that D articulates, leaving us to wonder whether to attend more to what D claims to believe or to deeper undertones within D.

274. Cf. Brown, *Tradition*, 374; Alon Goshen-Gottstein, "Promise," 97.

275. Similarly, it is possible that later readers understand an earlier text better than that text's first readers understood it. See E. D. Hirsch, *Validity*, 43. This is

especially the case in poetry and in scripture, as noted by Wilfred Cantwell Smith, *What Is Scripture*, 230.

276. Ibid., 148.

277. Congar, *Meaning*, 14.

278. Ratzinger, *Jesus*, xviii–xx. On the communal nature of biblical authorship in Catholic thought, see further Harrington's remarks in Brettler, Enns, and Harrington, *Bible and the Believer*, 87.

279. Schechter, *Studies (First)*, xxiv–xxv.

280. Though Gellman critiques my use of the Ropshitzer on the ground that I find an implication in his work unknown to the Ropshitzer, he is aware of the vitality of implication in religious tradition. In his own exploration of Rebbe Naḥman of Bratzlav, he states (Gellman, "Wellhausen," 205), "I am not about to claim that Reb Nachman reveals in this passage black on white what I have attributed to him. But it is alluringly close to what I think is implicit in his stance . . . (. . . I seek a hook, not a ground.)." It is not clear to me how my use of the Ropshitzer differs. Nonetheless, Gellman's clarity about the nature of his use of Rebbe Naḥman's teaching prompted me to add the exposition above and thus significantly improved my argument. In another article (Gellman, "Conservative"), Gellman advances some further critiques of my thesis, which I would like to address.

First, a central claim I make is that revelation at Sinai contains no specific laws or words, but it was nevertheless commanding—that is, in Gellman's fine summary of my position, "God's revelation had the force of a presence that put the Israelite nation under God's command, as a category of relationship to God, the details of 'command' to be worked out by the receivers of the revelation" (see Gellman, "Conservative," 52). Gellman claims, however, that it is not clear that the biblical documents really insist that the Sinai revelation be seen as commanding. Here Gellman neglects a point I made in my earlier article (Sommer, "Revelation," 450): "The responses of the Jewish people to revelation at Sinai, as presented in texts from the biblical period until the advent of the modern era, have unanimously expressed themselves in terms of law. From the consistency of these responses, we can learn that Jews understood the God manifest at Sinai not merely as a presence but as a presence that commands." Gellman's lack of attention to this aspect of my argument results more from my failing than his: I devoted only two sentences to this crucial point. It is for this reason that in following chapter I devote much more space to the centrality of command in the biblical and postbiblical texts.

Second, Gellman suggests that the historical status of the events at Sinai is not supported by biblical critical scholarship, and consequently that I ought not regard Sinai as a real event; instead, I should see it as a paradigm or a myth. For reasons I outlined earlier (in ch. 1, toward the end of the section, "Artifact Opposed to Scripture"), I do not agree with this assessment: there is no valid historical reason to regard the event at Sinai as fictional or merely paradigmatic. Archaeological and philological evidence cannot prove that the event in question occurred, but it can no more prove that it did not occur. All that philological study can do is help us see how different Israelites perceived or constructed the event differently; to some degree such study also helps us speculate on how those views developed over time. The notion of Sinai as paradigm occurs in the work of Hermann Cohen, but I strongly reject this notion, as I explain in n. 59 in ch. 3. Incidentally, in suggesting that my view requires us to see Sinai as paradigm, Gellman does something entirely legitimate: he uncovers an implication or logical ground of my own argument that I did not express, and which in fact I want to reject. I think that in this case he is incorrect, because in my opinion he misunderstands the nature and purview of archaeological and philological evidence. But the sort of claim he makes about an implication of my ideas is in no way objectionable.

Third, in "Conservative," 60–63, Gellman seems to think that the oldest texts describing the event at Sinai must describe it in the most accurate way, and that since the oldest poetic texts that mention theophany do not mention lawgiving, the event must not have been a legislative one. But there is no reason to presume that the oldest text that records a memory or interpretation of an event provides the most accurate or complete account. I can learn about the Second Temple period by reading Josephus, who was a contemporary (and participant) in many of the events he describes, and I can learn about it by reading the work of Shayye Cohen, who lived two thousand years later. Both are worth reading, but in many respects I will get a vastly more balanced, accurate, and comprehensive understanding of the historical period in question by reading Cohen. Poetic texts that discuss Sinai such as Judges 5.4–5 and Psalm 68.8–10 may well be older than E and P, but this does not mean that the former are more accurate than the latter.

Fourth, in both articles, Gellman rightly critiques my use of the term *contentless* for the revelation according to the participatory theology. In light of his careful analysis, it is clear that I used this term vaguely and in motley ways. Further, the term is not quite appropriate for Rosenzweig and Heschel; for Rosenzweig, we shall see in the next chapter, the command at Sinai contained some specific content, the command to love God. Consequently, I avoid the term in this book.

Finally, it is a pleasure to note that in all his interactions with me, from the time he first contacted me before he sent his articles to press and through preparations I made for a sabbatical in Israel, Yehudah has been a gracious intellectual sparring partner as well as a generous and helpful colleague. It is a privilege to thank him for his careful attention to my work, which has sharpened my thinking even as it allowed me to experience the upside of m. Avot 5.19.

Chapter 3. Command and Law

1. Shai Held, *Abraham Joshua Heschel*, 111–12.
2. See Goodman, *Secrets*, 167–69. For the view that Maimonides nevertheless believed that right opinions suffice to allow one a share in the world to come, see Shapiro, *Limits*, 5.
3. See Heschel, *TmH*, 2:123–298 (= *HT*, 407–501). Especially relevant to our concerns are 2:264–98 (= 478–501).
4. Kasher, *Torah Sheleimah*, 19:328–79.
5. Greenberg, *Studies*, 405–20; Cooper, "Imagining Prophecy," esp. 34–43.
6. See Viezel, "Divine Content," 391–93. Viezel makes clear that ibn Ezra believes that the wording of the Decalogue in Exodus was divine and that the wording of the Decalogue in Deuteronomy includes Moses's interpretive glosses and paraphrases. Viezel goes on to explain that according to ibn Ezra, the Decalogue in Exodus differs from the remainder of the Pentateuch, because the former contains God's actual words, whereas the rest of the Pentateuch contains a supralingual message from God that Moses transferred into Hebrew words. Viezel, "Rashbam on Moses' Role," 171–75, shows that Rashbam had a similar view: the Decalogue is divine language; Pentateuchal law in the first four books is a mix of divine and Mosaic language, but mostly the former; Pentateuchal narrative is also a mix, but largely Mosaic; Deuteronomy's laws are Moses's interpretations and clarifications of divine laws. Thus for both ibn Ezra and Rashbam revelation seems to have been at least in part verbal, though the text of the Pentateuch often includes Moses's paraphrases, expansions, or clarifications of verbal (and perhaps also non-verbal) revelations. See Viezel, "Divine Content," 397–98, and "Rashbam on Moses' Role," 175–76. An earlier example of this sort of approach occurs in Philo. On Philo's idea of Moses as interpreter and the Torah as his interpretation, see Najman, *Seconding Sinai*, 103–6. This approach also occurs in regard to the Book of Deuteronomy in the thought of Elie Benamozegh, as noted by Shapiro, *Limits*, 115 n. 172.
7. See Sommer, "Prophecy as Translation."
8. On the stenographic approach in classical Jewish thought more generally, see the collection of texts and extensive discussion in Heschel, *TmH*, 2:71–99 (= *HT*, 368–86), and Silman, *Voice*, 19–86. For examples of attitudes (both positive and negative) toward what some Christian thinkers call the "dictation theory" among modern Christian (especially British) thinkers, see McDonald, *Theories*, 212–85, 307–11.
9. Abraham Joshua Heschel aptly describes this theory as an attempt to "expand the notion of revelation in order to deny it." On such attempts by Spinoza, Schleiermacher, Blake, and early biblical critics, see Heschel, *Prophets*, 524–29 (the phrase just quoted appears on 525, referring specifically to Spinoza), as well as the discussion of "illumination" and "insight" theories and of Schleiermacher's influence, in McDonald, *Theories*, e.g., 234, 237, 253, 256, 264. On the pos-

sibility that prophets are inspired in the manner that all great poets and artists are inspired, and the implications of that view, see the trenchant discussion in Heschel, *Prophets*, 468–97, and cf. Geller, "Were the Prophets Poets?"

10. For an especially clear articulation of this notion, see S. R. Driver, *Introduction*, viii–xi, and, at greater length, Rowley, *Relevance*, 21–51, esp. 24–28 and 35, where he affirms that the Bible contains "the record of man's growing experience of God, and progressive response to God"—a comment that strongly parallels Heschel's approach. See further the discussion of Rowley in McDonald, *Theories*, 251–54. Von Rad, *Old Testament Theology*, 2:50, speaks of the prophetic office as "consisting on the one hand of binding commitments and on the other of liberties and powers." See further his chapter "The Prophet's Freedom," 2:70–79; on the interpretive nature of the prophet's task in moving from individual revelation to public proclamation, see especially 2:72–73.

11. See the discussion of "the ambiguity of revelation" in Ward, *Religion*, 21–25 and 343 (cf. 89–92 and 209–17), and the discussion of revelation as "interactive" in Brown, *Tradition*, 106–35, esp. 107 and 129. For predecessors, see in McDonald, *Theories*, the discussions of figures such as W. H. G. Thomas, 192–23; G. D. Barry, 239–40; H. Wheeler Robinson, 244–47; William Lee, 261–63; Frederick Watson, 277–76; James Orr, 174–76 and 279–80; and McDonald's own statement, 286–87. A comparable, but less far-reaching, attempt appears in Enns, *Inspiration*, esp. 17–21 and 167–73.

12. Ratzinger, *Jesus*, xix–xx. All but the first of the five models of revelation discussed by Dulles, *Models*, describe the Bible as being at least in part a human response to revelation.

13. Heschel, *TmH*, 2:264–98 (= *HT*, 478–501).

14. Rowley, *Relevance*, 47.

15. Cited in McDonald, *Theories*, 262.

16. On this term in relation to Heschel's own view of revelation, see Even-Chen, *Voice*, 83 and 183; in relation to Buber, see Amir, *Small Still Voice*, 179–80; on revelation as translation, or demanding translation, in Rosenzweig, see esp. Wolfson, "Light," 102–7. Viezel, "God's Revelation," at nn. 37 and 54, also uses this term to describe Radak's view of non-Mosaic prophecy and Maimonides's view of the Pentateuch. See also Uriel Simon, *Seek Peace*, 284, who stresses that the Torah is truthful and eternal, but that "it is phrased in the language of human beings who lived at a certain time, which is to say that it results from an adaptation at the level of language and ideas, an adaptation to the (limited) ability of those who receive it to understand it, to internalize it, and to live by its light." This statement recalls the comment of Ernst Simon that "we must view the mitzvot as an echo of the Lord's words (כהד דברי הגבורה)," translated and quoted by Mendes-Flohr, *Divided*, 345. (On the connection between views of the last two scholars I mention, see Proverbs 10.1a.) Without using the specific term translation, Fishbane presents essentially the same idea in *Sacred*

Attunement, 59. For the analogous suggestion that the record of revelation relates to the revelation itself as phenomenon relates to noumenon, see Kepnes, "Revelation," 208–16.

17. See Pannenberg, *Revelation*; Tillich, *Systematic Theology*, 1:120–22; the discussion of this model in Dulles, *Models*, 53–67. Of course, this approach is also significant in Jewish (and especially biblical) thought; see Fackenheim, *God's Presence*. On this notion in biblical and ancient Near Eastern thought including but not limited to Israelite literature, see Albrektson, *History*.

18. Similar ideas appear elsewhere in modern Jewish thought. See, e.g., Eisen, *Rethinking*, 88 and 283 n. 28, for the beginnings of an analogous idea in Mendelssohn.

19. Rosenzweig, *OJL*, 118, and Rosenzweig, *FRHLT*, 285.

20. See Batnitzky, *Idolatry*, 50–51, 111–12.

21. Rosenzweig, *Star* [Hallo], 176–78 = *Star* [Galli], 190–93. On the love of God as the central command in Rosenzweig, see Glatzer, "Introduction to *FRHLT*," xxiv–xxv; Eisen, *Rethinking*, 198–99; Amir, *Reason*, 136–38, 188–91, 289–90; Mendes-Flohr, *Divided*, 353–54.

22. Rosenzweig, *Star* [Hallo], 178 = *Star* [Galli], 192 = Rosenzweig, *Stern*, 198. Similarly, a few lines later, the younger Rosenzweig seems further from the idea of prophecy as translation, when he writes, "The prophet does not mediate between God and man, he does not receive revelation in order pass it on; rather, the voice of God sounds forth directly from within him, God speaks as 'I' directly from within him. . . . No sooner does his mouth open than God already speaks." On revelation as involving content, see also *Star* (Hallo), 405 (= Galli, 428): "Though as content of revelation and claim on the individual it is commandment, seen as world it is law." On the other hand, while that content, which essentially is a command to love God, is not necessarily verbal in nature, we can use language to summarize this content as I did earlier in this sentence.

23. Rosenzweig, *OJL*, 118.

24. Rosenzweig, *FRHLT*, 285.

25. Further, as Wolfson, "Light," 107, points out, in the final section of the *Star* Rosenzweig adumbrates an eschatological revelation that will articulate an "overcoming of word by image, the triumphant manifestation of the light that is beyond language." Haberman, "Franz Rosenzweig's," 325–26, maintains that the *Star* at certain points does imply that prophetic revelations (not only at Sinai but also to later biblical prophets) do include verbal content. On other precursors in Rosenzweig's work to his critique of Buber in "The Builders," see Batnitzky, *Idolatry*, 114–15.

26. The different phrasing in the *Star* and later writings may also result from the fact that, as Rosenzweig himself points out, attempting to define what exactly is the human element and what the divine in this dialogue is impossible. Rosenzweig expressed the view that Israel's election comes from God "but all the details of

the law come from man alone," but when he heard Nahum Glatzer make the same claim, he realized how problematic this phrasing is: "Can we really draw so rigid a boundary between what is divine and what is human? . . . The only matter of doubt is whether or to what degree this Law originating in Israel's election coincides with the traditional Jewish law. But here our doubt must be genuine doubt, which willingly listens to reason and is as willing to be swayed to as 'yes' as to a 'no'" (Rosenzweig, *OJL*, 119–20).

27. On the entirely human origin of the Bible's wording for Rosenzweig, see Rosenzweig, *Zweistromland*, 761. The point is obscured in the English translation in Buber and Rosenzweig, *Scripture and Translation*, 59, which leaves out a crucial sentence.

28. Rosenzweig, *Star* [Hallo], 199 (= *Star* [Galli], 321). In light of his definition of the content of revelation as a command to love God, it is not surprising that the exegetical section on his study of revelation in the *Star* focuses on the Song of Songs rather than Exodus 19–20 or Deuteronomy 4–5, or that Rosenzweig describes the Song of Songs (202) as "the focal book of revelation." Amir, *Reason*, 282, points out that in the *Star*'s discussion of Song of Songs, Rosenzweig focuses on the many imperative verbs expressing the lover's love, all of which speak to revelation as something that always occurs in a "now," a present moment.

29. My thanks to Neil Gillman for helping me see the ambiguity and variety in Heschel's work on this point and for encouraging me to think through this issue more carefully. See further Perlman, *Abraham Heschel's Idea*, 103–17, as well as Perlman, "Report."

30. Heschel, *God*, 274.

31. Ibid., 181–83.

32. Ibid., 264–65.

33. Ibid., 277 n. 22. Viezel, "Divine Content," 392–93, is more explicit; he shows that ibn Ezra's long commentary to Exodus 20.1 makes clear that the Decalogue in Exodus 20 contains God's words, while Deuteronomy 5 contains Moses's paraphrase of them.

34. Heschel, *God*, 274.

35. Ibid., 164. See also 265 (only one page later than a passage cited above suggesting that none of the wording is from heaven): "The Bible reflects its divine as well as its human authorship. . . . God borrowed the language of man and created a work such as no men had ever made." See further 180 and 244 for similar views.

36. Heschel, *Man's Quest*, 134 (= Heschel, *Moral*, 93). The sentence reappears as an either/or statement in his essay, "Toward and Understanding of Halacha," in ibid., 144: "*Mitzvot* . . . are expressions or interpretations of the will of God."

37. On Heschel's tendency to give evidence of both points of view, see further Eisen, "Re-Reading Heschel," 17, and Shai Held, *Abraham Joshua Heschel*, 108–12. Even-Chen, *Voice*, 83, captures the duality in Heschel's language quite well.

38. The exaltation of Moses over all other prophets is most characteristic of E and to a slightly lesser degree of D, but it is also evident in P and other biblical texts. See Blenkinsopp, *Prophecy and Canon*, 77–95. On views of Moses in J and E, see also Sommer, "Reflecting on Moses."

39. See, e.g., the reference to Duran and Rashi in Greenberg, *Studies*, 413, and further references and discussion in Heschel, *TmH*, 2:146–65 (= *HT*, 423–38).

40. On rabbinic debate concerning the extent of Moses's own contribution to Deuteronomy, see Heschel, *TmH*, 2:181–218 (= *HT*, 451–77).

41. Licht, *Commentary on the Book of Numbers XI–XXI*, 2:40.

42. This passage in Numbers entails a paradox with far-reaching implications for other reports of prophetic experience in the Bible. God's statement to Miriam and Aaron that no prophet other than Moses receives a clear-cut message from God is introduced through a direct address that seems clear cut! In other words, the divine words they are described as hearing deny the possibility that they could directly hear any divine words. (See ibid., 2:49; Milgrom, *Numbers*, 94.) If the statement in 12.6–8 is meaningful, then it follows that the phrase that introduces the statement ("He said") cannot be understood literally. The narrator in Numbers 12 does not hesitate to state that God spoke to Miriam and Aaron, even when the narrator goes on to explain that God did not literally speak to prophets like Miriam and Aaron. It seems to be a given that the words "God said," when not directed toward Moses, are intended rather broadly, to mean, "God issued a communication to the prophet, which the prophet had to interpret so that it could be rendered into human language." What is true of the author of Numbers 12 may well be true of many other biblical authors, including the prophets themselves.

43. On the term, see the brief discussion in Heschel, *TmH*, 1:276 (= *HT*, 308). The parallel passage in Mishnat Rabbi Eliezer 6 (page 115) reads not אספקלריות but מראות, a clear term for mirrors (but not, of course, a term for clear mirrors).

44. See Wolfson, *Through a Speculum*, 131, 133, 344 n. 56. On the mystical traditions' thematization of the אספקלריה as it relates to the comparison between Moses and other prophets, see ibid., *passim*, but esp. 26, 147–48, 151, 214.

45. Maimonides, *Guide*, I:54 = p. 123; see further Bland, "Moses," 52. In the Seventh Principle in the commentary to Mishnah Sanhedrin, Maimonides presents what seems a different view: all other prophets removed some but not all of the veils separating God from humanity, whereas Moses removed all the veils. And yet in the seventh chapter of the "Eight Chapters" introducing the commentary to Mishnah Avot, Maimonides states that Moses removed each veil save one, for even Moses's intellect remained tied to the material world. Using Exodus 33.18–23 as proof, Maimonides argues that Moses's apprehension of God was not perfect, though it was superior to that of all other prophets. On the contradiction between these two passages in the Mishnah commentary and the likelihood that we ought not attempt to reconcile them, see Kreisel, *Proph-*

ecy, 180–82, and further references there. This tension within Maimonides's Mishnah commentary recalls the difference between Numbers 12 and the midrashim that cite it: the Thirteen Principles (like *Mishneh Torah*, Yesodei Torah 7:6) resemble Numbers 12 in claiming that Moses differed from other prophets because he apprehended God directly while they apprehended God indirectly; the Eight Chapters (like the *Guide*) recall the midrashic texts in contending that Moses differed from other prophets because his indirect apprehension of God took place through one veil or mirror, while theirs involved many veils or mirrors. (On Moses's attainment of nonmaterial intellect in *Mishneh Torah*'s discussion, see Kreisel, 190.)

46. Kaplan, "I Sleep," 161, n. 50. Kaplan uses this term repeatedly of Maimonides's composition of the Torah; e.g., twice on 143, again on 144.

47. Goodman, *Secrets*, 187; Even-Chen, "I Appear," 212; Novak, *Tradition*, 44. Similarly, Reines, "Maimonides'," 355, speaks of Moses "creating the particular laws that reify the essence of the ideal law."

48. For the suggestion that Maimonides regards the difference between Moses and other prophets as a matter of degree rather than an essential difference, see especially Even-Chen, "I Appear," *passim*. This move is not unique to Maimonides within medieval Jewish thought; for example, the notion of a distinction between Moses and all other prophets is weakened in Gersonides, according to Samuelson, *Revelation*, 174.

49. Heschel, *God*, 160. Note also Heschel's explicit use of the partnership theme on page 274: "There is a partnership of God and Israel in regard to both the world and the Torah: He created the earth and we till the soil; He gave us the text and we refine it and complete it." Cf. Even-Chen, *Voice*, 83–84, who explains that for Heschel the Bible translates revelation from an experience to a concept (which doesn't encompass everything the experience encompasses). At 173, Even-Chen speaks of a partnership in which the human beings have to translate the divine will into the language of action or deed.

50. Heschel, *God*, 259–60. The same view is expressed in Heschel, *Prophets*, 624–25.

51. Heschel, *God*, 137.

52. Ibid., 252.

53. Ibid., 253.

54. The literature on correlational theology in Tillich's work is enormous. As good a place to start as any would be Tillich, *Systematic Theology*, 1:59–66. Note there especially his rejection of both the "supranaturalistic method" for understanding Christianity and the "naturalistic or humanistic method" in favor of a middle way reminiscent of the Heschel's approach to revelation. The supranaturalistic method recalls the stenographic model: it "takes the Christian message to be a sum of revealed truths which have fallen into the human situation like strange bodies from a strange world. No meditation to the human situation is possible. These truths themselves create a new situation before they can be received"

(1:65). The naturalistic or humanistic method "derives the Christian message from man's natural state. It develops its answer out of human existence, unaware that the human existence itself is the question" (1:65).

55. Hermann Cohen, *Religion*, 82, 98.

56. On the theme of correlations in Cohen, see Seeskin, *Autonomy*, 162–69, and Erlewine, "Reclaiming," 205. For a further development of this theme in Jewish philosophy, see Seeskin, *Autonomy*, 219–38.

57. Idel, "On the Theologization," 171.

58. On the connections between the theme of correlation in Heschel and modern Christian theologians including Tillich, see esp. Shai Held, *Abraham Joshua Heschel*, 84–93 (and, for crucial differences among them, see 262–64 n. 80).

59. Nonetheless, we should not overlook differences between Cohen's demythologizing understanding of revelation and Heschel's view, which puts more emphasis on the personhood of God. On these differences, see Erlewine, "Reclaiming," *passim*, esp. 185–86. Hermann Cohen, *Religion*, 86, contends that just as "spiritual succession was, in the course of political events, designated as an historical act in order that it might be considered a national one," so too in "proper, which is to say literary, history, criticism and correction appeared, which *transferred Sinai into the heart of man*. . . . The eternal . . . is removed from all sense experience, therefore also from all historical experience." This attempt to spiritualize revelation while minimizing its particularism marks Cohen off from both Heschel and Rosenzweig. Here we see why Cohen does not subscribe to the participatory theory of revelation as I describe it, and why (like Martin Buber) he is less relevant to the project of this book: Cohen breaks decisively from the historicity, specificity, and content of the revealed law. He idealizes Sinai, removing its significance from the event itself; for him, it matters little whether the event actually occurred, whereas for the participatory theory it is crucial that an event occurred in which both God and Israel participated. Cohen sees the Sinai narrative not as historical but as a symbolic representation of a moral argument concerning the relationship between God and humanity. For the rejection of a similar sort of idealization in Christian thought, see Ward, *Religion*, 197–200.

60. Idel, "On the Theologization," 171.

61. This summary of Idel's work comes from Garb, "Moshe Idel's Contribution," 20. For these themes, see esp. Idel, *Enchanted Chains*.

62. On Heschel's emphasis on Cordovero, see Kimelman, "Abraham Joshua Heschel's Theology," 217–19.

63. Heschel pointed to theurgical themes in the school of Rabbi Akiva in classical rabbinic texts; see Heschel, *TmH*, esp. 1:65–92, 1:232–37 (= *HT*, 104–26, 270–74, and see 113 n. 20, where Tucker notes Heschel's attention to this theme in his work on the Kotzker Rebbe). In emphasizing this theme not only in kabbalah (where, in Heschel's time, it was somewhat marginalized by Scholem's

school) but also among the rabbis (where modern scholars almost completely ignored it), Heschel evinces the great importance the theme held for him. Heschel's attention to this proto-kabbalistic element among the classical rabbis was decades ahead of his time in terms of Jewish scholarship. Several decades later, scholars such as Moshe Idel, Yehudah Liebes, Michael Fishbane, Elliot Wolfson, and Itamar Gruenwald began to claim that this core aspect of kabbalah of the second millennium had deep roots in classical rabbinic thought of the first. On Heschel as a predecessor to the revisionary work on kabbalah by these scholars, see Idel, "Abraham J. Heschel"; Lorberbaum, *Image*, 167; and esp. Kimelman, "Abraham Joshua Heschel's Theology." (Kimelman, 220, further notes respects in which Hermann Cohen is a key predecessor to Scholem's side in this debate on the origins of theurgy.)

64. Idel, "Theologization," 126. Idel introduces the concept of a correlational theology and the interplay of ascending and descending vectors in large part to emphasize the central role that theurgy plays both in kabbalah of the second millennium CE and in the kabbalah's first-millennium rabbinic predecessors. See ibid., esp. 171–73. On theurgy in kabbalah and its rabbinic forerunners, see further the more extended treatments in Idel, *Kabbalah*, 156–99, as well as Garb, *Manifestations*, and Lorberbaum, *Image*, 156–69. On the connection between theurgy and Heschel's emphasis on divine-human interdependence, see Kimelman, "Heschel's Theology," 220–27, 232–33.

65. Heschel, *God*, 291. Cf. Heschel, *Man Is Not Alone*, 248: "God is in need of man," as well as Heschel, *Moral*, 159. Heschel's phrasing echoes the notion that העבודה צרך גבוה in kabbalistic literature, on which see Green, "Abraham Joshua Heschel," 73.

66. Heschel, *Prophets*, 288. The concept of pathos is at the heart of *Prophets*; see esp. the first four chapters of part 2.

67. Heschel, *Man's Quest*, 136 (= Heschel, *Moral*, 93). In belittling the significance of symbols for religion, Heschel's correlational theology diverges in a crucial way from that of Tillich, for whom symbol becomes perhaps the central element of religious belief. In this emphasis Heschel also breaks away from Hermann Cohen. On this divergence from Tillich, see Mackler, "Symbols"; Shai Held, *Abraham Joshua Heschel*, 262–64, n. 80. On Heschel's negative attitude toward religious symbolism more generally, see Marmur, "In Search," 38–40 and literature cited there. On its early roots, see Kaplan and Dresner, *Prophetic*, 132 and (on the early and Hasidic roots of Heschel's stress on the effect of human behavior on God) 133.

68. See Idel, "Abraham J. Heschel," 92.

69. E.g., Heschel, *Moral*, 143–45, and also 91–95 (= Heschel, *Man's Quest*, 134–37).

70. Eisen, "Re-Reading Heschel," 32 n. 97, sees the phrase "to affect God" in *Man's Quest for God* as a regrettable lapse of Heschel's part; see too Petuchowski, "Faith," 392, 397. Eisen writes: "I think Heschel simply mis-spoke when he

said that the mitzvot 'affect God.' At no other point in his thought is anything remotely similar claimed. The meaning seems to be that 'mitzvot transcend reality,' that they have an 'ontological status' as the word of God. They 'affect God' in that God proclaimed them, and by doing so entered into a new relation with the world." Eisen discounts the phrasing as poorly chosen rhetoric, but I think that Heschel here is doing what he often does: repeating a central theme from the religion he has inherited while adapting it to the modern world. In this case, the religion he has inherited is Ḥasidism, with its kabbalistic emphasis on theurgy. He takes that theme very seriously, transforming it into the idea of God's longing for humanity, which, far from being a lapse, is one of the most characteristic motifs of his work. On the centrality of the theme of God's need for humanity in Heschel's work, see Shai Held, *Abraham Joshua Heschel*, 8–10, who further demonstrates (13–16, 22–24) the central role that God's dependence on the performance of *mitzvot* plays throughout Heschel's work, noting further significant ways Heschel transforms this older theme. On the Hasidic roots of this "dramatic sense of the cosmic importance of human deeds, which added so much to . . . the sense of divine/human partnership" in Heschel's work, see Green, "Abraham Joshua Heschel," 73–75.

71. See Rosenzweig, *Star* [Hallo], 410–11 (= *Star* [Galli], 433–44).

72. Idel, *Old Worlds*, 287 n. 14; see further 160–62. For a contextualization of this theme in Rosenzweig's thought more broadly, see Heinemann, *Ta'amei*, 2:233–35 (and on Rosenzweig's connection in this regard with Heschel and Buber, see 2:297 n. 185).

73. Idel, *Kabbalah*, 156–70, and cf. 181–82.

74. *Toledot*, 2:474.

75. The theme is central to all three volumes. For an overview, see esp. 1:238–41 (= *HT*, 274–78). The theme also receives detailed treatment in Silman, *Voice*, who analyzes two related approaches that speak of heavenly Torah (see 89–116 and 119–29, 140) and also describes an approach that moves in a completely different direction (21–30). The idea of a heavenly Torah with an earthly, verbal manifestation may be hinted at in Psalm 119, a late psalm that presents a proto-rabbinic piety. See the nuanced treatment in Reynolds, *Torah*, 124–46, esp. 133–36. An analogous distinction appears in the thought of Abraham ibn Ezra, who distinguished between the perfect content transmitted to Moses and the contingent verbal form Moses gave to that content in the Pentateuch. See Viezel, "Divine Content," 401–6.

76. See the discussions and many additional sources in Heschel, *TmH*, 2:8–12 (= *HT*, 325–28), and Urbach, *Sages*, 197–201. This notion has prerabbinic roots. Heschel points out that Philo already distinguished between the written Torah we know and the heavenly *logos* through which God created the world; see Heschel, 2:10–11 and n. 18 there.

77. *HT*, 275–76 nn. 34 and 39.

78. Heschel, *TmH*, 1:238–41 (= *HT*, 274–78). The sages' emphasis on the perfect correspondence between the heavenly and the earthly forms of Torah recalls Maimonides's belief that the Torah written by Moses reflects the pure intellectual overflow he received from heaven as perfectly as possible; see Reines, "Maimonides'," 354–58, but note the demurral in Kaplan, "I Sleep," 161 n. 50.

79. Heschel, *TmH*, 1:240, in my translation. Tucker (*HT*, 276–77) renders slightly differently. Where I suggest "lesser version," as the metaphoric sense of נובלת, Tucker supplies "surrogate," which, I think, does not convey the negative connotation that נובלת carries, a connotation clear to anyone who attempts to eat fruit that fell from a tree well before it ripened.

80. See Heschel, *TmH*, 2:3–32, esp. 10–11 (= *HT*, 321–40, esp. 326–27); see further the crucial passage in *TmH* 2:i–iii, which explains the main theme of the second volume (unfortunately, this is not translated in full by Tucker in *HT*). See also Heschel, *God*, 262–64, and Heschel's references to rabbinic and kabbalistic passages there.

81. The phrase does not appear in rabbinic literature, though the phrase תורה בשמים occurs in Midrash Shir Hashirim 8:15 and Midrash Mishlei 8:5. The distinction between these two Torahs recurs with different terminology in Fishbane, *Sacred Attunement*, 61–62, where Fishbane suggests the useful vocabulary of a Torah *from* God to which we have direct access and a primordial, pre-Sinaitic Torah *of* God, which is "the *torah kelulah*, whose reality throbs around the letters and words of the Torah from Sinai and reminds those with ears to hear that the immense 'Shall-Be' of God ever exceeds the written 'just this' of scripture." On the term תורה כלולה and its use in kabbalistic sources, see Scholem, "Revelation and Tradition," 294–95.

82. For these terms, Heschel, see *TmH*, 2:ii (= *HT*, 322, where Tucker translates them more freely than I do).

83. Many parallels are listed in Heschel, *TmH*, 2:22–23 and 2:28 n. 12 (= *HT*, 333–34 and 337 n. 71).

84. Scholem, "Revelation and Tradition," 294–95. At greater length, see Scholem, *On the Kabbalah*, 32–86; Idel, "Concept of Torah"; Idel, "Concepts of Scripture," 161–62 and 177 n. 36.

85. See Fishbane, *Garments*, 33–46; Scholem, "Revelation and Tradition," 292–303; and cf. the sources cited in Heschel, *TmH*, 2:32 nn. 31, 32 (= *HT*, 340 nn. 83, 84). The theme developed further after the *Zohar*. Shaul Magid shows that for many Lurianic kabbalists, the true meaning (Magid's use of the singular here is deliberate) of Torah existed before Sinai; thus "the entire Revelation [at Sinai] was the symbolic encoding of the ancient esoteric tradition of *tikkun*. ... Many kabbalists . . . worked under the assumption that their teaching preceded the Torah as we know it and believed that the Pentateuch was its symbolic representation. When they turn to exegesis, their intent is to de-symbolize Scripture in order to reveal its true nature . . . thus rendering the garment as symbol,

obsolete" (see Magid, "From Theosophy," 62 [and cf. esp. 42]). We see here an intimation of a radical devaluation of the revealed Torah we know.

86. On this widespread set of equations, see, e.g., Green, *Guide to the Zohar*, 123–24; Idel, "Concept of Torah," 71. On the identity of the supernal Torah that is *Hokhmah* in the *Zohar* with the black fire on white fire discussed by the classical rabbis, see Green, 124–25. On idea of heavenly Torah differing from earthly, see further, Even-Chen, *Voice*, 184, who follows Heschel in referring to Moshe Cordovero's *Pardes Rimonim*, Gate 21:6 (Heschel, *God*, 277 n. 12). Even-Chen shows that Heschel constructs his conception of Torah by utilizing the kabbalistic notion according to which the fullness of God's light is hidden in קליפות in this world, since that fullness cannot exist in its pure form in this world. Thus, the Torah of this world is not pure or full in the same way as the heavenly Torah. As Avraham Sommer reminds me, the notion of a Torah with content developing from an infinite but contentless Torah could be developed sephirotically as well: *Keter* (crown), the highest *sephirah*, has no particular content and is thus called אין ("Nothing"). The other Torahs emerge from *Keter*, becoming ever more specific as one moves down from the sephirotic tree. As Avi pointed out to me, kabbalists quote Job 28.12 (חכמה מאין תמצא ואי זה מקום בינה, "*Hokhmah* comes from *Ayin* . . .") to support this derivation of the supernal Torah. On his remark, see further Proverbs 15.20a.

87. This view is attributed to the Baal Shem Tov in Menahem Nahum of Chernobyl, *Sefer Me'or 'Einayim*, beginning of *Parashat Huqqat* (pp. 104–5), and elsewhere. See related Hasidic and mystical texts cited in Magid, "Modernity," 93 nn. 81 and 82. As Magid notes (94), the twentieth-century Hasidic leader Aaron (Areleh) Roth insists that apprehension of the inmost Torah is available only through faithful study of the exoteric garment that is the Torah of Moses; without this faithful study of the garment, the unity of Torah is destroyed. In adding this caveat to the Baal Shem Tov's dichotomy, it seems to me R. Areleh recognizes the powerful and, to him, dangerous implications of the notion that the Five Books reflect the divine Torah but do not constitute it.

88. Here I paraphrase an exegesis by my son, Avraham Sommer.

89. Deuteronomy 10.1–4 argued that God, not Moses, wrote the second set. D's revision or clarification of E here matches D's attempt to eliminate related ambiguities in E in chapters 19–20. Later Jewish exegetes do not unanimously accept D's reading, as the examples from Shemot Rabbah 47:2, Isaiah of Trani, *Moshav Zekeinim*, and other commentators discussed by Lieberman and Kasher (see n. 95 to ch. 2 earlier in this volume) show. Here, as in Deuteronomy 5.4, D's attempt to erase a participatory theory of revelation did not fully succeed.

90. On scribes' involvement not only with epistolary activities on behalf of the royal court or businessmen but also with religious settings, see van der Toorn, *Scribal*, 55–63, and Lenzi, *Secrecy*, 68–103.

91. Van der Toorn, *Scribal*, 111, 115.

92. Savran, *Telling*, 1–5; quotation from 110.

93. Ibn Ezra already hints that the freedom with which characters and narrators paraphrase carries implications regarding the nature of the wording of texts revealed to prophets. See Viezel, "Divine Content," 388–89.

94. This tendency is even more pronounced in biblical texts than in their counterparts from Mesopotamia and Canaan. Cassuto, *Biblical and Oriental Studies*, 2:29–32, notes that both Ugaritic and biblical narratives frequently employ repetitions, but the former are more likely to be verbatim or nearly verbatim than the latter. The same observation applies to Akkadian and Sumerian texts, in which repetitions resemble those of Ugaritic.

95. As noted by van der Toorn, *Scribal*, 325 n. 15.

96. For an exception, see Hurowitz, "Proto-Canonization," 38; on the gradual development of a stenographic theology of revelation in first millennium Mesopotamia, see van der Toorn, *Scribal*, 208–21.

97. On authority from Anu and Enlil, see the prologue to the Laws of Ḥammurapi, i:27, i:50; on command from Marduk, see v:14; on wisdom from Shamash, see the epilogue, xlviii:95 (edition with translation in Martha Roth, *Law Collections*, 76, 80–81, 134). See further Hurowitz, "Proto-Canonization," 35–36.

98. See, e.g., Rosenzweig, *Star* [Hallo], 177 (=*Star* [Galli], 190–91).

99. The congruence between this Rosenzweigian position and Menachem Mendel's dictum on the *aleph* was noted already by Gershom Scholem, *On the Kabbalah*, 30 n. 3.

100. Heschel, *Moral*, 139. The passage also appears in Heschel, *Man Is Not Alone*, 175. Italics in original.

101. Heschel, *God*, 185.

102. *OED* (3rd ed., online), s.v., "Religion," def. 3a. On the semantic drift of terms derived from the Latin *religio* in Western languages from definitions that originally stressed action and rite as much as belief to a definition concerned above all with faith, see Wilfred Cantwell Smith, *Meaning*, 19–50.

103. Heschel, *God*, 162. Even-Chen, *Voice*, 173, discusses Heschel's notion of a partnership, in which the human beings have to translate the divine will into the language of action and deed.

104. On the human origin of much of the system of *mitzvot*, see, e.g., Heschel, *God*, 302; see also the entire third volume of Heschel, *TmH* (= *HT*, 658–787).

105. Heschel, *Moral*, 144. His belittling of the notion of practice as custom is even more evident when he states, "Customs, ceremonies are fine, enchanting, playful. But is Judaism a religion of play?" (143).

106. I intend the term *peshat* as it has been used since the twelfth century: an interpretation that reads the language of a passage in keeping with the grammatical, syntactic, and stylistic norms of that language as it functions typically among human beings, and that reads a passage as a whole rather than atomistically. For this definition of *peshat*, see esp. Kamin, *Rashi's*, 14–15. This use of the term

is essentially that of Rashbam, even though Rashbam develops it from ideas found in a different form in the work of his grandfather, Rashi, as Kamin shows, at 266–74. See further on the term in Rashbam, Touitou, *Exegesis*, 98–176, esp. 110–12, and cf. on terminology and outlook his discussion on 238–56, and Robert Harris, "Jewish Biblical," 596–615, esp. 604–12.

107. See Frankel, *Land*, 126–27.

108. As Hoffman, "J's Unique," 54, notes, in P one occasionally finds cases that resemble J as well; that is, P contains both collections of law (as in E and D) and narratives presenting laws (as in J). On P's combination of law and narrative, see Chavel, "Second Passover."

109. This definition of the genre "Torah" is assumed by the opening paragraph of Rashi's commentary on the Pentateuch. On this narrative justification of law as central to both biblical and rabbinic culture, see Halivni, *Midrash, Mishna, and Gemara*. On the Torah's essential mixing of narrative and legislative material, see Schwartz, "Torah," 162–69. I capitalize the term *Torah* in this sense (viz., as the composite genre that mixes law and narrative so that the latter justifies the former) to distinguish it from the genre "torah," in the sense of a specific legal teaching or ruling, whether recorded for posterity (e.g., "This is the torah of the burnt offering" in Leviticus 6.2, "the torah of the nazirite" in Numbers 6.13) or issued in response to a specific query (e.g., the rulings referred to in Deuteronomy 17.8–11, Jeremiah 18.18, Malachi 2.7, Haggai 2.11–13).

110. Ibid., 197–98.

111. Frankel, *Land*, 104–13, argues that the Bible also contains a radically different account of the origin of the covenant between Yhwh and Israel in Joshua 24, which does not acknowledge the existence of a covenant from Sinai or Horeb. According to this chapter, Joshua rather than Moses mediated the covenant between God and the nation. In this fundamentally different version of Israel's history, there was no lawgiving at Sinai at all, and the law is not Mosaic, and yet, even here, Frankel notes (106), there is still a law (see verses 24–26). That chapter allows us to imagine a Judaism without Sinai and without Moses but not without the law.

112. See Zenger, "Wie und wozu," 67–77.

113. See the important comment in Rosenzweig's 1927 letter to Jacob Rosenheim in Rosenzweig, *Briefe und Tagebücher*, 1134 (= Buber and Rosenzweig, *Scripture and Translation*, 23). The point is similar to the more general comment in Hermann Cohen, *Religion*, 83, that traditional Judaism has no term for revelation but speaks instead of lawgiving (מתן תורה). On theophany as first of all lawgiving in biblical and rabbinic conceptions of the event, see Fraade, "Hearing and Seeing," 247.

114. On the development of this theory, see Schmid, "Emergence," and Römer, "How Many."

115. Baden, *Composition*, 128. Cf. Schwartz, "Torah," 217–18.

116. For one recent theory that gives a fine sense of the complexities, see Römer and Brettler, "Deuteronomy 34."

117. On the importance of this point and theological and historical ramifications, see James A. Sanders, *Torah and Canon*, 25.

118. The fact that third-century BCE Jews translated the name of the anthology into Greek as νόμος ("law") also suggests that the book was conceptualized first and foremost as law. Granted, one can wonder whether they were right to translate the term תורה as "law," rather than "instruction." (For such reservations, see, e.g., Heschel, *God*, 325–28, and Franks, "Sinai," 333–34, 346, 354.) The decision of the Septuagint translators to do so even though that "law" was not the most obvious choice evinces their view of the Pentateuch as a law book whose extensive narrative sections are present in order to serve the law, by justifying and encourage its observance.

119. Commentators began to note this problem in Maimonides work already during his lifetime. See Harvey, "Question," 63–74, and Halbertal and Margalit, *Idolatry*, 110. These voices have not entirely disappeared; for a recent critique of Maimonides's view on corporality as fundamentally non-Jewish, see Wyschogrod, *Body*, xiv–xv. On Maimonides's attempt to sublimate the Hebrew Bible's physical God, see Lorberbaum, *Image*, 27–78.

120. See Diamond, "Concepts." For Maimonides's rejection of what came to be kabbalistic notions of God, a rejection that is closely related to his reconceptualization of the Bible and midrashic literature, see Kellner, *Maimonides' Confrontation*.

121. For the notion that committed Jewish communities themselves decide what Jewish law is, see Shapiro, "Another Example," and Shapiro, "Marc Shapiro Replies." In the latter article, Shapiro clarifies his position in crucial ways, stating, "An unobservant community can never be an arbiter" (91 n. 4). See further 89–90 for the importance of a halakhically observant community as the ultimate decisor. Shapiro connects this position with Zechariah Frankel and to Solomon Schechter. See further Schechter, *Studies (First)*, xviii–xix; Heinemann, *Ta'amei*, 2:161–62, 173, 175–76, and, on the connection of peoplehood and religion in Israel, cf. 178–80; Louis Jacobs, *Principles*, 297 (for Jacob's own view on the matter, which closely resembles that of Frankel and Schechter, see Louis Jacobs, *Beyond*, 126).

122. A related issue involves the power and limitations of popular custom in Jewish law, on which see Elon, *Jewish Law*, 880–944, esp. 903–11; Joel Roth, *Halakhic Process*, 205–30.

123. Rosenzweig, *Briefe und Tagebücher*, 763–64. Cf. the distinction between "a halakhic system" and "*the* halakhic system" in Neil Gillman, *Sacred Fragments*, 59.

124. On Heschel's commitment to binding authority, see further Dresner, *Heschel, Hasidism*, 84–123; on the firm connection between revelation and command in Heschel, see also Perlman, *Idea*, 177 n. 49. Even-Chen, *Voice*, 33, discusses

Heschel's attempt to ensure that his emphasis on spirituality is not misread as implicitly endorsing antinomianism. Idel, quoting Heschel's characterization of kabbalists as those "want to feel and to enjoy [God], not only to obey, but to approach Him," (in Heschel, *Moral*, 164), points out that Heschel's "resort to the term 'not only to obey' assumes logically the importance of obeisance, posited as a given, which should culminate with a higher form of existence" (Idel, "Abraham J. Heschel," 84).

125. Heschel, *Moral*, 127–45.

126. See ibid., 143–45.

127. Even in this direct polemic, Heschel manages to remain surprisingly mild in temper. On this aspect of Heschel's oeuvre, see Harold Stern, "A. J. Heschel."

128. Heschel, *God*, 26, 162, 201, 213, 282, 286, 298–99 (cf. 216, 218, and 343–44), and, at greater length, chapters 32–35 there, as well as most of the third volume of Heschel, *TmH* (= *HT*, chapters 35–39). For a pithy summary of the centrality of command in not only in Heschel's philosophy of Judaism but also in his theological anthropology more broadly, see Heschel, *Who Is Man?* 111: "*I am commanded therefore I am.*"

129. See Heschel, *TmH*, 115–18 = *HT*, 731–36. For a fine guide to this theme in Heschel, see Gordon Tucker's remarks in ibid., 720–21.

130. Heschel, *TmH*, 60–62 = *HT*, 689–92.

131. See Heschel, *God*, 323, and also his remark in Heschel, *Moral*, 34: "Observance of the Law is the basis, but exaltation through observance is the goal." See further Even-Chen, *Voice*, 157–59. In regarding law as means rather than end, Heschel, like Rosenzweig, proves to be a successor to P rather than of E. For Heschel as for P, observance of the law allows the transcendent God to achieve the immanence that God so deeply desires.

132. For a banner example, see Goldberg, *Between Berlin*, 113–36. A fair but devastating critique of Goldberg's mendacious treatment of Heschel appears in Kaplan, "Review Essay: Between Berlin," xxi–xxvi.

133. Heschel, *God*, 282.

134. Ibid., 290.

135. Ibid., 274–75.

136. This insistence that what others see as two sides of a polarity are both crucial and are not in fact in tension is a hallmark of Heschel's thought; see Kimelman, "Heschel's Theology," 208, 234–35; Dresner, *Heschel, Hasidism*, 113–14. For another example, see Idel, "Abraham J. Heschel," 80. Similarly, for all Heschel's emphasis on personal religious experience, for him Judaism remains public and communal so that it can never be merely a matter of private choice, as noted by Jon Levenson, "Religious Affirmation," 35. Similarly, Levenson notes (41 n. 49) that as a reader, Heschel eschews subjectivist or relativist modes of reading, which are "quite alien to Heschel's theological agenda."

137. On the centrality of questions of authority in Rosenzweig's oeuvre, and not just in his discussions of law and command, see Batnitzky, *Idolatry*, 4–7.

138. Kurzweil, "Three Views," 296. A similar stress on the individual's choice regarding observance appears in Schoeps, "Franz Rosenzweig," 122, who maintains that the Rosenzweig did not universalize his own choice for observance but recognized the validity of other paths to Jewish commitment. Eisen, *Rethinking*, 189, characterizes Rosenzweig's approach to the commandments as "an evolving personal discipline, rather than a submission to divine decree or communal norm," and thus as religiously meaningful but not a matter of universal obligation. Kraut, "Approach," 58–61, reads Rosenzweig as having a "common sense" approach to halakhah in which Rosenzweig's attraction to halakhic practice was based not on theological concerns but on a "historical and emotional commitment to the Jewish people." Thus, Kraut makes Rosenzweig sound like Mordechai Kaplan (cf. Eisen, *Rethinking*, 200). For a view that elides the differences between Rosenzweig and Buber, see Brusin, "Rosenzweig's."

139. Mendes-Flohr, *Divided*, 355–56.

140. Eisen, *Rethinking*, 208. On Rosenzweig's commitment to autonomy, see further Mendes-Flohr, *Divided*, 350–51, 354.

141. See esp. the treatment in Heinemann, *Ta'amei*, 2:195–237, who (at 2:233) even locates Rosenzweig as in some respects to the right of Zechariah Frankel on this issue. See also Glatzer, "Introduction to *OJL*," 19–21; Samuelson, *Revelation*, 74–75 and 96; Kepnes, "Revelation," 231–32. Rosenzweig regards revelation as corresponding to the imperative in human speech and thus as essentially commanding (while creation corresponds to the indicative and redemption to the cohortative); see Batnitzky, *Idolatry*, 50, 112.

142. See Heinemann, *Ta'amei*, 2:223.

143. In Rosenzweig, *OJL*, 72–92; selections are also available in Rosenzweig, *FRHLT*, 234–42.

144. These include his famous exchange of letters with Martin Buber, available in Rosenzweig, *OJL*, 109–24, as well as his letter to Nahum Glatzer and three other friends found in Rosenzweig, *FRHLT*, 242–47. Another important source is a letter to Rudolph Hallo in Rosenzweig, *Briefe und Tagebücher*, 761–68 (not available in English; a Hebrew translation of this letter appears in Rosenzweig, *Mivḥar Iggerot*, 225–30). On commandment as the essential idea coming out of Bible, see also Rosenzweig's remark in Buber and Rosenzweig, *Scripture and Translation*, 134: "Biblical narrative seeks to be both revelatory message and commanding instruction. Only in commanding does it offer revelation; only as message does it teach."

145. As Heinemann notes, Rosenzweig "himself described his approach to the commandments as unfinished" (Heinemann, *Ta'amei*, 2:229, and see further 2:199). Rosenzweig recognized that upon completion of the *Star* the most pressing

problem he had to confront was the law (Rosenzweig, *Briefe und Tagebücher*, 761). Haberman, "Rosenzweig's," 325–27, shows that Rosenzweig's later writings move beyond what Rosenzweig came to regard as limitations in the *Star* with regard to the status of Jewish law. This is not to say that there is a contradiction between them; indeed Heinemann points out (2:210) respects in which basic elements of Rosenzweig's positive attitude toward theonomy are already to be found in the *Star*, but they come to full expression only in the later material. Batnitzky, *Idolatry*, 327, points out that in his 1925 essay "The New Thinking" (Rosenzweig, *PTW*, 109–38), Rosenzweig suggests reading the *Star* in reverse order, beginning with the discussion of the Jewish liturgical or communal year (book 3) then moving backward to the discussions of revelation (book 2) and creation (book 1). This order puts halakhic practice first and theory second, so that ritual practice contextualizes revelation and creation. This change in order—*mitzvot*, then theology—may reflect a fundamental shift in this thinking, a shift that the earlier Rosenzweig hoped for and that the later Rosenzweig would characterize as "growth."

146. Rosenzweig, *OJL*, 91.

147. For this reading, see also Haberman, "Rosenzweig's," 329. Against this approach, Amir, *Reason*, 295–97, maintains that what Rosenzweig proposes in "Builders" is not a temporary measure. But it seems to me that the audience of the essay and of the related letters has to be taken into account.

148. Rosenzweig, *OJL*, 123–24 (= Rosenzweig, *FRHLT*, 246–47).

149. Rosenzweig, *Briefe und Tagebücher*, 764.

150. Rosenzweig, *OJL*, 74. Cf. his letter to Hallo: "I am only at the beginning. What will come from this, I don't know, and don't want to know. I do hope and know that others are beginning, too" (Rosenzweig, *Briefe und Tagebücher*, 762).

151. Rosenzweig, *OJL*, 85–86.

152. See Mendes-Flohr, *Divided*, 354. For Rosenzweig not only does Israel respond to God's *Gebot* by creating *Gesetz*; it is just as important that *Gesetz* becomes *Gebot* when a Jew freely and lovingly adopts a law as her own. It is precisely then that humanly authored *Gesetz* becomes God's *Gebot*. See, e.g., Rosenzweig, *OJL*, 85–86 and 113, and Mendes-Flohr, *Divided*, 296.

153. Seeskin, *Autonomy*, 4, quoting from Kant, *Foundation*, 49.

154. Seeskin, *Autonomy*, 5.

155. Ibid., 6, 8, referring to Kant, *Foundation*, 65. Similarly, Batnitzky, *Idolatry*, 217, argues that "Rosenzweig contends that revelation makes human freedom truly possible."

156. Against reading Rosenzweig as exalting the individual over the community, see esp. Batnitzky's discussion in ibid., 70–72, and cf. 60 and 116. A similar argument regarding Heschel appears in Jon Levenson, "Religious Affirmation," 35.

157. See further Seeskin, *Autonomy, passim*, esp. his chapter on Maimonides, 90–118, as well as Levinas, *Beyond*, 142: "To be free is to do only what no one else can

do in my place. To obey the Most High is to be free." On Rosenzweig's defense of autonomy in traditional Judaism, see Mendes-Flohr, *Divided*, 295–96, and Heinemann, *Ta'amei*, 2:222. On autonomy and the law in Heschel, see Even-Chen, *Voice*, 82 and 156–57. For an important critique of glib misapplications of Kantian autonomy to religious authority more broadly, see Ward, *Religion*, 302–6.

158. Rosenzweig, *Briefe und Tagebücher*, 762.

159. Heschel, *Moral*, 133. Even-Chen, *Voice*, 154–55, notes a difference between Rosenzweig and Heschel on this point: for Heschel deed can precede intention, whereas Rosenzweig is more hesitant to act without the intention. But Rosenzweig does at times express admiration for actions that can help engender the intention; e.g., Rosenzweig, *OJL*, 122–23 (= Rosenzweig, *FRHLT*, 246–47).

160. Heschel, *Moral*, 133.

161. The study of Paul's attitudes toward the law constitutes a subdiscipline of its own. For a useful review of scholarship, see Tomson, *Paul*, 1–30. For the reading of Galatians 3.10–11 I summarize, see, e.g., Hübner, "Ganze"; Schreiner, "Paul and Perfect Obedience"; and, with greater respect for the subtlety and variations within Paul's view of the law, Stendahl, *Paul among Jews*, 80–81; Räisänen, *Paul and the Law*, 94–96. For Paul's more positive evaluation of observance of the law by Jews, see 1 Corinthians 7.17–20; see further works just cited by Stendahl, Räisänen, and Tomson, as well as Davies, *Paul and Rabbinic*, 69–72, and E. P. Sanders, *Paul, the Law* (who argues, at 74–81, that the impossibility of full obedience to the law should not be overstressed). In light of these scholars' recovery of a more positive attitude towards law in Paul, some would argue the contrast I draw above sets Rosenzweig and Heschel against Luther rather than Paul (or against Luther's Paul rather than Paul himself); cf. Davies, *Jewish and Pauline*, esp. 118, and Stendahl, *Paul among Jews*, 82–88.

162. On Heschel's association of perfectionism of works with Christian theology, and his pastoral use of a gentle critique thereof, see Coffin, *Once*, 289–90, cited in Kaplan and Dresner, *Prophetic*, 12.

163. Of course, in regard to Christology, it cannot be denied that many Ḥabad Ḥasidim of late have resembled Paul more closely than they resemble Rosenzweig or Heschel. See David Berger, *Rebbe*. On a difference between Heschel and the Lubavitch rebbe in regard to outreach and rabbinic authority, see Kaplan and Dresner, *Prophetic*, 138–39.

164. This dictum appears in, e.g., b. Yoma 85b, b. Sanhedrin 74a, b. Avodah Zarah 27b and 54a, Qohelet Rabbah 1:24, Tanḥuma Mass'ei 1.

165. Rosenzweig, *Briefe und Tagebücher*, 763.

166. See Elon, *Jewish Law*, 360–70; Joel Roth, *Halakhic Process*, 153–204; Halbertal, *Interpretive Revolutions, passim*.

167. One might challenge my assertion here by pointing toward the saying of R. Avdimi in Shabbat 88a, which could be read to question the validity of

Israel's acquiescence at Sinai. But the passage continues by affirming that the people's acceptance in Esther 9.27 provides the Torah with legal force in any event, so that Avdimi's suggestion has no practical impact of the fact of Israel's halakhic obligation.

168. In biblical Hebrew the verb בָּשַׁל means not "cook" (as in modern Hebrew) but "boil, cook in water." To harmonize the contradiction between two passages, traditionalist commentators have argued that the verb can mean merely "cook," but such a reading requires us to assume that the Pentateuch uses the verb in radically different senses in the Passover laws of Exodus 12.9 and Deuteronomy 16.7. As Fishbane, *Biblical Interpretation*, 136–37, notes, "This argument is both tendentious and circular." See also the useful treatment in Driver, *Deuteronomy*, 192–93.

169. 2 Chronicles 35.12 refers to "the Book of Moses," which, to judge by the several attempts Chronicles makes harmonize between the P laws and D laws, combines both priestly and deuteronomic laws. In other words, that "Book of Moses" is either the Pentateuch known to us or something very much like it. On the Chronicler's harmonizing in this passage, see esp. Fishbane, *Biblical Interpretation*, 136–37.

170. Reines, "Maimonides'," 355–57. See further Bland, "Moses," 64.

171. Translation from Abelson, "Maimonides," 54.

172. Ibid., 42–45; Kafaḥ, *Mishnah*, 139–40.

173. Rashi makes a assertion comparable to Maimonides's Eighth Principle in his commentary to b. Ḥullin 132b. Commenting on the statement of Rabbi Shimon that a priest who does not believe in Temple service (שאינו מודה בעבודה) receives no share in the priesthood and its emoluments, Rashi says that not believing in Temple service means that "one says in one's heart, 'They are worthless (דברי הבל הם), and God did not command us to offer sacrifices, but Moses made it up on his own (בדה מלבו).'" One might initially suggest that Rosenzweig's idea of a humanly authored *Gesetz* fits into this category of disbelief. But Rosenzweig argues neither that the laws are worthless nor that the authors of *Gesetz* made up laws entirely on their own. Rather, he maintains that the authors respond to a real command at Sinai. Furthermore, for him the practices the law requires are hardly worthless; when wholly embraced they become true expressions of a human's love for God as well as vehicles through which the human receives God's love.

174. See, e.g., Samuelson, *Revelation*, 229–30.

175. On authorship in the ancient world, see van der Toorn, *Scribal*, 27–49, and, more briefly, Schmid, "Authorship." On the inappropriateness of the idea of a pious fraud to biblical pseudepigraphy, see esp. Childs, *Introduction*, 132–35.

176. Bate, *Burden*; Bloom, *Anxiety* and *Map*.

177. Eliot, "Tradition and the Individual Talent."

178. Not all biblical texts claim that all law stems from Moses. Occasional verses (e.g., Daniel 9.9–10, Ezra 9.10–11, 2 Chronicles 29.25) refer to the law as having come to Israel through God's "servants, the prophets." The plural *prophets* in these verses shows that these authors do not regard all law as Mosaic. They evince a stage of Israelite belief prior to the crystallization of the idea that authoritative law is by definition Mosaic. See further Japhet, *From the Rivers*, 140. Similarly, Joshua 24.25–28 and 1 Samuel 10.25 attribute laws to Joshua and Samuel respectively; see Frankel, *Land*, 236–37. By providing a glimpse into an ancient Israelite attitude to the law that was not yet fully Mosaic, these verses show that Israelites did not attribute all law to Moses from the beginning of Israelite culture but tended to do so increasingly over time.

179. On evidence that psalms and eventually the whole Psalter were increasingly associated with David over time, see Sarna, "*Tehillim*," 8:444–45, and Wilson, *Editing*, 130–31, 136 and 155.

180. Attributions of specific teachings in rabbinic literature to a particular rabbi functioned the same way. Sacha Stern, "Attribution," 48, explains that "the typical phrase 'Rabbi X said' is not necessarily designed to indicate the author of the saying: it may refer to his disciple, to a later tradent, or even to some earlier authority." On pseudepigraphy in rabbinic literature, see further Sascha Stern, "Concept," and Bregman, "Pseudepigraphy."

181. Childs, *Introduction*, 135. Cf. Fishbane, *Garments*, 122.

182. Bregman, "Pseudepigraphy," 38, expresses the difference between modern and ancient views especially well: "In rabbinic thinking, the result of [an exegetical] inference seems more closely identified with the text or statement from which the inference is made than post-Enlightenment legal thinking would normally accept."

183. The literature on this subject is vast; an especially thoughtful and comprehensive study of the phenomenon of scribal transmission *cum* transformation with attention to the rich set of analogues available from both Mesopotamia and from Qumran can be found in Carr, *Formation, passim*, esp. 3–149. While Kaufmann, *Toledot*, shows repeatedly that modern scholars overestimate the extent to which scribes felt free to make major changes, that such changes were in principle possible and in fact did occur remains the case.

184. Students of oral literature and folklore know that certain kinds of texts have no author, and these include some written texts as well. Alan Dundes speaks of "the existence of different versions [of a text], none of which are a primary, authoritative source" (summary from Assis, "Author-ity," 10). This model will become important in our discussion of Oral Torah in the next chapter.

185. It is unclear to me whether my friends sent it to me because they thought I would not get tenure or because they were hinting they thought I am like God.

186. On this development throughout the ancient Near East in the middle and late first millennium BCE, see van der Toorn, *Scribal*, 27–49.

187. See Najman, *Seconding Sinai*, and Najman, *Past Renewals*, esp. ch. 3 for a fine overview of her approach, as well as the essays by various scholars in Brooke, Najman, and Stuckenbruck, *Significance of Sinai*.

188. Hayes, "*Halakhah*," provides a comprehensive study.

189. See Heschel, *TmH*, 3:36–38 (= *HT*, 671–72), and Even-Chen, *Voice*, 176–77.

190. Milgrom, *Leviticus 17–22*, 1368–69; see further Brettler, Enns, and Harrington, *Bible and the Believer*, 26–31.

191. On the ascription of the Temple stations to Moses and its relation to what Najman calls Mosaic discourse, see also Japhet, *From the Rivers*, 150.

192. Mosaic discourse subsumes diverse teachings and laws under the unifying rubric of Mosaic Law. A similar dynamic occurs in MT variant readings that replace an original plural תורות ("teachings, laws") with the singular תורה ("Pentateuch"); see Jeremiah 32.23, Ezekiel 43.11, 44.5; see also Brettler, Enns, and Harrington, *Bible and the Believer*, 28–29. Cf. the variation between an older plural (preserved in Samaritan, Peshita, and standard vocalized editions of Onkelos) and MT's singular form in Deuteronomy 33.10; see Begrich, *Gesammelte*, 233 n. 10; Fishbane, "*Tōrâ*," 8:472.

193. Cf. Milgrom, *Leviticus 17–22*, 1369–71. Cf. Sternberg, *Poetics of Biblical Narrative*, 77: the Pentateuch's linkage of writing and authority with Moses "implies . . . not that the author must be Moses but that he must be Moses-like."

194. Greenstein, "Understanding," 294. On the frequent use of "telescoping" in biblical historiography, see Malamat, "Proto-History," 307–8. Cf. Solomon, *Torah*, 314, who does not use the term but speaks of the notion of Torah coming from heaven as a myth of origin that "*interprets* our past, giving focus to episodes and developments . . . which . . . form a powerful, authoritative, timeless whole."

195. Ratzinger, *Jesus*, xx–xxi.

196. Kepnes, "Revelation," 225. Cf. the suggestive remarks of Jacob Wright, "Commemoration," 443–44 and 465 n. 23.

197. On the gradual development of the idea that the Torah is Mosaic and/or divine in origin, see Hurowitz, "Proto-Canonization," 33 n. 4, who explains: "According to 2 Kgs 22–23 . . . Deuteronomy, is simply designated ספר התורה, and part of it is called ספר הברית, with no specific attribution to Moses or God. This work is mentioned several times in these two chapters . . . but only in the last occurrence, in an evaluatory statement (23:25), is it specifically defined as תורת משה. The peculiarity becomes even more striking if we compare the parallel account in 2 Chr. 34 which at the very first mention of the discovery calls it ספר תורת ה' ביד משה. . . . If the account of the discovery and subsequent reform are predeuteronomistic, . . . the author may not have regarded the book found in the temple as a Mosaic composition. . . . [That] identification was made only by the [later deuteronomistic] redactor who added the evaluation of Josiah [in 23.25]." Similarly, Knohl, "Between Faith," 125, points out

passages as late as Ezra and Daniel that regard the laws of the Pentateuch as having been given by Moses and the prophets (Daniel 9.10–11) or even by unnamed "prophets" in the plural (see Ezra 9.10–12).

198. For additional parallels in rabbinic and medieval literature, see Kasher, *Torah Sheleimah Megillat Esther*, 248–49 §§75–77 and notes.

199. On this view of Moses's halakhic initiative and God's approval of it in classical rabbinic literature (which seems to undermine the ruling in b. Sanhedrin 99a, s.v. כי דבר ה' בזה), see Heschel, *TmH*, vol. 2: chs. 6, 8–9, and 11 (= *HT*, chapters 22, 24–26); Kasher, *Torah Sheleimah*, 19:333–42; and Fraade, "Moses and the Commandments," 411–13. For a useful overview, see Shapiro, *Limits*, 113–14.

200. From Nachman's *Liqqutei Moharan* (Jerusalem, 2002–3), pt. 1 §19:9. I quote from the translation by Gellman, "Wellhausen," 205.

201. Ibid.

202. As Rav explains in y. Berakhot 14c (9:8), the first verb is in the plural, to refer to the Jews' establishing the commandment. The second verb in the consonantal text of Esther is singular, to refer to God's subsequently accepting it. The verse is used to support this idea via a somewhat different interpretive route in b. Megillah 7a and b. Makkot 23b. See further sources referenced in Kasher, *Torah Sheleimah Megillat Esther*, 249, note to §77.

203. Cf. Louis Jacobs, *Principles*, 294–301. Jacob notes (296–97) that something analogous is already articulated in the work of Zechariah Frankel, for whom the acceptance of certain observances by the community of Israel is itself a form of divine revelation. (On this aspect of Frankel's thought, see also Heinemann, *Ta'amei*, 2:161–62, 173, 175–76.) It is crucial that for Frankel "the community" includes only those Jews committed to observing divine commands; people who do not observe the law are not involved in legislating it. But all those who do observe in effect also legislate (see Jacobs, 297, and cf. above n. 121). This approach, Jacobs notes, fits the comment of the sages in Midrash Tehillim 19:14 (to verse 8), according to which the fact that the law restores the soul is what makes it perfect, rather than the other way around.

204. For a vigorous defense of what I am calling ex post facto holiness in light of Jewish tradition, see esp. Louis Jacobs, *Beyond*, 106–31, in the chapter titled "The *Mitsvot*: God-Given or Man-Made?" We might sum up Jacobs's thesis by paraphrasing his title: humans made the *mitsvot*, and then God gave them. For the idea of what I am calling ex post facto holiness in the work of Rebbe Nahman of Bratslav, see the stunning discussion in Gellman, "Wellhausen," 205, and references there. The idea that what starts as a human innovation can acquire a divine status as generations go by is relevant not only to law but also to the status of scripture. Wilfred Cantwell Smith, *What Is Scripture*, 19, 230–31, speaks of humans elevating certain forms of language to the status of scripture precisely because they genuinely recognize transcendence in it. Similarly, Buber and Rosenzweig maintain that the Bible is sacred not only,

and perhaps not even primarily, because of its origins in divine revelation. Its humanly authored texts become sacred when its readers are open to the possibility of engaging in a dialogue with God through them. See Amir, *Reason*, 283, and cf. 286–87; Jonathan Cohen, "Concepts"; and Fishbane, *Garments*, 81–90 and 99–111.

Chapter 4. Scripture as Tradition

1. On the notion of scripture as a form of tradition among some Christian thinkers, see Brown, *Tradition*, *passim*, esp. 107–8. On the flexible nature of the boundary between scripture and tradition or text and commentary in most religions around the world, see Wilfred Cantwell Smith, *What Is Scripture*, 149–53, 204–6, as well as his discussion of amorphous and polymorphous scriptures, 126–27 and 299 n. 3. The basic idea of the Bible as a form of tradition was stated in passing in Fishbane, "The Hebrew Bible and Exegetical Tradition," 18, who notes its implication for biblical study: "The Bible is only tradition, in form and content, and . . . a proper analysis of its materials must take note of its composite character."

2. On the term itself, see Blidstein, "Concerning the Term," and also the critique of Blidstein by Rosenthal, "Oral Torah," 455–56 n. 30. According to Blidstein, in tannaitic times, the term seems to have been simply תורה שבפה, which was lengthened to תורה שבעל פה in amoraic Babylonia. The latter term's appearance in tannaitic texts (the baraita in b. Shabbat 31a, Avot deRabbi Nathan A15/B29) is a retrojection based on the later amoraic usage; it does not appear consistently in the manuscripts. See Blidstein, 496 n. 4.

3. The notion that more was given at Sinai than the biblical texts is not unique to rabbinic Judaism; the Book of Jubilees and the Temple Scroll from Qumran both claim to have been given to Moses at Sinai along with the Pentateuch. The difference between the Qumranic and rabbinic viewpoints is not whether the revelation included an additional teaching but whether that teaching was written or oral. See Werman, "Oral," 177–81.

4. On the term תורה as including the entire Tanakh, see Bacher, *Exegetische*, 1:197, 2:229, and Ben-Yehudah and Tur-Sinai, *Thesaurus*, 16:7704b. On the inclusion of the Prophets and Writings within that which was revealed as Written Torah, see, e.g., the Maharsha's commentary to b. Berakhot 5a (ד"ה אשר כתבתי); see further the sources cited in Heschel, *TmH*, 2:73–74 [= *HT*, 370–71] and Silman, *Voice*, 32–33.

5. On Nakh as essentially a single block, see Barr, *Holy Scripture*, 54–56; Barton, *Oracles*, 44, 91–92; Carr, *Writing*, 209–14, 225–34, 245–47. When some ancient Jewish works refer to the Law and the Prophets (e.g., 4 Maccabees 18.10–16), they clearly include Daniel, Psalms, and Proverbs in the latter category; see Solomon, *Torah*, 30.

6. See especially the very helpful presentations in Schäfer, *Studien*, 153–97, and Fraade, "Concepts." See further Rosenthal, "Oral Torah," 448–75; Safrai, "Oral Torah," 35–88, esp. 43–45, 56–60; Urbach, *Sages*, 286–314, esp. 304–5; Neusner, *What*. On the development of this notion and its relation both to prerabbinic Judaism and to the modern study of oral literature, see esp. Jaffee, *Torah*.

7. For example: When and why did it come to be written down? How did the memorizers and reciters of Oral Torah go about their work, and what elements of oral composition are evident in it? How do the works of Oral Torah compare to other oral traditions from around the world? For these topics, see the works of Jaffee, Safrai, and Schäfer in the previous note, as well as Lieberman, *Hellenism*, 83–99; Gerhardsson, *Memory*; Neusner, *Oral Tradition*, 61–100, 133–48; Elman, "Yerushalmi"; Werman, "Oral," 196; and the essays by Martin Jaffee, Steven Fraade, Elizabeth Shanks-Alexander, and Yaakov Elman in *Oral Tradition* 14, no. 1 (1999).

8. Levinas, *Beyond*, 137. For evocative portrayals of the multiplicity of voices in traditional Jewish commentary, see Greenstein, "Medieval," 214–15, 256–57, and Abigail Gillman, "Between Religion," 101–2. As both Greenstein and Gillman show, and Levinas hints, the physical layout of the printed page of a rabbinic Bible manages to convey a sense of polyvocality that is essential to Oral Torah.

9. See Halivni, *Peshat and Derash*, 163–67; Halivni, "Man's Role"; Rosenthal, "Oral Torah," 460–67.

10. See Schäfer, *Studien*, 162–63, and Jay Harris, *How*, 2. This basic idea is attributed to tanna'im in midrashic texts that were edited in the amoraic period; see the opinions of Rabbi Akiva in Sifra Beḥuqotai 8:13 and of Rabbi Nehemiah in Qohelet Rabbah 5:8.

11. On these passages, see Jaffee, *Torah*, 84–92.

12. On this passage as representing a nuanced minimalist conception of the revelation of Oral Torah, see Halivni, "Man's Role," 30–31, esp. n. 6. For other examples of a nonmaximalist approach to the revelation of Oral Torah, see Yannai's teaching and its explanation in y. Sanhedrin 6a (4:2) (which make clear that new halakhic decisions would be arrived at later than Moses's time); Seder Eliahu Zuṭa §2 (it is praiseworthy not merely to conserve Torah received at Sinai but to extend it, producing new things from it); Bemidbar Rabbah Ḥuqqat §4. On this theme in both classical rabbinic and Ḥasidic literature, see Elman, "R. Zadok," 7–12.

13. Mishnah and Tosefta do not employ the phrase הלכה למשה מסיני in a fully consistent manner, but they seem to mean by it a law distinct from scripture and not derived from scripture; see Hayes, "*Halakhah*," 74. Later texts use the phrase somewhat differently; nonetheless, the Babylonian Talmud and early tradents of the Jerusalem Talmud largely accept this distinction; see Hayes, 78, 110–11.

Various scholars argue that tanna'im regard the bulk of their own traditions to be of relatively recent origin; see Jaffee, *Torah*, 80; cf. Schäfer, *Studien*, 185, and Gruber, "Mishnah," 121–22.

14. Further, Azzan Yadin argues that texts associated with Rabbi Yishmael tradition radically limit the authority of what became known as Oral Torah; for these texts, scripture and exegesis of scripture are the only source of authority, and authoritative traditions parallel to and independent of scripture are all but non-existent. See Yadin, "Rabbi Ishmael," and Yadin, *Scripture*. Nonetheless, as Yadin points out, this attitude was marginalized in rabbinic tradition, so that Yadin can characterize it as radically unrabbinic.

15. On the rabbis' increasing tendency to attribute material to Sinaitic revelation, see Halivni, *Revelation*, 54–63; and Kraemer, "Formation," 616–27. This tendency is evident in the increasing importance of the phrase הלכה למשה מסיני in later Amoraic texts (especially Babylonian ones, which tend to use the phrase on a wholesale level to bolster rabbinic law in general); see Hayes, "*Halakhah*," esp. 67 n. 13, and 96–102.

16. E. P. Sanders, *Jewish Law*, 97–130, maintains that the earliest rabbis did not believe in a revealed Oral Torah and viewed their nonbiblical legal traditions as distinct from laws revealed at Sinai. It remains the case that early rabbis had nonbiblical traditions they regarded as ancient and authoritative, even if they were not Sinaitic. Hence they had a notion of twofold teaching quite parallel to the later rabbinic doctrine of Oral Torah. For a recent defense of the notion that the doctrine of a revealed Oral Torah is pre-tannaitic, see Werman, "Oral," 175–87.

17. Bigman, "Ladder." On the religiously positive aspect of a revelation that causes perplexity and hence debate, see also Ward, *Religion*, 22–23.

18. On this medieval debate, see Halbertal, *People*, 54–64 and 161–62, nn. 40–41; Halbertal, "What Is," 101–2; Silman, *Voice*, 72–76; Halivni, *Peshat*, 163–67; Halivni, "Man's Role," 36–44; Elman, "R. Zadok," 1–5.

19. Distinctive but not unique. One may compare the rabbinic doctrine of two Torahs with the notions of *shruti* and *smriti* texts in Hinduism. To the extent that sunna in Islam and tradition in non-Protestant Christianities are understood to be divinely guided but not divinely authored, they, too, are comparable to Oral Torah among the rabbis. See Wilfred Cantwell Smith, *What Is Scripture*, 137–38, 204–6; Graham, "Scripture," 134a–b and 141b.

20. Finkelstein, *Siphre*, 408, notes that the midrash evidently read a text in which תורתך was plural This parallels the plural משפטיך in the first verset. Such a text is preserved in Samaritan manuscripts and Peshita, and in standard vocalized editions of Targum Onkelos (though not in the better manuscripts). For a defense of the plural reading, see Begrich, *Gesammelte*, 233 n. 10; Fishbane, "*Tôrâ*," 8:472. A similar shift from the plural (= "various teachings or laws") to

the singular (= "Pentateuch") occurs in various קרי\כתיב variants in the MT; see Brettler, Enns, and Harrington, *Bible and the Believer*, 28–29.

21. On the important role this passage plays in later rabbinic thought, see Heschel, *TmH*, 2:237–38 (= *HT*, 564–66).

22. Hebrew: מקרא, literally "reading," but usually rendered "scripture." As Rashi explains, the word here refers specifically to the Pentateuch, which one is commanded to read (לקרות) in its entirety, not the Nakh.

23. The assonance and rhyme linking the words מצוה and משנה may lead to their identification, as does the fact that the Mishnah explains what the commandments are and how correctly to observe them. On the origin of this linkage (which enters the manuscript tradition of b. Berakhot at a late date but appears in very early—indeed, late Second Temple—traditions), see Shweka, "Tablet," 353, and esp. references to Cana Werman's work in n. 67 there.

24. Printed editions read "Gemara" here rather than "Talmud." The variant does not affect our point, since the word *Talmud* when used as a title in rabbinic literature generally refers to the work we now call "Gemara" by itself, and not to Talmud in the current sense of "Mishnah combined with Gemara." See Bacher, *Exegetische*, 2:235.

25. One might argue that the term משנה in b. Berakhot 5a is not a title referring to the specific literary work of that name edited by Rabbi Judah (as I translated earlier) but a noun referring to orally repeated traditions generally; on this sense of the term, see ibid., 1:122–23; Ben-Yehudah and Tur-Sinai, *Thesaurus*, 7:3403; and Jaffee, *Torah*, 206 n. 50. In this broader sense, the term משנה is essentially synonymous with "Oral Torah"; cf. Gerhardsson, *Memory*, 27–28, 83, and Rosenthal, "Oral Torah," 455 n. 24. Similarly, the term תלמוד at the end of the passage (in the better manuscripts) would refer not to the works we now call Gemara but to rabbinic debates concerning the Oral Torah (Bacher, *Exegetische*, 1.201–2; Ben-Yehudah and Tur-Sinai, *Thesaurus*, 16:775–76). This translation of the two terms suggests a reading of the passage that differs slightly from the one I explore earlier, but my point remains unchanged or is perhaps amplified: Oral Torah (in this case, Oral Torah generally, not just the Mishnah of Rabbi Judah) precedes a segment of Written Torah.

26. The same is true of the alternative versions of this midrash in other rabbinic sources, even though the identification of the various components with words from the source verse differs. Thus, in Midrash Hagadol, Halakhot Gedolot, and early manuscripts of b. Berakhot itself, "tablets" are the Pentateuch, "Torah" is the Mishnah, "commandments" are the commandments, "which I wrote" are the prophets and Writings, and "to teach them" is the Talmud (= Gemara). For references to these and additional sources, see Kasher, *Torah Sheleimah*, 19.277 §108, and Aharon Shweka, "Tablets." (Some midrashic texts provide another interpretation, in which the Written Torah precedes the Oral Torah; see

Kasher, 19.278 §12. Even these, however, stress that both were given to Moses at Sinai.) Even in this older version of the teaching found in Midrash Hagadol, Halakhot Gedolot, and manuscripts of b. Berakhot, Oral and Written Torah are mixed together. Indeed, the fact that this version identifies "Torah" from the verse in Exodus with the main component of the Oral Torah (i.e., the Mishnah) underscores the point I am making: that the Oral Torah is no less a form of Torah than the Written Torah. Shweka argues that the version that became standard in printed editions ("Torah" = Pentateuch, "commandment" = Mishnah) was influenced by the rise of Karaism, but he also shows that the identification of "commandment" with Mishnah is much earlier and perhaps even prerabbinic, because it appears already in scholia to Megilliat Taanit.

27. Urbach, *Sages*, 290–92, makes a similar point about the story in Avot deRabbi Nathan A15/B29: Hillel's statement that there are two Torahs "contains not the slightest indication that the two *Tŏrôt* were differently evaluated. 'Just as you have accepted the one in faith [Hillel says there,] so accept also the other in faith.'" Against this view, E.P. Sanders, *Jewish Law*, 97–130, argues that Pharisees and early rabbis viewed their non-biblical traditions as having a lower status than laws clearly stated in scripture or derived exegetically from scripture. Even if Sanders is correct, this attitude weakens over time, as more and more of the Oral Torah comes to be seen as Sinaitic.

28. Cited in Kasher, *Torah Sheleimah*, 19.277 §108.

29. Printed in standard editions of the Ein Yaakov.

30. Available in standard editions of the Ein Yaakov.

31. The Gemara, according to *Ahavat Eitan*, is mentioned last because it was originally intended only for Moses's use, not for the whole nation.

32. The secondary texts (both Nakh and Gemara) come to elucidate the primary texts (Pentateuch and Mishnah). On the prophetic canon as supplementing and commenting on the Pentateuch in the view of both rabbinic Judaism and at least some of the scribes in the Second Temple period, see Blenkinsopp, *Prophecy and Canon*, 116–20 (and see further 125 on the Ketuvim as elucidating the nature and limits of prophecy).

33. On the theme of Oral Torah as the more beloved Torah in rabbinic texts, see Schäfer, *Studien*, 175–76; Urbach, *Sages*, 305; Kraemer, "Formation," 621.

34. On this passage and its parallels, see Jaffee, *Torah*, 142–43; Schäfer, *Studien*, 166–67; Urbach, *Sages*, 305.

35. On the relative place of Bible and Talmud in Jewish curricula, see Halbertal, *People*, 98–100; Kalimi, "Bibel und klassich-jüdische," 596, 604–6.

36. See Halbertal, *People*, 98–100; Ben-Sasson, *History*, 717.

37. The single exception involves curricula for girls among the ultra-Orthodox, which focus on Bible and shun Talmud, but by associating Bible with girls (I use this term advisedly), the ultra-Orthodox rabbis in question do not intend a compliment to the Bible. One might view the Yishmaelian exegetical tradi-

tion in the tannaitic midrashim as another exception (see n. 14, *supra*), because that tradition maintains that all Torah depends on and originates in the Written Torah. But what the this tradition regards as the content of Written Torah is largely identical to what other rabbis term *Oral Torah*.

38. See Neusner, "Oral Torah and Tradition," 60; Gruber, "Mishnah," 114. Only in the tannaitic midrashim and in amoraic literature does the notion of a dual Torah emerge. See Jaffee, *Torah*, 84–85; Neusner, *What*, 3–4.

39. Avot uses the term *Torah* to include what other texts call Oral Torah and Written Torah, or so the parallel (or explanatory) texts in Avot deRabbi Nathan make clear; see Herr, "Continuum," 47 n. 30, and cf. Jaffee, *Torah*, 84–85. This use of terminology shows up outside the Mishnah and Tosefta as well; so, for example, in the debate between Elazar and Yoḥanan in b. Gittin 60b and y. Peah 4a (2:6), on which see Kraemer, "Formation," 624–25. Similarly, Yadin, *Scripture*, 13–17, points out that the phrase אמרה תורה in halakhic midrashim sometimes introduces verbal citations from the Pentateuch, and at other times it introduces conclusions not found verbally in the Pentateuch but derived from it in other midrashic texts. These texts use the term Torah to refer both to actual verses from Written Torah and exegesis found in Oral Torah.

40. See the sources collected in Heschel, *TmH*, 3:45–47 (= *HT*, 677–79). Especially pertinent is the comment of Rabbi Akiva in Sifra Beḥuqqotai 8:13, on which see Silman, *Voice*, 26–27. See further the sources listed in Fraade, *From Tradition*, 226 n. 198.

41. On my translation of the terms in their broad sense rather than as titles of specific books, see ibid., 96, and cf. n. 44, *infra*. That some manuscripts read *midrash* rather than *talmud* also suggests that these terms here have their broad meaning. See the textual notes in Finkelstein, *Siphre*, 339, and Fraade, *From Tradition*, 244 n. 103.

42. On the notion that the two Torahs constitute a unity, compare the very similar idea expressed in the statement of the Second Vatican Council, *Dei Verbum*, ch. 2, §9: "There exists a close connection and communication between sacred tradition and Sacred Scripture. . . . Both of them, flowing from the same divine wellspring, . . . merge into a unity and tend toward the same end. . . . Both sacred tradition and Sacred Scripture are to be accepted and venerated with the same sense of loyalty and reverence." It is remarkable how well this statement could summarize the rabbinic texts under consideration here.

43. See Jaffee, *Torah*, 144–45, and Schäfer, *Studien*, 170, for parallels.

44. In translating *mishnah* and *talmud* in their general sense rather than as titles, I follow Jaffee, *Torah*, 145, and cf. 206 n. 50; so also Herr, "Continuum," 12:1442, and cf. Bacher, *Exegetische*, 1:122–23, 1:201–2. That questions asked by future students are included in revelation makes clear that the broad sense is intended; a question asked yesterday by a student is not in the Talmud, but they are part of *talmud* in the sense of a learned discussion of tradition.

45. The parallel text in Tanḥuma Ki Tissa 34 makes this explicit: "God anticipated that the nations of the world would later translate the Torah and read it in Greek and say, 'We are Israel!'" On the text's polemic, see Bregman, "Mishnah, Mystery." Not all rabbinic texts take this attitude, incidentally; see Schechter, *Aspects*, 133 and references there.

46. Cf. Gerhardsson's assertion that the rabbis distinguished between Oral and Written Torah merely as laws which had been transmitted in different ways, not as two different types or qualities of law (Gerhardsson, *Memory*, 26).

47. Alan Levenson, *Making*, 50.

48. Jay Harris, *How*, 226–27.

49. Ibid., 227 and 326 n. 47.

50. Similarly, Hirsch's suggestion that for forty years the Torah existed in oral form and that the parts that became Written Torah were first written down immediately before Moses's death simply restates the view of Reish Lakish in b. Gittin 60a, which I discuss briefly in the following paragraph of my the main text. An idea analogous to that of Hirsch appears in ibn Ezra's conception of the Pentateuch's authorship. According to ibn Ezra, Moses chose some aspects of God's supralingual revelation to be included in the Written Torah, while he put other aspects into the Oral Torah. For ibn Ezra, however, the two Torahs do differ in a crucial respect: with the exception of a few verses (e.g., Genesis 12.6, 22.15), the Pentateuch is limited to Moses's linguistic representation of the divine content he received from God, while rabbinic texts contain the rabbis' paraphrases and expansions, which are their representations of Moses's representation of the divine content. See Viezel, "Divine Content," 407.

51. Cf. Urbach, *Sages*, 305; Kraemer, "Formation," 621; Schwartz, "Origin," 247–51. Herr, "Oral Law," 12:1440, points out that written laws in ancient Israel really did depend on oral tradition. The notion of the primacy of oral tradition is not merely a midrashic trope but also a historical reality: the phrasing found in biblical law codes clearly refers back to the culture's commonly held legal practices, which preceded the written texts found in scripture. Yitzchak Hutner is a modern ultra-Orthodox thinker who also stresses the priority of Oral Torah over Written; see the discussion in Bigman, "Ladder," 10–16.

52. For the same point in Catholic theology, see Congar, *Meaning*, 13.

53. See Rashi *ad loc.*, ד"ה חתומה ניתנה. For additional rabbinic sources expressing this view, see Fraade, "Literary," 43.

54. Kraemer, "Formation," 624 and 626.

55. On the translation of ותיק as "keen-witted," see Golinkin, "Meaning," 53–58.

56. See Rashi to b. Gittin 60b (ד"ה רוב בכתב), who explains the logic behind R. Elazar's statement: exegetically derived laws are part of the Written Torah, while Oral Torah contains only laws spoken directly to Moses at Sinai that have no basis in scripture. See further the insightful analysis by Kraemer, "Formation," 624–26.

57. See Maharsha to b. Gittin 60b (רובה ד"ה), summarizing the logic behind R. Yoḥanan's statement: teachings derived by sages using midrash can be seen as Oral Torah. The opinions of Eliezer and Yoḥanan here are consistent with their opinions in b. Berakhot 11a in the standard printed editions, especially if by *mishnah* in that passage they mean "Oral Torah." However, the manuscript evidence is inconsistent; see Rosenthal, "Oral Torah," 467–68.

58. Cf. Jaffee, *Torah*, 54, 70, and Satlow, "Oral Torah," 264–67.

59. Thus, the purport of this passage is, as Finkelstein, in *Sifra: Introduction*, 152, writes, to "inform us that there are whole areas of the Torah without any basis in scripture . . . (viz., Oral Torah) . . . and it is important to accept them just as the Pharisees accepted them, one man learning them from the mouth of another."

60. For a defense of the translation I provide against this reading by Rashi, Maimonides, and Bartenura, see Epstein, *Introduction*, 2:520, and the parallel text in t. Ḥagigah 1:9. Ironically, the Gemara's rereading of the passage's final line fits the perspective of the Mishnah as a whole: after all, the Mishnah does not even recognize Oral Torah and Written Torah as distinct categories but speaks only of the overarching category of Torah. Similarly, the position of m. Ḥagigah 1:8 is closer to that generally found in the Gemara as a whole, for the Gemara generally prefers to root laws from the Mishnah in biblical exegesis.

61. Halivni, *Midrash, Mishna, and Gemara*, 93.

62. Modern scholars disagree on the extent to which the Mishnah views its laws as deriving from the Pentateuch; see Stemberger and Strack, *Introduction*, 141–45. This modern debate parallels a debate among the ancients; see Jay Harris, *How*, esp. 1–24. Those modern scholars who insist on a deeper scripturalization the Mishnah's law reenact the work of the Gemara and the halakhic midrashim.

63. Cf. Neusner, *Midrash in Context*, 135–36, and Elman, "R. Zadok," 15–16.

64. On the importance of the oral and aural aspect of scripture not only in Judaism but in religions around the world, see Smith, *What Is Scripture*, 7–9 and 376 s.v. "Oral/aural," and Graham, "Scripture," 137b–139a. Graham has devoted an entire volume to this issue: Graham, *Beyond*.

65. I arrived at these figures using Davka's *Judaic Classics Library*, version 2.2. My count is imprecise in various ways: it does not attend to manuscript evidence, and it does not include variations involving prefixed prepositions. But the contrast is clear.

66. The invention of the printing press had a profound effect on the ways people related to the Bible and conceptualized it. The availability of the Bible in easily searched and retrieved digital formats today is likely to have a significant effect on Jewish and Christian notions of scripture.

67. Leading scholars of rabbinic law articulate this view. See Elon, *Jewish Law*, 1:232–33; Joel Roth, *Halakhic Process*, 9; Hayes, "Rabbinic Contestations," 125; cf. Schweid, *Philosophy of the Bible*, 1:4.

68. See esp. Leibowitz, *Judaism*, 346–50, and cf. 337–38; Schwartz, "Origin," 246–52.

69. Significantly, Heschel chooses this quotation as the heading of an important subchapter in Heschel, *TmH*, 3:27 (= *HT*, 663).

70. Schwartz, "Origin," 246. On this use of the passage by the rabbis, see Elon, *Jewish Law*, 237–38, 279–80, 481–85, and Joel Roth, *Halakhic Process*, 115–16, 125–27.

71. Schwartz, "Origin," 250–51. Similarly, Levinson, *Legal Revision*, 32–33, points out that in spite of the many cases of legal reform found in the Bible, biblical texts refer openly to such reform remarkably rarely: in Ruth 4.7 and in the four priestly stories in which Moses requests legal clarification from God (Leviticus 24.10–23; Numbers 9.1–14, 15.32–36, 27.1–11, and 36.1–9), on which see Fishbane, *Biblical Interpretation*, 98–102; Chavel, "Second Passover"; Chavel, "Numbers 15." On the absence of an admission of legal change in biblical texts, see also Japhet, *From the Rivers*, 138.

72. For a similar discussion of the relationship between Oral Torah and its derivative, Written Torah, see Rosenberg, "Biblical Criticism," 113. A similar view appears in Heschel's work; see Even-Chen, *Voice*, 175. As a defense of tradition against overweening claims by scripture, these arguments are not new. They were expressed by Erasmus, the Catholic biblical scholar of the Reformation era, in his debate with Luther; see Legaspi, *Death*, 16. The rabbinic concept of a halakhah Moses received at Sinai (e.g., in the story in b. Menaḥot 89a/b. Niddah 72b) also shows that some laws claim authority exclusively from revelation at Sinai, not from scripture or scripture as interpreted by midrash.

73. On the meanings and implications of these categories, see Elon, *Jewish Law*, 207–23; Joel Roth, *Halakhic Process*, 13–48 and 153–204.

74. Elon, *Jewish Law*, 212–14.

75. Cf. Joel Roth, *Halakhic Process*, 47, and Elon, *Jewish Law*, 207–12. To some degree, Maimonides seems to define דאורייתא commandments more narrowly, so that does not include midrashically based laws, but his view not accepted; in fact subsequent halakhic authorities read his statements in a forced manner so as to make it closer to the standard view that midrashically based laws can be דאורייתא. See Elon, *Jewish Law*, 209 and 210 n. 98.

76. For a well-crafted statement of the Written Torah's authority in rabbinic literature, see Assis, "Author-ity," 16–18, who suggests that midrash, in contrast to pseudepigraphic literature of the Second Temple period, "position[s] itself as secondary and inauthentic" because it presents itself as an interpretation. But Assis goes on to maintain, rightly, that the midrash's self-effacement is more apparent than real.

77. See Yadin, "Rabbi Ishmael" and Yadin, *Scripture*.

78. See Wolfson, "Beautiful Maiden," 159–60.

79. See Japhet, *Ideology*.

80. See Driver, *Deuteronomy*, iii–xix; Levinson, *Deuteronomy and the Hermeneutics*; Veijola, *Moses Erben*; Eckart Otto, *Deuteronomium: Politische Theologie*. Cf. Weinfeld, *DDS*, 179–243.

81. Knohl, *Sanctuary*.

82. See, e.g., Sommer, *Prophet*; Boda, Floyd, and Mason, *Bringing*; Tooman and Lyons, *Transforming*.

83. For several examples of this type, see Zakovitch, *Introduction*, 20–34; for dozens, see Fishbane, *Biblical Interpretation*, 23–88.

84. See Zakovitch, *Introduction*, 25; Seeligmann, *Studies*, 284–85.

85. I take this example from Gesundheit, *Three Times*, 46–58, who provides a rigorous defense of the reading I sketch out quickly.

86. Verse 2 may originally have been located after the word לאמר in verse 3, for reasons that Ehrlich, *Randglossen*, 1:303–4, lays out clearly. The repetition of לכם in verse 2 is odd, and it is possible that the first לכם was added when the verse was (accidentally?) moved to follow verse 1. In that case, part of the verse was not originally in the second person. For another approach, see Gesundheit, *Three Times*, 50–51 n. 14 and 54–55.

87. The study of inner-biblical exegesis was pioneered in the middle of the twentieth century, especially in Kaufmann, *Toledot*, 4:291–93 (where he speaks of מדרש הלכה בעזרא), 327–29, 331–38, 341–42, 346–50 (where he speaks of מדרש התורה וראשית תורה שבעל פה), and Seeligmann, "Voraussetzungen"; Seeligmann, "Beginnings." Kaufmann and Seeligmann followed up on earlier studies, including Yellin, "Allusion"; Kaminka, *Meḥqarim*, 19–30, 52–56, 159–64; and Seidel, "Parallels." All these scholars embrace and expand an insight that goes back to the beginnings of *die Wissenschaft des Judentums*, whose founders—especially Leopold Zunz and Abraham Geiger—argued (as Schechter, *Studies [First]*, xvi, put it in regard to the former) that "certain portions of the Bible ... are, in fact, little more than a traditional interpretation of older portions of Scripture, adapted to the religious needs of the time." Schechter presaged the study of inner-biblical exegesis when he wrote, "The great fact remains that the best commentary on the Bible is the Bible itself" (Schechter, *Studies [Second]*, 36). In the wake of the influential work of Kaufmann and Seeligmann, other scholars contributed to this field: e.g., Sarna, "Psalm 89"; Muffs, *Love*, 9–48; Toeg, "Numbers 15:22–31—Midrash Halacha"; Rofé, "Move," "History," and "Ephraimite." The 1980s witnessed the publication of the first comprehensive studies of the phenomenon throughout the Hebrew Bible: Fishbane, *Biblical Interpretation*, and Zakovitch, *Introduction*. Since the 1980s the field has flourished, in the work both of Fishbane's students (e.g., Levinson, *Deuteronomy and the Hermeneutics*; Levinson, *Legal Revision*; Schniedewind, *Society*; Sommer, *Prophet*) and of others (e.g., Steck, "Prophetische Prophetenauslegung"; Schmid, *Schriftgelehrte*; Gesundheit, *Three Times*).

88. On the continuity of inner-biblical exegesis postbiblical exegesis, see Fishbane, *Garments*, 3–32, 64–78; Fishbane, "The Hebrew Bible and Exegetical Tradition," 15–30, esp. 17; Zakovitch, *Introduction*, 9–11, 131–35; Kugel, *Traditions*, 15–19, 895–96; Kugel, "Bible's Earliest." Cf. the elegant phrasing in Carasik, "To See," 257,

who, discussing the exegetical aspect of Deuteronomy 4, described that chapter as "the locus of the Bible's invention of itself."

89. Levinson, *Legal Revision*, 18.

90. Sonnet, *Book*, 27–28.

91. Ibid., 41–42 and *passim*, discusses the paradox the written horizon that Deuteronomy projects into the future for Moses's oral communication.

92. For a treatment of all these figures, see Elman, "R. Zadok," 10–11; Elman, "Nahmanides and Abarbanel." My thanks to Michael Balinsky for referring me to these fascinating articles. On Abarbanel's view of Deuteronomy as partially exegetical and the roots of this view in the thought of Yosef Hayyun, see further Viezel, "Moses' Literary License."

93. See *Zohar* 3:271a; Horowitz, *Shenei Luḥot* 162a, 383a. See the discussion of these passages in Heschel, *TmH*, 2:184–85 (= *HT*, 454–56). Benamozegh, *Em Lamiqra*, *ad* Deuteronomy 1.1, writes that Deuteronomy "is distinct from the other four books. . . . Because it is an explanation and supplement to some of the commandments that appear in earlier books, I call it the beginning of the writing of the Oral Torah in accordance with the needs of the time." My thanks to Aharon Shear-Yashuv for pointing me to Benamozegh. A similar approach appears in ibn Ezra's long commentary to Exodus 20.1. There ibn Ezra refers to the wording of the Decalogue in Deuteronomy 5 as mixing God's words found in the Exodus 20 with "Moses's interpretations" (פריושי משה) of them; see Viezel, "Divine Content," 392–93. Rashbam, too, speaks of Deuteronomy as containing Moses's interpretations; see Viezel, "Rashbam on Moses' Role," 172–73.

94. Hermann Cohen, *Religion*, 73.

95. Van der Toorn, *Scribal*, 156.

96. In addition to the works cited in n. 80 earlier in this chapter, see relevant sections in Fishbane, *Biblical Interpretation*, and Veijola, "Deuteronomistic Roots." For an analogous treatment of the Holiness Code in Leviticus, see Levinson, "Birth."

97. On this dialectic, cf. Scholem, "Revelation and Tradition," 284. For an example of the problematic bifurcation between scripture and tradition, see J. Z. Smith, "Canons." For a discussion that demonstrates the artificial nature of this bifurcation, see Levinson, *Legal Revision*, 1–2, 12–21.

98. This fact has significant implications for Jewish and Christian theologians who are considering the nature of their sacred texts and traditions, for it strengthens the hand of those who regard the border between scripture and tradition as fluid or lacking significance. Recent Catholic and, increasingly, Protestant thinkers have put forward the view that tradition is prior to scripture, and that the former encompasses the latter. Significantly, it is the work of modern biblical criticism that encouraged Protestant thinkers to see tradition as prior to scripture, since it taught them that Christian scripture itself is the product of the passing on and reshaping of traditions in the early church. See esp. Dulles,

Revelation, 70–72 and 80, and cf. Congar, *Meaning*, 16–17, 92–95. On the denial of tradition's secondary or derivative status in Christian theology, see further Brown, *Tradition, passim*, esp. the clear thesis at 1. The move toward seeing tradition as prior to scripture among Protestant thinkers carries a certain irony (as Kugel, *How*, 1–46, and Kugel, "Torah," 1004, has pointed out): the doctrine of *sola scriptura* led Protestant biblical scholars starting in the eighteenth century to construct methods for reading the Bible in its own cultural context free of tradition, but the scholarship that emerged from these methods had shown by the twentieth century that (against the grain of Protestant thought) tradition is prior to scripture. A similar irony emerged as neo-Orthodox Protestant scholars emphasized the biblical canon as providing a rule of faith, only to realize that the very diversity of the canon prevents it, on its own, from functioning as a rule; see Blenkinsopp, *Prophecy and Canon*, 142 and 147.

99. On the use of the term *torah* in the Tanakh, see Fishbane, "*Tôrâ*"; Liedke and Peterson, "Torah"; García-López, "Tôrāh"; Kugel, "Torah"; Solomon, *Torah*, 27–28; and the still-useful entry in BDB, 435–36.

100. Solomon, *Torah*, 25.

101. Begrich, *Gesammelte*, 236. On the dynamic and ad hoc nature of what eventually crystallized as the priestly texts, see Japhet, *From the Rivers*, 139–40. To be sure, the "torahs" found in Leviticus and Numbers were probably reduced to writing at an early period; they probably existed as distinct scrolls in Temple archives that were later brought together to form the P document; see Kaufmann, *Toledot*, 1:49–50, 76, and Milgrom, *Leviticus 1–16*, 383.

102. Schwartz, "Priestly Account," 132.

103. In Ezra-Nehemiah, *torah* can refer to the Pentateuch, whether in its current form or in an antecedent recension. In Ezra 3.2 the phrase "written in the Torah of Moses" clearly refers to material from P found in Leviticus, while in Nehemiah 13.1–3 "The Book of Moses" or "the Torah" which was read aloud includes Deuteronomy 23.4. Apparently, then, the Book of Ezra-Nehemiah uses the term *Torah of Moses* to refer to a work that included both P and D, or both Leviticus and Deuteronomy. That work is either the Pentateuch or something very much like it. See Liedke and Peterson, "Torah," 1421–22; García-López, "Tôrāh," 629–30; Blenkinsopp, *Ezra-Nehemiah*, 155; the helpful review of literature and balanced conclusion in Williamson, *Ezra, Nehemiah*, xxxvii–xxxix; and the nuanced discussion in Japhet, *From the Rivers*, 137–51.

104. In surmising that one should use the branches to build the booths, the author of Nehemiah was followed by many postbiblical commentators, on which see Milgrom, *Leviticus 23–27*, 2065. On the exegetical nature of the Nehemiah passage, see especially Kaufmann, *Toledot*, 4.325–36, Fishbane, *Biblical Interpretation*, 109–12; Rofé, "Research on Biblical Law," 491–92; Blenkinsopp, *Ezra-Nehemiah*, 291–92.

105. On the development of both interpretations and the exegetical reasoning behind them, see Sperber, "Commandment." Sperber shows that the rabbinic interpretation was known already in prerabbinic times (it is mentioned in Jubilees 16.29–31 and 2 Maccabees 10.6–7). But he also argues persuasively that the interpretation known from Nehemiah (which becomes the interpretive norm among Samaritans and Qaraites) is the older one.

106. Alternatively, one might argue that Nehemiah 8 is based on an altogether different version of the Pentateuch, but Milgrom, *Leviticus 23–27*, 2065, cogently refutes this possibility; cf. Kaufmann, *Toledot*, 4:326. Like Nehemiah 8.14–15, the text of Ezra 6.18 refers to a practice as "written in the Book of Moses," which is not mentioned in the Pentateuch at all; see Najman, *Past Renewals*, 78–79.

107. See the insightful summary in ibid., 80–86, esp. 83. The practice of attributing new legal practices to Moses's Torah occurs in other passages in Ezra-Nehemiah as well; it exemplifies the widespread practice that Najman, *Seconding Sinai*, *passim*, calls Mosaic discourse, the attribution of a new practice to the authoritative tradition symbolized by Moses. Thus, Ezra 9.1–2, 9.11–12, and 10.1–5 create a new law on the basis of a midrashic combination of Leviticus 18.27, Deuteronomy 7.3 and 23.1–8, whereas Nehemiah 13.1–3 creates a new law on the basis of an extension of the more limited law found in Deuteronomy 23.1–9. See Japhet, *From the Rivers*, 137–57, and Fishbane, *Biblical Interpretation*, 114–17, 126–28, and see already on the "halakhic midrash" in these passages Kaufmann, *Toledot*, 4:339. (In using the term *midrashic* to refer specifically to the creation of new law or narrative on the basis of the combination of verses from different books or distant parts of a single book, I follow Boyarin, *Intertextuality*.)

108. Jon Levenson, "Sources," 570. Cf. García-López, "Tôrāh," 620–21. On the expansive—but not infinitely expansive—concept of Torah in Psalm 119, see Reynolds, *Torah*, 105–46.

109. Cf. Jon Levenson, "Sources," 571: "Just as Scripture generates tradition, so does tradition generate Scripture. Neither can be said to have absolute chronological priority."

110. See Gitay, "Deutero-Isaiah: Oral or Written?" *passim*, and esp. 191, Niditch, *Oral*, esp. 99–130; van der Toorn, *Scribal*, 11–14; and Person, "Ancient"; but see also Schniedewind, *How*, 11–17, who argues that the gulf between orality and literacy ought not be understated. On the intertwining of oral and written representations of Deuteronomy in that book itself, see Sonnet, *Book*, 41–42. This intertwining remained the norm during the rabbinic and medieval eras; indeed, to some degree, it remains the case that for many people contact with scripture comes primarily through lectionary readings during worship. On the importance of this point, see Elsie Stern, "Concepts."

111. See Carr, *Writing*, 4–8 (quotes from 4, 5, and 7).

112. Silent reading occurred rarely in the Greco-Roman world, and it was sufficiently exceptional that it was commented on. See Gilliard, "More Silent Reading."

113. The importance of this verse for understanding the twofold nature of Torah as written and oral is recognized as early as the scholia to *Megillat Ta'anit*; see Noam, *Megillat Ta'anit*, 78, and Werman, "Oral," 185.

114. Hurowitz, "Spanning," 13–18; on Deuteronomy 31.19, see his comments on 21–22. Similarly, Elman, "Authoritative Oral Tradition," 20, points out, "Even texts that were to be learned by heart were still transmitted by writing and learned from tablets." These processes happened together, not apart. See further van der Toorn, *Scribal*, 11–16, 110–15, 228.

115. See Elman, "Authoritative Oral Tradition," 26, and van der Toorn, *Scribal*, 128–29.

116. Elman, "Authoritative Oral Tradition," 22–31; Hurowitz, "Spanning," 23–24. In some cases the oral tradition may have been the more authoritative; see van der Toorn, *Scribal*, 348 n. 59. For an Israelite example of suspicion of the purely written, see van der Toorn's discussion of Jeremiah 8.8–9 at 77, as well as Blenkinsopp, *Prophecy and Canon*, 37–38. On parallels between the notion of Oral Torah and the orality of ancient Near Eastern scribal practice generally, see van der Toorn, *Scribal*, 128; Hurowitz, "Spanning," 12–13.

117. Geoffrey Miller, *Ways*, 148.

118. Cf. Ong, "Before Textuality," 260: "Before writing, there is no functional distinction between a statement and an interpretation of a statement. Asked to repeat a statement that he or she has made, a person from an oral culture commonly gives not a word-for-word repetition of what he or she has said, but an interpretation." What Ong writes applies not only "before writing" but also in cultures where writing is merely a form of recording texts that are delivered orally.

119. Carr, *Writing*, 302, 305.

120. Halbertal, *People*, 3.

121. Carr, *Writing*, 11. Carr's entire book may be taken as a description of how what Halbertal calls formative canon worked in various ancient Near Eastern and Hellenistic cultures—that is, how the reading and transmission of texts shaped identity.

122. Of course, some Jews assert that the Written Torah's real meaning is found in the Oral, and thus in some theoretical way the Pentateuch remains normative. Such an assertion does not alter the claim I make here, which is that texts of the Oral Torah and Written Torah are canonical in basically similar ways when viewed from the vantage point of Halbertal's discussion of formative and normative canons.

123. Again, these beliefs and practices are often linked exegetically to the Written Torah, but they still may be classified as part of Oral Torah, or as part of both Torahs. One would not be able to know them without the Oral Torah.

124. On the importance of this point for a Jewish biblical theology, cf. Moshe Goshen-Gottstein, "Tanakh Theology," 626–27 and n. 40. In stating that halakhic decisions base themselves on texts from Oral rather than Written Torah, I do not deny that post-amoraic scholars have been interested in the relationship between halakhot and their exegetical sources in the Pentateuch; many works have addressed just that issue. But such scholars have not generally made *rulings* of Jewish law by referring directly to the Pentateuch; their activities have been academic, not legislative, in nature.

125. For example, the lectionary reading required on the New Year according to b. Megillah 30b is Leviticus 23.23ff., but in synagogues throughout the world for the past millennium the reading has come from Genesis 21–22. Similarly, according to b. Megillah 31a, we should read Leviticus 26 on fast days; in fact, we read from Exodus 32 (and, on the Ninth of Av, Deuteronomy 4). Conversely, new practices have been given the force of halakhah in post-talmudic times. An especially prominent example is the מחיצה, a barrier placed between men and women during prayer, which was not required and may even have been rare in rabbinic times, became an increasingly common custom in the Middle Ages, and was formally accorded the status of law only in the nineteenth century. See Golinkin, *Status*, 308–40.

126. Knoppers and Levinson, "How," 6.

127. Westbrook, *Law*, esp. chs. 1, 3, and 4 in vol. 1. Bottéro, *Mesopotamia*, 167, points out that the so-called Code of Ḥammurapi was not a systematic collection of positive law but a "treatise, with examples, on the exercise of judicial power." This judgment applies to all the legal collections from ancient Mesopotamia, Israel, and Asia Minor.

128. Chavel, "Biblical Law," esp. 227–28 and 237.

129. Knoppers and Levinson, "How," 6. This overuse of the term *normative* to describe scripture is exceedingly common; in addition to Halbertal, *People*, 3, see also Jon Levenson, "Religious Affirmation," 25: "Historical research into the Tanakh . . . puts a painful question to those who wish to affirm Judaism as a contemporary reality: How can a literature so variegated and contradictory speak with a normative voice today?" This widespread perception of pain among those who wish to embrace Tanakh as both artifact and scripture might vanish if only we recognize that in Judaism scripture is overwhelmingly formative and barely if at all normative.

130. On Exodus 21–23 as a literary collection whose goal is not legislative but educational and ideological, see Chavel, "Biblical Law," 248; on the same characteristic in P, see his comments on 255; and on this characteristic of the redacted Torah, see 268–69.

131. The practice of reciting Targum blurs the line slightly; on Targum as Oral Torah, see Safrai, "Oral Torah," 38–39, and Gerhardsson, *Memory*, 68–69. Rabbinic law takes pain to distinguish between the formal recitation of the biblical

text from a scroll and the less formal restatement in Targum, as Gerhardsson points out (68 nn. 3–5). Similarly, there are passages from rabbinic literature that are recited in the liturgy, but these always occur in preliminary rather than central services (e.g., before פסוקי דזמרה), and the rabbinic passages are not chanted in the formal and rule-bound manner as biblical texts.

132. On the importance of scripture as ritual object and not only object of study, see especially Graham, "Scripture," 139, and cf. the notion of scripture as human activity in Wilfred Cantwell Smith, *What Is Scripture*, 18 and *passim*. See further Wyschogrod, *Body*, xiv, who overstates the significance of the distinctions between Oral Torah and Written Torah while underestimating the importance of Oral Torah.

133. On ritual uses as one defining characteristic of scripture, see Wilfred Cantwell Smith, *What Is Scripture*, 140, cf. 70 and 181. On the crucial distinction between reading for understanding and reading for a ritual purpose, see Halbertal, *People*, 13–14. See also Seder Eliahu Zuṭa, end of chapter 2, and the discussion in Heschel, *TmH*, 3:43. Gordon Tucker writes in his note there (*HT*, 675 n. [40]) that, for those who believe that reading a scriptural text has ritual value regardless of the text's meaning or the reader's understanding of it, "the words of Torah have an inherent *value*. . . . It is what the words *are*, not just what they denote, that entitles and requires us to say a blessing before studying them. This is a classic formulation of the Akivan view on the words of Torah." This Akivan view is expanded among mystics of both the pre-kabbalistic and kabbalistic movements, on which see Idel, "Concepts of Scripture."

134. Van der Toorn, "Iconic Book," 228–48.

135. Ibid., 240–42. Contra Rashbam to Exodus 13.9, verses such as these refer to physical objects and are not intended as figurative language. See Weinfeld, *Deuteronomy 1–11*, 341–33. The seventh-century Ketef Ḥinnom amulets, which include the priestly benedictions know to us from Numbers 6.23–27, indicates that practices such as those Deuteronomy 6.6–9 prescribe were not merely theoretical or metaphorical. Further, these amulets show that the ritual use of texts was not limited to Deuteronomic documents but included Priestly documents as well. On the link between these amulets and the commandments found in Exodus 13 and Deuteronomy 6 and 11, see further Barkay, "Priestly Benediction," 74–76; Keel and Uehlinger, *Gods*, 366.

136. Van der Toorn, "Iconic Book," 242.

137. Granted, the study of Oral Torah can also be a ritual act; one may study Talmud not only to gain understanding but to obey the commandment to study—in effect, to gain merit. The notion of study (primarily of Oral Torah) as religious act is prominent in rabbinic Judaism, especially in the Lithuanian yeshiva movement. Nonetheless, this function of Oral Torah is not highlighted in Jewish liturgy. Jaffee, *Torah*, 155–56, points out that rabbinic works are Torah only insofar as they are taught orally; their written texts themselves have no

inherent value, unlike the written texts of the Tanakh. Differences between the ritual status of Oral and Written Torah emerge from the talmudic debate regarding the blessing recited before studying Torah. It is a given that one recites this blessing before studying the Written Torah, but the rabbis debate whether one must recite it before studying Oral Torah; see y. Berakhot 3c (1:8), b. Berakhot 11a, concerning which see Rosenthal, "Oral Torah," 467–75. The issue is further complicated by differing opinions concerning halakhic and aggadic material within Oral Torah. The conclusion of both Talmuds—that one must recite the blessing for both Written Torah and Oral Torah—supports the notion of the unity of the two Torahs; but the fact that the issue is debated points to a distinction between them.

138. Barton, *Oracles*, 91. A similar distinction is suggested in Barr, *Holy Scripture*, 59–60, 63, and cf. 1–22. This distinction calls to mind Yehezkel Kaufmann's differentiation between the Torah literature (ספרות התורה), which existed in pre-exilic times, and the Torah book (ספר התורה), which crystallized after the destruction of the First Temple; see Kaufmann, *Toledot*, 1:185–220. We may add that what Kaufmann calls Torah literature is Oral Torah, while the Torah book (i.e., the Pentateuch) is the beginning of a fixed Written Torah. Modern biblical criticism restores the former to a more prominent place.

139. On alternative views in rabbinic and medieval Judaism, Heschel, *TmH*, vol. 2, esp. 2:146–56 (= *HT*, chs. 17–33, esp. pp. 423–32), and the articles by Viezel in my bibliography. See further Perlman, *Abraham Heschel's Idea*, 119–33. On the implications of stenographic and other positions, see Silman, *Voice, passim*.

140. Wyschogrod, *Body*, xiv.

141. Cf. Halivni, *Peshat*, 163–67, and Halivni, "Man's Role," 29–49. Halivni identifies an opinion in rabbinic and medieval Jewish texts according to which "the halakhic system was not revealed at Sinai *in toto*, and the legal process must therefore remain vibrant and active" (*Peshat*, 164).

142. Granted, phenomena such as the בת קול are referred to in rabbinic literature, but this is not quite the same as prophecy and in any event is infrequent. See Sommer, "Did Prophecy," 35–45.

143. See especially b. Temurah 15b–16a for the idea that the repeated traditions (Mishnah) were corrupted by forgetfulness. For a summary of medieval views of the human elements in Oral Torah, see Halbertal, *People*, 54–72. The Oral Torah often refers to its own orality and the possibility of its consequent fallibility: take, for example, its careful listing of tradents (which reflects an attempt to forestall erroneous transmission, and hence an admission of the possibility) and its acknowledgment of doubts concerning the accuracy of oral transmission (e.g., חד אמר ... וחד אמר). Consequently, as Samuel Fleischacker reminds me, Oral Torah sees itself as responsible to Written Torah, while it sees Written Torah as responsible only to God. Biblical texts, in contrast, put much less emphasis on their self-referentiality, and at times they tend to mask

it (see, e.g., Levinson, "Human," 45, and Sommer, *Prophet*, 20–22). My thanks to Daniel Nevins for pointing out the relevance of this issue.

144. An interesting question I do not pursue here is whether the Nakh more closely resemble Pentateuch or Oral Torah in this regard. Shemot Rabbah 28:6 and Tanḥuma Yitro §11 teach that the prophecies of the classical prophets (found in the Nakh) and the teachings of the sages (found in Oral Torah) were revealed at Sinai; both, however, were made public much later.

145. Rabbinic scholars on occasion insist that Oral Torah can overturn Written Torah (see Tosefot to Qiddushin 16b and Ḥullin 88b). But these apparent exceptions should not be exaggerated. See Halivni, *Peshat*, 152–53, and sources cited there.

146. On the very rare cases in which Sages saw themselves as uprooting a biblical law on their own authority, see Heschel, *TmH*, 3:27–28 (= *HT*, 663–65, with especially useful notes by Tucker).

147. Congar, *Meaning*, 99–102, discusses the respective qualities of scripture and tradition in Catholic thought, coming to conclusions somewhat different from what I claim about Jewish tradition.

148. See Eliade, *Sacred*, 11–12; Eliade, *Patterns*, 1–33. J. Z. Smith, "Acknowledgments," critiques Eliade's notion of hierophany, but a careful reading of Eliade shows he anticipated and rebutted these critiques; see Sommer, *Bodies*, 195 n. 146.

149. Ong, "Before Textuality," 265, 267.

150. Ibid., 265: "Oral utterance is inevitably discourse, verbal exchange between two or more persons."

151. Ibid: "Reading . . . gives [textualized discourse] context, always related dynamically to the present even more than to the past."

152. Van der Toorn, *Scribal*, 206–7, 218, 231–32. See also Assis, "Author-ity," 19–20.

153. Not all scholars agree that Jews in the Second Temple period stopped believing in the possibility of new prophetic revelations. I defend the idea that prophecy ceased fairly early in this period; see Sommer, "Did Prophecy." For more recent overviews of the debate, with further bibliography, see Floyd and Haak, *Prophets*; L. Stephen Cook, *On the Question*. If the position against which I argue in that article is right, then the point I am making here could be stated even more strongly.

154. Some scholars warn against attempts to regard the Pharisees as proto-rabbis with a well worked-out doctrine of tradition distinct from scripture. Nevertheless, consistent descriptions of the Pharisees' attitude toward tradition appear in Josephus, the Gospels, and Paul. From these we can conclude that the Pharisees were already concerned with traditions passed on from earlier generations and distinct from scripture. See Baumgarten, "Pharisaic." Some scholars maintain that they did not emphasize the oral nature or Sinaitic origin of these traditions; see E. P. Sanders, *Jewish Law*, 97–130; Jaffee, *Torah*, 39–61, and cf. the similar but more moderate skepticism of Neusner, "Oral

Torah and Tradition," 69–70. Others critique this skepticism: Schäfer, *Studien*, 190–91; Baumgarten, "Pharisaic," *passim*; cf. Werman, "Oral," 175–87, and Gruber, "Mishnah," 113, 121–22. In any event the Pharisaic category of nonbiblical tradition is similar to Oral Torah: it consists of authoritative Jewish beliefs and practices not explicitly spelled out by scripture.

155. See the discussion of the Qaraite's סבל הירושה in Frank, "Karaite Exegesis," 115, and cf. Moshe Goshen-Gottstein, "Tanakh Theology," 627.

156. Satlow, "Oral Torah."

157. See Elman, "R. Zadok," 9. Cf. the very similar definition of tradition in Christian tradition in Dulles, *Revelation*, 77.

158. Kepnes, "Revelation," 224.

159. Congar, *Meaning*, 4. On the Jewish roots of the notion that tradition involves not only learning oral texts but imitating a master's life and habits, see further his comments on 17.

160. See Satlow, "Oral Torah," 265.

161. On this aspect of tradition, see Congar, *Meaning*, 112–13.

162. See Jaffee, *Torah*, 126–56, and Levinas, *Beyond*, 137.

163. See *supra* n. 152.

164. The theme of tradition as by definition a social process appears in the work of Cardinals Yves Congar and Avery Dulles; see, e.g., Dulles's remark in his introduction to Congar, *Meaning*, ix, and Congar's own formulations, e.g., 24.

165. Cf. Carr, *Writing*, 10: "Writing ... depersonalizes language, decontextualizes expressions, ... formalizes, generalizes, ... cutting [language] loose from the momentary and context-bound utterance." On the profound utility of communal reading practices for the cultivation of religious humility and thus for promoting openness to revelation, see Fishbane, *Garments*, 132–33.

166. Haym Soloveitchik, "Migration," and Haym Soloveitchik, "Rupture."

167. See *supra* n. 152.

168. On this aspect of the Yishmaelian school, see Yadin, *Scripture*.

169. Gottlieb, "Oral Letter," who quotes from his own translations of Mendelssohn's *Jerusalem* and Hirsch's *Nineteen Letters*. See further Eisen, *Rethinking*, 82–83, 87. On the oral and commentarial aspects of Mendelssohn's translation, see Abigail Gillman, "Between Religion," 111.

170. See Rosenzweig's essay "Scripture and Word," in Buber and Rosenzweig, *Scripture and Translation*, 40–46. On their goal of transforming the Bible from a book back into a voice, see Abigail Gillman, "Between Religion," esp. 97; cf. Fishbane, *Garments*, 107–8. For a kindred conception of scripture, see Wilfred Cantwell Smith, *What Is Scripture*, 17–18, 239.

171. Amir, *Reason*, 283, cf. 286, 287. See also Amir, *Small Still Voice*, 179–82.

172. Jonathan Cohen, "Concepts," 188.

173. Rosenzweig, *FRHLT*, xxxvii.

174. See Glatzer in ibid., II, 117–18. On the centrality of community in Rosenzweig's view of revelation and authority and its connection to his work at the *Lehrhaus*, see Batnitzky, *Idolatry*, 70.

175. On this aspect of modern biblical scholarship, see, e.g., Goldingay, *Theological Diversity* (esp. 1–166, with useful discussion of different types of diversity on 1–12); Brueggemann, *Theology*; Knohl, *Divine Symphony*; Carasik, *Bible's Many Voices*; and, more briefly, Sharp, *Wrestling*, 59–75.

176. Rosenzweig, *Star* [Hallo], 303–4 (= *Star* [Galli], 322–23).

177. Rosenzweig, *OJL*, 84, and cf. 74–76. See further Amir, *Reason*, 293.

178. Rosenzweig's letter to Jacob Rosenheim of March 21, 1927, in Buber and Rosenzweig, *Scripture and Translation*, 23–24. Rosenzweig sees the two Torahs as distinct entities that originate at different times; but they effectively become a unity when taken up by the committed Jew. Contrasting himself with Hirsch (to whom, surprisingly, my position in this matter is closer), Rosenzweig writes (23): "For Hirsch the oral Torah is a stream parallel to the written, rising from the same spring. For us it is the completion of the unity of the book as written through the unity of the book as read."

179. The term to which I refer (*wunderbar*, Rosenzweig, *Briefe und Tagebücher*, 2:1135) is rendered "miraculous" in Buber and Rosenzweig, *Scripture and Translation*, 23.

180. Heinemann, *Ta'amei*, 2:217.

181. Heschel, *God*, 274.

182. Ibid., 273.

183. Heschel, *TmH*, 3:27–29 (= *HT*, 663–66).

184. Heschel, *God*, 26, and see further 160.

185. Ibid., 265. Heschel does not state this openly. He writes, "The event [of revelation to a prophet] is divine, but the formulation is done by the individual prophet. According to this conception, the idea is revealed; the expression is coined by the prophet." Only when one checks the note attached to these sentences (277 n. 22) does the reader see that the event to which Heschel refers is the lawgiving at Sinai and that he depends on ibn Ezra's discussion of the Decalogue's two versions, one in Exodus and one in Deuteronomy. Heschel takes ibn Ezra's interpretation as evidence for the Mosaic phrasing of at least one of these versions.

186. Ibid., 185.

187. The midrash appears in various texts, including Midrash Tehillim (Buber) 90:12. For additional citations, see Heschel, *TmH*, 2:22–23 and 2:28 n. 12 (= *HT*, 333–34 and 337 n. 71).

188. Scholem, "Revelation and Tradition," 294–95. Fishbane, *Sacred Attunement*, 62, suggests a similar idea when he avers that Oral Torah is based not just on scripture but just as importantly on the supernal Torah: the תורה כלולה, he maintains, "is the theological reality to which the disciples of Moses

[throughout the ages] respond, knowingly or not, when they bring the exigencies of life into the domain of the Written Torah, and transform both scripture and life reciprocally. The result of such attentiveness is the Oral Torah."

189. Scholem, *On the Kabbalah*, 50. Italics in original.

190. See Mendes-Flohr, *Divided*, 344–50 and 361 n. 21.

191. Translated and quoted in ibid., 344–45.

192. On Heschel's arrival in London, see Kaplan and Dresner, *Prophetic*, 289; on his arrival in Berlin, see 100.

193. Scholem himself downplays the similarity between his thought and Heschel's. In Gershom Scholem, *On Jews*, 274, he critiques Heschel for evading the tension between punctual and ongoing conceptions of revelation, a critique that ignores Heschel's complex treatment of these notions—whose alleged contradiction, we shall see in the following chapter, Heschel resolves by proposing that revelation is not ongoing but eternal from a divine point of view, even as it is an event from a human point of view. See my discussion in ch. 5 of this volume and nn. 58–60 there. On another similarity between the early views of both thinkers (involving the place of symbolism in Jewish mystical tradition) and their increasing disagreement over time, see Idel, "Abraham J. Heschel," 93–95; on their similarities and differences as scholars and thinkers, see also 80 and 95–100. As Kimelman, "Abraham Joshua Heschel's Theology," 210–20, points out, Heschel's writings on kabbalah and Ḥasidism present a massive polemic against Scholem's approach, though Heschel does not criticize Scholem by name. On Scholem's reaction, see Kimelman's remark on 224 n. 68. Kimelman further notes (218 n. 44) that through the work of Moshe Idel, Yehuda Liebes, and their students, Heschel's approach has won the upper hand in the department Scholem founded, an irony that prompts Kimelman to cite Esther 7.8aβ, to we might add Jeremiah 6.14aβ–b.

194. Schechter, *Studies (First)*, xiv–xv.

195. Catholic and Jewish scholars face remarkably similar tools and opportunities as they attempt to relate their scriptures, respectively, to the teachings of the magisterium and the church and to the apprehensions of כלל ישראל (or, as Schechter felicitously rendered it, Catholic Israel); see ibid., xviii–xix. For both groups of interpreters, the tension between scripture and tradition recedes, because the boundary separating scripture and tradition is subordinate to an overarching unity. Problems that seem vexing from Protestant points of view in light of the doctrine of *sola scriptura* (e.g., the relationship between a description of biblical thought and constructive theology) turn out to be nonissues for Jewish, Catholic, and (in all likelihood) Eastern Orthodox theology. (In noting these similarities between Jewish and Catholic reading of the Bible, I do not intend to ignore significant differences, such as those discussed in Brettler, Enns, and Harrington, *Bible and the Believer*, 67–72 and 118–24.) On tradition as a protective force that preserves what historical and philologi-

cal criticism might otherwise corrode in scripture alone, see the discussion of Maurice Blondel in Congar, *Meaning*, 26–28. Even some Protestant thinkers embrace tradition as a central source of religious authority; one thinks of the Wesleyan quadrilateral, for example. For a recent Protestant (in any event, Anglican) thinker who does so, see Brown, *Tradition*, esp. 106–67. (Brown explains the difference between his view of tradition and the views among Catholic theologians on 366.) A similar warmth to tradition is implied in James Barr's work; see especially his approving discussion of Brown in Barr, *Concept*, 586–604. A comparable position appears in the work of Manfred Oeming, who emphasizes the need for dynamic, back-and forth discussion between biblical texts and later theology; see Oeming, *Gesamtbiblische Theologien*, esp. 235–37, and similar views in Patrick D. Miller, *Way*, 297–309; Brown, *Tradition*, 111. For a discussion of the reemergence of tradition alongside scripture in Protestant thought, see Dulles, "Reflections," 67–74.

196. Schechter, *Studies (First)*, xii.
197. Cf. Assis, "Author-ity," 20–21. Indeed, rabbinic literature suggests that this sort of mixed literature is preferable to religious literature that is more closely tied to the divine: "A sage is preferable to a prophet" (b. Bava Batra 12a).

Chapter 5. Event, Process, and Eternity

1. Graham, "Scripture," 134a–b, and cf. 141b, lays out respects in which rabbinic texts fit his definition of scripture. See also the discussion of Talmud as "para-scripture" in Wilfred Cantwell Smith, *What Is Scripture*, 204–6, and Sommer, "Scriptures," 3–4.
2. I borrow the phrase from the aptly chosen title of Schorsch, *Canon without Closure*.
3. Here we see a difference between Judaism and Catholicism, in spite of their common emphasis on tradition alongside scripture. For both, scripture emerges out of tradition, and the faithful have access to scripture only through tradition. But Catholic authorities embrace all three of these pillars. More readily than most of their rabbinic counterparts, they enthusiastically affirm that tradition develops through the help of the Holy Spirit. See the treatment of revelation and scripture promulgated during the Second Vatican Council, *Dei Verbum*, ch. 2, and the discussion of the Holy Spirit as a transcendent subject or active carrier of tradition in Congar, *Meaning*, 51–58 and 99–100. But see the important qualification in 99 n. 20: Congar maintains that traditions formed during the historical life of the church, as opposed to those dating to the time of the apostles, benefit from divine assistance but not inspiration (see further 127 on different types of Catholic tradition). On tradition as a form of revelation in Christianity, see also Brown, *Tradition*, 112–35.
4. Heschel, *TmH*, esp. 3:23–29, 36–8, 49–82 (= *HT*, esp. 658–63, 671–72, 680–700), addresses the question of whether new ideas (חידושים) can result from

something akin to revelation. See further Silman, *Voice, passim.* Ross, *Expanding*, works elegantly on three levels. It is a study of the relationship of feminism and Orthodoxy. It is also a study of the thought of Abraham Isaac Kook and its implications for late-twentieth-century Orthodoxy. Finally, and most importantly for our purposes, it is a study of the relationships among revelation, interpretation, tradition and innovation in rabbinic, medieval, and early modern Jewish thought.

5. One would more typically translate שלמות as "wholeness" or "completeness," but the English table of contents at the back of Silman's volume renders it "perfection."

6. For a positive evaluation of human forgetfulness by a modern ultra-Orthodox thinker, see Hutner, *Paḥad*, third essay on Hanukkah. See further Bigman, "Ladder," 10–14, and Silman, *Voice*, 140. On the religious value of perplexity, see Ward, *Religion*, 22.

7. The second and third positions work well with the idea that prophetic revelation continues in Judaism after the biblical period, and thus it is not surprising that Heschel often speaks of divine inspiration enduring into the Middle Ages; see Heschel, *Prophetic Inspiration* (though see Shai Held, *Abraham Joshua Heschel*, 133–34, for evidence of the opposite position elsewhere in Heschel's work). But it is also possible for Jewish thinkers to agree with the rabbinic doctrine that prophecy ended in the early Second Temple period while maintaining that the development of Jewish tradition enjoys a subprophetic form of divine guidance. On attenuated, subprophetic forms of divine communication in Second Temple, rabbinic, and medieval Jewish cultures in which the belief that full-fledged prophecy had ceased, see Sommer, "Did Prophecy," 39–41; for further bibliography, see n. 153 in ch. 4.

8. On this debate see the literature cited in nn. 114–19 in ch. 2.

9. One might attempt to resolve this contradiction by asserting that different levels within D have different views, and that some of the older strata within D did not know of a forty-year wait between revelation at Ḥoreb and Moses's speeches in Deuteronomy. But not every contradiction should be taken as evidence of multiple authorship. The consistent pattern of emphasizing "today" throughout Deuteronomy (see main text, immediately following) suggests that tension between punctuality and eternity is a core aspect of D's religious worldview. For arguments against seeing this tension as reflecting multiple authors or redactors, see George Adam Smith, *Book of Deuteronomy*, 80.

10. One may argue that this reading works for the canonical Book of Deuteronomy, but that originally Deuteronomy 5 was not preceded by Deuteronomy 1–4. Indeed, almost all modern scholars agree that Deuteronomy 1.1–4.40 were added a later stage in the book's evolution. Even so, it remains clear that chapter 5 represents itself as speech Moses delivers toward the end of his career, not a speech shortly after the revelation itself; otherwise Moses would not have reminded his audience (5.2) that God spoke with Israel "at Ḥoreb." If the people

were still at Horeb, this reminder would be senseless. Moreover, even outside the introductory material in 1.1–4.40 the main stratum of D that includes chapter 5 refers to the forty years in the wilderness; see 8.2 and 29.4. Similarly, 9.1 makes clear that the main body of Deuteronomy is imagined as being uttered immediately before the nation enter Canaan.

11. Dillmann, *Die Bücher Numeri, Deuteronomium und Josua*, 265, and Driver, *Deuteronomy*, 83, argue plausibly that the "parents" that 5.3 has in mind are not the generation who left Egypt (the actual biological parents of the people who stand on the plains of Moab to hear this speech) but the patriarchs, Abraham, Isaac and Jacob, to whom Deuteronomy often applies the term אבותיכם (4.31, 4.37, 7.8, 7.12, and 8.18). Even if this is so, the passage in 5.2–3 remains boldly counterfactual as it insists that the people listening to Moses's speech were present at the creation of the covenant at Horeb. Rather than MT's אבותינו, LXX reads אבותיכם (πατράσιν ὑμῶν), which in fact would refer to the actual parents of the generation about to enter the land.

12. As Dillmann, *Die Bücher Numeri, Deuteronomium und Josua*, 239, notes, in 1.30 LXX omits the phrase "before your eyes," perhaps because of its historical anachronism; but throughout the whole of D's discourse, Moses regards the generation addressed as sharing the experiences of their forebears.

13. Ibid., 265.

14. Weinfeld, *Deuteronomy 1–11*, 238.

15. Hermann Cohen, *Religion*, 76.

16. On the neo-Assyrian origin of this motif, see Weinfeld, *DDS*, 104–5.

17. Dillmann, *Die Bücher Numeri, Deuteronomium und Josua*, 380.

18. Cf. the similar teaching of R. Joshua ben Levi in b. Berakhot 21b, according to which teaching one's child the Torah returns one to the event at Horeb, and that it is for this reason that Deuteronomy can speak to its audience as having been there.

19. In b. Berakhot 63b Judah ben El'ai makes precisely this point in relation to the word *today* in Deuteronomy 27.9.

20. The numbers vary slightly when one looks at the versions (Samaritan and LXX add *today* to "which I command you" at 4.2), but the point about the importance of command occurring "today" remains the same or becomes stronger.

21. On the relationship between the voices of Moses and Yhwh in Deuteronomy (which are sometimes blurred there), see Sonnet, *Book*, 38–40. As Sonnet points out in his notes, this blurring already bothered the ancient versions.

22. A similar rhetorical move occurs in the H stratum of P, which (Joosten, *People and Land*, 45–47 and 196–97, shows) employs several techniques to create a parallel between the Israelites in the desert addressed within the narrative and Israelites in the Land addressed by the H narrative.

23. This forty-year delay in D between Moses's receipt of the law and his passing it to the nation is discussed in all the standard literature. For an especially clear presentation of the issues, see Frankel, *Land*, 79–85. Frankel further argues

(85–96) that an earlier kernel of D made no reference to revelation at Ḥoreb, and that for this kernel the only lawgiving occurred in Moab, shortly after the exodus; in this conception, there was no long period of wandering in the desert, so that Exodus, lawgiving, and entry into the land occurred in quick succession. Frankel's closely argued thesis strikes me as difficult to confirm, and probably unlikely in light of D's constant dependence on E's plotline as suggested by Haran, *Ha'asufah*, 2:157–58 and 198–200, and demonstrated by Baden, *J, E, and the Redaction*, 99–195. In any event the D traditions as preserved in Deuteronomy do repeatedly posit a lengthy gap between revelation and Moses's lawgiving. If Frankel is correct, then the original kernel of D regards the specifics of the law as entirely Mosaic and not divine in origin; see Frankel's fascinating discussion, 91–94. In Frankel's reading, the earlier kernel adopts what I call a participatory theology of revelation, in contrast to D itself.

24. See Haran, *Ha'asufah*, 2:158–60.

25. On the distinction between the two covenants in Deuteronomy 28.69, see Rofé, *Deuteronomy*, 193.

26. Franks, "Sinai," 352.

27. Sonnet, *Book*, 181, and see further 140–47. On the complex interaction of oral and written in this passage, see 117–82.

28. Polzin, *Moses*, 64–65; Levinson, *Deuteronomy and the Hermeneutics, passim*; Levinson, *Legal Revision*, esp. 89–94; Levinson, *Right Chorale*, 265–75. The irony is also noted in Fishbane, *Biblical Interpretation*, 263, and in George Adam Smith, *Deuteronomy*, 58, who points out that Jeremiah 8.8–9 may be a complaint about Deuteronomy's legal revisions—in which case Jeremiah effectively agrees with the principle found in Deuteronomy 4.2 and 13.1 and criticizes D for ignoring it! It is also possible, however, that Jeremiah complains there about the very idea of reducing the law to writing and thus limiting its oral character; see van der Toorn, *Scribal*, 77.

29. I borrow phrasing from the apt title of the last chapter of Levinson, *Legal Revision*, 89, "The Canon as Sponsor of Innovation."

30. Ibid., 90–91.

31. On the camouflaging of innovation, see ibid., 48–49. On the differences among these forms of inner-biblical exegesis, see Sommer, *Prophet*, 10–18, 20–31. Sonnet, *Book*, 47–48, suggests that not only the redactor of the Pentateuch as a whole but also Deuteronomy itself undermines the camouflaging, since at Ḥoreb God entrusts Moses with the task of not merely repeating God's law in Moab but teaching it, which may provide Moses with latitude to rephrase the Torah he received forty years earlier.

32. Scholars debate whether Deuteronomy's reading of its predecessors is primarily exegetical or revisionary—that is, whether Deuteronomy intends only to clarify and update the older sources (so that D presumes that it will be read alongside E), or whether it intends to replace them (so that once one has Deuteronomy,

one need not—indeed, should not—continue reading E). For the former view, see Eckart Otto, "Mose der erste"; Najman, *Seconding Sinai*. For the latter point of view, see Haran, *Ha'asufah*, 2:157–58; Levinson, *Deuteronomy and the Hermeneutics*; Stackert, *Rewriting, passim*, and esp. 209–25. While the latter point of view seems far more likely to me (see esp. the arguments against the former in Stackert, 211–22, and in Grossman, "Beyond the Hand," 300), in the end the Deuteronomy gained a place alongside the texts it reworks rather than instead of them. Thus, the situation that Otto and Najman propose, though probably not intended by D, became the reality.

33. On the tensions between the admonitions of 4.2 and 13.1, on the one hand, and the final form of the Pentateuch with its record of legal diversity, on the other, see Krüger, "Gesetz und Weisheit," 8–9.

34. Thus, while in the literary context of D the phrase משנה תורה in Deuteronomy 17.18 refers to the physical copy of the law that the king writes, one can plausibly argue that within the redacted Pentateuch it means "this repetition of the law"—viz., Deuteronomy itself, as LXX and the rabbis understood it.

35. Similarly, D's attempt to camouflage the background of its own laws was in fact inconsistent, because it occasionally employs citation formulas referring back to earlier Pentateuchal sources. See Fishbane, *Biblical Interpretation*, 163–64, and cf. Milgrom, "Profane Slaughter," esp. 3–4.

36. See George Adam Smith, *Deuteronomy*, 58 (ad 4.2), and cf. Tigay, *Deuteronomy*, 176; Gersonides's commentary to 18.18; and (on these prophetic successors as practicing *Rechtsprophetie*) Blenkinsopp, *Prophecy and Canon*, 43–44. On the tension between 13.1 and 18.18, see esp. Polzin, *Moses*, 57–65, who argues persuasively that the Mosaic voice in 13.1 is subordinated to the divine voice in 18.18.

37. See Maimonides's *Guide* II:39–40 as well as Kreisel, *Prophecy*, 257–58, and Goodman, *Secrets*, 85–87.

38. See Tigay, *Deuteronomy*, 43–44, who further points out that both verses prohibiting addition to or subtraction from D's law occur in contexts emphasizing that Israelites can pray only to Yhwh. This suggests that the verses intend not a blanket prohibition against legal development generally but stringency regarding the worship of only one God specifically; this is a core point concerning which no change whatsoever can be tolerated.

39. The possibility that ancient texts intend this topos less literally than modern readers might assume becomes stronger in light of Josephus's many references to it. He claims he does not supplement or shorten the biblical accounts that form the basis for his narratives in *Jewish Antiquities* (e.g., at *Ant.* 1.17, 2.234, 4.196–98, 10.218, 20.261), even though by its very nature as a retelling the *Antiquities* does so liberally on every page. See Feldman's discussion in Josephus, *Judean Antiquities 1–4: Translation and Commentary*, 3:7–8. What ancient texts mean by this sort of phrasing is that they are loyal to the essence or theme of the source, not that they make no alterations.

40. For a similar argument regarding texts from the New Testament, see Congar, *Meaning*, 33–35.

41. Joel Roth, *Halakhic Process*, 157.

42. One could render the verb as "add, append," translating: "a great voice, and He added nothing to it."

43. Jonathan: קל רב דלא פסיק; Neofiti and marginalia: קל תקף ולא פסק \ קל רב ולא פסיק; Geniza fragments: קל תלי דלא פסיק.

44. See further Heschel, *TmH*, 3:36 (= *HT*, 671).

45. For this verb, see Esther 9.28 and Isaiah 66.17.

46. Similarly, we have seen that D emphasizes a stenographic theory of revelation but also refers repeatedly to the laws that Moses gave the people, phrasing that might leave the impression that the specifics of this law were Moses's composition (e.g., 4.44–45. 11.8, 12.28). On the Mosaic origin of the law in the original kernel of D, see Frankel, *Land*, 91–94.

47. On the unresolved but productive tension throughout the biblical canon between the fixity inherent in canon and the freedom characteristic of prophecy and of interpretation, see Blenkinsopp, *Prophecy and Canon*, 94–95, 116–29, 147, 150–52, and *passim*. He shows that canon depends for its authority on prophecy, but insofar as the canon delimits the number of authoritative texts, it also devalues prophecy. This would be a self-contradiction in the very concept of canon, if not for the fact that canon, because it is rooted in prophecy, encourages its own expansion.

48. Heschel, *TmH*, 3:35 (= *HT*, 670).

49. Rosenzweig, *Star* [Hallo], 177 (= *Star* [Galli], 191). The German occurs in Rosenzweig, *Stern*, 197–98. Yehoyada Amir describes this passage as "the heart of *The Star*" (personal communication): the entire book until this point prepares us specifically for this passage, and rest emerges from it.

50. Rosenzweig, *OJL*, 85 (= Rosenzweig, *Zweistromland*, 707). Glatzer translates *Heutigkeit* as "living reality"; I alter this to the more literal "today-ness."

51. Rosenzweig, *OJL*, 79.

52. Rosenzweig, *Star* [Hallo], 177 (= *Star* [Galli], 191;) German in Rosenzweig, *Stern*, 197–98).

53. Heschel, *God*, 213–15, citing Tanḥuma (Buber) Yitro 7, b. Berakhot 63b, and Rashi to Exodus 19.1, as well as Deuteronomy 6.6, 11.13, and 26.16. (Some of these are quoted at greater length in Heschel, *TmH*, 3:35 = *HT*, 670, along with *Zohar* 179b.) We may doubt that the authors of Exodus 19.1 meant to convey the idea the midrash attributes to them, but on the basis of our discussion above it is clear that the authors of Deuteronomy did mean to convey this message. The midrashic reading of the verse from Exodus lays out the *peshat* of Deuteronomy.

54. The connection of *Heutigkeit* and command has been widely noted: see Heinemann, *Ta'amei*, 2:211–12; Glatzer's comments in Rosenzweig, *FRHLT*, xxiv; Mendes-Flohr, *Divided*, 298–99, 353–55; Eisen, *Rethinking*, 198–200;

Samuelson, *Revelation*, 71 and 79; Amir, *Reason*, 134–35; Franks, "Sinai," 352; Fishbane, *Garments*, 101–2.

55. Heschel, *Prophets*, 551.

56. Heschel, *God*, 208–9.

57. Ibid., 138; see also Heschel, *TmH*, 3:36–39 (= *HT*, 671–72).

58. Cf. the discussions of event and process in Heschel, *God*, 209–11, and of two types of time in Heschel's thought in Even-Chen, *Voice*, 125–27. See further Shai Held, *Abraham Joshua Heschel*, 229–33, who is more inclined than I to find this tension in Heschel's thought unresolved. Held's discussion is especially useful for its explanation of the connection between Heschel's insistence on the punctuality and historicity of revelation on the one hand and Heschel's rejection of Enlightenment assumptions that the divine is by definition universal and unchanging (see 129–30 and 274 n. 162).

59. Heschel, *God*, 215. He makes a similar point in Heschel, *TmH*, 2:i (the relevant sentences are not translated by Tucker in *HT*).

60. Even-Chen, *Voice*, 122–23 and 103, where Even-Chen speaks of the Sinai event as both a one-time event, the very highpoint of human history, and also a non-punctual occurrence, since the goal of the Jewish people is always to arrive at Sinai.

61. Wolfson, "Light," 95–96, 102.

62. Even-Chen, *Voice*, 103.

63. On this crucial difference between Maimonides and Heschel, see ibid., 62–63, 102.

64. Heschel, "On the Holy Spirit," available in English in Heschel, *Prophetic Inspiration*. See further Even-Chen, *Voice*, 103–13. So far as I can discern, Heschel, *God*, 205, and Heschel, *Sabbath*, 96, flatly contradict the position found in "On the Holy Spirit."

65. For scholarly discussion on the decline of prophecy, see n. 153 in ch. 4.

66. Even-Chen, *Voice*, 176.

67. In other respects Cohen's concept of Sinai resembles that of Rosenzweig and Heschel. Hermann Cohen, *Religion*, 76, 78–79, stresses that revelation takes place "today" (see further Seeskin's remarks in "How," 30). Cohen champions an idealization of revelation, in which revelation is always taking place today—and he claims this idealization begins already in the Torah itself. But Cohen treats this theme in a manner radically different from Heschel and Rosenzweig. Seeskin, *Autonomy*, 163–64, notes that "Cohen does not view revelation as an event that took place in the desert thousands of years ago but as an archetype of God's relation to humanity. He is part of a tradition that takes external revelation as a myth whose purpose is to express the idea of internal revelation." Thus, we might term Cohen's position Bulthmannian, because he attempts to demythologize Sinai. Heschel refuses to demythologize, even as he sees the historical event as having an enduring archetypal significance; similarly, for

Rosenzweig, revelation is a particular and miraculous historical event or events, not an archetype; see Batnitzky, *Idolatry*, 44.

68. I take these terms from Heschel, *God*, 275.

69. The notion that two interpretations of ולא יסף convey a single idea rather than opposing each other also emerges from a consideration of Shemot Rabbah 28:6 (= Tanḥuma Yitro 11), according to which post-Mosaic prophets received their individual revelations not during their lifetimes but before their birth, when they were at Sinai. The midrash supports this assertion by quoting Deuteronomy 5.22. Which sense of the verse does the midrash intend here? One might think at first that the targumic reading (God's voice never stopped) is intended, since the midrash speaks of post-Sinaitic prophets. But as Kugel, "Torah," 999, points out, according to this midrash "in essence Sinai was the only divine revelation to man." Thus, the rabbis may just as well have intended the non-targumic understanding: God's voice did not continue—even to later prophets.

70. See the reference to Avraham Azulai's *Ḥesed Le'avraham* in Heschel, *TmH*, 3:37 (= *HT*, 671).

71. Wolfson, "Light," 94.

72. Literally: "Past and future apply to humans but to God this does not apply."

73. Heschel of Apt, *Oheiv Yisrael* to *Parashat Ki Teizei*, quoted in Heschel, *TmH*, 3:37; translation from *HT*, 672.

74. See additional references in Heschel, *TmH*, 3:36–38 = *HT*, 671–72.

75. On the curriculum and intensity of the youthful Heschel's studies in Poland, see Kaplan and Dresner, *Abraham Joshua Heschel*, 26–28, 38–48 (and note the significance of *Shenei Luḥot Habrit* in particular, at 46).

76. See Isaiah Horowitz, *Shenei Luḥot Haberit*, 25a–b (Amsterdam edition of 1648) = 1:18b–19a (Warsaw edition of 1930). A brief section from the beginning of this passage is quoted in Heschel, *TmH*, 3:37 (= *HT*, 671). See further Horowitz, 192a (Amsterdam) = 2:38b col. 1 (Warsaw).

77. Isaiah Horowitz, *Shenei Luḥot Haberit*, 25a = 18b.

78. See, e.g., Mekhilta, Yitro §9; Shemot Rabbah 5:9 and 29:1; Pesiqta DeRav Kahana Baḥodesh Hashelishi, end of §12. Further references in Kasher, *Torah Sheleimah*, 15:109 §240.

79. Isaiah Horowitz, *Shenei Luḥot Haberit*, 25a = 18b.

80. Ibid., 25b = 19a.

81. On the rabbinic notion of ירידת הדורות or הידרדרות הדורות (the decline of the generations), see b. Shabbat 112b and parallels.

82. Cf. Gershom Scholem, *On Jews*, 270, who notes both the audacity of the idea that every Jew received a personal revelation at Sinai and the limits that the notion of tradition imposes on it.

83. Rosenzweig, *Star* [Hallo], 303–4 (= *Star* [Galli], 322–23).

84. On Rosenzweig's respect for custom (מנהג) and his view of Jewish tradition as dynamic, see Heinemann, *Ta'amei*, 2:214–19.

85. Ibid., 218–19, who points out that Rosenzweig was not afraid to judge what was truly torah (and hence Sinaitic) and what was a passing fancy (and hence contingent and non-Jewish) on the basis of sense and feeling.

86. See the selections by these authorities in Litvin, *Sanctity*, 115, 119, and 139. As Lawrence Schiffman notes in ibid., xxxiv–xxxv, Soloveitchik regards separate areas for men and women as a biblical command and the physical barrier or מחיצה as a rabbinic ordinance, whereas Feinstein regards both as biblical in origin.

87. See Golinkin, *Status*, 317–21 (on the biblical era), 321–27 (on the talmudic era), and 327–28 (on the Middle Ages), along with his brief discussion of ahistorical positions of Feinstein and Soloveitchik, 312–16.

Chapter 6. A Modern Jewish Approach to Scripture

1. Many Jewish philosophers and theologians who turn to biblical texts assume that biblical criticism is irrelevant or even inimical to their project. A recent example is Hazony, *Philosophy*. In spite of his intention to challenge the distinction between reason and revelation and to recover biblical texts as humanistically exciting and philosophically provocative, Hazony devotes almost no attention to modern biblical scholars who elucidate the history of ideas in biblical texts and the ways these texts construct meaning. Much the same can be said of Schweid, *Philosophy of the Bible*. Similarly, Novak, *Natural*, 31–61, makes almost no reference to biblical critics who discuss the relationship of biblical texts and natural theology; e.g., Barr, *Biblical Faith*, and Collins, "Biblical Precedent." Novak does refer a single time to Barton, "Natural"; this is one of four references Novak makes to modern biblical scholarship in the 106 footnotes found in his chapter on biblical texts.

2. Recent works that are especially successful in thematizing the Bible's multivocality include Goldingay, *Theological Diversity*; Brueggemann, *Theology*; Knohl, *Divine Symphony*; and Carasik, *Bible's Many Voices* (and note especially Carasik's happy summary of this matter on 18). For a briefer discussion, see Sharp, *Wrestling*, 59–75.

3. Joseph B. Soloveitchik, *And from There*, 145–46.

4. Zakovitch, "Book."

5. For sensitive descriptions of the multiplicity of voices in traditional Jewish commentary, see Greenstein, "Medieval," 214–15, 256–57, and Abigail Gillman, "Between Religion," 101–2.

6. See Levinas, *Beyond*, 137.

7. By Joel Baden's count (personal communication), P accounts for 47 percent, and D for 17 percent. Disagreement concerning a verse here or a phrase there will not change these figures substantially, even for recent scholars who reject the classical Documentary Hypothesis and the neo–Documentary Hypothesis.

8. Sommer, *Bodies*, 12–57 and 179–213.

9. Idel, *Kabbalah*, 138–40; the quoted phrasing is at 139.

10. On the thoroughly anthropomorphic conception of God throughout the Bible, see Kaufmann, *Toledot*, 1:221–44; von Rad, *Old Testament Theology*, 1:145, 219, 237, 287, 366; Mark Smith, *Origins*, 87–88; Hendel, "Aniconism," 207–8; Muffs, *Personhood*, 31; Sommer, *Bodies*, 1–10. On the consistently anthropomorphic conception of God throughout rabbinic literature, see Alon Goshen-Gottstein, "Body"; Lorberbaum, *Image*, 14–22, 292–335; cf. Gershom Scholem, *On the Mystical Shape*, 34–35.

11. Greenberg, *Studies*, 422–23. Similarly, Maimonides cites Deuteronomy approvingly more than any book in the *Guide*. He cites Genesis roughly as often as Deuteronomy in the *Guide*, but in a great many of those cases, his purpose is to explain away Genesis's many anthropomorphisms, whereas he cites Deuteronomy for more positive reasons. See the indexes in Maimonides, *Guide*, 646–54.

12. For other examples of how compositional analyses allow us to discern parallels between biblical and postbiblical Jewish thought that otherwise are obscured, see Sommer, "Reflecting on Moses," and Sommer, "Dialogical," 43–50; Knohl, "Between Voice."

13. Shaye J. D. Cohen, *Significance*, 46.

14. Halbertal, *People*, 45.

15. This feature of the Pentateuch is well-nigh unique in its ancient Near Eastern context. Scribes produced most large works of Mesopotamian literature by combining originally separate sources and supplementing them with scribal additions (as demonstrated throughout Tigay, *Empirical Models*), but these large works do not display the constant doublets and outright contradictions so characteristic of the Pentateuch. Because the Pentateuch looks so radically different from Gilgamesh, Enuma Elish, and Hammurapi's Laws, it is likely that the process of its redaction differed from theirs. In this respect, an alleged weakness of the neo-Documentarian approach of Haran, Schwartz, and Baden (concerning which see n. 14 in ch. 1)—namely, the unusual model they propose for the Pentateuch's redaction—is in fact one of its strengths: the Pentateuch's compilers largely preserved the sources they used intact, whereas most ancient Near Eastern redactors rework their sources as they combine them. Appropriately, Schwartz and his school propose a highly unusual form of editing for a highly unusual composition.

16. On the link between rabbinic exegesis and the complex layering of biblical texts as recovered by modern biblical scholars, see Greenberg, *Al Hammiqra*, 345–49, and Jon Levenson, *Hebrew Bible, the Old Testament*, 53–56.

17. On these shifts of emphasis in modern Jewish cultures, see, e.g., Amir, *Small Still Voice*, 187–91, 200–201; Alan Levenson, *Making*, 122–25. For a good example of this anti-rabbinic aspect of the return to Bible, see Ben-Gurion, "Bible." Amir, *Small Still Voice*, 193, further notes that many of these thinkers privileged a highly specific, limited and, to my mind, not fully representative selection of prophetic

texts in their return to the Bible. Amir, *Reason*, 284, also points out that while Hermann Cohen and Rosenzweig diverge from this anti-rabbinic trend, in this regard both these thinkers recall Moses Mendelssohn and S. R. Hirsch. See also Alan Levenson, *Making*, 36–37, 42–44 (where he notes complexities of Mendelssohn's case and the extent to which later German Jews oversimplified his approach by neglecting his emphasis on rabbinic tradition), 49–55, 62–63, and (concerning Benno Jacob), 67–71. On the return to Bible in the work of religious German-Jewish thinkers of the late eighteenth and early nineteenth centuries, see also Edward Breuer, *Limits*; and Gottlieb, *Jewish Protestantism*.

18. For a definition of the term, see n. 106 in ch. 3. On my endorsement of *derash* as a biblical critic, cf. Simon, *Seek Peace*, 43, who rightly points out that careful thinking about biblical criticism in a religious Jewish context leads not to conflict between *peshat* and *derash*, but rather to a mature *peshat* that knows its own limitations.

19. My proposal recalls Rashbam's approach to *peshat* and diverges from ibn Ezra's. For Rashbam, *derash* and *peshat* are legitimate but distinct modes of Jewish thought. They are parallel, and therefore they never intersect and never compete with each other, especially in regard to halakhah. (See Maori, "Approach"; Touitou, *Exegesis*, 110, 177–78). Similarly, in light of my discussion of Oral Torah, both *peshat* and *derash* are legitimate expressions of Oral Torah—the former, an expression of the oldest form of Oral Torah (to wit, the Bible), and the latter, an expression of younger forms. Ibn Ezra, in contrast, is a hermeneutic monist. He denies the validity of *derash* and champions *peshat* alone—with the result that he resorts to stretched arguments when he wants to accept the rulings of Oral Torah as genuinely a part of the Written Torah. See Simon, "Rabbi Abraham Ibn Ezra as Exegete."

20. Cf. Samuelson, *Revelation*, 219.

21. As Heschel, *God*, 213, teaches: "The root of Jewish faith is ... not a comprehension of abstract principles but an inner *attachment to sacred events*; to believe is to remember, not merely to accept the truth of a set of dogmas." See further Carasik, *Bible's Many Voices*, 17, who notes "the many places ... where the Bible seems to *demand* that it be questioned."

22. My thanks to Gregg Stern for encouraging me to articulate my thinking in this matter. It may be helpful for me to sketch out a specific example that fleshes out the theoretical statement above. In what ways do the fluidity traditions I discuss in *The Bodies of God* matter to me as a religious Jew? I do not suggest that a Jew must believe that God is physically present in this rock and that bush, but not in other ones. Rather, I insist that the fluidity tradition is a guiding voice. It helps me to realize how uncanny, strange, incomprehensible, yet nearby, or potentially nearby, the God of Judaism is. Fluidity traditions aid me in ways that anti-fluidity traditions (P, D, Rambam) do not, and indeed on their own hinder.

23. Kugel, "Two Introductions," 145. See also Fraade, "Moses and the Commandments," 416.

24. Cf. Barton, *Oracles*, 150.

25. In fact, as Robert Harris has emphasized to me, the rabbis give no evidence that they even have a concept of the narrative unit we call "the Binding of Isaac." Only in the Middle Ages, when Jewish interpreters began thinking about longer textual units, does this concept appear in Jewish literature. The phrase appears only twice in midrashic literature: Tanḥuma (Buber), Vayyera §46 and Aggadat Bereshit §38. Moreover, even there, it refers not to a particular narrative unit but to what happened to Isaac in verse 9.

26. Thus, as Kugel, *In Potiphar's*, 255, notes, "Our present midrashic collections are somewhat deceiving, since they seem to constitute running commentaries on entire biblical books, whereas in fact most are anthologies of individual, verse-centered comments strung together by the editor."

27. See Fishbane, *Garments*, 124.

28. On the importance of memorization in midrash and its connection to midrash's verse-centeredness, see Kugel, "Two Introductions," 146–47.

29. A possible exception to this statement can be seen in m. Megillah 4:4, which rules that *haftarah* readings can skip from section to section within a biblical book but not from one book to another. This shows that Jewish law sees the unit of book as having at least some significance. The fact remains that rabbinic hermeneutics, like all ancient Jewish hermeneutics, never confronted the unit of book.

30. For a brief description of these cycles, see Stemberger and Strack, *Introduction*, 262–64, and Elbogen and Heinemann, *Jewish Liturgy*, 129–38. Some modern synagogues have introduced a triennial cycle that is even more disjunctive than its ancient counterpart.

31. Exegetical debate plays a much smaller role in nonrabbinic Judaisms of the ancient world. In Qumran, for example, the act of interpretation, at least by the Teacher of Righteousness, was regarded as inspired (see, e.g., Habakkuk Pesher 7:2–4), and therefore recording several possible interpretations was unnecessary. Precisely because the rabbis saw their readings as human in origin and fallible, they engaged in debate regarding correct understandings of biblical verses. See Fraade, *From Tradition*, 3–5, 9, 13.

32. See Mulder, "Transmission," 116–21, and Zafren, "Bible Editions." These studies are crucial for understanding Jewish conceptions of scripture. Zafren's listing of early printed editions shows that only about 13 of the 142 Hebrew editions of biblical texts and commentaries printed between 1469 and 1528 contained the full Tanakh. The way early Hebrew printers responded to the market's demand shows that above all Jews wanted editions of the Pentateuch with its commentaries; to a lesser extent, they wanted other biblical texts chanted in synagogue; and to some degree they also wanted copies of the Psalter. Zafren's study covers

the first century of printed Bibles; similar tendencies endured until the twentieth century, when Zionism and other factors encouraged the proliferation of small one-volume editions of the whole Tanakh—though a visit to a traditional Hebrew bookstore will show that to this day multivolume editions with commentary, most often consisting of the Pentateuch alone (or Pentateuch with prophetic lectionaries), remain exceedingly common.

33. On the use of this dictum in the Talmud itself, see Sagi, *Elu*, 10–24. In the remainder of his book, Sagi investigates varied understandings of this dictum in later rabbinic cultures, medieval and modern alike. See also the astute observations of Braiterman, "Elu Ve-Elu," who critiques the sloppy use of this dictum among liberal Jewish theologians and postmodern thinkers alike. See further Schweid, *Philosophy of the Bible*, 1:35. For an especially interesting medieval discussion relevant to our concerns, see the section titled מעלת אלו ואלו דברי א-להים חיים in Isaiah Horowitz, *Shenei Luḥot Haberit*, 199a of the 1648 edition from Amsterdam = 1:43a of the 1930 Warsaw edition. On varied attitudes toward legal pluralism and its limits in classical rabbinic literature (e.g., its lesser prominence in the Jerusalem Talmud as opposed to the Babylonian), see Hidary, *Dispute*.

34. See y. Pe'ah 4a (2:6), y. Ḥagigah 2d (1:8), b. Megillah 19b, Shemot Rabbah Ki Tissa 47:1; Wayiqra Rabbah 22:1; Qohelet Rabbah 1:29 and 5:6.

35. Halbertal, *People*, 64, and see further 161–62, notes 40–41; and cf. Safrai, "Oral Torah," 49. For a different view of the *Ritba*, see Halivni, "On Man's Role," 43–44.

36. See Fraade, "Moses and the Commandments," 402–9.

37. On the interplay between the perception of scripture as a unity and scripture's diversity in rabbinic interpretation, cf. Fishbane, *Garments*, 123–24.

38. On this negative attitude toward controversy, see Halbertal, *People*, 54–63; Halbertal, "What Is," 101–2; Silman, *Voice*, 72–76; Halivni, *Peshat*, 163–67; Halivni, "On Man's Role," 36–44; Elman, "R. Zadok," 1–5. On Heschel's reaction to this point of view, see Even-Chen, *Voice*, 164–65.

39. See Robert Harris, "Jewish Biblical," 604–12; Robert Harris, "Concepts"; Kamin, *Rashi's*, 14–15; Touitou, *Exegesis*, 126–34. Analogous trends emerged a few centuries earlier among Jews in the Arabic-speaking world, though without quite the same emphasis on the unity of local textual context; see Polliack, "Concepts." On precursors to a contextual approach late talmudic sources, especially in Babylonia, see Hayes, "Displaced," esp. 255–62 and 286–89.

40. Japhet, "Major," esp. 43–44, 57, and Breuer and Gafni, "Jewish Biblical Scholarship," 296–302.

41. On the differences between Rashi and Rashbam regarding *peshat*, see Kamin, *Rashi's*, 266–74.

42. For a fine example of both modes on a single page, see b. Shabbat 30b (ד"ה רב יהודה בריה דרב שמואל), in which the earlier Hebrew comment about

Qohelet is centrifugal while the later Aramaic statement is centripetal. See further Frankel, *Land*, 387–88.

43. See esp. Schwartz, "Torah," 211–18.

44. Baden, *Composition*, 221–28. Cf. Schweid, *Philosophy of the Bible*, 1:36, though Schweid makes the unwarranted assumption that the redactor wants the reader to harmonize what the redactor left contradictory. Alter, *Art*, 131–54, and Greenstein, "Equivocal," maintain that the redactor purposefully combines some stories in such a way that each one retains some identity. Thus, Greenstein remarks, "If the text that we accept as the final product contains discernible discrepancies between one verse and another, we do not presume that the redactor had attempted to remove them but failed. Rather, we allow that the redactor may have been well aware if the inconsistencies and desired to leave them in the text" (117). While Greenstein speaks here specifically of Genesis 37, his observation applies to the entire Pentateuch.

45. On the logic of אלו ואלו in the biblical canon generally, see also Blenkinsopp, *Prophecy and Canon*, 94–95. On biblical books' lack of emphasis on their own textual unity, see also Heinemann, *Darkhei*, 56–57.

46. Kaufmann, *Toledot*, 4:291–93 (where he speaks of מדרש הלכה בעזרא), 327–29, 331–38 (on the contract in Nehemiah 10–11 as a product of midrashic interpretation of texts from the Torah), 341–42, 346–50 (where he speaks of מדרש התורה וראשית תורה שבעל פה). See further Japhet, *From the Rivers*, 137–51, and multiple examples in Fishbane, *Biblical Interpretation*, 107–62. Ezra-Nehemiah's assumption of the Pentateuch's unity is ironic, since Ezra-Nehemiah itself is less a book than a loosely organized—indeed, we might even say unorganized—compilation book of early Second Temple documents. It can be compared, in terms of genre and organization, to a source book or course reader, perhaps one whose binding fell out.

47. See ibid., 194–97; Carr, "Method"; Gesundheit, *Three Times*, 12–43.

48. Ibid., 36–37.

49. On this understanding of midrash, see esp. Boyarin, *Intertextuality*, and, more briefly, Sommer, "Concepts of Scriptural Language."

50. Gesundheit, *Three Times*, 44–95.

51. Jon Levenson, "Religious Affirmation," 40. Levenson's comments on Heschel at 39–40 could describe Rosenzweig just as well.

52. In Buber and Rosenzweig, *Scripture and Translation*, 23; I add explanations in brackets. On Rosenzweig's unifying readings, see Amir, *Small Still Voice*, 181, and Amir, *Reason*, 284–85, who shows that Rosenzweig believes the religious reading of the editorial unity recalls the approach of classical midrash. In believing this, Rosenzweig is, I think, fundamentally unaware of the atomistic nature of midrashic reading.

53. Childs, "Old Testament as Scripture," 711, 715.

54. See ibid.; Childs, *Introduction*; Childs, *Biblical Theology of the Old and New*. For a useful overview and contextualization of Childs's method, see Perdue, "Old

Testament," 109–14, 215–16. For a subtle and sympathetic discussion of Childs's exegetical and theological proposals, see Seitz, *Word*, 102–9. For critical appraisals, see Barton, *Reading*, 77–103; Barr, *Concept*, 378–438; Sommer, "Scroll," Sommer, Review of Childs, *Isaiah*.

55. On the role of the *Mitte* in biblical theology, see Barr, *Concept*, 337–44.

56. Eichrodt, *Theology*.

57. von Rad, *Old Testament Theology*. Although von Rad claimed to reject the idea of a *Mitte* (see 1:114 and 2:362; Ollenberger, Martens, and Hasel, *Flowering*, 121), it is not quite the case that he in fact did so. The notion of salvation pervades his work: it serves as the criterion according to which he makes exegetical and critical judgments. A telling example is his insistence on the existence of a Hexateuch that ends with salvation in the form of the entry into the land under the leadership of Joshua (= Jesus = "Yhwh saves"). Further, Barr, *Concept*, 47, 339–40, and Carr, "Passion," 1–2, show that von Rad's emphasis on transmission and transformation (or, to phrase it differently, God's self-revelation in history) serves as a *Mitte*, though this *Mitte* involves a process rather than a theme.

58. Terrien, *Elusive Presence*.

59. However, Brueggemann, *Theology*, represents a liberal Protestant attempt to read the Bible's theological diversity as religiously instructive. For an evangelical attempt to do so, see Enns, *Inspiration*, 71–112. See further Barton, "Unity"; Goldingay, *Theological Diversity*.

60. On the tendency of Christian readers to harmonize and universalize, and hence to disregard much of the available biblical evidence, see Brueggemann, *Theology*, 327. On the evolution in Western Christianity (starting in the late first millennium and culminating in the Reformation) of the tendency to view the Bible as scripture rather than as a collection of scriptures, see Wilfred Cantwell Smith, *What Is Scripture*, 13–14, 53–54. Smith demythologizes this view, showing how unusual it is in the history of religions (see 126–27). In light of Smith's work, it becomes clear that the assumption of Childs and his followers that canon entails first and foremost unity is just that: an assumption, not a natural or inevitable feature of scripture. It is a historically conditioned view that reflects not the world of the canonizers (as Barr, *Holy Scripture*, 49–74, 130–71, notes) but the post-Gutenberg, post-Reformation era in which Childs worked.

61. In defense of Rosenzweig, it should be noted that at least to some the degree the unity of which he speaks is ultimately a unity of scripture together with tradition, and thus a unity that encompasses multivocality. See Batnitzky, *Idolatry*, 125–27.

62. For a similar approach, see Frankel, *Land*, 385. On the religious irrelevance of questions regarding authorship, see Brettler's remarks in Brettler, Enns, and Harrington, *Bible and the Believer*, 54–55.

63. On the notion that committed Jewish communities determine not only what Jewish law is but also what Judaism is, see references in n. 121 to ch. 3.

64. One could just as well read the text source-critically to arrive at the conclusion Rosenzweig articulates. In fact, Amir, *Reason*, 303 n. 6, points out that in the *Star* Rosenzweig in fact provided a lengthy reading of Genesis 1 by itself—in other words, of P's account, without its J counterpart.

65. The tendency of Rosenzweig's biblical exegeses to ignore the religiously interesting distinctions that are highlighted when we differentiate among the Bible's authors and schools is equally evident in Heschel, *Prophets*. There, as Jon Levenson, "Religious Affirmation," 43–44, notes, "the thinking and experience of all the prophets tend to run together in a blur . . . By paying close attention to the distinctive voice in each prophetic collection as recovered through critical study, Heschel could have . . . helped uncover yet another facet of the *shiv'im panim la-torah*, the seventy facets of the Torah, of which the Jewish tradition speaks." But, Levenson shows, Heschel did not do so. This is ironic, since the unattempted project Levenson describes would have fit quite well with Heschel's theology. My own work (in this book, in *Bodies of God*, and elsewhere) might summed up as an attempt to fill this lacuna in Heschel's work and thus to provide a deeply Heschelian reading of Bible absent in Heschel's own writings.

66. Buber and Rosenzweig, *Scripture and Translation*, 23.

67. For a similar use of higher criticism as witness to the centrality of a unanimously attested tenet, see Frankel, *Land*, 382, who points out that despite the diversity of biblical views concerning the land, "one never finds . . . a biblical conception of Israel's final destiny as a people that does not somehow incorporate . . . national life in the land as an ultimate ideal."

68. Rosenzweig, *Zweistromland*, 734.

69. Sommer, *Prophet*, 132–51.

70. See esp. Boyarin, *Intertextuality*.

71. On this often neglected aspect or source criticism, see Barton, *Nature*, 43–44.

72. Through the dialectic of Oral Torah (rather than through the fixity of Written Torah) revelation continues and knowledge of God grows, according to R. Zadok of Lublin; see Elman, "R. Zadok," 19–20. On the positive role of uncertainty (which leads to the centrifugality so characteristic of Oral Torah) in Jewish thought according to R. Zadok, see further Elman's comments, at 20.

73. See Simon, "Religious Significance," and Garfinkel, "Applied *Peshat*." The significance of this confluence of articles by Simon and Garfinkel for a project concerned with the *aleph* that was a sound of silence is self-evident. On the use of the parallel between *peshat* and modern critical scholarship, along with the limitations of the parallel, see Japhet, "Major," esp. 50–53, 60.

74. Satlow, "Oral Torah," 264–67.

75. See Japhet, "Tension"; Lockshin, "Tradition or Context?"; Halivni, *Peshat and Derash*, 169–71; Touitou, *Exegesis*, 117–21, 177–88. On the analogous problem in Radak's work, see Yitzhak Berger, "Peshat," and Grunhaus, *Challenge*, 123–42.

76. Mordechai Breuer goes further: when he distinguishes between what source critics call J and E, he intends to allow us to hear distinct voices of God. See

"Making Sense of Scripture's Plain Sense" and "The Divine Names and Attributes," in Mordecai Breuer, *Pirqei Bereshit*, 1:11–19 and 48–54, and the discussion in Carmy, "Concepts."

77. Cf. Maori, "Approach," 49: "There are seventy facets to the Torah, and *peshat* is one of them. If 'Torah is light' (Prov. 6:23), then the facet of *peshat*, too, must be enlightening."

78. For an example of such a recovery of biblical voices that turn out to show significant points of contact with later Jewish texts, compare my treatment of Deutero-Isaiah's view of kingship in Sommer, *Prophet*, 84–88, 112–19, with the discussion of the Amidah prayer's attitude toward kingship in Kimelman, "Daily Amidah" and Kimelman, "Messiah." For examples of *peshat* readings that problematize midrashic readings in religiously productive ways, see Simon, "Religious Significance," 56–60, and see the use of Greenberg's classic study of capital punishment, "Some Postulates of Biblical Criminal Law" (= Greenberg, *Studies*, 25–41), in Garfinkel, "Applied *Peshat*," 26. On the mutually challenging and beneficial relationship between biblical texts and later tradition in Christianity, see Brown, *Tradition*, esp. 1–2; Oeming, *Gesamtbiblische Theologien*, 232–41; Goldingay, *Theological Diversity*, 97–133; and Congar, *Meaning*, 125, who, while emphasizing the importance of tradition in Catholic thought, also explains that "the Magisterium and the Church must continually return to the point of origin. . . . In doing this they are reimmersed in a plenitude greater than themselves; there is *more* in the original source than in the stream it feeds" (and see further 160–61). For an explication of the religious significance of *peshat*, see Fishbane, *Sacred Attunement*, 65–68, 71–74, especially his crucial reminder that "reading for the *peshat* sense involves a subjugation of the self to the words of the text as they appear. . . . It is an exercise in the patient subordination of the self to the otherness of the language which has been selected by the author" (66, 71).

79. As Hillel Ben-Sasson put it to me (personal communication), in the participatory theology, revelation "produces on man a normative claim, which man in turn is entrusted with molding into a more elaborate content, a content which will always be asymptotic to the Absolute, never quite reaching it."

80. Various thinkers have recognized that what I call the translation theory entails the imperfection of prophecy. See the discussion of H. H. Rowley, Karl Barth, Emil Brunner, and Frederick Watson, in McDonald, *Theories*, 252–53, 257, and 278, as well as Rowley, *Relevance*, 28. On scholastic precursors to this idea, see McDonald, *Theories*, 255 n. 1. The theme of scripture's fallibility—and of tradition as a revelatory response to this fallibility—is developed esp. by Brown, *Tradition*, 54–55, 159, 165–66, 366, 374–75, and also by Ward, *Religion*, 25, 92 (cf. 44). In contrast, the teaching of *Dei Verbum* (the Dogmatic Constitution on Divine Revelation promulgated during the Second Vatican Council) seems to move away from this possibility when it states, "As the substantial Word of God became like to men in all things 'except sin' (Heb. 4:15), so the

words of God, expressed in human language, are made like to human speech in every respect except error." As Harrington notes in Brettler, Enns, and Harrington, *Bible and the Believer*, 87, however, many Catholic scholars and authorities acknowledge that scripture is not inerrant in issues of history or physical science; but it remains inerrant in what pertains to salvation—which I assume includes issues of ethics. Thus, the Catholic Church's approach recalls the idea of R. Yishmael that scripture speaks in the language of human beings and thus needs to be understood in its cultural context, but it does not draw the conclusion I draw from scriptures' status as part of a mixed human-divine tradition. In spite of the many similarities between modern Jewish and Catholic views of scripture, here we see a clear difference between my proposal and a recent teaching of the Church's Magisterium. Similarly, Enns, *Inspiration*, represents an evangelical attempt at constructing something like a participatory theology, according to which scripture, like Jesus, is both human and divine; but because Enns uses this analogy to suggest that scripture can be seen as 100 percent human and also 100 percent divine (see esp. his reference to Chalcedon, 17), it seems to me he cannot acknowledge that the Bible's humanity entails religious and moral flaws. In fact, he accords no attention to such flaws.

81. Wilfred Cantwell Smith, "Thoughts," 41 and 49.

82. Here we see a difference between the participatory theology in Rosenzweig and Heschel and the understanding of revelation in the work of Martin Buber. Kepnes, "Revelation," 213–16, describes all three of these thinkers as viewing Torah and law as a phenomenalization of the noumenal experience that is revelation. For Buber, Kepnes shows, this phenomenalization (or, as I term it, *translation*) debases the original I-thou experience of revelation into an I-it relationship. For Rosenzweig and Heschel, the phenomenolization need not function in so negative a way. See also Samuelson, *Revelation*, 175, and Even-Chen, *Voice*, 82–84 and 183, both of whom critique Buber for regarding the introduction of content to the contentless revelation as a step toward idolatry or anthropomorphism. See further Amir, *Small Still Voice*, 179–80.

83. See Sagi, "Punishment"; Lamm, "Amalek"; Josef Stern, "Maimonides on Amaleq"; Greenberg, *Hassegullah*, esp. chs. 1 and 3; Greenberg, "Problematic"; Solomon, *Torah*, 121–25; Halbertal, *Interpretive Revolutions*, 42–68.

84. Witness the use of verses concerning Amalekites and Canaanites among late-twentieth-century Kahanists. This use is unambiguously erroneous from the point of view of ancient, medieval, and modern halakhic literature, yet it flourishes within some Orthodox communities.

85. As Wilfred Cantwell Smith, "Thoughts," 41, points out, the scriptures of other religions all contain comparable ethical imperfections.

86. Cf. Oeming, *Gesamtbiblische Theologien*, 235–37; Brown, *Tradition*, 1, 374–75.

87. Schechter, *Studies (First)*, xvii.

88. Kaplan, "I Sleep," 145, 139–40. Bland, "Moses," 64, makes a similar point.

89. See ch. 2, n. 10.

90. Heschel, *God*, 266–73; quotation from 268.

91. Cf. Even-Chen, *Voice*, 184, who points out that Heschel connects the kabbalistic notion that the fullness of God's light is hidden in shells in this world to his conception of Torah. The Torah of this world is not pure or full in the same way as the heavenly Torah.

92. See also Heschel, *God*, 264 at nn. 17 and 18. Cf. 260, where Heschel states, "The share of the prophet manifested itself not only in what [the prophet] was able to give but also in what he was unable to receive. . . . It is incorrect to maintain that all words in the Bible originated in the spirit of God. The blasphemous tirades of Pharaoh, the rebellious utterances of Korach, the subterfuge of Ephron, the words of the soldiers in the camp of Midian, emanated from the spirit of man." Here, too, Heschel plays with the idea of a fallible scripture, but ends up pulling back by identifying the harsh voices not with the biblical authors but with characters those authors condemn. Perlman, "'As a Report,'" 36, attributes to Heschel the notion that the Torah "never was and never will be a perfectly formed text. What it was and will be is the most profound vehicle for transmitting meaning from God." Perlman follows Heschel in moving immediately from the reference to something less than perfection to a description of its incomparable profundity. Shai Held, *Abraham Joshua Heschel*, 119–24, seeks hints in Heschel's oeuvre of a realization of scripture's imperfection, and he notes how the interpretive practices Heschel encourages can imply a recognition of the need to correct flaws. While Held sensitively builds on implications of various statements by Heschel, Heschel himself does not confront the issues as frankly as Held does. On Heschel's occasional admissions that religion can be a force for evil, see Held, 238–39 n. 84.

93. The preambles occur on the page following the table of contents to the second volume of Heschel, *TmH*. They do not appear in the English translation (*HT*). The quotation also appears at a crucial moment in Heschel, *God*, 274.

94. See Halivni, *Revelation*; see also Halivni, *Peshat*, 132–36, 148–54.

95. See, most famously, the essay "Why Jews Are Not Interested in Biblical Theology," in Jon Levenson, *Hebrew Bible, the Old Testament*, 33–61.

96. Cf. ibid., 38. On the attempt of some Jewish biblical scholars encourage greater attention to the Bible, see Brettler in Brettler, Enns, and Harrington, *Bible and the Believer*, 22.

97. See Sommer, "Dialogical."

Conclusion

1. The productive tension between continuity and innovation (or normative order and interpretive freedom, or tradition and change) has been at the heart of the covenant since the biblical period. See Blenkinsopp, *Prophecy and Canon*,

passim, esp. 1–2 and 116–20, who calls this tension "a constituent element in the origins of Judaism" (2). Echoing Max Weber, Blenkinsopp insightfully explains that the Jewish biblical canon itself is "a way of maintaining a balance between law and prophecy, institution and charisma, the claims of the past and those of the future" (116).

2. Muffs, *Love*, 9–48.

3. Levinson, *Legal Revision*, 89, 90, 92.

4. See not only Levinson's *Legal Revision*, but also *Deuteronomy and the Hermeneutics*, *Right Chorale*, and *More Perfect*, among others.

5. See the discussion in ch. 3 concerning פוק חזי and committed communities defining Judaism and references in nn. 121 and 122 there. On the centrality of community in all issues involving revelation and authority for Rosenzweig, see Batnitzky, *Idolatry*, 60, 70–72, 116.

6. Harman Grossman points out to me that my use of Rosenzweig's distinction here might be productively compared to an argument in Dworkin, *Taking Rights Seriously*, 134–36. Discussing constitutional law in the United States, Dworkin suggests that in order to be true to the founders' "conceptions" (analogous to *Gebot*), one must be prepared from time to time to deviate from their "concepts" (analogous to *Gesetze*).

7. Sommer, *Bodies*, 62–68.

8. Most modern scholars date the shift from a religion centered on animal sacrifice to one oriented toward prayer and textual recitation to the late first century CE. They see this shift as resulting from the forced acquiescence of the rabbinic movement in Yavneh to the reality that the Second Temple had been destroyed. In fact this shift began some seven centuries earlier. It was not four Roman legions under Titus and Vespasian who were responsible for the beginnings of this development but the Levite scribes who authored Deuteronomy.

9. Levinson, *Legal Revision*, 48.

10. Jon Levenson, *Resurrection and the Restoration*, 217–18 and 185–87. On the rabbis' discomfort with radical legal changes (especially in the Babylonian Talmud but also to a significant degree in the Jerusalem Talmud), see Hayes, "Rabbinic Contestations," who notes that in spite of occasional hyperbolic narratives valorizing rabbinic authority (e.g., the story of Akhnai's oven in b. Bava Meṣia 59b), the Babylonian Talmud consistently resists admitting that the rabbis could overturn biblical laws. For another corrective to most scholars' overemphasis on rupture and innovation, see Steven Weitzman, *Surviving*. Weitzman demonstrates that ancient Jewish claims to stability and traditionalism are better founded than modern scholars have recognized.

11. In Levitical terms: I am with Jon, not Bernie, on this one.

12. Levinson, *Legal Revision*, 27–28.

13. See the discussion of ex post facto holiness in chapter 3 and references there. The discussion in Louis Jacobs, *Beyond*, 113–31, under the heading "From Man-Made Institutions to Divine Commands," is especially useful.

14. Levinson, *Legal Revision*, 29. Cf. 48.

15. E.g., Genesis 6–9; Exodus 32–34; 1 Samuel 15; 2 Samuel 7; Hosea 11. On the theme of God's fallibility in Hebrew scripture, see Sonnet, "God's Repentance."

16. This principle is rooted in rabbinic exegesis of Deuteronomy 17.8–11. See Elon, *Jewish Law*, 237–38, 279–80, 481–85; Joel Roth, *Halakhic Process*, 115–16, 125–27.

17. Cf. Louis Jacobs, *Principles*, 299–300, who notes that the Middle Way leads to an observance that is less scrupulous and more flexible. See also Eisen, "Re-Reading Heschel," 16–17, and Fishbane, *Sacred Attunement*, 60, on the origin of religious revision and development in the overflow of the divine that is manifest throughout the generations in what Fishbane calls the תורה כלולה.

18. See the discussion of committed communities defining Judaism in ch. 3 and references in n. 121 there.

19. Schechter, *Studies (First)*, xviii–xix. Congar, *Meaning*, 162–63, summarizes an analogous position in Catholic theology, for which scripture, tradition, and the Church, which consists not only of its hierarchy but is "a public institution, common to all and assisted as such by the Holy Spirit . . . [which institution] is also a fraternity, a family." See further Congar's discussion, 51–82, and especially his treatment of the faithful as subjects or carriers of active tradition, 72–77.

20. Cf. the words of my own teacher in his wise discussion of human and divine avatars of revelation: "Too soon do we close the terrifying gap between the divine infinity and a human world of words; too incautiously do we transform the *mysterium tremendum* into the *fascinosum* of social celebrations and familiarity" (Fishbane, *Garments*, 129).

21. On the diachronic nature of the community within which Jews read scripture, see Wilfred Cantwell Smith, *What Is Scripture*, 25–26.

22. Heschel, *Moral*, 142: "Without solidarity with our forebears, the solidarity with our brothers will remain feeble. The vertical unity of Israel is essential to the horizontal unity of the Community of Israel." Cf. Louis Jacobs, *Principles*, 299–300.

23. Scripture, when not learned from an authoritative master, is arguably not scripture at all. See Wilfred Cantwell Smith, *What Is Scripture*, 138, 144. Cf. Rosenzweig's remark, quoted by Glatzer in Rosenzweig, *FRHLT*, xxxvii, that as a youth he read the Bible "without the help of tradition, hence without revelation."

24. Cf. Rosenzweig, *OJL*, 75–76: "We accept as teaching what enters us from out of the accumulated knowledge of the centuries in its apparent and, above all, in its real contradictions. We do not know in advance what is and is not Jewish teaching; when someone tries to tell us, we turn away in unbelief and anger." Our inability to know in advance what is and is not teaching may account for the tradition's decision, going back at least to the redaction of the Pentateuch, to preserve minority or outdated opinions whose inclusion marks them as Torah in spite of their antiquated status. As Gershom Scholem, "Revelation and Tradition," 290, points out, tradition "maintains the contradictory views with astounding seriousness and intrepidity, as if to say that one can never know

whether a view at one time rejected may not one day become the cornerstone of an entirely new edifice." Cf. Halbertal, *People*, 51–54.

25. According to this notion, Jews may produce a text that God embraces as sacred and then gives to Israel. See ch. 3 nn. 198 and 202.

26. Selected, tendentiously, from the poems "Achshav Bara'ash," in Amichai, *Achshav Bara'ash*, 183, and "Melon Horay," in Amichai, *Patuaḥ*, 58. In using Amichai's secular poetry in the religious way that I do, I enact Kronfeld's thesis (in "Allusion," 159) that Amichai is the latest in "a long list of God's critics whom, like Job and Levi Yitzhak of Berdichev, the tradition has managed to pull into the mainstream."

Bibliography

Abelson, J. "Maimonides on the Jewish Creed." *JQR* 19 (1906): 24–58.

Abraham of Minsk. *Ahavat Eitan*. [In Hebrew.] Cited from standard (Vilna) editions of the *Ein Yaakov*.

Albrektson, Bertil. *History and the Gods*. Lund: CWK Gleerup, 1967.

Albright, William Foxwell. "The Song of Deborah in the Light of Archaeology." *Bulletin of the American Schools of Oriental Research* 62 (1936): 26–31.

———. *Yhwh and the Gods of Canaan: An Historical Analysis of Two Contrasting Faiths*. Garden City: Doubleday, 1968.

Alter, Robert. *The Art of Biblical Narrative*. New York: Basic Books, 1981.

———. *The Five Books of Moses: A Translation with Commentary*. New York: W. W. Norton, 2004.

Amichai, Yehuda. *Achshav Bara'ash*. [In Hebrew.] Jerusalem: Schocken, 1968.

———. *Patuah Sagur Patuah*. [In Hebrew.] Jerusalem: Schocken, 1998.

Amir, Yehoyada. *Reason out of Faith: The Philosophy of Franz Rosenzweig*. [In Hebrew.] Tel Aviv: Am Oveid, 2004.

———. *A Small Still Voice: Theological Critical Reflections*. [In Hebrew.] Tel-Aviv: Yedi'ot aharonot, 2009.

Anderson, Gary. "Biblical Origins and the Problem of the Fall of Man." *Pro Ecclesa* 10, no. 1 (2001): 17–30.

———. *The Genesis of Perfection: Adam and Eve in Jewish and Christian Imagination*. Louisville: Westminster John Knox Press, 2001.

———. "Necessarium Adae Peccatum: An Essay on Original Sin." *Pro Ecclesia* 8, no. 3 (Summer 1999): 319–37.

———. "To See Where God Dwells: The Tabernacle, the Temple, and the Origins of the Christian Mystical Tradition." *Letter and Spirit* 4 (2008): 13–45.

Assis, Amit. "Author-ity." *Mafte'akh* 2 (2011): 1–28.

Aster, Shawn Zelig. *The Unbeatable Light: Melammu and Its Biblical Parallels*. Münster: Ugarit-Verlag, 2012.

Bacher, Wilhelm. *Die exegetische Terminologie der jüdischen Traditionsliteratur.* Hildesheim: Georg Olms, 1965.

Baden, Joel. *The Composition of the Pentateuch: Renewing the Documentary Hypothesis.* New Haven: Yale University Press, 2012.

———. "The Continuity of the Non-Priestly Narrative from Genesis to Exodus." *Biblica* 93 (2012): 161–86.

———. "Identifying the Original Stratum of P: Theoretical and Practical Considerations." In *The Strata of the Priestly Writings: Contemporary Debate and Future Directions*, ed. Sarah Shectman and Joel Baden, 13–29. Zürich: Theologischer Verlag Zürich, 2009.

———. *J, E, and the Redaction of the Pentateuch.* Tübingen: Mohr Siebeck, 2009.

———. *The Promise to the Patriarchs.* New York: Oxford University Press, 2013.

Barkay, Gabriel. "The Priestly Benediction on the Ketef Hinnom Plaques." [In Hebrew.] *Cathedra* 52 (1989): 37–76.

Barr, James. *Biblical Faith and Natural Theology.* Oxford: Oxford University Press, 1993.

———. *The Concept of Biblical Theology.* Minneapolis: Fortress Press, 1999.

———. *The Garden of Eden and the Hope of Immortality.* Minneapolis: Fortress Press, 1993.

———. *Holy Scripture: Canon, Authority, Criticism.* Philadelphia: Westminster Press, 1983.

Barton, John. "Alttestamentliche Theologie nach Alberz?" *Jahrbuch für biblische Theologie* 10 (1995): 25–34.

———. "Natural Law and Poetic Justice in the Old Testament." *Journal of Theological Studies* 30 (1979): 1–14.

———. *The Nature of Biblical Criticism.* Louisville: Westminster John Knox Press, 2007.

———. *Oracles of God: Perception of Ancient Prophecy in Israel After the Exile.* London: Darton, Longman and Todd, 1986.

———. *Reading the Old Testament: Method in Biblical Study.* Rev. ed. Louisville: Westminster John Knox Press, 1996.

———. "Should Old Testament Study Be More Theological?" *Expository Times* 100 (1989): 443–48.

———. "Unity and Diversity in the Biblical Canon." In *The Unity of Scripture and the Diversity of the Canon*, ed. John Barton and Michael Wolter, 11–26. Berlin: De Gruyter, 2003.

Bartor, Assnat. "Seeing the Thunder: Narrative Images of the Ten Commandments." In *The Decalogue in Jewish and Christian Tradition*, ed. Henning Graf Reventlow and Yair Hoffman, 13–31. New York: T & T Clark, 2011.

Bate, Walter Jackson. *The Burden of the Past and the English Poet.* New York: Harvard University Press, 1970.

Batnitzky, Leora. *Idolatry and Representation: The Philosophy of Franz Rosenzweig Reconsidered.* Princeton: Princeton University Press, 2000.

Baumgarten, A. I. "The Pharisaic Paradosis." *HTR* 80 (1987): 63–77.

Begrich, Joachim. *Gesammelte Studien*. Munich: Kaiser Verlag, 1964.

Bekhor Shor, Josef. Biblical commentaries. [In Hebrew.] Cited from *Mikra'ot Gedolot Haketer*, ed. Menahem Cohen. Multiple vols. Ramat Gan: Bar Ilan University Press, 1992–.

Benamozegh, Elie. *Em Lamiqra*. [In Hebrew.] 5 vols. Livorno: Chez L'Auteur, 1863.

Ben-Gurion, David. "The Bible in Its Own Light." [In Hebrew.] In *Studies in the Bible*. Tel Aviv: Am Oveid, 1969.

Ben-Sasson, H. H., ed. *A History of the Jewish People*. Cambridge: Harvard University Press, 1976.

Ben-Yehudah, E., and H. Tur-Sinai. [In Hebrew.] In *Thesaurus Totius Hebraitatis*. 8 vols. Jerusalem: Ben Yehudah Society, 1908–59.

Berger, David. *The Rebbe, the Messiah, and the Scandal of Orthodox Indifference*. London: Littman Library of Jewish Civilization, 2001.

Berger, Yitzhak. "Peshat and the Authority of Ḥazal in the Commentaries of Radak." *AJSR* 31 (2007): 41–59.

Bigman, David. "A Ladder upon the Earth, Whose Top Reaches the Heavens." *Conversations: The Journal of the Institute for Jewish Ideas and Ideals* 11 (2011): 1–18.

Bird, Phyllis. *Missing Persons and Mistaken Identities. Women and Gender in Ancient Israel*. Minneapolis: Fortress Press, 1997.

Bland, Kalman. "Moses and the Law According to Maimonides." In *Mystics, Philosophers and Politicians: Essays in Jewish Intellectual History in Honor of Alexander Altman*, ed. Jehuda Reinharz, Daniel Swetschinski, and Kalman Bland, 49–66. Durham: Duke University Press, 1982.

Blenkinsopp, Joseph. *Ezra-Nehemiah: A Commentary*. Philadelphia: Westminster Press, 1988.

———. *Prophecy and Canon: A Contribution to the Study of Jewish Origins*. Notre Dame: University of Notre Dame Press, 1977.

———. *Sage, Priest, Prophet: Religious and Intellectual Leadership in Ancient Israel*. Louisville: Westminster John Knox Press, 1995.

Blidstein, Jacob (Gerald). "Concerning the Term 'Torah Shebe'al Peh'." [In Hebrew.] *Tarbiz* 42 (1973): 496–98.

Bloom, Harold. *The Anxiety of Influence: A Theory of Poetry*. 1973. London: Oxford University Press, 1975.

———. *A Map of Misreading*. Oxford: Oxford University Press, 1975.

Blum, Erhard. "The Decalogue and the Composition History of the Pentateuch." In *The Pentateuch: International Perspectives on Current Research*, ed. Thomas Dozeman, Konrad Schmid, and Baruch Schwartz, 289–301. Tübingen: Mohr Siebeck, 2011.

———. *Studien zur Komposition des Pentateuch*. Berlin: De Gruyter, 1990.

Boda, Mark, Michael Floyd, and Rex Mason, ed. *Bringing out the Treasure: Inner Biblical Allusion in Zechariah 9–14*. London: Sheffield Academic Press, 2003.

Bottéro, Jean. *Mesopotamia: Writing, Reasoning, and the Gods*, trans. Zainab Bahrani and Marc Van De Mieroop. Chicago: University of Chicago Press, 1992.

Boyarin, Daniel. *Intertextuality and the Reading of Midrash*. Bloomington: Indiana University Press, 1990.

Braiterman, Zachary. "Elu Ve-Elu: Textual Difference and Sublime Judgement in *Eruvin* and Lyotard." In *Textual Reasonings. Jewish Philosophy and Text Study at the End of the Twentieth Century*, ed. Peter Ochs and Nancy Levene, 206–13. Grand Rapids: William B. Eerdmans, 2003.

Bregman, Marc. "Mishnah, Mystery and the LXX." In *Continuity and Renewal: Judaism in Eretz Israel during the Byzantine-Christian Era*, ed. Israel Levine, 333–42. Jerusalem: Dinur Center and Jewish Theological Seminary, 2004.

———. "Pseudepigraphy in Rabbinic Literature." In *Pseudepigraphic Perspectives: The Apocrypha and Pseudepigrapha in Light of the Dead Sea Scrolls*, ed. Esther G. Chazon, Michael Stone, and Avital Pinnick, 27–41. Leiden: Brill, 1999.

Brettler, Marc Zvi. "'Fire, Cloud, and Deep Darkness' (Deuteronomy 5:22): Deuteronomy's Recasting of Revelation." In *The Significance of Sinai: Traditions about Sinai and Divine Revelation in Judaism and Christianity*, ed. George J. Brooke, Hindy Najman, and Loren T. Stuckenbruck, 15–27. Leiden: Brill, 2008.

———. *How to Read the Bible*. Philadelphia: Jewish Publication Society, 2005.

Brettler, Marc Zvi, Peter Enns, and Daniel J. Harrington. *The Bible and the Believer: How to Read the Bible Critically and Religiously*. New York: Oxford University Press, 2012.

Breuer, Edward. *The Limits of Enlightenment: Jews, Germans, and the Eighteenth-Century Study of Scripture*. Cambridge: Harvard University Center for Jewish Studies, 1996.

Breuer, Edward, and Chanan Gafni. "Jewish Biblical Scholarship between Tradition and Innovation." In *Hebrew Bible/Old Testament. The History of Its Interpretation, III: From the Renaissance to the Enlightenment*, ed. Magne Saebø, 262–303. Göttingen: Vandenhoeck & Ruprecht, 2012.

Breuer, Mordechai. "Dividing the Decalogue into Verses and Commandments." In *The Ten Commandments in History and Tradition*, ed. Ben-Zion Segal and Gershon Levi, 291–330. Jerusalem: Magnes Press, 1990.

———. *Pirqei Bereshit*. [In Hebrew.] 2 vols. Alon Shevut: Tevunot, 1999.

Brongers, H. A. "Bemerkungen zum Gebrauch des adverbialen *wᵉ'attāh* im Alten Testament (Ein Lexikologischer Beitrag)." *VT* 15 (1965): 289–99.

Brooke, George J., Hindy Najman, and Loren T. Stuckenbruck, ed. *The Significance of Sinai: Traditions about Sinai and Divine Revelation in Judaism and Christianity*. Leiden: Brill, 2008.

Brown, David. *Tradition and Imagination: Revelation and Change*. Oxford: Oxford University Press, 1999.

Brown, F., S. R. Driver, and C. Briggs. *A Hebrew and English Lexicon of the Old Testament*. Oxford: Oxford University Press, 1907.

Brueggemann, Walter. *Praying the Psalms: Engaging Scripture and the Life of the Spirit.* 2d ed. Eugene: Cascade, 2007.

———. *Theology of the Old Testament: Testimony, Advocacy, Dispute.* Minneapolis: Fortress Press, 1997.

Brusin, David. "Rosenzweig's Approach to Jewish Law." *Reconstructionist* 40, no. 5 (1974): 7–12.

Buber, Martin, and Franz Rosenzweig. *Scripture and Translation,* trans. Lawrence Rosenwald. Bloomington: Indiana University Press, 1994.

Carasik, Michael. *The Bible's Many Voices.* Philadelphia: Jewish Publication Society, 2014.

———. "To See a Sound: A Deuteronomic Rereading of Exodus 20:15." *Prooftexts* 19 (1999): 257–65.

Carmy, Shalom. "Concepts of Scripture in Mordechai Breuer." In *Jewish Concepts of Scripture: A Comparative Introduction,* ed. Benjamin D. Sommer, 267–79. New York: New York University Press, 2012.

Carpenter, J. E., and G. Harford-Battersby. *The Hexateuch According to the Revised Version.* 2 vols. London: Longmans, Green, and Co., 1900.

Carr, David. "Controversy and Convergence in Recent Studies of the Formation of the Pentateuch." *RelSRev* 23, no. 1 (January 1997): 22–31.

———. *The Formation of the Hebrew Bible: A New Reconstruction.* New York: Oxford University Press, 2011.

———. "Method in Determination of Direction of Dependence: An Empirical Test of Criteria Applied to Exodus 34, 11–26 and Its Parallels." In *Gottes Volk am Sinai: Untersuchungen zu Ex 32–34 und Dtn 9–10,* ed. Matthias Köckert and Erhard Blum, 107–40. Gütersloh: Chr. Kaiser Gütersloher Verlaghaus, 2001.

———. "Passion for God: A Center in Biblical Theology." *HBT* 23 (2001): 1–24.

———. *Reading the Fractures of Genesis: Historical and Literary Approaches.* Louisville: Westminster John Knox Press, 1996.

———. *Writing on the Tablet of the Heart: Origins of Scripture and Literature.* New York: Oxford University Press, 2008.

Cassuto, Umberto (Moshe David). *Biblical and Oriental Studies.* Jerusalem: Magnes Press, 1973.

———. *A Commentary on the Book of Exodus.* Jerusalem: Magnes Press, 1952.

Chavel, Simeon. "Biblical Law." [In Hebrew.] In *The Literature of the Hebrew Bible: Introductions and Studies,* ed. Zipora Talshir, 227–92. Jerusalem: Yad Ben-Zvi Press, 2011.

———. "Numbers 15, 32–36—A Microcosm of the Living Priesthood and Its Literary Production." In *The Strata of the Priestly Writings: Contemporary Debate and Future Directions,* ed. Sarah Shectman and Joel Baden, 45–55. Zürich: Theologischer Verlag Zürich, 2009.

———. "The Second Passover, Pilgrimage, and the Centralized Cult." *HTR* 102 (2009): 1–24.

Childs, Brevard. *Biblical Theology of the Old and New Testaments: Theological Reflection on the Christian Bible*. Minneapolis: Fortress Press, 1993.

———. *Exodus. A Commentary*. London: SCM Press, 1974.

———. *Introduction to the Old Testament as Scripture*. Philadelphia: Fortress Press, 1979.

———. "The Old Testament as Scripture of the Church." *Concordia Theological Monthly* 43 (1972): 709–22.

———. "Psalm Titles and Midrashic Exegesis." *Journal of Semitic Studies* 16 (1971): 137–50.

Clements, Ronald E. *God and Temple: The Idea of Divine Presence in Ancient Israel*. Oxford: Basil Blackwell, 1965.

Coffin, William Sloane. *Once to Every Man: A Memoir*. New York: Atheneum, 1977.

Cohen, Hermann. *Religion of Reason out of the Sources of Judaism*, ed. Steven S. Schwarzschild and Kenneth Seeskin, trans. Simon Kaplan. Atlanta: Scholars Press, 1995.

Cohen, Jonathan. "Concepts of Scripture in Martin Buber and Franz Rosenzweig." In *Jewish Concepts of Scripture: A Comparative Introduction*, ed. Benjamin D. Sommer, 179–202. New York: New York University Press, 2012.

Cohen, Shaye J. D. *The Significance of Yavneh and Other Essays in Jewish Hellenism*. Tübingen: Mohr Siebeck, 2010.

Collins, John J. *The Bible after Babel: Historical Criticism in a Postmodern Age*. Grand Rapids: William B. Eerdmans, 2005.

———. "The Biblical Precedent for Natural Theology." *JAAR* 45, supp. (1977): B35–B67.

———. *Introduction to the Hebrew Bible*. Minneapolis: Fortress Press, 2004.

———. "The Zeal of Phinehas: The Bible and the Legitimation of Violence." *JBL* 122 (2003): 3–21.

Commentary magazine, ed. *The Condition of Jewish Belief*. New York: Macmillan, 1966. (Originally published as *Commentary* magazine's special issue in August 1966, vol. 42, no. 2.)

Congar, Yves. *The Meaning of Tradition*, trans. A. N. Woodrow. San Francisco: Ignatius Press, 2004.

Cook, L. Stephen. *On the Question of the "Cessation of Prophecy" in Ancient Judaism*. Tübingen: Mohr Siebeck, 2011.

Cook, Stephen L. "Theological Exegesis of Genesis 22: A Case Study of Wrestling with a Disturbing Scripture." In *Staying One, Remaining Open: Educating Leaders for a 21st-Century Church*, ed. Richard Jones and J. Barney Hawkins IV, 125–38. New York: Morehouse Publishing, 2010.

Cooper, Alan. "Biblical Studies and Jewish Studies." In *The Oxford Handbook of Jewish Studies*, ed. Martin Goodman, Jeremy Cohen, and David Sorkin, 14–35. Oxford: Oxford University Press, 2002.

———. "Imagining Prophecy." In *Poetry and Prophecy: The Beginnings of a Literary Tradition*, ed. James Kugel, 26–44. Ithaca: Cornell University Press, 1990.

Cross, Frank Moore. *Canaanite Myth and Hebrew Epic: Essays in the History of the Religion of Israel*. Cambridge: Harvard University Press, 1973.

Crüsemann, Frank. *The Torah: Theology and Social History of Old Testament Law*, trans. Allan W. Mahnke. Minneapolis: Fortress Press, 1996.

Davies, W. D. *Jewish and Pauline Studies*. Philadelphia: Fortress Press, 1984.

———. *Paul and Rabbinic Judaism*. Rev. ed. New York: Harper & Row, 1967.

Davis, Ellen F. "Losing a Friend: The Loss of the Old Testament to the Church." In *Jews, Christians, and the Theology of the Hebrew Scriptures*, ed. Alice Ogden Bellis and Joel Kaminsky, 83–94. Atlanta: Society of Biblical Literature, 2000.

Day, John N. *Crying for Justice: What the Psalms Teach Us about Mercy and Vengeance in an Age of Terrorism*. Grand Rapids: Kregel Publications, 2005.

de Vaux, Roland. "Ark of the Covenant and Tent of Reunion." In *The Bible and the Ancient Near East*. Garden City, NY: Doubleday, 1971.

Dei Verbum. The Dogmatic Constitution on Divine Revelation, promulgated by Paul VI during the Second Vatican Council (Rome, 1965). http://www.vatican.va/archive/hist_councils/ii_vatican_council/documents/vat-ii_const_19651118_dei-verbum_en.html.

Diamond, James. "Concepts of Scripture in Maimonides." In *Jewish Concepts of Scripture: A Comparative Introduction*, ed. Benjamin D. Sommer, 123–38. New York: New York University Press, 2012.

Dietrich, M., O. Loretz, and J. Sanmartín. *The Cuneiform Alphabetic Texts from Ugarit, Ras Ibn Hani, and Other Places*. Münster: Ugarit Verlag, 1995.

Dillmann, August. *Die Bücher Numeri, Deuteronomium und Josua*. 2d ed. Leipzig: S. Hirzel, 1886.

Dillmann, August, and Victor Ryssel. *Die Bücher Exodus und Leviticus*. Leipzig: S. Hirzel, 1897.

Dorff, Elliot. *The Unfolding Tradition: Jewish Law after Sinai*. Rev. ed. New York: Aviv Press, 2011.

Dorff, Elliot, and Arthur Rosett. *A Living Tree: The Roots and Growth of Jewish Law*. Albany: State University of New York Press, 1988.

Dozeman, Thomas. *God on the Mountain*. Atlanta: Scholars Press, 1989.

———. "Masking Moses and Mosaic Authority in Torah." *JBL* 119 (2000): 21–45.

Dozeman, Thomas, Konrad Schmid, and Baruch Schwartz, ed. *The Pentateuch: International Perspectives on Current Research*. Tübingen: Mohr Siebeck, 2011.

Dresner, Samuel H. *Heschel, Hasidism, and Halakha*. New York: Fordham University Press, 2002.

Driver, S. R. *The Book of Exodus*. Cambridge: Cambridge University Press, 1911.

———. *Deuteronomy*. 3rd ed. Edinburgh: T & T Clark, 1902.

———. *Introduction to the Literature of the Old Testament*. New York: Meridan, 1956.

Dulles, Avery. *Models of Revelation*. New York: Doubleday, 1983.

———. "Reflections on 'Sola Scriptura.'" In *Revelation and the Quest for Unity*, 67–74. Washington, DC: Corpus Books, 1968.

———. *Revelation and the Quest for Unity*. Washington, DC: Corpus Books, 1968.

Dworkin, Ronald. *Taking Rights Seriously*. Cambridge: Harvard University Press, 1977.

Ehrlich, Arnold. *Randglossen zur hebräischen Bibel*. Leipzig: J. C. Hinrichs, 1908–14.

Eichrodt, Walther. *Theology of the Old Testament*, trans. J. A. Baker. 2 vols. Philadelphia: Westminster Press, 1961–67.

Eidevall, Göran. "Sounds of Silence in Biblical Hebrew: A Lexical Study." *VT* 62 (2012): 159–74.

Eisen, Arnold. "Re-Reading Heschel on the Commandments." *MJ* 9 (1989): 1–33.

———. *Rethinking Modern Judaism Ritual, Commandment, Community*. Chicago: University of Chicago Press, 1998.

Elbogen, Ismar, and Joseph Heinemann. *Jewish Liturgy: A Comprehensive History*, trans. Raymond P. Scheindlin. Philadelphia: Jewish Publication Society; New York: Jewish Theological Seminary, 1993.

Eliade, Mircea. *Patterns in Comparative Religion*, trans. Rosemary Sheed. New York: World Publishing Company and Meridian, 1963.

———. *The Sacred and the Profane: The Nature of Religion*, trans. Willard R. Trask. New York: Harcourt Brace Jovanovich, 1959.

Eliot, T. S. "Tradition and the Individual Talent." In *Selected Prose of T. S. Eliot*, ed. Frank Kermode, 37–44. London: Faber and Faber, 1975.

Elman, Yaakov. "Authoritative Oral Tradition in Neo-Assyrian Scribal Circles." *JANES* 7 (1975): 19–32.

———. "Nahmanides and Abarbanel on the Book of Deuteronomy as Revelation." In *Ḥazon Naḥum: Studies in Jewish Law, Thought, and History Presented to Dr. Norman Lamm*, ed. Yaakov Elman and Jeffrey Gurock, 229–50. New York: Yeshiva University Press, 1997.

———. "R. Zadok HaKohen on the History of Halakha." *Tradition* 21, no. 4 (1985): 1–26.

———. "Yerushalmi Pesaḥim, Tosefta Pisḥa, and the Problem of Orality." In *Introducing Tosefta*, ed. Harry Fox and R. Meacham, 123–80. Hoboken: Ktav, 1999.

Elon, Menachem. *Jewish Law: History, Sources, Principles*, trans. Bernard Auerbach and Melvin Sykes. Philadelphia: Jewish Publication Society, 1994.

Enns, Peter. *Inspiration and Incarnation: Evangelicals and the Problem of the Old Testament*. Grand Rapids: Baker Academic, 2005.

Epstein, Jacob Nahum. *Introduction to Mishnaic Text*. 2 vols. [In Hebrew.] Jerusalem: Magnes Press, 1948.

Erlewine, Robert. "Reclaiming the Prophets: Cohen, Heschel, and Crossing the Theocentric/Neo-Humanist Divide." *JJTP* 17 (2009): 177–206.

Evans, J. Martin. *Paradise Lost and the Genesis Tradition*. Oxford: Clarendon Press, 1968.

Even-Chen, Alexander. "'I Appear to Him in a Mirror; in a Dream I Speak to Him; but Not So with My Servant Moses; throughout My Household He Is

Trusted': Moses' Prophecy in the Writings of Maimonides and Maimonides as a Second Moses." [In Hebrew.] *Meḥqerei Yerushalayim Bemaḥshevet Yisrael* 18–19 [= *The Path of the Spirit: The Eliezer Schweid Jubilee Volume*, ed. Yehoyada Amir] (2005): 181–214.

———. *A Voice from the Darkness: Abraham Joshua Heschel Between Phenomenology and Mysticism.* [In Hebrew.] Tel Aviv: Am Oveid, 1999.

Fackenheim, Emil. *God's Presence in History: Jewish Affirmations and Philosophical Reflections.* New York: HarperCollins, 1972.

Fine, David. "Solomon Schechter and the Ambivalence of Jewish *Wissenschaft.*" *Judaism* 46 (Winter 1997): 3–24.

Finkelstein, Louis, ed. *Sifra on Leviticus.* Vol. 1, *Introduction.* [In Hebrew.] New York: Jewish Theological Seminary, 1989.

———, ed. *Siphre ad Deuteronomium cum Variis Lectionibus et Adnotationibus.* [In Hebrew.] New York: Jewish Theological Seminary, 1992.

Fischer, L. R., and F. B. Knutson. "An Enthronement Ritual at Ugarit." *Journal of Near Eastern Studies* 28 (1969): 157–67.

Fishbane, Michael. *Biblical Interpretation in Ancient Israel.* Oxford: Clarendon Press, 1985.

———. *The Garments of Torah: Essays in Biblical Hermeneutics.* Bloomington: Indiana University Press, 1989.

———. "The Hebrew Bible and Exegetical Tradition." In *Intertextuality in Ugarit and Israel,* ed. Johannes C. de Moor, 15–30. Leiden: Brill, 1998.

———. *Sacred Attunement: A Jewish Theology.* Chicago: University of Chicago Press, 2008.

———. *Text and Texture: Close Readings in Selected Biblical Texts.* New York: Schocken, 1979.

———. "*Tôrâ.*" [In Hebrew.] In *Encyclopaedia Biblica,* 8:470–83. Jerusalem: Mosad Bialik, 1955–88.

Floyd, Michael H., and Robert D. Haak, ed. *Prophets, Prophecy, and Prophetic Texts in Second Temple Judaism.* New York: T & T Clark, 2006.

Fox, Everett. *The Five Books of Moses.* New York: Schocken Books, 1995.

Fraade, Steven. "Concepts of Scripture in Rabbinic Judaism: Oral and Written Torah." In *Jewish Concepts of Scripture: A Comparative Introduction,* ed. Benjamin D. Sommer, 31–46. New York: New York University Press, 2012.

———. *From Tradition to Commentary: Torah and Its Interpretation in the Midrash Sifre to Deuteronomy.* Albany: State University of New York Press, 1991.

———. "Hearing and Seeing at Sinai: Interpretive Trajectories." In *The Significance of Sinai: Traditions about Sinai and Divine Revelation in Judaism and Christianity,* ed. George J. Brooke, Hindy Najman, and Loren T. Stuckenbruck, 247–68. Leiden: Brill, 2008.

———. "Literary Composition and Oral Performance in Early Midrashim." *OrTr* 14 (1999): 33–51.

————. "Moses and the Commandments: Can Hermeneutics, History, and Rhetoric Be Disentangled?" In *The Idea of Biblical Interpretation: Essays in Honor of James L. Kugel*, ed. Hindy Najman and Judith Newman, 399–422. Leiden: Brill, 2004.

Frank, Daniel. "Karaite Exegesis." In *Hebrew Bible/Old Testament—The History of Its Interpretation. I/2: The Middle Ages*, ed. Magne Saebø, 110–38. Göttingen: Vandenhoeck & Ruprecht, 2000.

Frankel, David. *The Land of Canaan and the Destiny of Israel: Theologies of Territory in the Hebrew Bible*. Winona Lake: Eisenbrauns, 2011.

Frankfort, Henri H., and Henriette A. Frankfort. "Myth and Reality." In *The Intellectual Adventure of Ancient Man: An Essay on Speculative Thought in the Ancient Near East*, 3–27. Chicago: University of Chicago Press, 1977.

Franks, Paul. "Sinai since Spinoza: Reflections on Revelation in Modern Jewish Thought." In *The Significance of Sinai: Traditions about Sinai and Divine Revelation in Judaism and Christianity*, ed. George J. Brooke, Hindy Najman, and Loren T. Stuckenbruck, 333–54. Leiden: Brill, 2008.

Freedman, David Noel, ed. *Anchor Bible Dictionary*. 6 vols. New York: Doubleday, 1992.

Friedman, Richard Elliott. *The Disappearance of God: A Divine Mystery*. Boston: Little, Brown, 1995. Republished as *The Hidden Face of God*. New York: HarperCollins, 1997.

————. *Who Wrote the Bible?* San Francisco: HarperCollins, 1987.

Friedman, Shamma. "Rambam and the Talmud." [In Hebrew.] *Dinei Yisrael* 26–27 [Mordechai Akiva Friedman Jubilee Volume] (5769–70): 315–26.

————. "What Does Mount Sinai Have to Do with the Sabbatical Year?" [In Hebrew.] *Sidra* 24–25 (2010): 387–426.

Frisch, Amos. "The Concept of Kingship in Psalms." *Shnaton: An Annual for Biblical and Ancient Near Eastern Studies* 19 (2009): 57–75.

Fromm, Erich. *You Shall Be as Gods: A Radical Interpretation of the Old Testament and Its Tradition*. New York: Holt, Rinehart and Winston, 1976.

Garb, Jonathan. *Manifestations of Power in Jewish Mysticism: From Rabbinic Literature to Safedian Kabbalah*. [In Hebrew.] Jerusalem: Magnes Press, 2005.

————. "Moshe Idel's Contribution to the Study of Religion." *Journal for the Study of Religions and Ideologies* 6 (2007): 16–29.

García-López, F. "Tôrāh." In *Theologisches Wörterbuch zum Alten Testament*, ed. G. Johannes Botterweck and Helmer Ringgren, 8:597–637. Stuttgart: Kohlhammer, 1970–2000.

Garfinkel, Stephen. "Applied *Peshat*: Historical-Critical Method and Religious Meaning." "Comparative Studies in Honor of Yochanan Muffs." Special issue, *JANES* 22 (1993): 19–28.

Geller, Stephen. *Sacred Enigmas: Literary Religion in the Hebrew Bible*. London: Routledge, 1996.

———. "Some Sound and Word Plays in the First Tablet of the Old Babylonian *Atraḥasis* Epic." In *The Frank Talmage Memorial Volume*, ed. B. Walfish, 1:63–70. Haifa: Haifa University Press, 1992.

———. "Were the Prophets Poets?" *Prooftexts* 3 (1983): 211–21.

Gellman, Jerome (Yehudah). "Conservative Judaism and Biblical Criticism." *CJ* 59 (2007): 50–67.

———. "Wellhausen and the Hasidim." *MJ* 26 (2006): 193–207.

Gerhardsson, Birger. *Memory and Manuscript: Oral Tradition and Written Transmission in Rabbinic Judaism and Early Christianity.* Lund: C. W. K. Gleerup, 1961.

Gerondi, Nissim (Ran). Talmudic commentaries. [In Hebrew.] Cited from standard (Vilna) editions of the Babylonian Talmud.

Gertz, Jan Christian, Konrad Schmid, Angelika Berlejung, and Markus Witte. *T&T Clark Handbook of the Old Testament*, trans. Linda M. Maloney. London: T & T Clark, 2012.

Gersonides, Levi. Biblical commentaries. [In Hebrew.] Cited from *Mikra'ot Gedolot Haketer*, ed. Menahem Cohen. Multiple vols. Ramat Gan: Bar Ilan University Press, 1992–.

Gesundheit, Shimon. "Das Land Israels als Mitte: Einer jüdischen Theologie der Tora Synchrone und diachrone Perspektiven." *ZAW* 123 (2011): 325–35.

———. *Three Times a Year.* Tübingen: Mohr Siebeck, 2012.

Gilliard, Frank. "More Silent Reading in Antiquity: *Non Omne Verbum Sonabat.*" *JBL* 112 (1993): 689–94.

Gillman, Abigail. "Between Religion and Culture: Mendelssohn, Buber, Rosenzweig and the Enterprise of Biblical Translation." In *Biblical Translation in Context*, ed. Frederick Knobloch, 179–94. Bethesda: University Press of Maryland, 2002.

Gillman, Neil. *Sacred Fragments: Recovering Theology for the Modern Jew.* Philadelphia: Jewish Publication Society, 1990.

Ginsberg, H. L. *The Israelian Heritage of Judaism.* New York: Jewish Theological Seminary, 1982.

Gitay, Yehoshua. "Deutero-Isaiah: Oral or Written?" *JBL* 99 (1980): 185–97.

Glatzer, Nahum. "Introduction to *FRHLT.*" In *Franz Rosenzweig: His Life and Thought*, ed. Nahum N Glatzer, ix–xxxviii. New York: Schocken Books, 1961.

———. "Introduction to *OJL.*" In *On Jewish Learning*, by Franz Rosenzweig, ed. Nahum N. Glatzer, 9–24. New York: Schocken Books, 1965.

Goldberg, Hillel. *Between Berlin and Slobodka: Jewish Transition Figures from Eastern Europe.* Hoboken: Ktav, 1989.

Goldingay, John. *Theological Diversity and the Authority of the Old Testament.* Grand Rapids: William B. Eerdmans, 1987.

Golinkin, David. "The Meaning of the Concepts *Watiqin, Watiq*, and Talmid Watiq in the Book of Ben Sira and Talmudic Literature." [In Hebrew.]. *Sidra* 13 (1997): 47–60.

———. *The Status of Women in Jewish Law: Responsa.* Jerusalem: Schechter Institute of Jewish Studies, 2012.

Goodman, Micah. *The Secrets of* The Guide to the Perplexed. [In Hebrew.] Or Yehudah: Dvir, 2010.

Goshen-Gottstein, Alon. "The Body as Image of God in Rabbinic Literature." *HTR* 87 (1994): 171–95.

———. "The Promise to the Patriarchs in Rabbinic Literature." In *Divine Promises to the Fathers in the Three Monotheistic Religions*, ed. Alviero Niccacci, 60–97. Jerusalem: Franciscan Printing Press, 1995.

Goshen-Gottstein, Moshe. "Tanakh Theology: The Religion of the Old Testament and the Place of Jewish Biblical Theology." In *Ancient Israelite Religion. Essays in Honor of Frank Moore Cross*, ed. Patrick D. Miller, Paul Hanson, and S. Dean McBride, 617–44. Philadelphia: Fortress Press, 1987.

Gottlieb, Michah. *Jewish Protestantism: Translation and the Turn to the Bible in German Judaism.* New York: Oxford University Press, forthcoming.

———. "Oral Letter and Written Trace: Samson Raphael's Defense of the Bible and Talmud." *JQR*, forthcoming.

Graham, William A. *Beyond the Written Word: Oral Aspects of Scripture in the History of Religion.* Cambridge: Cambridge University Press, 1987.

———. "Scripture." In *Encyclopedia of Religion*, ed. Mircea Eliade, Charles Adams, et al., 13:133–45. New York: Macmillan, 1987.

Green, Arthur. "Abraham Joshua Heschel: Recasting Hasidism for Moderns." *MJ* 29 (2009): 62–79.

———. *A Guide to the Zohar.* Stanford: Stanford University Press, 2004.

Greenberg, Moshe. *Al Hammiqra Ve'al Hayyahadut.* [In Hebrew.] Tel Aviv: 'Am 'Oveid, 1984.

———. "Exodus, Book of." In *Encyclopaedia Judaica*, 6:1050–67. Jerusalem: Keter, 1971.

———. *Hassegullah Vehakkoaḥ.* [In Hebrew.] Oranim: Hakkibbutz Hameuhad, 1985.

———. "A Problematic Heritage: The Attitude Toward the Gentile in the Jewish Tradition—An Israel Perspective." *CJ* 48, no. 2 (Winter 1996): 23–35.

———. *Studies in the Bible and Jewish Thought.* Philadelphia: Jewish Publication Society, 1995.

———. *Understanding Exodus.* New York: Behrman House and the Melton Research Center of the Jewish Theological Seminary, 1969.

Greenstein, Edward. "An Equivocal Reading of the Sale of Joseph." In *Literary Interpretations of Biblical Narratives*, ed. K. R. R. Gros Louis, 2:114–25, 306–31. Nashville: Abingdon, 1974–82.

———. "Interpreting the Bible by Way of Its Ancient Cultural Milieu." [In Hebrew.] In *Understanding the Bible in Our Times: Implications for Education*, ed. Maria Frankel and Howard Deitcher, 61–73. Jerusalem: Magnes Press, 2003.

———. "Medieval Bible Commentaries." In *Back to the Sources*, ed. Barry Holtz, 213–59. New York: Summit Books, 1984.

———. "Understanding the Sinai Revelation." In *Exodus: A Teacher's Guide*. 2d ed., ed. Ruth Zielenziger, Marcia Lapidus Kaunfer, Barry Holtz, and Miles Cohen, 273–317. New York: Melton Research Center of the Jewish Theological Seminary, 1994.

Grossman, Maxine. "Beyond the Hand of Moses: Discourse and Interpretive Authority." *Prooftexts* 26 (2006): 296–301.

Gruber, Mayer. "The Mishnah as Oral Torah: A Reconsideration." *Journal for the Study of Judaism in the Persian, Hellenistic, and Roman Periods* 15 (1984): 112–22.

Grunhaus, Naomi. *The Challenge of Received Tradition: Dilemmas of Interpretation in Radak's Biblical Commentaries*. New York: Oxford University Press, 2013.

Haberman, Joshua O. "Franz Rosenzweig's Doctrine of Revelation." *Judaism* 18 (1969): 320–36.

Halbertal, Moshe. *Concealment and Revelation: Esotericism in Jewish Thought and Its Philosophical Implications*, trans. Jackie Feldman. Princeton: Princeton University Press, 2007.

———. *Interpretive Revolutions in the Making*. [In Hebrew.] Jerusalem: Magnes Press, 1997.

———. *People of the Book: Canon, Meaning, and Authority*. Cambridge: Harvard University Press, 1997.

———. *Rambam*. [In Hebrew.] Jerusalem: Merkaz Zalman Shazar, 2009.

———. "What Is the *Mishneh Torah*? Codification and Ambivalence." In *Maimonides after 800 Years: Essays on Maimonides and His Influence*, ed. Jay M. Harris, 81–111. Cambridge: Harvard University Center for Jewish Studies 2007.

Halbertal, Moshe, and Avishai Margalit. *Idolatry*, trans. Naomi Goldblum. Cambridge: Harvard University Press, 1992.

Halivni, David Weiss. *Midrash, Mishna, and Gemara: The Jewish Predilection for Justified Law*. Cambridge: Harvard University Press, 1986.

———. "On Man's Role in Revelation." In *From Ancient Israel to Modern Judaism: Intellect in Quest of Understanding: Essays in Honor of Marvin Fox*, ed. Jacob Neusner, Ernest S. Frerichs, and Nahum M. Sarna, 2:29–49. Atlanta: Scholars Press, 1989.

———. *Peshat and Derash: Plain and Applied Meaning in Rabbinic Exegesis*. New York: Oxford University Press, 1991.

———. *Revelation Restored: Divine Writ and Critical Responses*. Boulder: Westview Press, 1997.

Haran, Menahem. *The Bible and Its World: Selected Literary and Historical Studies*. [In Hebrew.] Jerusalem: Magnes Press, 2009.

———. *Ha'asufah Hamikra'it: Tahalikhei Hagibush 'Ad Sof Yemei Bayit Sheini Ve-Shinuye Haṣurah 'Ad Motsa'ei Yemei Habeinayim*. [In Hebrew.] 3 vols. Jerusalem: Mosad Bialik and Magnes Press, 1996 and 2004.

————. *Temples and Temple Service in Ancient Israel: An Enquiry into the Character of Cult Phenomena and the Historical Setting of the Priestly School.* Oxford: Clarendon Press, 1978.

Harris, Jay M. *How Do We Know This? Midrash and the Fragmentation of Modern Judaism.* Albany: State University of New York Press, 1995.

Harris, Robert. "Concepts of Scripture in the School of Rashi." In *Jewish Concepts of Scripture: A Comparative Introduction,* ed. Benjamin D. Sommer, 102–22. New York: New York University Press, 2012.

————. "Jewish Biblical Exegesis from Its Beginnings to the Twelfth Century." In *The New Cambridge History of the Bible,* vol. 2, *From 600 to 1450,* ed. Richard Marsden and E. Ann Matter, 596–615. Cambridge: Cambridge University Press, 2003–9.

Hartman, David, and Charlie Buckholtz. *The God Who Hates Lies: Confronting & Rethinking Jewish Tradition.* Woodstock: Jewish Lights, 2011.

Harvey, Zev. "The Question of God's Non-Corporeality in Maimonides, Abraham of Posquières, Crescas and Spinoza." [In Hebrew.] In *Studies in Jewish Thought,* ed. Sarah Heller-Wilensky and Moshe Idel, 63–78. Jerusalem: Magnes Press, 1989.

Hayes, Christine. "Displaced Self-Perception: The Deployment of Minim and Romans in B. Sanhedrin 90b–91a." In *Religious and Ethnic Communities in Later Roman Palestine,* ed. Hayim Lapin, 249–89. Bethesda: University Press of Maryland, 2006.

————. "*Halakhah le-Moshe Mi-Sinai* in Rabbinic Sources: A Methodological Case Study." In *The Synoptic Problem in Rabbinic Literature,* ed. Shaye J. D. Cohen, 61–118. Providence: Brown Judaic Studies, 2000.

————. "Rabbinic Contestations of Authority." *Cardozo Law Review* 28 (2006): 123–41.

Ḥazzekuni (Hezekiah ben Manoah). *Commentary on the Torah,* ed. Ḥayyim Dov Chavel. [In Hebrew.] Jerusalem: Mosad Harav Kook, 1988.

Hazony, Yoram. *The Philosophy of Hebrew Scripture.* New York: Cambridge University Press, 2012.

Heinemann, Isaac. *Darkhei Ha-Aggadah.* [In Hebrew.] Jerusalem: Magnes Press, 1970.

————. *Ta'amei Hamitzvot Besifrut Yisrael.* [In Hebrew.] 2 vols. Jerusalem: Jewish Agency and Horeb, 1993 and 1996.

Held, Moshe. "A Faithful Lover in an Old Babylonian Dialogue." *Journal of Cuneiform Studies* 15 (1961): 1–26.

Held, Shai. *Abraham Joshua Heschel: The Call of Transcendence.* Bloomington: Indiana University Press, 2013.

Hendel, Ronald. "Aniconism and Anthropomorphism in Ancient Israel." In *The Image and the Book: Iconic Cults, Aniconism, and the Rise of Book Religion in Israel and the Ancient Near East,* ed. Karel van der Toorn, 205–28. Leuven: Peeters, 1997.

———. "The Exodus in Biblical Memory." *JBL* 120 (2001): 601–22.

———. "Leitwort Style and Literary Structure in the J Primeval Narrative." In *Sacred History, Sacred Literature: Essays on Ancient Israel, the Bible, and Religion in Honor of R. E. Friedman*, ed. Shawna Dolansky, 93–109. Winona Lake: Eisenbrauns, 2008.

Herr, Moshe David. "Continuum in the Chain of Torah Transmission." [In Hebrew.] *Zion* 44 [= Yitzhak F. Baer Memorial Volume] (1979): 43–56.

———. "Oral Law." In *Encyclopaeida Judaica*, ed. Cecil Roth and Geoffrey Wigoder, 12:1439–42. Jerusalem: Keter, 1972.

Heschel, Abraham Joshua. *God in Search of Man: A Philosophy of Judaism*. New York: Farrar, Straus and Giroux, 1955.

———. *Heavenly Torah as Refracted through the Generations*, ed. and trans. Gordon Tucker. New York: Continuum, 2005.

———. *Man Is Not Alone: A Philosophy of Religion*. New York: Farrar, Straus & Young, 1951.

———. *Man's Quest for God: Studies in Prayer and Symbolism*. New York: Scribner, 1954.

———. *Moral Grandeur and Spiritual Audacity: Essays*, ed. Susannah Heschel. New York: Farrar, Straus & Giroux, 1996.

———. "On the Holy Spirit in the Middle Ages." [In Hebrew.] In *Alexander Marx Jubilee Volume*, 175–208. New York: Jewish Theological Seminary, 1950.

———. *Prophetic Inspiration after the Prophets: Maimonides and Other Medieval Authorities*, ed. Morris M. Faierstein. Hoboken: Ktav, 1996.

———. *The Prophets*. New York: HarperCollins, 2001.

———. *The Sabbath: Its Meaning for Modern Man*. New York: Farrar, Straus & Young, 1951.

———. *Torah min Hashamayim B'aspaqlarya shel Hadorot*. [In Hebrew.] 3 vols. London: Soncino; New York: Jewish Theological Seminary, 1965 and 1990.

———. *Who Is Man?* Stanford: Stanford University Press, 1965.

Heschel of Apt, Abraham Joshua. *Oheiv Yisrael*. [In Hebrew.] Zhitomir: Defus Hashutafim Nikhdei Harav Mislavita, 1863.

Hidary, Richard. *Dispute for the Sake of Heaven: Legal Pluralism in the Talmud*. Providence: Brown Judaic Studies, 2010.

Hirsch, E. D., Jr. *Validity in Interpretation*. New Haven: Yale University Press, 1967.

Hirsch, Samson Raphael. *Der Pentateuch übersetzt und erläutert*. Frankfurt am Main: J. Kaufmann, 1899.

Hoffman, Adina, and Peter Cole. *Sacred Trash: The Lost and Found World of the Cairo Geniza*. New York: Schocken, 2011.

Hoffman, Shuvi. "J's Unique Approach to Law and Narrative." [In Hebrew.] MA thesis, Hebrew University, Jerusalem, 2007.

Hoffmeier, James K. *Ancient Israel in Sinai: The Evidence for the Authenticity of the Wilderness Tradition*. New York: Oxford University Press, 2005.

————. *Israel in Egypt: The Evidence for the Authenticity of the Exodus Tradition.* New York: Oxford University Press, 1997.

Holcomb, Justin, ed. *Christian Theologies of Scripture: A Comparative Introduction.* New York: New York University Press, 2006.

Horowitz, Isaiah. *Shenei Luḥot Haberit.* [In Hebrew.] Amsterdam, 1648; Warsaw, 1930.

Horowitz, Naftali Tzvi (Ropshitzer). *Zera' Qodesh.* [In Hebrew.] Jerusalem: N.p., 1954.

Hundley, Michael B. *Keeping Heaven on Earth: Safeguarding the Divine Presence in the Priestly Tabernacle.* Tübingen: Mohr Siebeck, 2011.

Hurowitz, Victor Avigdor. "'Proto-Canonization' of the Torah: A Self-Portrait of the Pentateuch in Light of Mesopotamian Writings." In *Study and Knowledge in Jewish Thought,* ed. Howard Kreisel, 31–48. Beersheva: Ben-Gurion University of the Negev Press, 2006.

————. "Spanning the Generations: Aspects of Oral and Written Transmission in the Bible and Ancient Mesopotamia." In *Freedom and Responsibility: Exploring the Challenges of Jewish Continuity,* ed. Rela Mintz Geffen and Marsha Bryan Edelman, 31–49. Hoboken: Ktav, 1998.

Hutner, Yitshak. *Paḥad Yitshak Kuntres Ve-Zot Hanukkah.* Brooklyn: Gur Aryeh, 1964.

Hübner, Hans. "Das Ganze und das eine Gesetz: Zum Problemkreis Paulus und die Stoa." *Kerygma und Dogma* 21 (1975): 239–56.

ibn Ezra, Abraham. Biblical commentaries. [In Hebrew.] Cited from *Mikra'ot Gedolot Haketer,* ed. Menahem Cohen. Multiple vols. Ramat Gan: Bar Ilan University Press, 1992–.

Idel, Moshe. "Abraham J. Heschel on Mysticism and Hasidism." *MJ* 29 (2009): 80–105.

————. "The Concept of the Torah in Heikhalot Literature and Its Metamorphoses in Kabbalah." [In Hebrew.] *Jerusalem Studies in Jewish Thought* 1 (1981): 23–84.

————. "Concepts of Scripture in Jewish Mysticism." In *Jewish Concepts of Scripture: A Comparative Introduction,* ed. Benjamin D. Sommer, 157–78. New York: New York University Press, 2012.

————. *Enchanted Chains: Techniques and Rituals in Jewish Mysticism.* Los Angeles: Cherub Press, 2005.

————. *Kabbalah: New Perspectives.* New Haven: Yale University Press, 1988.

————. *Old Worlds, New Mirrors: On Jewish Mysticism and Twentieth-Century Thought.* Philadelphia: University of Pennsylvania Press, 2010.

————. "On the Theologization of Kabbalah in Modern Scholarship." In *Religious Apologetics—Philosophical Argumentation,* ed. Yossef Schwartz and Volkhard Krech, 123–74. Tübingen: Mohr Siebeck, 2004.

Jacobs, Irving. *The Midrashic Process: Tradition and Interpretation in Rabbinic Judaism.* Cambridge: Cambridge University Press, 1995.

Jacobs, Louis. *Beyond Reasonable Doubt.* London: Littman Library of Jewish Civilization, 1999.

———. *Principles of the Jewish Faith, an Analytical Study*. New York: Basic Books, 1964.

———. *A Tree of Life: Diversity, Flexibility, and Creativity in Jewish Law*. Oxford: Oxford University Press, 1984.

Jaffee, Martin. *Torah in the Mouth: Writing and Oral Tradition in Palestinian Judaism, 200 BCE–400 CE*. New York: Oxford University Press, 2001.

Japhet, Sara. *From the Rivers of Babylon to the Highlands of Judah: Collected Studies on the Restoration Period*. Winona Lake: Eisenbrauns, 2006.

———. *The Ideology of the Book of Chronicles and Its Place in Biblical Thought*. Frankfurt: Peter Lang, 1989.

———. "Major Trends in the Study of Medieval Jewish Exegesis in Northern France." *Trumah* 9 (2000): 43–61.

———. "Some Biblical Concepts of Sacred Space." In *Sacred Space: Shrine, City, Land—Proceedings of the International Conference in Memory of Joshua Prawer*, ed. Benjamin Kedar and R. J. Zwi Werblowsky, 54–72. New York: Macmillan, 1998.

———. "The Tension between Rabbinic Legal Midrash and the 'Plain Meaning' (Peshat) of the Biblical Text—An Unresolved Problem? In the Wake of Rashbam's Commentary on the Pentateuch." In *Sefer Moshe: The Moshe Weinfeld Jubilee Volume*, ed. Chaim Cohen, Avi Hurvitz, and Shalom M. Paul, 403–25. Winona Lake: Eisenbrauns, 2004.

Jeremias, Jörg. *Theophanie: Die Geschichte einer alttestamentlichen Gattung*. 2nd ed. Neukirchen: Neukirchener Verlag, 1977.

Jindo, Job. "Concepts of Scripture in Yehezkel Kaufmann." In *Jewish Concepts of Scripture: A Comparative Introduction*, ed. Benjamin D. Sommer, 230–46. New York: New York University Press, 2012.

Jobling, David. "Myth and Its Limits in Genesis 2.4b–3.24." In *The Sense of Biblical Narrative: Structural Analyses in the Hebrew Bible II*. Sheffield: Department of Biblical Studies, University of Sheffield, 1978.

Joosten, Jan. "Covenant Theology in the Holiness Code." *Zeitschrift für altorientalische und biblische Rechtsgeschichte* 4 (1998): 145–64.

———. *People and Land in the Holiness Code: An Exegetical Study of the Ideational Framework of the Law in Leviticus 17–26*. Leiden: Brill, 1996.

Josephus, Flavius. *Judean Antiquities 1–4: Translation and Commentary*, ed. Steve Mason, trans. and commentary by Louis H. Feldman. Leiden: Brill, 2004.

Joüon, P., and T. Muraoka. *A Grammar of Biblical Hebrew*. Rome: Pontificium Institutum Biblicum, 1991.

Kalimi, Isaac. "Die Bibel und die klassich-jüdische Bibelauslegung. Eine Interpretations- und religionsgeschichtliche Studie." *ZAW* 114 (2002): 593–610.

Kamin, Sarah. *Rashi's Exegetical Categorization in Respect to the Distinction between Peshat and Derash*. [In Hebrew.] Jerusalem: Magnes Press, 1986.

Kaminka, Armond. *Meḥqarim*. [In Hebrew.] Tel Aviv: N.p. 1938.

Kaminsky, Joel S. *Yet I Loved Jacob: Reclaiming the Biblical Concept of Election*. Nashville: Abingdon Press, 2007.

Kant, Immanuel. *Foundation of the Metaphysics of Morals*, trans. Lewis Beck. Indianapolis: Bobbs-Merrill, 1959.

Kaplan, Edward K., and Samuel H. Dresner. *Abraham Joshua Heschel: Prophetic Witness*. New Haven: Yale University Press, 1998.

Kaplan, Lawrence. "'I Sleep, but My Heart Waketh': Maimonides' Conception of Human Perfection." In *The Thought of Moses Maimonides: Philosophical and Legal Studies*, ed. Ira Robinson, Lawrence Kaplan, and Julien Bauer, 130–66. Lewiston: E. Mellen Press, 1990.

———. "Review Essay: Between Berlin and Slobodka." *Da'at* 35 (1995): v–xxxiv.

Kasher, Menahem M. *Torah Sheleimah Megillat Esther*. [In Hebrew.] Jerusalem: Noam Aharon, 1994.

———. *Torah Sheleimah*. 48 vols. [In Hebrew.] Jerusalem: Beit Torah Sheleimah, 1979.

Kaufmann, Yehezkel. *Toledot Ha-Emunah Ha-Yisraelit*. [In Hebrew.] 4 vols. Jerusalem: Mosad Bialik; Tel Aviv: Devir, 1937–56.

Kautzsch, E. *Gesenius' Hebrew Grammar*, trans. A. E. Cowley. 2d ed. Oxford: Oxford University Press, 1910.

Keel, Othmar, and Christoph Uehlinger. *Gods, Goddesses, and Images of God in Ancient Israel*. Minneapolis: Fortress Press, 1998.

Kellermann, Diether. *Die Priesterschrift von Numeri 1, 1 bis 10, 10. Literarkrit. u. traditionsgeschichtl. untersucht*. Berlin: De Gruyter, 1970.

Kellner, Menachem Marc. *Dogma in Medieval Jewish Thought: From Maimonides to Abravanel*. Oxford: Oxford University Press, 1986.

———. *Maimonides' Confrontation with Mysticism*. Oxford: Littman Library of Jewish Civilization, 2006.

———. "Maimonides, Crescas, and Abravanel on Exod. 20:2. A Medieval Jewish Exegetical Dispute." *JQR* 69 (1979): 129–57.

———. *Must a Jew Believe Anything?* Oxford: Littman Library of Jewish Civilization, 2006.

Kepnes, Steven. "Revelation as Torah: From an Existential to a Postliberal Judaism." *JJTP* 10 (2000): 205–37.

Khan, Geoffrey. "Biblical Exegesis and Grammatical Theory in the Karaite Tradition." In *Exegesis and Grammar in Medieval Karaite Texts*, ed. Geoffrey Khan, 127–49. Oxford: Oxford University Press, 2001.

Kieckhefer, Richard. *Theology in Stone: Church Architecture from Byzantium to Berkeley*. Oxford: Oxford University Press, 2004.

Kimelman, Reuven. "Abraham Joshua Heschel's Theology of Judaism and the Rewriting of Jewish Intellectual History." *JJTP* 17 (2009): 207–38.

———. "The Daily Amidah and the Rhetoric of Redemption." *JQR* 79 (1988–89): 165–97.

———. "The Messiah in the Amidah: A Study in Comparative Messianism." *JBL* 116 (1997): 313–20.

Kislev, Itamar. "Numbers 36:13, the Transition between Numbers and Deuteronomy, and the Redaction of the Torah." In *Tziporah Talshir Festschrift*, forthcoming.

Klawans, Jonathan. "Ritual Purity, Moral Purity, and Sacrifice in Jacob Milgrom's Leviticus." *RelSRev* 29 (2003): 19–28.

Knohl, Israel. "Between Faith and Criticism." [In Hebrew.] *Megadim* 33 (2001): 123–26.

———. "Between Voice and Silence: The Relationship Between Prayer and Temple Cult." *JBL* 115 (1996): 17–30.

———. *The Divine Symphony: The Bible's Many Voices*. Philadelphia: Jewish Publication Society, 2003.

———. *The Sanctuary of Silence: The Priestly Torah and the Holiness School*. Minneapolis: Fortress Press, 1995.

Knoppers, Gary, and Bernard Levinson. "How, Where, When, and Why Did the Pentateuch Become the Torah?" In *The Pentateuch as Torah: New Models for Understanding Its Promulgation and Acceptance*, ed. Gary Knoppers and Bernard Levinson, 1–19. Winona Lake: Eisenbrauns, 2007.

Koehler, Ludwig, Walter Baumgartner, Johann Jakob Stamm, Benedikt Hartmann, Ze'ev Ben-Hayyim, Eduard Yechezkel Kutscher, and Philippe Reymond. *The Hebrew and Aramaic Lexicon of the Old Testament*, trans. M. E. J. Richardson. Leiden: Brill, 2001.

Kornfeld, W., and H. Ringrren. "קד״ש." In *Theological Dictionary of the Old Testament*, ed. H. Ringgren C. Botterweck, and H.-J. Fabry, various translators, 15 vols., 12:521–45. Grand Rapids: William B. Eerdmans, 1974–2006.

Kraemer, David. "The Formation of Rabbinic Canon: Authority and Boundaries." *JBL* 110 (1991): 613–30.

Kratz, Reinhard. "Der Dekalog im Exodusbuch." *VT* 44 (1994): 205–38.

Kraut, Benny. "The Approach to Jewish Law of Martin Buber and Franz Rosenzweig." *Tradition* 12 (1971): 49–71.

Kreisel, Howard. *Prophecy: The History of an Idea in Medieval Jewish Philosophy*. Dordrecht: Kluwer Academic Publishers, 2001.

Kronfeld, Chana. "Allusion: An Israeli Perspective." *Prooftexts* 5 (1985): 137–63.

Krüger, Thomas. "Gesetz und Weisheit im Pentateuch." In *Auf den Spuren der schriftgelehrten Weisen (FS J. Marböck)*, ed. I. Fischer, U. Rapp, and J. Schiller, 1–10. Berlin: W. de Gruyter, 2003.

———. "Die Stimme Gottes: Eine ästhetisch-theologische Skizze." In *Gottes Wahrnehmungen: Festschrift Helmut Utzschneider*, ed. S. Gehrig and S. Seiler, 41–65. Stuttgart: Kolhammer, 2009.

———. "Sündenfall? Überlegungen zur theologischen Bedeutung der Paradiesgeschichte." In *Beyond Eden: The Biblical Story of Paradise (Genesis 2–3) and Its Reception History*, ed. Konrad Schmid and Christoph Riedweg, 95–109. Tübingen: Mohr Siebeck, 2008.

Kugel, James. "The Bible's Earliest Interpreters." *Prooftexts* 7 (1987): 269–83.

———. *How to Read the Bible: A Guide to Scripture, Then and Now*. New York: Free Press, 2007.

———. *The Idea of Biblical Poetry: Parallelism and Its History*. New Haven: Yale University Press, 1981.

———. *In Potiphar's House*. San Francisco: Torch, 1990.

———. "Some Unanticipated Consequences of the Sinai Revelation: A Religion of Laws." In *The Significance of Sinai: Traditions about Sinai and Divine Revelation in Judaism and Christianity*, ed. George J. Brooke, Hindy Najman, and Loren T. Stuckenbruck, 1–13. Leiden: Brill, 2008.

———. "Torah." In *Contemporary Jewish Religious Thought: Original Essays on Critical Concepts, Movements, and Beliefs*, ed. Arthur A. Cohen and Paul Mendes-Flohr, 995–1005. New York: Scribner, 1987.

———. *Traditions of the Bible: A Guide to the Bible as It Was at the Start of the Common Era*. Cambridge: Harvard University Press, 1998.

———. "Two Introductions to Midrash." *Prooftexts* 3 (1983): 131–55.

Kuhl, Curt. "Die 'Wiederaufnahme'—ein literarkritisches Prinzip?" *ZAW* 64 (1952): 1–11.

Kurzweil, Zvi. "Three Views on Revelation and Law." *Judaism* 9 (1960): 292–98.

Lambdin, Thomas. *Introduction to Biblical Hebrew*. New York: Charles Scribner's Sons, 1971.

Lamm, Norman. "Amalek and the Seven Nations: A Case of Law. Vs. Morality." In *War and Peace in the Jewish Tradition*, ed. Lawrence Schiffman and Joel Wolowelsky, 201–38. New York: Yeshiva University Press, 2004.

Legaspi, Michael C. *The Death of Scripture and the Rise of Biblical Studies*. Oxford: Oxford University Press, 2010.

Leibowitz, Yeshayahu. *Judaism, the Jewish People, and the State of Israel*. [In Hebrew.] Jerusalem: Schocken, 1975.

Lenzi, Alan. *Secrecy and the Gods: Secret Knowledge in Ancient Mesopotamia and Biblical Israel*. Helsinki: Neo-Assyrian Text Corpus Project, 2008.

Levenson, Alan. *The Making of the Modern Jewish Bible: How Scholars in Germany, Israel, and America Transformed an Ancient Text*. Lanham: Rowman & Littlefield, 2011.

Levenson, Jon. *Creation and the Persistence of Evil: The Jewish Drama of Divine Omnipotence*. San Francisco: Harper and Row, 1988.

———. *The Hebrew Bible, the Old Testament, and Historical Criticism. Jews and Christians in Biblical Studies*. Louisville: Westminster John Knox Press, 1993.

———. "Religious Affirmation and Historical Criticism in Heschel's Biblical Interpretation." *AJSR* 25 (2000–2001): 25–44.

———. *Resurrection and the Restoration of Israel: The Ultimate Victory of the God of Life*. New Haven: Yale University Press, 2006.

———. *Sinai and Zion: An Entry Into the Jewish Bible*. San Francisco: Harper and Row, 1987.

———. "The Sources of Torah: Psalm 119 and the Modes of Revelation in Second Temple Judaism." In *Ancient Israelite Religion: Essays in Honor of Frank Moore*

Cross, ed. P. D. Miller, P. D. Hanson, and S. D. McBride, 559–74. Philadelphia: Fortress Press, 1987.

Levinas, Emmanuel. *Beyond the Verse: Talmudic Readings and Lectures*, trans. Gary Mole. London: Athlone, 1994.

Levine, Baruch. *Numbers 1–20: A New Translation with Introduction and Commentary*. New York: Doubleday, 1993.

———. "On the Presence of God in Biblical Religion." In *Religions in Antiquity: Essays in Memory of Erwin Ramsdell Goodenough*, ed. Jacob Neusner. Leiden: Brill, 1968.

Levinson, Bernard. "The Birth of the Lemma: The Restrictive Reinterpretation of the Covenant Code's Manumission Law by the Holiness Code in Leviticus." *JBL* 124 (2005): 617–39.

———. *Deuteronomy and the Hermeneutics of Legal Innovation*. New York: Oxford University Press, 1997.

———. "The Human Voice in Divine Revelation." In *Innovations in Religious Traditions*, ed. Michael Williams, Collett Cox, and Martin Jaffee, 35–71. Berlin: De Gruyter, 1992.

———. *Legal Revision and Religious Renewal in Ancient Israel*. New York: Cambridge University Press, 2008.

———. *A More Perfect Torah: At the Intersection of Philology and Hermeneutics in Deuteronomy and the Temple Scroll*. Winona Lake: Eisenbrauns, 2013.

———. *The Right Chorale: Studies in Biblical Law and Interpretation*. Winona Lake: Eisenbrauns, 2011.

Lewis, Theodore. "Divine Fire in Deuteronomy 33:2." *JBL* 132 (2013): 791–803.

Licht, Jacob. *A Commentary on the Book of Numbers I–X*. [In Hebrew.] Jerusalem: Magnes Press, 1985.

———. *A Commentary on the Book of Numbers XI–XXI*. [In Hebrew.] Jerusalem: Magnes Press, 1991.

———. "The Revelation of God's Presence at Sinai." [In Hebrew.] In *Studies in the Bible and Ancient Near East Presented to Samuel Loewenstamm*, ed. Y. Avishur and J. Blau, 1:251–67. Jerusalem: Rubenstein, 1978.

Lieberman, Saul. *Hellenism in Jewish Palestine*. New York: Feldheim, 1950.

Liedke, G., and C. Peterson. "Torah." In *Theological Lexicon of the Old Testament*, ed. Ernst Jenni and Claus Westermann, trans. Mark E. Biddle, 3:1415–22. Peabody: Hendrickson Publishers, 1997.

Lipman, Asher Isaiah. *'Or Yesha'*. [In Hebrew.] New York: Beit Hillel, 1984.

Litvin, Baruch, ed. *The Sanctity of the Synagogue: The Case for Mechitzah— Separation between Men and Women in the Synagogue—Based on Jewish Law, History, and Philosophy, from Sources Old and New*. 3rd. ed. Hoboken: Ktav, 1987.

Lockshin, Martin. *Rashbam's Commentary on Exodus: An Annotated Translation*, ed. and trans. Martin I. Lockshin. Illustrations by Channa Lockshin. Atlanta: Scholars Press, 1997.

———. "Tradition or Context? Two Exegetes Struggle with Peshat." In *From Ancient Israel to Modern Judaism: Intellect in Quest of Understanding: Essays in Honor of Marvin Fox*, ed. Jacob Neusner, Ernest S. Frerichs, and Nahum Sarna, 2:173–86. Atlanta: Scholars Press, 1989.

Loewenstamm, Samuel E. "The Formula 'At That Time' in the Introductory Speeches in the Book of Deuteronomy." [In Hebrew.] *Tarbiz* 38 (1969): 99–104.

———. "The Trembling of Nature during the Theophany." In *Comparative Studies in Biblical and Ancient Oriental Literatures*, 172–89. Kevelaer Neukirchen-Vluyn: Butzon & Bercker Neukirchener Verlag, 1980.

Lorberbaum, Yair. *The Image of God: Halakhah and Aggadah.* [In Hebrew.] Tel Aviv: Schocken, 2004.

———. "On Contradictions, Rationality, Dialectics, and Esotericism in Maimonides's *Guide of the Perplexed.*" *Review of Metaphysics* 55 (2002): 711–50.

Mackler, Aaron. "Symbols: Reality, and God, Heschel's Rejection of a Tillichian Understanding of Religious Symbols." *Judaism* 40 (1991): 290–300.

Magid, Shaul. "From Theosophy to Midrash: Lurianic Exegesis and the Garden of Eden." *AJSR* 22 (1997): 37–75.

———. "Modernity as Heresy: The Introvertive Piety of Faith in R. Areleh Roth's *Shomer Emunim.*" *Jewish Studies Quarterly* 4 (1997): 74–104.

Maimonides, Moses. *The Guide of the Perplexed*, trans. Shlomo Pines. Chicago: University of Chicago Press, 1963.

———. *Mishnah 'im Peirush Mosheh Ben Maimon: Tirgem Me'aravit 'al Pi Ketav Hayad Hameqori Vehosif Mavo Vehei'arot*, ed. and trans. Yosef Kafaḥ. [In Hebrew.] 6 vols. Jerusalem: Mosad Harav Kook, 1963–67.

———. *Mishneh Torah.* [In Hebrew.] 7 vols. Bnai Brak: Hoṣa'at Shabbetai Frankel, 1975–2005.

Malamat, Abraham. "The Proto-History of Israel: A Study in Method." In *The Word of the Lord Shall Go Forth: Essays in Honor of David Noel Freedman*, ed. Carol Meyers and Murphy O'Connor, 301–13. Winona Lake: Eisenbrauns, 1983.

Maori, Yeshayahu. "The Approach of Classical Jewish Exegetes to *Peshat* and *Derash* and Its Implications for the Teaching of Bible Today," trans. Moshe Bernstein. *Tradition* 21, no. 3 (1984): 40–53.

Marcus, Ahron. *Der Chassidismus: Eine kulturgeschichtliche Studie.* Pleschen: Jeschurun, 1901.

Marmur, Michael. "In Search of Heschel." *Shofar* 26 (2007): 9–40.

McDonald, H. D. *Theories of Revelation: An Historical Study 1860–1960.* London: George Allen and Unwin, 1963.

Menahem Nahum of Chernobyl. *Sefer Me'or 'Einayim.* New York: Twersky Brothers, 1952.

Mendes-Flohr, Paul. *Divided Passions: Jewish Intellectuals and the Experience of Modernity.* Detroit: Wayne State University Press, 1990.

Mettinger, Tryggve N. D. *The Dethronement of Sabaoth: Studies in the Shem and Kabod Theologies.* Lund: Almqvist and Wiksell, 1982.

Meyers, Carol. *Discovering Eve: Ancient Israelite Women in Context*. New York: Oxford University Press, 1988.

Milgrom, Jacob. *Leviticus 1–16: A New Translation with Introduction and Commentary*. New York: Doubleday, 1991.

———. *Leviticus 17–22: A New Translation with Introduction and Commentary*. New York: Doubleday, 2000.

———. *Leviticus 23–27: A New Translation with Introduction and Commentary*. New York: Doubleday, 2001.

———. *Numbers*. Philadelphia: Jewish Publication Society, 1989.

———. "Profane Slaughter and a Formulaic Key to the Composition of Deuteronomy." *HUCA* 47 (1976): 1–17.

Miller, Geoffrey. *The Ways of a King: Legal and Political Ideas in the Bible*. Göttingen: Vandenhoeck & Ruprecht, 2011.

Miller, Patrick D. *The Way of the Lord: Essays in Old Testament Theology*. Grand Rapids: William B. Eerdmans, 2007.

Moberly, R. W. L. "Election and the Transformation of Ḥērem." In *The Call of Abraham: Essays on the Election of Israel in Honor of Jon D. Levenson*, ed. Gary Anderson and Joel Kaminsky, 67–89. Notre Dame: University of Notre Dame Press, 2013.

Muffs, Yochanan. *Love and Joy: Law, Language and Religion in Ancient Israel*. New York: Jewish Theological Seminary; Cambridge: Harvard University Press, 1992.

———. *The Personhood of God. Biblical Theology, Human Faith and the Divine Image*. Woodstock: Jewish Lights, 2005.

Mulder, M. J. "The Transmission of the Biblical Text." In *Mikra: Text, Translation, Reading and Interpretation of the Hebrew Bible in Ancient Judaism and Early Christianity*, ed. M. J. Mulder. Philadelphia: Fortress Press, 1988.

Myers, David N. *Resisting History: Historicism and Its Discontents in German-Jewish Thought*. Princeton: Princeton University Press, 2003.

Na'aman, Nadav. "The Exodus Story: Between Historical Memory and Historiographical Composition." *Journal of the Ancient Near Eastern Religions* 11 (2011): 39–69.

Naḥmanides, Moses. Biblical commentaries. [In Hebrew.] Cited from *Mikra'ot Gedolot Haketer*, ed. Menahem Cohen. Multiple vols. Ramat Gan: Bar Ilan University Press, 1992–.

Naidoff, Bruce. "A Man to Work the Soil: A New Interpretation of Genesis 2–3." *JSOT* 5 (1978): 2–14.

Najman, Hindy. *Past Renewals: Interpretative Authority, Renewed Revelation, and the Quest for Perfection in Jewish Antiquity*. Leiden: Brill, 2010.

———. *Seconding Sinai: The Development of Mosaic Discourse in Second Temple Judaism*. Leiden: Brill, 2003.

Neher, André. *The Exile of the Word, from the Silence of the Bible to the Silence of Auschwitz*, trans. David Maisel. Philadelphia: Jewish Publication Society, 1981.

Neusner, Jacob. *Midrash in Context: Exegesis in Formative Judaism*. Philadelphia: Fortress Press, 1983.

———. "Oral Torah and Tradition: Defining the Problematic." In *Method and Meaning in Ancient Judaism (Volume 1)*, 59–78. Missoula: Scholars Press, 1979.

———. *Oral Tradition in Judaism: The Case of the Mishnah*. New York: Garland, 1987.

———. *What, Exactly, Did the Rabbinic Sages Means by "The Oral Torah"?* Atlanta: Scholars Press, 1998.

Nicholson, Ernest W. "The Decalogue as the Direct Address of God." *VT* 27 (1977): 422–33.

———. *The Pentateuch in the Twentieth Century: The Legacy of Julius Wellhausen*. Oxford: Clarendon, 1998.

Niditch, Susan. *Oral World and Written Word: Ancient Israelite Literature*. Louisville: Westminster John Knox Press, 1996.

Nihan, Christophe. "The Priestly Covenant, Its Reinterpretations, and the Composition of 'P.'" In *The Strata of the Priestly Writings: Contemporary Debate and Future*, ed. Sarah Shectman and Joel S. Baden, 87–134. Zürich: Theologischer Verlag Zürich, 2009.

Noam, Vered. *Megillat Ta'anit: Versions, Interpretation, History with a Critical Edition*. [In Hebrew.] Jerusalem: Yad Ben Zvi, 2003.

Noth, Martin. *The Deuteronomistic History*, trans. David J. A. Clines. Sheffield, England: JSOT Press, 1991.

———. *Exodus, a Commentary*, trans. John Bowden. Philadelphia: Westminster Press, 1962.

Novak, David. *Natural Law in Judaism*. Cambridge: Cambridge University Press, 1998.

———. *Tradition in the Public Square: A David Novak Reader*, ed. Randi Rashkover and Martin Kavka. Grand Rapids: William B. Eerdmans, 2008.

Oeming, Manfred. *Gesamtbiblische Theologien der Gegenwart: Das Verhältnis von AT und NT in der Hermeneutischen Diskussion Seit Gerhard von Rad*. Stuttgart: Verlag W. Kohlhammer, 1985.

Ollenberger, Ben, Elmer Martens, and Gerhard Hasel. *The Flowering of Old Testament Theology: A Reader in Twentieth-Century Old Testament Theology, 1930–1990*. Winona Lake: Eisenbrauns, 1992.

Ong, Walter. "Before Textuality: Orality and Interpretation." *OrTr* 3 (1988): 259–69.

Otto, Eckart. *Das Deuteronomium: Politische Theologie und Rechtsreform in Juda und Assyrien*. Berlin: De Gruyter, 1999.

———. "Mose der erste Schriftgelehrte: Deuteronomium 1,5 in der Fabel des Pentateuch." In *L'Ecrit et l'Esprit: Études d'histoire du texte et de théologie biblique en hommage à Adrian Schenker*, ed. Dieter Böhler, Innocent Himbaza, and Philippe Hugo, 152–59. Göttingen: Vandenhoeck & Ruprecht, 2005.

Otto, Rudolf. *The Idea of the Holy: An Inquiry into the Non-Rational Factor in the Idea of the Divine and Its Relation to the Rational*, trans. John W. Harvey. London: Oxford University Press, 1923.

Pannenberg, Wolfhart, ed. *Revelation as History*, trans. David Granskou. New York: Macmillan, 1969.

Paran, Meir. *Forms of the Priestly Style in the Pentateuch: Patterns, Linguistic Usages, Syntactic Structures*. [In Hebrew.] Jerusalem: Magnes Press, 1989.

Pardee, Dennis. "The Ba'lu Myth." In *Canonical Compositions from the Biblical World*. Vol. 1 of *The Context of Scripture: Canonical Compositions from the Biblical World*, ed. William W. Hallo and K. Lawson Younger, 241–74. Leiden: Brill, 1997.

Paul, Shalom. *Studies in the Book of the Covenant in Light of Cuneiform and Biblical Law*. Leiden: Brill, 1970.

Perdue, Leo. "Old Testament Theology since Barth's *Epistle to the Romans*." In *Biblical Theology: Introducing the Conversation*, ed. Leo Perdue, 55–136, 285–99. Nashville: Abingdon Press, 2009.

Perlman, Lawrence. *Abraham Heschel's Idea of Revelation*. Atlanta: Scholars Press, 1989.

———. "'As a Report about Revelation, the Bible Itself Is a *Midrash*.'" *CJ* 55, no. 1 (2002): 30–37.

Person, Raymond. "The Ancient Israelite Scribe as Performer." *JBL* 117 (1998): 601–9.

Petuchowski, Jakob. "Faith as the Leap of Action: The Theology of Abraham Joshua Heschel." *Commentary* 25, no. 5 (May 1989): 390–97.

Polliack, Meira. "Concepts of Scripture among the Jews of the Medieval Islamic World." In *Jewish Concepts of Scripture: A Comparative Introduction*, ed. Benjamin D. Sommer, 80–101. New York: New York University Press, 2012.

Polzin, Robert. *Moses and the Deuteronomist: A Literary Study of the Deuteronomistic History, Part One: Deuteronomy, Joshua, Judges*. Bloomington: Indiana University Press, 1980.

Potok, Chaim. *In the Beginning*. New York: Alfred A. Knopf, 1975.

Propp, William. *Exodus 19–40: A New Translation with Introduction and Commentary*. New York: Doubleday, 2006.

Radak. Biblical commentaries. [In Hebrew.] Cited from *Mikra'ot Gedolot Haketer*, ed. Menahem Cohen. Multiple vols. Ramat Gan: Bar Ilan University Press, 1992–.

Rashbam. Biblical commentaries. [In Hebrew.] Cited from *Mikra'ot Gedolot Haketer*, ed. Menahem Cohen. Multiple vols. Ramat Gan: Bar Ilan University Press, 1992–.

Rashi. Biblical commentaries. [In Hebrew.] Cited from *Mikra'ot Gedolot Haketer*, ed. Menahem Cohen. Multiple vols. Ramat Gan: Bar Ilan University Press, 1992–.

———. Talmudic commentaries. [In Hebrew.] Cited from standard (Vilna) editions of the Babylonian Talmud.

Ratzinger, Joseph (Pope Benedict XVI). *Jesus of Nazareth: From the Baptism in the Jordan to the Transfiguration*, trans. Adrian J. Walker. New York: Doubleday, 2007.

Räisänen, Heikki. *Paul and the Law*. Tübingen: J. C. B. Mohr, 1983.

Regev, Eyal. "Priestly Dynamic Holiness and Deuteronomic Static Holiness." *VT* 51 (2001): 243–61.

Reines, Alvin. "Maimonides' Concept of Mosaic Prophecy." *HUCA* 40–41 (1969–70): 325–61.

Reischer, Yaakov. *Iyyun Yaakov.* [In Hebrew.] Cited from standard (Vilna) editions of the *Ein Yaakov.*

Rendsburg, Gary. "The Date of the Exodus and the Conquest/Settlement: The Case for the 1100's." *VT* 42 (1992): 510–27.

Rendtorff, Rolf. *The Canonical Hebrew Bible: A Theology of the Old Testament*, trans. David E. Orton. Leiden: Deo, 2005.

———. *The Problem of the Process of Transmission in the Pentateuch*, trans. John J. Scullion. Sheffield: JSOT Press, 1990.

———. "Rabbinic Exegesis and the Modern Christian Bible Scholar." In *Canon and Theology*, ed. and trans. Margaret Kohl, 17–30. Minneapolis: Fortress Press, 1993.

Reynolds, Kent Aaron. *Torah as Teacher: The Exemplary Torah Student in Psalm 119.* Leiden: Brill, 2010.

Robinson, H. Wheeler. *Inspiration and Revelation in the Old Testament.* Oxford: Clarendon, 1946.

Rofé, Alexander. *Deuteronomy: Issues and Interpretation.* London: T & T Clark, 2002.

———. "Ephraimite versus Deuteronomistic History." In *Storia e tradizioni di Israele: Scritti in onore di J. Alberto Soggin*, ed. Daniele Garrone and Felice Israel, 221–35. Brescia: Paideia, 1991.

———. "The History of Israelite Religion and the Biblical Text: Corrections Due to the Unification of Worship." In *Emanuel. Studies in Hebrew Bible, Septuagint and Dead Sea Scrolls in Honor of Emanuel Tov*, ed. Shalom Paul, Robert Kraft, Lawrence Schiffman, Weston Fields, and Eva Ben-David, 759–93. Leiden: Brill, 2003.

———. *Introduction to the Literature of the Hebrew Bible.* Jerusalem: Simor, 2009.

———. "The Move towards the Study of Torah at the End of the Biblical Period: Joshua 1:8; Psalm 1:2; Isaiah 59:21." [In Hebrew.] In *The Bible in Light of Its Interpreters: Memorial Volume for Sarah Kamin*, ed. Sara Japhet, 622–28. Jerusalem: Magnes Press, 1994.

———. "Research on Biblical Law in Light of the Historical-Philological Method." [In Hebrew.] *Mishpatim* 13 (1984): 477–96.

Rosenberg, Shalom. "Biblical Criticism in Modern Jewish Religious Thought." [In Hebrew.] In *The Bible and Us*, ed. Uriel Simon, 86–119. Ramat Gan: Scribner, 1979.

Rosenthal, Avraham. "Oral Torah and Torah from Sinai—Theory and Practice." [In Hebrew.] *Meḥqerei Talmud* 2 [= Talmudic Studies Dedicated to the Memory of Professor Eliezer Shimshon Rosenthal] (1993): 448–89.

Rosenzweig, Franz. *Briefe und Tagebücher*, ed. Rachel Rosenzweig, Edith Rosenzweig-Scheinmann, and Bernhard Casper. Haag: Martinus Nijhoff, 1979.

———. *Franz Rosenzweig: His Life and Thought*, ed. Nahum Glatzer. New York: Schocken Books, 1961.

———. *Mivḥar Iggerot Veqit'ei Yoman*, ed. Rivka Horwitz. [In Hebrew.] Jerusalem: Mosad Bialik, 1987.

———. *On Jewish Learning*, ed. Nahum N. Glatzer. New York: Schocken Books, 1965.

———. *Philosophical and Theological Writings*, ed. and trans. Paul Franks and Michael Morgan. Indianapolis: Hackett, 2000.

———. *The Star of Redemption*, trans. Barbara E. Galli. Madison: University of Wisconsin Press, 2005.

———. *The Star of Redemption*, trans. William W. Hallo. Boston: Beacon Press, 1972.

———. *Der Stern der Erlösung*. Haag: Martinus Nijhoff, 1976.

———. *Zweistromland: Kleinere Schriften zu Glauben und Denken*, ed. Reinhold und Annemarie Mayer. Dordrecht: M. Nijhoff, 1984.

Ross, Tamar. *Expanding the Palace of Torah: Orthodoxy and Feminism*. Waltham: Brandeis University Press, 2005.

Roth, Joel. *The Halakhic Process: A Systemic Analysis*. New York: Jewish Theological Seminary, 1986.

Roth, Martha. *Law Collections from Mesopotamia and Asia Minor*. Atlanta: Scholars Press, 1997.

Rowley, Harold H. *The Relevance of the Bible*. London: James Clark, 1942.

Römer, Thomas. "How Many Books (Teuchs): Pentateuch, Hexateuch, Deuteronomistic History, or Enneateuch?" In *Pentateuch, Hexateuch, or Enneateuch: Identifying Literary Works in Genesis through Kings*, ed. Thomas Dozeman, Thomas Römer, and Konrad Schmid, 24–42. Atlanta: Society of Biblical Literature, 2011.

Römer, Thomas, and Marc Brettler. "Deuteronomy 34 and the Case for a Persian Hexateuch." *JBL* 119 (2000): 400–419.

Safrai, Shmuel. "Oral Torah." In *The Literature of the Sages, Part One*, ed. Shmuel Safrai, 35–119. Philadelphia: Fortress Press, 1987.

Sagi, Avi. *Elu Va-Elu: A Study on the Meaning of Halakhic Discourse*. [In Hebrew.] Tel Aviv: Ha-Kibbutz Ha-Me'uḥad, 1996.

———. "The Punishment of Amalek in Jewish Tradition: Coping with the Moral Problem." *HTR* 87 (1994): 323–46.

Sakenfeld, Katharine Doob, ed. *The New Interpreter's Dictionary of the Bible*. Nashville: Abingdon Press, 2006–9.

Samuelson, Norbert M. *Revelation and the God of Israel*. New York: Cambridge University Press, 2002.

Sanders, E. P. *Paul, the Law, and the Jewish People*. Philadelphia: Fortress Press, 1983.

———. *Jewish Law from Jesus to the Mishnah: Five Studies*. London: SCM Press; Philadelphia: Trinity Press International, 1990.

Sanders, James A. *Torah and Canon.* Philadelphia: Fortress Press, 1972.

Sanders, Seth. "Old Light on Moses' Shining Face." *VT* 52 (2002): 400–406.

Sarna, Nahum, ed. *Olam Hatanakh: Tehillim.* 2 vols. [In Hebrew.] Tel Aviv: Dodezon-Itti, 1995.

———. *Exodus.* Philadelphia: Jewish Publication Society, 1991.

———. "Psalm 89: A Study in Inner Biblical Exegesis." In *Biblical and Other Studies*, ed. Alexander Altmann, 29–46. Cambridge: Harvard University Press, 1963.

———. "*Tehillim, S. Tehillim.*" [In Hebrew.] In *Encyclopaedia Biblica*, 8:437–62. Jerusalem: Mosad Bialik, 1955–88.

Sasson, S. D., ed. *Sefer Moshav Zekeinim.* [In Hebrew.] London: Letchworth, 1959.

Satlow, Michael. "Oral Torah: Reading Jewish Texts Jewishly in Reform Judaism." In *Platforms and Prayerbooks: Theological and Liturgical Perspectives on Reform Judaism*, ed. Dana Evans Kaplan, 261–70. Lanham: Rowman and Little, 2002.

Savran, George W. *Encountering the Divine: Theophany in Biblical Narrative.* London: T & T Clark, 2005.

———. *Telling and Retelling: Quotation in Biblical Narrative.* Bloomington: Indiana University Press, 1988.

Schäfer, Peter. *Studien zur Geschichte und Theologie des Rabbinischen Judentums.* Leiden: Brill, 1978.

Schechter, Solomon. *Aspects of Rabbinic Theology.* New York: Schocken, 1961.

———. "Leopold Zunz." In *Studies in Judaism: Third Series*, 82–142. Philadelphia: Jewish Publication Society, 1924.

———. *Seminary Addresses and Other Papers.* New York: Burning Bush Press, 1959.

———. *Studies in Judaism, First Series.* Philadelphia: Jewish Publication Society, 1896.

———. *Studies in Judaism, Second Series.* Philadelphia: Jewish Publication Society, 1908.

Schmid, Konrad. "Authorship." In *Encyclopedia of the Bible and its Reception*, vol. 3. Berlin: Walter de Gruyter, 2010.

———. "The Emergence and Disappearance of the Separation Between the Pentateuch and the Deuteronomistic History in Biblical Studies." In *Pentateuch, Hexateuch, or Enneateuch: Identifying Literary Works in Genesis through Kings*, ed. Thomas Dozeman, Thomas Römer, and Konrad Schmid, 11–24. Atlanta: Society of Biblical Literature, 2011.

———. "Genesis and Exodus as Two Formerly Independent Traditions of Origins for Ancient Israel." *Biblica* 93 (2012): 187–208.

———. *Schriftgelehrte Traditionsliteratur: Fallstudien zur innerbiblischen Schriftauslegung im Alten Testament.* Tübingen: Mohr Siebeck, 2011.

Schniedewind, William. *How the Bible Became a Book: The Textualization of Ancient Israel.* Cambridge: Cambridge University Press, 2004.

———. *Society and the Promise to David: The Reception History of 2 Samuel 7:1–17.* New York: Oxford University Press, 1999.

Schoeps, Hans-Joachim. "Franz Rosenzweig und seine Stellung zum jüdischen Gesetz." *Theologische Literaturzeitung* 80 (1955): 119–24.

Scholem, Gershom. *On Jews and Judaism in Crisis: Selected Essays*, ed. Werner J. Dannhauser. New York: Schocken Books, 1976.

———. *On the Kabbalah and Its Symbolism*, trans. Ralph Manheim. New York: Schocken Books, 1996.

———. *On the Mystical Shape of the Godhead: Basic Concepts in the Kabbalah*, trans. Joachim Neugroschel. New York: Schocken Books, 1991.

———. "Revelation and Tradition as Religious Categories in Judaism." In *The Messianic Idea in Judaism*, 282–303. New York: Schocken, 1971.

Schorsch, Ismar. *Canon without Closure: Torah Commentaries*. New York: Aviv Press, 2007.

Schreiner, Thomas. "Paul and Perfect Obedience to the Law: An Evaluation of the View of E. P. Sanders." *Westminster Theological Journal* 47 (1985): 246–48.

Schwartz, Baruch. "The Case for E." Paper presented at the Conference of the Society for Biblical Literature, Toronto, November 2002.

———. "The Giving of Torah: The Contribution of Biblical Criticism to Understanding the Concept in the Past and the Present." [In Hebrew.] In *Jewish Thought and Jewish Belief*, ed. Daniel Lasker, 21–31. Beersheva: Ben Gurion University, 2012.

———. *The Holiness Legislation: Studies in the Priestly Code*. [In Hebrew.] Jerusalem: Magnes Press, 1999.

———. "The Holiness of Israel in the Torah." [In Hebrew.] In *Qoves Hug Beit Ha-Nasi Le-Tanakh U-Le-Meqorot Yisrael*, 17–26. Jerusalem: Beit Ha-Nasi, 5757.

———. "The Horeb Theophany in E: Why the Decalogue Was Proclaimed." Paper presented at the conference of the Society for Biblical Literature, San Antonio, Texas, November 2004.

———. "'I Am the Lord' and 'You Shall Have No Other Gods' Were Heard from the Mouth of the Almighty: On the Evolution of an Interpretation." [In Hebrew.] In *The Bible in Light of Its Interpreters: Sarah Kamin Memorial Volume*, ed. Sara Japhet, 170–97. Jerusalem: Magnes Press, 1994.

———. "The Origin of the Law's Authority: 'Grundnorm' and Its Meaning in the Pentateuchal Traditions." [In Hebrew.] *Shnaton Ha-Mishpat Ha-Ivri* 21 (2000): 241–65.

———. "The Pentateuch as Scripture and the Challenge of Biblical Criticism: Responses among Modern Jewish Thinkers and Scholars." In *Jewish Concepts of Scripture: A Comparative Introduction*, ed. Benjamin D. Sommer, 203–29. New York: New York University Press, 2012.

———. "The Priestly Account of the Theophany and Lawgiving at Sinai." In *Texts, Temples, and Traditions. A Tribute to Menahem Haran*, ed. Michael V. Fox, Victor Avigdor Hurowitz, Avi Hurvitz, Michael L. Klein, Baruch J. Schwartz, and Nili Shupak, 103–34. Winona Lake: Eisenbrauns, 1996.

―――. "The Torah—Its Five Books and Four Documents." [In Hebrew.] In *The Literature of the Hebrew Bible: Introductions and Studies*, ed. Zipora Talshir, 161–226. Jerusalem: Yad Ben-Zvi Press, 2011.

―――. "What Really Happened at Mount Sinai?" *Bible Review* (October 1997), 21–46.

Schweid, Eliezer. "Biblical Critic or Philosophical Exegete? The Influence of Hermann Cohen's *The Religion of Reason* on Yehezkel Kaufmann's *History of Israelite Religion*." [In Hebrew.] In *Massu'ot: Studies in Qabbalah and Jewish Thought in Memory of Professor Efraim Gottlieb*, ed. Michal Oron and Amos Goldreich, 414–28. Jerusalem: Mosad Bialik, 1994.

―――. *The Philosophy of the Bible as Foundation of Jewish Culture*, trans. Leonard Levin. 2 vols. Boston: Academic Studies Press, 2008.

Seeligmann, Isac Leo. "The Beginnings of Midrash in the Books of Chronicles." [In Hebrew.] *Tarbiz* 49 (1980): 14–32.

―――. *Studies in Biblical Literature*, ed. Avi Hurvitz, Emmanuel Tov, and Sara Japhet. [In Hebrew.] Jerusalem: Magnes Press, 1996.

―――. "Voraussetzungen der Midraschexegese." *Supplements to VT* 1 (1953): 150–81.

Seeskin, Kenneth. *Autonomy in Jewish Philosophy*. New York: Cambridge University Press, 2001.

―――. "How to Read *Religion of Reason*." In Hermann Cohen, *Religion of Reason out of the Sources of Judaism*, ed. Steven S. Schwarzschild and Kenneth Seeskin, trans. Simon Kaplan, 21042. Atlanta: Scholars Press, 1995.

―――. *Searching for a Distant God: The Legacy of Maimonides*. New York: Oxford University Press, 2000.

Seforno, Ovadia. Biblical commentaries. [In Hebrew.] Cited from *Mikra'ot Gedolot Shemot*. Vienna, 1859; Jerusalem: Eshkol, 1976.

Seidel, Moshe. "Parallels between the Book of Isaiah and the Book of Psalms." [In Hebrew.] *Sinai* 38 (1955–56): 149–72, 229–42, 272–80, 333–55.

Seitz, Christopher. *Word without End: The Old Testament as Abiding Theological Witness*. Grand Rapids: William B. Eerdmans, 1998.

Shapira, Anita. *The Bible and Israeli Identity*. [In Hebrew.] Jerusalem: Magnes Press, 2005.

Shapiro, Marc. "Another Example of Minhag America." *Judaism* 39 (1990): 148–54.

―――. *The Limits of Orthodox Theology: Maimonides' Thirteen Principles Reappraised*. Oxford: Littman Library of Jewish Civilization, 2004.

―――. "Marc Shapiro Replies." *Judaism* 40 (1991): 89–93.

Sharp, Carolyn. *Wrestling the Word: The Hebrew Scriptures and the Christian Believer*. Louisville: Westminster John Knox Press, 2010.

Shweka, Aharon. "The Tablets of Stone and the Law and the Commandment." [In Hebrew.] *Tarbiz* 81 (2013): 343–66.

Silman, Yochanan. *The Voice Heard at Sinai: Once or Ongoing?* [In Hebrew.] Jerusalem: Magnes, 1999.

Simon, Uriel. "Rabbi Abraham Ibn Ezra as Exegete." [In Hebrew.] *Sinai* 62 (1968): 113–26.

———. "The Religious Significance of the Peshat," trans. Edward Greenstein. *Tradition* 23, no. 2 (1988): 41–63.

———. *Seek Peace and Pursue It: Pressing Questions in Light of the Bible, and the Bible in Light of Pressing Questions.* [In Hebrew.] Tel Aviv: Yedi'ot Aḥronot and Sifrei Ḥemed, 2002.

Ska, Jean-Louis. *Introduction to Reading the Pentateuch,* trans. Pascale Dominique. Winona Lake: Eisenbrauns, 2006.

Smith, George Adam. *The Book of Deuteronomy.* Cambridge: Cambridge University Press, 1950.

Smith, J. Z. "Acknowledgments: Morphology and History in Mircea Eliade's *Patterns in Comparative Religion.*" *History of Religions* 39 (2000): 315–51.

———. "Canons, Catalogues and Classics." In *Canonization and Decanonization: Papers Presented to the International Conference of the Leiden Institute for the Study of Religions (LISOR), Held at Leiden, 9–10 January 1997,* ed. Arie van der Kooij, 295–311. Leiden: Brill, 1998.

Smith, Mark. "The Baal Cycle." In *Ugaritic Narrative Poetry,* ed. Simon Parker, 81–180. Atlanta: Scholars Press, 1997.

———. *The Origins of Biblical Monotheism: Israel's Polytheistic Background and the Ugaritic Texts.* New York: Oxford University Press, 2001.

———. "'Seeing God' in the Psalms: The Background to the Beatific Vision in the Hebrew Bible." *Catholic Biblical Quarterly* 50 (1988): 171–83.

Smith, Mark, and Wayne Pitard. *The Ugaritic Baal Cycle,* vol. 2. Leiden: Brill, 2009.

Smith, Wilfred Cantwell. *The Meaning and End of Religion.* San Francisco: Harper & Row, 1978.

———. "Thoughts on Transcendence." *Zeitschrift für Religions- und Geistesgeschichte* 42 (1990): 32–49.

———. *What Is Scripture? A Comparative Approach.* Minneapolis: Fortress Press, 1993.

Solomon, Norman. *Torah from Heaven: The Reconstruction of Faith.* Oxford: Littman Library of Jewish Civilization, 2012.

Soloveitchik, Haym. "Migration, Acculturation, and the New Role of Texts in the Haredi World." In *Accounting for Fundamentalisms: The Dynamic Character of Movements,* ed. Martin Marty and R. Scott Appleby, 197–235. Chicago: University of Chicago Press, 1994.

———. "Rupture and Reconstruction: The Transformation of Contemporary Orthodoxy." *Tradition* 28 (1994): 82–95.

Soloveitchik, Joseph B. *And from There You Shall Seek,* trans. Naomi Goldblum. Jersey City: Ktav, 2008.

Sommer, Benjamin D. *The Bodies of God and the World of Ancient Israel.* New York: Cambridge University Press, 2009.

———. "Concepts of Scriptural Language in Midrash." In *Jewish Concepts of Scripture: A Comparative Introduction*, ed. Benjamin D. Sommer, 64–79. New York: New York University Press, 2012.

———. "Dating Pentateuchal Texts and the Perils of Pseudo-Historicism." In *The Pentateuch: International Perspectives on Current Research*, ed. Thomas Dozeman, Konrad Schmid, and Baruch Schwartz, 85–108. Tübingen: Mohr Siebeck, 2011.

———. "Dialogical Biblical Theology: A Jewish Approach to Reading Scripture Theologically." In *Biblical Theology: Introducing the Conversation*, ed. Leo Perdue, 1–53, 265–85. Nashville: Abingdon Press, 2009.

———. "Did Prophecy Cease?" *JBL* 115 (1996): 31–47.

———, ed. *Jewish Concepts of Scripture: A Comparative Introduction*. New York: New York University Press, 2012.

———. "Prophecy as Translation: Ancient Israelite Conceptions of the Human Factor in Prophecy." In *Bringing the Hidden to Light: The Process of Interpretation—Studies in Honor of Stephen A. Geller*, ed. Diane Sharon and Kathryn Kravitz, 271–90. Winona Lake: Eisenbrauns, 2007.

———. *A Prophet Reads Scripture: Allusion in Isaiah 40–66*. Stanford: Stanford University Press, 1998.

———. *Reclaiming the Bible as a Jewish Book: The Legacy of Three Conservative Scholars (Yochanan Muffs, Moshe Greenberg, and Jacob Milgrom)*. New York: Jewish Theological Seminary, forthcoming.

———. "Reflecting on Moses: The Redaction of Numbers 11." *JBL* 118 (1999): 601–24.

———. "Revelation at Sinai in the Hebrew Bible and Jewish Theology." *Journal of Religion* 79 (1999): 422–51.

———. Review of B. Childs, *Isaiah. A Commentary. Biblica* 83 (2002): 579–83.

———. "Scriptures in Jewish Tradition, and Tradition as Jewish Scripture." In *Jewish Concepts of Scripture: A Comparative Introduction*, ed. Benjamin D. Sommer, 1–14. New York: New York University Press, 2012.

———. "The Scroll of Isaiah as Jewish Scripture, or, Why Jews Don't Read Books." In *Society of Biblical Literature 1996 Seminar Papers*, 225–42. Atlanta: Scholars Press, 1996.

———. "Translation as Commentary: The Case of the Septuagint to Exodus 32–33." *Textus: The Annual of the Hebrew University Bible Project* 20 (2000): 43–60.

Sonnet, Jean-Pierre. *The Book within the Book: Writing in Deuteronomy*. Leiden: Brill, 1997.

———. "God's Repentance and 'False Starts' in Biblical History." In *Congress Volume Ljubljana 2007*, ed. André Lemaire, 469–94. Leiden: Brill, 2010.

Speiser, Ephraim. "The Durative Hithpaʻel: A Tan- Form." *JAOS* 75 (1955): 118–21.

Sperber, David. "The Commandment 'And You Shall Take unto Yourselves . . .' on the Sukkot Holiday and Its Development." [In Hebrew.] *Sidra* 15 (1999): 167–79.

Stackert, Jeffrey. "Distinguishing Innerbiblical Exegesis from Pentateuchal Redaction: Leviticus 26 as a Test Case." In *The Pentateuch: International Perspectives on Current Research*, ed. Thomas Dozeman, Konrad Schmid, and Baruch Schwartz, 370–86. Tübingen: Mohr Siebeck, 2011.

———. *Rewriting the Torah: Literary Revision in Deuteronomy and the Holiness Legislation*. Tübingen: Mohr Siebeck, 2007.

Steck, Odil Hannes. "Prophetische Prophetenauslegung." In *Wahrheit der Schrift-Wahrheit der Auslegung: Eine Zurcher Vorlesungsreihe zu Gerhard Ebelings 80. Geburtstag Am 6. Juli 1992*, ed. H. F. Geiber, H. J. Luibl, W. Mostert, and H. Weder, 198–244. Zürich: Theologischer Verlag, 1992.

Steiner, Richard. "דת and עין: Two Verbs Masquerading as Nouns in Moses' Blessing (Deuteronomy 33:2, 28)." *JBL* 115 (1996): 693–98.

Stemberger, G., and H. L. Strack. *Introduction to the Talmud and Midrash*, trans. M. Bockmuehl. Edinburgh: T & T Clark, 1991.

Stendahl, Krister. "The Bible as a Classic and the Bible as Holy Scripture." *JBL* 103 (1984): 3–10.

———. *Paul among Jews and Gentiles, and Other Essays*. Philadelphia: Fortress Press, 1976.

Stern, Elsie. "Concepts of Scripture in the Synagogue Service." In *Jewish Concepts of Scripture: A Comparative Introduction*, ed. Benjamin D. Sommer, 15–30. New York: New York University Press, 2012.

Stern, Harold. "A. J. Heschel, Irenic Polemicist." *Proceedings of the Rabbinical Assembly* 45 (1983): 169–77.

Stern, Josef. "Maimonides on Amaleq, Self-Corrective Mechanisms and the War against Idolatry." In *Judaism and Modernity: The Religious Philosophy of David Hartman*, ed. Jonathan Malino, 359–92. Aldershot: Ashgate, 2004.

Stern, Sacha. "Attribution and Authorship in the Babylonian Talmud." *JJS* 45 (1994): 28–51.

———. "The Concept of Authorship in the Babylonian Talmud." *JJS* 46 (1995): 183–95.

Sternberg, Meir. *The Poetics of Biblical Narrative: Ideological Literature and the Drama of Reading*. Bloomington: Indiana University Press, 1985.

Strauss, Leo. "How to Begin to Study the *Guide of the Perplexed*." In Moses Maimonides, *The Guide of the Perplexed*, trans. Shlomo Pines, xi–lvi. Chicago: University of Chicago Press, 1963.

Sukenik, Eliezer, Moshe David (Umberto) Cassuto, Shemuel Aḥituv, Hayyim Tadmor, and Benjamin Mazar, ed. *Encyclopaedia Biblica*. 9 vols. [In Hebrew.] Jerusalem: Mosad Bialik, 1950–88.

Terrien, Samuel. *The Elusive Presence: Toward a New Biblical Theology*. San Francisco: Harper and Row, 1978.

Textual Reasoning: The Journal of the Postmodern Jewish Philosophy Network 8, no. 2 (November 1999).

Thucydides. *The Peloponnesian War: The Crawley Translation Revised*, ed. T. E. Wick. New York: Modern Library, 1982.

Tigay, Jeffrey, ed. *Empirical Models for Biblical Criticism*. Philadelphia: University of Pennsylvania Press, 1985.

———. *Deuteronomy*. Philadelphia: Jewish Publication Society, 1996.

Tillich, Paul. *On Art and Architecture*, ed. John and Jane Dillenberger, trans. Robert Sharlemann. New York: Crossroad, 1989.

———. *Systematic Theology*. Chicago: University of Chicago Press, 1951–63.

Toeg, Aryeh. *Lawgiving at Sinai*. [In Hebrew.] Jerusalem: Magnes Press, 1977.

———. "Numbers 15:22–31—Midrash Halacha." [In Hebrew.] *Tarbiz* 43 (1973): 1–20.

Tomson, Peter J. *Paul and the Jewish Law: Halakha in the Letters of the Apostle to the Gentiles*. Minneapolis: Fortress Press, 1990.

Tooman, William, and Michael Lyons, ed. *Transforming Visions: Transformations of Text, Tradition, and Theology in Ezekiel*. Eugene: Pickwick Publications, 2010.

Touitou, Elazar. *Exegesis in Perpetual Motion: Studies in the Pentateuchal Commentary of Rabbi Samuel Ben Meir*. [In Hebrew.] Ramat Gan: Bar Ilan University Press, 2005.

Urbach, Ephraim E. *The Sages: Their Concepts and Beliefs*, trans. Israel Abrahamson. Jerusalem: Magnes Press, 1975.

———. "The Search for Truth as a Religious Imperative." [In Hebrew.] In *The Bible and Us*, ed. Uriel Simon, 13–27. Ramat Gan: Devir, 1979.

van der Toorn, Karel. "The Iconic Book: Analogies between the Babylonian Cult of Images and the Veneration of the Torah." In *The Image and the Book: Iconic Cults, Aniconism, and the Rise of Book Religion in Israel and the Ancient Near East*, ed. Karel van der Toorn, 228–48. Leuven: Peeters, 1997.

———. *Scribal Culture and the Making of the Hebrew Bible*. Cambridge: Harvard University Press, 2009.

Veijola, Timo. "The Deuteronomistic Roots of Judaism." In *Sefer Moshe: The Moshe Weinfeld Jubilee Volume: Studies in the Bible and the Ancient Near East, Qumran, and Post-Biblical Judaism*, ed. Chaim Cohen, Avi Hurvitz, and Shalom M. Paul, 459–78. Winona Lake: Eisenbrauns, 2004.

———. *Moses Erben: Studien zum Dekalog, zum Deuteronomismus, und zum Schriftgelehrtentum*. Stuttgart: Kohlhammer, 2000.

Viezel, Eran. "The Divine Content and the Words of Moses: R. Abraham Ibn Ezra on Moses' Role in Writing the Torah." [In Hebrew.] *Tarbiz* 80 (2012): 387–407.

———. "God's Revelation to the Biblical Authors in the Writings of R. David Kimhi." [In Hebrew.] *Shnaton: An Annual for Biblical and Ancient Near Eastern Studies*, forthcoming.

———. "Moses' Literary License in Writing the Torah: Joseph Hayyun's Response to Isaac Abrabanel." [In Hebrew.] In *Zer Rimonim: Studies in Biblical Literature and Jewish Exegesis Presented to Prof. Rimon Kasher*, ed. Michael Avioz, Elie Assis, and Yael Shemesh, 603–19. Atlanta: Society of Biblical Literature, 2013.

———. "Rashbam on Moses' Role in Writing the Torah." [In Hebrew.] *Shnaton: An Annual for Biblical and Ancient Near Eastern Studies* 22 (2013): 167–88.

von Rad, Gerhard. *Old Testament Theology*, trans. David Stalker. 2 vols. Edinburgh: Oliver and Boyd, 1962–65.

———. *Studies in Deuteronomy*, trans. David Stalker. London: SCM Press, 1953.

Ward, Keith. *Religion and Revelation: A Theology of Revelation in the World's Religions*. Oxford: Clarendon Press, 1994.

Watson, Wilfred G. E. *Classical Hebrew Poetry: A Guide to Its Techniques*. Sheffield: Sheffield Academic Press, 1984.

Watts, James W. "Psalm 2 in the Context of Biblical Theology." *HBT* 12 (1990): 73–91.

Weinfeld, Moshe. "The Covenant of Grant in the Old Testament and in the Ancient Near East." *JAOS* 90 (1970): 184–203.

———. *Deuteronomy 1–11*. New York: Doubleday, 1991.

———. *Deuteronomy and the Deuteronomic School*. Oxford: Clarendon Press, 1972.

———. "God the Creator in Gen. 1 and the Prophecy of Second Isaiah." [In Hebrew.] *Tarbiz* 37 (1968): 105–32.

———. "Kāḇôḏ, כבוד." In *Theological Dictionary of the Old Testament*, ed. H. Ringgren C. Botterweck, and H.-J. Fabry, various translators, 15 vols., 7:22–38. Grand Rapids: William B. Eerdmans, 1974–2006.

———. *The Promise of the Land the Inheritance of the Land of Canaan by the Israelites*. Berkeley: University of California Press, 1993.

———. "Theological Currents in Pentateuchal Literature." *Proceedings of the American Academy for Jewish Research* 37 (1969): 117–39.

Weingreen, Jacob. *From Bible to Mishna: The Continuity of Tradition*. Manchester: Manchester University Press, 1976.

Weisbaum, M., ed. *Yalqut Menahem*. [In Hebrew.] Jerusalem: Machon Siftei Tsadiqim, 1986.

Weiss, Meir. *Scriptures in Their Own Light: Collected Essays*. [In Hebrew.] Jerusalem: Mosad Bialik, 1988.

Weitzman, Steven. *Surviving Sacrilege: Cultural Persistence in Jewish Antiquity*. Cambridge: Harvard University Press, 2005.

Wellhausen, Julius. *Die Composition des Hexateuchs und der historischen Bücher des Alten Testaments*. Berlin: Georg Reimer, 1899.

———. *Prolegomena to the History of Ancient Israel*, trans. J. Sutherland Black and Allan Menzies. New York: Meridan, 1957.

Werman, Cana. "Oral Torah vs. Written Torah(s): Competing Claims to Authority." In *Rabbinic Perspectives: Rabbinic Literature and the Dead Sea Scrolls Proceedings of the Eighth International Symposium of the Orion Center for the Study of the Dead Sea Scrolls and Associated Literature, 7–9 January, 2003*, ed. Steven D. Fraade, Aharon Shemesh, and Ruth A. Clements, 175–97. Leiden: Brill, 2006.

Westbrook, Raymond. *Law from the Tigris to the Tiber: The Writings of Raymond Westbrook*, ed. Bruce Wells and Rachel Magdalene. Winona Lake: Eisenbrauns, 2009.

Wevers, John. *Exodus (Septuaginta: Vetus Testamentum Graecum Auctoritate Academiae Scientiarum Gottingensis Editum)*. Göttingen: Vandenhoeck & Ruprecht, 1991.

White, Marsha C. *The Elijah Legends and Jehu's Coup*. Atlanta: Scholars Press, 1997.

Williamson, H. G. M. *Ezra, Nehemiah*. Waco: Word Books, 1985.

Wilson, Gerald. *The Editing of the Hebrew Psalter*. Chico, California: Scholars Press, 1985.

Wolfson, Elliot. "Beautiful Maiden without Eyes: Peshat and Sod in Zoharic Hermeneutics." In *Midrashic Imagination: Jewish Exegesis, Thought, and History*, ed. Michael Fishbane, 155–203. Albany: State University of New York Press, 1993.

———. "Light Does Not Talk but Shines: Apophasis and Vision in Rosenzweig's Theopoetic Temporality." In *New Directions in Jewish Philosophy*, ed. Aaron Hughes and Elliot Wolfson, 87–148. Bloomington: Indiana University Press, 2010.

———. *Through a Speculum That Shines: Vision and Imagination in Medieval Jewish Mysticism*. Princeton: Princeton University Press, 1994.

Wright, David P. *Inventing God's Law: How the Covenant Code of the Bible Used and Revised the Laws of Hammurabi*. New York: Oxford University Press, 2009.

Wright, Jacob. "The Commemoration of Defeat and the Formation of a Nation in the Hebrew Bible." *Prooftexts* 29 (2009): 433–73.

Würthwein, Ernst. "Elijah at Horeb: Reflections on I Kings 19.9–18." In *Proclamation and Presence: Old Testament Essays in Honour of Gwynne Henton Davies*, ed. J. Durham and J. Porter, 152–66. Macon: Mercer University Press, 1983.

Wyatt, N. *Religious Texts from Ugarit*. London: Sheffield Academic Press, 2002.

Wyschogrod, Michael. *The Body of Faith: Judaism as Corporeal Election*. New York: Seabury Press, 1983.

Yadin, Azzan. "Rabbi Ishmael, 4QMMT, and the Origins of Legal Midrash." *Dead Sea Discoveries* 10 (2003): 130–49.

———. *Scripture as Logos: Rabbi Ishmael and the Origins of Midrash*. Philadelphia: University of Pennsylvania Press, 2004.

Yellin, David. "Allusion." [In Hebrew.] In *The Writings of David Yellin: Biblical Studies*, ed. E. Z. Melammed, 210–13. Jerusalem: Reuven Mass, 1983.

Zafren, Herbert. "Bible Editions, Bible Study and the Early History of Hebrew Printing." *Eretz-Israel* 16 (1982): 240–51.

Zakovitch, Yair. "The Book of the Covenant Interprets the Book of the Covenant— The Boomerang Phenomenon." [In Hebrew.] In *Texts, Temples, and Traditions: A Tribute to Menahem Haran*, ed. Victor Avigdor Hurowitz Michael V. Fox, and Avi Hurvitz, 383–403. Winona Lake: Eisenbrauns, 1996.

———. *An Introduction to Inner-Biblical Interpretation*. [In Hebrew.] Even-Yehuda: Reches, 1992.

———. "Qol Demamah Daqah." [In Hebrew.] *Tarbiz* 51 (1982): 329–46.

————. "Scripture and Israeli Secular Culture." In *Jewish Concepts of Scripture: A Comparative Introduction*, ed. Benjamin D. Sommer, 299–316. New York: New York University Press, 2012.

Zenger, Erich. *Am Fuß des Sinai: Gottesbilder der Ersten Testaments.* Düsseldorf: Patmos, 1993.

————. *A God of Vengeance? Understanding the Psalms of Divine Wrath*, trans. Linda. Maloney. Louisville: Westminster John Knox Press, 1996.

————. "Wie und wozu die Torah zum Sinai kam: Literarische und theologische Beobachtungen zu Exodus 19–34." In *Studies in the Book of Exodus: Redaction—Reception—Interpretation*, ed. Marc Vervenne, 265–88. Leuven: Peeters, 1996.

Zimmerli, Walther. "Sinaibund und Abrahambund." In *Gottes Offenbarung: Gesammelte Aufsätze zum Alten Testament*, 205–16. Munich: C. Kaiser, 1963.

Subject Index

A locator in **boldface** indicates the page where the entry term is defined. This index lists scholars when I discuss them as primary sources (i.e., as thinkers in their own right) but not when I discuss them as secondary sources (e.g., when they comment on a passage or historical developments).

Abraham ben David of Posquières (Rabad), 70, 211
Abraham of Minsk (*Ahavat Eitan*), 152–53
alpeh of *anokhi*, 89–90, 96, 101, 118
Amalekites, 27, 236, 248
Amichai, Yehudah, 250–51, 364n26
amora'im, **148**–50, 152, 171, 175
animal sacrifice, 54, 243, 362n8
antinomianism, 101, 125–26
Apter Rebbe. *See* Heschel, Abraham Joshua of Apt
artifacts, **11**
artifactual approach, 11–15, 22–23
attributions. *See* pseudepigraphy
aurality. *See* orality-aurality
authority: law and, 43–44, 50, 245; revelation and, 2–4, 6–9, 30–31, 43–44, 159, 245, 268n45, 274n88, 330n72; sources, 168–69, 217
avataras, 213–14

Baal, 34–35, 91–93
Benamozegh, Elie, 165, 300n6, 332n93
Benedict XVI (Pope). *See* Ratzinger, Joseph (Pope Benedict XVI)
Bible/biblical literature, 2–10, 13, 186–87, 352n15; approach to/study

of, 11–26, 218–19, 258n17, 261n37, 261n40, 262nn43–44, 352–53n17 (*see also* artifactual approach; biblical scholarship and studies; scriptural approach); exegetical aspects, 64, 161–64, 283n163; Judaism/the Jewish people and, 18–19, 21–22; as oral or written, 159, 210, 237; origins and composition of, 27–28, 253n4, 260n33 (*see also* revelation); poetry in, 47, 271–72n74; on revelation, 7, 209. *See also* Pentateuch; Torah
biblical criticism and critics, **3**, **11**, **255n8**; modern, 23–25, 211; Protestant, 22, 230, 263n45, 357n60; Rosenzweig on relationship to religious sages, 232; synchronic and diachronic dimensions, 256n8. *See also* Bible/biblical literature; source criticism and critics
biblical theology, 5, 14, 23, 239–40, 256n9. *See also* correlational theology; Jewish thinkers and Jewish thought; participatory theology/theory
Brown, David: on fallibility of scripture, 359n80, 360n86; on

Brown, David (*continued*)
implication, 297n274; on importance of tradition, 322n1, 333n98,
343n195, 359n78; on revelation as
interactional, 103, 301n111; on tradition as revealed, 343n195
Buber, Martin, 3, 36, 94, 129, 234; approach to scripture, 179–81, 228–29,
264n9; on revelation, 254n10,
360n82
Bultmann, Rudolph, 349n67

Canaanite culture and Canaanites,
27–28, 34–35, 91–92, 236
canon and canonicity, 7–9, 70–72, 156,
170–75, 233, 335n122, 348n47; forma-
tive/normative, 170–72; interpretative aspects, 164; Jewish, 124–25,
147–48, 152; multiplicity of, 227
centrifugal approach, 218–22, 226
centripetal approach, 218, 222–26
Christian theologians, 103, 359–60n80.
See also Brown, David; Congar,
Yves; *Dei Verbum*; Dulles, Avery;
Erasmus; Luther, Martin; Paul;
Ratzinger, Joseph; Second Vatican
Council; *sola scriptura*; Tillich,
Paul; Ward, Keith
Chronicles (book), 224, 227
Cohen, Hermann, 66, 110, 165, 192,
259–60n22, 306n59, 349–50n67
command (divine/heavenly), 119–21,
135–38, 200–201. See also *Gebot*
(divine command)
commandedness, 100–101, 200–202
commanding presence, 90, 94, 118, 122
commandments, 6–7, 101, 131–35, 160;
Heschel's view, 111–12, 118–19, 132–
34, 307n67; Rosenzweig's view (*see*
Rosenzweig, Franz: on law, *ḥiyyuv*,
and commandment); transmission
of, 77–80, 289–90n212. *See also* "love
God" command

communications, heavenly, 102–3, 106–7,
117. *See also* divine-human communication; prophecy as translation
communities, as determiners of Jewish
law, 125–26, 242–43, 247–50, 313n121.
See also *puq ḥazi*
Congar, Yves, on implication, 97; on
nature of tradition, 178, 340n164,
363n19; on relationship of scripture
of tradition, 328n52, 332–33n98,
339n147, 348n40; on scripture and
tradition protecting each other,
262n43, 342–43n195, 359n78; on
tradition and Holy Spirit, 343n3
Conservative Judaism, *passim*
continuity and innovation, 241–44,
248–51, 361–62n1, 362n10. *See also*
tradition
correlational theology, 110–13, 245,
305–6n54
covenant, 47, 56–57. *See also* hierarchical
aspects, 248–49; *ḥiyyuv* (covenantal
obligation); law and, 46–47, 56,
63–64, 242–43, 245–46; revelation
and, 190–96
Covenant Code (Exodus 21–23), 101, 162,
226–27, 287n190
Creation narratives, 229, 231
cult centralization. *See* animal sacrifice

Davidic promise, 20
D document/source, 64, 66, 344–45nn9–
13; conception of law's purpose,
71–73; on the covenant, 190–96;
Deuteronomy and, 64, 68–74,
285n180; on God, 72, 214; on lawgiving, 64, 68–74, 196–99, 285n180,
345–46n23; as replacement for E,
65, 226, 346–47n32; on revelation,
68–70, 190–95, 286n181, 286n184; on
revelation as durative or non-
durative, 190–99. *See also* Deuteronomy (book)

Decalogue, 65, 74, 273n86; origins of, 35, 48–50, 115–16, 310n89; as summary of Covenant Code, 277n115; transmission of, 37–41, 43, 77–80, 289–90n212

Dei Verbum, 327n42, 343n3, 369n80

deities, bodies of. *See* divine embodiment

de'oraita and *derabbanan*, 160

derash interpretation, 217, 353nn18–19. *See also* midrash and midrashic approach

Deuteronomistic insertions, 282n156

Deuteronomy (book), 71, 120–21, 173; exegetical nature of, 64, 283nn163–64; influence of E, J, and P, 283–84n166; as Oral Torah, 164–65, 332n93; as precursor to Maimonides, 70–72, 197–98, 215, 253n11. *See also* D document/source

divine embodiment, 213–16. See also *kabod*

divine-human communication, 36, 52–53, 55–56, 103; direct, 67, 284–85n175; nature of, 60, 94 (*see also* silence); at the Tent of Meeting, 59–60, 280–81n139; visual, 58. *See also* God; Moses; *qol* (voice, thunder, "obedience")

divine-human contact, 41–42, 62, 68–69, 282n155

divine-human partnership, 29, 112, 307–8n70

divine immanence/presence, 56–57, 279n127, 288n203; lethal nature of, 282n155; managing, 62, 71–72, 112, 278nn122–24

divine pathos, 111

divine sovereignty, 9. *See also* authority

divine speech. *See* God; *qol* (voice, thunder, "obedience")

divine will, 246

Documentary Hypothesis, **16**, 45, 257–58n14. *See also* neo-Documentary Hypothesis; redaction/redactor of Pentateuch; source criticism and critics

Dulles, Avery, 301n12, 302n17; on nature of tradition, 340n164; on relationship between tradition and scripture, 332n98, 340n157, 343n195

E document/source, 46–48, 271n71; conception of law's purpose, 56–57, 73–74; on covenant, 56; Decalogue and, 48–50; distinction between command and law, 119–21; as encouraging questions about lawgiving, 47–53, 59, 73–74; on revelation and lawgiving, 49–50, 69, 101, 286n181; on timing and location of lawgiving, 55–56, 73

Egyptian bondage, 258n18

Eliade, Mircea, 175

Elijah the Tishbite, 91–93

Elohistic document/source. *See* E document/source

Erasmus, 330n72

eternity and eternal present, 200–204, 207

exegesis, 64, 170, 283n163; inner-biblical, 161–65, 179–81, 211, 225, 242–44, 331n87; midrashic, 218–19, 221. *See also* biblical criticism and critics; biblical scholarship and studies; *derash* interpretation; *peshat* (contextual and linguistic interpretation)

Exodus (book), 42–44, 119–21, 282n156

Expanding the Palace of Torah, 343–44n4. *See also* Ross, Tamar

ex post facto holiness, 144–45, 321–22n204. *See also* communities, as determiners of Jewish law

Ezra-Nehemiah (books), 166–67, 333n103

fallibility. *See* scripture, fallibility of; "troubling texts"

firewall mentality, 22, 261n37

Fishbane, Michael, 301–2n16, 322n1, 340n165, 363n20; on religious value of *peshat*, 359n78; on *torah kelulah*, 309n81, 309n85, 341–42n188, 363n17

Five Books of Moses. *See* Pentateuch

fluidity model/tradition, 213–15, 353n22

Frankel, Zechariah, 313n121, 321n203

Gebot (divine command), **118**–19, 121, 200–201, 243, 247

gentiles. *See* nations (gentiles)

Gerondi, Nissim (Ran), 150, 152–53, 221–22

Gesetze (laws), **118**–19, 121, 243, 247, 318n173

God, 18, 82, 213–14; Israel's response to, 125–26; nature of, 27–34, 63, 71–72, 213–16, 245; self-identification/disclosure, 30, 35, 41, 95, 99–101, 104 (*see also* revelation); speech/voice of, 79–80, 82–84, 249, 285n179, 290n213 (see also *qol* (voice, thunder, "obedience")). See also *kabod*; *under various* "divine" *entries*

grace, fall from, 19–20

Graham, William, 255n6; 330n64, 337n132

The Guide of the Perplexed, 80–88, 137–38, 290–91n215, 304–5n45

guiding words (*Leitwörter*), **36**, 58, 193–96, 200–201. See also *qol* (voice, thunder, "obedience")

Ḥabad Ḥasidim, 133–35

halakhah, malleability of, 206–8, 245–49. *See also* lawgiving; midrash, halakhic; the law(s)

Halivni, David Weiss, 238–39

Ḥammurapi's Law Code, 117

Hamnuna (Rav), 77–78

Hebrew Bible. *See* Bible/biblical literature

Heschel, Abraham Joshua, 2–4, 128, 358n65; on action and commandments, 111–12, 118–19, 307n67; correlational theology and, 110–11; on halakhah and *ḥiyyuv*, 127, 132–33, 138, 279n131, 313–14n124; on lawgiving and revelation, 6–8, 29, 100–101, 105–6, 112–14, 120–21, 200–204, 253n2, 341n185; on Oral Torah, 183, 185; on participatory theory, 109, 305n45 (*see also* correlational theology); on prophecy, 202; Scholem, Gershom and, 185, 342n193; on scripture, 228, 238, 361n92; and theurgy, 112–13, 314n131

Heschel, Abraham Joshua of Apt, 204–5

Hexateuch, 124–25

hierophanies, 175

Hirsch, Samson Raphael, 155–56, 180, 328n50

historical criticism. *See* biblical criticism and critics

historiography, role of, 259–60n22

hitpaʿel construction, 60

ḥiyyuv (covenantal obligation), **6**–7, 121–22, 125–29, 135, 201–2. *See also* covenant; the law(s)

holiness, 288n203. *See also* ex post facto holiness

holistic approach, 222–24

Ḥoreb and Ḥoreb narratives, 66, 120, 190–96. *See also* Sinai and the Sinai experience

Horowitz, Isaiah, 205–8

Horowitz, Naftali Tzvi (of Ropshitz), 89–91, 96, 101, 295n258

Hutner, Yitzchok, 4, 150

ibn Daud, Abraham, 222

ibn Ezra, Abraham, 76, 253n4, 300n6, 303n33, 308n75, 311n93, 328n50, 332n93

Idel, Moshe, 110–12, 116, 214, 245, 342n193

identity formation, 17, 172, 335n121

implications, unrealized/unstated (concept), 95–98, 297n274, 298–99n280
Ishbili, Yom Tov (Ritba), 150, 221–22
Israelite religion, 65–66, 72, 141, 213, 224, 261n34; influence of Canaanite religion, 92–93; shift from sacrifices to prayer, 362n8. See also covenant

Jacobs, Louis, 2, 43, 321–22nn203–4, 363n17
J document/source, 61–64, 73–74, 281n148, 283n158; law and commandment, 63–64
Jewish communities. See communities, as determiners of Jewish law
Jewish thinkers and Jewish thought, 2–3, 43, 106–9, 125, 132–35, 150, 165; classic, 221–23; German Jewish, 179–80; modern, 15–16, 101–3, 175; on Oral Torah, 180–86; on theology (see also biblical theology; Israelite religion; participatory theology/theory), 23–25, 28–29, 209; on tradition, 188–89, 209–10. See also implications, unrealized/unstated (concept); under individual names
Joshua (book and person), 27, 124–25, 152–53, 312n111
Joshua ben Levi, 78–79
Judah bar Ilai, 222
Judaism: alleged discontinuity from the Bible, 18–19, 21–24, 26, 210, 260n24; centrality of law, 9, 121, 125–26, 232 (see also halakhah; Sinai and the Sinai experience; the law(s)); continuity with the biblical period, 212, 218; covenantal law and (see covenant); See also Israelite religion

kabbalah, 111; correlational theology and, 110; theurgy and, 57, 111–13, 306–7nn63–64; Torah and, 114–15, 184–85; view of sephirot (manifestations), 214–15

kabod, 53–55, 58–59, 62–63, 276nn101–2, 279–80nn132–33
Kant, Immanuel, 131–32
Kook, Abraham Isaac, 4, 150, 344n4

lawgiving, 56–57, 73–75, 288n202; durative versus non-durative, 56, 73–74, 190–97, 199–205, 277n116, 277–78nn118–19; location of, 55–56, 59–60, 73–74; mediation and, 59, 69–70; view of D and Deuteronomy, 64, 68–71, 285n180; view of E, 84–85; view of P, 57–59, 112. See also Decalogue; revelation
the law(s), 46–47, 118, 121–22, 242–45; authority and, 50, 122, 144–45, 171, 244–45; centrality of, 9, 121–26, 232, 312n111, 312n113, 313n118; as distinct from command, 118–21, 135–39; earthly (see Torah); non-Mosaic, 312n111, 319n178, 320–21n197; observance of, 57, 112, 247–48 (see also communities, as determiners of Jewish law). See also Decalogue; halakhah; ḥiyyuv (covenantal obligation)
legal pluralism, 221
Leitwörter. See guiding words (Leitwörter)
Lipman, Asher Isaiah, 89–90
"love God" command, 104–5, 118, 302n21
Luther, Martin, 317n161, 330n72

Maimonides, Moses, 44, 70, 72, 287n190; Commentary to the Mishnah, 87, 138, 304–5n45; Deuteronomy (book) as precursor to, 70–72, 197–98, 215, 352n11; on law, 101, 109, 137–38; minimalist position, 80–89, 101; on Moses, 84, 109; on nature of God, 82–84, 215; on Torah, 84, 109, 237, 292n237. See also Guide of the Perplexed; Mishneh Torah; "Thirteen Principles"

manumission, 20–21
Masoretic Text (MT), 133, 226
maximalist interpretations, 75–76, 99, 212, 246–47. *See also* Deuteronomy (book); stenographic theory
mediation, 59, 280n138. *See also* Moses
Mekhilta deRabbi Shimon Bar Yoḥai, 41–42
memorization. *See* orality-aurality
Menaḥem Mendel of Rymanov, 89–91, 93, 294n252, 295n254, 297n269
Mendelssohn, Moses, 180, 223, 279n128, 302n18, 352–53n17
midrash, halakhic, 158
midrash and midrashic approach, 218–22, **225**, 233, **334n107**. See also *derash* interpretation
minimalist interpretations, 77–94, 96, 99–101, 246, 248, 289–90n212, 290n213; Elijah and, 91–94; Horowitz, Naftali Tzvi (of Ropshitz) and, 96; Maimonides and, 80–89, 101; Menaḥem Mendel of Rymanov and, 96. *See also* participatory theology/theory; prophecy as translation
Miqra'ot Gedolot, 211–12, 221
Mishnah, 70, 148, 152–54, 157–58, 171, 216–17
Mishneh Torah, 70, 287n190, 304–5n45, 307n190
mitzvah. See commandments
Moab, covenant at, 194–96
Mosaic discourse, **141**–43, 208, 334n107
Moses, 15, 50–53, 84; access to God, 52–53 (*see also* divine-human communication); the law and, 85–87, 122, 139, 319n178; Maimonides's view of, 84, 109; as mediator, 32, 36–40, 43–44, 48–53, 59, 67, 84–85, 122; as prophet, 58, 106–8, 279–80n133, 304n42, 304–5n45; role in Sinai narrative, 53–55, 63, 82–84; as translator, 88, 106–9, 120, 294n247. *See also* tablets of the law

Mount Ḥoreb, 91–92. *See also* Ḥoreb and Ḥoreb narratives
multivocality. *See* Oral Torah: multiplicity/nature of

Naftali Tzvi Horowitz of Ropshitz. *See* Horowitz, Naftali Tzvi (of Ropshitz)
Naḥmanides, 161, 165
Naḥman of Bratslav, 145
narrative justification for law, 64, 136, 242, 313n118; as definition of the genre *torah*, 123, 312n109; presence in all four Pentateuchal sources, 122–23, 231–32
nations (gentiles), 263–64n1, 328n45
Near East, ancient: the Bible and, 3, 21–22, 255n4, 255–56n8; context (setting) and culture, 5, 19–21, 24, 34–35, 47, 92, 177, 255n4, 263n46; deities, 213; prophets and prophecy, 116; scribal practices, 116–18, 169–71, 318n175, 319n183, 335n121, 352n15. *See also* Canaanite culture and Canaanites; Ḥammurapi's Law Code
neo-Documentary Hypothesis, 45, 63, 254n5, 255, **257–58n14**, 270n67, 352n15

obligations. See *ḥiyyuv* (covenantal obligation)
Old Testament, 13. *See also* Bible/biblical literature
orality-aurality, 159, 176–80, 220; Sinai experience and, 33, 58, 66–68, 90, 284n174; textuality and, 168, 170
Oral Torah, 146–53, 176–77, 236–39, 322n2; authority of/revelation and, 172, 174, 178, 188, 217, 222, 244–45, 323–24nn13–16, 338–39n143; blurring of boundary with Written Torah, 151–61, 165, 325–26nn25–27, 327n42; Deuteronomy as, 164–65; multiplicity/nature of, 149–50, 221–22, 323n8;

peshat and, 234–35; Priestly source as, 166; primacy of, 156, 328n51; ritual status of, 337–38n137; view of Jewish thinkers, 180–86. *See also* Written Torah; tradition

Otto, Rudolph, 62, 284n174, 363n20

participatory theology/theory, **2**, 7–8, 50, 147, 151, 161, 181–82, 239; Elijah and, 91–94; E source and, 99, 120; law and, 9, 121, 245–50; Moses and, 88; P source and, 59–60; revelation and, 1–3, 31, 42–44, 52, 241, 248–50, 253n3. *See also* minimalist interpretations; prophecy as translation

Paul, 133, 317n161

P document/source, 53–59, 73–74, 112, 214, 275n100; law as theurgy in, 57, 112–13; lawgiving as mediated, 59–60; on location of lawgiving, 55–56; as Oral Torah, 166; on revelation as durative, 56, 73, 190

Pentateuch, 2, 171–73; authority of, 44; centrality of law in all four sources, 9, 124–25, 232, 313n118; contradictions in/disunity of, 212–13, 216–17, 223–26, 352n15; origins/composition of, 15–16, 45; ritual status of, 173. *See also* Masoretic Text; Samaritan Pentateuch

peshat (contextual and linguistic interpretation), 217, 223, 234–35, **311–12n106**, 353nn18–19, 355n41, 359n78

Pharisees, 177, 339–40n154

polyvocality. *See* Oral Torah: multiplicity/nature of

Priestly source. *See* P document/source

prophecy as translation, 7–8, 100, 102–3, 301n10, 301n16; imperfection of, 359–60n80; Moses and, 88, 106–9, 120, 294n247; revelation and, 113–17, 235–36. *See also* minimalist interpretations; participatory theology/theory

prophets/prophecy, 102, 177, 339n153, 344n7; ancient Near Eastern, 116; authentication of, 58, 279–80n133, 289n205, 304–5n45; Heschel's view, 202; participatory theory and (*see* prophecy as translation); as poets/poetry, 102–3; postbiblical, 177, 338n142, 339n153, 344n7; stenographic theory, 102–3

Proto-Rabad, 70–71, 73, 120, 212, 287n188

pseudepigraphy, 139–40

puq ḥazi, 126, 247. *See also* communities, as determiners of Jewish law

qiyyemu veqibbel. *See* ex post facto holiness

qol (voice, thunder, "obedience"), 35–36, 65–68, 79–81, 92, 94, 272n79; durative and non-durative aspects, 199–205, 350n69; non-verbal, 42–43; as voice and/or noise, 48–50, 90

Qol Gadol Velo Yasaf (*Voice*), 2, 189

Rabad. *See* Abraham ben David of Posquières (Rabad)

Rabbi Akiva, 40

Rabbi Tarfon, 133

Rabbi Yishmael, 40

Rambam. *See* Maimonides, Moses

Ramban. *See* Naḥmanides

Rashbam, 76, 234–35, 253n4, 300n6

Rashi, 102, 223, 318n173

Ratzinger, Joseph (Pope Benedict XVI), 97–98, 143–44, 301n12

reading (as calling out loud), 168–69

redaction/redactor of Pentateuch, 72–75, 197, 217–28, 230–31; acceptance of contradiction by, 136–37, 223–24, 352n15; Rosenzweig's view, 229–33. *See also* Documentary Hypothesis

reductionism, **18**, 259n21, 259n22

Resh Lakish, 253–54n4

revelation, 3, 100–101, 166–68, 178, 190, 254n6; authority and, 2–4, 6–9,

revelation (*continued*)
30–31, 43–44, 159, 245, 268n45,
274n88, 330n72; collaborative and
participatory, 1–2, 31, 42–44, 52, 241,
248–50, 253n3; durative versus non-
durative, 56, 73–74, 190–97, 199–205,
277n116, 277–78nn118–19; as an
experience of God, 42, 44, 74, 82–83,
90, 166 (*see also* theophanies);
lawgiving and, 124, 246, 312n113;
nature of, 74–76, 94–95, 120, 203,
222, 298–99n280; Oral Torah and,
178, 181–82; other religions and,
294–95n253; telescoping of, 143. *See
also* God: self-identification/dis-
closure; Heschel, Abraham Joshua;
Ḥoreb and Ḥoreb narratives;
Rosenzweig, Franz; Sinai and the
Sinai experience
Ropshitzer Rebbe. *See* Horowitz, Naftali Tzvi (of Ropshitz)
Rosenheim, Jakob, 228. *See also* Rosenzweig, Franz: correspondence
Rosenzweig, Franz, 2–4, 103–4; on
autonomy, 131–32; correspondence,
57, 104, 129, 130, 134, 228, 231, 233,
315n144; on divine-human dialogue,
302–3n26; on law, *ḥiyyuv,* and commandment, 57, 118, 121, 126, 128–35,
138–39, 279n128, 315n138, 315–16n145;
on lawgiving, 200–204, 207–8; on
Oral Torah, 182–83, 341n178; on
redactor of Pentateuch, 229–33;
on revelation, 6–8, 29–30, 57, 118,
120–21, 195–96, 302n22; on scripture, 180–81, 228–33, 237–38
Ross, Tamar, 189, 343–44n4
Rymanover Rebbie. *See* Menaḥem
Mendel of Rymanov

Samaritan Pentateuch, 226
Schechter, Solomon, 2, 98, 186, 237; on
continuity of Bible and rabbinic
literature, 26; idea of Catholic
Israel, 247–48, 313n121; on source
criticism, 26, 263n50
Scholem, Gershom, 110, 114–15, 184–85,
341–42n188, 342n193
scribes and scribal practices, 116–18,
140–41, 162, 168–71, 177, 211, 242–43,
318n175, 319n183, 335n121, 352n15
scriptural approach, 22, 24–25, 28, 255n2,
257n13, 258n16. *See also* Bible/
biblical literature: approach to/
study of
scripture, 11; aurality of, 159, 220;
centrifugal approach, 218–22, 226;
centripetal approach, 218, 222–26;
fallibility of, 151, 186–87, 235–39,
248, 359–60n80, 361n92; as forma-
tive/normative, 170–72, 336n129;
interpretation of (*see* maximalist interpretations; midrash and
midrashic approach; minimalist
interpretations); Jewish conception of, 354–55n32; as ritual object,
173, 337nn132–33; as tradition, 8–9,
25–26, 146–47, 154, 161, 166, 232–33,
322n1; unrealized/unstated implications of, 98. *See also* tradition;
Written Torah
Second Vatican Council, 261, 327n42,
343n3, 369n80
sephirot (manifestations), 115, 214–15
sexism in the Bible, 28
Shenei Luḥot Haberit, 205–7
silence, 92–94, 99–101, 115, 118,
296–97n264
Silman, Yochanan, 2, 189
sin, original, 19–20
Sinai and the Sinai experience, 9, 41–43,
123, 246–47, 266n25; aurality of, 33,
58, 66–68, 90, 284n174; centrality of,
30, 39, 241, 268n45; memories/per-
ceptions of, 45–46, 79–80; narrative
of, 30–42, 53–54, 57, 72; visuality of,
42, 58, 61, 66–68. *See also* Ḥoreb and
Ḥoreb narratives; revelation

slavery and slaves, 20–21, 196, 248–49

Smith, Wilfred Cantwell, 97, 255n1, 255n6, 311n102, 321n204, 357n60, 363n21; on fundamentalist readers, 258n17; on scripture as oral, 329n64, 340n170; on scripture as ritual object, 337nn132–33; on scripture and tradition, 298n275, 322n1, 363n23; on troubling texts, 236, 264n4

sola scriptura, 22, 333n98, 342–43n195

Soloveitchik, Joseph, 208, 210–11

sounds, 35–36. *See also* orality-aurality; *qol* (voice, thunder, "obedience")

source criticism and critics, 3, 18–19, 209, 254n5, 255–56n8, 261–62n41, 351n1; origins of, 15–16; religious exegesis and, 10–12, 16–18; theology and, 24–25, 258–59n19. *See also* Documentary Hypothesis; neo-Documentary Hypothesis; redaction/redactor of Pentateuch

speech, divine, 44. *See also* communications, heavenly; divine-human communication; God

Spinoza, Baruch, 6, 279n128, 300n9

The Star of Redemption, 104–5, 112, 207; on *Gebot*, 118, 200–201; on law, 129, 315–16n145; on prophecy/revelation, 302n22, 302n25; on revelation and Song of Songs, 303n28

stenographic theory, 2; of prophecy, 102–3; rejection of, 80, 87; of revelation, 2–3, 30, 36–37, 43–44, 51–53, 253–54n4. *See also* maximalist interpretations; Torah

supersessionism, 21–24, 210

Tabernacle. *See* Tent of Meeting/tent shrine

tablets of the law, 50–53, 115–16, 120, 274n90, 287n189

Talmud. *See* Oral Torah

tanna'im, 148–50, 171, 175, 177, 323–24n13

Targums, 199, 336–37n131

Ten Commandments. *See* Decalogue

Tent of Meeting/tent shrine, 53–55, 276n110; instructions for building, 58, 280n135; as location of lawgiving, 59–60

texts: ancient, 3–6, 117–18, 168–69, 347n39 (*see also* biblical scholarship and studies); as artifacts, 11–15, 23; role of, 179; sacred, 11–15, 22, 146, 321–22n204 (*see also* Bible/biblical literature)

theology. *See* biblical theology; Christian theologians; correlational theology; Jewish thinkers and Jewish thought; participatory theology/theory

theophanies, 61–62, 276n110; Canaanite model, 34–35, 47; comparison of, 92–93, 296–97n264, 296n262; Horeb (*see* Horeb and Horeb narratives); imagery, 33–35, 42, 53–55, 66–68, 266n21, 266n25, 276n101; Sinai (*see* Sinai and the Sinai experience)

theurgy, 57, 111–13, 134, 145, 306–7nn63–64, 307–8n70, 314n131

thinkers, modern, 3–6. *See also* Christian theologians; Jewish thinkers and Jewish thought; *under individual names*

"Thirteen Principles," 87–89, 138, 293n242, 293–94n245

Tillich, Paul, 65, 110, 284n169, 305–6n54, 307n67

today (guiding word), 193–96, 200–201

Torah, 5, 75; authority of, 43, 244; earthly and heavenly versions, 113–18, 308n75, 309n81, 309–10n85, 310nn86–87, 342n188; evolution of, 241, 249–50, 363–64n24; as genre, 123; origin of, 1, 7–8, 16, 85–89, 174–75, 292n237 (*see also* Moses; participatory theology/theory; stenographic theory), 292–93n241; redaction of (*see* redaction/redactor of Pentateuch); revelation

Torah (*continued*)
  of (*see* revelation); study of, 178–79,
    181–82 (*see also* Bible/biblical litera-
    ture); "troubling texts," 28. *See also*
    narrative justification for law; Oral
    Torah; Pentateuch; Written Torah
torah (teachings, revelation), 166–68
Torah min Hashamayim, 113–15, 253n2
Tosafot and tosafists, 222–24
Tosefta, 154
tradition, 8–9, 138, 178, 342–43n195;
    change and, 97, 242–44, 248–51,
    361–62n1; dialogical aspects, 210;
    Oral Torah and, 146; postbiblical,
    188–89; as response to revelation,
    29–30; scripture and, 25–26, 147, 154,
    156, 161, 165–66, 198, 217, 332–33n98;
    view of Jewish thinkers, 209–10.
    See also Brown, David; Congar,
    Yves; Dulles, Avery; Erasmus; Oral
    Torah; Ratzinger, Joseph; scripture;
    Smith, Wilfred Cantwell

"troubling texts," 28, 236–38. *See also*
    scripture, fallibility of

Ward, Keith, 103, 257n12, 359n80; on
    autonomy, 317n157; on historical
    criticism and faith, 259n29; 306n59;
    on revelation as perplexing, 271n68,
    288n201, 301n11, 344n6; on revela-
    tion as symbolic
writing process, 170
Written Torah, 146–48, 184, 210; au-
    thority/revelation of, 172 (*see also*
    revelation); blurring of bound-
    ary with Oral Torah, 151–61, 165,
    325–26nn25–27, 327n42; as subset of
    Oral Torah, 156, 170. *See also* Oral
    Torah; scripture; tradition

Zadok Ha-Kohen, 4, 164–65, 358n72
Zera' Qodesh, 89–90
Zohar, The, 112, 115, 214–15, 217
Zunz, Leopold, 26

Index of Ancient and Medieval Sources

The following index includes pages that discuss various ancient and medieval texts but does not include locations where a verse or chapter is cited in passing.

Tanakh

GENESIS

2–3	19
12.2	12
16.10–11	190
22.1	219–20

EXODUS

3–4	123
3.3	66
3.6	61
4.5	66
4.9	66
4.12	66
4.15	66
4.19	66
4.24–26	64
4.25	66
4.36	66–67
5.24	66–67
7.16	248
7.26	248
8.16	248
9.1	248
9.13	248
10.3	248
12	162, 190, 227, 232
12.5	136
12.8	136
12.9	137
12.10	225
12.12–14	227
12.22–24	227
16.4–5, 16–30	64
17	248
17.7	281n148
18	226
19–34	271n71
19–24	30–35, 46, 119–20
19–20	35–37, 41–45, 49, 52, 67, 69–70, 76, 81, 91, 99
19	42, 81, 94, 200, 212, 272n75
19.1–2a	54
19.2–6	272n77
19.3	32
19.3–6	47
19.5	36
19.9b	281n148
19.11	32, 61, 65–66
19.12	32
19.12–13	62
19.16	33, 36
19.18	32–33, 62
19.18–19.19	273n86
19.19	33, 36, 38, 48–50, 76
19.20	32

EXODUS (*continued*)

19.21	66
19.21–22, 24	62
19.23	32
19.24	42
19.24–25	32
19.25	38–39, 268–69n47
19.25–20.2	39
20–23	196–97
20	42, 101
20.1	32, 38–39, 48–49, 65, 68, 76, 79, 90, 104–5
20.1–17	41
20.2	77, 105
20.2–6	77, 81
20.3	77
20.3–6	77
20.4	274n87
20.4–6	77
20.18	36–38, 40, 42, 48–49, 62, 68, 76, 81, 90–91, 93, 267n38, 273n86
20.18–19	38
20.18–21	38, 48, 68, 77–78, 273n86
20.18–22	32–33, 37, 41
20.21	50
20.22	274n87
20.23–23.33	37–38, 47, 56, 63
20.24–25	243
21–23	101, 162, 226
21.2–6	20, 196
21.6	21
21.7–11	196
22.24	162
23.14–19	225
24	41–42, 45, 62
24.1	42
24.2	42, 63
24.3	169
24.3–7	47, 72
24.7	169
24.9	62
24.10	32, 61, 63, 65–66
24.11	65
24.12	50
24.15–17	53
24.15b–16	54
24.16–17	58
24.16–18a	54
24.17	65–66
25–31	280n135
25.1–31.17	54
25.8–9	58
25.9	66
25.22	56, 60, 72
25.40	58, 66
26.30	66
27.8	66, 280n135
31.18	50, 52, 54, 115
32.9	61
32.15–16	50–51
32.16	54, 115
32.19	115
32.26–28	61
33.11	52
33.18	63
33.19–34.6	92
33.21–22	63
33.23	61, 63
33	53, 101
34	101, 120, 226, 232
34.1	51–52
34.2–3	63
34.5–7	241
34.5–8	63
34.10	63
34.10–11	63
34.12–17	63
34.18–26	63, 225
34.27	63, 122
34.28	51–53, 92
34.29–35	54
34.29	58
35–40	280n135
35.1–40.32	54
40.33–38	54
40.38	66

LEVITICUS

1.1	54, 60
1.2–7.38	54
6.2	166
7.37	166
8.1–10.20	55
9.23–24	61
11–25	55
16	60
19.11	65
23.15	225
23.40	167
23.42	167
24.10–11	65
25.39–43	20
25.42	248
25.55	248
26	55
26.1–2	214
27	55

NUMBERS

3.5–10	142
5–6	55
7.89	59
8.4	66
9.1	114
9.15	276n101
9.15–23	276n110
12	53, 107–8
12.6–8	107
12.8	52
14.14–19	241
18.6–7	142
27.5	55
31.21	166
33.1–2	166

DEUTERONOMY

generally	164–65
1–31	64
1.5	283n163
1.9–17	226
1.33–39	191, 195

4–5	54, 64, 66, 71, 94, 99
4	193, 284n174
4.1–9	71
4.2	191, 196, 198
4.10–15	65
4.12	65, 81, 91
4.15	65
4.15–16	66
4.26	32
4.33	67
4.38	225
5	67, 69–70, 212
5.1	193
5.2–3	191–92, 199
5.2–27	67
5.3	193, 195
5.4	68, 91
5.4–5	68–69
5.5	69–70, 76, 120, 286n184
5.6	104
5.22	68, 190, 199, 202, 204–5
5.23–27	62
5.23–31	68
5.24	68, 193
5.24–31	226
5.25	68, 76
5.27	195
5.31	68
6.4	105
6.4–5	66
6.5	13, 104
6.6–9	173, 337n135
7	27
7.5	214
7.9–10	241
8.2–4	195
9.4–5	225
11	194
11.2–8	195
11.13	194
11.18–20	173, 337n135
12–26	63, 162, 165, 197
12	243
12.3	214

DEUTERONOMY (*continued*)

12.20	225
13.1	191, 196, 198
14.18	225
15.12–18	196
16.2	136
16.6–7	136
15.12–18	20
15.21–22	214
17.8–11	159
18.12	225
18.15–19	197, 268n45
18.16	68
18.18	76, 197
20	27
21.18–21	28, 136
24.1–4	198
25	248
25.17–19	27, 236
26.16–18	194
26.17	194
27	195
27.1–7	226
27.26	133
28.69	195
29.1–8	71
29.4	195
29.9	193
29.9–14	192, 207
29.11–12	193
29.13–14	193
31.9–13	196
31.10–13	66
31.19	169
33.2–4	34
33.3–4	62
33.4	77–78
33.10	151
33.15	62

JOSHUA

13–22	153
24	312n111

24.24–26	125
24.25–28	121

JUDGES

5.4–5	123

I SAMUEL

10.25	121

2 SAMUEL

14.13	60

I KINGS

18–19	91–93
19.7	91–92
19.9	93
19.11–12	92
19.11–13	92–94, 100
19.12	93, 115
19.15–18	93

ISAIAH

6.1–5	63
9–11	20
44.28–45.6	18

JEREMIAH

36.32	117

EZEKIEL

I	276n101
1.24	94
1.25	94
2.2	60
8–11	214
18	241
43.6	60

JONAH

4.2	241

HABAKKUK

3.3–6	34, 123

PSALMS

2	20
29.4	205
50.1–7	34, 123
65.2	94
68.8–10	33, 123
72	20
99.8	241
103.8–10	241
114	34, 123
119	168

JOB

4.16	94

SONG OF SONGS

generally	303n28
1.2	78–79

LAMENTATIONS

5.21	208

ESTHER

9.20–32	144
9.23	144
9.27	144–45, 250, 317–18n167

EZRA

1.1–11	18
2	18
3.2	140
3.10	140

NEHEMIAH

8	167
8.14–15	167
9.13	32, 224
10.1–40	142

2 CHRONICLES

23:18	140
30.16	142
35.13	137
36.22–23	18

Mishnah

PE'AH

2:6	150

ḤAGIGAH

1:8	157–58, 167

EDUYOT

8:7	150

AVOT

2:15–16	133
3:3–4	179
3:18	113
5:19	209

YADAYIM

4:3	150
4:4	28

Tosefta

SUKKAH

3:1–2	150

QIDDUSHIN

5:6	28

SANHEDRIN

11:2	28

Babylonian Talmud

BERAKHOT

5a	152, 325n25
28a	28
45a	126, 247
63b	179

SHABBAT

31a	151
87a	145
146a	193

ERUVIN
13b   221
14b   126, 247

YOMA
54a   28

MEGILLAH
7a   144, 245
19b   149

ḤAGIGAH
6a–b   56, 190, 277–78n119
11b   158

YEBAMOT
49b   108
62a   145

NEDARIM
22b   152
39b   113

SOṬA
10b   199

GITTIN
6b   221
60a   156
60b   153, 157

QIDDUSHIN
66a   157

SANHEDRIN
71a   28
96b–99a   20

HORAYOT
8a   79

SHEVUʿOT
39a   193

MAKKOT
23b   144, 245
23b–24a   77

MENAḤOT
29b   150
35b   126, 247

Jerusalem Talmud
PEʾAH
4a (2:6)   149, 153, 156, 193, 249

ḤAGIGAH
2d (1:8)   149, 151

Midrash
MEKHILTA DERABBI SHIMON
19:9   222

MEKHILTA DERABBI YISHMAEL
Baḥodesh §2 222
Baḥodesh §9 76
Vayyisaʿ §1 150

MIDRASH TEHILLIM
90:12   114
93:3   113

SIFRA
Beḥuqqotai 8:12 151
Shemini 1:9   150

SIFRE DEVARIM
§48   150
§306   154
§351   150–51

BERESHIT RABBAH
1:1   113
1:4   113
17:5   113
55   219–20

SHEMOT RABBAH

28:6	193, 350n69
33:7	77
47:1	149, 154, 156, 24

WAYIQRA RABBAH

1:14	108
11:7	159
22:1	149, 156, 193, 249

BEMIDBAR RABBAH

| 19:33 | 145 |

SHIR HASHIRIM RABBAH

| 1:13 | 78 |

RUTH RABBAH

| 4:5 | 144, 245 |

QOHELET RABBAH

1:29	149, 156, 193, 249
5:6	149, 156, 193, 249
11:12	114

BERESHIT RABBATI

Lekh Lekha 17:19   77

PESIQTA RABBATI

| 22:5 | 78 |

AVOT DERABBI NATHAN

A 15/B 29 [31a–b]   151

TANḤUMA

Niṣṣavim §4   193

TANNA DEVEI ELIYAHU ZUṬA

| 2:1 | 238 |

Medieval Works

GUIDE OF THE PERPLEXED

I:54   305–6n45

I:65–67	279n65
I:65	82–83
II:33	80–83
II:36	86
II:37	86
II:39	198, 347n37
II:40	86
II:45	86
II:48	82–83
III:27	86
III:39	87

MISHNEH TORAH

Foundations of Torah 7:6	305n45
Laws of Kings 5:4	28
Laws of Repentance 3:8	88

MAIMONIDES'S COMMENTARY ON THE
MISHNAH

To Hagigah: 1:8	158
To Avot: Eight Chapters	305n45
To Sanhedrin: Thirteen Principles:	
Seventh Principle	304–5n45
Eighth Principle	87–89
Ninth Principle	138

ZOHAR

| 3:152a | 114 |
| 3:271a | 332n93 |

New Testament

HEBREWS

| 8.13 | 13 |

GALATIANS

| 3.10–11 | 133 |

ROMANS

| 2.25 | 133 |
| 3.23 | 133 |